The Contemporary Hollywood Reader

We are all experts about Hollywood. We have to be, given its iconic power as the global source of so much entertainment. Designed to add to students' existing expertise as movie-goers, *The Contemporary Hollywood Reader* enables them to enter into thematic, critical, artistic, economic, and political debates on Hollywood.

The Contemporary Hollywood Reader is a dynamic selection of scholarly writings on Hollywood from the post-World War II period onwards, divided into three sections, each with contextualizing introductions from the editor. The sections, Production, Text, and Circulation, address all the major perspectives on Hollywood, allowing equal attention to the field, in both thematic and disciplinary senses.

In this collection, Toby Miller offers a plural, open guide to major scholarly tendencies in writing about Hollywood, with a mixture of familiar and less familiar works. While the *Reader* draws on research undertaken within US–UK film or cinema studies, it also ventures further afield, bringing together the most stimulating materials available on the subject.

Contributors include:

Michael Patrick Allen, Suman Basuroy, Sarah Berry, Denise D. Bielby, William T. Bielby, Erwin A. Blackstone, Gary W. Bowman, Lucia Bozzola, Subimal Chatterjee, Susan Christopherson, Rosemary J. Coombe, A. L. Cradock, Martine Danan, G. Escamilla, Kelly Gates, Douglas Gomery, Bill Grantham, Thomas H. Guback, Ed Guerrero, Janet Harbord, Jeffrey D. Himpele, Robert E. Kapsis, I. Kawachi, Paul Kerr, Barry King, Noel King, Geoff Lealand, Francis L. F. Lee, Anne E. Lincoln, Philippe Meers, Tania Modleski, Chon Noriega, Scott R. Olson, Tom O'Regan, Pope Pius XII, S. Abraham Ravid, Shari Roberts, R. L. Rutsky, Allen J. Scott, Jack Shaheen, Cheng Shao-Chun, JoEllen Shively, Charles S. Tahiro, Justin Wyatt, and Ruth Zanker.

Toby Miller is Professor of Media & Cultural Studies at the University of California, Riverside. His teaching and research cover media, sport, labor, gender, race, citizenship, politics, and cultural policy. Toby is the author and editor of over 30 volumes, and has published essays in over 100 journals and books. His current research covers the success of Hollywood overseas, the links between culture and citizenship, and anti-Americanism.

The
Contemporary Hollywood
Reader

Edited by

Toby Miller

Routledge
Taylor & Francis Group

LONDON AND NEW YORK

First published 2009
by Routledge
2 Park Square, Milton Park, Abingdon, Oxon OX14 4RN

Simultaneously published in the USA and Canada
by Routledge
270 Madison Avenue, New York, NY 10016

Routledge is an imprint of the Taylor & Francis Group, an informa business

Typeset in Perpetua and Bell Gothic by
RefineCatch Limited, Bungay, Suffolk
Printed and bound in Great Britain by
CPI Antony Rowe, Chippenham, Wiltshire

British Library Cataloguing in Publication Data
A catalogue record for this book is available from the British Library

Library of Congress Cataloging in Publication Data
A catalog record for this book has been requested

ISBN 10: 0–415–45225–2 (hbk)
ISBN 10: 0–415–45226–0 (pbk)

ISBN 13: 978–0–415–45225–0 (hbk)
ISBN 13: 978–0–415–45226–7 (pbk)

Contents

About the editor

TOBY MILLER IS CHAIR of the Department of Media & Cultural Studies at the University of California, Riverside. He is the author and editor of over 30 volumes, and has published essays in over 100 journals and books, many related to Hollywood. His books are: *The Well-Tempered Self: Citizenship, Culture, and the Postmodern Subject* (Johns Hopkins University Press, 1993); *Contemporary Australian Television* (University of New South Wales Press, 1994—with Stuart Cunningham); *The Avengers* (British Film Institute, 1997/Indiana University Press, 1998); *Technologies of Truth: Cultural Citizenship and the Popular Media* (University of Minnesota Press, 1998); *Popular Culture and Everyday Life* (Sage, 1998—with Alec McHoul); *SportCult* (University of Minnesota Press, 1999—edited with Randy Martin); *A Companion to Film Theory* (Blackwell, 1999—edited with Robert Stam); *Film and Theory: An Anthology* (Blackwell, 2000—edited with Robert Stam); *Globalization and Sport: Playing the World* (Sage, 2001—with Geoffrey Lawrence, Jim McKay, and David Rowe); *Sportsex* (Temple University Press, 2001); *Global Hollywood* (British Film Institute/Indiana University Press, 2001—with Nitin Govil, John McMurria, and Richard Maxwell); *A Companion to Cultural Studies* (Blackwell, 2001—edited); *The Television Genre Book* (British Film Institute/Indiana University Press, 2001—associate editor, editor Glen Creeber); *Cultural Policy* (Sage, 2002—with George Yúdice); *Television Studies* (British Film Institute/ University of California Press, 2002—edited, associate editor Andrew Lockett); *Critical Cultural Policy Studies: A Reader* (Blackwell, 2003—edited with Justin Lewis); *Television Studies: Critical Concepts in Media and Cultural Studies* (Routledge, 2003—5 volumes—edited); *Spyscreen: Espionage on Film and TV from the 1930s to the 1960s* (Oxford University Press, 2003); *Global Hollywood* (Chu Liu, 2003—with Nitin Govil, John McMurria, and Richard Maxwell); *Política Cultural* (Gedisa, 2004—with George Yúdice); *International Cultural Studies: An Anthology* (Blackwell, 2005—associate editor, editors Ackbar Abbas and John Nguyet Erni); *Global Hollywood 2* (British Film Institute/University of California Press, 2005—with Nitin Govil, John McMurria, Richard Maxwell, and Ting Wang); *El Nuevo Hollywood: Del Imperialismo Cultural a las Leyes del Marketing* (Paidós, 2005—with

Nitin Govil, John McMurria, and Richard Maxwell); *A Companion to Cultural Studies* (Blackwell, 2006—edited); *Cultural Policy* (Tartu Chu Liu, 2006—with George Yúdice); *Cultural Citizenship: Cosmopolitanism, Consumerism, and Television in a Neoliberal Age* (Temple University Press, 2007); and *Makeover Nation: The United States of Reinvention* (Ohio State University Press, 2008). Simplified Chinese translations of *Cultural Policy* (Nanjing University Press), *Global Hollywood* (Hua Xia), *A Companion to Cultural Studies* (Nanjing University Press), *A Companion to Film Theory* (China Radio & Television), and *Global Hollywood 2* (China Radio & Television) are in press. He is the editor of *Television & New Media*, co-editor of *Social Identities*, and editor of the Popular Culture and Everyday Life series for Peter Lang. Previously he was editor of the *Journal of Sport & Social Issues* (1996–99), co-editor of *Social Text* (1997–2001), co-editor on the Web of *Blackwell/Polity Cultural Theory Resource Centre* (1998–2002), and co-editor of the Cultural Politics book series for University of Minnesota Press (1997–2001), the Film Guidebooks book series for Routledge (1999–2002), and the Sport and Culture book series for University of Minnesota Press (1997–2006). He has been a Visiting Media Scholar at Sarai, the Centre for the Study of Developing Societies in Delhi; Distinguished Faculty Visitor at the Center for Ideas and Society, University of California, Riverside; Becker Lecturer at the University of Iowa; Queensland Smart Returns Fellow at the Queensland University of Technology; Honorary Professor at the University of Queensland's Center for Critical and Cultural Studies; and CanWest Fellow at the Alberta Global Forum. *Sportsex* and *A Companion to Film Theory* have been *Choice* Outstanding Titles.

Acknowledgments

MANY THANKS TO PENNY BUSHEY, Natalie Foster, Julene Knox, Jim McKay, Rebecca O'Connor, Brandy Quarles, Andrew Watts, Charlie Wood, and everyone at Taylor & Francis and elsewhere involved in the production of the book.

The following were reproduced with kind permission.

Part 1A Structure

Robert E. Kapsis. "Hollywood Genres and the Production of Culture Perspective." *Current Research in Film: Audiences, Economics, and Law vol. 5*. Ed. Bruce A. Austin. Norwood: Ablex, 1991. 68–85. Reproduced with permission of Greenwood Publishing of Greenwood Publishing Group, Inc., Westport, CT.

Janet Harbord. "Digital Film and 'Late' Capitalism." From *Media and Cultural Theory*. Ed. James Curran and David Morley. London: Routledge, 2006. 263–74. Copyright © 2006 Routledge. Reproduced by permission of Taylor & Francis UK.

Douglas Gomery. "Economic and Institutional Analysis: Hollywood as Monopoly Capitalism." *Understanding Film: Marxist Perspectives*. Ed. Mike Wayne. London: Pluto Press, 2005. 168–81. Reproduced with permission.

Erwin A. Blackstone and Gary W. Bowman. "Vertical Integration in Motion Pictures." *Journal of Communication* 49, no. 1 (1999): 123–39. Reproduced by kind permission of Wiley-Blackwell Publishing.

Part 1B Artists

Denise D. Bielby and William T. Bielby. "Women and Men in Film: Gender Inequality Among Writers in a Culture Industry." *Gender and Society* 10, no. 3 (1996): 248–70. Copyright © 1996 Sociologists for Women in Society. Reprinted by permission of Denise Bielby and SAGE Publications.

Anne E. Lincoln and Michael Patrick Allen. "Double Jeopardy in Hollywood: Age and Gender in the Careers of Film Actors, 1926–1999." *Sociological Forum* 19, no. 4 (2004): 611–31. Reproduced by kind permission of Wiley-Blackwell Publishing.

First published as "The *Twilight Zone* of Contemporary Hollywood Production," by Charles S. Tahiro, from *Cinema Journal* 41, no. 3, pp. 27–37. Copyright © 2002 by the University of Texas Press. All rights reserved.

First published as " 'The Lady in the Tutti-Frutti Hat': Carmen Miranda, a Spectacle of Ethnicity," by Shari Roberts, from *Cinema Journal* 32, no. 3, pp. 3–23. Copyright © 1993 by the University of Texas Press. All rights reserved.

Lucia Bozzola. " 'Studs Have Feelings, Too': Warren Beatty and the Question of Star Discourse and Gender." *Masculinity: Bodies, Movies, Culture*. Ed. Peter Lehman. Copyright 2001 by Taylor & Francis Goup LLC – Books. Reproduced with permission of Taylor & Francis Group LLC – Books in the format Textbook via Copyright Clearance Center and by kind permission of the author.

Barry King. "The Star and the Commodity: Notes Towards a Performance Theory of Stardom." *Cultural Studies* 1, no. 2 (1987): 145–61, Taylor & Francis Ltd, http://www.informaworld.com, reprinted by permission of the author and publisher.

Part 1C Globalization

Cheng Shao-Chun. "Chinese Diaspora and Orientalism in Globalized Cultural Production: Ang Lee's *Crouching Tiger, Hidden Dragon*." *Global Media Journal* 4, no. 6 (2005). Reproduced with permission.

Ruth Zanker and Geoff Lealand. "New Zealand as Middle Earth: Local and Global Popular Communication in a Small Nation." *Popular Communication* 1, no. 1 (2003): 65–72, Taylor & Francis Ltd, http://www.informaworld.com, reprinted by permission of the authors and publisher.

Allen J. Scott. "Hollywood and the World: The Geography of Motion-Picture Distribution and Marketing." *Review of International Political Economy* 11, no. 1 (2004): 33–61, reprinted by permission of the author and publisher.

Reprinted from *Geoforum* 37, no. 5, Susan Christopherson. "Behind the Scenes: How Transnational Firms are Constructing a New International Division of Labor in Media Work," pp. 739–51. Copyright 2006 Elsevier Ltd, with permission of Elsevier.

Part 2A Genre

Sarah Berry. "Genre." *A Companion to Film Theory*. Ed. Toby Miller and Robert Stam. Oxford: Blackwell, 2004. 25–44. Reproduced by kind permission of Wiley-Blackwell Publishing.

Paul Kerr. "Out of What Past? Notes on the B *film noir*." *The Hollywood Film Industry: A Reader*. Ed. Paul Kerr. London: Routledge & Kegan Paul, 1986. 221–44. Copyright © 1986 Routledge & Kegan Paul. Reproduced by permission of Taylor & Francis Books UK.

Part 2B Pleasure

Pius XII. (1957) *Miranda Prorsus: Encyclical Letter on Motion Pictures, Radio and Television*. Libreria Editrice Vaticana. Copyright © Libreria Editrice Vaticana 1957. Reprinted with permission.

First published as "Serious Pleasures: Cinematic Pleasure and the Notion of Fun," by R. L. Rutsky and Justin Wyatt from *Cinema Journal* 30, no. 1, pp. 3–19. Copyright © 1990 by the University of Texas Press. All rights reserved.

First published as "Lost in the Funhouse: Noel King Responds to R. L. Rutsky and Justin Wyatt," by Noel King from *Cinema Journal* 31, no. 3, pp. 56–62. Copyright © 1992 by the University of Texas Press. All rights reserved.

First published as "Throwing Shade in the Kingdom," by R. L. Rutsky and Justin Wyatt from *Cinema Journal* 31, no. 3, pp. 63–66. Copright © 1992 by the University of Texas Press. All rights reserved.

Part 2C **Representation**

Ed Guerrero. "A Circus of Dreams and Lies: The Black Film Wave at Middle Age." *The New American Cinema*. Ed. Jon Lewis. Durham: Duke University Press, pp. 328–52. Copyright 1998, Duke University Press. All rights reserved. Used by permission of the publisher.

G. Escamilla, A. L. Cradock, and I. Kawachi. "Women and Smoking in Hollywood Movies: A Content Analysis." *American Journal of Public Health* 90, no. 3 (2000): 412–14. Reprinted with permission from the American Public Health Association.

Tania Modleski. "A Rose is a Rose? Real Women and a Lost War." *The New American Cinema*. Ed. Jon Lewis. Durham: Duke University Press, pp. 125–45. Copyright 1998, Duke University Press. All rights reserved. Used by permission of the publisher.

Chon Noriega. "Citizen Chicano: The Trials and Titillations of Ethnicity in the American Cinema, 1935–1962." *Social Research* 58, no. 2 (1991): 413–38. Reproduced by kind permission of the author.

Jack Shaheen. "Reel Bad Arabs: How Hollywood Vilifies a People." *Annals of the American Academy of Political and Social Science* 588, no. 1, pp. 171–93, copyright © 2003, American Academy of Political Science and Social Science. Reprinted by permission of SAGE Publications and the author.

Part 3A **Distribution**

Jeffrey D. Himpele. "Film Distribution as Media: Mapping Difference in the Bolivian Cinemascape." *Visual Anthropology Review* 12, no. 1 (1996): 47–66, Taylor & Francis Ltd, http://www.informaworld.com, reprinted by permission of the author and publisher.

Martine Danan. "Marketing the Hollywood Blockbuster in France." *Journal of Popular Film and Television* 23, no. 3, pp. 131–40, 1995. Reprinted with permission of the Helen Dwight Reid Educational Foundation. Published by Heldref Publications, 1319 Eighteenth St., NW, Washington, DC 20036–1802. Copyright 1995.

"How Critical are Critical Reviews? The Box Office Effects of Film Critics, Star Power, and Budgets." Reprinted with permission from *Journal of Marketing*, published by the American Marketing Association, by Suman Basuroy, Subimal Chatterjee, and S. Abraham Ravid, vol. 67, no. 4 (2003), pp. 103–17.

Part 3B **Audiences**

JoEllen Shively. "Cowboys and Indians: Perceptions of Western Films Among American Indians and Anglos." *American Sociological Review* 57, no. 6 (1992): 725–34. Reprinted with permission.

Philippe Meers. " 'It's the Language of Film!': Young Film Audiences on Hollywood and Europe." Eds. Richard Maltby and Melvyn Stokes, *Hollywood Abroad: Audiences and Cultural Exchange*, 2007. © 2007 BFI Publishing. Reproduced with permission of Palgrave Macmillan.

Francis L. F. Lee. "Cultural Discount and Cross-Culture Predictability: Examining the Box Office Performance of American Movies in Hong Kong." *Journal of Media Economics* 19, no. 4 (2006): 259–78, Taylor & Francis Ltd, http://www.informaworld.com, reprinted by permission of the author and publisher.

Part 3C   Government

Rosemary J. Coombe. "The Celebrity Image and Cultural Identity: Publicity Rights and the Subaltern Politics of Gender." *Discourse* vol. 14, no. 3. Copyright © 1992 Wayne State University Press, with permission of Wayne State University Press and the author.

Thomas H. Guback. "Government Support to the Film Industry in the United States." *Current Research in Film: Audiences, Economics and Law Vol. 3.* Ed. Bruce A. Austin. Norwood: Ablex, 1987. 88–104. Reproduced with permission of Greenwood Publishing of Greenwood Publishing Group, Inc., Westport, CT.

Kelly Gates. "Will Work for Copyrights: The Cultural Policy of Anti-Piracy Campaigns." *Social Semiotics* 16, no. 1 (2006): 57–73, Taylor & Francis Ltd, http://www.informaworld.com, reprinted by permission of the author and publisher.

Part 3D   Globalization

Tom O'Regan. "Cultural Exchange." *A Companion to Film Theory.* Ed. Toby Miller and Robert Stam. Oxford: Blackwell, 2004. 262–94. Reproduced by kind permission of Wiley-Blackwell Publishing.

Scott R. Olson. "The Globalization of Hollywood." *International Journal on World Peace* 17, no. 4 (2000): 3–17. Reprinted with permission.

Bill Grantham. "America the Menace: France's Feud with Hollywood." *World Policy Journal* 15, no. 2 (1998): 58–66. Reproduced by kind permission of the author.

Whilst every effort has been made to trace copyright holders and obtain permission, this has not been possible in all cases. Any omissions brought to our attention will be remedied in future editions.

Introduction

WE ARE ALL EXPERTS about Hollywood. We have to be, given its iconic power as the global source of so much entertainment. So why another book about it? *The Contemporary Hollywood Reader* is designed to add to your existing expertise as a watcher of Hollywood movies so that you can enter thematic, critical, artistic, economic, and political debates about this bizarre bazaar of extravagant fun, folly, and industry. It's a supplement to your own knowledge.

I've tried in this collection to offer a plural, open guide to major scholarly tendencies in writing about Hollywood. That has meant going beyond the specialized materials you might expect to read if you are enrolled in film school, or communications, or cinema studies, or law school, or media studies, or American studies. So rather than aiming to satisfy entirely people who run courses on Hollywood in a history department; or courses on genre in a film department; or courses on the effect of watching cinema in a public-health department; or parents and students who want to know about major issues of pleasure and policy in US culture, I have sought to borrow from all these desires, all these disciplines, all these preoccupations, all these systems of knowledge, all these methods, all these shibboleths, myths, truths, fears, and pronouncements. Does this mean that no individual reader of this volume will be satisfied? Perhaps. But they will certainly be surprised and, I hope, challenged. My wish is that students will find something here to make them think in an informed way about the most pervasive and powerful art form of the twentieth century, with continuing relevance to the twenty-first.

The Contemporary Hollywood Reader is a selection of pre-published work on mainstream US film, divided into three parts, with brief contextualizing introductions. The parts are:

1. PRODUCTION
2. TEXT
3. CIRCULATION

This organization permits equal attention to Hollywood from all major perspectives, in both thematic and disciplinary senses. Unlike the study of literature, which is mostly about texts; or TV, which is mostly about production and circulation, Hollywood is generally taught and researched with attention to all these contexts: production, text, and circulation. This volume covers these topics across the academic fields that address them: cinema or film studies, communications, media studies, geography, sociology, economics, anthropology, history, literature, law, and other arms of the human sciences.

The *Reader* is restricted to the period since World War II, for three reasons. First, space does not permit a comprehensive consideration of the full Hollywood century. Second, much teaching and research is divided at 1946 or thereabouts, because Hollywood's way of making films changed markedly with the simultaneous advent across the US landscape of televisualization, trust-busting, and suburbanization. Production and audiences were transformed, thanks to new technology and new forms of state intervention: TV re-emerged after a forced hiatus during hostilities; the Supreme Court encouraged the film studios to end vertical integration of production, distribution, and exhibition; and the GI Bill encouraged white men to buy homes in the suburbs and multiply.

In keeping with the seven decades of time that the *Reader* covers, a sense of history runs through many pieces, and my introductions will come prior to each section in order to locate it within key moments and debates. As a backdrop, I hope you will bear in mind this sketch of the material relations that describe a screen text's life through script development, pre-production, production, post-production, marketing, distribution, exhibition and reception. Film remains at the apex semiotically, but not financially:

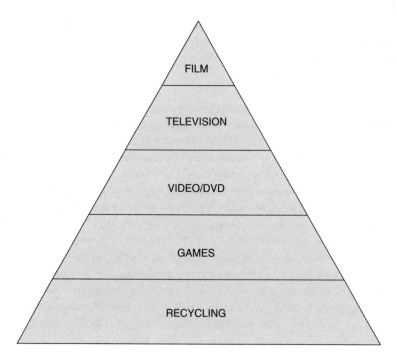

Figure I.1

Hollywood film is the site of origin for these other forms and has the most venerable status, so it is at the top. Video and television have the most popularity and games the most revenue, so they come next and broaden out the diagram. Recycling is at the bottom, with the newest stature and potentially greatest economic effect, by recycling film stock from old movies as polyester, or metals retrieved from old computers and televisions.

Then there are the various processes that go into the creation and life of Hollywood texts—numerous complex methods of conceiving, managing, promoting, and understanding each film on its wayward journey from script development to legal download. Although some of these processes happen sequentially, they frequently overlap, and so this diagram emphasizes the dynamic and controlling role of capital—finance, labor, and management—in each moment of the life of the text.

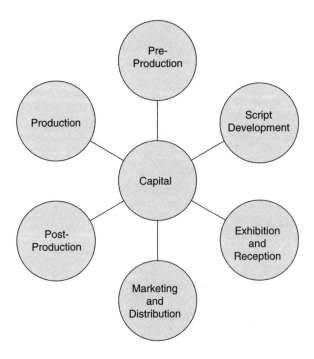

Figure I.2

If you want to understand Hollywood, it's advisable to keep these diagrams in your virtual back pocket. They're a good reality check as you immerse yourself in the methodologically and politically diverse essays to come.

PART 1

Production

INTRODUCTION

HOW DOES HOLLYWOOD MAKE MOVIES?
We can represent the labor process like this (NICL stands for the New International Division of Cultural Labor):

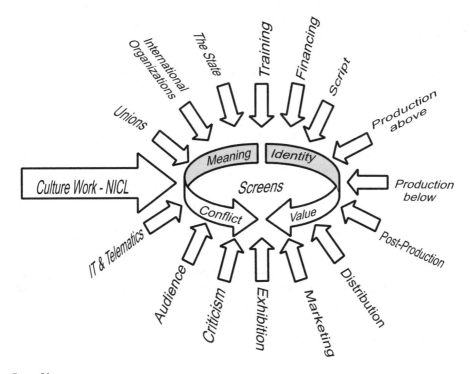

Figure P1

People are working to generate the meaning and the physicality of each Hollywood movie, whether they are sitting in coffee shops in west LA tapping away on battered laptops to produce scripts, lining up in suburban Canberra to buy a ticket, or waiting in stylish Coyoacan for a download to finish. This is not always a functional, easy process—conflicts, values, and identities are as relevant to what is made and how it is interpreted as managerial control and marketing power are. In the various parts of this *Reader*, it is important to recall the interconnected but relatively autonomous nature of the work we do, whether as interns on a movie set or watchers at home.

Hollywood work is forever being transformed by both new technologies and new work relations. For example, the advent of digital technology has diminished the prior necessity for editors to keep a vast array of information under control as they ploughed through analogic changes. Non-linear editing permits randomness as workers gain skills in the latest machines— and lose them in the latest narratives. And there are key distinctions between primary and secondary labor markets. In the primary market, such as working for the major broadcast networks in the US, employment may be relatively regular and workers receive benefits and pensions. In the secondary market, of cable networks and small production houses, peripheral employees are caught in perennial uncertainty and lack anything beyond contingent wages. For some this is a story of loss, for others it is about transition—and in cheerleading versions, it is hailed as a celebration of autonomy.

In the **Structure** section, Robert E Kapsis examines the role of genre in making and promoting Hollywood, while Janet Harbord's chapter looks at how Hollywood business practices have changed with the advent of digital technologies. As you read their essays, bear in mind both the pyramid and the circular diagrams from the Introduction as you ponder where, how, and by whom meaning is made through the cinema. You will be assisted in this project by Douglas Gomery's political–economic analysis of the Hollywood system and Erwin A Blackstone and Gary W Bowman's exemplification of how to trace and represent the industry's business model. Hollywood is an institution as well as a set of texts and people, and we need to comprehend it if we want to intervene in it as critics, scholars, citizens, consumers, or producers.

The **Artists** section brings this analysis down to the level of people working in the industry—to the experiences and representations of workers, from off-screen personnel to on-screen stars. Hollywood is characterized, of course, by the social inequalities that afflict economic life. Denise D Bielby and William T Bielby have studied gender inequality among Hollywood writers and offer some fascinating insights. For their part, Anne E Lincoln and Michael Patrick Allen's longitudinal survey examines how age and gender affect stardom. They analyze the period from before the advent of sound to the turn of our new century, while Charles S Tahiro looks at a specific event, the tragedy surrounding the filming of *Twilight Zone* and its implications for labor protection in the industry. The section concludes with two historical–textual case studies, of Carmen Miranda and Warren Beatty, with Shari Roberts and Lucia Bozzola, respectively, analyzing these icons of Latin femininity and Anglo masculinity; and Barry King's political–economic take on stars as commodities.

Globalization again blends specific and more general chapters. Cheng Shao-Chun problematizes the notion of Hollywood as "American" by analyzing Ang Lee's career. Ruth Zanker and Geoff Lealand consider how New Zealand/Aotearoa experiences Hollywood. Moving to more general applications, Allen J Scott examines the geography of filmmaking, and Susan Christopherson highlights transnational screen labor.

Chapter 1

Robert E. Kapsis

HOLLYWOOD GENRES AND THE PRODUCTION OF CULTURE PERSPECTIVE (1991)

FILM GENRES CAN BE DEFINED AS BROAD forms of popular expression, such as Westerns, gangster films, musicals, horror films, romantic comedies, science fiction films, and psychological suspense thrillers that contain predictable combinations of features (cf. 25, 38, 39).[1] The dominant theoretical orientation of most sociological and historical studies of film genres and cycles is that they in some way reflect some aspect of society. According to this viewpoint (henceforth referred to as "the reflection of society perspective"), shifts in film content reflect changes in audience taste preferences which are, in turn, linked to major shifts in the structure of society. The underlying assumption of many studies in this tradition is that popular films are a more or less accurate mirror of social structure, because by choosing the films it attends, the audience reveals its preferences to film studios and distributors which, in turn, passively produce and finance films reflecting audience desires. Siegfried Kracauer's *From Caligari to Hitler* (30) was a pioneering effort in viewing film content as a reflection of the psychological tendencies of a nation as a collectivity.

The reflection approach has also been applied to American cinema. Three important studies are *The Six-Gun Mystique* by John Cawelti (14), *Sixguns and Society* by Will Wright (47), and *Hollywood Genres* by Thomas Schatz (39). All three studies are preoccupied with the mythical qualities of Hollywood genres.[2] In addition, each book treats genre films primarily as symbolic reflections of the society and historical period in which they are created. Wright, for example, describes changes in the content of popular Hollywood westerns between 1930 and 1970, from a concern for solitary heroes fighting it out with villains for the sake of the weak but growing community (which Wright calls the "Classical Plot" western) to a preoccupation with elite bands of heroes, who fight not for the community which they have rejected but to affirm themselves as professionals (which Wright calls the "Professional Plot" western). According to Wright, this structural progression in the western is the result of a profound change in American economic institutions occurring at roughly the same time, from a free market (the gunfighter as *homo economicus*) to a corporate economy (the gunfighter as technocrat).

Theoretically more ambitious than Wright or Cawelti, Schatz's approach to genre promises to deliver more—to show how genre development reflects not only changes in the wider society but also the way the film industry routinely conducts business. Unfortunately, in the individual chapters devoted to specific genres, such as the Western, screwball comedy, and musicals, Schatz falls back to a societal reflection orientation or simply to describing individual films in relation to the generic form, largely ignoring the role of the Hollywood studio system. What is needed is a study which examines how the industrial process, independent of changes in audience taste preferences, influences both the short- and long-term development of Hollywood genres.

In contrast to the reflection viewpoint, there is what has been termed the production of culture perspective. Developed by sociologists, this orientation is less polemical than either the more general critique of the mass media developed by the Frankfurt School (see, e.g., 22, 32) or recent neo-Marxist criticisms of classical Hollywood films (e.g., *Cahiers du cinéma's* collective text on John Ford's *Young Mr. Lincoln* [11]; but see Buscombe's [10] critique of Marxist attempts to relate the products of Hollywood to the industry which produced them). The production of culture viewpoint begins with the observation that the nature and content of all cultural products (including film) are influenced by or embedded in the immediate organizational, legal, and economic environments in which they are produced (13, 36, 42). The various milieux of symbolic production examined from this perspective have included book publishing, television, popular music, painting, and more recently film (see 7, 35, 42 for good overviews of this work).[3]

A sizable body of literature in this tradition has concentrated on mass media organizations, showing how the complex interorganizational network of production companies, distributors, mass media gatekeepers, and retailers influence the production and dissemination of a wide range of cultural commodities (see, for example, 17, 20, 21). A recurring theme in the literature on television and the movies is that because of uncertainty over the future tastes of the audience, the production process characteristically involves interpersonal conflict between producers, directors, script writers, and distribution executives over what the audience will like or accept (12, 16, 17, 26, 27).

In addition to interorganizational relationships, there are also a number of other extra-artistic factors—the market, pressure groups and censorship, statute law and government regulations, and new technologies which have influenced the production of popular culture independent of actual shifts in audience taste preferences (see 36). Consider, for example, markets. Changes in the types of theatrical films made may result from shrinking or expanding markets having little to do with actual changes in audience desires. One of the most conspicuous developments in Hollywood since the late 1960s has been the production of movies primarily for teenagers and young adults, that is, a shift away from making films for a truly mass audience. That American film studios have become less willing to back films dealing with serious social themes reflects what is now a deeply entrenched belief among film packagers, namely, that Hollywood's core market—young people—are simply not interested in such films.

In this chapter, I will apply a production of culture perspective to Hollywood genre film production. There are two major reasons why I believe this approach is an essential tool for examining Hollywood film genres. First, the very existence of genre films and cycles is a product of the film industry's attempt to overcome the problem of uncertainty, that is, of not knowing the future tastes of the mass audience. To reduce this uncertainty, the movie studios, like other mass entertainment industries, fall back on notions about "live or dead genres, doomed formats, cycles that come and go" (17, p. 23).

A second reason for applying this perspective to Hollywood filmmaking relates to the existence of a complex network of interorganizational relationships which mediates between the movie production company and the consumer. Which genres finally get made depends on how organizational gatekeepers at various stages of the film production process assess the product in relation to their perception of the audience's future tastes. For example, film production companies often make films from which marketing executives then determine which generic label is most appropriate for promotion the film. While the audience and, by extension, society have some indirect influence on film content via ticket sales, that influence is filtered through the in-house conflicts and interorganizational decisions that shape what films are made and get released.

In this chapter I will examine the boom and bust cycle that movie genres periodically go through. My objectives are three-fold: (1) to show that genre film production is vastly different during the boom phase of a cycle than when a genre is in decline; (2) to determine the extent to which cyclical change is independent of changes in audience taste preferences; and (3) to explore the relative impact of three factors—markets, pressure groups, and media gatekeepers on the emergence, persistence, and decline of film cycles.

During the boom phase of a film cycle, dozens of films of a particular genre are released or re-released each year while dozens more are either in pre-production, production, or post-production. One factor that might affect the duration of a film cycle is the perception of how markets (audiences) might respond to the genre. According to many movie industry observers, for a genre boom period to emerge and persist, there must be strong indications that the genre will thrive in at least two of the three major theatrical markets—domestic, foreign, and ancillary (such as sales to network and cable television and videotape playback). A second condition to be examined is the impact of pressure groups organized against the genre. A number of historical studies have documented how pressure groups have caused popular genres to either disappear or change their basic formulas (sec 8, 34).[4] The third condition to be explored here is the role of media gatekeepers.[5] I hypothesize that in order for a film cycle to persist, media gatekeepers must regularly provide stories about the genre, and feature interviews with persons connected with film projects that are examples of the form. When a genre is no longer perceived as "newsworthy" by the media, it may lose its appeal to audiences as well.

To explore the cyclical nature of genre film production, I will examine post-1978 developments in the horror genre. In late 1978, a new horror cycle emerged which would last until around 1983.

RESEARCH PROCEDURES

Between February 1981 and January 1986, I interviewed marketing, production, and acquisition executives, senior story editors, and readers at Universal, Twentieth Century-Fox, Paramount, MGM, Columbia, Embassy, and Shapiro Entertainment, and asked them about their views on audiences, genre pictures, and film cycles. During the exploratory phase of the research, personal contacts largely determined which film organizations were selected. When my focus shifted to horror films, the organizations I selected (e.g., Universal, Paramount, Embassy, and Shapiro Entertainment) were those which at that time figured prominently in the production and/or distribution of such films. During the project's first year, I gathered detailed information on the pre-production, filming, post-production, and marketing of several low-budget horror films. For one of the films examined, *Halloween II*, two members of my West Coast research staff were on the set every day during the film's six week shooting schedule and gathered detailed field notes on the shooting of the film. During

post-production, we interviewed members of the cast and crew (including the online producer, director, and cinematographer) in order to gain an understanding of the routine
factors which influence the content of genre films (e.g., changes in the way the potential
audience is perceived). Executives from Universal Studios involved in the marketing and
advertising of the film were also interviewed. Subsequently, I interviewed artistic and
financial decision makers involved in other recent horror films. Additional valuable information about the horror cycle of the early 1980s was drawn from the newspaper and magazine
clipping services at the Margaret Herrick Library of the Academy of Motion Picture Arts
and Sciences in Beverly Hills and from the major trade papers of the film industry, especially
Variety and *The Hollywood Reporter*.

1979–80: HORROR BOOM PERIOD

Horror[6] has been one of the most enduring of Hollywood film genres. The decade of the
1970s was no exception. Three top grossing films, *The Exorcist* (1973), *Jaws* (1975), and
Halloween (1978), probably did more than anything else to assure that the horror film genre
during the 1970s and early 1980s would enjoy the kind of long-term popularity it had
experienced throughout the 1930s. The enormous success of *The Exorcist*, for example,
resulted in each major studio reaching out to make another film about demonic possession.
But by fall 1978, the popularity of such films had already peaked. Horror films were leaving
studios in the red, and it would have come as no surprise had Hollywood temporarily
stopped making them altogether. The meteoric arrival of the low-budget horror film
Halloween in October 1978 after the genre had supposedly peaked, assured that movie studio
executives would continue to back horror film projects. *Halloween* earned over $50 million
in box office receipts after costing under $400,000 to produce. And it performed well in
both domestic and foreign markets.

Film companies—first the minors and then the majors—were quick to cash in on
Halloween's success. Film executives extracted from *Halloween* the elements or formula
believed to have been responsible for its success: (1) the male psychopathic killer terrorizing
teenage girls in their social milieu (the world of babysitters, prom queens, and camp
counselors), and (2) the graphic depiction of blood and violence (indeed, more explicit than
permitted at that time on prime time television). Over the next two years film companies
produced a large number of films so similar to *Halloween* in style and content that a new
subgenre of horror emerged, what has been termed "knife-kill," "splatter," or "slasher"
movies. From *Prom Night* and *Friday the 13th* to *Terror Train* and *Friday the 13th Part II*, each
film contained successively more graphic depictions of violence, blood, and gore. The "slice
and dice" horror film had been born.

Other types of horror films also went into production during this period (e.g., ghost
stories, werewolf stories, etc.), reflecting the film industry's view that more traditional
forms could be revived and rejuvenated by beefing up the violence and through startling
special effects. In addition, recent horror film "cult" classics were reissued, such as *Night of
the Living Dead, The Texas Chain-Saw Massacre* and *The Last House on the Left*.[7] Indeed, by late
1979, a horror genre boom period had emerged which would last roughly until early 1981.

Between 1979 and 1981, horror films performed strongly in both domestic and foreign
markets. In 1978 only nine horror films earned at least one million dollars in domestic
rentals. That rate doubled and tripled over the next two years. Seventeen horror films in
1979 and 26 in 1980 topped the million dollar mark.[8] Over the same period foreign
production of horror films dramatically increased—from only 23 new films starting production in 1978 to 33 in 1979 and 55 in 1980. Another indication that a bullish market for

horror had arrived is that roughly one-fourth of all movies screened and pitched at the international sales events at Cannes, Milan, and Los Angeles were horror films (43, 45; see Tables 1.1 and 1.2).

During this period, horror projects received considerable coverage from the mass media. Executives at Pickwick/Maslansky/Koenigsberg (PMK)—a public relations firm whose horror film clients during the horror boom included directors Brian De Palma,

Table 1.1 Horror film performance*

Year	Film Rentals
1970	$ 6,500,000
1971	19,000,000
1972	31,500,000
1973	6,500,000
1974	80,000,000
1975	166,500,000
1976	73,000,000
1977	118,000,000
1978	109,000,000
1979	204,000,000
1980	168,000,000
1981	133,000,000
1982	227,000,000
1983	107,000,000

* Source: Adapted from *Variety*, January 25, 1984, p. 36

Table 1.2 Horror film production*

Year	U.S.	Foreign	Total
1970	22	71	93
1971	57	88	145
1972	83	106	189
1973	39	76	115
1974	21	50	71
1975	22	36	58
1976	43	37	80
1977	28	33	61
1978	35	23	58
1979	38	33	71
1980	66	55	121
1981	70	45	115
1982	34	35	69
1983 (est.)	35	25	60

* Pictures are dated by the year filming commences, not year of eventual release. The 1970, 80 data have been updated from *Variety's* November 19, 1980 chart to include recently discovered films and backdate releases to their earlier production date. Comedy horror spoofs and other borderline fantasies are omitted from the yearly totals. Source: *Variety*, January 25. 1984, p. 36.

George Romero, and John Carpenter, producer Debra Hill, and actress Jamie Lee Curtis—reported that at the height of the horror craze, media gatekeepers "were all jumping on our horror films," that is, were willing to plug them in various ways. Said account executive Katie Sweet, "We really got involved with the whole business of horror after *Halloween* . . . We started handling John Carpenter and for whatever reason we became the office for handling a lot of this genre of film" (personal interview, fall 1981). According to Sweet, at the height of the horror boom period, PMK could bring together many of its clients working in horror and have them talk to the media about their work. For example, one night on NBC's now defunct *Tomorrow Show*, Rona Barrett moderated an entire segment which brought together horror directors John Carpenter and George Romero to discuss their work. "In those days," recalled Sweet, "there was ease in getting the media to cover horror; it was just not that difficult."

Another characteristic of this horror boom period was that there were no organized crusades against horror films. In fact, for a short time, it became chic to like horror—a trend traceable to the rise of auteur theory in the late 1960s as well as to the attempts of high-culture critics in the 1970s to apply self-sufficient and self-referential aesthetic criteria (derived from high-culture criticism) to popular genres. One outcome of this shift in critical standards was that by the late 1960s a number of the films of popular genre filmmakers, such as Alfred Hitchcock and Howard Hawks, were considered works of art (see 28). This tendency was broadened during the 1970s to include other popular genre filmmakers as well. Indeed, at the start of the horror boom period of the late 1970s, critics who ordinarily regarded horror with disdain were arguing that with the right director (e.g., Hitchcock in *Psycho*), a work of considerable artistry could be achieved within that genre. *Newsweek*'s critic David Ansen praised John Carpenter's *Halloween* as "a superb exercise in the art of suspense . . . From the movie's dazzling prologue in 1963 to its chilling conclusion in 1978, we are being pummeled by a master manipulator" (4, p. 116). Apparently, the prestigious literary magazine, the *New Yorker*, agreed with this assessment because in the winter of 1980 it featured a lengthy profile of Carpenter (41).

Fear No Evil is a horror film that was conceived in 1979, shot in 1980, and released in early 1981. The circumstances surrounding the evolution of this film illustrate how the favorable climate for horror between 1979 and 1981 affected filmmaking at that time.

In the fall of 1978 Frank La Loggia, the director of *Fear No Evil*, started work on a love story but ended up with a horror movie. At that time, according to La Loggia, "Horror films were doing very well and we were looking for a first project that our money people could get behind, and so we developed an idea for a horror fantasy, approached them with that, and were able to raise about a half million dollars" (personal interview, fall 1981).

With that money the director was able to complete principal photography for the film but still needed about $250,000 to add the visual and sound effects. So he took the picture in rough cut form to Avco Embassy—a major distributor of horror films at that time—which agreed to supply the money to complete the film. Recalled the executive who subsequently advised the director on the project, "The sales department thought they could take it to Cannes and get $1 million right off the top in foreign rentals" (31, p. 4). Convinced that it was a safe investment, Avco agreed to cover post-production costs, but with certain strings attached.

Avco Embassy executives wanted more shots of high school kids at school because they believed they could sell the film from the exploitative angle of kids in danger. Yet the film's story line had really little to do with kids in jeopardy. The film centers on three arch angels—Michael, Gabriel, and Raphael—who periodically return to earth in the guise of humans to do battle with the latest incarnation of Lucifer, the fallen angel. The premise of *Fear No Evil* is that Lucifer comes to earth in the form of a high school student who is then pursued by the arch angels. According to La Loggia, in the film's original form, the high school environment was not central to the story. "We included that environment because the horror films that were making it theatrically seemed to revolve around high school kids. When we brought the film to Avco the first time, they found the high school setting the most appealing aspect of the picture." Therefore, Avco insisted that the high school element be more dominant and that more blood and guts be added whenever possible. The director had shot several scenes involving high school kids that were absent from the rough cut form that Avco saw. Recalled La Loggia, "I'd shot the material primarily as a safeguard and sure enough when they began to ask for it, it was a good thing we had it around, because not having the footage might have jeopardized the deal. That's just the way they were thinking at the time." More relevant than how audiences were thinking at the time of the horror boom period was how studio executives were thinking about that audience.

By early fall 1980, it appeared to some well placed industry observers that the domestic market was once again saturated with horror and that the low-budget horror film was on a downslide (19). Accordingly, worried marketing executives concentrated on positioning the horror films that were already finished, releasing them when national or regional markets were not already glutted with horror.

1981–82: BOOM OR BUST? THE BACKLASH AGAINST HORROR[9]

In January of 1981, the next wave of horror started with Avco Embassy's *Fear No Evil* and *Scanners*. *Fear No Evil* opened in Florida and Texas on January 16 and, according to its director, did "fantastic business." The film's good showing in the South did not escape the notice of the other studios. In a matter of weeks, many of the other horror films that had been sitting on the shelves were released. "We took the first step in the water," said La Loggia. "The water was fine and everybody else came in." By the time *Fear No Evil* opened in New York in February, for example, *Scanners* and *Maniac* had already opened, and *My Bloody Valentine* was to premier the next week. Soon to follow were *Blood Beach, The Boogey Man*, and the re-release of *The Texas Chain Saw Massacre*.

The 1981 mini-boom in horror provoked a media backlash. Leading the assault of the critics were Chicago reviewers Gene Siskel and Roger Ebert, who devoted an entire "Sneak Previews" television show to denouncing knife-kill movies, while (paradoxically) defending Carpenter's handling of similar material in *Halloween*. The Siskel–Ebert complaints focused on both the explicit and exploitative violence of these films as well as on their rampant misogyny (the victims often were independent young women who, the films implied, were asking for it). Other critics and journalists quickly followed suit (newspaper clipping file, Academy of Motion Picture Arts and Sciences, Beverly Hills). Indeed, by later 1982, many newspapers and national magazines had stopped reviewing low-budget horror films altogether.[10]

The critical attack on low-budget horror movies extended to big-budget productions which are more dependent on the good will of critics and other journalists as they seek a broader appeal. Most of the big-budget horror films released in 1981 and 1982 (e.g., *Ghost Story, Cat People*, and *The Thing*) received terrible reviews. They also performed poorly at the box office. Failing to attract a broader audience, these films received most of their business from fans of low-budget horror (newspaper clipping file, Academy of Motion Picture Arts and Sciences, Beverly Hills).

It also became more difficult for horror films to get free media coverage, reflecting not merely the backlash or crusade against horror but that "horror" was no longer perceived as "newsworthy." One might expect free publicity for any type of genre film to be easier to obtain earlier in a cycle than later. According to public relations executive Neil Koenigsberg who I interviewed in 1981, "You can no longer go in and say, 'Oh we have this horror picture.' " He then cited as a hypothetical case the prospects of getting *Life* magazine to do a story on John Carpenter's *The Thing*—a horror film that was scheduled for release the summer of 1982. Because it's perceived as a horror film, a production story wouldn't get published. What might work, Koenigsberg said, is a story about "this incredible career of a young person named John Carpenter. Look at the career and look at what makes him tick, because that means eventually getting into *The Thing*."

An additional assault against horror films came from the Classification and Rating Administration (CARA) of the Motion Picture Association of America which assigns the ratings to theatrical films. Richard D. Heffner, the chairman of CARA, admitted to me in 1981 that since the arrival of the slasher films in 1978, his office had gotten tougher on violence. Some movies, said Heffner, that received an R rating three years ago would get an X rating today. One movie that received the dreaded X on its first screening for CARA was the sequel to *Halloween*. Heffner admitted that the version of the film CARA first saw was not as violent as some of the earlier films in the "slasher" series that had received an R. But, he stressed, this had nothing to do with punishing the sequel because the original had spawned the slasher cycle, as the film's producers had alleged, but because CARA's stand-ards had stiffened over the last few years. CARA's harder line, Heffner was quick to point out, reflects what the board perceives as changing parental attitudes toward violence. CARA is not a moral agent imposing its position on the film industry, he said, but a "barometer" of the country's changing moral climate.

Despite the chill, horror films continued to be made. The difference was that now skittish directors and producers started to put some distance between themselves and the genre. An early indication came in late October 1981 when critic Stephen Farber hosted a weekend "Harvest of Horror" course at UCLA. At the opening session, Farber apologized to his students for the failure of a number of invited guests to show up and discuss their work. "We had invited Christopher Lee," said Farber at the time, but "he decided he no longer wanted to be associated with horror films. He felt that he had transcended the genre."

Farber went on to cite similar reactions from other people in the industry he had contacted. Filmmaker Paul Schrader, who was completing his remake of *The Cat People*, told Farber that his film wasn't horror but "a phantasy in the tradition of Cocteau." Many producers insisted their movies were "suspense thrillers," "supernatural tales," "intense psychological dramas"—anything but horror films (field notes, October 30, 1981).

Producer Edward Feldman is typical of those who worked on horror projects during the 1981–82 down-turn period who called horror by any other name. "Horror to me always connotes a low-budget maneuvering of the audience," he said. "It is graphically violent. It appeals to a much lower educational level" (personal interview, Fall 1981). According to David Madden, who was feature story editor at Twentieth Century-Fox when we inter-viewed him in fall 1981, Feldman's film, *The Sender*, was Fox's only horror project then in development. Not surprisingly, Feldman disagreed with Madden's characterization of his film—insisting that his unfinished picture was more suspenseful than graphically violent:

> There is much more intellectual violence. It's more in your mind and in your emotional state. You don't see people chopping people up. You walk a fine line in these kinds of movies. If you don't intellectualize a little and make them more a dramatic vehicle, as *The Exorcist* or *The Shining*, you've got what is known as a "quick-in and quick-out movie," which opens in a thousand theaters and you pray for one or two good weekends. We're trying to make a movie that has some substance.

In the spring of 1980 when plans to make a sequel to *Halloween* got underway, the boom in low-budget horror films was in full swing. However, by the fall of 1981, when *Halloween II* was about to be released, industry uncertainty about the marketability of horror had become widespread and the media backlash against horror films had reached its zenith. The making of this film illustrates that audience uncertainty among filmmakers and studio marketing people intensifies as it becomes less and less clear whether the genre cycle in question will continue to boom or suddenly bust.[11]

According to its producers, the challenge of *Halloween II* was to make a film that would end the slasher cycle but would not be as bloody as recent films in the genre. The game plan was to create a thriller or suspense film rather than simply a horror film. The director, Rick Rosenthal, said he was hired for *Halloween II* because of his work on a short which "was not a horror film but a psychological thriller." Co-producer Debra Hill concurred that the premise of the sequel as with the original was to build fear and suspense— Hitchcockian virtues—rather than repulse the audience with graphic displays of blood and guts. At the same time, the filmmakers recognized that because of recent developments in the horror genre, the sequel would have to be more graphic and violent than the original. Indeed, the original script was most compatible with this strategy, calling for no less than a dozen grisly killings.

After shooting the film, the director was given about five weeks to prepare his cut or version of the film. Once his rough cut (minus a sound track) was completed, the producers, still unsure about what audiences hoped to find in their film, proceeded to show the unfinished film to high school students, soliciting their opinions. And, according to one of the producers, the students wanted more blood and guts. As the director described it, the producers became scared that there wasn't enough blood and gore in their film, so they went out and shot a few new scenes that were extremely violent. Although the rough-cut version of the film did include a dozen or so brutal killings, none of the victims was a teenage girl. Killing off at least one teenage girl had become a staple of the genre. So a new scene was shot and inserted early in the picture depicting the fatal slashing of a high school girl. Also, the producers drastically shortened several scenes where there were no immediate payoffs, that is, where no gory killings occurred.

Late in the film, one of the female characters is trying to escape from the killer. She gets in a car, tries to start it, can't start it, and gets out. In the director's original cut, the scene lasts several minutes and functions to build suspense in the audience. "It goes on and on and on when I cut it," the director told us (personal interview, Fall 1981). "The viewer is supposed to think, 'Oh shit, the car doesn't start' and then you say 'Wait a minute. This isn't a scene bout a car not starting. He's in the back seat. Get out! Get out of the car!' And just when you are saying, 'Oh, no! He's coming out of the back seat,' she gets out of the car." According to the director, because there was no payoff in the scene, that is, the girl was not brutally murdered, the producers shortened it. In the final version, she gets in and out of the car in a matter of seconds—not long enough for the audience to say, "Look Out!"

Halloween II was a big success at the box office but nearly all reviews of it were strongly negative. In fact, the vast majority of horror films released in 1981 and 1982 were panned, including several that many of today's critics admire (e.g., *Deadly Blessing*, 1981; *The Thing*, 1982; and *The Entity*, 1982; see newspaper clipping file, Academy of Motion Picture Arts and Sciences, Beverly Hills). One of John Carpenter's best films, *The Thing*, was "reviled by critics as loathsome, disgusting and horrible" (37). Despite the backlash, horror remained a potentially big winner at the box office. While film rentals for horror were somewhat down in 1981, they climbed to an all-time high in 1982.

1983: BUST

Horror films performed badly at the box office in 1983, a trend which has continued right up to the present. Domestic film rentals declined by over 50 percent from 1982 levels. "In absolute dollar terms, not correcting for inflation," reported *Variety* (45), "this represented the worst performance for shock pictures since 1976" (see Table 1.1). In addition, none of the horror films released by independent producers earned over five million dollars, while virtually all the big-budget horror films flopped. In fact, the only commercially successful films were the moderately budgeted and well-publicized projects from the major distributers (*Jaws 3D, Psycho II, Cujo, The Dead Zone*, and *Christine*). And even these films enjoyed only a modest success at the box office. What happened?

Contrary to the reflection thesis, the sudden collapse of a genre may result from shrinking or expanding markets having little to do with actual shifts in audience taste preferences. As mentioned earlier, current studio practices dictate that in order for most film deals to be consummated, there must be some degree of certainty that the movie will perform well in at least two of the three major markets—domestic, foreign, and ancillary. That the domestic market for a particular genre may be good is no guarantee that film studios will back future projects in that genre. Thus, if a type of genre film remains popular with American audiences but fails overseas, Hollywood will schedule fewer such films for production in the future, especially if the ancillary market for such films is limited.

The sudden bust of horror films in 1983 is largely explained by the perceived failure of the genre overseas two years earlier and Hollywood's subsequent decision to start pulling out of horror. This decision is reflected in the relatively few number of American-made horror films that went into production in 1982—less than half the figure for 1981 (see Table 1.2). Also note in Table 1.2 that the decline in the production of foreign-made horror films started in 1981—one year before the decline of American-made horror films. Indeed, the 1981 decline of horror in foreign territories was interpreted by a number of industry observers as a signal to pull out of horror. "It was the overseas market that sent the signal," explained Leonard Shapiro, President of Shapiro Entertainment, who during the early 1980s was vice-president of film acquisitions and marketing services at Avco Embassy. "That market dried up six months before the U.S. market did. So the writing was definitely on the wall that the making of horror film deals was in for a slow-down period" (personal interviews, fall 1981 and winter 1986).

Yet horror remained popular with American audiences in 1982. As we recall, horror film rentals were higher that year than for any other year (see Table 1.1). A record 31 horror films earned at least one million dollars in domestic rentals in 1982 compared to 22 in 1981 and 26 in 1980 at the height of the horror craze. But because of Hollywood's decision before 1982 to start cutting back drastically in the production of horror, 1983 found relatively few new horror films available to American audiences. Indeed, *Variety* (45. p. 3) reported that of the 51 new horror films released during 1983, "over half (some 27 titles) were shelved pictures actually filmed in 1981 or earlier and dumped on the market at this time." One might speculate that if audiences in 1983 had been offered a fresher product, the horror genre would have survived longer than it did. Moreover, the dismal performance of horror in 1983 suggests that genre films need to be produced in sufficient numbers in order to create a sense that they are the hallmark of a group (generational or subcultural) consciousness.

The media backlash against horror may also have influenced Hollywood's decision to cut back on horror. However, its influence was probably small compared to the market constraints described above. Filmmakers working in horror are willing to risk a hostile press. "I make films for audiences, not critics," said Debra Hill, line producer of the *Halloween* series (personal interview, Fall 1981). "It is a business. I'm not dumb." And for distributors of horror, media ads or spots are more important than reviews as a means of selling their films. Thus, the reluctance of certain newspapers and magazines during the height of the backlash to publish movie ads depicting explicit violence may have discouraged some film companies from competing in the horror sweep stakes (see 26).

IMPLICATIONS AND FINAL REMARKS

The research reported in this chapter has implications for the scholarly debate about the role of the audience in popular culture production (see 13, pp. 97–115). Are audiences active or passive? This debate is important because of its concern about who is responsible for the content and quality of a society's popular entertainment. According to the reflection of society perspective, Hollywood's audience is sovereign because by choosing the films it attends, the audience reveals its preferences to the Hollywood studios which, in turn, passively produce films reflecting audience desires.[12] By contrast, the research on Hollywood genre filmmaking reported here supports the production of culture perspective by suggesting that the audience's influence is more passive since it is filtered through conflicting perceptions of the audience's future tastes, other in-house conflicts, and interorganizational decisions regarding expanding and contracting markets. For example, early in the genre boom period we found that the secondary audience was a more important force in influencing a director's or producer's decision regarding content than their image of the primary audience. That is, more relevant than how audiences were thinking at the time of the genre boom period was how studio executives were thinking about that audience. During the making of *Fear No Evil*, studio executives acted as if they knew what the audience wanted. Later in the cycle, uncertainty intensified as it became problematic whether the genre craze would continue or suddenly bust. Under these conditions, as exemplified in the discussion of *Halloween II*, conflicting images of audience expectations emerged which affected the overall coherence of the emerging film.

This chapter assessed the role of markets, media hype, and pressure groups as constraints on genre film production. Two other constraints that have been important in the development of movie genres should be briefly noted here.

Innovations in film technologies have influenced the artistic conditions within which films have evolved. Hollywood's conversion to sound movies in the late 1920s, for example, proved to be a catalyst in the evolution of certain movie genres such as the musical and the gangster film. As Schatz (39) points out, "synchronous sound affected both the visual and editing strategies of gangster movies. The new audio effects (gunshots, screams, screeching tires, etc.) encouraged filmmakers to focus upon action and urban violence, and also to develop a fast-paced narrative and editing style" (39, p. 85). Technological innovations have also affected the horror film. Recent advances in special makeup effects partially explain why the depiction of explicit violence and gore became the vehicle for innovation within the horror cycle described in this chapter. Of course, this argument presupposes that behind the technological advances was the search for heightening the means of sensationalism.

Another important constraint, especially on long-term genre development, which has received surprisingly little scholarly attention, is the competition between Hollywood and other sources of entertainment, such as television, Broadway, and the recording industry. As mentioned earlier, Wright attributed the post-1950 decline of the "classic plot" western and the rise of the "professional plot" formula during the same period to a shift in popular ideology brought about by the transformation in American society from a free market to a planned economy. If Wright's reflection interpretation is sound, then, the TV western should have undergone a parallel development during the same period. It did not. The classical plot western remained the dominant TV western format throughout the 1960s. In an effort to differentiate its product from the TV western, Hollywood experimented with several different western formats, culminating in the eventual commercial success of the professional plot western and other types of theatrical westerns that displayed more graphic depictions of violence than was then permitted on network television. Examining recent developments in other genres from this perspective might also prove especially fruitful. Consider, for example, the Hollywood musical. Many of the classical movie musicals of the early 1950s (e.g., *Singin' in the Rain* and *Bandwagon*) glorified Hollywood as the great inheritor of the spirit of musical entertainment while criticizing other sources of musical entertainment, such as Broadway and television. By contrast, post-1975 Hollywood musicals (e.g., *Footloose* and *Purple Rain*) tend to be less critical of alternative sources of popular entertainment. I suspect that this development is in someway related to the fact that movie production since the early 1970s has become more firmly entrenched in the economic and industrial complex that produces other forms of mass culture. Showing how changes in the nature of competition between Hollywood and other entertainment centers involved in producing similar generic forms have dramatically affected both the long-term and short-term development of movie genres and cycles could open up a whole new area for future research in the popular arts.

Notes

1   Genre films depict familiar, basically one dimensional characters enacting a predictable story line within a familiar social setting. By contrast, non-genre films generally involve central characters who we relate to more as unique individuals than in terms of previous film experiences and these unique individuals progress through nonconventionalized conflicts toward a not easily predictable resolution (cf.39).

2   Consider the following passage from Schatz which is typical of this approach:

> Throughout this study we have discussed Hollywood film genres as formal strategies for renegotiating and reinforcing American ideology. Thus genre can be seen as a form of social ritual. Implicit in this viewpoint is the notion that these ritual forms contribute to what might be called a contemporary American mythology. In a genuine "national cinema" like that developed in Hollywood, with its mass appeal and distribution, with its efforts to project an idealized cultural self-image, and with its reworking of popular stories, it seems not only reasonable but necessary that we seriously consider the status of commercial filmmaking as a form of contemporary mythmaking. (39, p. 261)

3   In the past decade, film scholars have become increasingly interested in exploring the relationship between the industrial structure of Hollywood and the content of Hollywood feature films (see 1, 2, 3, 9, 15, 23, 24, 29, 33, 40). Still, the bulk of recent industrial, legal, and commercial histories of the American film industry fail to systematically examine how business and economic interests influence the production and aesthetic practices of the films themselves (e.g., 5, 6, 18).

4   Since the inception of motion pictures at the turn of the century, groups of concerned citizens have attacked the popular medium, perceiving it as a potential threat to the established order. Fearing government censorship, the film industry imposed its own controls on film content. The National Review Board, the Hays Office, the Production Code Administration, and the Classification and Rating Administration were all manifestations of the film industry's attempt, during different historical periods, to regulate film content on its own without government interference. Pressure from the Catholic Legion of Decency, for example, triggered the strict enforcement of the production code during the mid-1930s, resulting in the sudden disappearance of the then popular gangster genre.

5   As Hirsch (20) points out, the role of mass media gatekeepers is especially important in cultural industries, such as the movie business, where both demand uncertainty is high and formal vertical integration has been made formally illegal. "Cultural products provide 'copy' and 'programming' for newspapers, magazines, radio stations, and television programs; in exchange, they receive 'free' publicity. The presence or absence of coverage, rather than its favorable or unfavorable interpretation is the important variable here" (20, p. 647).

6   The basic formula of the horror film is that normality is threatened by the Monster. This formula encompasses the entire range of horror films "being applicable whether the Monster is a vampire, a giant gorilla, an extra terrestrial invader, an amorphous gooey mass. . . . a child possessed by the Devil" (46) or a human psychotic or schizophrenic.

7   Another indication of an environment conducive to horror film production is that many young filmmakers who were looking for an opportunity to direct their first feature film were handed horror projects, while veteran filmmakers who were still recovering from a string of commercial failures (e.g., John Frankenheimer, Paul Schrader, and Sidney Furrel) found work in horror. Directors Wes Craven and Tobe Hooper, who had offended the Hollywood establishment a decade ago with *The Last House on the Left* and *The Texas Chain Saw Massacre* respectively, suddenly found themselves employable again.

8   The rate of change in the profitability of horror is only slightly reduced after controlling for ticket price inflation.

9   An earlier version of this section appeared in Kapsis (26).

10   According to *Variety*, "With the glut of product on the market, and the reluctance of both indies and major distribs to hold press screenings for violent (and gory) films most national and New York publications have stopped reviewing low-budget horror pictures" 144. p. 71.

11   For a detailed account of the making of *Halloween II* see Kapsis (27).

12   A key flaw in this argument is that the audience presumably "votes" by paying at the box office. Yet paying does not tap the reasons for attendance nor, importantly, subsequent levels of enjoyment.

References

1.   Allen, J. "The Film Viewer as Consumer." *Quarterly Review of Film Studies* 5, Fall 1980, pp. 481–499.

2.   Allen, R. C. and Gomery, D. *Film History Theory and Practice*. New York: Alfred A. Knopf, 1985.

3.   Altman, R. "A Semantic Syntactic Approach to Film Genre." *Cinema Journal* 23, 1984, pp. 6–18.

4.   Ansen, D. "Trick or Treat." *Newsweek*, December 4, 1978, pp. 116, 120.

5.   Balio, T. (Ed.), *The American Film Industry*. Revised Edition, Madison: University of Wisconsin Press, 1985.

6.   Balio, T. *United Artists: The Company Built by the Stars*. Madison: University of Wisconsin Press, 1976.

7.   Becker, H. S. *Art Worlds*. Berkeley: University of California Press, 1982.

8.   Bergman, A. *We're in the Money*. New York: New York University Press, 1971.

9.   Bordwell, D., Staiger, J. and Thompson, K. *The Classical Hollywood Cinema: Film Style & Mode of Production to 1960*. New York: Columbia University Press, 1985.

10.   Buscombe, E. "The Idea of Genre in the American Cinema." *Screen* 11, 1970, pp. 33–45.

11.   "Young Mr. Lincoln de John Ford." *Cahiers du Cinéma* August 1970, pp. 29–47.

12.   Cantor, M. G. *The Hollywood TV Producer: His Work and His Audience*. New York: Basic Books, 1971.

13.   Cantor, M. G. *Prime-Time Television: Content and Control*. Beverly Hills: Sage, 1980.

14.   Cawelti, J. G. *The Six-Gun Mystique*. Bowling Green, Ohio: Bowling Green Popular Press, 1971.

15.   Davies, P. and Neve, B. (Eds.), *Cinema, Politics and Society in America*. Manchester, England: Manchester University Press, 1981.

16.   Gans, H. J. "The Creator Audience Relationship in the Mass Media: An Analysis of Movie Making." In B. Rosenberg and D. White (Eds.), *Mass Culture: The Popular Arts in America*. New York: Free Press, 1957, pp. 315–324.

17.   Gitlin, T. *Inside Prime Time*. New York: Panthcon, 1983.

18.   Gomery, D. "The American Film Industry of the 1970s: Stasis in the New Hollywood." *Wide Angle* 5, 1983, pp. 52–59.

19.   Harmetz, A. "Quick End of Low-Budget Horror Film." *New York Times*, October 2, 1980, section 6, p. 15.

20.   Hirsch, P. M. "Processing Fads and Fashions: An Organization-set Analysis of Cultural Industry Systems." *American Journal of Sociology* 77, 1972, pp. 639–659.

21.   Hirsch, P. M. "Occupational, Organizational and Institutional Models in Mass Media Research." In P. Hirsch, P. Miller, and F. G. Kline (Eds.), *Strategies for Mass Communication Research*. Beverly Hills: Sage. 1978, pp. 13–42.

22.   Horkheimer, M. and Adorno, T. W. *Dialectic of Enlightenment*. New York: Herder and Herder, 1972.

23.   Jowett, G. *Film: The Democratic Art*. Boston: Little, Brown, 1976.

24.   Jowett, G. and Linton, J. M. *Movies as Mass Communication*. Beverly Hills: Sage, 1980.

25.   Kaminsky, S. M. *American Film Genres*. New York: Dell, 1974.

26.   Kapsis, R. E. "Dressed to Kill." *American Film*, March 1982, pp. 52–56.

27.   Kapsis, R. E. "Hollywood Filmmaking and Audience Image." In S. Ball-Rokeach and M. Cantor (Eds.), *Media, Audience, and Social Structure*. Beverly Hills: Sage, 1986, pp. 161–173.

28.   Kapsis, R. E. "Hitchcock: Auteur or Hack—How the Filmmaker Reshaped His Reputation Among the Critics." *Cineaste* 14, 1986, pp. 30–35.

29.   Kerr, P. "Out of What Past? Notes on the B Film Noir." *Screen Education*, 1979/80, pp. 45–65.

30.   Kracauer, S. *From Caligari to Hitler: A Psychological History of the German Film*. Princeton: Princeton University Press, 1947.

31.   "Devil and Mr. LaLoggia." *Los Angeles Times*, Calendar Section, November 9, 1980, p. 4.

32.   Marcuse, H. *One-Dimensional Man: Studies in the Ideology of Advanced Industrial Society*. Boston: Beacon, 1964.

33.   May, L. *Screening Out the Past*. New York: Oxford University Press, 1980.

34.   Parker, J. J. "Organizational Environment of the Motion Picture Sector." In S Ball-Rokeach and M. Cantor (Eds.), *Media, Audience, and Social Structure*. Beverly Hills: Sage, 1986, pp. 143–160.

35.   Peterson, R. A. "Revitalizing the Culture Concept." *Annual Review of Sociology* 5, 1979, pp. 137–166.

36.   Peterson, R. A. "Five Constraints on the Production of Culture: Law, Technology, Market, Organizational Structure and Occupational Careers," *Journal of Popular Culture* 16, 1982, pp. 143–153.

37.   Pollock, D. "Carpenter: Doing His 'Thing' Despite Critics." *Los Angeles Times*. Calendar Section, July 9, 1982, pp. 1, 8.

38.   Rosenblum, B. "Style as Social Process." *American Sociological Review* 43, 1978, pp. 422–438.

39.   Schatz, T. *Hollywood Genres, Formulas, Filmmaking, and the Studio System*. Philadelphia: Temple University Press, 1981.

40.   Sklar, R. *Movie-Made America*. New York: Random House, 1975.

41.   Stevenson, J. "Profiles" (John Carpenter). *New Yorker*, January 28, 1980, pp. 41–42.

42.   Tuchman, G. "Consciousness Industries and the Production of Culture." *Journal of Communication* 33, 1983, pp. 330–341.

43.   "Fear 'Stalk & Slash' Horror." *Variety*, May 26, 1982, pp. 7, 36.

44.   "Incredible Shrinking Horror Market." *Variety*, February 16, 1983, pp. 7, 24.

45.   "Horrid Year for Horror." *Variety*, January 25, 1984, pp. 3, 36.

46.   Wood, R. "Return of the Repressed." *Film Comment* July, 1978, pp. 25–32.

47.   Wright, W. *Sixguns and Society: A Structural Study of the Western*. Berkeley: University of California Press, 1975.

Chapter 2

Janet Harbord

DIGITAL FILM AND "LATE" CAPITALISM: A CINEMA OF HEROES? (2006)

'Unfortunately, the only thing "late" about capitalism is that it has rather inconveniently failed to disappear on schedule.'

(D.N. Rodowick 2001: 206)

'A certain nostalgia for cinema precedes its "death". One doesn't – and can't – love the televisual or the digital in quite the same way.'

(Mary Ann Doane 2002: 228)

'CINEMA'S HUNDRED YEARS appear to have the shape of a life cycle: inevitable birth, the steady accumulation of glories, and the onset in the last decade of an ignominious, irreversible decline.' So starts Susan Sontag's impassioned, polemical essay 'A century of cinema'. According to this account, cinema and its attendant sensibility, cinephilia, are lost objects.[1] The tone of Sontag's account is stirring, mournful and nostalgic, leaving a sense of the present as simply inadequate. The essay leaves open the possibility that new films may inspire, yet such objects will be 'heroic violations of the norms and practices which now govern moviemaking everywhere in the capitalist and wouldbe capitalist world'. The valiant heroic, according to Sontag, is our only stand against a system of production that has transformed the art of cinema into a culture propelled by corporate profit, with the blockbuster film and its cynical franchise of serial films the most obvious example. Sontag's is a criticism of fatigue in the face of so-called 'late capitalism', yet notable for its own predictable narrative of restitution, whereby the critic restores order through courageous acts of commentary. In so doing, cultural criticism becomes a peculiarly protectivist practice where the polarities (of good–bad, noble–cynical) stay firmly in place. The more complex and contradictory aspects of film culture in the present are paradoxically lost in this heroic struggle, along with questions of what cultural criticism can achieve, and how it might define and approach an object of study at a moment of rapid transformation.

Sontag is not the only commentator to reach for the sententious, and nor is 'late' capitalism the only threat to cinema on the critical horizon. A similar sense of cinema reaching an end is found most notably in a parallel (and overlapping) discourse whose focus is technology. The arrival of the digital age for cinema has, as John Belton argues, been a slow inauguration (Belton 2002). Emerging in the cinema of the 1970s in special effects, digitalisation has leaked into various areas of film production, distribution and exhibition in barely discernable ways. It is only in a wave of millennial anxiety that digitalisation has come to be positioned as the antihero about to slay the collective experience of film viewing. Belton sounds a cautious note about what digitalisation may signify, but other commentators tread less circumspectly. With the uptake of digital distribution systems streaming films straight into the home, it is argued, for example in the collection of essays edited by Jon Lewis, the direct distributor–consumer relationship has repositioned cinema as an optional mediation of these positions. And with the refurbishment of homeview technologies to create an ambient viewing space in the front room (the scale and dimension of screens, surround sound, additional and interactive DVD features) the particular experience of cinema-going is potentially eclipsed. As Lewis comments, 'We can now envision a not so distant future in which we will never have to leave our houses to see a movie' (Lewis 2001: 3).

The peculiar convergence of technological and economic development at the end of the twentieth century provides a situation where the prognosis, for both film and cinema, is unclear. Interpretations of the 'condition' of filmmaking in this moment vary widely. On the one hand, there is a sense in which the transmutation of a studio system of film production into a vertically and horizontally integrated web of multinational corporations is the final phase in an exhausted capitalist cycle. In an article that echoes Sontag's fatigue in the face of such cynicism, Christopher Sharrett declares the contemporary an epoch of 'hyperinflation', characterised by 'the endless repetition of narrative formulas' which lay bare the 'wasteland' of the entertainment industry (Sharrett 2001: 319). In a further intertextual twist, Paul Arthur argues that the emergence of apocalyptic disaster films signifies 'the most resonant and deeply ambivalent expressions of the studio system's looming obsolescence' (Arthur 2001: 342). Within this genre, and this historical moment, what is most feared is also mostly vividly imagined and expressed. On the other hand, the ability of the film industry to transform, to adopt a new corporate presence, or corporeality in the manner of the Terminator, characterises the present. Hollywood as a global enterprise has, according to Miller *et al.*, manœuvred, shifting its focus from material production to virtual control through attention to copyright (Miller *et al.* 2001). In this account, the demise of the cinema and the emergence of new technologies are not threats to the industry, but conversely opportunities to permeate new markets (through the facilities of digital distribution), and engender new film cultures in the provision of software and content for homeview.

Within these competing accounts of the life and potential death of cinema, however, is an elision of the different film cultures that exist. Whilst most accounts concern themselves with the texts of global Hollywood, it is erroneous to generalise the condition of a dominant film industry for all film production. In addition to global Hollywood, a European tradition of art house filmmaking (mourned by Sontag), troubled by its dependent relationship to nation states, provides a different form of film culture. There is also a tradition of cinema from outside of the West, framed by Paul Willeman historically as Third Cinema and now marketed euphemistically as World Cinema, providing another facet. In addition, independent cinema, a convergence of avant-garde and new-wave filmmaking, exists largely outside of cinematic culture, utilising the space of the gallery and/or websites. Each of these forms of film culture exist alongside each other, providing competing definitions of what cinema is and how it can be practised. It is a competition of physical resources, a struggle over visibility played out through marketing, distribution and sites of exhibition. And each film culture connects us to a different sense of scale and space: Hollywood trades in the epic (in terms of story, screen image, diegetic world), offering a connection to a global, transcendental cinema. World Cinema connects us to the space of the nation, with fictional constructs set in recognisable locations. Art house and avant-garde cinema is often located in the realm of the subjective. These distinctions between film cultures and their relationship to space and scale are crude mappings, which are in many instances more nuanced and complex. Yet in posing questions about change, the concept of plural film cultures offers a schematic way of thinking about individual films within specific traditions, and of film cultures acting interrelationally.

This chapter provides an analysis of how digital technology has been used variously to further the distinctions between film cultures, to emphasise particular features and further demarcate cinematic traditions. Here, technology is precisely not a determining force inevitably operating on film, nor a temporal marker that spells the end of cinema. Rather, digital technology is more usefully envisaged as part of the material condition of cinema that affords opportunities for innovation. In a climate in which the new and the distinct are key factors in a competitive marketplace, digitalisation facilitates the development of film cultures as different from one another. The demarcation of difference most obviously resides in the film text itself, and what follows is an analysis of film cultures and their relationship to change via textual features. Yet, I want to suggest that textual differences are connected to the circuits of distribution and the sites of consumption of each culture. The digital facilitates historical differences between such cultures, and throws into relief the diverse trajectories that films, as objects, travel.

EPIC FILM

To conceive of the present as a moment of change immediately creates a repression of the ongoing unfolding of time and the concomitant everyday transformation of objects and practices. The epic cinema of the present, which has attracted attention partly through its sheer exuberance of scale, was itself a reaction to the emergence of television in the 1950s and the decline in cinema attendance in the late 1960s. Reflecting back to this moment, cinema was reinvented as a theatre of spectacle in order to better distinguish its culture from that of the living room.[2] This form of cinema has slowly evolved as an experiential practice, a visceral experience of spectacle and bodily involvement. Alongside the development of the cinematic theatrical experience in the 1970s and 1980s, the site of the cinema was reconfigured through the lens of consumer choice: the multiplex pluralised film choice within one location (Friedberg 1993), aligned cinema with other consumer practices and positioned it at the margins of city life (Harbord 2002).

The relocation of cinema and the simultaneous redefinition of the scale of film are changes facilitated by digital technology. The transformation of scale has impacted on the narratives and formal structures of the films themselves: the digital has furthered a culture of spectacle and immediacy through the creation of fantastical worlds and the effects of superhuman efforts. The narrative structure is characterised by the mythic quest, a journey that involves the hero overcoming obstacles, encountering key archetypal characters, and returning with the elixir, the prize of a precious object or a metaphysical reward such as self-knowledge. As Sean Cubitt remarks of these films, 'Narrative is diminishing in importance (hence the ubiquity of the mythic quest), while diegesis, the imaginary worlds created by films, becomes more significant' (Cubitt 2002: 26). The epic spectacle film is characterised either by revisiting an historical world or creating an imaginary future, temporal locations that allow other diegetic worlds to be constructed. Scott Bukatman refers to the synergy of the science fiction genre and digital technology as an obvious partnership at a moment in which film becomes 'a multimedia, global consciousness' (Bukatman 1998: 249). Digital special effects are key to the creation of projected worlds, whilst science fiction lends a reflexive edge to the discourse of technology. *The Matrix* is a film that illustrates this eloquently, set in the future in 'a world where anything is possible' (Morpheus). In *The Matrix*, it is not only the fabric of the world that is facilitated by the digital, but also the identity of the hero. Neo is a character whose power resides in the superhuman abilities of fighting. Synthesising styles of martial arts and conventional (Western) fighting skills, Neo is a creation of digital effects, of midair kicks, passages of flight and wallwalking. As Leon Hunt has noted, where martial arts films relied on a notion of authenticity of performance, *The Matrix* offers pleasure in the performance of the virtual, the artificial, the technologically mediated body (Hunt 2002: 195).

Digital technology has profoundly impacted on the process of production, not always in an economy of production but also in large budget films, creating another dimension to post-production. Over one hundred digital artists were employed in the production of *The Matrix* to work on action sequences. As a text, it is a hybrid of analogue and digital formats, a hybridity that thoroughly permeates the film: the text is a *mélange* of East/West cultural influences, and works across the binaries of human/machine, the real/the virtual. Located in a virtual world where humans are deceived into thinking that this is 'real', the protagonists are our doubles; just as the film is a constructed world that we enter, suspending disbelief, so the characters enter a virtual world to play out the fight for humanity. Yet, despite the reliance on digital form, the film exercises a paradoxical relation to technology. The virtual world within the film (the matrix itself) is a clinical place, governed by a rationality best signified by the computer code. Pat Mellencamp comments on the metatextual relationship to technology thus: '*The Matrix* enacts the contradictions of contemporary technology – it decries the effects of technology on humanity, while at the same time deploying the most advanced technologies to make its point in dazzling, moneymaking images' (Mellencamp 2002: 85). Whilst global Hollywood constantly triumphs the human over the machine in narrative terms, its transformation of film production into a system of virtual ownership (through copyright and the integration of film production and distribution) in fact mimics the matrix more closely than might be imagined.

HISTORY IN ONE BREATH

If the digital is used to create fantastical worlds in a mythic past or fantastical future in global Hollywood film, it is put to another use in the tradition of art house film. Alexander Sokurov's *Russian Ark* uses the properties of digitalisation to evoke a sense of a nation, and equally to create a formally innovative film: *Russian Ark* is a film without an edit. Located and literally shot within the Hermitage museum in St Petersburg, *Russian Ark* is a rendering of history situated in place. Here, the museum itself is a time capsule, an ark having weathered time to preserve cultural artefacts of past ages. The film is shot in one long take; a steady cam travels through an assortment of rooms (35 in total) to return to specific historical moments. History is presented in tableau form, a series of set pieces of 'great' historical moments spanning four centuries. Unlike the epic historical film, in *Russian Ark* the individual is largely absent from the frame. We ostensibly follow a French aristocrat through the opulent halls in a discovery of all that has endured of Russia's post-Renaissance culture. Yet, character is insignificant; the continuous movement of the camera comes to stand in for an embodied point of view. This is cinema travelling, through time and space. Where montage offers and controls a range of perspectives, reactions, exchanges, *Russian Ark* pursues a slow contemplative gaze.

In many ways, *Russian Ark* has been constructed on principles opposing those of Hollywood. It denies the centrality of character, of plot, of a narrative structure punctuated by obstacles and culminating in triumph over adversity. It is a film that meanders without a sense of purpose. Its subject matter resides in a particular historical context, a reflexive return to a time that is pre-revolutionary Russia, forging lost connections with a European culture, with a past that is both buried and preserved. If, as Cubitt argues, history as a discursive text is foreclosed in spectacle film, *Russian Ark* unlocks the past as ill-fitting moments, resistant to a cohering narrative of progress or a determining social fatalism. Here, history is a series of hieroglyphic set pieces, jumbled together; the perpetual motion of the camera as it enters yet another room stumbles upon another scenario, creates the experience of history as dream. And in the haunting quality of a dream, another history is summoned by the film, of Eisenstein, a 'master' of Russian cinema. Eisenstein's fascination with cinematic form was located in the cut, the montage of attractions, a concept that was defined and redefined throughout his life.[3] If *Russian Ark* recalls the filmic past through its negation of montage, it is not simply a project in opposition to Eisenstein. Montage in *Russian Ark* is eliminated as a cut, an act of splicing and forging new relations dialectically with the material of film. Yet the edit returns spatially as each room entered situates the viewer in a different context; this 'spatial edit' requires the viewer to make links between the various tableaux rather than between shots.

The duration of the film as a single take, producing history as an act of exhalation, distinguishes *Russian Ark* from its predecessors. It also marks it out in the contemporary as technologically innovative work. Shot with the Sony high-definition camera, the F900, the film was launched as 'the first high definition Russian movie' (producer Andrey Deryabin). The F900, launched at Cannes 2000, created a shift in digital production, providing the first image to compare in quality to 35 millimetre film. Thus digital stock, like video before it, provided extended duration of shooting. But unlike video the quality of image was sustained. Recorded straight onto hard disc, there is a suggestion that the film some-how returns to a *cinéma vérité*, the product of one shoot located in real time and space, and with real actors (over 4,500 people participated in the shoot). However, in post-production the film was considerably altered with special effects: the effect of candlelight, for exam-ple, was added to scenes. *Russian Ark* was then transferred to film for distribution and exhibition.

Digital technology in this context provides a novelty, an innovative filmic experience, which allows Sokurov to make it new. Whilst in interviews the director has stated repeatedly that the project of the film was to engage with art and not technology (the computer still hasn't come up with anything of its own), reviews and marketing materials foreground the technological as breathtaking innovation. The facilities of digital production have allowed this film to define a niche in the marketplace. Receiving major funding from the Russian Federation Ministry of Culture, *Russian Ark* is a national film, concerned with a specific past and located in a national context.[4] It reflexively returns us to questions of Russian identity, culture, heritage, and to a certain extent invites us on a disembodied tour of a tourist site. The premiere of the film in Russia took place in May 2003, during the celebration of St Petersburg's 300th anniversary, with a parallel link celebration taking place in Paris. In the USA, the premiere was held in Washington at the National Arts Gallery, and was attended by the Russian ambassador. Clearly, the film had an ambassadorial role, promoting Russian culture of a pre-revolutionary era. Its circuit of distribution included major festivals of key global cities following its spectacular premiere at Cannes, including Delhi, Helsinki, Milan, New York, São Paolo, Tokyo and Toronto. If we see the film as an object with a life of its own, defined by a trajectory through these global centres, we begin to see how aesthetics, technology and film cultures are imbricated. The distinction of the text's aesthet-ics (here facilitated by a particular use of digital technology) ties it to its path of circulation and to certain sites of reception.

The use of digital technology facilitates a particular type of film culture, its textual specificities putting it in dialogue with a tradition of formally innovative filmmaking. Moreover, the innovative dimension of the film, relying on digital technology, facilitates a sense of national cinema. In contrast to the epic scale of Hollywood spectacular films, *Russian Ark* is marketable through its relationship to place and history. Its success therefore is embedded in the conditions of late capitalism where the monopoly on film distribution and exhibition dominates the market, yet a national, state-funded project finds a specialised circuit of distribution.

DIGITAL STORYTELLING IN 4/4 TIME

The final example of the effects of digital technology on film cultures comes from the independent sector, an ill-defined culture of filmmaking, which draws on traditions of formal experimentation and avant-garde practice. The term 'independent' contains many of the paradoxes of a tradition that perceives itself to be separate. In the current climate it is unclear whether independence in filmmaking is attained through a separation from state funding or commercial sponsorship. It raises the question of how culture can be independent from its material conditions of production. Yet it also signals a consciously fierce rejection of filmmaking being put to the service of other interested bodies or other uses (such as a film's relationship to other media texts or products). In so doing, it places critical emphasis on the process of filmmaking itself, an independence from concerns other than the material form of film and its practices.

Timecode is a film of four simultaneously run stories each filling a quarter of the screen. The film is given coherence by spatial location, a map of a part of a city where events take place. Shot with four mobile camera units, *Timecode* borrows from video surveillance and documentary *vérité*, yet its structural composition defies a realist aesthetic. The grammar that is forged in this film is one of simultaneity, the ability to see events, situations and characters impacting on each other. Where the conventional three act structure creates ellipses in the narrative, sustaining the linear structure of story by moving between narratives, removing the surplus ineffectual material so that the film moves toward moments of enlightenment, *Timecode* reduces this emphasis on moments of knowledge. In a chaos of complex happenings, the effort for the spectator is to track events in the various windows. The director, Mike Figgis, articulates the structural properties of the film in terms of music, a conceptualisation of the script that prioritises the synchronicity of events rather than the unfolding of story: 'I had to have four separate stories going at the same time. I decided to use paper, a string quartet format where each bar line represented one minute of real time.' Where scriptwriting manuals teach a craft of plotting, of placing events and active questions in ways that will 'pay off', here there is a sense of sparseness of structure and an accumulation of significant detail. In *Timecode* we are presented with a surplus of information and detail that culminates in moments of collision. In place of progression in the three act structure we have coexistence; instead of the sequential the simultaneous; in place of influence and enlightenment we have collision and conflict. Where the mythic quest leads purposefully toward conclusion, *Timecode* creates a grammar of images and sounds that defy clarity of purpose or outcome.

Critical attention to the innovative qualities of *Timecode* have focused on two aspects: its continuous take (like *Russian Ark*), and its splitscreen format. Lev Manovich places *Timecode* neatly into his theory of new media reproducing old media (Manovich 2001, 2002). Here *Timecode* repeats the original distinction between a cinema of spectacle (Méliès) and a cinema of realism (Lumière brothers), by providing an aesthetic of realism to counter the fantasy world of Hollywood film. Yet this conceptualisation refuses both the textual detail of the film, and the extratextual dimensions that impact on its form. To take the textual features first, *Timecode* is not an unmediated representation of reality, but a film that constructs a particular form of parallel narratives, a visual interface of simultaneous events and a sound text that steers attention through the audial. These features are not merely a reproduction of a tradition of documentary or reality TV aesthetics, but a construction of fictional worlds where the inter-relationship of people, and their impact on one another, is the subject of the film. In many ways, *Timecode* has a metarelationship to the technical means of its representation: in the film, technology is implicated in the nature of human interaction. Whilst the split screen images present a world of increasingly proximate lives, and technology masters the distances that exist, the film communicates a profound failure of communication between characters. Despite our networks of sophisticated contact, face-to-face encounters are brutal, language obfuscates rather than enlightens characters and communication misfires.

There are two scenes in the film where technology mediates relationships to obfuscate communication. In one scene, a sound device (a bug) is placed in the bag of a character, ostensibly to act as a surveillance mechanism. Her partner suspects that she is having an affair. Listening to events from the distance of her car, what she hears is the soundtrack of a pornography film playing in the background of a meeting between the two characters she suspects. We are privy to the visual information that her partner is indeed having an affair, and about to engage in sex, yet the sound here is from another film. The scene complicates our notions of the real, of what is being communicated and simultaneously miscommunicated: her suspicions are confirmed but through the relay of misinformation. A second moment of disjunction occurs in the final moments of the film when a woman calls her partner on a mobile phone. The conversation is about a reunification, and a meeting is planned for that evening. Yet her partner has been shot and lies bleeding to death. Thus, mobile technologies facilitate an immediacy of communication, but not clarity. Technology is not simply a tool for communication across distance; it creates possibilities for particular relationships where partial knowledge is the result, leading to obfuscation rather than enlightenment.

In addition to the textual reflexivity to technology, the form of the film experiments with the relationship between viewer and text. Sound is deployed in the film to structure our relationship to the text; in the cinematic version of the film, the volume of each window moves up and down as the dramatic tension rises within that particular frame. Despite the fantasy of watching four frames simultaneously, sound is used to control our vision. It is a directorial device, yet it also presents the more philosophical proposition that to comprehend the simultaneity of events and their inter-relationship is beyond possibility. At moments the film allows a leaking of sound from different windows creating something like white noise, sounds competing for a form of address and tipping over into aural assault. In contrasting moments, non-diegetic music rides over the sound from all four windows, relieving the spectator of the task of bringing together the narrative segments. Where, in the tradition of filmmaking, sound is sublimated to the image, in *Timecode*, sound is our means of orientation, of navigation. This feature of the film becomes more pronounced in its version as a DVD. Here, the potential for the viewer to select which story to follow, and the tantalising prospect of the four windows of images, is opened out. In digital format, sound becomes a selection, a choice for the viewer to make, to move between the different stories by tuning in to any of the four sound channels.

Once again, technology needs to be connected to material conditions of circulation, of the life of film as an object. The use of digital technology in *Timecode* transforms the conventional features of film: the single screen, the language of editing, the primacy of the image are conventions radically challenged. But the life span of *Timecode* also stakes out the transformation of the object as it moves through various release windows, as it becomes embedded in other contexts. In a phenomenological sense, film does not simply stay the same, but is transformed by its life as a DVD. The film is situated alongside other intertextual material, is one object on a menu of related choices, and takes film viewing into a more interactive sphere. This suggests that we need to attend to the various ways in which we engage with film in its various stages of life. To frame the debate simply as innovation or stasis, cinema or home view, polarises the field as inflexible and exclusive positions. Just as there is more than one form of cinema, there are various forms of viewing/using film in a range of locations. This pluralisation of cinema cultures, sites of viewing and viewing practices, however, undoubtedly threatens the powers of critical analysis. Rather than resort to the heroic, we may need to trace more particularly the lives of objects, and their trajectories through the networks that constrain and enable them.

Declining the heroic

Bruno Latour, an anthropologist of science and technology, writes, 'The moderns have a peculiar propensity for understanding time that passes as if it were really abolishing the past behind it' (Latour 1991: 68). Latour's project is to establish the error of thinking about change in linear terms, of dividing time into neat periods (modernism, postmodernism, 'late' capitalism), and placing objects within each historical configuration. For Latour, such divisions are acts of purification, whilst objects, such as films, are hybrid forms, constituted by a mix of resources drawn from different moments. Film, for example, draws on Greek traditions of drama, Renaissance notions of perspective, nineteenth-century traditions of spectacle. Digitalisation does not affect a radical break or aesthetic disjunction from earlier forms. Rather, the digital contributes to new hybrids of cinematic culture, which might return to earlier cultural traditions in the forging of the 'new'. Interactivity, to offer another example, is an ancient cultural relationship between 'creator' and 'audience' in the tradition of oral storytelling. The 'new' in new media is then the realisation of a particular mix of components, which in turn shape and are shaped by the particular traditions of film cultures. Rather than polarise the past and present, and to create radical disjunctions of an epic scale, our understanding of the digital is more fruitfully traced through local details of emergence, in smaller textual features and film cultures. What we are experiencing is less than a technological revolution and more of an incremental cultural shift and remix.

In place of an analytical discourse of heroism, a more useful term for thinking through such developments might be the emerging ecologies of film, a term used by O'Regan and Goldsmith to think the relationship between old and new media. Ecology suggests a shift in scale from a distant panoramic view of change, like the opening establishing shot of a film, to a more local investigation of particular forms. To think of film cultures as emerging ecologies signals an approach to cultural change that regards the object in the context of its environment. That is, the study of film in its interaction with and on other objects. Cinema is, as Sontag notes, undergoing a transformation as a set of practices (both production and consumption) that were largely set down a century ago. Yet it is also experiencing reassembly in perhaps less predictable and not totally mournful ways. If Thomas Elsaesser is right, 'the digital is not only a new technique of post-production work and a new delivery system or storage medium, it is the new horizon for thinking about cinema' (Elsaesser 1998: 227). How we think that horizon remains a critical task.

Notes

1   For further discussions of cinephilia and its significance in the end of cinema debate, see Paul Willeman (1994) and Mary Ann Doane (2002). Doane writes, 'It is arguable that cinephilia could not be revived at this conjuncture were the cinema *not* threatened by the accelerating development of new electronic and digital forms of media' (228).

2   *Star Wars* in 1977 is credited in many accounts as the emergence of large-format special effects cinema. The evolution of effects under digitalisation can be measured in both quality and quantity. Lucas's company, Industrial Light and Magic, returned to the 'original' *Star Wars* text and digitally remastered it to radically upgrade effects quality (1997). The latest component in the franchise, *The Phantom Menace*, is comprised of 95 per cent digitally written frames.

3   Eisenstein's essay 'The montage of film attraction' appears in *Selected Works*, vol. 1, *Writings 1922–34*, ed. and trans. Richard Taylor, London: BFI, 1988.

4   *Russian Ark* was funded also by ARTE, the German–French channel, Filmboard Berlin Brandenburg, Filmforderung Hamburg, among others; there were around fifty financial partners. The state Hermitage retained authorship rights.

References

Arthur, Paul (2001) 'The four last things: history, technology, Hollywood, apocalypse', in J. Lewis (ed.) *The End of Cinema as We Know It*, London: Pluto Press, pp. 342–55.

Belton, John (2002) 'Digital revolutions?' *October* 100: 98–114.

Bukatman, Scott (1998) 'Zooming out: The end of offscreen space', in J. Lewis (ed.) *The New American Cinema*, Durham: Duke University Press, pp. 248–68.

Cubitt, Sean (2002) 'Spreadsheets, sitemaps and search engines: why narrative is marginal to multi-media and networked communication, and why marginality is more vital than universality', in M. Rieser and A. Zapp (eds) *New Screen Media: Cinema/Art/Narrative*, London: BFI, pp. 3–13.

Doane, Mary Ann (2002) *The Emergence of Cinematic Time: Modernity, Contingency, the Archive*, Cambridge, MA, and London: Harvard University Press.

Eisenstein, Sergei (1988 [1924]) 'The montage of film attraction', in *Selected Works*, vol. 1, *Writings 1922–34*, ed. and trans. R. Taylor: London: BFI, pp.39–58.

Elsaesser, Thomas (1998) 'Digital cinema: delivery, event, time', in Thomas Elsaesser and K. Hoffman (eds), *Cinema Futures: Cain, Abel or Cabel?* Amsterdam: University of Amsterdam Press, pp. 210–29.

Friedberg, Anne (1993) *Window Shopping: Cinema and the Postmodern*, Berkeley: University of California Press.

Harbord, Janet (2002) *Film Cultures*, London, Thousand Oaks, Delhi: Sage.

Hunt, Leon (2002) ' "I know Kung Fu!" The martial arts in the age of digital reproduction', in G. King and T. Krywinska (eds) *ScreenPlay: Cinema/Videogames/Interfaces*, London and New York: Wallflower Press, pp. 194–205.

Latour, Bruno (1991) *We Have Never Been Modern*, trans. Catherine Porter, Cambridge, MA: Harvard University Press.

Lewis, Jon (ed.) (2001) *The End of Cinema as We Know It*, London: Pluto Press.

Manovich, Lev (2001) *The Language of New Media*, Cambridge, MA, and London: MIT Press.

Manovich, Lev (2002) 'Old media as new media: cinema', in D. Harries (ed.) *The New Media Book*, London: BFI, pp. 209–18.

Mellencamp, Pat (2002) 'The Zen of masculinity – rituals of heroism in *The Matrix*', in J. Lewis (ed.) *The End of Cinema as We Know It*, London: Pluto Press, pp. 83–94.

Miller, Toby, Govil, Nitin, McMurria, John and Maxwell, Richard (2001) *Global Hollywood*, London: BFI.

O'Regan, Tom and Goldsmith, Ben (2002) 'Emerging global ecologies of production', in D. Harries (ed.) *The New Media Book*, London: BFI, pp. 92–105.

Rodowick, D.N. (2001) *Reading the Figural, or, Philosophy after the New Media*, Durham and London: Duke University Press.

Sharrett, Christopher (2001) 'End of story: the collapse of myth in postmodern narrative film', in J. Lewis (ed.) *The End of Cinema as We Know It*, London: Pluto Press, pp. 319–31.

Sontag, Susan (2001) 'A century of cinema', in *Where the Stress Falls*, New York: Picador USA, pp. 117–22.

Willeman, Paul (1994) *Looks and Frictions: Essays in Cultural Studies and Film Theory*, Bloomington and Indianapolis: Indiana University Press.

Wyatt, Justin (1994) *High Concept: Movies and Marketing in Hollywood*, Austin: University of Texas Press.

Chapter 3

Douglas Gomery

ECONOMIC AND INSTITUTIONAL ANALYSIS: HOLLYWOOD AS MONOPOLY CAPITALISM (2005)

K ARL MARX WROTE AS A POLITICAL economist and, while neoclassical-based theories have come to dominate the world, we ought not forget the history, debates and critical tools which Marxism offers, particularly in relation to Hollywood as a textbook example of monopoly capitalism. I am not downplaying Marxism's important component in the history of cultural criticism, but simply going back to the basics of economics. The motion picture industry in capitalism is just that: a collection of businesses seeking profit and power. I shall not simply reformulate Marxist economics, but seek to position Marxist economics at the centre of a debate in film studies. Hollywood defines for our world images and sounds of ideology, class, race and gender – from the basis of corporations. And has done so for most of the twentieth century.

THE CORPORATION

Many still believe that the studios are controlled by banks and Wall Street. This 'financial control' is no longer an appropriate framework for understanding the history of the US film industry. V.I. Lenin's *Imperialism: The Highest Stage of Capitalism*, first published in 1916, is well known; less familiar is Lenin's source for his idea of financial control, Rudolph Hilferding's *Das Finanzkapital*, published in Vienna in 1910. It was the Soviet's success in 1917 which popularised and gave substantial credence to the concept of financial control. Indeed Lenin had placed financial control as one of the five pillars of modern capitalism.[1]

Marxist economist Paul Sweezy, for one, argues that in the US the dominance of financiers ended with the Great Depression, replaced by corporate hegemony. Sweezy agrees that financial control did exist between 1890 and 1930, as bankers helped to form new companies, and then moved to occupy a position on boards of directors. Financial capital became a component of a new power complex rather than simply the directing hand. The corporation with many options for raising money could operate without banks, and thus became the centre of capitalist economy. Thus Sweezy asserts, since the 1930s, bankers occupied secondary, not primary, roles in the US economy. Sweezy argues that the primary unit for economic analysis should be the corporation.[2]

Thus we need to concentrate on the ownership, management, and operation of the large Hollywood corporations which have dominated the US studio system since 1930. We can see this change as early as the coming of sound. The major studio corporations were able to stand up to the most powerful corporation in the US at the time – the American Telephone and Telegraph (AT&T) – because through their trade association, the Motion Picture Producers and Distributors Association (MPPDA), they colluded and collectively opposed all attempts by AT&T to raise prices and seize a greater share of the sound movie profits. In fact the studio corporations gained a measure of power they had given up under the original licence agreements of 1928. Specifically, the film monopolists by 1936 paid lower (not higher) prices for sound equipment and service from AT&T.[3]

STATE SUPPORT

Once the dominant corporations came to be as a result of the coming of sound, the state supported them. Through the National Industrial Recovery Act (NIRA) of 16 June 1933, the federal government sanctioned and supported the monopolistic behaviour of the large motion picture corporations at the expense of the small exhibitors and producers. Title I of the Act established a National Recovery Administration (NRA) to institute and supervise codes for 'fair competition' to promote cooperation and hopefully push the US out of the Great Depression. The administration of Franklin Roosevelt assumed that the dominant trade association of each industry would author the code. In exchange for a government-approved code, each industry became exempt from prosecution under all anti-trust laws. The law (and the administration's attitudes) clearly favoured the preservation of the monopolistic status quo.[4] The Motion Picture Producers and Distributors Association, more common known as the Hays' Office, became Hollywood's organ for self-regulation.

The Hollywood corporate oligopolists quickly embraced the NRA. They rightly saw it as an opportunity to obtain a legal sanction for their monopoly power. Ten days before the US Congress even passed the legislation, the Hays' Office offered its first proposal: pool all production and distribution under a single governmental commissioner. The government passed. Thus two weeks later the Hays' Office proposed a second plan: reinstate the monopolistic practices utilised in 1929–30, the peak period of industry earnings. Since they would be hurt by such behaviour, the small, unaffiliated exhibitors, through their trade association, the Allied States Association of Motion Picture Exhibitors (Allied States) set forth their own plan. In brief, Allied States recommended that all current and proposed monopolistic behaviour be outlawed. There was little doubt the Hays' group's code would be accepted; the only question was could Allied States exact any concessions. The struggle began in July 1933 and ended in November when President Roosevelt signed the motion picture code. The Hays' group conceded only on the issue of the ability of labour to organise. The corporations were so confident of their power they felt that labour organising would prove little hindrance to their power and profits. They were right.[5]

In sum, the US federal government, through the National Industrial Recovery Act of 1933, openly sanctioned the monopolistic behaviour of the large firms in the motion picture industry. Instead of the informal collusion which had existed throughout the 1920s, open and explicit collusion and exploitation took place, free from any threat of anti-trust action. Thus it was strong action by the state which increased the profits of the movie monopolists and guaranteed strict barriers to entry, at a point of the most severe economic downturn of the twentieth century. Moreover this analysis of the NRA hardly scratches the surface of state–film industry interaction. We know little, for example, about the tax laws, or special tariffs imposed by the state.

OWNERSHIP AND MANAGEMENT

The studio corporations have always been hard to manage. They are always profitable in the long run, but running them scientifically has proven a failure. Consider the case of RKO in the 1930s. Throughout the 1930s in a condition of receivership, RKO remained a major studio. RKO as a corporate enterprise had a reputation for a rocky financial history and failed to attain through most of its corporate life any kind of financial solvency. With the entry of Floyd B. Odlum into the corporation as a stockholder in 1936, RKO was to see what is generally considered its most profitable period – which ended when Odlum sold his interests to Howard Hughes.

To do a case study of RKO in the 1930s, the historian needs to focus upon market relations under monopoly capitalism – looking for tendencies towards maximising profits, accumulating capital and systematically avoiding risks. Changes inside RKO should follow major structural changes in monopoly capitalism: the emergence of the corporate man (as outlined by Baran and Sweezy), an elaboration of a complex authority, hierarchy and bureaucracy, the proliferation of competition in new directions – internally – as a result of a non-price competitive system, namely cost reduction and innovation.

During the mid-1930s, the chief way that RKO in particular and the studios in general found to accumulate capital, maximise profits and avoid risks was through a sophisticated oligopoly in which they agreed on the rules to keep out competition, and yet tried to outgross each other so as to maximise profits – but with minimum risk. One of the more obvious corporate internal structural changes occurs in management. Control of the corporation no longer rests in outside individuals or interests but, as Baran and Sweezy suggest, real power is held by insiders whose careers are tied up with the corporation. Perhaps Henry Ford himself best summed up this new era of capitalistic management that from 1930 on characterised the studio system:

> Modern corporation or joint-venture capitalism has replaced tycoon capitalism.
> The one man band owner-manager is fast being replaced by a new class of
> professional managers, dedicated more to an advancement of the company than
> to the enrichment of a few owners.[6]

Since the 1930s the corporations known as Hollywood have had a series of new owners/managers – who replaced the entrepreneurs who built the new enterprises (exemplified by Adolph Zukor, Marcus Loew and William Fox), and their successors in the 1930s like Odlum who tried to operate corporations like business scientists. Odlum took RKO, which was almost out of business, and remade it as a major company. Odlum was a self-made utilities lawyer whose major instrument to success was Atlas Corporation. Odlum bought up depressed companies like RKO, turned them around, and then sold out for his profits. Odlum managed, as a result, to make the impressive figure of $100 million in the middle of the Depression. By 1935, his statisticians were studying RKO.[7]

In 1936, Odlum bought a large chunk of RKO's depressed stock. Between 1936 and 1943 he relied on a hierarchy of intermediaries who operated RKO. Odlum spearheaded the reorganisation of RKO. His statisticians found RKO was a mass of separate units – mostly theatres – independently working organisations who seemed hardly to take notice of each other. RKO had always been an uneasy amalgam of corporate bosses (RCA, NBC, Westinghouse Electric, its theatre circuit) whose shifting managements had resulted in very shifting policies. The result was a vast over-duplication of jobs, executives and responsibilities. Odlum's central aim in reorganisation was to wipe out this duplication, simplify through centralisation and hierarchise the corporate structure. For example, in 1936 RKO had approximately 80 active subsidiaries and affiliated companies. Odlum truly for the first time merged them.[8]

Odlum selected a Chicago corporate reorganisation lawyer Leo Spitz – who would stay until the reorganisation had been completed. Spitz's replacement was Peter Rathvon, an Atlas executive, Odlum's chief assistant. He then hired industry veterans Ned Depinet and Charles Kroener. Both had experience in distribution and sales, where the money entered the system – as was happening at Warners, Paramount and Loew's.[9]

This centralisation and bureaucratisation of authority worked well, and RKO thrived. Like others before and after, the one area Odlum would fail to add some business science to was production. While the chain of hierarchy and bureaucracy could be established in the distribution and exhibition areas, the production department at RKO – as was the case through the corporate history of Hollywood – basically could not be routinised. Odlum then simply found a buyer, Howard Hughes, and cashed in. He also proved that while the studio system could be run like a factory, it was not a factory but a flexible system, and needed someone to innovate the system to solve this vexing production problem.[10]

LEW WASSERMAN: THE CREATOR OF MODERN HOLLYWOOD

As Hollywood adapted to the TV era, Lew Wasserman of Universal led the way. Beginning as an agent, Wasserman moved into independent television and film production and took over a whole studio, Universal, in 1962. During the following two decades, Wasserman showed the film industry how to use a flexible system of production and distribution, deal with television, and in the process reinvent itself. Five achievements rank Wasserman as the leading executive of his age.

First, Wasserman initiated independent production, based in Hollywood. As an agent he 'sold' his clients as corporate properties, and turned MCA (parent company of the Universal studio) into the leading independent producer of radio, television and film. James Stewart and Alfred Hitchcock were allied with Universal as 'independents', able to package their own projects, yet always dependent on the studio for distribution and release.

Second, Wasserman accumulated a library of film titles to then sell to broadcast TV, pay TV, and then exploit again as the home video era commenced. He even bought a film library from Paramount, and so initiated a new era in which studios prospered by milking long-term value from their libraries of older films (and TV shows).

Third, Wasserman pioneered movies made for television even as Universal produced and syndicated half-hour and hour-long broadcast television shows. With TV movies Universal became the largest network supplier of network broadcast television programming, reaching a crest in 1977 by providing *Roots*, the most popular TV show of its era.

Fourth, with his broadcast TV base providing the dependable profit streams, Wasserman returned to the feature film and pioneered the blockbuster motion picture, dominating an era from the pioneering exploitation of *Jaws* (Steven Spielberg 1975) through to the then record-setting *E.T.: the Extra-Terrestrial* (Steven Spielberg 1982).

Fifth, Wasserman's final innovation in business practice would through the late 1970s fundamentally redefine feature filmmaking. He coupled mass saturated advertising of the film on prime-time television with simultaneous bookings in new shopping mall cineplexes across the United States with the release of *Jaws* in 1975. The film created a sensation and with it Universal initiated the era of blockbuster feature film, and forever altered the Hollywood filmmaking and distribution landscape. Advertising on television became the key to turning a feature film into a blockbuster, enabling the studio distributor to milk millions and millions of dollars from 'ancillary rights'.

Jaws was not the first film sold by and through broadcast television, but its million dollar success proved that that strategy was the one that would redefine Hollywood. The Wasserman-led Universal money-making machine reached its climax and closure with *E.T.* in 1982, bringing the company that was languishing two decades earlier revenues that needed to be measured in the billions of dollars. Lew Wasserman showed the Hollywood oligopoly how to reinvent itself during the 1960s and 1970s.[11]

LATE TWENTIETH-CENTURY HOLLYWOOD

Twentieth-century cinema ended on 19 May 1999 with the premiere of George Lucas's much awaited *Star Wars: Episode I – The Phantom Menace*, a tribute to Wasserman's innovations. Two weeks before the premiere, fans were purchasing tickets – 22 years after Lucas's original *Star Wars* had opened. For his $115 million cost, producer and director George Lucas took 90 per cent of the money Twentieth Century Fox collected from box office revenues – after a distribution fee. Toymaker Hasbro paid Lucas a quarter of a billion dollars in licensing fees plus stock options; PepsiCo agreed to spend $2 billion to promote *Episode I – The Phantom Menace* and two future sequels along with its soft drinks. Pepsi guaranteed at 3,000 screens across the US to sell toys and other merchandise in the lobby. (Indeed even before the movie premiered retailers reported selling out of the new toys and action figures.) Collectors stood for hours so they could get figurines of one of the movie's villains, Darth Maul, and Wall Street bid up the prices of toy stocks. This motion picture defined popular entertainment for the early summer of 1999, as no event could. Such was the power of Hollywood motion pictures.[12]

Star Wars: Episode I – The Phantom Menace opened to a record $28.5 million worth of tickets sold the first day, as buyers filed in front of theatres, and overwhelmed the telephone, and internet, circuits. That it set such a record was hardly news; the only question was how long would the revenue keep flowing in? The answer?: well into the twenty-first century. The latest edition of *Star Wars* represented the economic power of Hollywood. With its distribution by one of the Big Six studios, there was no way – even with its $1.15 million cost, that *Star Wars: Episode I – The Phantom Menace* would not make vast profits. Theatre owners signed to play it for months; pay TV longed for its video release; home video retailers knew that it should make them profits later in the year 2000. Twentieth Century Fox, a core member of Hollywood's six dominant firms, had turned out another myth-making product shaping class, race, gender and ideology.[13]

While heralded a rich and powerful man, George Lucas alone could not distribute his epic; he needed Twentieth Century Fox. He also needed pay TV networks, and home video retailers to exploit the expected multiple streams of revenues. Prior to 1950, movie theatres were the lone source of revenues. Then came additional revenues from reshowings on broadcast television, then Hollywood added multiple venues on cable TV, and finally got a significant boost from home video rental and sales. Indeed, by the mid-1990s domestic box office takings in the US and Canada ranked only the equivalent of domestic and foreign home video sales and rentals. Domestic and foreign pay TV ranked next, with domestic broadcast and basic cable coming further behind.

But with all this additional money pouring into the system, still only six major studios gathered the bulk of it. Whatever the venue – theatrical, cable TV, or home video – the locus of the production and distribution of most of the films most people saw as the twentieth century ended continued to be Hollywood in general, six major studios in particular. In a profile of a former, powerful Hollywood agent, Michael Ovitz, Lynn Hirschberg of *The New York Times* put it best:

> Hollywood is a small community – there are only six big movie studios, four
> big TV networks, and three big talent agencies. [The people who own and run
> these organisations] talk to one another every day. They confide, they feud, they
> forgive, they do business together, they vacation together.[14]

As the twenty-first century commenced, the Hollywood film industry remained a closed
oligopoly of the Big Six – (in alphabetical order) Disney (owned by The Walt Disney
Corporation), Paramount Pictures (owned by Viacom), Sony Pictures (owned by Sony),
Twentieth Century Fox (owned by News Corporation), Universal Pictures (owned by
Seagram/Vivendi), and Warner Bros. (owned by Time Warner). All competed to produce
and release the top hits, but all cooperated to make sure the game remained only
among themselves. Who was on top which year varied, but only the Big Six premiered
possible blockbuster hits in multiplex theatres during the 1990s – and well into the twenty-
first century.

A TITANIC EXAMPLE

1998 saw a record year for going to the movies as the Hollywood industry reaped the
benefits of *Titanic* (James Cameron), which was released late in 1997. By the end of 1998
Titanic had grossed some $600 million in the US from patrons in theatres alone. So popular
was *Titanic* that it was still collecting theatrical revenues even as the film spectacular was
being released in its video versions. The $7 billion collected in theatres in the US and Canada
set a record, some 9 per cent greater than the year before. Attendance also jumped more
than 5 per cent, to nearly 1.5 billion tickets sold.[15]

The Big Six profess to bet millions of dollars each summer (and Christmas) and this
leads to intense competition between them across production, distribution and presentation.
The blockbuster system also guarantees larger than normal profits for the members of the
Big Six oligopoly as long as they are able to keep new companies from entering into this
prescribed game of blockbuster making. They alone could exploit the system of movie
making and viewing.

Indeed, the defining moment of the past decade came when Twentieth Century Fox
and Paramount delivered the much-delayed, much-maligned *Titanic*. Costing between $220
million and $240 million, *Titanic* was considered too long, too expensive, and too accident-
prone. But by year's end it already had grossed $134 million, on its way to a worldwide
record. The very executives who had earlier scaled back their spending and their expectations were now even more perplexed. As we know now, all the delay and a story often-told
made no difference. The film grossed more than any in history.[16]

In the end, the Big Six remain firmly in place, and even as new releases were being
hammered into place, there always existed an optimism based on the fact they and they alone
were members of an exclusive club – one where long-term failure was almost impossible.
Summer would lead to autumn when (like spring following the Christmas season) Big Six
executives could launch their more artistically ambitious projects. But they knew summer,
like Christmas, meant go-for-broke, when the big movie-going audiences were out there,
wallets in hand. Summer was blockbuster time. Most of the movies that would be released
in summer had been in the works for years – a glimmer in a filmmaker's eye. All desired
to make the next *Titanic*.

THE BIG SIX AND MERGER MANIA

Indeed, a new Warners commenced with the new decade of the 1990s with the $15 billion consolidation of Time and Warner, bringing this Hollywood studio into the centre of the largest media company in the world. In 1993 Viacom acquired the Paramount studios, Rupert Murdoch's Twentieth Century Fox studio expanded from his original 1986 takeover, and a newcomer – Sony – took Columbia Pictures and reorganised it as Sony Entertainment. In 1995 Canadian liquor giant Seagram bought the massive entertainment colossus MCA, and renamed the entertainment giant after its centrepiece – the Universal studio. Seagram would at the beginning of the next century sell out to France's Vivendi. The vast profits that are available from owning a member of the Big Six have driven this merger mania. New owners wanted in.

However, Vivendi's attempts to buy into Hollywood via Universal have ended in failure. Despite their size and the exclusivity of the club, its members can be vulnerable as Vivendi have now found and Matsushita before them. Thus it surprised no one that in June 2003, Edgar Bronfman Jr, head of Seagram, former owner of Universal, was seeking to line-up a team of investors in his quest to regain the assets Vivendi had acquired in 2000. As Vivendi subsequently plunged into turmoil and its share price collapsed, that deal came to be seen by many as a major blunder by Bronfman. He could – in the summer of 2003 – redeem his family's name by buying about 70 per cent of the Vivendi entertainment assets, leaving Vivendi a small stake so it could avoid heavy taxes in the deal. The entertainment assets include the Universal Music Group; Vivendi Universal Entertainment, which owns the cable networks USA and Sci-Fi Channel; the Universal Pictures movie studio; a TV production business; and a stake in the theme park business. Selling those properties would leave Vivendi, based in Paris, with holdings that include the European wireless company Cegetel and the French pay television company Canal Plus. The Vivendi story shows that despite the size and exclusivity of the club, members can be vulnerable – especially companies from other countries.

Yet with all these takeovers and changes the structure of the industry has changed little. These six Hollywood operations – Warner, Paramount, Twentieth Century Fox, Sony, Disney and Universal – still define the world's dominant motion picture makers and distributors. Although many fans look back to the 1930s and 1940s as the golden age of the movie business, in fact the end of the twentieth century was the era when the Big Six achieved its greatest power and profitability. Pretenders, as analysed below, try to enter; none have succeeded, although the DreamWorks SKG experiment continues. Dozens have tried and failed, so the odds against DreamWorks SKG are long indeed. Indeed, through the 1980s and 1990s MGM had virtually dropped out, unable to match the power of the Big Six.

THE MPAA

Business strategies came and went. The oligopoly remained. During the 1990s this six-member oligopoly retained tight and firm control. The movie business oligopoly in Hollywood was one of the tightest in the media business. Two scholars looked at the position in 1994 and concluded that 'An examination of concentration ratios indicates that high levels of concentration exist in most of the [media] industry segments' and were surely correct for motion pictures, and so this industry deserves our close attention.[17]

We can most easily see oligopoly power in the activities of the Big Six's trade association – the Motion Picture Association of America (hereafter the MPAA) – where the six deal with common concerns from rating films to smoothing the way for international distribution and protecting their valuable copyrights around the world. While critics of the film industry usually focus only on the MPAA's ratings system, its long-time head, Jack Valenti, earns his $1 million a year salary by helping the Big Six expand revenues from around the world. Indeed Valenti can more often be found abroad, far from his home office in Washington, DC, two blocks from the White House. While Valenti's total Association budget ($60 million per annum it is estimated) would make and market a single modest blockbuster, the Big Six know it is money well spent – protecting their turf and expanding their markets.[18]

They collude. The studios joined together to cooperate, even to the point of co-producing expensive feature films, Twentieth Century Fox and Paramount's co-financing of *Titanic* being the key example. In the end the game is profit maximisation. Since these are the only six players in town, the worries are not about losing money in the long run, but about maximising profits. So the studios spend enormous efforts to craft hits in their theatrical runs so that the revenues will be as high as possible, all the while trying to keep costs as low as possible. Such has been the case since Universal's Lew Wasserman pioneered the blockbuster strategy with the release of *Jaws*.

Through the MPAA, the Big Six cooperated on common issues, which then freed them – and them alone – to pursue the blockbuster like *Titanic*, which could set in motion such a vast array of profit-making deals. The revenue flows seemed to never cease. For example, because of its fabulously successful theatrical re-release in February and March 1997, Fox's *Star Wars* trilogy regained its crown as the top-grossing set of films. Add in the moneys from foreign revenues, pay TV, home video, and broadcast TV, as well as merchandising tie-ins, and *Star Wars* stands as a multi-billion property, fully amortised, with millions more expected in the future from further re-releases.

CONCLUSION

Thus through the last two decades of the twentieth century the Big Six took on new owners, or management teams, and still remained the 'majors'. Year in, year out they controlled between 80 and 90 per cent of the expanding movie business in the US and a bit less in the rest of the world. Every few years a couple of bold pretenders – during the 1980s Orion Pictures and New World – emerged to challenge the Big Six, but none ever survived after creating only a modest hit or two. No challenger has survived in the long haul, although as the 1990s were ending DreamWorks SKG was mounting a serious challenge. In the real Hollywood industry, the dozens of independent producers have no choice but to distribute their films through one of the six major studios if they wish to maximise their return on investment, and if they want the largest possible audience to see their work.

Thus in its almost ten-year history DreamWorks SKG founders Steven Spielberg, former Disney executive Jeffrey Katzenberg and billionaire David Geffen could not join the exclusive Hollywood oligopoly. Despite occasional hits like *Saving Private Ryan* (Steven Spielberg 1998), the company could never build its own studio lot and had to rent space at Universal City. DreamWorks might distribute its films in the US, but for world distribution, it depended upon its patron Universal.[19]

DreamWorks was to have been a fully integrated studio, with a full slate of movies, television, music and multimedia. But with the exception of the hit ABC comedy *Spin City* and an also-ran record division, the company is almost entirely dependent on new-release movies, many of which are co-produced with other studios. In 2000, DreamWorks had a total box office haul of $670 million for ten features, but the public was distracted by its Oscar winner, *Gladiator* (Ridley Scott). A more costly blockbuster – *A.I.*, a Steven Spielberg epic – failed. DreamWorks lacked other dependable revenue streams such as TV advertising or a film library. For DreamWorks, 'it's crucial to keep the lights on', says an executive with close ties to the studio.[20]

DreamWorks shows that a studio cannot be dependent just on making films. It must have power in distribution and presentation – theatrical and television and video – as well. In 2001, with little fanfare, Steven Spielberg, partner for DreamWorks, announced that they have renewed their distribution agreement with Universal Studios. Spielberg stated 'This alliance is particularly gratifying for me because Universal has been an important part of my life for 32 years.' While Jeffrey Katzenberg stated 'Dreamworks and Universal have a five-year history that has seen both companies grow a great deal.'[21] DreamWorks was best understood as a subsidiary of Universal, not as a new member of the exclusive studio system club.

Notes

1   V.I. Lenin, *Imperialism: The Highest Stage of Capitalism* (Peking: Foreign Languages Press, 1975 [1916]); Rudolf Hilferding, *Das Finanzkapital* (Berlin: Dietz Verlag, 1947 [1910]).

2   Paul M. Sweezy, *The Theory of Capitalist Development* (New York: Monthly Review Press, 1970), pp. 239–53 and Paul A. Baran and Paul M. Sweezy, *Monopoly Capital* (New York: Monthly Review Press, 1966), pp. 1–78.

3   J. Douglas Gomery, 'The Coming of Sound to the American Cinema: A History of the Transformation of an Industry', Unpublished Ph.D. dissertation, University of Wisconsin-Madison, 1975, pp. 406–29.

4   Bernard Bellush, *The Failure of the NRA* (New York: W.W. Norton & Company, 1975), pp. 52–5; Ellis W. Hawley, *The New Deal and the Problem of Monopoly* (Princeton: Princeton University Press, 1966), pp. 53–72.

5   *Variety*, 6 June 1933, p. 7; *Variety*, 13 June 1933, p. 5; *Variety*, 20 June 1933, p. 5; *Variety*, 27 June 1933, p. 4; A.B. Moment, *The Hays Office and the NRA* (Shawnee, OK: Shawnee Printing Company, 1935), pp. 1–35; Michael Conant, *Anti-trust in the Motion Picture Industry* (Berkeley: University of California Press, 1960), p. 85; Will H. Hays, *The Memoirs of Will H. Hays* (Garden City, NY: Doubleday, 1955), p. 448.

6   Baran and Sweezy, *Monopoly Capital*, p. 17; see also p. 30.

7   *Saturday Evening Post*, 11 June 1937, p. 34.

8   *Variety*, 25 November 1936, p. 7; *Variety*, 22 November 1941, p. 5.

9   *New York Times*, 19 June 1942, p. 27; *New York Times*, 20 June 1942, p. 8; *Variety*, 4 March 1942, p. 2.

10   *Variety*, 4 March 1942, p. 2; *Variety*, 22 December 1943, p. 33; *Fortune*, May 1953, p. 212.

11   See Douglas Gomery, 'Hollywood Corporate Business Practice and Periodizing Film History', in Steve Neale and Murray Smith (eds), *Contemporary Hollywood Cinema* (London: Routledge, 1998), pp. 47–57.

12   Joseph Periera, 'Star Wars Merchandise Launch Draws Thousands of Shoppers on the First Day', *Wall Street Journal*, 4 May 1999, p. B13; Ron Grover, 'The Force Is Back', *Business Week*, 26 April 1999, pp. 74–8; Bruce Orwall and John Lippman, 'From Creator of "Star Wars", a New Legal Force', *Wall Street Journal*, 10 March 1999, pp. B1, B6.

13   'As "Star Wars" Opens, Many Gauge Payoff', *Wall Street Journal*, 20 May 1999, p. B2; Bruce Orwall and John Lippman, 'Return of the Franchise', *Wall Street Journal*, 14 May 1999, pp. B1, B6; Thomas E. Weber and Stephanie N. Mehta, 'Web, Telephone Prove No Match for "Star Wars" ', *Wall Street Journal*, 13 May 1999, p. B1.

14   Lynn Hirschberg, 'Michael Ovitz Is On the Line', *New York Times Magazine*, 9 May 1999, p. 49.

15   See the latest edition of the *International Motion Picture Almanac* (New York: Quigley Publishing Company) for a concise review of the year for the Hollywood major studios.

16   Leonard Klady, 'H'wood's B. O. Blast', *Variety*, 5–11 January 1998, pp. 1, 96.

17   See Alan B. Albarran and John Dimmick, 'Concentration and Economics of Multiformity in the Communication Industries', *The Journal of Media Economics*, vol. 9, no. 4 (1996), pp. 41–50.

18   Dyan Machan, 'Mr. Valenti Goes to Washington', *Forbes*, 1 December 1997, pp. 66, 68, 69–70; Paul

Karon, 'MPAA's 75th Year Under Fire', *Variety*, 22–28 September 1997, pp. 11, 16; web site <www.mpaa.org> (last accessed 15 May 2003).

19   'DreamWorks SKG', in Tracy Stevens (ed.), *2001 International Motion Picture Almanac* (La Jolla, CA: Quigley Publishing, 2001), p. 639.

20   Mark Lacter, 'Mr. Nice Guy', *Forbes*, 16 April 2001, p. 56.

21   *DVD News*, 23 April 2001, vol. 5, no. 15, p. 1.

Chapter 4

Erwin A. Blackstone and Gary W. Bowman

VERTICAL INTEGRATION IN MOTION PICTURES (1999)

THE MOTION PICTURE INDUSTRY has continued to draw attention because of vertical integration. Recently, vertical integration of production-distribution and first-run exhibition seems to have increased. Standard and Poor's (1997) reported that distributors began returning to theater ownership in the 1980s, and that they now have ownership stakes in about 2,300 U.S. screens or about 8% of the nationwide total (p. 7). The possible loss of competition, with attendant problems such as higher prices and restricted choice, is a concern. On the other hand, vertical integration may involve substantial gains to consumers and to the industry. The achievement of such gains is the central thesis of this paper.

Currently, most first-run motion pictures are exhibited in theaters that are independent of the producers and distributors of the films. In the 1930s and prior to the *Paramount* decision of 1948, vertical integration was the norm. Concerns associated with ease of entry into the first-run film industry were part of the reason for the *Paramount* decision (for a discussion of *Paramount* and its aftermath, see Crandall, 1975; for a general history of the industry, see Litman, 1990).

In this essay we develop a model to understand better the impact of vertical integration of production-distribution and exhibition of first-run movies. Our model suggests that vertical integration of the first-run movie industry might result in, for example, a 30% lower admission price, which could cause a doubling of audiences and higher total admission revenue. Even if the films and theaters were unchanged after vertical integration, the change in incentives resulting only from vertical integration could cause this admission price decline. Further, the higher profits resulting from the lower price might be invested by rivalrous oligopolists to increase the quality and number of the now more profitable first-run films and theaters. This would further expand the audience. Of course, a bigger filmmaking budget does not ensure a better film. However, better writers, directors, actors, sets, or locations tend to cost more.

Accordingly, a bigger budget would be expected to increase the chance of success. Even if the gains from vertical integration were far smaller, their existence would mean that vertical integration may be desirable despite concerns about competition in general and entry in particular. Of course, many factors, such as growth of population and alternative forms of entertainment, affect movie attendance and revenues. Our analysis evaluates the effect of vertical integration in addition to (not instead of) these factors.

MODEL OF MOVIE PRODUCTION, DISTRIBUTION, AND FIRST-RUN EXHIBITION

Vertical integration

Perfect competition and its attendant marginal cost pricing would generally price products efficiently, including those moving from firm to firm as they flow vertically through various competitive stages of production to consumers. However, if one stage of product production were monopolized, the consumer would have to pay a price for the final product that is above marginal cost. If two stages of production were monopolized by separate monopolists, then the price paid by the consumer would be even further above marginal cost. Yet, if those two stages of production were controlled by a single monopolist, the price paid by the consumer would generally fall (to that paid when only one stage of production were monopolized), and the profits of the single monopoly controlling two stages would be greater than the combined profits of the two monopolists who each controlled one stage of production. In short, vertically integrating monopolists tend to raise their combined profit, to reduce consumer price, and to increase economic efficiency. However, introducing perfect competition at all stages of production would reduce consumer prices even further, and maximize economic efficiency. Of course, some vertical integration may be needed to achieve production and transaction economies in any event.

Although neither the producer-distributor nor the exhibitor stage of production in movies is monopolized, at each stage there is significant differentiation of product across the oligopolists. The means that each oligopolist has pricing discretion. Each oligopolist faces a demand curve that slopes downward, although not as steeply as it would be if that firm were a monopoly. Therefore, the monopoly argument noted above can apply. Vertically integrating a producer-distributor and an exhibitor can lead to lower prices, which would cause bigger audiences, higher admissions revenues, and higher profit. Indeed, when speaking generally about vertical integration Waldman and Jensen (1998) said, "public policy should encourage as much vertical integration as possible where successive market power exists" (p. 409).

Consequently, whenever there is successive market power in any industry, vertical integration can be expected to cause the newly integrated firm to choose a lower price to become more profitable. This does not depend on a special case. It depends only on the notion that firms seek profit and on the existence of successive market power, which seems to exist in the producer-distributor stage of motion pictures and in the exhibition stage.

The motion picture industry currently shows moderate degrees of concentration at all stages. For example, Litman (1995) found that in 1992 the Herfindahl Index for the production-distribution stage was 1600 (p. 201). This means that there was the equivalent of 6.25 equal-size firms in the industry, clearly an oligopoly. The industry's concentration suggests that these firms have market power. For 1996, Standard and Poor's (1997) reported the share of the top 10 distributors to be 95.6% of box office revenues (p. 7). Standard and Poor's (1991) noted that the top 10 released 184 films in 1990 (p. L33). The imperfect substitutability among films is also seen in the statement that "those pictures . . . are the most expensive ones and are risky because many are scheduled to compete against each other. Not all of them can be hits" ("Hollywood Prepares for a Hot Summer," 1992, p. B1).

In the exhibition stage, the relevant loci of competition are local markets that show moderate concentration. In Detroit, which Litman (1990) described as fairly typical of metropolitan areas around 1990, the top two chains had 51% and the top four chains had 71% of the 255 screens (p. 198). In Philadelphia, there were five movie chains. Litman (1995) noted that "in most localities, therefore, the consumer is faced with a handful of oligopolists" (p. 207). Further, *The Christian Science Monitor* reported that mergers in New York City and elsewhere may be limiting moviegoer's choices and increasing prices ("Of Movies and Big Mergers," 1998). There is evidence that, at least at the exhibition stage, collusion has been a problem. Collusion, of course, is more likely to be successful where only few firms exist, the prevailing situation in local exhibition.

The movie industry, then, can be regarded as a producer-distributor oligopoly in which firms have market power selling to an exhibitor oligopoly in which firms also possess market power. Therefore, vertical integration would be expected to cause the integrated firm to choose to reduce price in all cases, but the amount of the reduction would depend on the particular circumstances. Below, we compute the reduction in price and the increase in audience for a typical successful film.

One important feature of the first-run movie industry is that, at the distribution and exhibition stages of a film, the marginal cost of another copy of the film or of another seat in the theater is small (perhaps almost zero). Although marginal cost may be low, entry into film production-distribution or into exhibition does not seem to be easy. Therefore, the marginal cost pricing cannot cover all (or possibly any) of the costs. This is similar to television programming and might suggest a role for public provision (like public television), but the focus of this essay is privately funded and produced first-run movies.

Low or zero marginal cost at various stages of production in first-run movies naturally implies that competition at those stages is imperfect at best, because perfect competition suggests that price equals marginal cost. Perhaps, partly as a consequence of this and of transactions efficiencies (discussed below), even before 1948, when eight studios were competing to some degree, the industry had evolved largely into one with vertically integrated firms. The special nature of cost in the movie industry is one reason why the model of perfect competition does not apply.

The 1948 *Paramount* antitrust case (*United States v. Paramount Pictures*, 1948) required vertical dissolution in the production and exhibition of first-run movies. According to Litman (1995), the five largest film producer-distributor companies then operated 70% of the first-run theaters in the 92 cities with a population of at least 100,000, and 60% of the theaters in cities with a population between 25,000 and 100,000 (p. 199). The decision emphasized concerns that vertical integration made entry of firms difficult because it was argued, the entrant would need simultaneously to enter production, distribution, and exhibition.

In recent years, television and cable television have provided additional competition for production and exhibition of entertainment shows that are imperfect substitutes for first-run movies. This should lessen the concern about entry in the industry, but it should also decrease the gains from vertical integration. Below we provide some estimates of those gains in terms of profits to the industry and lower prices to movie patrons and suggest that some additional vertical integration may be desirable.

We regard the production of movies to be an oligopoly with differentiated products. Movies are imperfect substitutes. For example, although at a point in time action-adventure movies compete with each other, they seem to be imperfect substitutes. Therefore, each faces a downward sloping demand curve. The exhibition of movies is another oligopoly in which the products may be differentiated by content of the film and by the geographic location and other characteristics of the theater. Thus, each theater showing a given movie is regarded, at a minimum, to have location convenience to nearby customers and to have, at least in principle, some potential pricing flexibility that is not eliminated by other theaters showing the same film. Even if there were some price differences across theaters showing the same film, all audience members would not go to the theater with the lowest price.

Firms seem to have the capacity of fairly easy entry into the production of movies (although perhaps not into distribution) so that economic profits are approximately zero. If this is so, higher revenues to these producers of first-run films can be expected to generate additional or better (i.e., higher budget) films, or both, for the reasons discussed previously. Once a film is made, it is unique. Therefore, we consider the distributor of that film to be an oligopolist with a differentiated product (with very low marginal cost), and each of the exhibitors of that film to be an oligopolist with a geographically differentiated product (with very low marginal costs). Although the distributor of a given film may choose to lease to one of several oligopsonists in a local area, once chosen, that oligopsonist has geographic market power in his or her neighborhood for people wishing to see that film. Indeed, if the exhibitor is a chain, it may be the only (monopoly) exhibitor of that movie in the city. Further, entry into local exhibition may be somewhat difficult because the best locations will already be taken. Such market power and entry barriers may explain, in part, the acquisition of many exhibitors (Vogel, 1994, p. 294).

We assume that the pricing and associated audience size of one film at a theater has negligible impact on future films at that theater (in effect, zero cross-elasticity of demand) and on the rental arrangements that the theater may negotiate on future films. Before 1948, temporal price discrimination, in the form of additional theater releases of a film, may have involved significant cross-elasticity between releases. A potential moviegoer could then have substituted a second-run viewing in a theater for a first-run viewing by waiting a while. Now, subsequent releases are generally television or video rental. We regard these as having negligible cross-elasticity with theater releases because viewing at home may require a longer wait, is a different experience from going out to a theater, and may require ownership of a video recorder as well as a television. For a given film at a given time, we regard the cross-elasticity between theater chains to be essentially zero. In fact, generally, only one chain has a film (see *United States v. Capitol Service Inc.*, 1983). We also recognize that some theaters (mainly in large cities and suburbs) are more valuable than other theaters. For example, Vogel (1994) noted that, in the early 1990s, the top one third of screens accounted for about 65% of total theater revenue (p. 77).

Consider as Case 1, the situation in which a vertically integrated producer-distributor-exhibitor has refreshments in its theaters. Here, the refreshment, which we shall call "a box of popcorn" for linguistic convenience, is a perfect complement in consumption with viewing a movie. With each ticket there is exactly one box of popcorn. Imagine that a movie patron pays a single price for admission and a box of popcorn. The profit of the producer-distributor-exhibitor is equal to the sum of the revenues at each of m theaters (Quantity x Price at each theater) minus the cost at each theater and minus the cost of producing and distributing the movie. Refreshments are indeed an important revenue source. For example, Guback (1987) noted that, at indoor theaters, approximately 25% of expenditures are on refreshments (p. 64). Similarly, Standard and Poor's (1997) put the estimate at 25% to 30% for theaters in the U.S. and Canada (p. 3). There seems to be strong complementarity between popcorn and movies. We feel that the assumption of perfect complementarity is an approximation to reality and is close enough to yield useful insights.

Pricing choice in a typical theater of the vertically integrated operation at point B is shown in Figure 4.1. The quantity (at point B) that maximizes profit is the point at which the marginal revenue curve and marginal cost curve meet. Price (at point B) is then found by going up to the demand curve. If a business owner with a sense of the market and cost chooses price according to his or her business interest, then profit maximization is implied. Marginal cost of another patron includes the marginal cost of theater capacity in the long

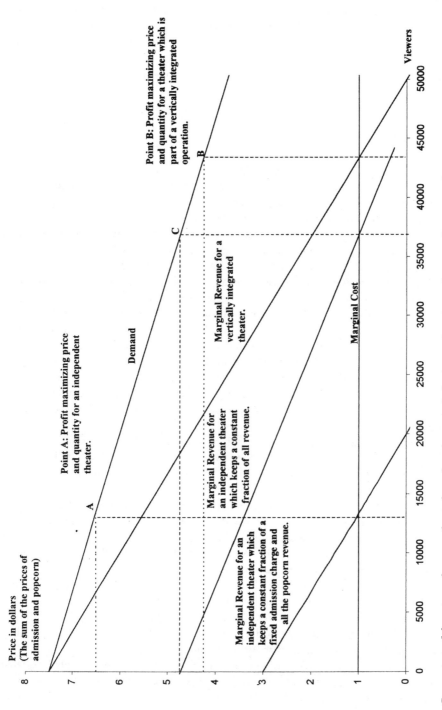

Figure 4.1 Comparison of the price and output of an independent theater and of a theater that is part of a vertically integrated operation. A general case.

run, but only the marginal cost of popcorn in the short run. Recall that with each admission there is exactly one box of popcorn. There are no additional costs of production and distribution associated with an additional patron at this theater. The demand curve slopes downward, which indicates that, at lower prices, there will be more viewers (more tickets and popcorn sold). The marginal revenue curve shows the extra revenue that is generated by an additional viewer. It is below the price shown on the demand curve because additional viewers can be obtained only by lowering the price to all viewers. Improvements in the quality of the movie or of the theater would result in shifting the demand curve outward so that, at any given price, there would be more viewers.

Independent theaters

The cost to the producer-distributor of allowing another theater to exhibit a film is small. Price discrimination across theaters is important because theaters differ substantially in their size and sometimes in their bargaining power. The typical rent is a fraction, perhaps as much as 90%, of theater admission revenues.[1] This form of rent shifts more of the risk associated with unknown revenue size to the producer-distributor, who is likely to be in possession of more information about the film characteristics and likely appeal and would seem to lower contracting costs. The theater owner may not even have seen the film.

For linguistic convenience, we have generally used the word *theater* to be a theater with one screen unless otherwise noted. There seem to be some economies of scale in the exhibition of a given movie because more seats in front of a given screen would seem to lower the average cost per admission. This would, of course, tend to limit the number of locations at which a given film could be exhibited in a neighborhood. However, there seem to be economics of scope in the exhibition of several films at a given location. Guback (1989) stated that "The cost of operating . . . three screens is not necessarily three times . . . one screen" (p. 65). We shall assume that cross-elastic effects between different films at one exhibition location have no effect on the pricing choice for a given film as analyzed in this essay.

Consider, as Case 2, the situation in which a producer-distributor contracts with m independent exhibitors who share revenues with the producer-distributor and who have refreshment in their theaters. Consider first the simple, but very uncommon, case in which the independent theater owner retains only a share of all revenues, including popcorn revenues. The profit of each of the theater owners is equal to the quantity of Tickets Sold × Price, including admission and popcorn, per ticket minus the cost of operating the theater and minus the producer's share of the revenues. The pricing choice of a typical independent theater at point C is shown in Figure 4.1. At this point, the quantity is the point at which the marginal revenue curve crosses the marginal cost curve. The demand curve at point C shows the price at this quantity. The demand curve and marginal cost curves relevant for this independent theater profit maximizer are the same as the vertically integrated profit maximizer would use if he or she were operating the same theater.

However, the respective marginal revenue curves differ. Because the independent theater owner gets some constant share of all the theater revenue, the marginal revenue for the independent is that constant share of the marginal revenue of the vertically integrated theater owner. Thus, these two marginal revenue curves cross the Q-axis at the same point, but up to that point the independent's marginal revenue curve is always lower. Therefore, the independent theater will always choose a smaller quantity of viewers, charge a higher price, and take in less total revenue than the vertically integrated theater. Because the marginal revenue is positive at these quantities, lower quantity implies lower total revenue.

Further, the combined profit for both the producer-distributor and the exhibitor that is generated by the independent theater is less than the profit of the vertically integrated theater. This is so because the profit maximization choice of the integrated theater maximizes the combined profit. With rivalry among vertically integrated producer-exhibitors, that profit might be spent for more or better movie production and for theater improvement.

Consider next the more complicated, but common, case in which the independent theater owner retains all the popcorn revenue, but only part of the admission revenue. Although the theatergoers care only about the sum of the admission and popcorn prices (with each ticket there is exactly one box of popcorn), the theater owner cares very much about the relative size of these two components. If there are no constraints for her in terms of the components, she will set the admission price at zero. Although this might be technically feasible, it would mean zero revenue for the producer-distributor. Therefore, we shall assume that there is a floor on the admission price. Vogel (1994) noted, in referring to this differential interest in low admission prices that "there have been situations (e.g., the releases of *Superman, Annie*, and a few Disney films) in which minimum per-capita admission prices have been suggested by the distributor to protect against children's prices that are too low" (p. 75). Also, producer-distributors often try to combat the practice of theater owners giving away free admission passes. A floor in admission prices would contribute to inflexible prices. The subsequent numerical example for a typical theater includes consideration of different floors and different revenue shares.

The equilibrium for the independent theater owner is shown as point A in Figure 4.1. At point A the profit maximizing quantity is the point of the intersection of the marginal revenue and marginal cost curves. The price for this quantity is found on the demand curve. The demand and marginal costs appropriate here are the same as appropriate for vertical integration and for the independent theater that shares all revenue. However, the marginal revenue curve is now lower than for either of these two previous situations. In fact, the marginal revenue curve now is parallel, but is lower by the producer-distributor's share of the fixed admission price to that of the vertically integrated theater. These curves are developed in an application below. The independent theater at point A will always choose the highest of the three prices, together with the smallest quantity of viewers, the lowest revenue, and lowest combined profit. The independent theater at point C will always choose the midlevel price, together with midlevel quantity, midlevel revenue, and midlevel profit. The vertically integrated theater owner at point B will always choose the lowest price, together with the highest quantity of viewers, the largest revenues, and the highest combined profit.

APPLICATION OF THE MODEL TO THE CURRENT MOVIE INDUSTRY SITUATION

We seek to measure the possible gains from vertical integration of a successful movie (i.e., lower price, larger audience, greater total revenue, and more profit or resources for additional movies). Of course, less popular movies would gain less from vertical integration in terms of expansion of audience and greater resources for additional movies. However, vertical integration generates the same price decrease and same percentage audience increase, regardless of the movie's popularity or the number of theaters in which it is shown. By applying our framework to the current industry situation, we get an approximation to an upper bound for the gains from vertical integration (some of these gains may be achievable by vertical contracts). For a successful movie, the current industry situation may be characterized as follows. As described below, the exact magnitude, but not the nature, of our results depends on this characterization.[2]

1.   Typical (average) admission price is approximately $5.
2.   Typical refreshment revenues are 30% of admission revenues. Therefore, the box of popcorn, has an approximate price of $1.50.
3.   Profits on refreshments (popcorn) are 50%; thus the approximate marginal cost of popcorn is $.75.
4.   Typical successful first-run theater revenues are roughly $66,666,666. The producer-distributor may get 90% of the theater revenues.
5.   Given 1 and 4 above, there are 13,333,333 tickets sold.
6.   If the film is shown in 1,000 theaters, the typical theater sells 13,333 tickets.
7.   The marginal cost of seating for a movie is $.25. This is intended to be a conservative (small) value. Smaller values for marginal cost make the independent exhibitor and the vertically integrated operation more similar in pricing and other ways. Because our analysis suggests large differences, the use of conservative marginal cost tends to understate our result.[3]

With the above information and the assumption that the typical independent theater owner is profit maximizing, we can construct Figure 4.2, which shows her equilibrium. If the theater owner generally has a sense of her market and prices according to her business interest, then profit maximization is implied. This logic, together with the above information about the typical movie (i.e., marginal cost = $1, price = $6.50, quantity of tickets = 13,333, and marginal revenue = marginal cost) allows us to infer the location and slope of the demand curve. We extended this curve as a linear approximation to make comparisons with vertical integration.

The profit-maximizing independent theater owner chooses the quantity at which the marginal revenue curve crosses the marginal cost curve and then finds the price on the demand curve. We know from the characteristics of the typical movie above that the marginal cost curve is a horizontal line at $1, and that the marginal revenue curve must cross marginal cost at the quantity of 1,333 viewers. Further, the marginal revenue line, which must be a straight line because the demand curve is a straight line, must start on the vertical axis $4.50 below where the marginal revenue of a vertically integrated theater would start, because the producer-distributor gets $4.50, which is 90% of the $5 admission price. Finally, the vertically integrated theater's marginal revenue must start on the vertical axis where the demand curve starts and must be twice as steep as the demand curve. This, and a little algebra, allow us to find the demand curve and the two marginal revenue curves (see Figure 4.2). The resulting slope of the demand curve is shown on Figure 4.2 to be −1/13333. The negative slope is a property of almost all demand curves and shows that lowering (or raising) price causes customers to purchase more (or less). In part this reflects the other forms of entertainment among which the movie patron can choose as movies become a relatively better, or worse, buy. This buyer response to change in price is also important to the theater owner who needs to use it in conjunction with cost information to determine what price is in her business (profit) interest.

The independent theater owner's equilibrium is point A of Figure 4.2. The equilibrium price (admission and popcorn) is $6.50, with a quantity of 13,333. This yields $60,000 ($4.50 Cost Per Ticket × 13,333 Tickets) in payment to the producer-distributor and, at most, theater owner profit of $13,333 ($6.50 − $4.50 − $.75 − $.25 Per Ticket × 13,333 Tickets). Because there seems to be declining average cost in theater operation, the use of marginal cost in place of average cost overstates profit in the preceding sentence. Indeed,

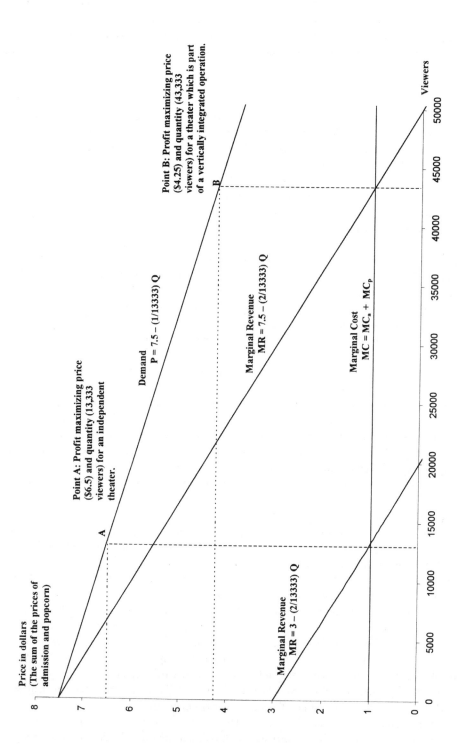

Price in dollars
(The sum of the prices of
admission and popcorn)

Point A: Profit maximizing price
($6.5) and quantity (13,333
viewers) for an independent
theater.

Demand
P = 7.5 − (1/13333) Q

Point B: Profit maximizing price
($4.25) and quantity (43,333
viewers) for a theater which is part
of a vertically integrated operation.

Marginal Revenue
MR = 7.5 − (2/13333) Q

Marginal Cost
MC = MC$_a$ + MC$_p$

Marginal Revenue
MR = 3 − (2/13333) Q

Viewers

Figure 4.2 Comparison of the price and output of an independent theater and of a theater that is part of a vertically integrated operation. A numeric example.

profit may well be zero. The profit-maximizing quantity is the one at which marginal revenue equals marginal cost. Marginal revenue for the theater owner is the sum of marginal revenue from admission (10% of the $5 admission fee, which is fixed at a $5 floor) and marginal revenue from popcorn ([$7.5–$5] − [2/13,333]Q). Marginal cost is $1, which is the sum of the marginal cost of admission associated with capacity ($.25) and the marginal cost of popcorn ($.75).

Figure 4.2 also shows the profit-maximizing equilibrium that would result if a vertically integrated operation took over the same independent theater. Equilibrium for the vertically integrated theater is shown as point B. The quantity is found at the point at which the marginal cost curve, which is the same as that of the independent theater, crosses the marginal revenue curve. This is substantially higher than that of the independent theater. Therefore, the quantity is much greater than that of the independent theater. Price is found on the demand curve at the relevant quantity. Point B is found under the assumption that the theater taken over stays the same in all characteristics except size (i.e., seating capacity). Thus, price and other comparisons are in the context of the same character of theater. The equilibrium price at point B (with vertical integration) is $4.25. This is two thirds of the $6.50 of the independent exhibitor. Theater attendance is up over threefold.[4] The theater's contribution to production and distribution costs is $127,499 with vertical integration compared to $60,000. That is a 112% increase, with theater-retained profits the same. This seems to be quite a substantial improvement. Prices for movies are cut by one third, and there are 112% more funds available for more profit, or for more and better, or at least more expensive, movies. Even if the gains are smaller than our model suggests, they raise questions about the merits of discouraging vertical integration in the movie industry.

The above gains resulting from moving from an independent theater's equilibrium at point A of Figure 4.2 to that theater's vertically integrated equilibrium at point B can be expressed in terms of the increase in both consumer and producer surplus. The increase in consumer surplus is a measure of the dollar value of gain to movie patrons resulting from the price reduction. It is not a measure of consumer savings. Indeed, at the lower prices, they have increased their attendance and are spending more on movies. Theater revenues are up. Change in producer surplus is basically a measure of change in profit. Consumer surplus is increased by $63,750 per theater, whereas producer surplus is increased by $67,500. It may seem paradoxical that prices are down and profits are up. However, for almost any product or service if prices are very high, so few units may be sold that there is little profit. Even if a monopoly exists, it is logically possible to price too high to maximize profit. Thus, the reduction of deadweight loss (i.e., the sum of the changes in consumer and producer surplus) resulting from vertical integration is the rather substantial sum of $131,250 per theater. With 1,000 theaters, the gain becomes $131,250,000 per film for vertical integration for just one movie. However, the gain would be less if there were nonzero, cross-elastic demand among a town's theaters showing this same film.

Further, in an oligopolistic industry like movie production, if each of the existing producers became vertically integrated and lowered prices, then the gain per producer would be much less than the gain for only one vertically integrated producer. Indeed, Cooter and Ulen (1997) reported a price elasticity of demand for all movies of −3.67 (p. 25). If we use this elasticity with a linear demand curve, and start from point A of Graph 2, then the per-theater reduction of deadweight loss is $64,134. This is approximately one half the $131,250 reduction when just one theater vertically integrates.

The magnitude of the gains from vertical integration depends on the typical theater and typical successful movie numbers that we employed, but other results do not. If the size of total revenues from a first-run movie were different, or if the number of theaters were different, then the $6.50 price for independent theaters and the $4.25 price for vertically integrated theaters, and the over threefold increase in attendance, would not change. However, if the share of the fixed $5 admission price that goes to the producer-distributor were to become .8 (instead of .9), the $6.50 price of the independent theater would imply a different demand curve. It would be associated with a $4.50 (not $4.25) price for vertically integrated theater and a 2.33-fold (not 3.25-fold) increase in attendance. Indeed, as the producer-distributor share falls by .1, the associated vertically integrated theater price rises by $.25. The percentage attendance increase declines until, with a zero share, the independent and integrated theater prices are, of course, the same.

If we had started with an independent theater admission charge of $7 (not $5), the results are essentially the same in percentages as in Figure 4.2. Here, when refreshment revenues are still 30% of admission revenues, our box of popcorn is now approximately $2 (with marginal cost $1), and the marginal cost of a patron is $1.25. The independent theater price is thus $9, including admission and popcorn. In the situation in which the independent theater kept 10% of the fixed admission charge, the vertically integrated theater would price at $5.85 for admission and popcorn. That is a 35% decrease, and the theater would enjoy a 317% increase in the number of patrons. The percentage changes are virtually the same as those in Figure 4.2.

DISCUSSION

Our argument that movie attendance could increase dramatically with lower prices does imply a fairly elastic demand. The estimate reported in Cooter and Ulen (1997) is, in fact, fairly elastic (p. 25). Further, the growth of television, cable, and other entertainment sources tends to increase demand elasticity or consumer sensitivity to movie prices. Additional substitutes make demand more elastic. When movies were "the only game in town," demand elasticity was lower. Finally, lower prices may take some time to induce the responsiveness we have suggested.

There is some evidence that separating production-distribution from exhibition reduced the number of films produced. This is consistent with our model. Vogel (1994) stated that, "Soon after the distribution-exhibition split had been effected, studios realized that it was not longer necessary to supply a picture every week, and they proceeded to substantially reduce production schedules" (p. 32). Television also began to be a competitive force at the same time, so definitive conclusions are difficult.

Our argument that both the number and quality of films are likely to increase is also consistent with the experience of rival oligopolies. Nonprice competition is likely to increase as oligopolists with additional profits try to expand their market shares. As Waldman and Jensen (1998) stated, "Depending on the level of effective competition, oligopolists may or may not have profits available to invest in R and D" (p. 350). Because of the fairly low concentration in the production industry and the current level of profitability, the increase in profits should promote more and better films. Profits could of course be used in other areas (e.g., cable), but as long as resources used in movies promise additional profit, the improved financial position of the integrated companies should encourage such activities. Whether additional resources will improve movie quality is arguable. However, we believe that additional expenditure will tend to do so and will certainly increase the number of films.

The model does not formally include contracting costs between the producer-distributor and the independent theater. The product about which they negotiate is unique (i.e., a soon-to-be-released movie). The producer-distributor has been involved in the whole creation process and any associated market research, whereas the theater owner may not have seen the movie. Every theater owner would have to redo the evaluation process, which would occur only after vertical integration. The producer-distributor has a limited interest in sharing only optimistic information about the new film. Further, there is usually substantial uncertainty, even on the producer-distributor's side, about how well the film will do.

A movie rental fee of some fixed number of dollars per week paid by the independent theater owner would shift all the risk onto the party (i.e., independent theater-owner) who probably has less ability to bear it, except for large theater chains, and less information. Not surprisingly, such rental fees are unusual. As noted, the more common form is a percentage—perhaps as much as 90%—of admission revenues to the producer-distributor. The fixed rental fee, although perhaps virtually impossible in practice, is much more efficient, because it leaves the theater owner with all the marginal gains from cutting price and from improving the theater.

As Coase (1960) has argued, contracts can be an alternative to integration. Long-term exclusive contracts in which the independent theaters agree to take all the movies of a producer-distributor might generate results like those of vertical integration, but might also run afoul of the *Paramount* decision. Weaker agreements would involve high monitoring costs. Chisholm (1993), in analyzing contract length of actor-studio arrangements, suggested that 7-year contracts were common prior to the *Paramount* decision of 1948 (p. 150). She also observed that vertical integration in theater ownership lowered transaction cost and uncertainty of exhibition of the film and increased the studio incentive for a long-term contract with an actor.

The transactions between the producer-distributor and the independent theater owners of a given exhibition market have been prone to collusive price-setting called "splits." This is an example of transactions costs that may arise in the absence of vertical integration. Splits refer to a situation in which the theater owners in an area agree among themselves to take turns bidding for films so that only one theater owner would bid for a given film. This may be motivated in part by the uncertainty about film popularity discussed above. Also it can be extremely profitable because the supply of already produced movies to one of very many exhibition markets is likely to be very inelastic. Splits, thus, seem to reduce the returns to the producer-distributors and provide a motivation for vertical integration.

Splits seem to have been tolerated by the U.S. Justice Department until approximately 1978. Since then, the practice has been successfully prosecuted (e.g., *U.S. v. Capitol Service, Inc.*, 1983). Ornstein (1995) argued that splits may be efficient and mutually beneficial to the distributor and exhibitors, and that, in part, they may capture gains that would result from vertical integration. In any event, vertical integration would eliminate the split problem.

A vertically integrated movie producer might not have enough films to keep a theater fully occupied. Also there may be some towns that are so small that they would not be able to support as many theaters as there would be (or are) producers of films. In either case, the theaters would probably not operate as outlets for only one producer. Indeed, these theaters would be, in part, like nonvertically integrated theaters. This is partially why the price and output calculations shown in Figure 4.2 represent an upper bound.

Since the mid-1980s, some movie industry vertical (re)integration apparently has been permitted by the antitrust authorities. If such permission were known to be industrywide and were free of constraints, our analysis predicts that there would be extensive vertical merging.

Movie rentals and movies on television are similar to additional theater runs of past decades. The analysis presented in this paper might seem to recommend the extension of vertical integration to producer-distributor-exhibitor-movie-rental operator. Some characteristics of this last stage of integration make it different from first-run exhibition. The economies of scale in the exhibition of a first-run movie in a given neighborhood mean that the exhibitor has some market power, even if he or she is not the only one in town showing that film. This market power is why vertical integration can create the incentive to lower price, which increases audience and revenues. To the extent that movie rental operators are highly competitive, as they seem to be, they do not have market power. However, the issue of availability of new popular films for rental seems to be a problem. Customers often cannot find a copy of new popular movies at their video stores. The *Wall Street Journal* has reported that Blockbuster Video, with almost 30% of the retail video sales, is moving from the existing system of purchasing videotapes for $65 from the studio (i.e., producer-distributor) to a system of revenue sharing, with an initial $8 to the studio ("Blockbuster Seeks," 1998). Therefore, Blockbuster will be acquiring more copies of new popular films. This is important to studios. The article further reported that studio home-video revenue for 1997 was $4.85 billion, compared to studio domestic box-office revenue of $3.08 billion. However, Standard and Poor's (1997) noted that "theatrical success influences a film's future reception and value in ancillary markets" (p. 15).

CONCLUSION

Our model suggests that vertical integration is likely to result in lower prices, bigger audiences, and more and better films in nicer theaters. Application of the model to the present industry situation suggests vertical integration may, at most, result in a one-third lower price for first-run movies, a tripling of audience size for the same movies, and the same number and quality, but not size, of theaters. Vertical contracts may be able to achieve some of these gains, but there will be lower contracting cost with vertical integration.

Vertical integration may lead to more and better films and better theaters, as well. This result is based on the presumption that the movie production-distribution industry is a rivalistic oligopoly in which the initially higher profit from vertical integration would be spent on films. If vertical integration somehow reduced competitiveness by making entry more costly, then these gains might be completely offset by horizontal restraints. However, vertical integration, other things being equal, does seem to offer important advantages to the motion picture industry and to the moviegoing public.

Notes

1   See, for example, *United States v. Capitol Service* (1983). The Court noted, "Typical percentage rental terms are calculated on the basis of '90/10 versus the floor.' Under this formula, the exhibitor pays to the distributor for each week of playtime the higher of (a) 90% of the gross box office income after the theater's 'house allowance' has been deducted, or (b) a percentage of the gross box office without any deductions (the 'floors')" (p. 137). Sometimes exhibitors must pay guarantees. This transfers some risk to the exhibitor. The Academy of Motion Pictures's reference department in Beverly Hills, California, suggests that the rent might be as high as 90% (personal communication, February 6, 1995).

2   There is enormous variation in the success of first-run movies. Cross-sectional estimation (across films) of demand relationships is complicated by the fact the demand curve for a hit film is shifted to the right, or rotated to the right, by perhaps 100 times that of a flop movie. We have chosen to analyze a typical hit movie in order to get some notion of the magnitude of gains that could occur from vertical integration. Of course, variation in success also implies risk. Future research might formally model risk in this context. We discuss risk below.

3   For estimates for the price and revenues for a typical movie, see Guback (1987), Vogel (1994), U.S. Department of Commerce (1992), and Standard and Poor's (1991, 1993, 1997). For example, the Department of Commerce reported an average ticket price of $4.75 in 1990. Standard and Poor's

(1997) suggested an average ticket price of $4.55 for 1997 (p. 1). Guback referenced refreshment share and margins. Standard and Poor's showed that the average revenue for each of the top 25 movies in 1990 was $94 million. We took $66.66 million (approximately two thirds), as a rough estimate of first-run exhibition revenues. Standard and Poor's (1997) reported that 1996 films financed by major distributors averaged approximately $40 million in production cost and $20 in distribution and advertising cost (p. 15). In 1996 there were 421 new releases by U.S. film companies (DRI/McGraw-Hill, Standard and Poor's, U.S. Department of Commerce/International Trade Administration, 1998, pp.32–33). The Capitol case cited above and Standard and Poor's (1997) indicated that producer-distributors often get 90% of marginal theater revenues. The Academy of Motion Pictures's reference department suggested that, at most, a 90% share for hit movies. Standard and Poor's (1993) reported that the average movie in 1992 earned revenues of about $11 million (p. L20).

4   If Graph 2 were constructed for the average film (one-sixth revenues) rather than for the typical successful film, the horizontal axis (i.e., Quantity) would have each demarcation labeled with numbers one-sixth as big. The prices and percentage quantity increases would remain the same.

References

Blockbuster seeks a new deal with Hollywood. (1998, March 25). *Wall Street Journal*, pp. B1, B6.

Chisholm, D. C. (1993). Asset specificity in motion-picture contracts. *Eastern Economic Journal*, *19*, 113–155.

Coase, R. (1960, October). The problem of social cost. *Journal of Law and Economics*, *3*, 1–44.

Cooter, R., & Ulen, T. (1997). *Law and economics*. Reading, MA: Addison-Wesley.

Crandall, R. W. (1975). The postwar performance of the motion-picture industry. *Antitrust Bulletin*, *20*(2), 49–88.

DRI/McGraw-Hill, Standard and Poor's, and U.S. Department of Commerce/International Trade Administration. (1998). Entertainment: Motion pictures. *U.S. Industry and Trade Outlook '98*, 32–3, 32–4. New York: McGraw-Hill.

Guback, T. (1987). The evolution of motion picture business in the 1980s. *Journal of Communication*, *37*(2), 60–77.

Hollywood prepares for a hot summer. (1992, April 8). *Wall Street Journal*, p. B1.

Litman, B. R. (1990). The motion picture entertainment industry. In W. Adams (Ed.), *The structure of American industry* (pp. 183–216). New York: Macmillan.

Litman, B. R. (1995). Motion picture entertainment. In W. Adams & J. Brock (Eds.), *The structure of American industry* (9th ed., pp. 197–221). Englewood Cliffs, NJ: Prentice Hall.

Of movies and big mergers. (1998, April 16). *Christian Science Monitor*, pp. 1, 18.

Ornstein, S. (1995). Motion picture distribution, film splitting and antitrust policy. *Hastings Communications and Entertainment Law Journal*, *17*, 415–444.

Standard and Poor's. (1991, March 14). Leisure time: Film entertainment. *Standard and Poor's Industry Surveys*, pp. L29–L36.

Standard and Poor's. (1993, March 11). Leisure time: Film entertainment. *Standard and Poor's Industry Surveys*, pp. L17–L20.

Standard and Poor's. (1997, October 2). Movies & home entertainment. *Standard and Poor's Industry Surveys*, pp. 1–32.

United States v. Capitol Service, Inc. 568 F. Supp. 134 (1983).

United States v. Paramount Pictures, 334 U.S. 131 (1948).

U.S. Department of Commerce (1992). Entertainment. In *U.S. Industrial Outlook 1992* (pp. 31–1–31–6). Washington, DC: U.S. Government Printing Office.

Vogel, H. L. (1994). *Entertainment industry economics*. New York: Cambridge University Press.

Waldman, D. E., & Jensen, E. (1998). *Industrial organization theory and practice*. Reading, MA: Addison–Wesley.

1B ARTISTS

Chapter 5

Denise D. Bielby and William T. Bielby

WOMEN AND MEN IN FILM: GENDER INEQUALITY AMONG WRITERS IN A CULTURE INDUSTRY (1996)

IN PREVIOUS RESEARCH, WE (Bielby and Bielby 1992) documented how unstructured labor market arrangements in the television industry generate a process of "continuous disadvantage," whereby women television writers are disadvantaged relative to men throughout their careers, regardless of their previous accomplishments in the industry. This model proved to be a better representation of the data than the model of "cumulative disadvantage," whereby men and women begin their careers with more or less similar opportunities, but women encounter a "glass ceiling," falling further and further behind their male counterparts over time. That research also rejected the hypothesis that the level of gender inequality among writers in the television industry had declined throughout the 1980s.

In our 1992 article, we argued that five distinctive features of the organization of production sustained this pattern of gender inequality among television writers: (1) the employment relation is based on short-term contracting for the duration of a specific project; (2) the quality and commercial viability of the completed work cannot be unambiguously evaluated based on technical and measurable features of the finished product, but it can only be evaluated post hoc; (3) career success is largely dependent on a writer's current reputation among a small group of "brokers" who match creative talent with commercial projects; (4) reputations are based on perceptions of an artist's success in currently fashionable styles or genres; and (5) the overwhelming majority of those who make decisions about matching creative talent to commercial projects are men. Given the skewed sex-ratio, women's marginal location within networks of decision makers, and the high levels of ambiguity, risk, and uncertainty surrounding employment decisions, social similarity and gender stereotypes are likely to have a strong impact on employment decisions. Indeed, empirical results of that study show that compared to male television writers of similar age, experience, and track record, women earn 11 to 25 percent less throughout their careers (Bielby and Bielby 1992).

This research examines whether a similar pattern of gender inequality exists among writers for feature film. There are good reasons to expect that the findings for television will apply to the feature film industry as well. The overall structure of the two industries is quite similar—what DiMaggio (1977) calls "centralized brokerage administration" and Faulkner and Anderson (1987) describe as "recurrent short-term contracting." Each of the five distinctive characteristics of television production apply to feature film as well.

However, there are differences between film and television production in their organization and business contexts, and some of these differences may be of consequence for labor market dynamics of writers and other "culture workers." First, the levels of ambiguity, risk, and uncertainty facing producers in feature film are substantially greater in the film industry than in television. Production costs are many times higher than in television, and predicting which film projects will become hits is much more difficult than in television. In their study of the film industry, Baker and Faulkner (1991, 286) observe, "Filmmaking is a tenuous enterprise. It occurs in a business and technical environment characterized by high stakes, risk, and uncertainty. It requires substantial investments of financial capital for properties, artists, and support personnel. And it entails high personal and career risks."

Compared to television network programmers, risk-adverse production executives in feature film might be more likely to imitate prior successful projects and to rely on rules of thumb that tend to typecast women writers. For example, no one wants to be the first to develop a script from a woman writer for a big-budget action-adventure film. In a recent interview, Callie Khouri, who won an Academy Award for her script for *Thelma & Louise*, put it this way:

> There is a certain stigma, I think that there is a set of expectations that women write a certain type of picture, so you don't look for an action movie that's written by a woman. You don't look for a thriller. There are certain types of movies that you don't expect to be written by a woman. People still call things "women's pictures." If it has a female audience then there is always a somewhat derogatory connotation to a so-called woman's picture. (Danquah 1994)

Carolyn Shelby who wrote *Class Action* has expressed similar sentiments:

> You come in with an action project, and they see you're a woman, and you can see it's not something they're comfortable with. They're thinking "small picture" rather than *Terminator 2* when you're sitting there talking to them. (Voland 1992)

Second, the level of uncertainty facing the writers themselves is greater in feature film than in television. Several thousand episodes of network, cable, and syndicated television series are produced in the United States each year, and the writers on the staff of a successful series can generally count on being employed for an entire season if not the series' entire run. In contrast, a film project is a one-shot deal, and only about 300 feature films are released domestically in the United States each year. At the same time, tens of thousands of individuals aspire to careers as screenwriters, and they register about 36,000 scripts or script treatments with the Writers Guild of America each year. In short, the labor market for film appears much more competitive than that for television writers, and as a result the barriers faced by women might be more formidable as well.

Third, in television, successful writer-producers (also known as "hyphenates") can become powerful brokers in the industry, gaining autonomy in running their own shows and negotiating long-term development deals. Women hyphenates such as Diane English, Linda

Bloodworth-Thomason, Beth Sullivan, and Marcy Carsey have joined the ranks of male writer-producers such as Steven Bochco, Aaron Spelling, and Stephen J. Cannell in the industry elite. As research for the Writers Guild of America, West, shows, when women become writer-producers of ongoing series, the number of women writers employed increases substantially (Bielby and Bielby 1987, 1989, 1993). In feature film, in contrast, very few women have joined the ranks of top writers during the same period. Moreover, elite film writers might be very well paid, but unless they also direct, they have virtually no say in the production process. In the absence of arranging a writer-director hyphenate combination for film projects, writers find themselves pitted against directors over creative control of a film's final form (Baker and Faulkner 1991; Cox 1995; Robb 1994).

Although the factors noted above are likely to generate greater gender inequality in feature film than in television, other differences between the two industries suggest a lesser degree of typecasting by gender of screenwriters compared to television writers. First, genre categories are much more highly institutionalized in television than in feature film. Although film genres such as "action-adventure," "romantic comedy," and "adult drama" are widely recognized, television genres are much more highly institutionalized in the organizational structures of the studios and networks. For example, each of the broadcast networks has separate development divisions for drama, comedy, daytime, and so on, whereas genre distinctions are not built into the film divisions of the major studios (Bielby and Bielby 1994). In television, female executives are likely to be segregated into divisions dealing with female-typed genres (e.g., television movies and miniseries, children's programming, daytime programming), whereas—at least officially—a woman vice president of production at a film studio is not charged with working within a specific film genre. And by 1990, women accounted for nearly one third of the executives in the ranks of vice president or higher in the production divisions of the major film studios (Bernstein 1990).

Second, in television, advertising revenues are sold on the basis of the demographic composition of the audience. In television, *who* is watching can be as important as *how many* people are watching. For example, an action-adventure series in development at a network might be targeted to an 18- to 35-year-old male audience, and advertising rates might be set based on a network guarantee regarding the size of the audience within that age/gender group. In contrast, a film's profitability depends on the number of people who pay to view it. Although the film might be developed to appeal to a younger male audience, a ticket purchased by a 45-year-old woman earns the studio the same amount as one bought by a 19-year-old man. Thus, the less intense age/gender targeting of film audiences may reduce the incentive to typecast writers by gender. On the other hand, there is a tremendous amount of typecasting of "on screen" talent in feature film, where there is a widely held belief that a female star cannot successfully carry a big budget film. In the words of one studio head:

> It's almost impossible for a female to "open" a movie now. It just doesn't work. People don't come. A movie like *Ghost* succeeded conceptually, on its own terms, not because of Demi Moore. (Dutka 1990, 8).

Thus, it is reasonable to assume that the often explicit devaluation of female talent on screen carries over to a devaluation of women's contributions to film off screen.

Overall, the similarities between television and feature film are probably more consequential than the differences. Although distribution channels differ, the same large corporations—the major studios—dominate production in both TV and film, and with the advent of new technologies of production and distribution, the distinctions between the two sectors of the entertainment industry are increasingly blurred. To a significant extent, the two sectors draw on the same pool of writers; in any given year, about one third of those writing for feature film are also employed in television. Thus, we expect the structure and dynamics of labor markets in the two sectors to be largely similar, although on balance, if there is a detectable difference in the levels of gender inequality, we expect it to be somewhat larger in film than in television.

Below, we first present an overview of women writers' participation in feature film from the silent era to the present, relying on both historical scholarship and quantitative data from the membership files of the Writers Guild of America, West. Then we describe the data, measures, models, and hypotheses used to assess alternative models of gender inequality in labor market dynamics among film writers. Following the presentation of our results, we discuss the implications of our findings for gender inequality in the mass media and in culture industries more generally.

WOMEN WRITERS' PARTICIPATION IN FEATURE FILM FROM THE SILENT ERA TO THE AGE OF THE BLOCKBUSTER

Film writing is one of the few professional occupations in which a labor force with a substantial female presence has been displaced by men. Many of the most successful early scenarists, as screenwriters of the silent film era were called, were women (Francke 1994; McCreadie 1994). The highest-paid writer of the 1920s was Frances Marion, whose silent credits include *Humoresque, Stella Dallas,* and *Love,* and who went on to write the sound films *The Champ* and *Dinner at Eight* (Schwartz 1982). Although definitive statistics are not available, estimates of the gender composition of screenwriters during the silent era (from the early 1900s to 1927) range from 50 percent (Martin and Clark 1987) to 90 percent (McCreadie 1994), and it is generally agreed that women screenwriters played a major role in establishing the narrative form and conventions of the film scenario (Francke 1994).

The process whereby screenwriting was transformed from a profession with substantial opportunities for women to one that became male dominated appears similar to that described by Tuchman (1989) in her account of the masculinization of authorship of the Victorian novel. Tuchman's evidence indicates that before 1840 at least half of all novelists were women. She argues that the occupation of novelist was a relatively lucrative "empty field" for woman of the educated classes at this time, albeit one with relatively low prestige. Over the next half century, men "invaded" the empty field, drawn to the profession as demand increased and the field became more lucrative. Moreover, the centralization and rationalization that accompanied the industrialization of the publishing industry placed men in control of production and distribution. The transformation of authorship into "men's work" was legitimated ideologically in the late nineteenth and early twentieth century, as the narrative form of the novel was redefined as a valued cultural object, and a critical double standard was applied that valued the contributions of male novelists over women.

Tuchman suggests that the same process of invasion, redefinition, and institutionalization should be apparent in other professions that experience masculinization, even when the transformation occurs rapidly. The transformation of screen-writing in the late 1920s and early 1930s appears to fit this pattern. With the advent of sound movies in 1927, those with a talent for storytelling—playwrights, novelists, journalists—were recruited to Hollywood in large numbers (Beranger 1950; Schwartz 1982). The Depression accelerated the trend toward consolidation of production that began in the 1920s, so that by the early 1930s the financing, production, distribution, and exhibition of feature films was dominated by eight vertically integrated corporations: Warner Brothers, RKO, Twentieth Century Fox, Paramount, MGM, Universal, Columbia, and United Artists (Stanley 1978). This consolidation was accompanied by a rationalization of production, including writing. Under the studio system, the role of the scenarist had become elaborated, subdivided, and formalized (Staiger 1983). Within the story department of each studio, a story editor had responsibility for identifying viable literary properties for producers and would supervise a dozen or so script readers who would evaluate books, plays, stories, or treatments for their cinematic potential. Studios generally relied on their own staff of screenwriters to write the actual scripts, with others such as continuity clerks and script clerks doing much of the routine work in processing the filming of a script (Work Projects Administration, American Guide Series 1941).

Some of the more established women writers of the silent era continued to thrive under the studio system (Francke 1994; McCreadie 1994; Schwartz 1982). Among them were Frances Marion, who was a founding member and first vice president of the Screen Writers Guild (the predecessor of the Writers Guild of America), and Anita Loos, whose credits range from *Intolerance* (1916) to *Gentlemen Prefer Blondes* (1953). However, the male "invasion" of the profession was an accomplished fact by the mid-1930s. Membership statistics from the Writers Guild of America, West, show that women accounted for less than 15 percent of those working as screenwriters in the late 1930s (see Figures 5.1 and 5.2). In sharp contrast to the early years of the industry—when the lines dividing production roles were fluid and women moved with relative ease across the tasks of scenarist, editor, director, and producer—under the studio system, women writers were likely to be assigned to administrative or support roles such as reader or script supervisor (Francke 1994) or as "corpse rougers" who "brightened the dialogue of other people's scripts" (Mary McCall, Jr., quoted in McCreadie 1994, 111).

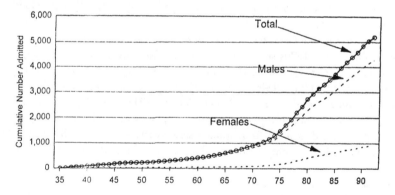

Figure 5.1 Cumulative number of screenwriters admitted to WGA, West, by gender, 1935–1992.

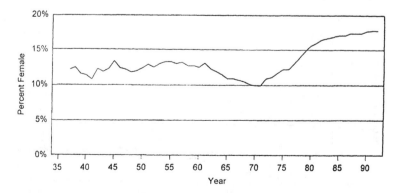

Figure 5.2 Gender composition of the cumulative membership, screenwriter members of the WGA, West, 1936–1992.

The institutionalization of the male invasion of the screenwriting profession was legitimated by the typecasting of women writers. Women's work on story adjustments, scene polishes, and dialogue rewrites was regarded as the "tyranny of the woman writer" by male writers of the time (Frances Marion, cited by McCreadie 1994, 28). Studio chiefs believed women were especially well suited for writing for "women's films," for writing dialogue for female stars, and for infusing the "women's angle" into films more generally (Francke 1994). Of course, the reality is quite different; women screen writers have been associated with successful scripts in every film genre, and many "women's films" have been scripted by men.[1] But the ideology that women's talents are best suited for women's themes or female stars (an ideology shared by many women writers themselves) legitimates the notion that outside of narrow genres and specialties, screenwriting is men's work.

With men's dominance of screenwriting fully institutionalized, the decline of the studio system and the trend toward independent production during the 1950s had little impact on women's representation among screenwriters. From the 1950s through the early 1960s, women continued to constitute about 12 to 13 percent of those entering the screenwriting profession. Perhaps not coincidentally, the decline in women's representation among new screenwriters from 1962 through 1971 to its lowest level in the history of the industry (see Figure 5.3) corresponds exactly with the era feminist film critic Molly Haskell (1987, 323) calls "the most disheartening in screen history" regarding the portrayals and prominence of women.

Not until the early 1970s is there a noticeable increase in women's representation among those entering the profession: from 1972 to the present, women have accounted for about one in five screenwriters qualifying for membership in the Writers Guild (Figure 5.3). It is not clear what accounted for the modest upturn in women's representation in the early 1970s. On the one hand, feminist themes were beginning to appear in commercially successful films of the 1970s such as *Klute* (1971), *Alice Doesn't Live Here* (1974), *A Woman Under the Influence* (1974), and *An Unmarried Woman* (1977),[2] and women in the industry began organizing to advance their interests through groups such as Women in Film and the Women's Committee of the Writers Guild of America. These developments may have both encouraged talented women to pursue careers in the industry and persuaded producers to be more open toward material from women screenwriters. On the other hand, the early 1970s also marked the beginning of the "blockbuster" era, which greatly increased the financial risk involved in pursuing projects with potential box office sales in excess of $100 million (Baker and Faulkner 1991). Increasingly, the "blockbuster" mentality encouraged producers to seek out established directors, writers, and actors who have track records of consistent success and forgo serious consideration of writers who seek to transcend proven

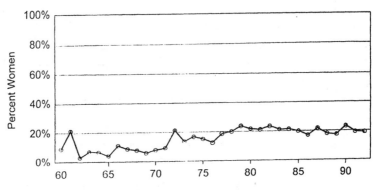

Figure 5.3 Women as a percentage of screenwriters admitted to WGA, West, annually, 1960–1992.

formulae and established genres. As a result, the salaries of a small group of elite screen-writers have been bid up to levels in excess of $750,000 per film, while the gap in career trajectories between this group and other screenwriters widens. *Daily Variety* analyst Paul F. Young observes:

> Why the red carpet? Studio executives and agents unanimously agree that a writer can't "open" a film like a star. But veteran agents and producers alike say the trend to shop at Tiffany reflects the paranoia felt by studio executives who don't read much themselves, or who fear rocking the corporate boat. Says one high-profile producer, "I can't get the studio to pay a writer *less* than $750,000. It makes them nervous." Another producer with a studio deal explains, "They think an expensive writer will get it right the first time. And if he doesn't, the executive has protected himself by using a pre-approved writer" (Young 1995, 5, 18).

Our quantitative data on film writers' employment and earnings cover the years 1982 to 1992. This period is of interest because of potentially countervailing forces affecting the careers of women writers. On the one hand, by the mid-1980s the talent guilds for writers, directors, and actors were issuing statistical studies documenting women's underrepresenta-tion in the industry, and the industry press began giving widespread coverage to the issue of gender discrimination. And as noted above, during the same period, women were finally moving into the top executive ranks of the motion picture studios, paralleling women's gains in management in other sectors of the economy. On the other hand, men's dominance of screenwriting (and all other aspects of the industry) had been fully institutionalized for half a century, and the business environment of the period appears not to be conducive to innova-tive ways of reaching out to groups previously excluded by the industry. Given these countervailing if not contradictory trends, it is not surprising that many feminist film analysts look on the past decade as "the age of ambivalence" (Haskell 1987; also see Francke 1994). Our data allow us to bring systematic quantitative evidence to bear on the question of whether efforts to challenge men's institutionalized dominance are beginning to create new opportunities for women writers.

An overview of trends in employment and earnings of screenwriters suggests that women writers are encountering an impenetrable glass ceiling in the era of the blockbuster. From 1982 through 1992 there was no perceptible change in the gender composition of those employed in screenwriting; women accounted for about 18 percent of employed screenwriters throughout this period. (In comparison, according to 1990 census statistics, women account for 49.5 percent of all authors in the United States.) Figure 5.4 shows gender differences in earnings trends over the same period. While the gender gap in median earnings closed modestly from the mid-1980s to the early 1990s, in both absolute and relative terms the gap at the 90th percentile is significantly greater in the early 1990s than it was in 1982. In other words, among the industry's most successful screenwriters, women are falling further behind their male counterparts.

These descriptive statistics tell just part of the story. For example, one cannot tell from these statistics whether the closing of the gender gap in median earnings is simply attribut-able to the increasing levels of experience of women screenwriters. Nor can one compare the career trajectories of men and women screenwriters who enter the industry at the same time. With multivariate analyses we can explore the dynamics of disadvantage faced by women film writers that generate the overall trends. How great is the disadvantage faced by women writers—in terms of employment and earnings—compared to men with similar qualifications and track records? Do labor market dynamics generate a pattern of

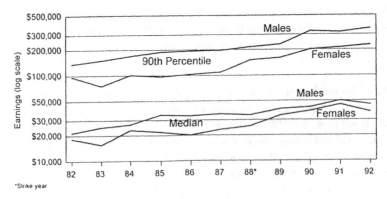

Figure 5.4 Gender differences in earnings among employed screenwriters at median and at 90th percentile, 1982–1992.

"cumulative disadvantage" whereby men and women begin their careers with more or less similar opportunities, but with women subsequently encountering a "glass ceiling" as the careers of their male counterparts take off? And finally, is the magnitude of women's disadvantage declining over time as more women move into positions of power and authority in the industry?

DATA, MEASURES, AND MODELS

The data for our study describe the employment and earnings trajectories of 4,093 screen-writers who were employed at least once during the period from 1982 through 1992. These data are from the employment and membership records of the Writers Guild of America, West (WGAW). Each quarter, guild members report earnings from all employment covered by the "MBA," the WGAW's major collective bargaining agreement with producers. Because virtually all active producers are signatory to the MBA, these earnings declarations cover nearly all writing for feature films produced in Hollywood.

In their earnings declarations, members report total earnings; employing organization; type of employment; whether the writing is for screen, television, radio, or pay-TV; the title of the film, series, or program; and its length. In most cases, writers also report whether they worked on a first draft, polish, final draft, revision, and so forth.

Our model is a pooled cross-section time series specification of the form:

$$Y_{ict} = a + b_1 X_i + b_2 W_{it} + Z_c + d_t + e_{ict} \qquad (1)$$

where Y_{ict} is log earnings for the ith individual in cohort c in year t, and cohort is defined as year admitted to membership in the Writers Guild of America. Attributes of individuals that do not vary over time (e.g., minority status) are included in X_i and individual traits that vary over time (e.g., years of experience) are included in W_{it}. The term Z_c captures effects on earnings that are unique to a specific cohort over time, while d_t captures year-specific effects on earnings. The disturbance, e_{ict} is assumed to have a mean of zero and constant variance and to be uncorrelated with the other independent variables.

Minority status is represented by a binary variable coded 1 for minority writers and 0 otherwise. Gender is coded 1 for females, 0 for males. Work experience is measured in two ways. The first is years of membership in the WGAW. Because less than half of all writers are employed in any given year, years of membership does not equal years of employment experience. Consequently, in some models we also include binary variables for lagged employment status one, two, and three years prior to year t.

Age is measured as year t minus year of birth. Year effects are captured by 10 binary variables, with 1982 as the reference category. Cohort effects are captured by two binary variables, the first coded 1 for those admitted to the WGAW prior to 1971 and the second coded 1 for those admitted between 1971 and 1975. Finally, because many writers work in both television and film, our models include a binary variable coded 1 if the writer received earnings from work in television during year t.

Descriptive statistics reporting gender differences in age, experience, and employment appear in Table 5.1. On average, women screenwriters employed at least once between 1982 and 1992 are younger and have fewer years of experience than their male counterparts.

Table 5.1 Means by gender on age, experience, employment, and minority status, WGA West members employed at least once in film, 1982–1992

Variable	Metric	Female Means (N = 752)	Male Means (N = 3,341)
Cohort (year admitted to WGA)			
Pre-1971	0–1	0.064	0.155
1971–75	0–1	0.094	0.110
1976–80	0–1	0.243	0.226
1981–85	0–1	0.258	0.196
1986–90	0–1	0.270	0.251
1991–92	0–1	0.070	0.062
Years experience in 1992		10.5	12.8
Age in 1992			
<30	0–1	0.025	0.032
30–39	0–1	0.262	0.257
40–49	0–1	0.460	0.369
50–59	0–1	0.141	0.160
60–64	0–1	0.020	0.051
65+	0–1	0.040	0.080
Age NA	0–1	0.052	0.052
Employed in film, 1992	0–1	0.359	0.379
Employed in TV, 1992	0–1	0.309	0.290
Employed (TV or film):			
1982	0–1	0.360	0.392
1983	0–1	0.390	0.412
1984	0–1	0.408	0.433
1985	0–1	0.457	0.479
1986	0–1	0.489	0.509
1987	0–1	0.517	0.534
1988 (strike year)	0–1	0.495	0.508
1989	0–1	0.539	0.552
1990	0–1	0.553	0.594
1991	0–1	0.555	0.571
1992	0–1	0.552	0.559
Minority status	0–1	0.035	0.030

Just more than one third of the men and women screenwriters were employed in feature film in 1992, and about 30 percent were employed in television. Finally, Table 5.1 shows that writers of color are virtually absent in the industry, accounting for just more than 3 percent of the screenwriters employed from 1982 through 1992. Indeed, because so few women of color are employed to write for feature film (only 26 over the 11-year period), our statistical models are not able to provide reliable estimates of the interaction of race and gender as they influence the earnings of screenwriters.

CUMULATIVE VERSUS CONTINUOUS DISADVANTAGE: HYPOTHESES

Table 5.2 summarizes our hypotheses regarding the determinants of earnings under alternative conceptualizations of labor market dynamics. The main effects of gender, experience, and control variables are assumed to be the same across models. Each assumes a net negative effect of being female, effects of years of experience that increase at a decreasing rate, and positive effects of prior employment and earnings.

The three models of labor market dynamics, "cumulative disadvantage," "continuous disadvantage," and "declining disadvantage," are differentiated by their implications for interaction effects by gender. We choose between the cumulative disadvantage and continuous disadvantage models based on interaction effects between gender and experience, between gender and prior employment, and between gender and prior earnings.

The cumulative disadvantage model assumes that access to opportunity early in the career pays off more for men than for women. As a result, the gender gap in wages is expected to increase with experience. In other words, according to the cumulative disadvantage model, the net returns to experience are expected to be lower for women than for men (i.e., a negative interaction between gender [coded 1 for female] and the experience variables). Similarly, if women have more volatile careers and find it difficult to sustain career success from year to year, then the impact of prior earnings and employment should be lower for women than for men. Accordingly, the cumulative disadvantage model also

Table 5.2 Hypothesized effects of independent variables on earnings for different models of labor market dynamics

Variable	Cumulative Disadvantage	Continuous Disadvantage	Declining Disadvantage
Female	−	−	−
Experience (years in industry)	∩	∩	∩
Lagged employment	+	+	+
Lagged earnings	+	+	+
Gender interactions			
Female by			
Experience	−	o	?
Lagged employment	−	o	?
Lagged earnings	−	o	?
Year	?	?	−

NOTE: Hypothesized relationships: + = hypothesized positive relationship, − = hypothesized negative relationship, ∩ = hypothesized curvilinear relationship (increasing at a decreasing rate), ? = no relationship hypothesized.

predicts a negative interaction between gender and the lagged employment and earnings variables.

In contrast to the cumulative disadvantage model, the continuous disadvantage model implies a pervasive bias against women that affects them equally through all stages in their careers. Under the continuous disadvantage model, the earnings disparity between men and women at entry is neither greater nor worse than at later stages in the career. According to this model, the shape of the earnings trajectory over the course of a career is the same for men and women, but women start their careers with a substantial earnings "penalty" and never catch up. Thus, the continuous disadvantage model implies *no* interaction between gender and measures of experience, prior employment, and prior earnings; but it implies a strong "main effect" of gender, with women earning significantly less than men with similar levels of experience.

Neither the cumulative disadvantage nor the continuous disadvantage model provides an explicit prediction about trends over time in the aggregate gender gap in earnings. Over time and net of all other factors in these two models, the earnings gap between men and women might be increasing, decreasing, or not changing at all. In contrast, according to the model of declining disadvantage, there is a trend toward an erosion of gender barriers and a resulting decline in the gender gap in earnings over time. According to this model, whether the underlying dynamic is one of cumulative or continuous disadvantage, forces are at work that are slowly but surely dismantling the sources of that disadvantage. Thus, the declining disadvantage model predicts that the impact of gender declines over time (a negative interaction between gender [coded 1 for female] and year).

In sum, if we find strong evidence of lower returns among women than among men in the effects of experience, prior employment, and prior earnings (i.e., negative interactions between gender and each of these traits), then the cumulative disadvantage model will be favored over the continuous disadvantage model. In contrast, if there is a large net effect of gender but no interaction of gender with measures of experience, prior employment, or prior earnings, then the continuous disadvantage model will be favored. Regardless of the outcome of this comparison, a large negative interaction of female-by-year will provide evidence of declining disadvantage, that is, an erosion of gender barriers over time.[3] Absence of such an interaction will suggest that the barriers faced by women writers have persisted throughout the 1980s and into the early 1990s, despite women's increasing representation in positions of power and responsibility, and despite increased attention to the problem of gender bias in the industry.

FINDINGS FROM MULTIVARIATE MODELS

We choose between the cumulative and continuous disadvantage models of gender inequality in labor market dynamics based on whether there are interactions between gender and measures of experience, prior employment, and prior earnings, and we evaluate the declining disadvantage model based on whether there is a negative interaction between gender and year. Accordingly, our analytic strategy is to estimate and contrast models with and without gender interactions and to assess whether statistically significant gender interactions correspond to the patterns hypothesized by the cumulative and declining disadvantage models as summarized in Table 5.2. To fully exploit the longitudinal data, we estimate and test models under three alternative specifications. The first specification (Models 1 and 2) includes our measure of experience, but not lagged employment and lagged earnings. This specification has the advantage of exploiting all 11 years of data from 1982 through 1992, reflecting the earnings trajectories of the 4,093 writers who worked at least once during that period. The second specification (Models 3 and 4) adds binary variables for whether a writer was employed in years t-1, t-2, and t-3. Because data on employment are not available for years prior to 1982, estimates for this specification are based on a shorter time span, from 1985 through 1992, and pertain to the 3,645 writers who worked at least once during this period. The final specification (Models 5 and 6) includes effects of earnings in years t-1 and t-2 and is limited to writers with at least one employment spell of three consecutive years between 1983 and 1992 (i.e., nonzero earnings in years t, t-1, and t-2). Accordingly, the results of this specification apply to a select subgroup of 1,606 more successful writers with relatively continuous employment histories in the industry.

Results for the first two specifications (Models 1 through 4) appear in Table 5.3 and for the third specification (Models 5 and 6) in Table 5.4. The results for the models with no gender interactions (Models 1 and 3 in Table 5.3) show a substantial net disadvantage faced by women writers compared to men of similar age, experience, minority status, and recent employment history. Evaluated at the mean, the effect of being female of −.282 in Model 1 corresponds to a net gender gap in earnings of 25 percent, and the effect of −.234 in Model 3 corresponds to a net gender gap of 21 percent. Thus, if there were no gender interactions, we would conclude that women writers face an earnings penalty of 21 to 25 percent throughout their careers. However, because results reported below reveal significant gender interactions, the 21 to 25 percent estimate of the earnings penalty represents an average across a gender gap in earnings that is in fact contingent on the amount of experience screenwriters have in the industry.

Table 5.3 Determinants of earnings among all employed film writers 1982–1992[a]

Variable	Model 1	Model 2	Model 3	Model 4
Cohort				
Pre-1971	0.163**	0.140*	0.532**	0.506**
1971–75	−0.057	−0.062	0.246**	0.240**
Year				
1983	0.046	0.066	—	
1984	0.205**	0.214	—	
1985	0.330**	0.368**	—	
1986	0.372**	0.420**	0.047	0.061
1987	0.471**	0.515**	0.150**	0.167**
1988 (strike year)	0.485**	0.494**	0.103**	0.081
1989	0.596**	0.596**	0.283**	0.258**
1990	0.702**	0.706**	0.413**	0.387**
1991	0.776**	0.792**	0.450**	0.426**
1992	0.777**	0.782**	0.436**	0.403**
Age 30–39	−0.063	−0.067	−0.159**	−0.164**
Age 40–49	−0.186**	−0.192**	−0.236**	−0.242**
Age 50–59	−0.548**	−0.554**	−0.448**	−0.455**
Age 60–64	−0.864**	−0.881**	−0.725**	−0.741**
Age 65+	−1.074**	−1.088**	−0.928**	−0.945**
Age NA	−0.329**	−0.337**	−0.272**	−0.281**
Experience	0.0795**	0.0854**	0.0017	0.0073
Experience squared	−0.0016**	−0.0018**	−0.0003*	−0.0004**
Female	−0.282**	−0.045	−0.234**	−0.203*
Minority	−0.243**	−0.207*	0.010	0.018

TV employment	−0.274**	−0.301**	−0.171**	−0.215**
Lag TV employment			−0.024	−0.019
Employed—lag 1	—	—	0.495**	0.515**
Employed—lag 2	—	—	0.435**	0.424**
Employed—lag 3	—	—	0.479**	0.474**
Interactions, Female by				
Experience	—	−0.0374**	—	−0.0389**
Experience^2	—	0.0010**	—	0.0010**
1983	—	−0.118	—	—
1984	—	−0.066	—	—
1985	—	−0.240	—	—
1986	—	−0.293	—	−0.067
1987	—	−0.290	—	−0.114
1988	—	−0.072	—	0.123
1989	—	−0.021	—	0.148
1990	—	−0.046	—	0.150
1991		−0.116		0.137
1992		−0.053		0.191
TV employment	—	0.173*	—	0.256**
Minority	—	−0.250	—	−0.069
Employed—lag 1			—	−0.097
Employed—lag 2			—	0.057
Employed—lag 3			—	0.048
Constant	9.823	9.788	9.789	9.786
Root mean squared error	1.393	1.392	1.300	1.299
R^2	0.081	0.084	0.186	0.188
N (person-years)	14,439	14,439	11,296	11,296

Tests	df	F ratio	df	F ratio
All interactions	14	2.009*	14	2.271**
Experience interactions	2	6.793**	2	5.741**
Lag employment interactions	—	—	3	0.727
Year interactions	10	1.042	7	1.497

a. Pooled cross-sectional time-series regression models, ordinary least squares estimates. Dependent variable is log earnings.

* $p < .05$; ** $p < .01$.

Table 5.4 Determinants of earnings among film writers employed in three consecutive years, 1985–1992[a]

Variable	Model 5	Model 6
Cohort		
Pre-1971	0.074	0.049
1971–75	0.078	0.071
Year		
1986	−0.142*	−0.141*
1987	−0.060	−0.068
1988 (strike year)	−0.130*	−0.136*

(Continued Overleaf)

Table 5.4 Continued

Variable	Model 5	Model 6
1989	0.030	0.002
1990	0.117*	0.127*
1991	−0.085	−0.122*
1992	−0.069	−0.117
Age 30–39	−0.023	−0.023
Age 40–49	−0.119	−0.120
Age 50–59	−0.220**	−0.221**
Age 60–64	−0.393**	−0.397**
Age 65+	−0.274**	−0.280**
Age NA	−0.068	−0.068
Experience	0.0050	0.0096
Experience^2	−0.0001	−0.0002
Female	−0.039	−0.060
Minority	0.009	0.010
TV employment	−0.244**	−0.279**
Lag TV employment	0.122**	0.129**
Employed—lag 3	0.062*	0.062*
Log earnings—lag 1	0.518**	0.519**
Log earnings—lag 2	0.267**	0.263**
Interactions, female by		
Experience	—	−0.0405*
Experience squared	—	0.0011*
1986	—	0.021
1987	—	0.084
1988	—	0.071
1989	—	0.198
1990	—	−0.058
1991		0.302*
1992		0.347*
Minority	—	−0.039
TV employment		0.248**
Employed—lag 3	—	0.0472
Log earnings—lag 1	—	−0.0189
Log earnings—lag 2	—	0.019
Constant	2.526	2.556
Root mean squared error	0.968	0.967
R^2	0.500	0.502
N (person-years)	5,049	5,049

Tests	df	F ratio
All interactions	14	1.708*
Experience interactions	2	3.072*
Lag earnings interactions	2	0.134
Year interactions	7	1.84

a. Pooled cross-sectional time-series regression models, ordinary least squares estimates. Dependent variable is log earnings.

* $p < .05$; **$p < .01$.

Overall, the results support the model of cumulative disadvantage. First, in each instance, a global test of the gender interactions rejects the null hypothesis of no interaction (see row labeled "all interactions" at the bottom of Tables 5.3 and 5.4). Models 2, 4, and 6 (with interactions) provide significant improvement in fit over Models 1, 3, and 5 (without interactions), respectively. Second, specific tests of the gender-by-experience interactions reject the null hypothesis of no interaction in all three comparisons (see row labeled "experience interactions" at the bottom of Tables 5.3 and 5.4). In each instance, the estimated parameters for the linear and quadratic experience effects imply that earnings increase with experience at a decreasing rate for men, and the gender-by-experience interaction implies that the rate of earnings growth is slower for women than for men (or even negative for women). In other words, the gender gap in earnings grows as screenwriters move through their careers, even after controlling for gender differences in prior career success. The pattern of cumulative disadvantage with years of experience is portrayed in Table 5.5, based on the main and interaction effects of gender and experience estimated in Models 2, 4, and 6. Although the precise pattern depends on whether prior employment and earnings are controlled, Table 5.5 shows that for each model the net gender gap in (log) earnings increases dramatically with years in the industry. At career entry, the gender gap in earnings is as low as 4 to 6 percent (and not statistically significant according to the estimates of the main effects of gender in Models 2 and 6). But the results in Table 5.5 show that within five years of career entry, the gender gap in earnings grows to 20 percent or more, and by the fifteenth year the gap is on the order of 40 percent or more.

Although the gender gap in earnings increases with years in the industry, we find no evidence that the effects of prior employment on earnings are greater for men than for women (see row labeled "lag employment interactions" at the bottom of Table 5.3 and "lag earnings interactions" in Table 5.4). Nor do the results in Tables 3 and 4 show any evidence of declining disadvantage, because the gender-by-year interaction is not statistically significant. That is, there is no statistical evidence that the disadvantages faced by female screenwriters are declining over time. In each instance, we fail to reject the null hypothesis of no gender-by-year interactions (row labeled "year interactions" at the bottom of Tables 5.3 and 5.4).[4] In short, with respect to the impact of gender on earnings, consistent with research on television writers (Bielby and Bielby 1992), the structure of disadvantage was essentially static during the 1980s and early 1990s. The apparent decline in the gender gap in median earnings shown in Figure 4 is actually a spurious trend generated by shifts over time in the number of years of experience women screenwriters have relative to men.[5]

Table 5.5 Estimates of cumulative disadvantage: net effect of gender on log earnings at different levels of industry experience

Years of Experience	Model 2 No Lags	Model 4 Net of Lag Employment	Model 6 Net of Lag Employment, Earnings
0 Years	−0.045	−0.203	−0.060
1 Year	−0.081	−0.241	−0.099
5 Years	−0.207	−0.373	−0.235
10 Years	−0.321	−0.492	−0.356
15 Years	−0.386	−0.561	−0.422
20 Years	−0.402	−0.581	−0.433

In sum, our findings support a model of cumulative disadvantage whereby the gender gap in earnings grows with years of experience in the industry. Women writers in the industry face gender barriers that reduce their earnings substantially compared to men of similar age and experience, and these barriers increase the longer they work as screenwriters. We also found no evidence that the barriers faced by women screenwriters are eroding over time. Our confidence in these results is reinforced by two features of our analysis. First, by using a pooled cross-section design, we are exploiting both intra- and interindividual variation, and with such large sample sizes we certainly would have detected substantively significant interactions by year had they existed.[6] Second, the pattern of coefficients for the control variables is consistent with what we know about the structure of the labor market for screenwriters. Year effects increase monotonically. Older writers face a net disadvantage, consistent with descriptive statistics for the industry (W. Bielby and D. Bielby 1993) and with findings for television writers (D. Bielby and W. Bielby 1993). Minority writers are disadvantaged according to models 1 and 2, although the other models show this to be largely mediated by differences between minority and nonminority writers in prior employment and earnings.[7] Finally, the effect of work in television is negative in all our models, consistent with the notion that writers achieving success in television are less likely to be pursuing film work, where the odds of success are much lower.

CONCLUSION

Women compose about half of those who are classified as authors by the U.S. Census, but the screenwriting profession is more than 80 percent male. Those women who are able to break into the profession experience a process of cumulative disadvantage: the longer they work in the industry, the more their earnings lag behind their male counterparts. It has not always been this way. In the early years of the industry, women participated fully in the writing of film narratives and were among the highest-paid scenarists in the industry. However, in the late 1920s and 1930s, the profession went through a transition that Tuchman (1989) has described as the "empty field" phenomenon. As filmmaking became industrialized and rationalized, men dominated key roles in corporate channels of production, distribution, and exhibition. As screenwriting became more lucrative, men entered the profession in large numbers, and their dominance was legitimated by an ideology that valued men's contributions across the board but considered women's talent as appropriate only for a narrow range of genres. By the end of the 1930s, male dominance of the profession was fully institutionalized, and with the exception of a slight upturn in the early 1970s, women's representation among screenwriters has changed little over the last half century.

The typecasting of women writers seems as prevalent today as it was when "women's pictures" were at the height of their popularity in the 1930s and 1940s. Bettye McCartt, a prominent Hollywood talent agent, describes her encounters with typecasting as follows:

> When we get a call for a writer, they'll say, "Who do you have who can write an action-adventure piece?" If I suggest a woman, well they laugh at me. There are certain genres where a woman won't even be considered. By the same token, they'll call and say, "What woman writers do you have for a piece on so-and-so" (Writers Guild of America, West 1990, 12).

Although we have no quantitative data on the extent of typecasting of women writers, it is easy to imagine how it generates a pattern of cumulative disadvantage. The typical woman writer is likely to break into the industry writing material that is either currently fashionable or viewed by producers as appropriate for a woman writer, and she is paid at a rate comparable to that for a new male writer (Guild minimums under the collective bargaining agreement place a floor on compensation of novice writers). But as her career progresses, the woman writer's opportunities are limited to a narrow range of genres, whereas her male counterpart faces no such limitations. Even if she achieves a modest degree of success as a screenwriter, her long-term marketability is vulnerable to the inevitable cycles in the popularity of specific genres in the way that a male writer's is not. Such a dynamic is consistent with anecdotal accounts from women writers and their agents, and it is with our empirical findings of cumulative gender disadvantage in earnings, even when women writers are compared to men who have similar patterns of employment and earnings over a three-year period.

Among feature film writers, a gender gap in earnings emerges and widens over the course of writers' careers. Our earlier research (Bielby and Bielby 1992) detected a different dynamic in the labor market for television writers. For them, there is a substantial earnings gap at career entry that persists throughout the career. The two patterns probably reflect different routes to career entry in film and television. In film, there are more ways for both male and female aspiring writers to participate at the periphery of the labor market (e.g., by selling an option on a story or treatment, by doing a rewrite or "polish" on a screenplay). Typically, both male and female film writers start at the margins of the industry, and although few succeed beyond that level, men have better prospects for breaking into the ranks of successful writers of feature film, and success breeds success once they do. In contrast, the market for television writers is more highly structured. An aspiring writer either participates by gaining access to the interconnected social network of writer-producers, studio development executives, and network programmers or does not participate at all. In that kind of market, women writers are likely to face a substantial disadvantage from the very beginning.

Despite the somewhat differing dynamics of cumulative versus continuous disadvantage, it is important to recognize that there is substantial gender stratification in both segments of the industry, and in neither film nor television have we found any evidence of a decline since the early 1980s in the barriers faced by women writers. The similarities in the organizational, business, and labor market arrangements in television and film are no doubt more important than the differences in understanding the nature of those barriers. Short-term contracting in a context of ambiguity, risk, and uncertainty encourages the reliance on closed social networks of interpersonal ties and the use of informal, subjective criteria for the hiring and evaluation of writers and other creative workers. A large body of social research demonstrates that these are precisely the conditions under which gender stereotypes reinforce structural barriers to women's career advancement (Bielby 1992; Deaux 1984; Eagly and Wood 1982; Williams and Best 1986), especially when there is no system for holding those responsible for decisions about hiring and compensation accountable for doing so in a way that is free from bias (Salancik and Pfeffer 1978; Tetlock 1985). So in one sense, our findings are exactly what one would expect from established theories of gender inequality in the workplace. At the same time, prevailing theories of gender-segregated job ladders and a bureaucratically legitimated gendered division of labor (Acker 1990) are less relevant to television, film, and related media industries than they are to the corporate, government, blue-collar, and pink-collar settings that have been the focus of most research on gender inequality in the workplace. Although there is some research and theory on how gender is created and reinforced symbolically in the workplace (Cockburn 1985; Hearn and Parkin 1983; Hochschild 1983), none of it addresses how it occurs in mass culture industries that deliberately and self-consciously attempt to reflect and trade on cultural idioms about gender. The women and men who finance, write, produce, market, and distribute feature films and television programming are "doing gender" in a way that simultaneously shapes the work experiences and opportunities of those who participate in the industry and determines the images of gender consumed by a global audience. Mass culture industries are sites where symbolic representations of gender are literally produced, and they provide new challenges to the way we understand gender inequality in organizations. Our research highlights the importance of attending to the industrial context, social networks, organizational arrangements, and the symbolic content of the commodities produced to fully understand the barriers to women's full participation in the production of media narratives.

Notes

1   Even feminist film critics are vulnerable to these stereotypes. McCreadie (1994) suggests that the rise of "women's films" in the 1940s opened new opportunities for women writers, which then declined with the demise of that genre in the postwar period. But Writers Guild of America, West membership statistics suggest that women's representation among screenwriters remained steady at about 13% from the mid-1930s to the early 1960s (Figure 2). Thus, although it is widely believed that women are best suited for writing almost exclusively for women's films, for approximately three decades, women's representation among screenwriters remained constant regardless of the dominant genre of the day.

2   None of these films was written by a woman.

3   Strictly speaking, if the cumulative disadvantage model is favored over the model of continuous disadvantage, then a process of declining disadvantage would imply a three-way interaction between time, gender, and the effects of experience, prior employment, and prior earnings.

4   Although the hypothesis that the year-by-gender interaction coefficients are jointly zero cannot be rejected, the point estimates seem to suggest a pattern of declining gender effects over time. To examine this possibility, we replaced the 10 binary interaction terms, female × (year—1982). This provides a more powerful 1 degree of freedom test of the hypothesis that the gender gap in earnings declined linearly from 1982 to 1992. However, even with this more powerful test, the null hypothesis of no interaction could not be rejected.

5   From the early 1980s to the early 1990s, there was a substantial shift in employment favoring younger writers. So by the end of the period covered by our study, the industry was relying more heavily on writers who were just launching their careers. Because the gender gap in earnings is smaller among writers who are early in their careers, this trend has the effect of attenuating the bivariate association of gender and earnings, even though the net gender gap, controlling for experience, is not shrinking.

6   Moreover, inspection of collinearity diagnostics indicated that our failure to detect interaction is not due to inflated levels of sampling variation and covariation.

7   As noted above, because so few minority women are employed as screenwriters, we are unable to obtain reliable estimates of the interaction of minority status and gender. In each of our models, the interaction of female by minority status is negative (substantially so in model 1), suggesting that minority women face additional barriers. However, due to the small number of cases, the test of the interaction has very little power, and even a substantial gender-by-minority status interaction would fail to be detected as statistically significant in our models.

References

Acker, Joan. 1990. Hierarchies, jobs, bodies: A theory of gendered organizations. *Gender & Society* 4:139–58.
Baker, Wayne E., and Robert R. Faulkner. 1991. Role as resource in the Hollywood film industry. *American Journal of Sociology* 97:279–309.
Beranger, Clara. 1950. *Writing for the screen.* Dubuque, IA: W.C. Brown.
Bernstein, Sharon. 1990. But is there hope for the future? *Los Angeles Times*, 11 November, 9, 82–3.
Bielby, Denise D., and William T. Bielby. 1993. The Hollywood "graylist"? Audience demographics and

age stratification among television writers. In *Current research on occupations and professions (Creators of Culture)*, vol. 8, edited by Muriel G. Cantor and Cheryl Zollars. Greenwich, CT: JAI.

Bielby, William T. 1992. The structure and process of sex segregation. In *New approaches to economic and social analyses of discrimination*, edited by Richard Cornwall and Phanindra Wunnava. New York: Praeger.

Bielby, William T., and Denise D. Bielby. 1987. *The 1987 Hollywood writers' report: A survey of ethnic, gender and age employment factors*. West Hollywood, CA: Writers Guild of America, West.

——— . 1989. *The 1989 Hollywood writers' report: Unequal access, unequal pay*. West Hollywood, CA: Writers Guild of America, West.

——— . 1992. Cumulative versus continuous disadvantage in an unstructured labor market. *Work and Occupations* 19:366–489.

——— . 1993. *The 1993 Hollywood writers' report: A survey of the employment of writers in the film, broadcast, and cable industries for the period 1987–1991*. West Hollywood, CA: Writers Guild of America, West.

——— . 1994. "All hits are flukes:" Institutionalized decision-making and the rhetoric of network prime-time program development. *American Journal of Sociology* 99:1287–1313.

Cockburn, Cynthia. 1985. *Machinery of dominance*. London: Pluto Press.

Cox, Dan. 1995. WGA cuts into DGA territory. *Daily Variety* 246:1, 26.

DiMaggio, Paul. 1977. Market structure, the creative process, and popular culture: Toward an organizational reinterpretation of mass culture theory. *Journal of Popular Culture* 11:433–51.

Dutka, Elaine. 1990. Women and Hollywood: It's still a lousy relationship. *Los Angeles Times*, 11 November, 8, 85–8.

Danquah, Mari. 1994. Crashing the glass ceiling: Women writers in Hollywood. *The Journal of the Writers Guild of America* 7:12–7.

Deaux, Kay. 1984. From individual differences to social categories: Analysis of a decade's research on gender. *American Psychologist* 39:105–15.

Eagly, Alice H., and W. Wood. 1982. Inferred sex differences in status as a determinant of gender stereotypes about social influence. *Journal of Personality and Social Psychology* 43:915–28.

Faulkner, Robert R., and Andy B. Anderson. 1987. Short-term projects and emergent careers: Evidence from Hollywood. *American Journal of Sociology* 92:879–909.

Francke, Lizzie. 1994. *Script girls: Women screenwriters in Hollywood*. Bloomington: Indiana University Press.

Haskell, Molly. 1987. *From reverence to rape: The treatment of women in the movies*, 2d ed. Chicago: University of Chicago Press.

Hearn, Jeff, and P. Wendy Parkin. 1983. Gender and organizations: A selective review and critique of a neglected area. *Organization Studies* 4:219–42.

Hochschild, Arlie R. 1983. *The managed heart: Commercialization of human feeling*. Berkeley: University of California Press.

McCreadie, Marsha. 1994. *Women who write the movies*. New York: Birch Lane Press.

Martin, Ann, and Virginia Clark. 1987. *What women wrote: Scenarios, 1912–1929*. Cinema History Microfilm series. Frederick, MD: University Publications of America.

Robb, David, 1994. Writers Guild, DGA in clash over credits. *The Hollywood Reporter* 334: 1, 94.

Schwartz, Nancy Lynn. 1982. *The Hollywood writers' wars*. New York: Knopf.

Salancik, Gerald R., and Jeffrey Pfeffer. 1978. Uncertainty, secrecy, and the choice of similar others. *Social Psychology* 41:264–6.

Staiger, Janet. 1983. "Tame" authors and the corporate laboratory: Stories, writers, and scenarios in Hollywood. *Quarterly Review of Film Studies* 8 (Fall):33–45.

Stanley, Robert. 1978. *The celluloid empire: A history of the American motion picture industry*. New York: Hastings.

Tetlock, P. E. 1985. Accountability: The neglected social context of judgment and choice. In *Research in organizational behavior*, vol. 7, edited by L. L. Cummings and B. M. Staw. Greenwich, CT: JAI.

Tuchman, Gaye. 1989. *Edging women out: Victorian novelists, publishers, and social change*. New Haven, CT: Yale University Press.

Voland, John. 1992. The sun also rises: Confronting discrimination in the entertainment industry. *The Journal of the Writers Guild of America* 5:9–12.

Williams, John E., and Deborah L. Best. 1986. Sex stereotypes and intergroup relations. In *Psychology of intergroup relations*, edited by S. Worchel and W. G. Austin. Chicago: Nelson-Hall.

Work Projects Administration, American Guide Series. 1941. *Los Angeles: A guide to the city*. New York: Hastings.

Writers Guild of America, West. 1990. Women in Hollywood. *The Journal of the Writers Guild of America* 3:10–15.

Young, Paul F. 1995. Scripters caught in studio squeeze. *Daily Variety* 247:5, 18.

Chapter 6

Anne E. Lincoln and Michael Patrick Allen

DOUBLE JEOPARDY IN HOLLYWOOD: AGE AND GENDER IN THE CAREERS OF FILM ACTORS, 1926–1999 (2004)

INTRODUCTION

Sociologists have explored ascriptive inequality in terms of life–outcome disparities, but explanations of these outcomes and the mechanisms that produce them have been limited (Reskin, 2003). The effects of such ascriptive characteristics as gender and race on occupational outcomes have been well documented. However, the effects of other ascriptive characteristics, such as age, on these same outcomes remain largely unexplored (Riley, 1987). One of the most important theoretical questions raised by the research on ascriptive inequality involves the concept of "double jeopardy." Specifically, this concept asserts that devalued ascriptive characteristics may interact with one another with respect to certain outcomes: for example, the effects of gender and race interact in such a way that African-American women earn less than one would expect from the combined direct effects of gender and race (Collins, 1990; King, 1988). By extension, this concept implies that other ascriptive characteristics, such as gender and age, may interact with one another with respect to similar outcomes. For example, it has been argued that older women experience double jeopardy to the extent that their health is worse than would be predicted by the combined direct effects of gender and age.

(Chappell and Havens, 1980)

O NE OCCUPATION IN WHICH the issue of double jeopardy has been raised in terms of the effects of gender and age on career outcomes is film acting. This is ironic since film acting was one of the first high-income, high-status occupations in the United States to achieve high levels of gender integration, due largely to the narrative demands for heterosexual romantic relationships in most films (Bordwell et al., 1985). Indeed, film acting was one of the few elite occupations in which women were often paid as much as men. For example, 5 of the 10 highest paid film stars in 1938 were women (Rosten, 1941:342). Despite these indications of early gender equality in film acting, some evidence suggests that gender inequalities currently exist in the profession that are inextricably bound up with the issue of aging. Celebrated female stars, such as Meryl Streep, have complained that their careers in film are shorter than those of their female predecessors and that they are paid much less than men (Dutka, 1990). These claims are bolstered by recent research conducted by the Screen Actors Guild (1999) which found that, at all levels of acting, women appear as lead characters in fewer films than men and earn half as much as their male counterparts. Other research has found additional gender and age disparities in two measures of professional achievement in the field—receipt of Academy Awards (Gilberg and Hines, 2000; Levy, 1990a; Markson and Taylor, 1993) and appearances in the Quigley *Motion Picture Herald* poll of "Top Money-Making Stars" (Levy, 1990b).

Although the findings of these studies are suggestive, these researchers have not explicitly examined the concept of double jeopardy within film acting. Indeed, an analysis of the careers of film actors provides a unique opportunity to investigate the concept of double jeopardy by disentangling the direct and interactive effects of gender discrimination and age discrimination on career outcomes. Given the public nature of film acting, the available archival data permit a longitudinal analysis of actors' careers over relatively long periods of time. Moreover, these data permit us to compare the careers of actors over several decades. Consequently, we can obtain a rare longitudinal perspective on the direct and interactive effects of gender and age on the careers of film stars at different points in the history of the American film industry.

A great deal of research has focused on inequality in the workplace, but hardly any has focused on the joint effects of gender and age discrimination on the careers of those in elite professions. Indeed, there have been very few longitudinal studies of changes in ascriptive inequality in specific professions. The study of an individual profession, such as film acting, allows a detailed investigation of the gendered aspects of aging on different occupational outcomes. Although acting is a highly specialized occupation, such an analysis might have implications for the differential effects of aging on the careers of women and men in any number of elite professions that require a public presentation of self, such as lawyers, television journalists, business executives, public officials, and entertainers of all kinds. Ultimately, the results may suggest career trends in other occupations, regardless of their visibility (Morrow *et al.*, 1990). Last but not least, some understanding of the gendered effects of aging in film acting is important because film actors serve as important role models (Herzog and Gaines, 1991; Stacey, 1991), especially with respect to the appropriateness of certain gender roles (Dyer, 1998; Signorielli, 1989; Wexman, 1993). As Bielby and Bielby (1996:267) observe, "Mass culture industries are sites where symbolic representations of gender are literally produced, and they provide new challenges to the way we understand gender inequality in organizations."

THEORETICAL ISSUES AND HISTORICAL CONTEXTS

Sociological investigations of inequality on the basis of ascribed characteristics have proceeded in relative isolation from each other. This isolation stems from an assumption that the causes of ascriptive inequality differ for each attribute (Reskin, 2003). For example, the explanation for racial discrimination is often assumed to be different from the explanation for discrimination on the basis of gender. The resulting "balkanization" of theories has hampered stratification research to the extent that the effects of different ascriptive characteristics are studied in a sort of "social vacuum" to the detriment of a broader theory of stratification. The sociologies of aging and gender have not been immune to this segmentation (Moen, 2001). As a result, mainstream sociological theory has generally ignored the gendered nature of the process of aging (Arber and Ginn, 1991). This theoretical gap persists despite increasing evidence in recent empirical research on gender in the sociology of aging (McMullin, 1995; Riley, 1987) that the effects of aging are not homogeneous with respect to gender. However, the theoretical complexity of combining these two attributes may be the reason that no joint conceptual framework has been developed (Levy, 1988).

One attempt to account theoretically for the interactive effects of multiple ascriptive characteristics is the notion of "double jeopardy," a concept first introduced to describe the combined effects of sexism and racism on the experiences of black women (King, 1988). Scholars have since hypothesized a more general formulation in which gender and other social characteristics such as race and social class operate simultaneously in a nonadditive manner to affect various life outcomes. When these characteristics are devalued, the proposition asserts that joint effects of two or more of the characteristics are more deleterious than the sum of their separate effects. To this end, it has been argued that the interactive effects of gender and age represent a form of double jeopardy (Chappell and Havens, 1980) that puts older women at a greater disadvantage than their male counterparts in all aspects of life, ranging from psychological problems to economic difficulties. Thus far, however, double jeopardy has remained a largely untested theoretical concept. Most empirical studies have been cross-sectional, and the few longitudinal studies have yielded inconsistent empirical evidence (Ferraro and Farmer, 1996; Markridge et al., 1984).

If the concept of double jeopardy is valid, it would be particularly important with regard to the position of men and women in the economic system. However, very few longitudinal studies have examined the differential effects of aging on the careers of men and women (Warren et al., 2002), especially within a single occupation. Because of the public nature of their careers, film actors are an ideal population to study empirically the intersection of gender and age in an elite occupation. Additionally, many studies ignore gender differences in labor force participation or assume that the careers of men are continuous, while those of women are more sporadic due to family requirements (Lorence and Mortimer, 1989). In the acting profession, however, neither women nor men have continuous careers in the traditional sense. Acting careers consist of a series of separate film projects. The concept of a sex-differentiated labor market, in which women have qualitatively different career patterns than men (Simpson et al., 1982), is simply not applicable to actors. Moreover, unlike most other occupations, film acting has historically been highly gender-integrated. Finally, archival information permits a longitudinal examination of the effects of gender and aging on actors' careers as well as a historical comparison of the ways the effects of these variables have changed over the past several decades in response to developments in the film industry and in American society.

The careers of actors have undoubtedly been affected by historical changes in the organization of production within the film industry. The most significant change has been the decline of the "studio system," which was the dominant mode of film production from the late 1920s until the early 1950s. Under this system, the major studios were vertically integrated, controlling the production, the distribution, and, to a large extent, the exhibition of films (Bordwell et al., 1985). Given the industrial logic of this system, both male and female stars were typically placed under long-term contracts. As a result, the studios had an incentive to invest in the careers of their stars. Indeed, studios often produced specific films, known in the industry as "star vehicles," for each of their major stars on a regular basis. Not surprisingly, then, women comprised 50 percent of the top ten box office draws from 1932 to 1938, as reported by exhibitors in the Top Ten Poll of Money-Making Stars (Quigley Publications, 1994). While women starred in all film genres in the 1930s and 1940s, they were typically cast in serious dramas and even more prominently in musicals and romantic melodramas. So-called "women's films," which portrayed strong heroines involved in melodramatic situations, were also popular in the 1930s and 1940s (Balio, 1993). Conversely, men were typically cast in Westerns and adventure films (Schatz, 1997).

The careers of both male and female stars were adversely affected by the decline of the studio system after the Paramount decision by the Supreme Court in 1948, which forced the major studios to divest themselves of their theaters. This event, coupled with the rise in competition for audiences from television, led the studios to cancel their long-term contracts with stars. Beginning in the 1950s, almost all of the major talent involved in the production of films was contracted for single projects (Faulkner and Anderson, 1987). Studios no longer developed films for specific female stars. At the same time, there was a shift in the types of films being produced in Hollywood. The careers of female stars may have been adversely affected by changes in the audience and consequent changes in the popularity of different film genres. Musicals have declined in popularity in recent decades, and "women's films" virtually disappeared in the 1950s. During the 1970s, roles for women all but vanished with the arrival of the "buddy film," which focused on "macho exploits and homoerotic bonds" (Quart and Auster, 2002:109). Since the 1970s, adventure films have become the most popular film genre (Levy, 1989). These films typically have few, if any, significant parts for women. For example, one of the first highly successful adventure films of this period, *Jaws* (1975), starred three men.

Recent studies of character portrayals in film and television have demonstrated that male actors are more prevalent than female actors, especially in leading roles (Bazzini *et al.*, 1997; Screen Actors Guild, 2002). One explanation of this pattern is that producers believe that a film with a female star is unlikely to earn enough money to recoup its costs (Bielby and Bielby, 1996). Similarly, studies of ageism in television have found that television actors have become younger in the last two decades (Davis, 1980; Gerbner, 1998). Research conducted by the Screen Actors Guild (1999) suggests a double jeopardy effect for female actors, who experience aging differently from male actors during the course of their careers. For example, although 43 percent of Americans are over the age of 40 (U.S. Bureau of the Census, 2000), women over age 40 received only 24 percent of all female roles cast in television and film, while men over age 40 received 37 percent of all male roles. The Screen Actors Guild (2002) also noted that obtaining roles in feature films posed an even greater challenge for female actors over the age of 40. Clearly, the demand for actors diminishes as they age, especially if they are women. In fact, the term "older" is now popularly being used to describe male actors over the age of 40 and female actors over the age of 30 (Michaelson, 1993). Thus, the interaction between age and sex may result in a "double standard about aging that denounces women with special severity" (Sontag, 1979:464). Indeed, empirical research suggests that gender and age discrimination in the film and television industries extends even to screenwriters (Bielby and Bielby, 1992, 1993, 1996; Falk and Falk, 1997).

Some evidence also suggests that even the most successful film stars are not immune to this double jeopardy effect. One source of systematic historical information is the Top Ten Poll of Money-Making Stars conducted every year by the *Motion Picture Herald* (Quigley Publications, 1994). The results of this poll of theater owners indicate that women have significantly shorter periods as top draws on box office charts than do men (Levy, 1989). While 26 men have had more than 5 years of commercial popularity as measured by this poll, only five women have achieved that distinction (Levy, 1990b). Disparities also exist in the peer recognition afforded by the Academy Awards. Women are nominated for and win Oscars at a significantly younger age than men (Gilberg and Hines, 2000; Markson and Taylor, 1993). In fact, youth was the most powerful criterion for women who won the Best Actress award, while middle age was the best predictor for male Best Actor winners (Markson and Taylor, 1993). It appears that a sort of "revolving door" for young female actors has developed, to the detriment of older female actors (Jacobs, 1989). This pattern is not entirely new. In his comparison of the major film stars of the 1940s with those of the 1930s, Schatz (1997:363) notes that "the ranks of top stars would be predominantly male, and female stars would tend to be considerably younger than their male counterparts."

On the basis of these theoretical and empirical observations, this research expects to find a pattern of "double jeopardy" for female actors in the Hollywood film industry in comparison to male actors. This theoretical model is consistent with the findings of Bielby and Bielby (1992) with respect to the effects of "cumulative disadvantage" within the film and television industries. Both models assert that interactive effects between gender and age systematically disadvantage older women. In general, we expect that women will appear in fewer films than men and have fewer leading roles than men. We also expect that the disparity between male and female actors will become more pronounced as a result of the differential effects of aging. Moreover, because of the decline of the studio system and shifts in the popularity of certain film genres, this disadvantage has probably become even more pronounced overtime. In short, we anticipate that the process of cumulative disadvantage has become marked in recent years, resulting in more "durable" careers for male actors than for female actors (Levy, 1990b).

SAMPLE AND DATA

In order to assess these theoretical issues, this research examines in detail the careers of a large sample of leading actors in Hollywood films over a period of more than seven decades. A sample of 318 stars (168 men and 150 women) was compiled from a number of film reference publications, including *Screen World*, the *Motion Picture Guide* (Nash and Ross, 1999), the Internet Movie Database (http://www.imdb.com), the American Film Institute list entitled "400 Greatest Actors," and two comprehensive directories of film actors (Shipman, 1989; Truitt, 1983). These actors appeared in a total of 14,922 film roles between 1926 and 1999, an average of 46.9 films over the course of their careers.

Because they are more popular and more prominent than other actors, stars may be expected to have the greatest influence upon film audiences. For the purposes of this research, actors were considered to be stars if they were billed as one of the top two "leads" in at least six major films. Of the 318 actors in our sample, 73 percent qualified as "stars" in the first 5 years of their careers. More lenient criteria would have included many less popular and less influential actors. However, this sample purposely focuses on the careers of stars who, by virtue of their celebrity, enjoyed greater rewards and autonomy than most actors. At the same time, we must note that not all of the actors in this sample had long careers. Indeed, 14 of the 318 stars had careers that spanned less than 15 years.

This research focuses on those stars who appeared primarily in major films, also called A-list films within the industry, that involve "top talent" in all facets of production. These films involve the talents of the most accomplished actors, writers, and directors in the industry. In the 1930s, major film studios also produced a large number of B-list films that played in theaters after A-list films in double features. These films were usually shorter than A-list features, had much smaller budgets, and featured less accomplished and celebrated talent. Today, the equivalent of a B-list film is the "straight-to-video" film, which never achieves a major theatrical release. Therefore, actors who appeared primarily in B-list films, such as Gene Autry and Tom Mix, were excluded from this study. In addition, because this research examines only leading actors, well-known supporting actors like Walter Brennan and Agnes Moorehead were similarly excluded from the analysis.

The careers of many stars of silent films were truncated because they were not able to make a successful transition to sound films. Indeed, the introduction of sound is a major turning point in the history of film production. The first "talkie," *The Jazz Singer*, was released in 1927, and within 2 years every major American studio had converted to sound. Consequently, this analysis focuses only on the careers of stars whose careers began after 1925, just before the advent of the sound era. Furthermore, in order to study their careers until they reached the age of 40, we had to limit the analysis to those stars whose careers covered a span of at least 25 years. Thus, actors like Marilyn Monroe and James Dean, who died prematurely, are excluded from the analysis. Correspondingly, actors whose first films were released after 1975 were not included in the analysis. In addition, this research is limited to actors who starred primarily in American films; thus, it excludes actors who starred mainly in foreign films, such as Catherine Deneuve and Alec Guinness. However, foreign actors who appeared predominantly in American films, such as Anthony Hopkins and Sean Connery, are included.

We compiled data on each film role in which each actor appeared during the first 25 years of his or her careers, including ranking in the credits. Thus we were able to trace the career trajectories of these actors, both in terms of the number of film roles in which they appeared and their star billing in those roles at each point in their careers. For the purposes of this analysis, the careers of actors are assumed to begin with their first credited role in a film. The number of films in which an actor appears over a period of time must be interpreted with some caution. Certainly, popular actors are likely to make more films than other actors. However, the opportunities are affected by the number of films released each year. Stars who began their careers in the 1930s appeared in more films than contemporary stars simply because the film industry produced more films then than it produces today. Moreover, the number of film appearances per year does not tell us whether an actor had a leading or supporting role in any given film. The relative ranking of actors in the credits of a film is an important measure of their overall market power and their importance in a given film. First billing typically goes to the most popular actor, who characteristically plays the lead role in that film. However, because star billing is ordinal, it is difficult to summarize the importance of an actor over several films.

To address this problem, we used the ordinal data on the film credit rankings to create an interval measure of the "star presence" of each actor in each film. This transformation was achieved using the "inverse-rank" function. We can measure the "star presence" of an actor in a film by obtaining the inverse of their ordinal rank in the credits for that film as follows:

$$p_i = \frac{1}{r_i}$$

where r_i is the rank of the actor among the acting credits for a film i and p_i is the star presence of that actor in that film. The rationale for employing the "inverse-rank" function to transform ordinal data on star billing into interval data on star presence is indirect. The relationship between rank and magnitude has been observed in a number of different empirical contexts. For example, when scientists are ranked in terms of the number of citations to their work, the second-ranked scientist typically receives one-half of the citations received by the first-ranked scientist, and the third-ranked scientist usually receives one-third of the citations received by the first-ranked scientist. This relationship between magnitude and rank order, which was proposed independently by Pareto and Zipf (Price, 1976), has also been found to describe the distributions of cities, words, incomes, and firms. Separate analyses, which are not presented for sake of brevity, indicate that star presence scores of major stars in 1938 were positively correlated with their incomes and with the number of articles published about them in general-interest periodicals.

In the context of this research, the application of the power function provides a simple and meaningful transformation of star ranking into star presence in a given film. An advantage of this measure is that star presence can be averaged over a number of roles. An actor who appeared in two films might get second billing in one and third billing in the other in the same year. Using the power rule, we can transform these ordinal rank data into the following interval data:

$$p_1 = \frac{1}{2} = 0.500 \quad \text{and} \quad p_2 = \frac{1}{3} = 0.333$$

These star presence scores can then be averaged: an actor who received second billing in one film and third billing in another in the same year would have an average star presence of 0.417 for that year. If that same actor had received top billing in both films, his or her average star presence for that year would have been 1.00. The value of this measure ranges from a theoretical minimum that approaches 0 to a maximum of 1. The average star presence measure also has the advantage of being mathematically independent of the number of film roles received by an actor.

We can demonstrate the utility of these two measures of the career trajectory of a film star by a simple example. Figure 6.1 presents a graph of the first 10 years of the career of Bette Davis, from 1931 to 1940, in terms of both the number of film roles she received each year and her average star presence each year. In 1931, she appeared in three films and was billed third, fifth, and seventh, resulting in an average star presence score of 0.225 for that year. In contrast, of the four films she appeared in during 1939, she was ranked first in three and second in one, resulting in an average star presence score of 0.875 for that year. A comparison of these two measures gives two different views of a career. In the first 5 years of her career, Bette Davis appeared in an average of 5.4 films per year, but her average star presence score was 0.563. In the next 5 years of her career, she appeared in an average of only 3.2 films per year but her average star presence score was 0.900 out of a possible 1.0. Although beginning to appear in fewer films, Bette Davis was becoming a bigger star.

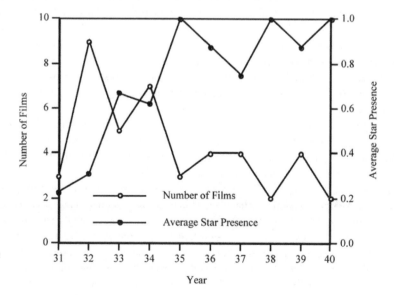

Figure 6.1 Number of films and average star presence of Bette Davis, 1931–1940.

No study has examined virtually the entire careers of actors in this manner. The only comparable research is a study conducted by Levy (1989) of the 10 most popular stars each year as identified by the Motion Picture Herald Poll of exhibitors. However, because only 129 stars have been identified by this poll in its 65-year history, Levy was not able to draw many conclusions regarding the combined effects of gender and age on the careers of film stars in general. Similarly, other research has examined the age at which actors achieve certain honors, such as receiving an Academy Award nomination (Gilberg and Hines, 2000; Levy, 1990a; Markson and Taylor, 1993). Consequently, these studies focus only on the peer recognition or commercial success that some actors achieve at some point and do not consider their entire careers. However, these studies suggest that measures of achievement may be important in analyzing the careers of film stars.

The present analysis examines the effect of several independent variables on the number of film roles and star presence accorded actors during their careers. To test assertions of double jeopardy, the gender and age of the actors are certainly the primary predictors. In order to avoid introducing a bias into the age variable, in the case of child stars, the analysis includes only the film roles they received after they turned 16. In addition, findings from the studies of professional achievement of actors mentioned above prompted the tabulation of the cumulative number of Academy Award nominations, if any, that actors had received at each point in their careers. We should also note that, until relatively recently, very few stars have been members of racial or ethnic minority groups. Consequently, no such comparisons are possible in this analysis.

RESULTS

The theory being proposed argues that age has a differential effect on the careers of male and female stars. However, a cursory examination of the data reveals that their careers were also affected by historical trends in the film industry. The number of feature films produced by the American film industry declined steeply during World War II. Moreover, after the advent of television and the divestiture of theaters by the major studios following the Paramount decision in 1948, the film industry never regained its former production levels, which diminished the careers of film actors. In the time period from 1926 to 1942, the film stars in the sample received an average of 2.97 film roles each year, but between 1943 and 1999 they received only 1.22 film roles each year. The correlation between a dummy variable representing the post-1942 time period and the number of film roles received by stars each year is −0.418. Consequently, the following analyses include two dummy variables, one representing female actors and another representing the post-1942 time period. This research employs multivariate statistical techniques to disentangle the effects of age, gender, and time period on the careers of actors. Specifically, the pooled time-series data can be analyzed using generalized least-squares regression techniques (Kmenta, 1986). This technique corrects for the serial correlation between the errors of prediction overtime, a common problem in regression analyses of time-series data.

The results of three regression models for number of film roles each year are presented in Table 6.1. Model 1 examines the main effects of age, gender, time period, and the cumulative number of Academy Award nominations on the number of film roles received by an actor each year. As expected, age, being female, and the post-1942 time period have significant negative effects on that number. Conversely, the cumulative number of Academy Award nominations received by an actor has a positive effect on the number of film roles received. Model 2 examines the main effects of these same variables, as well as the interaction effects between age, gender, and time period on the number of film roles received by

Table 6.1 Generalized least-squares analysis of the effects of age, gender, time period, and Oscar nominations on number of film roles

Independent variables	Model 1	Model 2	Model 3
Age	−0.0370*** (0.0023)	−0.0577*** (0.0058)	−0.0548*** (0.0069)
Gender (female = 1)	−0.7216*** (0.0654)	0.1389 (0.1526)	0.9672 (0.3519)
Oscar nominations	0.0846*** (0.0175)	0.0849*** (0.0173)	0.0853*** (0.0173)
Time period (post-1942 = 1)	−1.3904*** (0.0508)	−2.9434*** (0.2018)	−2.8379*** (0.2472)
Gender × age		−0.0334*** (0.0041)	−0.0414*** (0.0115)
Gender × Time period		0.7374*** (0.1071)	0.4800 (0.3629)
Age × Time period		0.0388*** (0.0055)	0.0357*** (0.0069)
Gender × Age × Time period			0.0086 (0.0115)
Constant	4.3037*** (0.0908)	5.0937*** (0.2030)	4.9985*** (0.2399)
R^2	0.377	0.405	0.404
ρ	0.143	0.137	0.136
N	7950	7950	7950

*** $p < 0.001$.

stars. The effects of all three interactions between age, gender, and time period on the number of film roles are significant, but only the interaction between gender and age is in the expected direction. Model 3 examines the main effects of these variables, their two-way interactions, and the three-way interaction between age, gender, and time period on the number of film roles received by each star. The three-way interaction term is not statistically significant.

We can use these same techniques to disentangle the effects of the individual characteristics of actors on their average star presence each year. The results of three models are presented in Table 6.2. As before, Model 1 examines the main effects of age, gender, time period, and the cumulative number of Academy Award nominations on the average star presence of an actor. As expected, age, being female, and the post-1942 time period have significant negative effects on the average star presence of an actor each year, while the cumulative number of Academy Award nominations received has a positive effect on the performer's average star presence. Model 2 examines the main effects of these same variables, as well as the interaction effects between age, gender, and time period on average star presence. The effects of all three interactions between age, gender, and time period on average star presence are significant and negative. Model 3 examines the main effects of these variables, their two-way interaction effects, and the three-way interaction between age, gender, and time period on average star presence. As expected, the interaction effect of age, gender, and time period on average star presence is significant and negative.

In general, a comparison of the multivariate statistical analyses presented in Tables 6.1 and 6.2 reveals both similarities and differences in the effects of age, gender, and time period on the number of film roles received by an actor and on the average star presence of an actor. Being female, being older, and working in the post-1942 time period clearly have significant, negative main effects on the careers of actors. Moreover, Model 2 shows a significant interaction effect between gender and age with respect to both number of films and average star presence. This initially suggests that older female actors are subjected to the "double

Table 6.2 Generalized least-squares analysis of the effects of age, gender, time period, and Oscar nominations on average star presence

Independent variables	Model 1	Model 2	Model 3
Age	−0.0035*** (0.0006)	0.0151*** (0.0016)	0.0119*** (0.0019)
Gender (female = 1)	−0.1632*** (0.0164)	0.4001*** (0.0418)	0.1297 (0.0973)
Oscar nominations	0.0554*** (0.0047)	0.0628*** (0.0047)	0.0622*** (0.0047)
Time period (post-1942 = 1)	−0.0881*** (0.0141)	0.4090*** (0.0561)	0.2871*** (0.0687)
Gender × Age		−0.0129*** (0.0011)	−0.0037 (0.0032)
Gender × Time period		−0.1041*** (0.0296)	0.1933 (0.1010)
Age × Time period		−0.0143*** (0.0015)	−0.0107*** (0.0019)
Gender × Age × Time period			−0.0099** (0.0032)
Constant	0.6845*** (0.0247)	0.0112 (0.0560)	0.1197 (0.0662)
R^2	0.283	0.224	0.231
ρ	0.108	0.110	0.111
N	7950	7950	7950

** $p < 0.01$; ***$p < 0.001$.

jeopardy" effects of age and gender and disadvantaged, both in terms of number of film roles and in terms of average star presence, compared to older male actors. However, differences between the tables in the three-way interaction effect of age, gender, and time period point to a more complex relationship. This variable is either not significant, with regard to number of film roles, or negative and significant, with regard to average star presence. This finding warrants more careful scrutiny.

Clearly, the results of the regression models presented in Tables 6.1 and 6.2 are very difficult to interpret due to the inclusion of several interaction terms. It is difficult to trace the effects of each of the independent variables on the dependent variable because the interpretation of the constituent variables changes with the inclusion of each additional interaction term. For example, age has a main effect on the number of film roles and star presence of an actor, but it also has interaction effects on these variables resulting from its first-order interactions with both gender and time period separately and its second-order interaction with gender and time period conjointly. As a result, the coefficients of the interaction variables estimate conditional relationships. It is entirely possible for the main effects of the independent variables on a dependent variable to be nonsignificant at this level. Therefore, the total effect of age on the number of film roles received by an actor must be calculated from the additive effects of four variables.

Perhaps the best way to simplify the interpretation of these models is to graph the expected values of the dependent variables derived from these multivariate statistical models for the different values of the independent variables. The resulting graphs illustrate the cumulative effects of age for both male and female stars on each dependent variable during the period from 1926 to 1942 and the period from 1943 to 1999. Figure 6.2 graphs the relationship between age and the number of film roles received each year by male and female actors for both time periods. Stars in the period between 1926 and 1942 obviously received more film roles when they were younger than they did in the period between 1943 and 1999. This is attributable to the fact that the American film industry produced more films

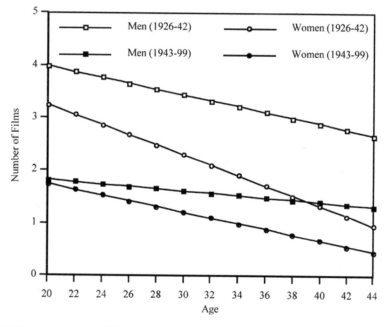

Figure 6.2 Expected number of films by men and women stars with one Academy Award nomination by age and time period.

each year prior to 1943 than it did afterward. Note also that the number of film roles that actors received declined as they aged in both time periods and that this decline is much more precipitous for female stars than it is for male stars in both time periods. In terms of the number of film roles received each year, female stars in the time period from 1926 to 1942 were at a substantial disadvantage in comparison to male stars when they were young, and this disparity increased dramatically as they grew older. Conversely, during the time period from 1943 to 1999, female stars were not especially disadvantaged in comparison to male stars when they were young, but they became progressively more disadvantaged as they aged.

A similar graph of the relationship between age and average star presence for both male and female stars during both time periods is presented in Figure 6.3. The gender differences between actors, in terms of their average star presence, are relatively small when they are young in both time periods. Recall that average star presence is not necessarily related to the number of film roles received each year. During the time period between 1926 and 1942, the difference between male and female stars in terms of their average star presence remained relatively small as they aged. Female stars lost their small advantage over male stars, but the average star presence of both sexes increased as they grew older. In contrast, the relationship between age and average star presence is much different for stars in the period from 1943 to 1999. Once again, female stars had a small advantage over male stars when they were young, but they became increasingly disadvantaged as they aged. Male stars were able to maintain their average star presence as they grew older, while the average star presence of women declined precipitously.

CONCLUSIONS

This research has examined the theoretical utility and empirical validity of the concept of "double jeopardy" with respect to gender and age as it pertains to the careers of film actors.

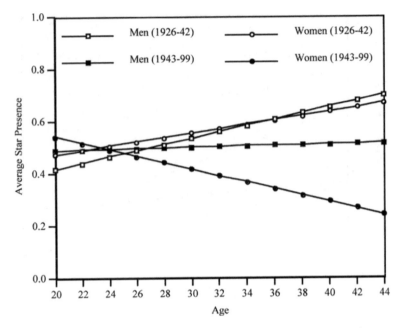

Figure 6.3 Expected star presence for men and women stars with one Academy Award nomination by age and time period.

In many respects, this occupation is ideally suited for such an analysis because of the wealth of detailed longitudinal data on the careers of a relatively large number of actors over the past several decades. At the same time, our analysis reveals the inherent complexity of any analysis of this issue. The concept of "double jeopardy" implies that significant interaction effects exist between gender and age with respect to occupational outcomes in addition to their main effects. This analysis reveals that actors receive fewer film roles and have less star presence as they grow older. It also reveals that women receive fewer roles and have less star presence than men. These differences persist even after controlling for the cumulative number of Academy Award nominations they have received at each point in their careers. We also find consistent empirical evidence of a "double jeopardy" effect inasmuch as the disparity between men and women with respect to film roles and star presence increases with age. However, the effects of this double jeopardy have apparently diminished somewhat since 1943 with respect to number of film roles, even though they have remained relatively constant with respect to average star presence.

In general, these results lend some credence to the concerns raised by female stars like Meryl Streep, albeit with some qualifications. Despite the relatively stable career trajectories experienced by most contemporary stars, aging clearly has a gendered impact upon their careers. Female stars appear in significantly fewer films and have a lower average star presence than male stars. Moreover, women are subject to "double jeopardy" inasmuch as the disparities in the number of film roles and the average star presence of male and female stars increase as they age. However, it does appear that the "double jeopardy" effects of age and gender on the number of film roles received by an actor have become less pronounced in recent decades. Conversely, the "double jeopardy" effects of age and gender on the average star presence of actors have not changed appreciably overtime. Altogether, these results suggest a relatively stable pattern over the past several decades in which female stars have more modest careers than their male counterparts and that this gap increases as they age.

These results also suggest a number of alternative explanations for these observed differences in the careers of male and female film stars. One is that these differences reflect the preferences of film producers. Another is that film producers are simply acting in accordance with their beliefs about the composition and preferences of film audiences. Although the film industry did not conduct systematic research on its audience until 1945, the implicit assumption of producers prior to that time was that the composition of the film audience mirrored the composition of the population. However, with the introduction of audience research, producers discovered that, largely as the result of the growth of television, the film audience was much younger than the population. Many producers still hold this belief despite recent research indicating that the film audience has become older in recent years. Specifically, the share of the film audience between ages 16 and 24 dropped from roughly 50% in 1968 to 33% in 1989 (Krämer, 1999:99). It has since dropped to 29% (Motion Picture Association, 2002:6). Moreover, contrary to the conventional wisdom of most producers, men and women attend films in roughly the same numbers and have done so consistently for decades. Consequently, the differences in the careers of male and female actors cannot be attributed to the gender composition of the film audience.

Why, then, do female performers age differently than male stars? Attractiveness, particularly to a male audience, may be one reason. Levy (1989) found that one-quarter of the popular female stars identified in the Motion Picture Herald Poll were models prior to beginning their acting careers, whereas none of the men had been models. Further, in his assessment, "the vast majority of women could be described as attractive, often extremely beautiful; by contrast, about half the male stars have not been handsome by any convention" (Levy, 1990b:250). These findings provide support for the assertion by Sontag (1979:473) that "a woman's fortunes depend, far more than a man's, on being at least 'acceptable' looking."

The importance placed on the physical appearance of women is hardly limited to film acting. For example, researchers (e.g., Deutsch et al., 1986) have found that, although the perceived attractiveness of both men and women decreases with age, evaluations of the femininity of women decrease, while evaluations of the masculinity of men are unaffected by age. More generally, researchers (Kite et al., 1991) have discovered that older women are rated as less feminine than younger women. Thus, despite evidence that men and women undergo similar psychological experiences as they age (Gove et al., 1989), the physical processes of aging may affect them differently. These processes have implications for the careers of both men and women, given that attractiveness has been found to positively affect the promotion decisions of personnel professionals (Morrow et al., 1990). Thus, there is every reason to believe that the effects of declining youth on the career opportunities of women may not be restricted to the acting profession. Women in professions that require a public presentation of self, such as law (Saporta and Halpern, 2002) or business, may suffer these effects to some extent. Indeed, the negative interaction effect of being a woman and being older is consistent with the concept of a "glass ceiling" with respect to managerial promotions (Maume, 1999).

These findings also have implications that go far beyond the differences between the careers of men and women in a high-status and high-income occupation. As noted at the outset, stars exert a pervasive influence on society as cultural role models. The very fact that most of the characters in films are men rather than women amounts to an "explicit devaluation of female talent on screen" (Bielby and Bielby, 1996:251) and an implicit cultural devaluation of women. This cultural devaluation of women is reinforced by the fact that they do not receive star billing as often as men. In short, films tell audiences that men are more important, in all kinds of contexts, than women. In addition, stars provide audiences with idealized images of masculinity and femininity. The problem, of course, is that men are allowed to age in film, and women are not. Male stars in their sixties are routinely cast as leads, even in physically demanding roles. Conversely, female stars are rarely cast as leads after they enter their forties. One consequence of this discrimination against older women is that male stars are often paired romantically with younger, often much younger, female stars. Unfortunately, the differential representation of men and women in film and television probably contributes to the cultural devaluation of older women in American society.

References

Arber, Sara, and Jay Ginn, 1991 "The invisibility of age: Gender and class in later life." *Sociological Review* 39: 260–291.

Balio, Tino, 1993 *Grand Design: Hollywood as a Modern Business Enterprise, 1930–1939*. New York: Scribner.

Bazzini, Doris G., William D. McIntosh, Stephen M. Smith, Sabrina Cook, and Caleigh Harris, 1997 "The aging woman in popular film: Underrepresented, unattractive, unfriendly, and unintelligent." *Sex Roles* 36: 531–543.

Bielby, Denise D., and William T. Bielby, 1993 "The Hollywood 'graylist?' Audience demographics and age stratification among television writers." *Current Research on Occupations and Professions* 8: 141–172.

——, 1996 "Women and men in film: Gender inequality among writers in a culture industry." *Gender and Society* 10: 248–270.

Bielby, William T., and Denise D. Bielby, 1992 "Cumulative versus continuous disadvantage in an unstructured labor market: Gender differences in the careers of television writers." *Work and Occupations* 19: 366–386.

Bordwell, David, Janet Staigner, and Kristin Thompson, 1985 *The Classical Hollywood Cinema: Film Style and Mode of Production to 1960*. New York: Columbia University Press.

Chappell, Neena L., and Betty Havens, 1980 "Old and female: Testing the double jeopardy hypothesis." *Sociological Quarterly* 21: 147–171.

Collins, Patricia Hill, 1990 *Black Feminist Thought: Knowledge, Consciousness, and the Politics of Empowerment*. New York: Routledge.

Davis, Richard H., 1980 *Television and the Aging Audience*. Los Angeles: University of Southern California Press.

Deutsch, Francine M., Carla M. Zalenski, and Mary E. Clark, 1986 "Is there a double standard of aging?" *Journal of Applied Social Psychology* 16: 771–785.

Dutka, Elaine, 1990 "Meryl Streep attacks hollywood's gender gap at SAG conference." *Los Angeles Times*, Aug. 3, p. 4.

Dyer, Richard, 1998 *Stars*. London: British Film Institute.

Falk, Ursula Adler, and Gerhard Falk, 1997 *Ageism, the Aged and Aging in America: On Being Old in an Alienated Society*. Springfield, IL: Charles C. Thomas.

Faulkner, Robert R., and Andy B. Anderson, 1987 "Short-term projects and emergent careers: Evidence from Hollywood." *American Journal of Sociology* 92: 879–909.

Ferraro, Kenneth F., and Melissa M. Farmer, 1996 "Double jeopardy to health hypothesis for African Americans: Analysis and critique." *Journal of Health and Social Behavior* 37: 27–43.

Gerbner, George, 1998, "Cultivation analysis: An overview." *Mass Communications and Society* 1: 175–194.

Gilberg, Michael, and Terence Hines, 2000 "Male entertainment award winners are older than female winners." *Psychological Reports* 86: 175–178.

Gove, Walter R., Suzanne T. Ortega, and Carolyn Briggs Style, 1989 "The maturational and role perspectives on aging and self through the adult years: An empirical evaluation." *American Journal of Sociology* 94: 1117–1145.

Herzog, Charlotte Cornelia, and Jane Marie Gaines, 1991 " 'Puffed sleeves before tea-time:' Joan Crawford, Adrian and women audiences." In Christine Gledhill (ed.), *Stardom: Industry of Desire*: 74–91. London: Routledge.

Jacobs, Jerry A., 1989 *Revolving Doors: Sex Segregation in Women's Careers*. Stanford, CA: Stanford University Press.

King, Deborah K., 1988 "Multiple jeopardy, multiple consciousness: The context of a black feminist ideology." *Signs* 14: 42–72.

Kite, Mary E., Kay Deaux, and Margaret Miele, 1991 "Stereotypes of young and old: Does age outweigh gender?" *Psychology and Aging* 6: 19–27.

Kmenta, Jan, 1986 *Elements of Econometrics*. New York: Macmillan.

Krämer, Peter, 1999 "A powerful cinema-going force? Hollywood and female audiences since the 1960s." In Melvyn Stokes and Richard Maltby (eds.), *Identifying Hollywood's Audiences: Cultural Identity and the Movies*: 93–108. London: BFI Publishing.

Levy, Emanuel, 1989 "The democratic elite: America's movie stars." *Qualitative Sociology* 12:29–54.

—— , 1990a "Stage, sex, and suffering: Images of women in American films." *Empirical Studies of the Arts* 8: 53–76.

—— , 1990b "Social attributes of American movie stars." *Media, Culture and Society* 12: 247–267.

Levy, Judith A., 1988 "Intersections of gender and aging." *Sociological Quarterly* 29: 479–486.

Lorence, Jon, and Jeylan T. Mortimer, 1989 "Job involvement through the life course: A panel study of three age groups." *American Sociological Review* 50: 618–638.

Markridge, Kyriakos S., Diane M. Timbers, and Scott J. Osberg, 1984 "Aging and health: A longitudinal study." *Archives of Gerontology and Geriatics* 3: 33–49.

Markson, Elizabeth W., and Carol A. Taylor, 1993 "Real versus reel world: Older women and the academy awards." *Women and Therapy* (Special Issue: Faces of Women and Aging) 14: 157–172.

Maume, David J., Jr., 1999 "Glass ceilings and glass escalators: Occupational segregation and race and sex differences in managerial promotions." *Work and Occupations* 26: 483–509.

McMullin, Julie, 1995, "Theorizing age and gender relations." In Sara Arber and Jay Ginn (eds.), *Connecting Gender and Ageing: A Sociological Approach*: 30–41. Buckingham, UK: Open University Press.

Michaelson, Judith, 1993 "Blacklist gone—Now it's a graylist, conferees believe." *Los Angeles Times*, Sept. 13, p. 2.

Moen, Phyllis, 2001 "The gendered life course." In Robert H. Binstock and Linda K. George (eds.), *Handbook of Aging and the Social Sciences*: 179–196. San Diego: Academic Press.

Morrow, Paula C., James C. McElroy, Bernard G. Stamper, and Mark A. Wilson, 1990 "The effects of physical attractiveness and other demographic characteristics on promotion decisions." *Journal of Management* 16: 723–736.

Motion Picture Association, 2002 *2002 Movie Attendance Study*. Encino, CA: Motion Picture Association of America.

Nash, Jay Robert, and Stanley Ralph Ross, 1999 *The Motion Picture Guide*. Chicago: Cinebooks.

Price, Derek J. D., 1976 "A general theory of bibliometric and other commutative advantage processes." *Journal of the American Society for Information Science* 27: 292.

Quart, Leonard, and Albert Auster, 2002 *American Film and Society Since 1945*. Westport, CT: Praeger.

Quigley Publications, 1994 *International Motion Picture Almanac*. New York: Quigley Publications.

Reskin, Barbara F., 2003 "Including mechanisms in our models of ascriptive inequality." *American Sociological Review* 68: 1–21.

Riley, Matilda White, 1987 "On the significance of age in sociology." *American Sociological Review* 52: 1–14.

Rosten, Leo C., 1941 *Hollywood: The Movie Colony, The Movie Makers*. New York: Arno Press.

Saporta, Ishak, and J. J. Halpern, 2002 "Being different can hurt: Effects of deviations from physical norms on lawyers' salaries." *Industrial Relations* 41: 426–466.

Schatz, Thomas, 1997 *Boom and Bust: American Cinema in the 1940s*. Berkeley and Los Angeles: University of California Press.

Screen Actors Guild, 1999 "Screen actors guild casting data finds ageism still a critical issue for American performers." Press Release, April 21.

—— , 2002 "Screen Actors Guild employment statistics reveal decrease in total number of TV/theatrical roles: Decline in roles for minorities." Press Release, July 1.

Shipman, David, 1989 *The Great Movie Stars*. London: MacDonald.

Signorielli, Nancy, 1989 "Television and conceptions about sex roles: Maintaining conventionality and the status quo." *Sex Roles* 21: 337–356.

Simpson, Ida Harper, Richard L. Simpson, Mark Evers, and Sharon S. Poss, 1982 "Occupational recruitment, retention, and labor force cohort representation." *American Journal of Sociology* 87: 1287–1313.

Sontag, Susan, 1979 "The double standard of aging." In Juanita H. Williams (ed.), *Psychology of Women: Selected Readings*: 462–478. New York: Academic Press.

Stacey, Jackie, 1991 "Feminine fascinations: Forms of identification in star-audience relations." In Janet Staiger (ed.), *The Studio System*: 141–163. New Brunswick, NJ: Rutgers University Press.

Truitt, Evelyn Mack, 1983 *Who Was Who on Screen*. New York: R. R. Bowker.

U.S. Bureau of the Census, 2000 *Resident Population Estimates of the United States by Age and Sex: April 1, 1990 to July 1, 1999, With Short-Term Projection to October 1, 2000*. Population Estimates Program, Population Division. Washington, DC: U.S. Government Printing Office.

Warren, John Robert, Robert M. Hauser, and Jennifer T. Sheridan, 2002 "Occupational stratification across the life course: Evidence from the Wisconsin longitudinal study." *American Sociological Review* 67: 432–455.

Wexman, Virginia Wright 1993 *Creating the Couple: Love, Marriage, and Hollywood Performance*. Princeton, NJ: Princeton University Press.

Chapter 7

Charles S. Tahiro

THE *TWILIGHT ZONE* OF CONTEMPORARY HOLLYWOOD PRODUCTION (2002)

THE "ACCIDENT"

IN THE EARLY-MORNING HOURS OF July 23, 1982, a film crew working in the Santa Clarita Valley on the outskirts of Los Angeles was shooting a scene for a film set during the Vietnam War. In one shot, a helicopter was meant to hover over the film's star, Vic Morrow, and two child extras. As the helicopter approached, a nearby hut built for the occasion was to explode. The charge for the explosion was set by professional technicians. The helicopter was flown by an experienced pilot.

After photographing the shot, the force of the explosion proved too great for the pilot to handle, sending the helicopter careening out of control. As it crashed to the ground, its rotors decapitated Morrow and the two children. The pilot survived the crash.

Under California labor regulations in effect at the time, the two children were working illegally, since the shoot took place later than the children were allowed to work. Fines totaling $62,375 were levied against the studio producing the film, Warner Bros., three other companies, and some individuals involved in the production.[1] Attention then shifted to assigning responsibility for the accident. Blame increasingly focused on the film's director, John Landis. Along with associate producer George Folsey, Jr., and unit production manager Dan Allingham, Landis was eventually tried for involuntary manslaughter. All three men were acquitted. The pilot of the helicopter lost his license but was not prosecuted. The completed *Twilight Zone Movie* included the scene that caused the accident, albeit without the decapitation.

One would expect, given their commitment to political evaluation, that academic media critics would study incidents resulting in the loss of life with at least the same level of interest given to gender and ethnicity. Yet an overview of such academically respectable media studies journals as *Screen*, with its stated commitment to leftist political causes,[2] the *Quarterly Review of Film and Television*,[3] with a similar commitment to "progressive" criticism, and this publication, *Cinema Journal*, the mouthpiece for an organization that has repeatedly positioned itself on the left of political issues, reveals a peculiar silence on fatal accidents like the decapitations on the set of *The Twilight Zone Movie*.

Had *The Twilight Zone Movie* incident been an isolated event, this reluctance would be understandable. Since such accidents are in fact common and integral to the logic of industrial filmmaking,[4] the failure of media studies scholars to address them suggests a rather odd definition of political responsibility. While a plausible explanation for this lack of attention to production realities could be found in the hypocrisies of academic criticism itself, this discussion will focus instead on the consequences of the structure and ideology of contemporary mass-media production. By necessity, this overview must be sketchy and superficial. A detailed study would run to book length. This article can, however, provide the contours for future debate.

THE PROBLEM

The first problem encountered by anyone interested in describing contemporary production is how to generalize about a system that in many ways seems to be a collection of exceptions. Working on a production or series of them and deriving conclusions from those experiences would be one way to gather information, but, of course, such involvement is neither encouraged nor rewarded by academia. Moreover, Hollywood is a notoriously closed community that does not respond well to outsiders poking their noses into its business.[5]

Unlike media studies journals, the popular and trade publications provide a wealth of information and a good starting point for debate. Whether the even-handed technical descriptions of individual productions in *American Cinematographer* or book-length histories of productions gone awry, like Steven Bach's *Final Cut: Dreams and Disaster in the Making of "Heaven's Gate"* and Julie Salamon's *The Devil's Candy: "The Bonfire of the Vanities" Goes to Hollywood*, there is plenty of material available for anyone wishing to read between the lines of self-consciously objective description.[6]

The daily press also provides resources. The *Twilight Zone* incident received considerable coverage in the *Los Angeles Times*, for example. The paper reported over several years on the investigation of the accident, the subsequent manslaughter trial, and the fallout from both. Its coverage also demonstrated the limits of such an approach. Treating the incidents leading to the acquittal as a series of atomized events, the various *Times* writers made no effort to understand the accident. Only Randall Sullivan in *Rolling Stone* tried to go a step further by interpreting events.[7] His conclusion, that Landis was chiefly responsible because he was the director, while too limited in scope nonetheless suggests the terms for a discussion.

What remains true of all these accounts is that they focus on individuals as the engines of contemporary production. This belief in the possibility of individual expression is shared by every person involved in filmmaking, from studio chiefs to dolly grips, from movie stars to caterers. This myth persists despite the contradictions offered by these workers' daily experiences, and despite the equally well-known reality that "freedom of expression" is always constrained by studio efforts to maximize market position and profits.[8]

The focus on auteurism is also significant in that this ideology influences material success. Had *The Twilight Zone Movie* been a hit, it would have enhanced John Landis's position in the industry and raised his critical reputation. This is the concrete, material manifestation of ideology: the financial success, the greater power, future employment, and critical attention the myth of artistic freedom and responsibility creates. Even if reviewers remain universally hostile to a successful director's work, a mantra like "a film by John Landis" repeated frequently enough eventually becomes self-confirming. It is, finally, not achievement that creates authorship but advertising.[9]

Accepted fully, of course, this ideology should lead to article titles such as "The Fatal Accident by John Landis" or, as Randall Sullivan expressed it, "The Auteur Theory of Homicide."[10] Instead, responsibility for breaking the law or for financial failure is diffused, muted, or deflected to the point of disappearance. This avoidance and obfuscation exonerate the director and hide the culpability of the studios, production company executives, and technicians who may have had a share in the accident. Responsibility gets suspended in the air between people's intentions and actions, obviously there—three people undeniably died—but conveniently vaporous and vague, still hanging around like secondhand smoke.

THE STRUCTURE

Responsibility hides easily in the nooks and crannies of modern Hollywood production, fragmented, elusive, a moving target. Indeed, the term "movie studio" today is little more than a figure of speech, a descriptive convenience to cover the irrational industrial, financial, artistic, and power practices that pass for rational organization. The companies that inherited their names and prestige from the high-studio days of the 1930s and 1940s may or may not be major "players" on the current film scene, but the only resemblance they have to their ancestors is the hierarchical decision-making practices that continue to predominate. (Most of them, for example, no longer even have physical facilities. When they need studio space, they rent it from other companies.)

Power has been reconfigured and made more complex, but it is certainly not more democratically distributed. Alongside the studios, for example, are the large agencies, which, while holding real power, probably hold less than is often supposed. Agencies depend on their list of clients. Because the larger ones run the gamut of talent from actors to writers to directors, more successful agents can "package" deals that bring these people together. (Whether they will work well together or make a decent movie is a secondary question.) Agents also have the power to see that projects do not get produced. If, for example, a popular actor's agent refuses to read the script for a project built on exploiting the performer's personality, the producers have to either find another less suitable actor or abandon the project.

Still, this considerable influence is limited by the agents' lack of control over budgets and finances and by the inconstancy of their "talent" (i.e., clients). Talent is handsomely rewarded financially and enjoys the double-edged perquisite of public attention in a way that studio executives and agents do not. This situation has the beneficial side effect for the agent and the producer of putting the talent on the front lines of responsibility. If a film is a success, all share in the rewards, including the otherwise ghostly executives poised to consume the fruits of productive labor. If a film is a failure, or if a fatal accident occurs on the set, only the artists are blamed. Their careers are put at risk, while the executives move to another studio.

Like that of the agencies that represent them, the power of artists is restricted by their lack of control over the budgeting process. While their "noes" can sink a project and their "yeses" can help one get produced, the decision to finance a film ultimately lies outside the artists' control. This is why so many successful stars, directors, producers, and writers form their own production companies. Particularly after a large popular success, it is common for studios to sign long-term contracts with successful talent, guaranteeing artists a certain number of "green lights" to produce proposed projects and executives financial security. Both guarantees are illusory, of course; one successful project does not assure future popularity, and in fact most long-term production deals are eventually bought up by studios when "hot" commodities prove to be lukewarm long-term investments.

For the most part, independent production companies put together the personnel who actually make films. These technicians and support staff are usually hired on contractual, one-time bases. Top-level contract laborers, such as cinematographers, editors, and designers, in turn subcontract their assistants and crews. For producers who sign guild agreements, all of these staff must be members of the unions that represent the interests of the actors, soundmen, grips, and myriad other filmmaking subprofessions.

With their exclusionary practices and conservative definitions of craft, guilds are indeed the semifeudal organizations their name suggests. At the lowest level of the power pyramid, union members are the only film workers forced to deal with capitalist realities. As runaway production and low-budget independent work break down their control over employment and film school graduates, trained in the technical arcana that were once craft labor's source of strength, enter the workforce without loyalties to the guilds, film unions experience the corrosive effects of economic competition that impact other industrial laborers. These unions nonetheless remain powerful, particularly with respect to major studio-financed productions.

However, unions can exercise power only negatively, by disrupting or thwarting a production. They have no control over what is produced. At best, unions can militantly defend their members' interests, although their behavior in this capacity is often colored by the need to ensure organizational survival at the expense of individual interest. It is common, for example, for unions to punish members for working on nonunion productions. In this sense, the power the guilds exercise over their members reflects the monopoly control exercised by the studios. The two parties are mutually dependent, if often antagonistic, forces. And, to the extent they use their limited power not to change the system but to exclude others and to guard their privileges, the guilds are profoundly conservative institutions.

There is another group of people, below the unions in the hierarchy, who are too low to be considered a meaningful part of the "power pyramid." These are the unemployed or underemployed staff. Not members of protective guilds, they comprise the eager labor pool, the "line waiting outside the door," of people being paid next to nothing or literally nothing, hoping for their "big break." These people go as far as their ambition and salesmanship allow. Some reach the pinnacles of Hollywood power. More lead lives of destitution, dying of hope. Consisting of students, hangers-on, parasites, semi- and no-talents, new arrivals to Los Angeles, and other hopefuls, these are the migrant laborers of Hollywood. They are just as ruthlessly exploited as their counterparts in agriculture and just as essential to the functioning of the system. The difference is that migrant workers *know* they are being exploited (and the public knows it too). The Hollywood lumpenproletariat, by contrast, is content to be on a first-name basis with fame and prefers that the public *not* know how thoroughly unglamorous its work is.

Many of the more successful people in Hollywood are major contributors to the Democratic Party, and most probably consider themselves politically progressive.[11] They would no doubt be shocked to hear themselves described as exploiters. In fact, the average Hollywood executive has a degree of control over his or her employees that the most rapacious robber baron would envy, yet few have any compunction about exercising that power. Part of this lack of conscience may result from the fact that many of these "executives" are stars and directors who head their own companies. They are perfectly comfortable cavalierly exercising power, because they are used to getting their way on a set. (For example, director Steven Spielberg was one of the producers of *The Twilight Zone Movie*, as was John Landis himself.)

Contemporary Hollywood's abysmal labor practices make the old-fashioned patriarchy of the studio days seem enlightened by comparison. The injustices of the mythical casting couch are nothing compared to the daily, mundane abuse of the average worker. Firing someone in a fit of pique is a regular occurrence, "interns" lucky enough to get paid are usually hired for less than a living wage, and none has a guarantee of a job after the internship is over. Secretaries are expected to work extra hours on short notice with no additional compensation, people who dare to put their private lives ahead of their jobs risk losing the latter, staff often find themselves training their own replacements, and on and on. Most of these practices are in violation of laws enacted by the very politicians these people have helped to rise to power, but no one dares to complain. Hollywood's code of silence is stricter than the Mafia's and just as difficult to break.

Most of the labor abuses in Hollywood derive from the thoroughly irrational nature of its business dealings. To give one small example, it is usual for the power elite of Hollywood (i.e., those in a position to make decisions) to take off the week between Christmas and New Year. It is therefore virtually impossible for a major deal to be closed that week except, perhaps, on the slopes at Aspen. Thus, the only event likely to happen in the offices of these people, except for those with something in production, is the compulsive hourly phone call from the boss, asking if anything has happened.

Under such circumstances, it would be sensible to give the office staff the week off. Even if something happens, nothing can be concluded until the bosses return, because they have deliberately structured their companies to make their presence indispensable. Instead, virtually all support staff are expected to work. The only objective explanation for this requirement is self-flattery. Executives can tell themselves and others that their staffs are so loyal that they show up during the holidays, or that they recognize how important it is to be there "in case" something comes up, or a million other nonsensical rationalizations. Of course, since just about all executives require this service of their staffs, it's a meaningless pose, but then, since it *is* true of just about every executive, such unnecessary "work" becomes a *requirement* of the job, even though *everyone knows* nothing will actually happen. It's a self-affirming cycle of bluff.

At the top of this heap of contradictions sits the "auteur" of industry, the multimillionaire entrepreneur who, because of the state of development of media companies, possesses power unusual for a large corporation. Journalist Emma Duncan notes:

> Few chief executives can match Rupert Murdoch, Ted Turner, or Sumner Redstone for guts, bloody-mindedness, and sheer aggression.
> There are two reasons for that. One is that show business naturally attracts big egos. The other is that the global entertainment business is still at the entrepreneurial stage of development, with companies run not by hired bosses, but by men who created them.[12]

Not surprisingly, the service class and contract workers receive the fewest financial rewards under this system, despite the repeated refrain that overpriced labor leads to excessive budgets. In fact, the real reason for the skyrocketing production costs is the "above-the-line" fees paid to directors, stars, writers, and producers, who demand such upfront payment because they expect the studios to cheat them out of their fair share of any profits.

Studios and the people who control them, while receiving little publicity from this or that hit, reap huge financial rewards, maintain copyrights over products, and control all distribution and exhibition.[13] To put financial realities in perspective, consider the example of the "disastrous" *Bonfire of the Vanities*. Warners' prestige release of 1990, *Bonfire* cost between $45 and $50 million to complete. Its box-office failure caused much public hand wringing by studio executives about "out-of-control" budgets. Nonetheless, that same year, Warner Bros.' studio head, Steven Ross, was the highest-paid executive in America, with reported earnings of $78.11 million (i.e., more than 50 percent more than the *entire budget* for *Bonfire*).[14] With compensation like that, talent and staff could be paid nothing and budgets would still be out of control.

By downplaying their stake in individual productions, studio executives exercise control, reap the greatest financial reward possible, and avoid responsibility for catastrophe when it occurs. By sanctioning, even exaggerating, the contributions of artists, studio executives shield their own activities from public scrutiny. They are thus rarely held as accountable as their equivalents in other corporations, since they can always point to the waywardness of talent as the reason for their failures.

Studio executives risk very little by playing up the "art" of film production. Even if artists increase their power and asking prices by being involved in successive hits, studio executives retain the ultimate power of "yea" or "nay." A film is "by" someone only if a studio finances it. The artists' degree of creative responsibility is secondary to the corporation's control of its assets, to its political and economic power.

THE WAR

When people gather finally to make a film, one of the most common and accurate analogies used to describe their activities, made by participants and onlookers alike, is to a war.[15] For example, consider Julie Salamon's description of the first day of principal photography on the set of *The Bonfire of the Vanities*:

> Despite the apparent casualness of the troops . . . the film world was as rigidly hierarchical as the military. Richard Sylbert had been right when he'd said that moviemaking was like war. The perfect war, in fact. There were uniforms and regiments and communications on walkie-talkies in code, middle-of-the-night maneuvers under grim conditions, and an overwhelming sense of mission. But all that got shot was film.[16]

This is more than dramatization about an industry addicted to hyperbole. It is a nearly literal description of the attitudes film workers shooting a film have toward the inconveniences of a physical world ceaselessly exploited in the service of spectacle and fiction. The war analogy nonetheless misses the extent to which the command structure on a set mirrors the overall hierarchy working behind the scenes. Brian DePalma may have been calling the shots in New York, but he was at most the field commander in a battle directed from Hollywood HQ. Salamon's description also provides no reasons for why filmmakers view the world antagonistically and the potential consequences of their attitudes.

Movie corporations have a double investment in the kind of large-scale special effects used in *The Twilight Zone Movie*. To distinguish its impersonally produced commodities from more distinctive fare, studios invest in pleasurable, spectacular surfaces to dress up recycled content. These spectacles then become the technical standard against which more individually compelling work is measured and found lacking. Since only corporations with access to mass capital are in a position to produce such images, the spectacular surface becomes one of the chief supports of the industry. (Ironically, in trying to distinguish these commodities from one another, both industry and criticism repeatedly emphasize what is thoroughly unoriginal about them, their literary content.)

At the same time, all films, in order to persuade, must convince as compelling illusions of real space. It is that capacity, structured in time, that distinguishes cinema from other media. Thus, the "great special effect," no matter how it is achieved, is so because of its capacity to persuade viewers momentarily that the event the effect represents "really" happened. That impact can be created only by measuring the manufactured effect against real space.

If the car must truly crash, if the building really has to collapse, or if the explosion must actually set the helicopter off course, then filmmaking is in a real war with the physical environment. That war is controlled and circumscribed, to be sure, but physical destruction is still the purpose of the exercise. Filmmakers producing such effects may not set out to kill people, but no one should be surprised if they do. Such "accidents" are a logical consequence of flirting with death, the promise just nearly averted. If we do not believe someone could be killed in these elaborate games of Chicken, the effects cease to compel as spectacle and thereby cannot provide exchange value for mediocre content.

THE ALTERNATE VERSION

Consider, then, this alternative description of the events leading to the deaths on *The Twilight Zone Movie*. A large movie company, seeking profit, wants to distinguish its product from that of its competitors. While it could diversify into alternative modes of production and expression, habit and proven success lead it to continue to invest in narrative-based two-hour spectacles. Since the spectacular image requires professional technicians, a large budget is required to produce that image. To ensure profit from such a potentially large investment, the studio hires "proven" writers, directors, and actors as a quasi-guarantee of its investment. Because of their demonstrated capacity to generate revenue, these workers insist on higher salaries, thus raising the budget that much more. This expense requires even more neutering of content and expression to attract the widest audience possible.

Given that both the studio and the audience have an ideological investment in the "realistic" image, if the script for *The Twilight Zone Movie* requires scenes of war, then, to a certain extent, the conditions of war will have to be reproduced on the set. If the script further describes an outdoor battle, then those conditions must be staged outdoors, probably on location. Once outside the controlled physical environment of a studio, physical hazards increase with the unpredictability of wayward environmental conditions.

On location, the crew photographing the scene is directed by someone who has been encouraged to believe he should create the most spectacular image his imagination and budget will allow. Indeed, he has a *responsibility* to create such an image, since special effects will help to distinguish his product from its competition. Since one law (forbidding child labor after hours) has already been broken, the precedent for ignoring constraints has been set. Not that such a precedent is necessary: in an environment in which participants view themselves as soldiers in a war, even if only a war to get the "best shot," legal niceties are not high priorities. In any event, actors, special-effects technicians, and pilots are, like the director, paid to do what they are told.

When an "accident" occurs and fatalities cannot be hushed up, there is an effort to fix blame. Because of the indifference of the critical community, this effort becomes strictly formal and legal, rather than moral or political. Thus, instead of trying to understand how and why three people were put in a position that resulted in their deaths, efforts were made to determine if laws were broken and, if so, who was legally responsible for the decision to break them. Where there is no contest, as in the fact that the children were clearly employed at a time when they should not have been, punishment is meted out within the guidelines established by statute.

Fines cover the breaking of a labor regulation. A criminal court determines responsibility for deaths. Since the ideology of singular creation and responsibility structures the thinking about film workers and studio executives and is fundamental to the legal system itself, the search for blame is directed toward finding the individuals responsible for the "accident." Since, thanks to auteurism, high-profile directors are most in the public eye, they logically become the major focus of any inquiry about criminal responsibility for activities on a set. This focus overlooks the structural dynamics that positioned individuals to be involved in such a situation. It contains responsibility by failing to shed light on the overall hierarchy of corporate command.

Thus, it makes legal sense to have tried Landis, Folsey, and Allingham as the individuals most directly responsible for the event. Having delivered a "not-guilty" verdict, the legal system becomes silent. It does not make moral sense, however, for the process to have stopped with the verdict. If we accept the logic of ascribing blame to individuals, and if Landis et al. were not guilty, who was? Unless attributing events to Divine Will (something the legal system may be willing to accept but that materialist critics should not), responsibility has to be located somewhere on earth and in human actions. And if the "not-guilty" verdict should be read as a recognition that individuals cannot be held responsible for accidents resulting from corporate decisions, why has the legal system not been reformed to allow corporations to be held criminally responsible? (Corporations already enjoy many of the legal privileges of individuals, such as the ability to hold copyright. Why then do they not have the same legal responsibilities?)

There is little likelihood that the legal system will be restructured to make corporations or the individuals who head them criminally responsible for actions performed while creating their products, except, of course, in the case of such economic crimes as fraud or embezzlement. One does not have to be a cynic, just a realist, to recognize that in a capitalist society laws are structured to benefit corporations and individuals with massed capital. If we doubt this, we should consider that exactly two years after the *Twilight Zone* accident, and reportedly partially inspired by it, the state of California's Department of Industrial Relations announced revisions to child-safety rules. Although spelling out in detail what was not permissible and considered dangerous, the new rules *increased* the number of hours children could legally be employed. The rationale for these revisions, as expressed by California Labor Commissioner C. Robert Simpson, was "to induce producers to stay in California."[17]

What the courts may not touch, we the critical community ought to consider. Therefore, to determine political responsibility for the *Twilight Zone* or any similar movie set accident, we need to ask some questions:

(1)   Who stood to gain the most?
(2)   Who authorized the project?
(3)   Who had ultimate authority for activities on the set?
(4)   Who continues to make money on distribution of the film?

As for our responsibilities as critics, we should ask:

(1)   Why are the deaths and maiming of film industry workers and the industrial practices that cause them less important than issues of representation pertaining to "political" criticism?
(2)   What degree of complicity does silence establish between the "critical" community and those responsible for such actions?
(3)   Is the most potent ideological deconstruction to be found in representation or in the attitudes of production itself?
(4)   To what extent does our nearly exclusive attention to industrial, commercial film-making as a subject help to perpetuate its coercive control over audiences and to suppress potential alternatives?

If such a call for an analysis of actions seems naive, consider the postscript to the *Twilight*

Zone story. Six years after the accident, long after the publicity for the manslaughter trial had died down, the only concrete expression of responsibility in the entire affair, the fines levied by the State of California's Occupational Safety and Health Administration against Warner Bros., Landis, and others were reduced from the initial total of $62,375 to $1,350.[18]

Divided by three, that's $450 per head.

Who's being naive?

Notes

1   As reported by Tracy Wood, "State Agency Slashes Fines in *Twilight Zone* Filming Deaths," *Los Angeles Times*, February 1, 1988, 16. According to Eric Malnic, director John Landis and three others were fined $5,000 apiece. Malnic. "4 Will Pay *Twilight Zone* Fines," *Los Angeles Times*, June 28, 1983, 1+.

2   See, for example, Sam Rohdie's editorial in *Screen* 12, no. 2 (summer 1971): 4–6.

3   See Jane Gaines and Michael Renov, "Preface," *Quarterly Review of Film and Video* 11, no. 1 (winter 1989): vii–viii.

4   For a look at some of the incidents in the early 1980s, see Michael London, "Safety First, Last, or if Ever?" *Los Angeles Times*, February 6, 1983, 1+. For a discussion of why such accidents are integral to Hollywood expression, see my *Pretty Pictures: Production Design and the History Film* (Austin: University of Texas Press, 1998).

5   Much of the following description of individual abuses is derived either from personal experience working in "the industry" or from anecdotal information relayed to me by others.

6   Steven Bach, *Final Cut: Dreams and Disaster in the Making of Heaven's Gate* (New York: Morrow, 1985), and Julie Salamon, *The Devil's Candy: "The Bonfire of the Vanities" Goes to Hollywood* (New York: Dell, 1991).

7   Randall Sullivan, "Death in the Twilight Zone," *Rolling Stone*, June 21, 1984, 31+.

8   It is debatable how accurate auteurism ever was as a description of classical Hollywood, but it has never been less accurate than it is today. Only a handful of contemporary American filmmakers have anything approaching a distinctive visual style, and only a few more have consistent thematic concerns. The rest are highly paid executors who rely on technicians and a lot of money to cover their basic lack of imagination. Many are graduates of film schools.

9   Films like *The Twilight Zone Movie*, with no distinction but their negative publicity, create unique marketing problems. See Jim Seale, "The Untouchables," *Los Angeles Times*, June 19, 1983, 1+, for a discussion of the difficulties publicity departments face in selling such films.

10 Sullivan, "Death in the Twilight Zone," 31.

11 See, for example, "Lexington," "The End of the Affair," *The Economist*, August 19, 2000, on the relationship between Hollywood and the Clinton administration.

12 Emma Duncan, "Wheel of Fortune: A Survey of Technology and Entertainment," *The Economist*, November 21–27, 1998, 56f.

13 The studio chief's anonymity may be giving way to the temptations of fame. See "Mr. Bronfman in Tinseltown," *The Economist*, November 21, 1998, 66–67, and particularly "Business as the New Rock and Roll," *The Economist*, November 28, 1998, 70. The latter article points out some of the dangers for executives who acquire too visible a public profile.

14 Salamon, *The Devil's Candy*, 419.

15 For an elaborated theoretical discussion of the relationship between film and military technology, see Paul Virilio, *War and Cinema: The Logistics of Perception*, trans. Patrick Camiller (London: Verso, 1989).

16 Salamon, *The Devil's Candy*, 113.

17 Gene Blake, "'Twilight Zone' Deaths Inspire New Child-Safety Rules," *Los Angeles Times*, June 23, 1984, 22.

18 Wood, "State Agency Slashes Fines in *Twilight Zone* Filming Deaths," 16.

Chapter 8

Shari Roberts

THE LADY IN THE TUTTI-FRUTTI HAT: CARMEN MIRANDA, A SPECTACLE OF ETHNICITY (1993)

IN THE YEARS FROM 1939 TO 1944, just prior to and during U.S. involvement in World War II, Carmen Miranda, the "Brazilian Bombshell," appeared in eight Hollywood musicals and two Broadway musical revues, all of which were highly successful. When Miranda's *Weekend in Havana* opened in 1941, it received top box office statistics for that week—over twice the amount achieved by *Citizen Kane*, which was in its second week.[1] The speed with which rival studios jumped on the Fox-Miranda bandwagon reflects the Latina actress's popularity and profitability. Miranda wannabes included Lina Romay, "Cugie's Latin Doll" of M-G-M; Margo of RKO; and Maria Montez of Universal; not to mention Acquanetta, the "Venezuelan Volcano," and Olga San Juan, the "Puerto Rican Pepperpot." Although not billed as the star in most of her musicals, Miranda was, according to the popular press, the "oomph that stops the show."[2] In fact, for her debut in the United States in *The Streets of Paris* on Broadway, Miranda's songs weren't listed in the program and she appeared for only six minutes, but she was still seen as "the outstanding hit of the show."[3] What was the attraction that brought such instant fame in the United States to an actress who never succeeded in exceeding her status as a specialty act? And what appeal did these films hold for female viewers, who comprised the majority of home-front audiences?

World War II created a home front containing a higher percentage of financially and otherwise independent women than had existed before the war, which helped contribute to the greater number of female film stars and female fans during wartime.[4] The musical, as the most popular wartime film genre, consequently offers a rich field in which to investigate issues of feminine representation and reception. Jane Feuer and others have read musicals as specifically resistant to typical Hollywood narrative positioning because of the direct address of the viewer by the performers during musical numbers, recalling more participatory modes of live entertainment.[5] Stars, whose appeal transcends their film roles, further serve to disrupt narrative in Hollywood cinema because they necessarily address fans directly through marketing and publicity.[6] In addition, the image of women in film has been explored by many theorists as a spectacle that can disrupt the typical narrative drive of Hollywood film.[7] The representation of women in films and related direct-address advertising during World War II was affected by the propagandistic attempts of the government, via Office of War Information film and advertising guidelines, to influence women's self-conception and consequential behavior.[8] Drawing on, but expanding and historicizing all of these claims, I argue that the complex figure of the World War II female musical star offers a juncture of all these modes of spectacle and direct address—for example, the musical number, the star, publicity and advertising, the feminine image in film, and World War II propaganda addressed to women. In particular, I want to explore what happens when this historically specific figure is also a spectacle of ethnicity.

In this essay I examine Miranda's conflicted star text through textual analysis of her films and through study of primary source materials, especially publicity and articles in fan magazines and newspapers. While exploring the ways historical fans may have understood, appreciated, and used Miranda, I link my reading of the historical and textual material on a single star to questions of feminine and ethnic representation and reception. While Carmen Miranda's parodic star text offers various negative images of Latin Americans and of women, her persona also reveals these images as stereotypes, allowing for negotiated readings by fans. Finally, I argue that Miranda's fans were drawn to an imagined masquerade performed by their star, which she was able to create through her performance of her own character as both feminine and ethnic excess, a spectacle that ultimately puts into question both feminine and foreign stereotyping.

To understand how Miranda was experienced and used by her contemporary audience, we need to explore her star text, which is comprised of many smaller, individual texts, including films, radio shows, concerts, publicity photos, and records, as well as interviews, articles, and reviews.[9] These individual texts combine to constitute the star through work that entails an integration and reading across possible elements—work that involves both chance and choice. We must read Miranda through her specific historical moment in order to approach audiences' understanding of the star text as a signifying system. For instance, during World War II, Axis powers—the Japanese, the Germans as represented by Hitler, and the Italians as represented by Mussolini—were portrayed in the popular press by ethnic stereotypings that stressed dark hair and dark skin.[10] Blond, therefore, came to be perceived as the most unquestionably "American" hair color, and it is not a surprise that Miranda's studio supported a golden blonde policy: all of Fox's female wartime stars—Betty Grable, Alice Faye, and Vivian Blaine—were uniformly blonde. To accommodate Miranda to this blonde "policy," she was ideologically linked and filmically paired with Betty Grable, the feminine, all-American "norm" posited by 20th Century-Fox. If Grable was the norm, Miranda was the allowable cultural Other for wartime Hollywood, playing the dark but comic and, therefore, unthreatening foil to all the gilded wartime female musical stars. The press and her North American fans saw Miranda as the "Ambassadress of good will from Latin America," "an unofficial envoy from a carefree country."[11]

When Miranda began her U.S. film career in 1940, the threat of war with Germany was growing. President Roosevelt promoted the Good Neighbor policy in an attempt to maintain hemispheric unity in the face of foreign invasion. This policy subsequently became a part of the Office of War Information guidelines for the film industry: "In the field of world policy, I would dedicate this nation to the policy of the Good Neighbor, the neighbor who resolutely respects himself, and, because he does so, respects the rights of others; the neighbor who respects his obligations and respects the sanctity of agreements in and with a world of neighbors."[12] John Hay Whitney, head of the Motion Picture Division of the Office of the Coordinator of Inter-American Affairs, urged that "wherever the motion picture can do a basic job of spreading the gospel of the Americas' common stake in this struggle [against "the menace of Nazism"], that job must and shall be done."[13] Films were not products of a simple, top-down application of the Motion Picture Bureau of the Office of War Information guidelines. Film studios did, however, in general, follow these guidelines—incorporating pro-U.S. involvement messages both directly and indirectly into films, urging spectators to buy war bonds in film credits, participating in the production of pro-U.S. newsreels and short subject films, and encouraging actors to participate in U.S.O. tours and Hollywood canteens. At the same time, filmic war support was not only patriotic but profitable. Any support that a studio, a film, or an actor gave to the war effort was publicized by the studio and also generally received free publicity from the press. For example, Fox might have distributed pin-up photos of Betty Grable free to servicemen, but any cost incurred was certainly made up in profits achieved as she became the most popular star of the wartime period.

The complicated relationship between the government and the studio industry also resulted in the Fox translations of the government's Good Neighbor policy into the Miranda "exotic locale" fantasies, which depicted harmonically exploitative relations between the United States and Latin American countries. Fox's implementation of the Good Neighbor policy is represented in the opening shots of *The Gang's All Here* (1943): the SS *Brazil* unloads the major exports of Latin America—sugar, coffee, fruit, and finally Miranda herself, Brazil's most important export. Following this number, the nightclub host comments, "Well, there's your Good Neighbor policy!" and Miranda proceeds to teach the audience the "Uncle Sam-ba."

According to contemporary articles, Miranda, "as an advertisement for Roosevelt's good-neighbor policy, . . . [was] worth half a hundred diplomatic delegations."[14] While, according to Bosley Crowther of the *New York Times*, Betty Grable was "abundantly qualified to serve as a ministress plenipotentiary to the Latin American lands," Miranda was the "ambassadress of Latin America." Through an exchange of good will orchestrated by these two women, Fox films achieved the illusion of international, economic, and personal harmony. The scenario established here was a falsely simplistic us/them, United States versus the foreign Other, dichotomy. It parallels the long-established Hollywood tradition of male-female opposition, set up by the film structure as a pleasantly false, surface opposition of inessential differences that may be easily resolved through the "universal language" of love, represented here through music. Almost every film of this particular Fox musical sub-genre, the wartime exotic fantasy musical, has for its plot the initial "problem" of an "American" and a Latino foreigner who fall in love but must resolve cultural differences (and often other plot conflicts) in order to marry. The gender difference overlays the ethnic and national differences, and the sexual resolution works to resolve all differences. The underlying assumption of this logic is that "it's a small world after all," that "under the skin" we are all *essentially* the same, and that any differences between cultures are only superficial and irrelevant. Cultural and ethnic differences are seen as problems that can and should be easily resolved.

The Miranda star text, which consistently pushes this concept of U.S.–Latin American harmony, is permeated by a breezy, one-to-one "translation"—an exchange of North-to-South American culture and vice versa through the universal language of music and dance. Many of the songs in Miranda's films involve a "getting to know you" theme in which the main characters representing Latin America and the United States demonstrate the ease with which one can *learn* another country's songs, dances, and language—can *acquire* another country's culture. For example, in *Down Argentine Way* (1940), Don Ameche first sings the title song in Spanish, then Grable provides an English rendition, and the performance ends with the couple's duet in both Spanish and English:

> You'll be as gay as can be
> If you can learn to "*Si, si*," like Aladdin
> For just as soon as you learn then you'll never return to Manhattan.
> When you hear, "*Yo te amo*," you'll steal a kiss and then,
> If she should say, "*Mañana*," it's just to let you know that you're gonna meet again.

The lyrics, which provide a handy guide to Spanish and Argentinean culture, demonstrate that cross-cultural harmony can be achieved with the ease and speed of a couple of choruses.

Extra-filmically, in a 1942 radio broadcast called, "Hello Americans: Brazil," Orson Welles and Carmen Miranda jointly introduce U.S. listeners to the people, culture, and music of Brazil.[15] Welles reminds the audience that "America" does not exclusively mean the United States: "That's a big word, America. It's easy to forget how much it means. . . . We need to remember that America is two continents. . . . We the people of the United Nations of America now stand together. We ought to know each other better than we do." Listeners learn that *surdo* means a drum in Portuguese, and they hear Welles and Miranda sing an ideologically, if not melodically, harmonious duet. Here, as in her films, Miranda helps an (authoritative) American explain that any transnational problems can be solved with a little simple translation. Inhabitants of Rio, or *cariocas*, are made to seem less alien through a comparison to "Hoosiers," the inhabitants of Indiana; and the samba is presented as "the old two-step, really, with a South American accent . . . roll up the parlor rug, grab your best girl, and see what you make of it." Through such "how-to" demonstrations, both within and beyond her films, Miranda's star text encourages the assumption that ethnic differences merely present surface agitations that can be assimilated into a U.S. discourse of unity.

The disturbing and complex political, economic, and cultural situation of the United States during wartime is not only explicitly referred to by Fox's "good neighbor" musicals but also clouded by the conscientious simplicity of these films. The government's desire to unify the Americas in the face of potential invasion by Axis nations arose from real fear occasioned by the United States' eventual entry into the war. However, it could have been only superficially and temporarily reassuring to imagine that international political differences—here, Northern and Latin America, but by extension the United States and Europe—could be resolved through a few songs and a few kisses.[16] Audiences, viewing eight of these Latin American fantasies in less than four years, were quite conscious of the soft-sell propaganda of the Fox wartime musicals. As *Time* magazine said of Miranda's fourth film, "*Springtime in the Rockies* ends with a song called 'Pan-Americana Jubilee' and attempts to be just that by whipping together (1) Latin America (Cesar Romero, Carmen Miranda and her band), (2) the U.S. (Betty Grable, John Payne, Harry James and his band), (3) Canada (large Technicolor hunks of Lake Louise, where the action takes place). The addition of an Eskimo and a penguin would have made the show still more hemispheric in scope."[17]

Roosevelt's Good Neighbor policy directly related to the United States' economic investments and military intervention in *Central* America, not South America. While Miranda was from Brazil, while her films were set in *South* America and her theme song was "*Sous* American Way," Miranda's banana-and-fruit hats refer most directly to the imported products of *Central* America and its "banana republics." As the quintessential "good neighbor," therefore, Miranda substituted for Central America and thereby helped displace good-neighbor relations onto South America for the wartime Fox fantasies.[18] Fox's *Down Argentine Way* presents a positive view of U.S. intervention in which Grable stands in for Uncle Sam, intervening in the affairs of Latin America, represented by Don Ameche's father, "for his own good." Don Ameche says, "the best thing we can do for him is not to interfere," but Grable insists, "we can't leave things in the mess they're in now"—a mess caused, we discover, by her father. Of course, Grable is ultimately right, and her intervention solves all the problems that have erupted in the film. This exclusively pro-U.S. message did not go unnoticed by "local industry, critics and a sampling of the public" in Argentina, who questioned why Argentines were "pictur[ed] . . . as operating a phoney race track, while the gents from the U.S. were the good folk."[19]

How Latin American film audiences received the U.S. musicals greatly interested the film industry since European audiences had vanished because of the war, and Hollywood attempted to exploit Latin American markets.[20] A *Variety* review of *Down Argentine Way* reflects the industry conception that the Latin American population would only be attracted by films with "familiar" subject material: "Picture's reception in the South American sector will provide studios with an angle on potentialities of upping income on big pictures which carry backgrounds of those countries (instead of European settings). . . . *Down Argentine Way* should click in a big way in the southern hemisphere."[21] U.S. film producers thought that by making "Latin" films they would appeal automatically to financially attractive Latin audiences, but the films created according to this naive premise reduce the different South and Central American countries to an homogenization.

In the same vein, and in true "democratic" spirit, Fox cast Miranda as a variety of Latin American nationalities—*Down Argentine Way, That Night in Rio*, and *Weekend in Havana*. She appears either as herself, Carmen, or as some stereotypically Latin persona—alternately Querida, Chiquita, Chita, Marina, Carmelita, and, in four films, Rosita. Casting Miranda as a generic, homogenized version of our "good neighbor" robs her of any claim to her actual heritage.[22] The Hollywood homogenization also undercuts Miranda's already established star status in Brazil on radio, records, and in films. Miranda had made at least 136 records with three different record companies and appeared in five full-length films and one full-length play in Brazil before arriving in the United States in 1939.[23] Although many contemporary articles (over)-credited her with between 300 and 400 Brazilian records and nine sold-out South American tours pre-Hollywood, Miranda was simultaneously presented as a naïve Latina, awed by North American culture.[24] *The New York Post* quotes Miranda: " 'De meedle [middle, stomach],' she said, 'he get too teeck in Nort America. Always I eat in dis contree. De eat is verree, verree good. I most stop him! . . . I walk in de street, . . . and my eyes dey jomp out of de head. Sotch life! Sotch movement! I like him verree, verree motch. De men dey all look at me. I teenk dat's lofflee and I smile for dem. . . . I know p'raps one honderd werds—prettee good for Sous American gerl, no? Best I know ten English werds— MEN, MEN, MEN, MEN, MEN and MONNEE, MONNEE, MONNEE, MONNEE, MONNEE!' "[25] Miranda was also occasionally reported as a talent "discovered" alternately by the Shuberts and/or by Sonja Henie for U.S. audiences.[26] By transmuting her from a Brazilian star into a newly discovered ingenue, Miranda's publicity works to reduce the potential threat an in-control ethnic female entertainer might hold for U.S. audiences.

Not surprisingly, the alteration of Miranda's specific ethnicity and the improvisation of cultural details for whatever Latin American country was highlighted in each film failed to wow the audiences or reviewers South of the Border. For instance, the assistant commercial attaché to the American Embassy in Buenos Aires condemned the ridiculous representation of Argentina in *Down Argentine Way*: "Carmen Miranda, a *Brazilian* star, sings in *Portuguese* a *Tin Pan Alley rhumba* which speaks of *tangos* and rhumbas being played beneath a *pampa* moon."[27] Cuban reviewers were offended by the presentation of Miranda as Cuban in *Weekend in Havana* (1941): "Carmen Miranda talks, not sings, . . . and stomps around, not dances, something imported from Rio that has a bit of Hawaiian mime. . . . Carmen does not dance anything Cuban in that 'Weekend' called Havanese."[28] The reviewers' complaints address directly the homogenization of Latin American cultures which results in the erasure of specific nationalities and cultures through the United States "melting pot" fantasy. *Sintonia*, an Argentine weekly, argued that the "United States goodwill drive . . . has taken on the characteristics of a spiritual blitzkrieg prepared in the arsenals of Yankee advertising." The Argentine paper expressed concern that "this good neighbor policy might become dangerous" because the "Yanqui cine" was "striking a blow" at the Argentine film industry by crowding local productions out of the marketplace.[29] The hierarchical nature of the U.S. fantasy of unity was transparent to these Latin American reviewers.

Of course, the blandly asserted us/them of North and South America that forms a united Americas in the Miranda musicals obscures the unmentioned, internal us/them within the United States. All the U.S. citizens who were domestic Others were not a part of Hollywood's ideal, mainstream WASP audience, were not represented by Betty Grable or Alice Faye, and were thereby excluded from the Good Neighbor fantasy of inclusiveness. For instance, Japanese-Americans confined in U.S. concentration camps and African-Americans were non-WASP populations who might not have seen these same Good Neighbor musicals due to exclusionist exhibition practices of censorship and segregation. Even the simple resolution of the U.S./Latin America split fails in that, although the blonde lead woman and the Latino lead man often end up together, Miranda is paired romantically only with men of the "same" ethnicity (Argentinean, Brazilian, or Cuban, depending on the movie). Moreover, this uni-ethnic affair functions as the comic foil to the serious romance of the main couple.

Finally, then, this Fox musical myth of the essential sameness of all people, regardless of gender, nationality, or ethnicity, optimistically articulated through the "universal" language of music, refers to, but also veils, several political and economic factors that contributed to the complex relationships both within the United States and between the United States and Latin America. Just as gender and sexuality cannot be reduced to the simplistic heterosexual, male/female terms of difference assumed in our society, the political and economic world situation during World War II was also irreducible to an uncomplicated dichotomy. The simplification of terrifyingly complex global turmoils to us/them terms would have seemed audacious to wartime audiences if presented as anything other than escapist musical entertainment.

While films starring Carmen Miranda are racist and reductive, Miranda herself appeals to modern audiences largely because she seems so excessive and outrageous, so clearly entertaining, so beautifully camp, especially when seen outside of her historical context. For her contemporary audiences, Miranda perhaps provided a more complex pleasure as fans appreciated her outrageous performances within their problematic film settings and alongside the tensions of home-front America. Feminist theorists have asked whether it is possible to represent women in a nonsexist way? I could ask whether it is possible to represent ethnicities in a nonracist way? Although some film anthologies have noted supposed progress in Hollywood studios' portrayal of Latinos due to their Good Neighbor implementation, by trading negative "lazy greaseball" stereotypes for positive "happy children" stereotypes, the Fox Latin America musicals clearly did not come close to escaping racist representation.[30] Given that Carmen Miranda's star matrix referred so obviously to the world war and to the United States' ongoing struggles with Latin America, one might ask how contemporary audiences achieved pleasure through her texts at all? Certain elements of Miranda's star text were emphasized and repeated in her films and extrafilmic publicity material, and the same elements were noted (with pleasure) by fans and reviewers. These elements centered on her look, especially her bright, multitextured outfits, and on her voice—that is, her singing voice as pure sound as opposed to any message she communicated.

All of Miranda's films during wartime were in Technicolor, which emphasized her vivid, brightly colored outfits, like those of "native" Latina girls, suggesting to some "the brash colors of tropical birds."[31] Not unusual with stereotypes of foreign women, the popular press described Miranda in terms of the physical, of the body—as wild, savage, and primitive, like an exotic animal, "enveloped in beads, swaying and wriggling, chattering macawlike . . ., skewering the audience with a merry, mischievous eye."[32] *Motion Picture* compared her to "a princess out of an Aztec frieze with a panther's grace, the plumage of a bird of paradise and the wiles of Eve and Lileth combined." Beyond the usual savage and bestial qualities, this fanzine suggests that the fall of man might also be attributable to Miranda.[33]

But what audiences loved most about Carmen Miranda was her extreme Otherness, especially the difference enunciated by her Other language; what they loved was that they could not understand her. As one *Collier's* review reads, "The songs were not listed in the program and nobody . . . had the faintest notion of what they were about. Precisely four words were intelligible, . . . which she repeated several times, . . . 'the Souse American Way.' These didn't mean much, either, but they implied that the South American way was very excellent indeed. . . . Nothing, though, could have been of less importance than her language."[34] *Life* magazine comments that "partly because there is no clue to their meaning except the gay rollings of Carmen Miranda's insinuating eyes, these songs, and Miranda herself, are the outstanding hit of the show."[35] Any language she might employ consists of those "universal" languages of the body. Miranda's songs are often nonsensical plays of sounds, words that do not signify in any language, such as "Chica Chica Boom Chick" or "I-Yi-Yi-Yi." Reviewers, confronted with Miranda's lack of words, are contaminated: unable to control her spectacle with their words, the medium that they normally control, they lose voice. Common tropes include expressing an inability to describe her performance and, alternately, imitating Miranda's comic speech patterns. One *Motion Picture* writer says Miranda "seengs song from Brazeel and her body sings with her. . . . If you've seen her, words are an anti-climax. If you haven't, keed! What you've missed!"[36]

Latina actresses in Hollywood films generally fit neatly within one of two stereotypes of the foreign Other: the exotic sex object (such as Delores Del Rio, the "female Valentino") or the ignorant comic actress (such as Lupe Velez, the "Mexican Spitfire"). Miranda is unique in that she initially straddled both categories: she was perceived by contempoary audiences as simultaneously sexy *and* comic, a vamp and a joke. The split created a tension between her hypersexualized *visual* presence available through performance as spectacle, foregounding her body, and her comic *oral* presence available through interviews, foregrounding her words, her "paprika English."[37]

Reviews of her first shows describe her as overwhelmingly sexy and sexual: "What it is that Carmen has is difficult to describe; so difficult, in fact, that dramatic critics have grown neurotic in their attempts to get it into words that would make sense and at the same time not brand them as mad sex fiends. Nevertheless, it must be attempted again. First, there is the impact of Carmen's costumes, . . . always covering her thoroughly with the exception of a space between the seventh rib and a point at about the waistline. This expanse is known as the Torrid Zone. It does not move, but gives off invisible emanations of Roentgen rays. [Her songs'] words are absolutely unintelligible to a North American . . ., but what the listener hears—or hopes he is hearing—is unmistakable."[38] Naming Miranda's mid-section the "Torrid Zone" conflates Latin Americans, or at least this Latin American woman, with her country, equating her "equator" with that of the planet's, the "torrid zone" of South America, where it's hotter than the rest of the planet and where the natives are stereotypically wilder, sexier, and more naked than other people. Another reporter refers to numerous contemporary articles which pointed directly, if euphemistically, to Miranda's sex appeal by commenting, "Call it 'oomph,' 'yumph,' or go way back to Elinor Glyn and call it 'it.' That's Miranda."[39]

At the same time, in the popular press, Miranda's foreign accent is emphasized by comic malapropisms and mispronunciations of English, suggesting that foreigners are incapable of good English and, by extension, promoting a "primitive," ignorant stereotype. The topics of Miranda's speech reported most often are "primal" subjects, topics related to primal needs and basic subsistence, such as money, food, or sex: " 'I say monee, monee, monee,' she told an amazed group on the boat before a single question had been asked. 'I say twenty words of English. I say yes and no. I say hot dog! I say turkey sandwich and I say grapefruit. . . . I know tomato juice, apple pie and thank you,' she says brightly. 'De American mens is like potatoes.' "[40] A *Newsweek* reviewer condescendingly and bizarrely describes her as "a Brazilian chanteuse . . . who with eyes dreamily closed and doubtless thinking of Dinty Moore's juicy hamburgers sings the softly romantic and insinuating songs of Rio."[41] In trying to peek "inside" Miranda, this critic cannot imagine a subjectivity behind her ethnic, feminine mask, except for this stereotype of raw, yet consumer-oriented, primal drives.

Only later, after her two U.S. stage shows and her first Hollywood movie, when she was incorporated into plots and made to speak her comic, pidgin English in the films (tempering her performative spectacle with narrative), does Miranda become *merely* comic, the non-sexual camp female grotesque, as she is remembered by today's fans. Miranda is presented in these later (still wartime) films simply as a grotesque comedienne, and her grotesqueness is emphasized both visually and orally. Visually, her costumes become distanced from her original explicitly Bahian costume: she wears a candy-cane costume in *Greenwich Village* (1944), and a battery-operated lighthouse costume in *Doll Face* (1945–46). Orally, she mixes Portuguese with comic malapropisms and mispronunciations of English, saying, for example, that she wears "lip-steak." In the only film in which she was given the romantic lead, *Copacabana* (1947), Miranda plays a dual role that enacts her typical position, fluctuating between a dark-haired, comic personality and that of a blonde, star-quality, glamorous, and refined *chanteuse*. The discarding of half of her original star appeal was due perhaps to audiences' inability to accept her contradictory, or double, image. One reason why Miranda's feminine star text failed to sustain the sexual/comic split past her first, noninte-grated shows in the United States is that a sexually attractive foreign Other would compete with the femine WASP norm posited by the studio in the figure of Betty Grable and the other Fox blondes. U.S.–Latin American harmony could be suggested by a marriage of North and South Americans, but only if the U.S. feminine star was presented as the single acceptable object of desire. The war film's job was not only to entertain the "boys" on the front but also to reinforce their ties to home; encouragement to look at foreign feminine Others as sexually desirable would be counterproductive to the studio's mission. Therefore, Miranda's inclusion in the plots necessitated a simultaneous segregation from the cross-national couple.

In addition, Miranda's star text has been the object of a continued love-hate relationship between the United States and Brazil, a symbol alternately accepted and rejected as a part of Brazilian national identity. Miranda's image influenced the formation of Brazil's multiracial self-identity as it was reconceptualized in the 1930s, inclusive of the large, disempowered African-Brazilian population, which asserted its presence partially through the acceptance of the music and dance traditions of samba. *Samba* and *candomblé*, music and religion, together constitute an integral part of black Brazilian culture. After the abolition of slavery in 1888 and the lifting of the ban against African religion and its music and rituals, newly freed black slaves established *favelas*, the destitute hillside African-Brazilian communities of Rio, and there developed the original samba *de morro*. Etymologically, "samba" stems perhaps from the Angola word *semba*, or prayer, and also *umbigada*, a euphemism for the touching of the genitals during the dance. With the introduction of the radio in Brazil in the 1920s, the samba proved profitable for record companies and quickly spread as a form of popular music throughout Brazil.[42] The original samba *de morro* evolved into the mellower samba popularized by singers such as Miranda from the 1930s forward.

The *candomblé* temples of Rio were established by women, freed slaves from Bahia, the sixteenth-century capital of Brazil. These women, Bahians, were stereotyped within Brazil as women with shawls, turbans, and flirtatious ways. In addition, "Their special relationship with the old continent was . . . recognized . . . They knew the religion, they had 'samba in the foot,' they had survived, and they kept the culture going."[43] To masquerade as a Bahian for Carnival was initially a tradition not only for women, but also for men. Miranda adopted this Bahian costume, which signified African religion, music, and tradition to Brazilians, as her trademark outfit, and it came to mean Brazil to North Americans via Fox's Bombshell. Thus Miranda's influence on Brazil's self-image affects U.S. perceptions of Brazil. In an interview, Miranda discussed the origin of her costume, which at least in 1941 was still available to fans not only as Brazilian but as African-Brazilian: "Her costumes were inspired by those of the Negroes in Bahia. Like any creator, she takes good ideas where she finds them and gives them new life. . . . In Bahia, the Negro girls walk to market, wide skirts flaring. . . . Carmen explains, 'An' wone boy, born in Bahia, make beeg song in Brazeel about theez Bahiana dress. An' I say, I will put theez dress an' seeng theez song. You can't put theez dress, they say, because theez dress only Negroes put. Bah!' She gave it the brush-off. 'I put, but in gold an' silk an' velvet, an' I seeng in Rio. One week before Shubert see me in Casino, I put this Bahiana dress.' "[44] Miranda's words foreground her authorship of her Brazilian star image, enacted seriously, in the manner of a carnival masquerade costume. In addition, Miranda imagines an anthropomorphized Brazil telling her, "You can't put theez dress . . . because theez dress only Negroes put," thereby high-lighting the way Brazil has traditionally denied its own black population and traditions.

Contemporary accounts of Miranda's much-publicized return "home" to Brazil in 1940 reveal the split between Brazilian and U.S. perceptions of the star. Brazilian news reports describe the reception of her performance as extremely negative, the crowd booing and whistling. Reviewers claimed Miranda had lost her voice, had changed her style and her soul: Miranda had become Americanized.[45] With typical savvy, Miranda incorporated this negative reaction into subsequent Rio performances by adding new songs such as "Disseram Que Voltei Americanisada" ("They Say I Came Back Americanized") and "Voltei P'ro Morro" ("I'm Back in the Morro"), thereby salvaging the remainder of her Brazilian tour. In the United States, however, where Miranda has come to represent Brazil/Latin America, most articles reported an unmitigated success for Miranda: the "South American Bombshell" returned to loving crowds, making Brazil and Brazilian people complicit with how North America imagined and distorted South America. For instance, a *New York Times* article reports that Miranda's arrival caused "one of the city's greatest ovations," adding the curious detail that most of the people in this fantasy crowd were women.[46]

While Miranda played a role in shaping a Brazilian national identity, she also affected U.S. wartime national identity negatively by aiding in popular conceptions of the United States and its role in international politics and its relationship to other countries. Miranda's star text, concomitant with the fad of samba in the United States, influenced the way Brazilian culture came to be understood and identified in the states. For instance, Orson Welles, in his "Hello Americans" broadcast, conflates Brazil with its musical tradition: "The music . . . is rich, deep, Brazilian. It comes rolling down to Rio from the hills, throbs in the streets, everybody dances to it. It's called samba. If you scramble the two words 'music' and 'Brazil' and then unscramble them again you end up with the word 'samba.' Also if you scramble a moderate number of Brazilians together and then unscramble them, you find out they've been dancing the samba. . . . Brazilian babies can beat out a samba rhythm before they can talk, and dance to samba before they can walk."[47] A reporter explains, in an article titled "Miss Miranda and the Samba Here for Good," that "the samba is a native Brazilian dance, introduced here by Miss Miranda. It is more than likely that the whole hemisphere will twirl to its rhythm."[48]

Miranda's star image later became a symbol for Tropicalism, the third phase of Cinema Novo, which parodied myths that represented Brazil as a tropical paradise, as in *The Heirs* (1969).[49] In 1968 Caetano Veloso, one of the movement's pop artists, wrote the song "Tropicalia," a manifesto for Tropicalism which ended with the words "Viva Carmen Miranda-da-da-da-da." Veloso explains, in a recent *New York Times* article, that "Tropicalismo appropriated [Miranda] as one of its principal signs, capitalizing on the discomfort that her name and the evocation of her gestures could create."[50] That Miranda's image still holds great emotional power for Brazil and still influences Brazilian self-perception and Brazilian identity was demonstrated recently in New York at a well-meant, although dramatically unsuccessful, attempt to free Miranda as a Brazilian artist from her Hollywood stereotyping.[51] (This failed resuscitation was performed by Arto Lindsay and other Brazilian performance artists, along with Laurie Anderson and Miranda's aging sister Aurora Miranda.)

On the one hand, Carmen Miranda's star matrix reinforces typical negative stereotypes of ethnic women by enacting a nurturing earth-mother cliché. By taking as her costume enormous flowers, fruits, and vegetables intermixed with exaggerated traditional Brazilian dress, Miranda becomes the image of an overflowing cornucopia of South American products, ripe, ready, and eager for picking by North American consumers. In addition, Miranda's comic element relies on the "primitive" qualities emphasized in her persona: her inability to speak (in English); her ignorance, stemming from language and cultural barriers; and her secondary status and inferiority. All of these exaggerated qualities contribute to negative conceptions both of "foreign" Others and of women. On the other hand, Miranda's appeal resides in the parody of these stereotypes. Because Miranda so exaggerates signifiers of ethnicity and femininity, her star text suggests that they exist only as surface, that they do not refer, and in this way Miranda can become sheer spectacle. For instance, the joy reviewers articulate about Miranda's lack of English stems partly from the illusion of masculine and American superiority but also from an enthusiasm for a freedom within or without language, the freedom allowed by songs when the listener has "no clue to their meaning"—the freedom experienced through the recognition of the artifice, as opposed to the essence, of social definitions of ethnicity and femininity.[52]

Carmen Miranda is exemplary as a musical star famous *as* spectacle, as excess, as parody or masquerade. Many recent feminist theorists have looked to fantasy scenarios, in particular to theories of spectatorial masquerade, as a way to enact or perform femininity and thereby throw into question concepts of feminine essence, opening alternative viewing options for female spectators.[53] Studies on masquerade attack the idea that an essential feminine exists prior to the concept of "woman" as constituted in any age. Masquerade mimics a socially constructed identity in order to conceal, but at the same time to indicate, the absence that exists behind the mask and ultimately to discover the lack of any "natural" gender identity. Similarly, ethnic masquerade works to undermine the concept of ethnic essence. An exploration of notions of the feminine and ethnic minorities in society at a very specific, complex historical moment can reveal possibilities for the use of masquerade by female spectators and other marginalized spectators in wartime society.

Miranda performs a femininity so exaggerated that it becomes comical, undercutting any threat that her female sexuality might pose but also calling into question society's assumptions about feminine essence. Additionally, while Hollywood representations of different ethnicities often draw on, emphasize, and contribute to stereotypical ethnic clichés and myths, Miranda's ethnic persona nears hysteria with its exaggeration. Miranda's costumes lampoon both feminine fashion and traditional and stereotypical Latin dress—stacks of accessories, shoes so high they impede walking, and cornucopia hats. Miranda's outfits suggest female sexuality in excess, revealing and accentuating her sexually invested body parts—the navel, breasts, and legs. Busby Berkeley's number "The Lady in the Tutti-Frutti Hat" in The Gang's All Here lampoons *both* U.S.–Latin American trade relations and notions of feminine sexuality through the casting of Miranda as the overseer of countless enormous, swaying phallic bananas buoyed up by lines of chorus girls who dance above other girls who have oversized strawberries between their legs. A New York Times reviewer notes that these "dance spectacles seem to stem straight from Freud and, if interpreted, might bring a rosy blush to several cheeks in the Hays office."[54] The "Tutti-Frutti Hat" number was censored in

Brazil.[55] Miranda's sexual excess extended beyond her film roles, most notably during a widely circulated 1941 scandal caused by a low-angle photo of Miranda dancing with Cesar Romero in which she is clearly naked beneath her swirling skirts. In response to the scandal, Miranda reportedly said, "Why should I be so foolish to dance weethout de pants?"[56]

At this point we may ask how can a racist and sexist stereotype be positive? And why would we want to pursue such a stereotype, why would we want to spend the time, energy, and perhaps misdirected pleasure on understanding this text? I believe that Miranda's appeal and fame resided in fans' perception of her as a producer of her star text, as in control of her own self-parody. Miranda's contemporary audience accepted and enjoyed her as a caricature, as a parody of herself, as a demonstration of masquerade. For instance, in 1943, after only four years in Hollywood, Busby Berkeley showcased Miranda in "The Lady in the Tutti-Frutti Hat." Miranda stands in front of a forced-perspective set painting, creating the illusion of an impossibly enormous banana hat and enunciating the ultimate, classic image of herself as parody. Further evidence of fan perception of Miranda as parodic text lies in the frequency with which she was and continues to be imitated by both women and men in drag, from Mickey Rooney in *Babes on Broadway* (1941) to Bugs Bunny in *What's Cookin', Doc* (1944) to Ted Danson in *Three Men and a Little Lady* (1990). She was the female character most impersonated by both gay and straight GIs, so that in 1944 a *Theatre Arts* writer reported that "cries of anguish can still be heard from harried Special Services officers who were tired of 'impersonations of Carmen Miranda.' "[57]

Unlike other entertainers who simply become the objects of parody, Miranda was presented in the discourse of the time as both subject and object of self-parody. To begin with, Miranda was known as the author of her own costume and her own image. The Bahian costume was not designed for her by Broadway or Hollywood designers. She first adopted it for her last Brazilian film, *Banana de Terra* (1938), in which she impersonates a Bahian woman for a performance of a song written by a Bahian composer, Dorival Caymmi. Articles and publicity commonly report that Miranda designed her own costumes and "turbans" and insisted on bringing her own musical accompaniment, the Bando da Lua, with her from Brazil.[58] Imogene Coca's popular parody of Miranda's "Sous-American Way" in the *Straw Hat Revue* was presented by the producers of Miranda's first U.S. theater show, *The Streets of Paris*, at the same time that Miranda appeared in this show. While flamboyant performers are commonly burlesqued, Miranda is perceived in contemporary articles as having a hand not only in the production of this parody but also in the manufacture of her own image. In this instance, the popular press publicized the fact that Coca learned to parody Miranda from Miranda herself: Coca told the papers that "she burlesqued herself for my benefit more than I'd ever dare."[59]

For all of her reported naive, cutely stupid remarks concerning "American mens" and other aspects of U.S. culture, Miranda occasionally reveals a more perceptive self behind her "primitive Other" persona. For instance, in 1939 she expresses irritation at North Americans' refusal to understand other cultures and our negative stereotyping of foreign Others: "I met an American girl in a doctor's office here and she say, 'Ees thees how a Brazilian womans look?' . . . as if I am supposed to have feathers in my hair like Indians. And she ask if in Brazil they have electric lights yet. HAH! . . . North Americans do not want to learn about other countries, especially their language. Yanquis expect us to learn their language instead."[60] Miranda demonstrates a sophisticated recognition of the profitability of her artificial persona in the following interview, in which she shows more insight into the appeal of her supposedly fragile grasp of (English) language than do her previously quoted U.S. reviewers: "She said that [her singing 'con movimientos'] was creation. . . . 'I feel like an artist,' she said. 'In Brazil I do the same thing. I sing in the same songs. But everybody knows what I sing. They comprehend the language. Nobody here knows what I sing. All they can do is understand from my tone. From my movement. It is a maravilla.' "[61] Miranda understood the advantage of her own ethnic masquerade. Miranda reveals in an interview that she is aware that, in Hollywood, a foreign "accent is an asset."[62] As a 1939 *Collier's* article on Miranda notes, "an actress or singer who murders English gets a lot more headlines than one who talks as though she had been brought up in Boston."[63]

At the World's Fair in 1939 Miranda won a Charlie McCarthy doll, a replica of Edgar Bergen's popular wooden alter ego. She expressed her delight in *controlling* her dummy, of playing Bergen to an image, a persona, detachable in the real perhaps but ultimately inescapable and integral to his popularity: " 'He is home, this Charlie,' she said. 'I push a button. I make him talk. He talks what I say. He is the artificial man, I can control him.' "[64] Miranda's supposedly ingenuous remarks about a doll won at a fair suggest self-knowledge on her part and an understanding of the way her self-created image has a life of its own in the popular imagination of the U.S. public. A further provocative revelation of agency behind the star persona comes at the end of a typical article on Miranda's life-style, in which the female journalist metaphorically steps back from her own reporting to question the recognized artifice of the Miranda façade. "There was a glint in her eye—I looked at her publicity man. . . . Carmen, are you kidding?" I find it significant that the only reporter to attribute to Carmen an awareness of the artificiality of her star image is a woman.

The press often reported Miranda's desire to appeal to a female audience, as in an article titled "No 'Men Only' for This Carmen": "She isn't happy unless she can please the wives and sweethearts, too."[65] In another article titled "Ladies Invited," Miranda is linked explicitly with female fans' role in the war effort.[66] Women readers are urged to "keep your hands soft," as Miranda does, in order to achieve hands as beautiful and expressive as are hers. The beauty tips, presented as direct advice from Miranda to female readers, are connected to the war effort since women's hands are needed to make "sweaters, or socks, or scarfs" for the army and bandages for the Red Cross, for which they may be rewarded with "a salute from the army . . . a bow from the Red Cross," and if lucky, "an engagement ring from you-know-who." Also, Miranda's costumes popularized a South American fashion trend for women's hats and shoes.[67] And consumers were urged, in a full-page 1939 advertisement that featured a glamour photo of Miranda, to "Do as Miss Carmen Miranda does, learn your foreign language at the Barbizon School of Languages, for better accent."[68] Miranda fans who perceived themselves as "foreign," and in this way identified with her, also imitated her. Fans encouraged to mimic Miranda through consumerism also recognized that a feminine or ethnic image bought, to wear or discard at will, was no more essential to their identity than any other beauty product. By applying cosmetics, donning hats, altering accents, fans physically perform the Miranda masquerade, highlighting for themselves the artificiality of the stereotypes that interpellate them in their everyday life.

This masquerade performed by consuming fans was also perhaps enacted during individual film-viewing experiences. By looking closely at a single film sequence, we can explore the insinuation of self-authorship in Miranda's film presence, to examine further the way she was understood by fans. The opening sequence of *Down Argentine Way*, in which Miranda sings "Sous American Way," provides a clear example of her appeal—her control over her own joke, her self-parody. Here in her first Hollywood performance, completely unintegrated with the film, Miranda appears in an excerptable clip which in fact works as a prologue for the film proper. She sings only in Portuguese and has no dialogue or interaction with the other film characters. The mainstream 1940 U.S. viewer must read her body . . . the "universal" language of her gestures and music—because she does not speak (English); she seems to be denied subjectivity. Miranda clearly knows how to "read" herself, however. She understands both her own body, along with the viewer, as well as her words; she is, moreover, in on the joke. Miranda's aural and visual presentation of herself as *out*-of-control excess is in fact a demonstration of her *hyper*control over her own voice and image. The knowingness she expresses in this clip indicates her own subjectivity, insinuating that she knows a secret to which the viewer will never have access.

Because Miranda controlled her own image, some fans were able to understand her stereotypical persona as manipulated by the star herself in a kind of masquerade and were thereby, through interpretation and fantasy, able to identify with her as one way to negotiate or cope with their own minority status in society. I want to clarify that I am neither trying to develop a theoretical move to *excuse* any negative stereotypes nor suggesting that *any* star can be understood to be performing a masquerade. For instance, this kind of relationship would be more difficult to imagine between a similarly racially stereotyped secondary star, such as Stepin Fetchit, and her fans. While Stepin Fetchit was, like Miranda, in control of his image, exploiting his character as a lazy, shuffling "coon," a "natural-born" comedian, in order to get film roles,[69] it is important that he was not seen by fans as in control of his own stereotype. Miranda could emerge from behind her character, using her own name and speaking in her first language of Portuguese instead of pidgin English,[70] but Stepin Fetchit was always Stepin Fetchit both on screen and stage and off. Fans would not know that his real name was Lincoln Perry nor that he could speak in a different manner or with different words than those used by his stammering, slow-witted character. No distance existed between the character and the star that would allow for masquerade. In addition, while Miranda's wink at the camera indicates understanding of the play and control of the show, Stepin Fetchit's performance remains consistently caught in the confines of a regressive racial stereotype, which would offer little appeal of identification for viewers. In more direct comparison to Miranda, none of the contemporary Latin American copycats, such as Lina Romay or Maria Montez, were able either to escape their stereotypes or to achieve control over their image. Importantly, none of these B-movie Miranda mimics ever neared her fame or her lasting power, indicating, perhaps, Hollywood fans' disinterest in the simpler stereotype.

In conclusion, while Miranda's parodic text works undeniably to reinforce regressive stereotypes of Latin Americans and of women, and to support racist and sexist conceptions of the dominant ideology, her text at the same time reveals them as stereotypes, allowing for negotiated or subversive readings by fans. For instance, the gay servicemen who turned Miranda into an immediate camp icon recognized her parody of gender roles and were able to use her text in impersonations at camp shows as an allowable expression of their subjectivity. Miranda's text could, in this way, be used to speak for particular marginalized minority audiences, including ethnic and female viewers.

By foregrounding excessiveness, Miranda's text addresses two of the most consistent marginalizations in the studio system and in wartime, as well as in our current society. Her star text speaks to the erasure of women—specifically women's sexuality—and of ethnic minorities. For a secondary star of forty-five years ago to be remembered so vividly seems quite unusual, but Miranda's is a still-current image for audiences. That the very elements of her persona that threaten to disturb the Hollywood studio system are precisely those for which she was and is still famous suggests that this disruptiveness is what has sustained her fame so vividly and for so long. What appealed to and continues to attract fans of Miranda is the double masquerade which insists on questioning both feminine essence and foreign stereotyping, and so offers resistant, alternative viewing options.

Notes

1   *Weekend in Havana* earned $25,000, *Citizen Kane* $9,000.

2   "New Shows in Manhattan," *Time*, 3 July 1939, 42.

3   "Broadway Likes Miranda's Piquant Portuguese Songs," *Life*, 17 July 1939, 34.

4   See, for instance, Michael Renov, *Hollywood's Wartime Woman: Representation and Ideology* (Ann Arbor: UMI, 1988), 34–35.

5   On the illusion of participatory entertainment, see Jane Feuer, *The Hollywood Musical* (Bloomington: Indiana University Press, 1982), 35; and Rick Altman, *The American Film Musical* (Bloomington: Indiana University Press, 1987), 350–64; on the musical as "attraction," see Tom Gunning, "The Cinema of Attraction: Early Film, Its Spectator and the Avant-Garde," *Wide Angle* 8, nos. 3–4 (1986): 63–70.

6   On stars, direct address, and spectacle see, for instance, Lea Jacobs and Richard deCordova, "Spectacle and Narrative Theory," *Quarterly Review of Film and Video (QRFS)* 7, no. 4 (1982): 293–303.

7   On the feminine image as spectacle, see Laura Mulvey, "Visual Pleasure and Narrative Cinema" (1975), in her *Visual and Other Pleasures* (Bloomington: Indiana University Press, 1989), 19.

8   Renov, *Hollywood's Wartime Women*; Renov, "Advertising/Photojournalism/Cinema: The Shifting Rhetoric of Forties Female Representation," *QRFS* 11, no. 1 (1989): 11.

9   I rely on studies on stars by Dyer and deCordova, especially Richard Dyer, *Stars* (London: BFI, 1979); Richard deCordova, "Dialogue," *Cinema Journal* 26, no. 3 (1987): 57; and deCordova, *Picture Personalities: The Emergence of the Star System in America* (Urbana: University of Illinois Press, 1990).

10   While the Japanese were caricatured as generic racial stereotypes in popular cartoons, Germans were represented by Hitler, and Italians by Mussolini. These racially stereotyped caricatures are self-evident in war-era cartoons, comics, propaganda films, and other material, as well as feature films. On cartoons, see for instance Michael S. Shull and David E. Wilt, *Doing Their Bit: Wartime American Animated Short Films, 1939–1945* (Jefferson, N.C.: McFarland, 1987), 33–35; for examples of poster propaganda, see Zbynek Zeman, *Selling the War: Art and Propaganda in World War II* (London: Orbis, 1978); on the representation of the Japanese during World War II see John W. Dower, *War Without Mercy: Race and Power in the Pacific War* (New York: Random House, 1986), 3–200.

11   In an effort toward brevity and variety—not because I have forgotten about Canada or Mexico—I occasionally use the adjective *North American* to indicate the United States. "Miss Miranda and the Samba Here for Good," *New York Herald Tribune*, 9 March 1941, sec. 6, 4.

12   George Black, *The Good Neighbor: How the United States Wrote the History of Central America and the Caribbean* (New York: Random House, 1988), 59.

13   Ibid., 69.

14   Wilella Waldorf, " 'The Streets of Paris' Opens at the Broadhurst Theatre," *New York Post*, 20 June 1939.

15   "Hello Americans: Brazil," CBS, 15 November 1942, part of a series, "Hello Americans," which ran from 1942–43. Tape recording available at the Museum of Television and Radio in New York.

16   Roland Barthes intimates the uneasy nature of this kind of surface equation of peoples and nationalities: "This myth of the human 'condition' rests on a very old mystification, which always consists in placing Nature at the bottom of History . . . to give to the immobility of the world the alibi of a 'wisdom' and a 'lyricism' which only make the gestures of man look eternal the better to diffuse them." Roland Barthes, "The Great Family of Man," in *Mythologies*, trans. Annette Lavers (New York: Noonday Press, 1972), 101–102.

17   "Springtime in the Rockies," *Time*, 9 November 1942, 96.

18   In an explicit Miranda-Banana Republic tie-up, the giant United Fruit Company (with operations in Cuba, Guatemala, Honduras, Costa Rica, Panama, and Colombia) modeled its "Chiquita Banana" character on Miranda at the height of her career in 1944—an ad campaign so successful that, for the first time, brand-name loyalty (for United Fruit) was attached to a generic fruit (the banana). Cynthia Enloe, *Bananas, Beaches, and Bases: Making Feminist Sense of International Politics* (Berkeley: University of California Press, 1990), 128–32.

19   "Latin Americans Urge Film Care," *Variety*, 6 November 1940, 1, 22.

20   See, for instance, *Variety*, 20 March 1940; and "New Film Cycles," *Newsweek*, 22 July 1940, 12.

21   "Down Argentine Way," *Variety*, 9 October 1940.

22   Miranda was born in Portugal; her family moved to Rio de Janeiro when she was a baby, and she

regularly identified herself with Brazilian culture in interviews. See, for instance, Obituary, *New York Times*, 6 August 1955, 15.

23   According to a retrospective on Miranda compiled by the Cinematic Museum of Modern Art from the Cinema Club of Rio de Janeiro and the Secretary of Tourism for the Government of Guanabara, Miranda made one record with Brunswick; sixty-nine with RCA-Victor; and sixty-six with Odeon. Her films were *A Voz do Carnaval* (1933); *Alô Alô, Brasil!* (1935); *Estudantes* (1935); *Alô, Alô, Carnaval!* (1936); and *Banana da Terra* (1938). She also appeared in the play *Vai dar o Que Falar* (1930).

24   See, for instance, "Brazil's Carmen Miranda to Make Debut in 'Streets of Paris,' " *New York Post*, 10 June 1939, 10.

25   Michel Mok, "Ogling New Yorkers, to Carmen Miranda, Are the Best Caballeros in Pan-America," *New York Post*, 23 June 1939, 11.

26   See, for instance, Henry F. Pringle, "Rolling Up from Rio," *Collier's*, 12 August 1939, 23; or, Waldorf, " 'The Streets of Paris.' "

27   Quoted in Martha Gil-Montero, *Brazilian Bombshell: The Biography of Carmen Miranda* (New York: Donald I. Fine, 1989), 97.

28   Ibid., 124.

29   *Sintonia*, 11 June 1941, quoted in Allen L. Woll, *The Hollywood Musical Goes to War* (Chicago: Nelson-Hall, 1983), 118.

30   See, for instance, Woll, *The Hollywood Musical*, 120.

31   *Current Biography* (1941): 586.

32   "New Shows in Manhattan," *Time*, 3 July 1939, 42.

33   Ida Zeitlin, "Sous American Sizzler," *Motion Picture*, September 1941, from the Billy Rose Collection.

34   Pringle, "Rolling Up," 23.

35   "Broadway Likes Miranda's Piquant Portuguese Songs," *Life*, 17 July 1939, 34.

36   Zeitlin, "Sous American Sizzler."

37   Miranda uses "paprika English," according to Louise Levitas in "Carmen Gets Unneeded Vocabulary," *PM*, 7 September 1941, 55.

38   Robert Sullivan, "Carmen Miranda Loves America and Vice Versa," *Sun News*, 23 November 1941, from the Billy Rose Collection.

39   "Carmen, Rio Style: This One Has a Last Name (It's Miranda) and She's the Good Neighbor Policy Itself," *Boston Evening Transcript*, 3 June 1939, from the Billy Rose Collection. Glyn was the popular Jazz Age novelist and screen writer who coined the term "it," which became Clara Bow's tag name.

40   Although many articles refer to this Miranda speech, this quote is from Pringle, "Rolling Up," 31.

41   George Jean Nathan, "The Streets of Toujours," *Newsweek*, 3 July 1939, 28.

42   See Alma Guillermoprieto, *Samba* (New York: Random House, 1990), 8–9, 52–53; and Gil-Montero, *Brazilian Bombshell*, 24–26.

43   Guillermoprieto, *Samba*, 52.

44   Zeitlin, "Sous American Sizzler."

45   Gil-Montero, *Brazilian Bombshell*, 106–107.

46   "Rio Hails Carmen Miranda," *New York Times*, 11 July 1941, from the Billy Rose Collection.

47   "Hello Americans," tape recording available at the Museum of Television and Radio in New York.

48   "Miss Miranda and the Samba," sec. 6, 4.

49   See Randal Johnson and Robert Stam, eds., *Brazilian Cinema* (New Jersey: Associated University Presses, 1982), 38–39.

50   Caetano Veloso, "Caricature and Conqueror, Pride and Shame," *New York Times*, 20 October 1991, sec. H, 34.

51   I saw this performance at the Brooklyn Academy of Music, 25 October 1991. Also see Julian Dibbell, "Notes on Carmen," *Village Voice*, 29 October 1991, 43, 45 [preview of the BAM *Carmen Miranda* performance].

52   Julia Kristeva's concept of the "semiotic" and chora, that which "does not yet refer . . . or no longer refers . . . to a signified object," that which is "anterior to naming," is helpful here, although her inability to imagine a disengagement from the symbolic without a simultaneous essentializing of the feminine is problematic. See Julia Kristeva, "From One Identity to Another," in *Desire in Language*, ed. Leon S. Roudiez, trans. Thomas Gora, Alice Jardine, and Leon S. Roudiez (New York, Columbia University Press, 1980), 133.

53   See Joan Riviere, "Womanliness as Masquerade," in (1929) *Formations of Fantasy*, ed. Victor Burgin, James Donald, and Cora Kaplan (New York: Routledge, 1989), 35–44. For the introduction of the concept into film studies, see Mary Anne Doane, "Film and the Masquerade: Theorizing the

Female Spectator," *Screen* 23, nos. 3–4 (September/October 1982): 74–87; "Masquerade Reconsidered: Further Thoughts on the Female Spectator," *Discourse* 11, no. 1 (1988–89): 42–54; and Claire Johnston, "Femininity and the Masquerade: Anne of the Indies," in *Psychoanalysis and Cinema*, ed. E. Ann Kaplan (New York: Routledge, 1990), 64–72. See also Stephen Heath, "Joan Riviere and the Masquerade," in *Formations of Fantasy*, 45–61.

54 "At the Roxy," *The New York Times*, 23 December 1943.

55 See Tony Thomas and Jim Terry, *The Busby Berkeley Book* (New York: New York Graphic Society, 1973), 152–54.

56 See, for instance, "Springtime in the Rockies," *Time*, 9 November 1942, 96; for photo, see Kenneth Anger, *Hollywood Babylon II* (New York: Dutton, 1984), 275.

57 Allan Bérube, *Coming Out under Fire: The History of Gay Men and Women in World War Two* (New York: Free Press, 1990; New York: Penguin, 1991), 89.

58 See, for instance, Sullivan, "Carmen Miranda Loves America"; Constance Palmer, "Not Half as Wild as You Think," *Silver Screen*, May 1947, 51; "Brazil's Carmen Miranda," 10.

59 "Miranda Will See Herself Burlesqued," *New York Herald Tribune*, 22 October 1939, from the Billy Rose Collection.

60 Candide, "Only Human," *Daily Mirror* (New York), 26 May 1939, from the Billy Rose Collection.

61 "Gestures Put It Over for Miranda," *New York World Telegram*, 8 July 1939, from the Billy Rose Collection.

62 Hyman Goldberg, "Miranda Clings to Souse American Accent—Brazilian Singer Fights Off Learning English," *New York Post*, 8 September 1941, from the Billy Rose Collection.

63 Pringle, "Rolling Up," 31.

64 "Gestures Put It Over for Miranda."

65 Sue Chambers, "No 'Men Only' for This Carmen," *The Milwaukee Journal-Screen and Radio*, 13 February 1944, from the Billy Rose Collection.

66 Gloria Mack, "Ladies Invited," *Photoplay*, January 1942, 84.

67 See, for instance, "Up From Rio" in "The Talk of the Town," *The New Yorker*, 28 October 1939, 15.

68 From the Billy Rose Collection.

69 See, for instance, correspondence from Stepin Fetchit to John Ford at the Lilly Library at the University of Indiana in Bloomington.

70 Press articles identified her as Carmen Miranda or, occasionally, as Maria da Cunha, as in "Springtime in the Rockies," *Time*, 9 November 1942, 96.

Chapter 9

Lucia Bozzola

"STUDS HAVE FEELINGS TOO": WARREN BEATTY AND THE QUESTION OF STAR DISCOURSE AND GENDER (2001)

"Hey, I'm a star, I'm a star."

—George Roundy

I think that everybody should see *Shampoo* if only to decide on the basis of first-hand evidence whether Warren Beatty is God's gift to women or merely an imaginative con man with a flair for self-promotion.

—Andrew Sarris, *Village Voice*, March 13, 1975

WARREN BEATTY IS AN ACTOR WHO WAS famous before his first film was released through, among other things, his highly publicized affair with Joan Collins. The discourse of his personal life preceded that of movie actor (Parker 1993, 37, 49–50). Warren Beatty as a star is just as famous for never talking about his personal life; the power over his cinematic image exercised as producer/writer/director extends to his private activities. The knowledge to be gained about his exploits (but not from him) further presents Beatty as a man in near-mythic control of his desirability to women. The "truth" behind his sex symbol status for those audience members who want to know might be gleaned from the interplay between movies and press stories but never from the source. Yet the sex symbol meaning of that offscreen private life combined with Beatty's onscreen penchant for playing men not in control render him a desired and acted-upon object, questioning the assumed relationship between "masculinity" and power, particularly in the realm of sexuality. The interplay between movies and metatext, especially in the films that (allegedly) intersect directly with Beatty's "private" life like *Shampoo* and *Love Affair*, underlines Beatty's image as a gender category breaker, in terms of his star persona and the posited audience relationship to that persona. The usual binary arrangement of sexual roles is broken down and redefined, revealing the binary's constructedness and the need to approach this type of male star from a different direction.

The representation of sexuality and desire in Hollywood film often rests on normative assumptions of what is "masculine" and what is "feminine" and how bodies, particularly star bodies, are treated accordingly.[1] With subjectivity assumed to be "male" and objectivity "female," the male star and his visibility have long been taken to exist in a dysfunctional relationship, with the male body often treated "as an object hiding in plain sight" as Dennis Bingham writes (1994b, 149). Steve Neale, for instance, states that Rock Hudson's objectification in Douglas Sirk's films is recuperated through his "feminization" at those moments (1993, 18); Steven Cohan asserts that William Holden's 1950s paratext of "normal" manhood could sufficiently offset the potential threat presented by Holden's objectified body in *Picnic* (1993, 223). Even Warren Beatty, whose body often seems to be front and center, literally as well as figuratively, manages, in Bingham's analysis, to avoid objectification. The paradoxical nature of this conclusion, and the nature of Beatty's star image as he himself addresses it, put into question the presumed gendered categories of subject and object that are used to maintain that this male body can hide "in plain sight." Indeed, it is the intersection of two star discourses in Beatty's image that destabilizes these assumed gender qualities, manifesting their mutability: the male star who is presented to be looked at expressly as a sexually desirable figure yet must maintain an idea of manhood, and the star in the post-studio era who has a large degree of agency over the formation of his image yet presents himself as an object for desire. The divide between "active" and "passive" and their gendered associations regarding sex and desire begins to collapse.[2] The categories of "male" and "female" vis-à-vis notions of desire need to be mapped out as the star discourse constructs them, rather than assuming that the star discourse inevitably conforms one way or the other.

The means for recuperating Holden's masculinity brings to the fore the strategy of reading a particular actor's films as one aspect of a larger discursive field, the "images in media texts" constituting the star (Dyer 1979, 10). The extratextual discourse constructs the star's sexuality through revealing the private life of the star, and therefore, according to Richard deCordova's use of Michel Foucault, the "secret" truth of the person and the connection of that truth to the star's films (1990, 140–41); a "truth" that is aimed at making the star conform to acceptable contemporary "norms" of heterosexuality, and is thus as much of a construct as the overall star image. The notion of a star's sexuality as a product of a network of discourses in turn invokes Foucault's model of the discursive production of "sexuality," and how it functions as a mechanism of power.[3] The sexualized body is paradoxically the subject of discourse "ad infinitum," while posited as the secret (35); knowing the secret of the body shifts the relationship of power. Returning to deCordova's notion of the star discourse locating the secret of the star's identity in the star's most private of lives, then, the dense intersection of relationships of sexuality, knowledge, and power are worked out across the site of the star's body, literally and figuratively. If a star "works" according to modes of masculinity or femininity that are considered "normative," then the star image abides by "strategic unities" constructing this norm, in or outside the films.[4] What is key here in the network of sexuality, knowledge, and power vis-à-vis the star is the instability inherent in that discursive construct. A star construct may abide by certain rules, but this does not mean that there will not be other star constructs that could break, and therefore alter, the rules.

The power/knowledge relationship figured by deCordova as the audience seeking to find out the star's secret points to the fact that in constructing a star's sexuality, the discursive network also constructs a receiver, mandating for whom the discourse exists, as well as who may appropriate that position. The question then becomes what investment does this audience have in this "truth": why, and ultimately if, they want to know. This issue regarding audience investment is raised in Bingham's essay (1994b) on Warren Beatty, as he concludes that Beatty offers a subjectivity that can only cause unease for the male spectator (174). If this is the case, then it must be asked who is not supposed to be caused unease by this construction; the answer in a hetero-norm culture is, of course, the elusive female spectator.

My aim here is not to try to theorize the female spectator, but to point out that the "man for woman's eyes" is a figure who foregrounds the notion of sexuality as a construction by destabilizing the accepted terminology.[5] Warren Beatty is quite the exemplar of the disruptive star body. Bingham is on the mark in his assertion that Beatty is a star who does not obey the accepted gender categories because the film texts and his own metatext do not seem to match in terms of a "mastery of the gaze," even though each is heavily invested in the other (1994b, 154). Rather than presume then that Beatty is a figure of "incoherence" because of mismatched gazes, however, I want to take as the issue the categories themselves and examine how they are constructed or reconstructed in his body (of work). As Peter Lehman asserts, "Our rigid notions of male-female difference are over-simplified," and the positions available for identification are "multiple, fluid and contradictory" in discourses involving the sexualized male body (1993, 8). The intersection of the texts in the discursive field that is "Warren Beatty" seems to announce that this is what women want, but in so doing, the construction of femininity invested therein comes under question. The problem-atization of the categories and the reliance on textual intersection to create meaning necessitate a "mapping" of the discursive fields that construct sexuality in Beatty's film *Shampoo*, with a few thoughts about his 1994 film *Love Affair* and its aftermath.

"GEORGE ROUNDY" = WARREN BEATTY?

While Beatty's extratextual discursive life has almost always managed to intersect with his films, the one film that provokes particular speculation about its closeness is *Shampoo*, featuring Beatty as a randy Beverly Hills hairdresser. Different publications note the snug fit, and attempt to draw Beatty out on the parallel. A gossip writer for the *New York Post* asked Beatty if he was "type-casting himself as the lady-killer" and then notes that Beatty "modestly" evades the answer (Winsten 1975, 22). An interview in *Viva* begins, "Although he'd be the last to admit it, Warren Beatty's new movie is alive with resonances from his own life" (Adler 1975, 40). The *Village Voice* also gets in on the act, with Tag Gallagher asking Beatty, " 'I get the idea there was an autobiographical element.' WB: 'Are you talking about sex?' TG: 'Yes.' " Beatty then proceeds to say that his answer would be "boring," since it is not a good question (1975, 60). Several of the reviews make reference to the parallels between the sex life of Beatty's character George Roundy, and Beatty's sex life as it had been documented in the media. The most critical reference is Jay Cocks's assertion in *Time* (1975, 4) that the film, produced and co-written by Beatty as well, could have been called "Advertisements for Myself."[6] Besides Beatty's narcissism, this highlights the control that Beatty exercised over the film and his representation in it. The difference between the quip in *Time* and Beatty's various ways of avoiding the question in interviews makes apparent the slippery nature of the question itself as a means for reaching the "truth" of the matter. The person who wants to know if this film is Beatty advertising himself would have to see the film, read the articles and decide, since Beatty has *not* denied that reading.

Beatty's character in *Shampoo*, along with the multiple relationships that circulate around him further the question of sex and the construction of sexuality; issues given particular real-life contemporary political currency as the 1960s and '70s women's move-ment sought to break down the constrictive ideas of what traditionally constituted "male" and "female" (Chafe 1977, 133). Along with this political context of instability, Beatty's assertion that he and co-writer Robert Towne wanted to explore a Don Juan, "hoping not to make the classical . . . Freudian analysis of Don Juan that requires that Don Juan has . . . hostile feelings towards women" (Gallagher 1975, 62) recalls Foucault's description of Don Juan as the ultimate sexual rule-breaker (1990). As a man whose life "overturned" the "two great systems conceived by the West for governing sex: the law of marriage and the order of desire," Don Juan epitomizes the disruptive potential of the Great Lover type (39–40). George is unquestionably a "stud," as Andrew Sarris noted, but he is a stud who lives up to the benign description, used in a 1961 profile on Beatty, of "catnip for the opposite sex," rather than a stud who wields his powers of attraction as a weapon (Muir, 100). In his pursuit of physical gratification, George sleeps with Felicia (the wife of a businessman, Lester, who may back a salon for George), Lorna (Lester and Felicia's teenage daughter), and Jackie (his ex-girlfriend and Lester's mistress). His own girlfriend, Jill, who is Jackie's best friend, rightfully complains that she is always last in line for his favors. Without setting out to, George manages to render starkly what a farce the only marriage in the film is. The order of desire that would favor the under-30 Jill as the proper mate for George, and ratify her wish to be with him only, is jettisoned as George moves from woman to woman, regardless of age or other relationships. As he admits, he "fucked 'em all," but not out of hostility toward them, or toward Lester for that matter.

The benign nature of George as stud and the rethinking of male and female roles continue in the figuring of the women around him as decidedly not passive, and George's own status as an object for their desires. Beatty exercises his subjectivity to play George, and as George, Beatty chooses to objectify himself, authoring his "amorphousness" and disrupting the traditional order of desire (active male and passive female, subject and object). To borrow Lehman's reworking of Laura Mulvey, "he not only [carries] the 'burden of sexual objectification,' but indeed wants to carry it" (1993, 6). Beatty himself draws attention to the problematic nature of the blanket assertion of passivity as female in the *Viva* interview when he states: "First of all, I don't think females are necessarily people who would lie on their backs and let things be done to them; it says a lot about the sex life of a man who thinks they are" (Adler 1975, 42). In *Shampoo*, each woman asserts power in her own way over George, offsetting the power of George's ability to seduce. Felicia asserts herself physically by pulling George into the ladies' room at the Nixon dinner; she is fiscally assertive in suggesting that George go to her husband to get money for a salon. Lorna and Jackie likewise state their demands with a clarity that leaves George speechless. George dodges Lorna's questions about whether he is "making it" with her mother, but when she asks, "You wanna fuck?" he pauses to consider. When Jackie announces to a table of Nixon supporters that what she really wants is to "suck [George's] cock," George is unable to talk her out of climbing under the table. Felicia's, Lorna's and Jackie's different means for demanding that George perform, or be performed on, reorder desire in terms of pursuer and pursued. Yet it is not a direct mirror/reversal that would seem to uphold the rules, since each woman has her own motives outside of George for demanding sex. He also initiates sexual encounters with Felicia and Jackie as well as being a willing participant all around. The relationships of power expressed through sex are not fixed in any of the circumstances.

Jackie's announcement at this election night dinner for Nixon supporters not only accentuates her position within a sex/power network, but also underscores the contemporary circumstances shaping that network. *Shampoo* is pointedly set on Election Day in 1968, a date that has extra resonance because of Nixon's resignation the summer before the film's release, and because of Beatty's own publicized involvement with George McGovern's presidential campaign (Parker 1993, 189–92). Jackie's raw, direct expression of sexual desire at a Nixon campaign VIP dinner encapsulates issues of sexual freedom at stake in the '70s women's movement, and the more general implications of the election (Chafe 1977, 121–22). Her demand evokes the clash of values inherent in an election contest between the conservative Nixon and Hubert Humphrey, who in Nixon's campaign rhetoric (regardless of what Humphrey's actual views may have been), "had a 'personal attitude of indulgence and permissiveness toward the lawless' " (Schell 1975, 21). Along with his status as a successful businessman and an active, albeit pragmatic, Nixon supporter, Lester uses the term "anti-establishment" as he tries to make sense of George's actions late in the film, aligning himself with the conservative order that consists of, among other things, fixed traditional gender roles. A 1975 view on 1968, however, doubly attests to the actual fluidity of those roles in a political matrix of power that is itself hardly fixed.

This flexibility of power and sex carries over into the relationship between George and Lester. While they correspond to opposing sides of the political spectrum (even though George never expresses what would be considered a political opinion), each has an aspect of power within the male/female relationship that the other does not, and each asks to share that power. George clearly possesses the physical power of attraction that the older Lester does not, but he also has the power of knowing what women think in general because of what he hears at the salon all day, and what the women around Lester think in particular. Lester listens attentively as George shares his own acquired wisdom—"We're always trying to nail 'em, and they know it. They know it, and they don't like it"—since Lester has no idea what Jackie and Felicia would "have against" him. He expresses genuine surprise when George informs him that Lorna hates her mother; the dynamics of their relationship never occurred to him, let alone what women think at all. What Lester does have, however, is the power of money. Lester uses his potential investment in George's salon to scold him with, "That's a helluva way to treat a business partner"; George loses Jackie to Lester because she likes to wake up "with the rent paid." George may know how women feel, but he loses out to Lester's power of security. This ending resonates with the 1968 Nixon victory, but the film's post-Watergate production and post-resignation release, as well as Lester's own ambivalence about his candidate, render this reversal of power in favor of Lester more complex than it might seem, undermining Lester's model of masculine power and privilege even as he succeeds. With this ending, however, the film also paradoxically asserts that what women do not want is the sort of man that Beatty is extratextually structured to be. *Shampoo* ultimately rejects the promiscuity inherent in the list of affairs that appears or is referred to in just about every Beatty article, along with the "mobility" described in a 1968 *Life* profile (Thompson, 86). He must be theirs alone and show the responsibility that commitment requires. Jill has the power to say no to him once she definitively knows that he spreads his favors around; Jackie leaves with Lester since she has no basis for believing that George will really take care of her.

"WARREN REALLY IS A SEX SYMBOL": BEATTY'S BODY AND THE GAZE

This intermingling of "subject" and "object" roles present in Jackie and Jill asserting their subjectivity to find a man who will take care of them or George as the seducer and seduced carries over into the physical presence of each in *Shampoo*. The use of the actors' bodies plays out the shifting roles of power in the construction of masculine and feminine as sexual entities that invite or evade a desiring look. While the women are "put on display" in certain ways, this display is usually offset by its conditions, evoking Neale's formulation of how the man avoids being seen as spectacle only through context (1993, 16–18). Goldie Hawn as Jill is always shown in either short nighties or mini dresses, but the camera never lingers on parts of her body. Lee Grant as the voracious Felicia is shown once in the opening scene without her top, but in a very dimly lit room; in the rest of the film she is fully covered or clothed, even during her sex scenes with George. Like Goldie Hawn, Julie Christie as Jackie wears revealing outfits, but the circumstances argue against an interpretation of exhibition to the viewer for its own sake. The dress she wears to the Nixon party has a high neck and long sleeves, but no back; the various reactions to the view of her body are emphasized over the view itself. When Jackie turns so that Felicia can see the full effect, the camera is positioned at a medium long distance from the characters, so that the shot shows Jackie from the side, George helpless in the middle and Felicia glaring at the view. At the orgy after the Nixon dinner, George and Jackie are shot in conversation from the front, so that she is covered while George in his unbuttoned shirt is teasingly visible, and there to be investigated.

This arrangement of bodies that reveals George more than Jackie is part of the overall organization of the film. George's central position in the web of sexual relationships is echoed by the order of which body is meant to be seen; his tight jeans and perpetually open shirts set off his body throughout the film. When he does Jackie's hair, she is in a towel, but George's upper body is as revealed by his tank top. His placement in the frame favors the view of his muscular arms, chest and back as he cuts her hair; when he stops to show her the results in the mirror, he is framed so that his head is not visible. There is no choice but to look at his body, as he is center-frame with Jackie. A scene in the salon of George straddling a client while he dries her hair with her head bent toward his groin keeps the action that is supposed to displace the exhibition of the male body overtly sexual. Finally, the only well-lighted displays of nudity among the principals are reserved for George in both of his sex scenes with Jackie; he is positioned both times so that his body covers hers as his own is made available for the viewer.

This discourse designed to enlighten the audience about Beatty's physical attributes— since, of course, it is Beatty on display—is also part of his press. A 1974 article in *Women's Wear Daily* describes Beatty's physical impact as he walks around the set of *Shampoo*: "He moves across the set in well-fitted blue jeans, a blue silk shirt unbuttoned low, a bright green scarf tied at the neck and loads of Indian jewelry. Female crew members stare. 'There's a lot of grabbing around here because Warren really is a sex symbol,' someone explains. 'He puts everybody in the mood to kiss everybody else' " (Winner, 12). Beatty does not efface the effect of his body on- or offscreen in order to preserve his status as a "man," questioning the assumed necessity of the strategy to maintain a semblance of heterosexuality. Despite the display of Beatty's body during sex with Jackie, the "manliness" of the act is verified by the more "normal" Lester's approving statement, "That's what I call fucking." Lester, who bears all of the accoutrements of male privilege including a Rolls, a big house, a mistress, and a body that avoids the gaze, believes George is a "fairy" because of his job and appearance; once he sees George in the act, however, Lester knows otherwise. The confirmed heterosexuality of this desirable male body on screen is echoed by the observation in the article that it is the female crewmembers who stare. It must be noted that what is not seen of Beatty is any full frontal nudity; if the representation of "phallic masculinity . . . depend[s] on keeping the male body and the genitals out of the critical spotlight," as Lehman (1993) suggests, then Beatty not only defies tradition by showing his body, but also retains his "manhood" by not revealing the physical sign (28). The knowledge that the female spectator, the female who would stare as Beatty walks across a set or read his non-answers about his sexual powers, can gain from the text of *Shampoo* is seeing that body in a very private moment, as well as watching him seduce and submit, but without the potentially disruptive revelation of the ultimate "truth." Seeing his body in the act is truth enough.[7]

Beatty's star image as something for women is reinforced by who does and does not understand why George is a "star" in his work. By writing George as a hairdresser, Beatty and Towne place George in a woman-oriented profession that exists to make women beautiful (objects). Yet at the same time, his attention is focused on fulfilling women's desires to be, somehow, better. Jill tells Jackie about how George woke her up in the middle of the night to do her hair and make her "the grooviest chick in town." Jill's response—"if you love me then I *am* the grooviest chick in town"—attests to the dual nature of George's talents. When George tells Felicia that he could have his own salon because "Hey, I'm a star, I'm a star," Felicia agrees that he would be a great "investment," since she also knows the appeal. The male loan officer at the bank, on the other hand, only wants to hear about financial references, not how many "heads" George cuts. Lester also expresses skepticism about George's "unusual trade," and accuses him of being "anti-establishment" because of his promiscuous life. Like Bingham's male spectator, the men are not "reassured" by George's presence, whereas the women all agree that "he's a great hairdresser," among other things.

The agency given to women by the presentation of a male body that is available for and will submit to their desire, as well as perform an act of improvement, is used against that male at the end of the film. In choosing to say no, Jill and Jackie have the final say in their relationships with George. The film closes with an image of George that differs from the rest of the film. He is alone, motionless, watching Jackie leave with Lester; Beatty is shot from behind and from the waist up, with his face and body position essentially denying one last look. It is at a moment of impotence that Beatty paradoxically obeys the order of the male not to be looked at. This end that denies the discourse of Beatty as "irresistible to women," and emphasizes George as being one more of a line of Beatty "schmucks" that includes Clyde and McCabe would seem to deny certain aspects of Beatty's metatext (Bingham 1994b, 165), but that would mean that the viewer would have to forget the rest of the film that devoted so much time to the display of George as an active symbol of sex and the breakdown of what "normally" constitutes "male" and "female." He is at his most powerful as a subject who has some agency when he is positioned as an object of female desire.

With this end, Jackie would seem to be placing herself as an object of male power and privilege, but it is her decision to do so based on a pragmatic assessment of the options. Beatty himself echoes this formulation of female as rational and male as sexual in another *Women's Wear Daily* article that asks, "Is Warren Beatty really a closet feminist?" because he asserts, " 'Well, I think I've always treated women as equals. . . . But I think men are more controlled by their libidos' " (Collins 1975, 16). In explicating the "male libido and its absurdities" as well as its attractions, Beatty presents a body that can be investigated and possessed without a complete loss of power for him or the female investigator; the relationship is fluid. Beatty makes himself available, while simultaneously controlling access to himself and hinting through his film texts that he cannot be the Powerful Male in spite of his career control. The woman can get a glimpse of the "secret" that Beatty withholds in interviews (though it is always brought up)—"You're asking me to talk about my sex life and I never have and I never will talk publicly about it"—seeing in the process that she has the power to turn it down if she chooses (Beatty qtd. in Collins 1975, 16). The rules are subject to change.

DON JUAN'S LOVE AFFAIR

The discourse of Beatty as sex symbol remains constant, even now, as an unavoidable part of his history as a star, despite his marriage and his turning sixty. But with the changes one must ask whether an audience still wants to know the secret as it has been altered to accommodate age, marriage, and family. The publicity surrounding the release of *Love Affair*, with Beatty co-starring with his wife, Annette Bening, in another remake of the Classical Hollywood romance *Love Affair* (1939)/*An Affair to Remember* (1957), not only relied on audience awareness of this history; it also reiterated it in various ways to sell the film through the proximity of film and life texts, in a manner similar to *Shampoo*. Among the requisite series of courtship shots in the film's trailer is the intentional mismatch of two scenes that alludes to audience knowledge about Beatty's life, as well as its knowledge that Bening also would have known before he married her in 1992. In the first, Beatty, lit softly in the style of Classical Hollywood "glamour" lighting, turns to Bening on an airplane and informs her that he has a reputation for rampant womanizing. The trailer cuts to Bening in reverse shot, but in an entirely different location, "replying" sarcastically, "I am *shocked* and *amazed*." This vignette also appeared frequently in the shorter television ads, emphasizing that part of the film's appeal was potentially "knowing" the "secret" of how a figure famous for his love life decided to settle down.

A joint appearance by the couple on Oprah Winfrey's talk show (for an overwhelmingly female studio audience) continued this mode of winking at the audience about Beatty's private life. Winfrey asked Bening if she ever thought, "So many women wanted Warren, but I got him," to which Bening sensibly replied, "No, of course not." Winfrey also asked both of them what "romantic things Warren does for Annette," as if this would contain the answer to the studio audience's prayers; a question he modestly tried to evade (he brings her flowers). With questions like this, a big entrance for Beatty twenty minutes after Bening that involved a standing ovation, and Winfrey addressing him as "Mr. Beatty" whereas Bening was simply "Annette," the program supported the discourse of Beatty as a big romantic star of long standing. This discourse was part of Dominick Dunne's profile in *Vanity Fair* that described Beatty as an "old-fashioned" movie star: "Think of Clark Gable, Gary Cooper, Cary Grant, those icons of another era . . . who were still kissing Marilyn Monroe and Audrey Hepburn and Doris Day long past kissing time and you begin to get the idea about Warren Beatty" (1994, 143). Among the descriptions of Beatty's life-changing reaction to meeting Bening, and Beatty's fatherly love for his daughter, Dunne still includes references to Beatty's romantic history, a dance with Kim Novak at a party in the 1960s that created palpable sexual tension, and the fact that Beatty's body is still trim (144, 203, 202). Beatty inadvertently raises the specter of his sexual appeal when, as he is listing the roles he did not originally see himself in, like Clyde, he says, "In *Shampoo*, I never thought of anyone but myself" (203). The appeal of seeing *Love Affair*, the publicity implies, is not only that of seeing a great romantic idol in an old-fashioned love story with his beautiful wife, but also of seeing the powerful seducer seduced, and maybe knowing the "secret" of the seduction. The constant that remains, along with Beatty's address to a female audience, is the woman who still has the power to resist his powers of seduction if she chooses, with a sarcastic quip in the case of the film trailer; a woman who entrances Beatty equally.

The tease of the publicity is verified by the opening of the film itself, through the establishment of the reputation of Beatty's character, Mike Gambril, a promiscuous sports figure whose profession recalls Beatty's prematurely dead quarterback from *Heaven Can Wait*, not to mention Beatty's own personal history as a high school jock. As Mike and his fiancée are celebrities, the news of his engagement is treated in a manner similar to the news of Beatty's engagement to Bening. A report on the TV tabloid program *Hard Copy* within the film shows actual paparazzi shots of Beatty with old girlfriends, doctored so that the women are not quite recognizable, to announce that one of the world's most durable bachelors has finally settled down. As if the various entertainment news reports reiterating Mike's reputation were not enough, he and his agent are stopped on their way out to Mike's car by a young pretty editing assistant who brings Mike his watch. As she tells Mike he forgot it in the editing room, she gives him a meaningful glance that is duly noted by his agent, who then asks him not to mess up his engagement. The line between Mike Gambril and Warren Beatty is blurred from the outset.

Even with this beginning that parades Beatty's sexual past one more time, the overtly sexual appeal of Beatty is displaced to overt romanticism in the film as well as in the publicity, in keeping with the extratextual events of marriage, age and the pre- and post-AIDS sexual and political climates of 1975 and 1994.[8] This difference in climate is acknowledged by Beatty himself in a New York *Newsday* interview, as he "muses aloud . . . 'Could *Love Affair* have been made fifteen, twenty years ago? . . . During the period of sexual and drug mayhem, the picture might have been a little less appealing' " (Pacheco 1994, 25). In a 1996 *Esquire* piece about the purported end of Hollywood's rapacious sexual culture, one of the professed reasons that "Don Juan" is "in turnaround" is simply "Warren Beatty is married," and no longer a purveyor of such hedonism (Hedley, 122). Whereas *Shampoo* features George/Beatty *in flagrante* several times, *Love Affair* shows that the relationship has been consummated through the strategic use of a dissolve from Beatty and Bening deciding to stay on board the ship they have been forced to take after their plane crash-lands on an island in the Pacific, to a close-up freeze-frame of Beatty and Bening kissing super-imposed over shots of the ship as it sails, accompanied by lush violins on the soundtrack. True to the film's trailer in spirit if not in actual dialogue, Bening's Terry McKay does not give in easily; when she finally does, it is not because she just wants to have sex with Mike, and he with her, but because they have fallen hopelessly in love.

The most notable event in this discourse surrounding the private life of Beatty in his films, however, is the reaction of the audience. In 1975, Beatty's orchestration of sexuality, which reworked the categories of what it was to be male and female by directly involving the construction of Beatty's own sexuality on and off the screen, was a hit.[9] The audience wanted to know. In 1994, however, the cinematic discourse about Beatty's "secret" life was rejected, despite the publicity and plot that promised some sort of revelation. According to the final analysis in the *New York Times*, two of the problems were directly related to the nature of Beatty's star discourse: "No one wants to see a married couple on screen" because "the sexual sparks don't fly," and "younger audiences were not especially interested in Mr. Beatty as a romantic lead."[10] The tease that attracted viewers to *Shampoo* failed.

While the film's critical and financial failure is one indication of the limits of Beatty's star image as a sex symbol, Beatty's curtailed presence in popular culture between 1994 and 1998 intimates that Beatty is at best a sex symbol with limited appeal, or perhaps is under no woman's desiring gaze at all (except, probably, his wife's), especially if that younger audience has no interest in Beatty that way. Peter Bart, in a 1996 article for the men's magazine *GQ*, sums up Beatty's problem on the cusp of age sixty: "He is suddenly a husband and father, not a lover-at-large. . . . Most daunting, as the utter failure of *Love Affair* (which Beatty produced as well as starred in opposite Bening) vividly demonstrated, he is no longer able to get away with playing the romantic lead" (78). This is not to say that there is a direct correspondence between the film's failure and Beatty's absence; he has taken long periods off between roles in the past. What is notable regarding these alterations in persona cited by Bart, however, is that when a potentially quite demystifying story about Beatty's body and sexual ability was published in 1995, there was very little public reaction vis-à-vis Beatty. In the book *You'll Never Make Love in This Town Again*, authored by several Hollywood prostitutes and women about town, one of the women deemed Beatty "nothing to write home about" either physically or sexually. Though the book appeared on the best-seller list, the revelation that Beatty was ostensibly not the Great Lover he is purported to be on screen and in gossip got almost no mention in the press. While *Esquire*'s "Don Juan in Turnaround" article (1996) includes Beatty's angry response to the book's "exploitation," "lies," and the alleged damage to his reputation, it is in the context of an argument with the book's publisher at a party (Hedley, 130). More important, the entire incident is relegated to the final pages of a ten-page article, superseded by the story of Don Simpson's life and death, and O.J. Simpson's take on the Hollywood "culture of whores" and sleaze.[11] The revelation simply does not matter as a revelation, nor is it worth first position in a story about 1990s sexual Hollywood. Since Beatty does not function as a visible star presence signifying sex *or* romance for an audience, who wants to know the "truth" of the person that much? In 1997, a *Marie Claire* piece on Beatty and Jack Nicholson posed the question, "Sexy at 60?" then suggested that since Beatty and Nicholson are turning 60, "for women the image of the Great Seducer needs adjustment"; even more so since Beatty is "in safe harbor, with a third baby on the way" (Howell 34, 37). There is no tease left in Beatty's private life.

The failure to incorporate a discourse on sexuality that abides by its own rules to question the categories of "masculine" and "feminine," subject and object, through positing a desirable male and a desiring female into a discourse that involves the "law of marriage" raises larger questions about the cultural apparatus surrounding the star discourse that go beyond the methodological intent of this essay. The seeming contradiction of Beatty stems from an organization of desire that does not abide by "normative" rules, yet it expresses a decidedly "normal" heterosexual desire, to the point of marriage and several children. The vicissitudes of Beatty's star discourse and its polymorphous construction of sexuality indicate a fluidity and a susceptibility to outside discourses that defy a set reading. When Beatty constructs a manhood that corresponds more to the "norm," the reception is very different from when he breaks the rules, putting into question what the "rules" are at any given time. In order to avoid a tendency toward all-encompassing assumptions about sexuality and power, the qualities attached to male and female need to be mapped out as they are constructed in the star discourse itself, whether it is in a particular event or a series over time, before they can be determined, rather than the reverse of stating what the categories are and then deciding if the star "fits." Indeed, as the construction of Beatty as fantasy sexual object is fading another consistent aspect of his star text was positioned to take its place with the release of *Bulworth* in 1998: politics—a traditional bastion of male power regardless of liberal or conservative stance.

Notes

1   See especially Mulvey 1988, 62–63, and Neale 1993, 17–18, for the early paradigms of Hollywood's representation of gender dictating that the male body "hides" from the gaze in order to preserve the norm of active male looking subject and passive female spectacularized object.

2   Rudolph Valentino is a clear antecedent in this regard. As both Miriam Hansen and Gaylyn Studlar assert, Valentino's image as a highly desirable man for women's eyes ultimately resisted recuperation into the "norm" of masculinity, rupturing the binary discourse of active/passive attached to gender in the realm of sexual desire. See Hansen 1986, 23; Studlar 1989, 31.

3   See Foucault 1990, especially 105–7.

4   This brings up the active/male passive/female binarism of Mulvey and Neale. Still, despite criticism that the sex assumed is male, Foucault's formulation suggests that this binarism is not the overriding rule of Power and the Father. For that criticism see, for example, de Lauretis 1987, 14–15; Fuss 1991, 107.

5   The need to recuperate the epistemological rupture of an "objectified" or "feminized" male body through the intervention of various discursive practices such as those suggested by Neale, Cohan, Studlar on Valentino, and Bingham on Jimmy Stewart points to the capacity for this type of star to cause this instability. See Studlar 1989, 26; Bingham 1994a, 24.

6   The other reviews include Kael 1975, 89; Michener 1975, 51; Sarris 1975b, 61.

7   Not that Beatty's physical sign of phallic masculinity has never been the object of public discourse. In an *Esquire* article titled "Beds" (Mansfield 1990) that consisted of a collection of quotes regarding Beatty's career in bed, Bianca Jagger and Mamie van Doren say, "It was very big," but Carole Mallory reports, "He's average in size but more friendly than most. It's not the size of Texas. More like the tip of Montauk" (156). Madonna nicely conflates size and performance when she tells the *Advocate* in 1991, "I haven't measured it, but it's a perfectly wonderful size" (Shewey 1991, 51). The woman in *You'll Never Make Love in This Town Again*, however, says nothing on the subject.

8   All of this could constitute its own more extensive study. It is the persistent intersection of film and

life texts to construct notions of sexuality that are of interest here, but these extratextual influences needed to be acknowledged, especially given the different reactions of audiences to the discourse.

9   With a gross of more than $20 million in the first three months of release, "Distrib says the film 'is already one of the company's biggest grossing films in its 50-year history.'" From "*Shampoo* a Columbia Clean-Up," 1975, 6.

10   Weinraub 1994, C19. A detail that has too many implications to analyze beyond what is here. It is not possible to determine exactly why from the *Times*, but the few articles on Beatty between 1994 and 1998 do suggest that age can be just as epistemologically disruptive for the male sex symbol as the female, even if it is ostensibly used more as a yardstick in certain pieces for how long Beatty has been around.

11   Simpson qtd. in Hedley 1996, 129. No comment.

Works cited

Adler, Dick. 1975. "Warren Beatty: The Star of *Shampoo* Lets Down His Hair." *Viva*, July 40ff.

Bart, Peter. 1996. "Warren Can Wait." *GQ*, April, 76–80.

Beatty, Warren, and Annette Bening. 1994. Interview with Oprah Winfrey. *The Oprah Winfrey Show*. ABC. WABC, New York. Oct. 21.

Bingham, Dennis. 1994a. *Acting Male*. New Brunswick: Rutgers University Press.

———. 1994b. "Warren Beatty and the Elusive Male Body in Hollywood Cinema." *Michigan Quarterly Review* 33 (winter): 149–76.

Chafe, William H. 1977. *Women and Equality: Changing Patterns in American Culture*. New York: Oxford University Press.

Cocks, Jay. 1975. "Blow Dry." *Time*, Feb. 24, 4–5.

Cohan, Steven. 1993. "Masquerading as the American Male in the 50s: *Picnic*, William Holden and the Spectacle of Masculinity in Hollywood Film." In *Male Trouble*, ed. Constance Penley and Sharon Willis, 202–32. Minneapolis: University of Minnesota Press.

Collins, Nancy. 1975. "Bad Boy Goes Good." *Women's Wear Daily*, Feb. 11, 16.

deCordova, Richard. 1990. *Picture Personalities: The Emergence of the Star System in America*. Chicago: University of Illinois Press.

de Lauretis, Teresa. 1987. *Alice Doesn't: Feminism, Semiotics, Cinema*. Bloomington: Indiana University Press.

Dunne, Dominick. 1994. "Love Story." *Vanity Fair*, Sept., 140ff.

Dyer, Richard. 1979. *Stars*. London: BFI Publishing.

Foucault, Michel. 1990. *The History of Sexuality, Vol. 1: An Introduction*. Trans. Robert Hurley. New York: Vintage Books.

Fuss, Diana. 1991. *Essentially Speaking*. New York: Routledge.

Gallagher, Tag. 1975. "Warren Beatty: The Stud as a Thoughtful Man." *Village Voice*, Feb. 24, 112, 60–62, 87.

Hansen, Miriam. 1986. "Pleasure, Ambivalence, Identification: Valentino and Female Spectatorship." *Cinema Journal* 25, 4 (summer): 6–32.

Hedley, Tom. 1996. "Don Juan in Turnaround." *Esquire*, September, 122–32.

Howell, Georgina. 1997. "Sexy at 60?: Warren & Jack." *Marie Claire*, Feb., 34–37.

Kael, Pauline. 1975. "Beverly Hills as a Big Bed." *New Yorker*, Feb. 17, 86–93.

Lehman, Peter. 1993. *Running Scared: Masculinity and the Representation of the Male Body*. Philadelphia: Temple University Press.

Mansfield, Stephanie. 1990. "Beds." *Esquire*, May: 151–57.

Michener, Charles. 1975. "Don Juan in Beverly Hills." *Newsweek*, Feb. 10, 51.

Muir, Florabel. 1961. "The New Great Lover." *The Sunday News*, Oct. 15, 100.

Mulvey, Laura. 1975. "Visual Pleasure and Narrative Cinema." *Screen* 16, 3 (autumn 1975). Reprinted in *Feminism and Film Theory*, ed. Constance Penley, 57–68. New York: Routledge, 1988.

Neale, Steve. 1983. "Masculinity as Spectacle." *Screen* 24, 6. Reprinted in *Screening the Male*, eds. Steven Cohan and Ina Rae Hark, 9–20. New York: Routledge.

Pacheco, Patrick. 1994. "Love Connection." *New York Newsday*, Oct. 16, 18ff.

Parker, John. 1993. *Warren Beatty: The Last Great Lover of Hollywood*. New York: Carroll & Graf Publishers.

Robin et al. 1995. *You'll Never Make Love in This Town Again*. Los Angeles: Dove Books.

Sarris, Andrew. 1975a. "The Blissful Servitude of Self-Indulgence." *Village Voice*, March 13, 71.

———. 1975b. "Studs Have Feelings Too." *Village Voice*, Feb. 24, 61.

Schell, Jonathan. 1975. *The Time of Illusion*. New York: Vintage Books.

"Shampoo a Columbia Clean-Up." 1975. *Variety* May 28, 6.

Shewey, Don. 1991. "The Saint, the Slut, the Sensation . . . Madonna." *Advocate*, May 7, 42–51.

Studlar, Gaylyn. 1989. "Discourses of Gender and Ethnicity: The Construction and De(con)struction of Rudolph Valentino as Other." *Film Criticism* 8, 2 (winter): 18–35.

Thompson, Thomas. 1968. "Under the Gaze of the Charmer." *Life*, April 26, 86–94.

Weinraub, Bernard. 1994. "This Year, Oscar Bets Won't Be Sure Ones." *New York Times*, November 29, C15ff.

Winner, Karin. 1974. "On Movies and Politics." *Women's Wear Daily*, May 24, 12.

Winsten, Archer. 1975. "Rages and Outrages." *New York Post*, March 3, 22.

Chapter 10

Barry King

THE STAR AND THE COMMODITY: NOTES TOWARDS A PERFORMANCE THEORY OF STARDOM (1987)

M Y PURPOSE IN WHAT FOLLOWS is to set the limits of a Marxist account of the star system in the popular cinema, which, in the West at least, is more or less coterminous with Hollywood. I take it that such an account must pay attention to the particularities of performance as a labour process, and the relations of production in which such a process occurs. This materialist thesis of the primacy of production relations over symbolic relations should not in itself be read as a denial of the particular effectivity of the symbolic, but I shall be unable to pursue such matters conclusively here. Evidently any consideration of the commodity form and the metabolism of exchange will be struck by the parallels between this process and signification proper. The work of Jean Baudrillard is a play on such parallelisms, which claims to show that the point of reference in the labour theory of value – use value – is in itself a social form, a signifier in the chain of signifiers imposed by bourgeois economy.[1] The extent to which this reading of Marx is valid is a question that cannot be addressed here.[2] Yet one can take consolation in the fact that the account offered limits itself very clearly to the terrain of political economy. If from the perspective of Baudrillard this constitutes a delineation of the 'terroristic' imposition of the illusion of reference on the 'play' of signifiers, this is precisely the spirit that animates the account here.

UNDERSTANDING THE STARS

If the ever-proliferating literature on stardom and celebrity can be symptomatized by a single characteristic, it would be that writers on stardom are seemingly obsessed with matters of signification – in the narrow Saussurian sense of the relationship between the sign and its referent – to the detriment of representation.[3] It is usual for those who wish to explain the 'meaning' of stardom to catalogue the presence of existential themes in its discourses. Such an operation, which takes as its point of reference the sphere of consumption, is usually combined with a thoroughgoing populism, whereby allusions to the problems of everyday life, especially adolescent everyday life, are seen as the credentials of the star as a popular hero. Such a form of analysis, while not necessarily invalid, nevertheless tends to preclude a consideration of how the discourses of stardom are constructed and activated in the first place. This emphasis, which is by no means the sole property of journalists, belletrists and vox-populizers but shows up in 'serious' writing, can be evidenced by a few citations.

Marianne Sinclair, in her introduction to *Those Who Died Young: Cult Heroes of the Twentieth Century*, argues that for teenagers of her generation Montgomery Clift, James Dean and Marlon Brando were 'living symbols of our rebellion, our scepticism, our yearning'. Such a profound indexicality – ever threatened, one takes it, by its implication in the specificities of time and place – finds its apotheosis when the bearer of meaning meets with an early death. 'No star or entertainer, however popular and famous, can really be considered a "myth" if he lives to a ripe old age and dies at ninety. Basically, these terms are reserved for stars who die young and tragically.'[4]

Make what one will of these claims overall, it is nevertheless clearly the case that physical decease becomes a kind of excuse for installing signality into the discourse of stardom – endowing the luckless victims with the resonances of common fate – and, more important, installing the biography of the star as the basic axiom of the social relationship between star and fan.[5] Such a formulation encapsulates one of the paradoxes of the populist view of stardom: sooner or later, the star as 'reflex' of audience needs becomes the archetype or the matrix of such needs. Such an exorbitation is doubtless forced upon those who wish to account for the 'meaning' of the star's popularity by the presumption that this meaning must reside in the star's 'personality'. For such a narrow point of reference to cohere at all requires a powerful suppression of semiosis, the difficulty of which is only demonstrated when one asks for an *exact* definition of the meaning of, for example, Marilyn Monroe. Physical termination writes out at least the prospect of change from the side of the bearer of the image, but a more comprehensive resolution is to be found in postulating that the star embodies some deep-seated – i.e. transhistorical – human essence. Thus, for example, Pete Townshend, combining the insider's authority with a few homely psychoanalyticisms, observes:

> Put more celestially, when we pursue perfection, in ourselves or in others, we are searching for God. A perfect father or mother, brother or sister, son or daughter – all are dreamed of in the demand for a psychotherapeutic placebo, often embodied in the image of a chosen star.[6]

But, as pointed out, such formulations are not exclusive to popular writers. For instance, Edgar Morin, arguably the first analyst to provide a systematic account of stardom, writes when dealing specifically with the 'star and us':

> The star is indeed a myth: not only a daydream but an idea-force. The characteristic of myth is to insert itself or incarnate itself somehow within life. If the myth of the stars incarnates itself so astonishingly within reality, it is because myth is produced by that reality, i.e. the human *history* of the twentieth century. But it is also because the human reality nourishes itself on the imaginary to the point of being semi-imaginary itself.[7]

Evidently no one with the kind of sociological sensibility that Morin exhibits elsewhere in the same text – 'James Dean has invented nothing: he has canonized and codified an ensemble of sumptuary laws which allows age class to assert itself' – is likely fully to endorse the vision of personal transcendence that is found in popular accounts. But, even so, such a formulation, with all its reifying grandeur, is not too far removed from the foregoing in counterposing the concrete particularity of the star to an entire social formation.

In recent times, as most readers will be aware, the main opportunity to explore the phenomenon of stardom has fallen to Richard Dyer. In *Stars*, Dyer is mainly concerned to detail the range of approaches to stardom and to set the limits of the field, but he does indicate clearly enough what his own position – to be laid out in greater length in a forthcoming book – would be.[8] For Dyer, the 'symbolic' power of the star – charisma – rests on the fact that his or her persona constitutes a condensation (in the Freudian sense of an unstable combination of contradictory themes or images) of the conflict between every-day experience and the normative protocols of the dominant ideology. Dyer's view of stardom amounts to a role-conflict theory, with certain categories of audience member – such as adolescents, blacks, women and gays – seen as particularly responsive to the contra-dictory play of meaning and identity implicit in the imagery of stars. Such responsiveness, Dyer argues, is based on the fact of exclusion – or, at least, the fact that inclusion is only at the cost of self-effacement – 'from the dominant articulacy . . . of adult, male, heterosexual culture'.[9] The infirmities of personal identity in relation to the 'official' norms are by no means the exclusive property of the groups or categories identified, Dyer argues. These may experience such infirmities more intensely – hence their apparent 'proneness' to star-worship – but, overall, stardom serves to dramatize a central crisis in 'bourgeois society': the presence of widespread 'uncertainty and anxiety concerning the definition of what a person is'.[10]

Even if one takes at face value the notion that bourgeois society ever posited a coherent definition of a person, there are a number of problems with Dyer's arguments. It is not at all clear how the 'subcultural' account of stardom fits in with his general theory of the star as 'charismatically' embodying the general crisis of the personal. At the very least, the latter position suggests that the 'dominant articulacy of adult, male, heterosexual culture' is less solid and pervasive than the subcultural phase of his theory implies. Nor is it entirely clear that these two themes can be synthesized: if the official norms of valid human agency are truly problematic, then it is difficult to see why subcultural groups especially suffer a trial of identity in relation to it as opposed to those who have embraced (or were socialized into the text of) such a definition. The answer that Dyer would give, no doubt, is that subordinate groups experience such contradictions as more oppressive. In view of the preponderant weight of institutional discrimination against women, blacks and gays, for example, there is a sense in which this is true. It is another matter to assume that there is a continuous problematic (not to mention a continuity of problem) of the personal between black and white, straight and gay, masculine and feminine experience.

There is little doubt that Dyer would not radically disagree with this kind of qualifica-tion, but the substantial point remains: how is it possible, if one situates the meaning of stardom at the level of the content of audience response, to offer a general theory of stardom? There are relatively few accounts of what kinds of interpretation various sub-groups place upon stars. Consequently, such a procedure must infer meaning from the general social conditions of such groups, and this is Dyer's procedure. The problem with this approach is that the specification of the star's persona becomes subject to overload and a dissemination of meaning.[11] Thus Jane Fonda's charisma 'can be accounted for not only in the reconciliation of radicalism and feminism with Americanness and ordinariness but also her ability to suggest (as a tomboy) redefinitions of sexuality while at the same time overtly reasserting heterosexuality'.[12]

This drift towards tautology – the star means nothing because she means everything – in my view results from the failure to define stardom as a form of agency deriving from the site of production. Thus, for example, Dyer details at some length some of the constitutive ingredients of a given star's performance, but these elements are treated overall as channels for the realization of persona. At no point are the specificities of the social relations of production in which performances occur and personae are represented subject to scrutiny.

At the most general level, such a result derives from the emphasis on consumption in Dyer's analysis – an emphasis which willy-nilly mirrors the governing imperatives of the capitalist media anyway: that the moment of consumption (realization of value) has onto-logical priority over the moment of production. More immediately, the failure to address the full materiality of performance as a determinant of stardom, while in itself an evidential weakness – stars are performers (of some kind, at some level of competence) before they are public 'symbols' – has a more serious consequence. It tends to erode the valuable contrast between subcultural readings of the star and the fact that there appears to be a residue of meaning that is never finally exhausted by such meanings. Such a residue points towards the need for a theorization of the impact of stardom at a level beyond wants and needs as content – a conception of the *form* of agency that stardom inscribes in re-presenting contents. It is because of Dyer's failure to theorize the latter that his notion of the role of the stars in defining the personal is left in a state of unfocused generality.

In what follows I want to preserve the contrast between the star as indicating something about the general form of social agency under capitalist social relations and the sphere of contents – essentially a sphere of experience in search of collectivizing embodiments.[13] This stems from the need to recognize that identification with stars often takes the form of an identification with a specific form of agency – with the star *per se* rather than with the narrative functions (characters) he or she re-presents. But, more specifically, I believe that there is a need to connect the form of the star more decisively with the capitalist relation-ships within which the star is 'born' and which he or she, by being born, sustains.

A COMMODITY AMONG COMMODITIES

It is a truism of the literature that the star system, whether in film, stage or the music business, develops out of and sustains capitalist relations of production and consumption. Not only is it possible to point to the fact that the star is central to the raising of finance, as the least problematic advance guarantee of a certain level of audience interest. It is also relatively easy to detail the various ways in which stars stabilize the process of representation itself by focusing a disparate range of specialisms and narrational inputs around a relatively fixed nucleus of meaning, which is given in advance of any specific instance of narration or, for that matter, context of production. Likewise the mobilization of publicity and advertising around the moment of consumption of film itself – not to mention the consumption of derived commodities such as fan magazines, fashions and consumer goods – relies on the star as the cybernetic monitor which returns all efforts to the same apparent core of meaning. Again, it is not difficult to cite instances of the efficacy of the star's persona as a means towards the accumulation of capital on the part of actors, who emerge from a labour market marked by chronic unemployment and underemployment to become in effect the propri-etors of their own image – for example, Clint Eastwood.

Such a set of processes, not without its moments of breakdown and contradiction, can be held to constitute the star *system*. The further delineation of this system is not my concern here.[14] Rather, I want to approach a more cellular aspect of this system: the formation of the performance commodity.

As a matter of fact, it is far from unusual for commentators on stardom to refer to the star as a commodity, but this usage invariably has a metaphorical rather than a substantive reference – indicating, at best, that aspects of the star's personality, or more exactly part of the star's anatomy read as indices of his or her personality, enter into the process of exchange. Such a reference, while partially justified by the fact that stars have a key role in imparting significance to material objects, such as vinyl, tapes and video/film formats, nevertheless fails to distinguish clearly enough between things as commodities and labour power as a commodity.

To make this clear it is necessary to enter into a brief exposition of value concepts as defined by Marx. It will be recalled that Marx defined the commodity as the 'simplest social form in which the labour product is represented in . . . [capitalist] society'.[15] A commodity proves on analysis to be the articulation of three determinants:

1   Use values – which indicate in general the material content of wealth, regardless of the form that wealth takes, and, specifically, the physical property or quality of a thing, usually a product of human labour, as useful in relation to human needs. Only under specific circumstances, when the production of use values is oriented towards the needs of others, rather than the needs of the direct producers, do use values assume a *commodity form*.

2   Value – the general substance underlying the metabolism of the production and exchange of commodities which determines the possibility of the relationship of equivalence or comparability between one commodity and another, despite the presence of profound differences in the concrete qualities of the commodities as *use values*. Such a substance is identified in the first instance as labour, and its magnitude is shown to be the function of an abstraction from the particularities of any concrete act of labour. Accordingly, the measure of value is revealed to be the socially necessary labour time required to produce the commodity, as an average expression of the relation between the actual duration of a given act of labour and the conditions of production overall.

3   Exchange value – the phenomenal form that *value* assumes under capitalist relations of production. A commodity manifests its value only in relation to other commodities – that is, in so far as its value is equivalent to the use value of some other commodity which in expanded commodity exchange is part of an entire string of equivalences. The operation of such a string of equivalences in the metabolism of exchange, in which each commodity shrugs off its particularity (its qualities as a use value), is the process that demonstrates that there is some underlying substance – value – that renders all commodities equatable as quantities despite their sensuous concrete qualities. Ultimately the extension of the process of exchange renders value in the form of a universal equivalent – a substance which by social convention is excluded from the chain of equivalences and appears instead as the natural form in which the value of all other commodities is expressed, in short as *money*. With the derivation of the money form, the manifestation of value as exchange value is complete.[16]

The analysis of the development of the commodity form, which in the immediate context of the analysis of capitalist relations has two aspects – use value and exchange value – in fact already contains the outline of the social relationships governing labour power as a commodity among commodities. In the first place, under such a system all products of human labour enter the process of exchange (and hence become commodities) only in so far as they lose their distinctive concrete particularity as things or processes and become exchange values, i.e. undifferentiated quanta of human labour. In other words, the character of commodities as use values is made socially visible only in so far as they take on exchange value or assume in immediate terms a market price. For such a relationship to pertain, it follows that labour activities in general have assumed an immediate, private character. Not only are the direct producers divorced from the direct consumers, so that use values cease to regulate the general (as opposed to, say, the household) economy, but the social usefulness of any concrete labour activity cannot be known in advance of the relation of exchange, wherein it only finds a reductive expression as an abstraction – a quantity of universal equivalent or *money*. The wage form constitutes from the side of consumption an expression of the same process whereby the use value of labour power as a commodity 'finds' expression, if at all, only as exchange value (the wage).[17]

The representational outcome of these processes is addressed by Marx in terms of the notion of commodity fetishism, which indicates the process whereby the social characteristics of human labour appear as the derivatives of the properties (some conventional, some material) of the products of labour. This is then characterized as producing a general framework of thought in which 'the definite social relations between men . . . assumes . . . the fantastic form of a relation between things'.[18] Such a process of reification not only encompasses the world of things and objects – its objective aspect – but, reaching into the consciousness of agents, leads them to perceive themselves as parcelled out between units of socially significant activity (labour power as a commodity) and the comprehensive particularity of their own being (personality) which appears as having only a *private* significance. Personality becomes in the metabolism of exchange, and at the point of production, a thing to be suppressed or reductively functionalized (i.e. the charm of the salesman or the politeness of the shop assistant) in the sale of labour power.[19] Finally, it is necessary to stress that fetishism is not based on a process of simple misrecognition or error but is a representational formation derived from the immediately given (empirical) surface of capitalist relations.[20] It appears, in short, to be the 'natural' state of capitalist social relations.

The key point I wish to draw from this synopsis is that the deployment of value concepts allows the identification of the manner in which labour power in general is represented under capitalism.[21] As will be apparent, not all forms of labour power are subject to this process of reduction to the same extent, but I would stand by the assertion that it is the tendential centre of their 'treatment' under extended commodity production.[22] Generally speaking, one might say that the *social* as opposed to the *private* destiny of the bearers of labour power under capitalism is to enter the process of exchange – find employment – and encounter a denial of their particularity. Such a denial is the individual expression, filtered through factors of race, class, gender, age and skill, of the twin reduction of private labour to general labour and concrete labour to abstract labour.

With these markers of the anthropology of work under capitalism in place, I can now approach the question of the formation of the performance commodity as a process subtended in this general representational space.

THE PERFORMANCE COMMODITY

At first sight, the star seems to constitute an exception to the process of fetishism. Contrary to the proposition that the representation of labour under capitalism is reduced to a state of depersonalized objectivity, the star stands as the resplendent, full centre of a personalized teleology, a place where the distinction between role and person is meaningless. Thus the very presence of the star within the heartland of cultural capitalism can be seen as a refutation of the pervasiveness of commodity fetishism. It is relatively easy to cite counter-instances which undermine this appearance of autonomy, which is the stuff of insider journalism.[23] But these accounts will not explain the persistence, the eternal recurrence of a notion of a realm of freedom centred on stardom and, by extension, celebrity.

If one is to remain faithful to the premises of commodity fetishism, it follows that one cannot dismiss this example of counter-fetishism as a mere *illusion*. On the contrary, it must be regarded as a reality at the level of appearance which provides the concrete material of the operations of advertising and promotion, not to mention its material effects at the point of sale. At a first approximation, let us note that Marx in fact holds two apparently opposing

views on the representational effects of commodity production: fetishism and personification, which is the reverse process whereby individuals become the embodiments of social
relations. But the contrast between fetishism and personification is not a fundamental difficulty because on Marx's account the latter, personification, arises only where individuals
have a place in the social division of labour as owners or managers of the reified moments of
capitalist production – capital and land – and, in the case of trade-union leaders, as monopolists of labour power.[24] The 'thing-like' facticity of capitalist productive relations is in
fact the precondition for those placed in positions of agency to invest such positions with an
'aura' of personality – always bearing in mind that such an aura has its objective limits set by
the subjectivity inscribed in the role.

At first sight, such a process might be held to account for the phenomenon of stardom.
Stars, after all, especially in contemporary times, have functioned as capitalists, setting up
production companies and profiting from the sale of their own personae. As such they
function as the 'happy inheritors' of the fruits of the collective labour power mobilized
around the capital deployed in film production, much the same as managers in industry. One
problem with this assimilation is that, certainly in the past and even today, many stars still
retain an employee status, selling their services on a 'freelance' basis to production companies within or contractually linked to the major producers. More decisively, perhaps, it is
still the case that, where a star is an owner of a production company, the rationale of such
ownership, or indeed the basic reason why the star is in such a position in the first place,
rests on his or her role in the actual process of production. Clint Eastwood is both the
proprietor of his persona and the seller of the services that this persona represents.
Whereas, in the former capacity, he and his fellow investors in Malpaso Productions might
wish to maximize short-term returns by flooding the market with Dirty Harry clones, as a
star, Eastwood the actor is concerned with preserving the long-term flexibility of the
services he offers: in short, in avoiding over-exposure.

Such considerations suggest caution in seeing the star as a personification of capitalist
agency. In the first place, the sustenance of the role of the star depends on the endorsement,
however mediated, of mass opinion. This reliance, with its associated populisms, means that
the general image of stardom is as a 'powerless élite' – a cadre of prominent personalities
whose effectivity is based on a necessary severance from the power structure.[25] This severance of the 'expressive' and the 'instrumental' may be more conventional than real, but the
presence of such a constraint, even if exceeded, is not in doubt. Ronald Reagan may use
actorly skills as President, but he cannot carry the instrumental burden of that office and
admit that he uses them.

But of more immediate concern than a need to court mass opinion is the fact that the
star is, in real terms, ambiguously located between capital and labour. As a freelance
employee active in a casual labour market reminiscent of manual trades, the star maintains
his or her position less through the exercise of above-average skills than through a personal
monopoly over his or her persona. It is from this position, I suggest, that the star can offer
not a metaphor but a *metonymy* for labour power in general. To understand this requires a
consideration of the performance commodity.

Cultural commodities in general can be distinguished from highly functionalized
commodities by the stress on prototypicality and uniqueness that marks even their mass
production. Obviously even highly functionalized commodities are culturally determined,
but these do not occupy a specific place in the division of labour where uniqueness and
'creativity' are prioritized or, obversely, serve a market where use values are more generalized, rather than truncated within the confines of strict functionality. Cultural commodities
have three broad forms: as unique objects, as reproducible objects and as non-material
performances. The key feature of performance as a labour process is its potential for a high

level of diversity, since as an unmediated event it does not materialize into a commodity with a delimited content or form before reception. As is well known, transcription technologies operate to stabilize performance and render it as a material object, freed from the time and place of the original event. But, before I consider the effects of the latter further, it is worth identifying what features of performance carry through from its basis in live events. One of the features of performance is that the distinction between the *process of labour* and the *product of labour* is hard to make – and this is so even when the event is transcribed. Strictly speaking, a performance is a labour process, exhibited for consumption regardless of whether the performers have a direct or mediated relationship with the audience. Another way to put this is to say that performance is not the production of a product but a service; and even then not a specific act of service as given by, say, a hairdresser, but a flow of services built around various values – spectacle, pleasure in physical and vocal mastery, social involvement, identification, communication of meaning, aesthetic and emotional patterns of affect, and so on.[26] Obversely, when productive activities which do result in definite material products are 'aestheticized' (e.g. basket-weaving and pottery), the labour process itself becomes as great if not a greater source of use values (delight in the craft process, etc.).

Such factors indicate that in the case of performance the reduction of concrete acts of labour to abstract general labour cannot have the same progressive effect as labour processes (whether skilled or unskilled) that produce a definite commodity or part of a commodity. As Baumol and Bowen observe, labour intensity, itself an expression of the complexity of the skills involved, remains a persistent feature of the performing arts.[27] Likewise the reduction of private labour to general labour cannot have the same progressive character as that which affects labour power in general, if only because performance *qua* performance never has a private character. The private labour of a dancer, musician or actor is not performance but practice. The elements of such an anterior activity clearly enter into the performance, but only as elements of signification in relation to the performance itself. Indeed, signs of practice – automatisms of movement, phrasing and speech – are generally regarded as a sign of deficiency in a performer, unless these have assumed some nostalgic value or entered into a performance context in which the performer is more important than the performance.

These observations, which strictly speaking rest on an individualistic model of performance, are only intensified in their grip if one considers that performance is invariably a collective event. This means that the concrete particularity of the labour process ramifies through a diversity of skill inputs, since each element of the performance is an ingredient of the whole and hence, in ideal circumstances, must achieve its particularity in order to function as a part of the totality. But matters go further than this, because obviously all performances involve a range of labour activities which are strictly speaking 'non-creative' – ticket selling, theatre cleaning, and so on. These latter take as their rationale the objectives of the performance and to that extent have an *aesthetic context* of application. This is to say nothing of general skills, like carpentry, that are developed for aesthetic purposes in set and props design, or the fact that in fringe productions many routine tasks are undertaken by the cast.

At first sight, therefore, the material properties of performance (it is a process rather than a thing, a service rather than a material production) mark it off from the general processes of commodity production. Viewed against the backdrop of labour in general, it exhibits a paradoxical nature: the labour power exercised in performance is *concrete* and yet *social*, in contrast to labour power in general, which remains private in its execution and loses all concrete particularity at the moment of its exchange. Yet, as it stands, this argument from the material features of performance is misleading to the extent that it considers the labour process of performance outside the social relationships imposed on performance by capitalism.

Marx's position on the extent to which the material specificity of the labour process in areas of 'aesthetic' labour determines the commodification process would seem at first sight to deny that it does. When such matters are addressed, it is mainly in respect of the issue of productive and unproductive labour – productive, that is, from the point of view of capital, as a contribution to the accumulation process. Such an issue, which essentially turns on the question whether or not services are paid for out of revenue as fees or occur as wage labour, renders the question whether labour is of a special kind at best irrelevant or, at worst, a lever for the denial that capitalist production relations can operate in the sphere of culture.[28] On the other hand, as the famous metaphor of the architect and the bee shows, Marx was fully aware of the 'creative conceptual' capacity of human labour power in general, of which aesthetic labour is a specialization. The point I wish to preserve from all this is that the materiality of performance imposes a limit on the extent to which capitalist relations can be imposed on aesthetic labour. What this means at its most fundamental is, as Michael Chanan puts it, that '*the full resources of real control over the labour process cannot be applied*. Something, however slight, escapes mechanization and automation, and capital has to resort to *formal and ideological* controls which induce a *subjective* automatism in the worker's exercise of judgement.'[29] But it is in the play-off between the real control and the formal control of the labour process that the performance commodity, the star, is formed, and the armature of that formation is transcription technology.

To exemplify these processes here, it is useful to deploy the perspective of Walter Benjamin's famous essay, 'The work of art in the age of mechanical reproduction'. According to Benjamin, the effect of film as a technology on the actor is to produce a 'shrivelling' of the 'aura' of his or her presence as a person, which is, on stage, inseparable from the aura of the character (e.g. Macbeth) that the actor represents. It is an effect of the capitalist organization of film production that the labour process of acting is both fragmented and automatized – rendered as an *effect* derived from the apparatus rather than from the actor – at the same time as the direct link with an audience is severed and the actor becomes more dependent on the camera as the point of address of his or her performance: 'While facing the camera he knows that ultimately he will face the public, the consumers who constitute the market. This market where he offers not only his labour, but also his whole self, his heart and soul, is beyond his reach.'[30]

This shrivelling of the aura of the person prompts the development of the cult of the movie star which offers instead 'the spell of the personality, the phony spell of the commodity'.[31] However one assesses the final validity of Benjamin's claims about the inherently demystificatory potential of film as technology, it is nevertheless clear that the basic impact of the standardized uses of film technology and technique is as he defines it. Yet it is by no means clear that the effects of the cinematic apparatus necessarily lead to the shrivelling of aura – unless, of course, one holds on to some metaphysics of presence. The filmed image of the actor, especially the leading player, and its insertion in an articulation of filmic time and space that prioritizes a person-centred schema of causality, can be argued to increase the massivity of the actor's presence in terms of both significance and cynosure.[32] More substantially, perhaps, Benjamin's connection between the process of 'shrivelling' and commodification, an obvious allusion to the reduction of concrete labour to abstract labour, is rendered as a straight contrast between the actor *qua* character and the persona. There are reasons to conclude, as I have argued elsewhere, that such relationships should be seen as triangulated around the contradictory positionalities of *character* as a notational entity, *personality* as the private biographical reality of the actor as a person pre-given in the host culture, and *persona* as the public image of the actor as a concrete person that is inferred from his or her screen presence and associated publicity.[33] The insertion of the persona into the interplay between the actor and the character is, as Benjamin perceives, the moment of commodification. However, he does not specify clearly enough that this occurs via the equation of persona with character at the point of casting, in the case of the star, and that off screen the actor's private personality is sedulously adapted to the screen persona. More decisive for our account is the process whereby this prioritization of the persona is achieved in performance.

One of the key features of film as a technology is that by means of editing (which is a pre- and post-shooting process mediated through the shooting script and the editing table) it facilitates a detailed control over performance. Such a facility, also found in video and sound recording, can be applied while still preserving the capacity to reinterpolate edited frag- ments back into a more compact, high-resolution form of the original. The original (a process, not a thing) can be, of itself, a concrete act of labour of some duration and complexity, or it can be a series of minimal units of verbal or physical behaviour. In either case it is possible within the limits of the material to effect a concerted reassembly which either imparts a new meaning to the performance or brings to greater effectivity the conception that was prioritized in its original execution. The overriding tendency in the Hollywood film has been to favour a mode of performance (not to mention a style of filming performances) that favours small units of behaviour – reacting rather than enacting – whose principle of coherence, in terms of narrative causality, time or space, is exterior to the process of performance itself. Such a process is most apparent, of course, in the vehicle wherein the principle of coherence is the persona of the star. But even actors in general find that in such circumstances the execution of a part is rendered motivationally meaningful (if at all) only in terms of the paradigmatic space of his or her private conception of character – the dynamics of portrayal becoming, primarily, the mobilization of the psychological and physical resources of the actor's private personality. This is why, if actors remain committed to the norm of impersonation, the techniques of Method acting are so in evidence.

By contrast – and in part this is also a function of the professional ideology of acting – the stage actor's execution of character is doubly articulated around, on the one hand, a conception of its place in the totality of the text, visible as unfolding alongside and through his or her performance, and, on the other, his or her private conception of character. One might say that for the stage actor the character remains a *pars totalis* – a moment of the whole – whereas for the Hollywood film actor it becomes the totality itself. The fact that film acting often occurs in isolation from the ensemble of performances, which are manifested only in post-production, merely compounds this tendency.

To this extent it is misleading to see the impact of film technology as leading to a shrivelling of the aura of the person, since its basic effect is to open up the discursive range of the personal within the context of commodity production. The expression of these relationships within acting – and others besides, such as the labour market for actors, the routines of casting and the requirement of a stable 'biographical' entity on which to hang publicity and the like – manifests itself as a discursive prioritization within performance. This prioritization emphasizes an approach to character portrayal in which the biographical resources of the actor are to be mobilized, rather than differentially suppressed. This approach I have called personification, which, by no happy accident, refers to the same mechanism on the side of labour power that Marx identified in relation to agents of capital.

In personification – and let us not forget that the actor is very often a willing party to such arrangements, but not necessarily so – the actor's exchange value is prioritized over his or her use value. An actor's use value is in general terms identified by the social division of labour – as a sign vehicle that can shed, suppress or articulate personal characteristics in order to materialize a narrational signified, a character. Naturally, it is possible to conceive

of uses of non-actors that satisfy the requirements of signification without requiring impersonation. But such uses are clearly not a refutation of the social function of acting *per se*. Nor,
for that matter, would they exhaust the requirements of versatility and skill acquisition
implicit in pursuing acting as a full-time occupation. Viewed in the context of an actor's use
value, personification represents the reduction of the concrete particularity of craft skills to
a fetishized linearity of function. To this extent it conforms to the reductive rendering of all
forms of labour under commodity production. However, as a process located within performance and articulated under the effectivity of Hollywood's use of film technology, this
reduction, so far as leading players are concerned, does not occur as an anonymizing process
that submerges personality under function. Rather, it constitutes a selective application of
the techniques of body maintenance, grooming, self-presentation, sedulous cultivation of
mannerisms, and so on, which at any given moment constitute the cultural ground of the
specific skills of actors, a ground which is articulated and modified by their practices. Such
a selection is based on validating the star (or the would-be star) as the proprietorial centre of
his or her image on screen. The dialogic process, wherein the actor develops a range of
behaviours off screen to complement the sedulous use of techniques before the camera that
ensure his or her place in the centre of filmic space as an attractive, luminous cinematic
object, constitutes *the performance strategy of the Hollywood star*. What needs to be emphasized
here is that this process, which relates to an ostensive mode of sign production, represents
the projection, always a contractually and institutionally guaranteed process, of the personal
qualities of one of the direct producers on to the material form taken by the totality of the
performance itself. If it is recalled that this 'fix' (always a proactive and retroactive result of
the deployment of the technology) is always occurring at the intersection of a multiplicity
of diverse concrete labours, then its reductiveness is plain.

In sum, the formation of the persona of the star accomplishes, from the side of labour
power, the same suppression of the fundamentally collective character of all productive
activity that enables the capitalist to appear as the demiurge of production. But the place of
the star is on the side of labour, as visibly an employee within the process of representation,
even if the star is also his or her own employer (not forgetting that the celebrity of the star
always rests in the last analysis on popular approval). These conditions mean that stardom
can be seen as returning to the level of the collective account as a signifier of the potency of
labour. In reality, the persona of the star is the moment of the performance commodity.

BACK TO APPEARANCES, BRIEFLY

The thrust of the foregoing was to establish the outline of a formal theory of stardom. Such a
formal theory is in the last analysis resolved into a relationship of representation: the star,
before all contents, can function as a metonymy for labour power and for what stands behind
this connection – that is, the sensuous, creative capacity of human labour power. Such a
theorization, if it can be sustained, will tell us why the star system finds a place in popular
consciousness, but not what the specific content of a star's popularity will be. Again, the
theorization offered here has confined itself to film stardom, though I believe it is possible to
discern how such an analysis might be applied, for example, to the rock star. Indeed, it seems
likely that the rock star, because he or she is involved more obviously in a discourse marked
by personal forms of address, represents an intensification of the process identified here.

I take it as relatively unproblematic to detail some of the reasons, at the level of content,
why the stars are popular: they occupy the centres of collective attention which impart a
scale of importance to what the star represents against the anonymous mass of consumers;
they are presented in an environment which, if demeaning as opposed to glamorous, is none

the less full of a decidedly human schema of causality arising from their interest as characters; they are glamorous and accomplished individuals who are highly rewarded and much admired, despite lowly or disparaged social origins in some cases; they carry the burden, given the powerful mimetic thrust of popular culture, of representing a seemingly more comprehensive view of everyday (or not so everyday) life than is available to those of us who remain within the confines of work and locales; they are very often beautiful human artefacts. None of the foregoing is intended to subvert the validity of such insights. Rather, it would claim that these effects are based on the manner in which stars enter popular consciousness – their as it were ontological threshold as public figures.

It is not difficult to see a connection between stardom as a form of labour that prioritizes personality and certain grades of employment (e.g. routine white-collar work, unskilled service work such as bar keeping and waiting) which require a 'scripted' personality for their execution.[34] Such a connection is only compounded by the fact that it is precisely in such areas of work that actors often find employment. Again, it is not difficult to see that the image of the star would have an attraction – as an assertion of denied experiences and values – for those in routine manual occupations. Such connections are in need of serious empirical study, but if confirmed might lead towards an occupational or class-related anthropology of stardom. The advantage of the account offered here is that it does ground itself in the materiality of performance and yet offers a way towards making such connections. Lastly, it is worth emphasizing again that the anonymous subjects of this analysis, the lower middle class and working class of Western capitalism and beyond, are themselves not fully integrated into the market economy because of the nature of the commodity production. As Offe and Wiesenthal put it:

> workers can neither fully submit to the logic of the market (first of all, because what they 'sell' on the market is not a 'genuine' commodity) nor can they escape from the market (because they are forced to participate, for the sake of their subsistence).[35]

From this angle of comparison, the star system can be seen as a recuperative play on what eludes commodification.

Notes

1   J. Baudrillard, *For a Critique of the Political Economy of the Sign* (St Louis: Telos Press, 1981), p. 131.
2   See E. Preteceille and J.-P. Terrail, *Capitalism, Consumption and Needs* (Oxford: Blackwell, 1985), pp. 30 ff.
3   See the relevant entries in T. O'Sullivan, J. Hartley, D. Saunders and J. Fiske, *Key Concepts in Communication* (London: Methuen, 1983).
4   M. Sinclair, *Those Who Died Young: Cult Heroes of the Twentieth Century* (London: Plexus, 1979), p. 13.
5   I take the term 'signality' from Volosinov; it denotes the imposition of an invariant, univocal meaning on the multi-accentuality of the sign. See V. N. Volosinov, *Marxism and the Philosophy of Language* (London: Seminar Press, 1973), p. 23.
6   F. and J. Vermorel, *Starlust: The Secret Fantasies of Fans* (London: Comet, 1985), p. 7. This text is mainly about fantasies of sexual possession and rock stars. It nevertheless reveals the extent to which fans do not distinguish between star image and real person.
7   E. Morin, *The Stars: An Account of the Star System in Motion Pictures* (New York: Grove Press, 1960), p. 183. Morin was the first to underline the connection between stars and commodity merchandising. Lately this has been proffered as a brave new insight. See C. G. Herzog, 'Puffed sleeves before teatime', *Wide Angle*, 6, 4 (1985), pp. 24–33.
8   R. Dyer, *Stars* (London: BFI Publications, 1979). The second edition of this text has been published

as a 'classic' in the field. Macmillan are shortly to publish Dyer's latest work on the subject, to be entitled *Heavenly Bodies*.

9 Dyer, op. cit., p. 37. Dyer also suggests, but without giving any indication how, that race and class should be included in the account. For an account of a black perception of Hollywood, see J. Baldwin, *The Devil Finds Work* (London: Corgi, 1976).

10 Dyer, op. cit., p. 183.

11 For an account based on form, see D. Robins and P. Cohen, *Knuckle Sandwich* (Harmondsworth: Penguin, 1978), pp. 96 ff.

12 Dyer, op. cit., p. 98.

13 Cf. E. Knoedler-Bunte, 'The proletarian public sphere and political organization', *New German Critique*, 4 (Winter 1974), p. 67.

14 For a further delineation, see, for example, B. King, 'The Hollywood star system', PhD thesis (University of London, 1984), or G. Kindem, *The American Movie Industry* (Southern Illinois University Press, 1982).

15 K. Marx, 'Marginal notes on Adolph Wagner's *Lehrbuch der politischen Ökonomie*', *Theoretical Practice*, 5 (1972), p. 50.

16 K. Marx, *Capital*, vol. 1 (Harmondsworth: Penguin, 1976), pp. 126–64. A very useful exposition can be found in D. Sayer, *Marx's Method* (Brighton: Harvester, 1979), and D. Harvey, *The Limits to Capital* (Oxford: Blackwell, 1982). For a different account, see J. Roemer's article in J. Roemer (ed.), *Analytical Marxism* (Cambridge: Cambridge University Press, 1986). Since the account I offer here is, ultimately, based on a model of class struggle at the point of production, value concepts are appropriate, as Roemer points out (see pp. 100–2).

17 See Marx, *Capital*, vol. 1, ch. 19, and H. Cleaver, *Reading Capital Politically* (Brighton: Harvester, 1979), pp. 71 ff.

18 Marx, *Capital*, vol. 1, p. 165.

19 See C. Wright Mills, *White Collar* (Oxford: Oxford University Press, 1951), especially ch. 8.

20 J. Mepham, 'The theory of ideology in *Capital*', *Working Papers in Cultural Studies*, 6 (1974). See also G. Lukács, *History and Class Consciousness* (London: Merlin, 1971).

21 See D. Elson, *Value: The Representation of Labour in Capitalism* (London: C.S.E. Books, 1980), pp. 123 ff.

22 Essentially, this entails the analysis of deskilling. For a recent summary of the debates, see P. Thompson, *The Nature of Work* (London: Macmillan, 1983).

23 Cf. T. W. Adorno, 'The culture industry reconsidered', *New German Critique*, 6 (Fall 1975), p. 14. For a recent account, see S. Garfield, *Expensive Habits: The Dark Side of the Music Industry* (London: Faber, 1986).

24 Marx, *Capital*, vol. 1, p. 1003. Also Marx, *Capital*, vol. 3 (Moscow: Foreign Languages Publishing House, 1962), pp. 797 ff.

25 F. Alberoni, 'The powerless élite', in D. McQuail (ed.), *Sociology of Mass Communications* (London: Collier Macmillan, 1969).

26 The best account is still R. Dyer, 'The meaning of *Tom Jones*', *Working Papers in Cultural Studies*.

27 W. Baumol and W. Bowen, 'On the performing arts: the anatomy of their economic problems', in M. Blaug (ed.), *The Economics of the Arts* (Oxford: Martin Robertson, 1976).

28 K. Marx, *Theories of Surplus Value* (London: Lawrence & Wishart, 1964), pt 1, pp. 164 ff.

29 M. Chanan, 'Labour power and aesthetic labour in film and television in Britain', *Media, Culture and Society*, 2 (1980), pp. 120–1.

30 W. Benjamin, *Illuminations* (London: Fontana, 1977), p. 233.

31 Ibid.

32 See D. Bordwell *et al.*, *The Classic Hollywood Cinema: Film Style and Mode of Production to 1960* (London: Routledge & Kegan Paul, 1985). The formulation here assumes, of course, that the actor has learnt the skills of playing to the camera.

33 B. King, 'Articulating stardom', *Screen*, 26, 5 (September–October 1985), which fills out in greater detail the relationships explored here.

34 Cf. E. Goffman, *The Presentation of the Self in Everyday Life* (Harmondsworth: Penguin, 1971).

35 Cited in Z. Bauman, *Memories of Class* (London: Routledge & Kegan Paul, 1982), p. 15. Bauman's discussion of the place of labour overall is useful.

Chapter 11

Cheng Shao-Chun

CHINESE DIASPORA AND ORIENTALISM IN GLOBALIZED CULTURAL PRODUCTION: ANG LEE'S *CROUCHING TIGER, HIDDEN DRAGON* (2005)

> One may ask: Are Ang Lee and his films Taiwanese? Chinese? American? Taiwanese American? Chinese American? . . . The lack of a clear answer to such questions indicates the very nature of transnational Chinese Cinema.
> — Sheldon Hsiao-peng Lu (1997a, p. 18)

ANG LEE'S *CROUCHING TIGER, HIDDEN DRAGON* (2000) is a cultural phenomenon. As a Mandarin martial arts costume drama, *Crouching Tiger, Hidden Dragon* is not only an international box-office hit, but also is highly acclaimed worldwide as a masterpiece. So far the box-office returns in the U.S. alone have reached 150 million dollars, making *Crouching Tiger, Hidden Dragon* the most profitable foreign film ever in the U.S. Its revenue has doubled Italy's *Life Is Beautiful* (1998), which was the most popular foreign feature film in the U.S. film history. *Crouching Tiger, Hidden Dragon* has made another record: it is the first Chinese film (including films made in Taiwan, Hong Kong, or China) to win Academy Awards (it won 10 nominations and four Academy Awards including Best Foreign Picture). Because of the staggering success of this film, Ang Lee, after winning the best director in the Golden Globe Awards and DGA (Directors Guild of America), was chosen as "the best American film director" by *Time* magazine (Corliss, 2001, p.55).

The international success of *Crouching Tiger, Hidden Dragon* and its relatively modest performance in two main Chinese markets, China and Hong Kong (Landler, 2001), raise a complex question about global cultural production and local cultural consumption. It needs a delicate explanation, considering the interaction of global media, political economy and specific interpreting practices with different cultural positioning.[1] In this essay, I try to answer more basic questions: First, with funding and crewmembers from different countries, and international promotion and distribution by a Hollywood studio, is *Crouching Tiger,*

Hidden Dragon "Chinese national cinema?" Secondly, what are the lessons *Crouching Tiger, Hidden Dragon* provides to the national/local cinema production? And why did a film by a Taiwan-born Chinese diaspora director and employing the Chinese martial arts genre become the most successful foreign feature film in the U.S.? In this essay, these questions will be answered first in terms of Ang Lee's auteurism.

A CHINESE DIASPORA DIRECTOR'S DREAM OF CHINA

> . . . .But you can't remove China from the boy's head, so I'm finding China now. That's why I'm making this movie [*Crouching Tiger, Hidden Dragon*] with these people, to talk about things we know and that particularly don't exist. Good old China.
>
> – Ang Lee quoted in Dupont 2000, p. 40.

As a second-generation Mainland Chinese displaced to Taiwan by the Chinese civil war in 1949, Ang Lee studied film and started his directorial career in the United States. Different from the work of Asian directors such as John Woo who immigrated to America and has been totally incorporated into the Hollywood film industry, or Wayne Wang who goes back and forth between Hollywood studio production projects and the English-language independent productions, Ang Lee's oeuvre can be divided into two main categories: the Mandarin-language productions and the English-language productions. The former includes his "father-knows-best" trilogy—*Pushing Hands* (1991), *The Wedding Banquet* (1993), and *Eat Drink Man Woman* (1994), and *Crouching Tiger, Hidden Dragon*. The second category includes *Sense and Sensibility* (1995), *The Ice Storm* (1997), *Ride with the Devil* (1999), and *The Hulk* (2003). Ang Lee seems always to oscillate between these two kinds of career, and the making of Mandarin-language films seems to be a cultural obligation for him (Hardesty, 2001, p. 21).

Although referring himself as a "Taiwanese" (Lee, 1999, p. ix; Hardesty, 2001, p. 21), Ang Lee admits that he has a serious identity crisis:

> To me, I'm a mixture of many things and a confusion of many things. . . . I'm not a native Taiwanese, so we're alien in Taiwan today, with the native Taiwanese pushing for independence. But when we go back to China, we're Taiwanese. Then, I live in the States; I'm a sort of foreigner everywhere. It's hard to find a real identity.
>
> (quoted in Berry 1993, p. 54.)

Yet, this confusion of identity, I would argue, only reflects Ang Lee's political identity crisis. In terms of cultural identity, he is very certain he is Chinese. When explaining the motive for making *Crouching Tiger, Hidden Dragon*, Ang Lee straightforwardly emphasizes this film is a fulfillment of his "dream of China." Three years ago, when Lee first went to Beijing, literally his "Motherland," his mother's hometown, he tried to find out if he could make a film there. The result was disappointing because everything was modern, and he said:

> I didn't see what I was looking for—it felt as if I were in a big Taipei. I had no thrill because that China does not exist anymore, either in Taiwan or America or here: it's a history. It's a dream that all the Chinese people in the world have, an impression. Gone with the wind.
>
> (quoted in Dupont, 2000, p. 40)

The audience can easily categorize *Crouching Tiger, Hidden Dragon* as a "Chinese film." However, there is a hesitation to pigeonhole this film as "Chinese national cinema." As Lu argues, Ang Lee's works are typical "transnational Chinese cinema." According to his criteria, Lu points out that transnational Chinese cinemas, like Zhang Yimou's *Raise the Red Lantern* (1991) and Chen Kaige's *Farewell My Concubine* (1993), are films that "were funded by foreign capital (Hong Kong, Taiwan, Japan, Europe), produced by Chinese labor, distributed in a global network, and consumed by an international audience," and they are dominated by global cultural production and consumption (Lu, 1997, p. 11). Lu argues, "It seems that Chinese *national* cinema can only be understood in its properly *transnational* context." And he goes on to articulate the transnational perspectives inscribed in Chinese cinemas:

> Transnationalism in the Chinese case can be observed at the following levels: first, the split of China into several geopolitical entities since the nineteenth century—the Mainland, Taiwan, and Hong Kong—and consequently the triangulation of competing national/local "Chinese cinemas," especially after 1949; second, the globalization of the production, marketing, and consumption of Chinese film in the age of transnational capitalism in the 1990s; third the representation and questioning of "China" and "Chineseness" in filmic discourse itself, namely, the cross-examination of the national, cultural, political, ethnic, and gender identity of individuals and communities in the Mainland, Taiwan, Hong Kong, and the Chinese diaspora; and fourth, a re-viewing and revisiting of the history of Chinese "national cinemas," as if to read the "prehistory" of transnational filmic discourse backwards.
>
> (Lu, 1997, p. 2)

Lu's analytical framework provides a pertinent perspective from which to analyze Ang Lee's four Mandarin-language works. I will argue that with the increasing globalizing of film production, Ang Lee's "transnational Chinese cinema" is a special kind of "national cinema" in the globalization era. I will use his international box office hit *Crouching Tiger, Hidden Dragon* as a example to analyze what Ang Lee inherits from traditional Chinese cinema and how he transforms it to cater to the international film market. In addition, I will also argue that Lee increasingly employs a more specific Oriental aesthetic and invokes more obvious "Chineseness" as the selling point of his Mandarin films in the international markets, including Chinese diaspora communities, and that this strategy culminates in *Crouching Tiger, Hidden Dragon*.

CULTURAL CHINA VS. CHINESE DIASPORA

Having gone through cultural displacement several times, Ang Lee has been always conscious of his Chinese diaspora identity in his Mandarin film making. According to William Safran's *Diasporas in Modern Societies: Myths of Homeland and Return* (1991), the "ideal type" definitions of diasporas are those who form "expatriate minority communities," and they have the following characteristics: 1. They are dispersed from an original "center" to at least two 'peripheral' places; 2. They maintain a "memory, vision, or myth about their original homeland"; 3. They "believe they are not—and perhaps cannot be—fully accepted by their host country"; 4. They see the ancestral home as a place of eventual return; 5. They are committed to the maintenance or restoration of the homeland; and 6. The group's consciousness and solidarity are "importantly defined" by this continuing relationship with the homeland (as cited in Clifford, 1994: 304–5).

Ang Lee's real-life experiences nearly duplicate each characteristic Safran delineated. Although he was physically displaced from Taiwan to the U.S., as a second-generation mainlander growing up in the milieu of identifying with the China Proper and de-Taiwanese cultural policies enforced by the ruling Nationalist Party (KuoMingTung) back then, Ang Lee symbolically and culturally went through two times displacements from his imaginary homeland—China. In this way, all four of Ang Lee's Mandarin-language films can be seen as a kind of homecoming.

Ang Lee's diaspora identity may best reflected by his political detachment from Taiwan and the apolitical subject matter in his works. It is not surprising that none of Lee's four Mandarin-language works has ever dealt with Taiwanese national identity which is the main characteristic defining Taiwan New Cinema (Chen, 2000). When Hou Hsiao-heien coped with the issue of Taiwanese national identity in his Taiwan Trilogy—*The City of Sadness* (1989), *The Puppetmaster* (1993), and *Good Men, Good Women* (1995), other second-generation Mainland Chinese directors also started to deal with the complex historical/political/cultural relationships between Taiwan and Mainland China, as seen in Edward Yang's *A Brighter Summer Day* (1991) and Wang Tong's *Banana Paradise* (1989). However, the common subject matter of Ang Lee's "father-knows-best" trilogy, *Pushing Hands, The Wedding Banquet*, and *Eat Drink Man Woman* is about the conflicts and differences between traditional "Chinese" culture and western (American) culture. Ironically, Taiwanese intellectuals seemed lenient toward the detachment of Ang Lee's works from Taiwanese social-political reality. As Chen (2000) explains, this is because no Taiwanese intellectual thinks of Ang Lee as a native Taiwan director. The funding of Ang Lee's "father-knows-best" trilogy came from Central Motion Picture Corporation. CMPC is the largest film producer in Taiwan and is owned by the ex-ruling KMT government, which served as a mouthpiece of the government's international propaganda for joining the United Nations. As Chen argues,

> It is no accident that the setting of both films (*Pushing Hands* and *The Wedding Banquet)* was New York, thus permitting the 'transnationalization' of TNC [Taiwan New Cinema] and '*Ang Lee*,' who has almost achieved the status of national hero since the release of *Sense and Sensibility* (1996). For the state [Taiwan], what matters is not so much the ideological content of the film, but whether it will disseminate the name of Taiwan.
>
> (Chen, 2000, p. 176)

Another implication for Ang Lee's Chinese diaspora identity is his using Chineseness to construct an imagined Chinese community. Chineseness is a set of cultural differentials which is adopted, by Chinese and other ethnic groups as well, to demarcate "Chinese" and "the other." These kinds of cultural boundaries have become naturalized to distinguish "Chinese" as an insulated ethnic community (Chow, 2000). These cultural differentials are functioned as nature, as Etienne Balibar argues:

> Biological or genetic naturalism is not the only means of naturalizing human behavior and social affinities. . . . *Culture can also function like a nature*, and it can in particular function as a way of locking individuals and groups *a priori* into a genealogy, into a determination that is immutable and intangible in origin.
>
> (as cited in Chow, 2000, p. 5)

Ang Lee once described his own experience of being Chinese in New York as follows:

Of course, I identify with Chinese culture because that was my upbringing, but that becomes very abstract; it's the idea of China. . . . And the sentiment of being Chinese is different in New York than it is in Taiwan or in China. Wherever you come from, whether it's China or Hong Kong or Taiwan, in New York, you're just Chinese; it's sort of generalized and merged, and people are drawn to each other by that abstract idea of being Chinese.

(quoted in Berry 1993, p. 54)

It is the daily life experience of being "Chinese" in New York City, the symbolic capital of the international world, that drives Ang Lee to invoke Chineseness in his films to define his identity. Ang Lee proves himself proficient at portraying Chineseness in his Mandarin-language productions. In his "father-knows-best" trilogy "Chineseness" is employed as a symbolic device, in a rather stereotypical way, to distinguish "the East/China" from "the West/America." In *Pushing Hands* and *The Wedding Banquet*, the cultural conflicts between "traditional"/"Chinese" and "modern"/"Western" cultures are the main dramatic tension through the narratives. In terms of the cultural signifier, everyone might agree that food and martial arts are two of the most universal representations of Chinese ethnicity, or Chineseness. In *Pushing Hands*, the protagonist is a martial arts (TaiChi) master from China who plans to live with his son in New York City, but the reunion is obstructed by the cultural difference between this Chinese old man and his Caucasian daughter-in-law. In this film, martial arts symbolize the wisdom of life—how to compromise with reality and to lead a peaceful life. At the same time, in *Pushing Hands* the dinner table is the locus where cultural confrontations take place. When the Chinese TaiChi master leaves home after a confrontation with his daughter-in-law, he lands in a Chinese restaurant to work as a dishwasher.

In *The Wedding Banquet*, the dramatic tension is centered on homosexuality and generational/cultural differences. But it is Chinese food and mealtimes, especially the wedding banquet sequence, that deploy the storyline and serve as an important symbolic device to imply the possible transgression between different national/sexual identities. *Eat Drink Man Woman* is a spectacle of Chinese gastronomy. The detailed depiction of the complex procedures in preparing and cooking Chinese cuisine is a vivid example of what Rey Chow called "self-exhibitionism" or "autoethnography" (Chow, 1995), and also a kind of "food pornography," defined by Sau-ling Cynthia Wong as

> making a living by exploiting the 'exotic' aspects of one's ethnic foodways. In cultural terms it translates to reifying perceived cultural differences and exaggerating one's otherness in order to gain a foothold in a white-dominated social system.
>
> (as cited in Ma, 1996, p. 198)

Wang Hui-Ling, the screenplay co-writer of *Eat Drink Man Woman*, admits that the profession of the protagonist in the original design is a tailor, and the later change into a chef was made by considering the international audiences' interest in Chinese food (Chen Bao-Xia, 1994).

Yet, even *The Wedding Banquet* in which Ang Lee tries to cover as many diverse "Chinese" identities as possible—Mainland China/Taiwan, young/elder, man/woman, heterosexual/homosexual—still presents the stereotypical images of the Chinese diaspora rather than a diverse Asian/Chinese American community. Gina Marchetti (2000) incisively points out that like Lee's *The Wedding Banquet*, most Asian American productions "deal less with the development of an Asian American identity among Chinese immigrants than with the creation of a transnational sense of Chinese identity" (p. 292). However, the traditional

Chinese (Mainland Chinese) family depicted in *Eat Drink Man Woman*, set in modern Taipei, rarely exists in modern Taiwanese reality. To a large extent, the family in this film is just a nostalgic imagining of a stereotypical traditional Chinese family.

After three modern family dramas, Ang Lee's fourth Mandarin-language production moves back to ancient China. *Crouching Tiger, Hidden Dragon* is about the conflict among three women and one man surrounding a legendary sword. The story line starts when Li Mu-Bai (Chow Yun Fat), a famous warrior, asks his longtime friend and unacknowledged love, swordswoman Yu Shu-Lien to give his Green Destiny sword to an aristocrat. Yu Shu-Lien (Michelle Yeoh) had inherited a convoy business from her father and remained single in honor of her deceased fiancé. Jen (Zhang Ziyi), the young daughter of Governor Yu, has secretly learned martial arts from her governess, Jade Fox. Jade Fox (Cheng Pei Pei) was an ambitious swordswoman who once offered her body in exchange for lessons in the highest martial arts from Li's master. But when Li's master finally refused to teach her martial arts she poisoned him and took cover as Jen's governess. Apprehensive about her upcoming arranged marriage, Jen longed for the freedom of a fighter's life. After she stole the Green Destiny Sword, a turmoil started.

In *Crouching Tiger, Hidden Dragon* the evocation of Chineseness is omnipresent. As a martial arts period drama set in the Qing dynasty, the film contains everything "Chinese" and exotic. By totally excluding the West from its narrative, this film has become a quintessential Orientalist fantasy. In analyzing the "father-knows-best" trilogy, Sheng-mei Ma criticizes Ang Lee's works as "Third-World international or festival films" shot in a "tourist-friendly" way and argues that "taken chronologically in the order of their release, the trilogy reveals an increasing propensity toward exotic travel in search of the Other rather than nostalgic lamentation over the loss of the self" (1996, p. 195). I agree with Ma's argument that Ang Lee's Mandarin-language productions are increasingly inclined to employ Orientalist aesthetics, and are more often seen as exotic spectacles to international audiences than before. However, besides the "pull" from a sophisticated calculation of how to make a hit in the world film market, I will contend that Ang Lee's anxious nostalgia for his imaginary homeland, China, also serves as the subjective "push" force lying under the increasingly exotic, or "Chinese," filmic aesthetics in his Mandarin-language production.

CHINESENESS: THE CULTURAL CHINA AND IMAGINED COMMUNITY

Contrary to the "political China," the transnational sense of Chinese identity implies a "cultural China." "Cultural China" is employed by Tu Wei-ming to elaborate on the contours of a symbolic universe "that both encompasses and transcends the ethnic, territorial, linguistic, and religious boundaries that normally define Chineseness" (1994, p. v). In the project of "cultural China," Tu tries to deconstruct the cultural authority of geopolitical China. He wants, instead, to "explore the fluidity of Chineseness as a layered and contested discourse, to open new possibilities and avenues of inquiry, and to challenge the claims of political leadership (in Beijing, Taipei, Hong Kong or Singapore) to be the ultimate authority in a matter as significant as 'Chineseness'" (1994, p. viii). Contrasting the monolithic and hegemonic essentialist national China discourse with "cultural China," Tu emphasizes that the periphery—the Chinese diaspora—can form a new cultural center of Chineseness. Tu uses "the living tree" as a metaphor to represent "cultural China": the Chinese diaspora is sprouting the most vigorous new branches and leaves from the root China.

Yet Ien Ang incisively criticizes cultural China as a project to deconstruct "the obsession with China." She claims, on the contrary, it represents "an overwhelming desire . . . to somehow maintain, redeem, and revitalize the notion of Chineseness as a marker of common culture and identity in a rapidly postmodernizing world" (2000, p. 288). Ien Ang argues that the organic metaphor of "the living tree" exactly illuminates the illusion of decentering an essentialist China implied by the "cultural China" project. Ang contends:

> Without roots, there would be no life, no new leaves. The metaphor of the living tree dramatically imparts the ultimate existential dependence of the periphery on the center, the diaspora on the homeland. Furthermore, what this metaphor emphasizes is continuity over discontinuity: In the end, it all flows back to the roots (2000, p. 289).

Using Ien Ang's critiques makes clear that what Ang Lee did in his Mandarin-language productions was merely going back to the root of "the living tree" and to use the most distinguished "Chineseness" to interpellate individuals as Chinese subjects and to build an "imagined community," an imagined China. Benedict Anderson's felicitous concept of "imagined communities" (1983) is well accepted in the field of national cinema studies, because it makes people rethink the nation, not as something taken for granted, but as a social and historical human construction.

Anderson emphasizes that communities are not to be distinguished by their genuineness, but by the style in which they are imagined. The nation is defined by shared characteristics and cultural codes among its national citizenry. This can explain why the stylistic mannerism of Chineseness in Ang Lee's Mandarin-language filmic narratives is significant in the imaging and imagining of China as a cultural community.

In his own words, Ang Lee describes *Crouching Tiger, Hidden Dragon* thus:

> The film [*Crouching Tiger, Hidden Dragon*] is a kind of dream of China, a China that probably never existed, except in my boyhood fantasies in Taiwan. . . . My team and I chose the most populist, if not popular, genre in film history—the Hong Kong martial arts film—to tell our story, and we used this pop genre almost as a kind of research instrument to explore the legacy of classical Chinese culture.
>
> (Lee, 2000a, p. 7)

Ang Lee continues:

> My desire to direct a martial arts film comes from nostalgia for classical China. The greatest appeal of the kung fu world lies in its abstraction. It is a conceptual world based on 'imagined China.' This world does not exist in reality and therefore is free from its constraints.
>
> (Lee, 2000b, p.116)

In this straightforward self–reflection, one can understand that for *Crouching Tiger, Hidden Dragon* to be a martial arts drama is not a contingency; instead, it is from Ang Lee's conscious choice.

MARTIAL ARTS GENRE: THE NOSTALGIA AND IMAGINATION OF CHINA

Genre is a special category to classify cultural objects. According to Allen (1989), genre attempts to interpret the dynamic relationship between texts and readers. It systematizes similarities among different texts so that a common language can be shared and an interpretive community of readers can be formed. In terms of *Crouching Tiger, Hidden Dragon*, the martial arts genre is a sophisticated choice. First of all, it is an obviously "Chinese"/ "exotic" genre to non-Chinese audiences. The stunning acrobatics and choreography, which were shown in Jackie Chan's films and the box-office hit *The Matrix*, are Oriental spectacles that proved to be a successful commercial formula to attract international audiences. In addition to the action part, the costumes, settings, and musical score all provide opportunities to construct an imagined "Chinese" world. Second, as Ang Lee specifies, the martial arts film is "the most populist, if not popular, genre in film history." "Populist" literally implies "comes from the people." Here, Ang Lee reminds us of the long tradition of the martial arts film genre in Chinese film history. In doing so, *Crouching Tiger, Hidden Dragon* tries to invoke Chinese audiences' collective memory of a specific national film culture.

In Chinese cinema, the martial arts genre is not only one of the most popular but also one of the earliest. Grown out of the unique tradition of the martial arts and popular martial arts literature, martial arts movies can be dated from the silent era of the 1920s in Shanghai. The genre's first box office hit was *Burning of the Red Lotus Monastery* (1928), which bred 18 sequels within three years. In the same period, martial arts films occupied 60 percent of the total production of films in Shanghai (Desser, 2000a, p.11). The martial arts genre can be divided into two categories: *Wuxia pian* (martial chivalry films/swordplay films) and kung fu films. The former dominated the screen until the 1970s when kung fu films were invented by superstar Bruce Lee. *Wuxia pian* emphasizes swordplay to distinguish itself from the fist fights of kung fu. Almost all *wuxia pian* are period films, historical epics, or action-spectaculars with colorful costumes (Desser, 2000a). Another difference between *wuxia pian* and kung fu films is that female characters, i.e. swordswomen, always occupy the center stage of the former. One explanation for this difference is that *wuxia pian* heavily relies on choreography and wirework to show the warriors' astonishing physical abilities, while kung fu is more realistic and highlights the spectacle of the masculine body. Specifically speaking, *wuxia pian* is the exact genre tradition drawn on by *Crouching Tiger, Hidden Dragon*. The reason Ang Lee chose the martial arts/*wuxia* genre for his fourth Mandarin-language production is because this special Chinese film genre can serve as a road map to guide him in returning to China, his imaginary hometown.

The martial arts film is the staple of the Hong Kong and Taiwan film industries. It is estimated that between the end of World War II and 1980, the Hong Kong film industry alone produced about a thousand martial arts films (Stokes and Hoover, 1999). Originally, Hong Kong's films were Cantonese-dialect productions, which appeared in the late 1930s. Many filmmakers fled to Hong Kong from the Mainland to escape the Japanese invasion during World War II. However, by the middle of the 1960s, the Hong Kong film industry powerhouse Shaw Brother Studio started to produce films in the Mandarin language (the official language of both People's Republic of China and Taiwan). After Shaw Brother Studio contracted with talented young directors such as King Hu and Chang Che with the release of productions like *Come Drink with Me* (King Hu, 1965) and *The One Armed Swordsman* (Chang Che, 1966), Mandarin martial arts movies dominated the Hong Kong and Taiwanese film industry for a decade (Desser, 2000a, p. 32–3).

Martial arts, per se, is a Chinese diaspora film genre. Though it originated in Mainland China, the fruition of the martial arts genre was only accomplished in Hong Kong and Taiwan. In terms of Mandarin-language *wuxia* productions, the two master directors Chang Che and King Hu are typical of the Chinese diaspora. They were forced to leave Mainland China when the Communists took over after 1949. Here, I want to go into a more detailed discussion of King Hu, not only because he is the only Chinese director of whom Ang Lee specified his personal admiration (Corliss, 2001, p. 55), but also because he forged his career as a Chinese diaspora director just as Ang Lee has done.

KING HU AND ANG LEE: TWO CHINESE DIASPORA DIRECTORS

King Hu (1931–1997) was one of the Mainland Chinese cinema talents who immigrated to Hong Kong after the 1949 Communist revolution. In 1966, he directed his first martial arts film, *Come Drink with Me*, and its commercial success and special aesthetics opened a new page for the Mandarin martial arts films. Afterwards, King Hu moved to Taiwan and made his signature works, such as *Dragon Gate Inn* (1967) and *A Touch of Zen* (1971). *Dragon Gate Inn* turned out to be one of the biggest box-office hits in the whole Asian Chinese film market (including Taiwan, Hong Kong and Southeast Asia Chinese communities), and the staggering aesthetics of *A Touch of Zen* made it the first Chinese film to garner an award at the Cannes Film Festival. In the 1980s, King Hu once again moved, this time to the United States where he tried to make a film about the early Chinese immigrants who built the railroads during the California gold rush, but lack of funding killed the project.

A Chinese born in Beijing who died in Taipei, King Hu built his reputation mainly on his Mandarin-language martial arts films (Stokes and Hoover, 1999; Desser, 2000a; Bordwell, 2000b). Hector Rodriquez points out that, derived from King Hu's experience of exile and cultural rootlessness, his martial arts films emanate from a nostalgic "craving for China," with elements like Chinese visual and performing arts and traditional ethical values (1998). These characteristics can also easily be found in Ang Lee's *Crouching Tiger, Hidden Dragon*.

In addition to his unique aesthetics, King Hu's works can be analyzed in terms of "national allegory." In his seminal essay, "Third-World Literature in an Age of Multinational Capitalism" (1987), cultural critic Fredric Jameson brings up the influential theory of "national allegory" to examine Third World cultural productions. He argues that every Third-World text is a kind of "national allegory," because "the story of the private individual destiny is always an allegory of the embattled situation of the public Third World culture and society" (p. 142). In a similar vein, Bordwell points out that martial arts films in King Hu's hands turned out to be a general national allegory:

> Hu used the Mandarin movie as an occasion to explore China's tragic history of state corruption. In a genre that spun out plots of private revenge and family loyalty, he elaborated political intrigues. . . . He gravitated to the Ming dynasty, a period in which venal cliques plotted against one another and cooperated only to oppress the people. He tried to capture China's confrontation with external invaders, like the Mongols and the Japanese, and portrayed the Ming as a period when Confucianism, Taoism, and Buddhism jostled one another (2000b, p. 255).

King Hu's martial arts films can be interpreted as nostalgia and as a political critique of China, a homeland he could never go back to because of the different political ideologies.

However, Hu is not the only Chinese director employing the martial arts genre to express concern about China's politics. In fact, the martial arts film is usually used as a national allegory to refer to China in a world political context. For example, in his brilliant *Once Upon a Time in China* series, Tsui Hark uses the legendary Chinese folk hero Wong

Fei-Hong as a nationalist icon who resists imperialist invasion. Wong Fei-Hong, a martial arts master, is depicted as a fighter who defends the Chinese cultural identity and Confucian humanistic ideals in the turmoil of modernization. These six films of the *Once Upon a Time in China* series, produced from 1990 to 1997, were employed by Tsui Hark as a symbolic device to reflect the political/cultural/social anxiety of Hong Kong toward the 1997 return to Mainland China (Stokes and Hoover, 1999). Another example of this national allegory concept is the legendary kung fu icon Bruce Lee. He always plays a furious nationalist defender fighting back imperialist invasions of China. In his analysis of Bruce Lee and the kung fu craze in the U.S., Vijay Prashad (2003) highlights the 1970s' political milieu of multi-ethnic anti-imperialism in which Bruce Lee's Chinese national hero image became a popular icon among Black and other minority groups. In this case, the martial arts film is not solely a Chinese national allegory but is transformed into an allegory for all the oppressed people worldwide.

Stephen Teo (1997) incisively maintains that the martial artist/actor's films produced a "cultural nationalism" expressing the Chinese diaspora's desire to "identify with China and things Chinese, even though they may not have been born there or speak its national language or dialects" (p.111). He points out that not only the genre itself, but the production and marketing of martial arts films are significant. Just as King Hu's Taiwanese productions took the Southeast Asia's film markets by storm, these films also mold "a kind of pan-Chinese internationalism within the region [Southeast Asia]" (as cited in Bordwell, 2000a, p.67). When Ang Lee talks about how he fulfills the image of the China of his childhood memory in martial arts films, he exactly refers to this unique Chinese diasporic film culture.

CROUCHING TIGER, HIDDEN DRAGON: THE TRADITIONAL HERITAGE AND TRANSFORMATION

In many ways, Ang Lee's *Crouching Tiger, Hidden Dragon* is a salute to King Hu's martial arts films. Like Hu, Ang Lee highlights women warriors of the martial arts genre. Cheng Pei Pei, one of the most famous martial arts actresses in the 1970s, who played the female warrior in King Hu's *Come Drink with Me*, also plays Jade Fox, the villain swordswoman in *Couching Tiger, Hidden Dragon*. The swordswoman impersonating a man in the fights in the inn and the bamboo swordplay scene remind the martial arts genre audiences of King Hu's works, *Dragon Gate Inn* and *A Touch of Zen*. The bamboo swordfight at the end of *Crouching Tiger, Hidden Dragon* is obviously paying homage to King Ku's classical bamboo fight scene in *A Touch of Zen*, described by David Bordwell (2000a, 2000b) as, "perhaps the most famous scene in all the new *wuxia pian*."

However, there are several critical differences between *Crouching Tiger, Hidden Dragon* and vintage King Hu's martial arts works. First of all, the national allegory as a political critique is totally missing in Ang Lee's martial arts remake. In his "father knows best" trilogy, the family serves as a symbol of Chinese traditional culture, and it is always in conflict with Western/American/modern culture which makes it possible to find a common national allegory in the trilogy. However, in *Crouching Tiger, Hidden Dragon* the Western/American/modern factors are totally wiped out, and the film is only a Chinese saga. Second, in contrast to King Hu's reticent portraying of the warriors' feats, Ang Lee pushes Orientalist aesthetics to its extreme. For example, the fighting sequences of *Crouching Tiger, Hidden Dragon* are what Rey Chow (1995) defines as the "self-exhibitionist spectacles." Taking the bamboo swordfight sequence for comparison, in Hu's *A Touch of Zen* the fighting is presented in abstract stylistic film aesthetics:

Apart from the acrobatics, the swordfight is filmed and cut in a daringly opaque way. Although each image is carefully composed, the editing makes the shots so brief that we merely glimpse the fighters' extraordinary feats.

(Bordwell, 2000b, p. 2)

On the contrary, the swordfight in *Crouching Tiger, Hidden Dragon* is presented as an astonishing depiction of the warriors' mythical feats. Relying on heavy wire work which could be erased by cutting-edge computer graphics techniques, Ang Lee could create incredible images of how two warriors drift down to pause effortlessly and fight violently on the gently bobbing bamboo branches. In a rooftop chase sequence at the beginning, the wire work enables the two women warriors to walk up the wall and literally in defiance of gravity.

Ang Lee seems very proud of the fighting scenes in this film. In his own words, he tried to make "the most incredible fight sequence you ever saw" (Hardesy, 2001, p. 22). Lee said he wanted to make the "action scenes play like choreographed dances" (2000b, p.116), so he "did a lot of vaulting wire work—more than Yuen Wo Ping [choreographer] ever did before" (2000c, p. 4). Yuen is a veteran martial arts film director and choreographer, whose works include Tsui Hark's *Once Upon a Time in China* (starring Jet Li), Jackie Chan's *Drunken Master*, and the international box-office hit *The Matrix*. Yet, the wire work in *Crouching Tiger, Hidden Dragon* exceeded anything he had done with this technique before.

Making fighting scenes like dance is nothing new to King Hu who once said, "I've always taken the action part of my films as dancing than fighting" (as cited in Stokes & Hoover, 1999, p. 90). Yet, when King Hu tried to beautify the warriors' feats he was careful to make them not seem implausible or like sheer fantasy. David Bordwell argues that Hu used a unique stylish aesthetics to conquer this dilemma of beautification and mystification, which Bordwell described as "richness through imperfection," and he goes on to explain it:

[A]ny such acts [feats] can be shown quite clearly if the director is able to spend time and money on wires and special effects. But special effects inevitably risk looking fake. Today this problem has still not been surmounted: wire-work often makes combatants look like they are being hauled and swung around. . . . The solution he [King Hu] found was to stress certain qualities of these feats— their abruptness, their speed, their mastery. And he chose to do so by treating these feats as only partly visible. . . . The recent *wuxia pian* techniques give us time to savor the outrageousness of the stunts, but Hu's glimpses tantalize rather than satisfy our appetite for action (2000b, pp. 118–120).

Compared with King Hu's abstraction of the fighting scene, Ang Lee's arrangement is simply "make-you-see-it-all." Distinguished from its basic Hollywood realistic narrative, all the fighting scenes in *Crouching Tiger, Hidden Dragon*—no matter whether the rooftop chase, the inn fighting sequence, the duel between two swordswomen, or the bamboo fight—flaunt the warriors' feats to a totally unrealistic extent. They are pure *magic* as most American critics describe this film. If King Hu's fighting scenes were consummated through the audiences' imaginations, Lee's literally extinguish any imagination through special effects and computer graphics. Devoid of the political national allegory, the fighting scenes of *Crouching Tiger, Hidden Dragon* are only *spectaclized spectacles*, or *self-exoticizing spectacles*, which are used to cater to the oriental gaze dominating the international film market.

CROUCHING TIGER, HIDDEN DRAGON: WHY ANG LEE AND WHY THE MARTIAL ARTS GENRE?

If we explain the production of *Crouching Tiger, Hidden Dragon* only through Ang Lee's auteurism, it will be a dangerous simplification of a complicated global cultural phenomenon. To further explore the cultural logic behind the production of *Crouching Tiger, Hidden Dragon*, let us begin with these simple questions: Why is the most successful foreign film in U.S. film history a Chinese film? Why was Ang Lee chosen to be the director? And why is this film a martial arts film?

First of all, how could a Chinese film like *Crouching Tiger, Hidden Dragon* be so overwhelmingly acclaimed by Western film critics and audience? In his *Screening China: Critical Interventions, Cinematic reconfigurations, and the Transnational Imaginary in Contemporary Chinese Cinema* (2002), Yingjin Zhang presents a detailed analysis of the operation of global cultural politics which makes the Chinese cinema a powerhouse of the international film industry. Klaus Eder, program organizer for the Munich International Film Festival, points out: "That is a surprising and admirable series of successes, which no other cinema has ever duplicated, at least not within the last two or three decades." (quoted in Zhang, 2002, p.16). According to Zhang, the staggering success of Chinese cinema (including Mainland China, Taiwan, and Hong Kong productions) is a contingent mixture of post-Cold War/post-Tiananmen international politics, the highlight in international film festivals, the box-office boom in Western art theaters, the Western academic interest of pursuing the Oriental cultural authenticity, and the dialectic interaction between global cultural industries and Chinese local filmmaking. Owing to the Chinese cinema craze in the international film market, it is not too surprising that *Crouching Tiger, Hidden Dragon*, a Chinese film, could take the international market by storm.

Second, why was Ang Lee assigned to direct *Crouching Tiger, Hidden Dragon*? The answer might be that Lee's previous work has proved not only that he is familiar with the *modus operandi* of both U.S. and Chinese (Taiwanese) film industries, but also that he knows how to make an international box office hit. In fact, Ang Lee's debut, *Pushing Hands*, was a coproduction between Taiwan's Central Motion Picture Company and New York's independent film production house Good Machine Company. Through Good Machine's sophisticated promotion strategy, Ang Lee's second film, *The Wedding Banquet*, garnered the Golden Bear Prize at the Berlin Film Festival and became an instant hit in art houses worldwide. Since then Lee not only has become a brand name on the film festival circuit but also has given a pull to Good Machine's solid footing in the U.S. film industry. Now, despite *The Hulk's* failure in the U.S. market, both Ang Lee and Good Machine have been on the list of the most-wanted among Hollywood film studios.

Ang Lee's long-time partnership with Good Machine is an interesting case of a reciprocal relationship between an artist and the managerial agency in the creative industry. Yet, a great part of the credit for Ang Lee's success has to be given to James Schamus, one of the co-founders of Good Machine Company. Almost all the screenplays of Lee's works— including his Mandarin-language productions *Crouching Tiger, Hidden Dragon, The Wedding Banquet*, and *Eat Drink Man Woman*—came from Schamus' writing, co-writing or revision. It is no exaggeration to say that James Schamus serves as the informant of American culture to Ang Lee's successful career.

Third, why were the martial arts, or specifically the *wuxia pian*, genre chosen for *Crouching Tiger, Hidden Dragon*? Compared to kung fu films which were best represented by Bruce Lee's powerful cinematic image, the *wuxia* films are a martial arts sub-genre less familiar to Western audiences. However, in the 1990s the *nijutsu* (a Japanese martial art emphasizing the mythical feats of the warriors, which is more like *wuxia* than kung fu) appeared in American comic books such as *The Teenage Mutant Ninja Turtles* and achieved an astonishing popularity. In addition, the emergence of the home video game mania around 1985, aroused by the Japanese company Nintendo's starting to provide software in the market, made Asian martial arts a household item in the popular culture in the U.S. Consequently, as video game culture was incorporated by the film industry, more and more martial arts special effects were showing on both the big and small screen. This martial arts mania culminated in the box-office megahit *The Matrix* (1999) (Desser, 2000b, p. 89–90), choreographed by Yuen Wo Ping, who did *Crouching Tiger, Hidden Dragon* as well.

This might make some sense of why *Crouching Tiger, Hidden Dragon* was well accepted by U.S. audiences. However, creating a film which will be loved both by the critics and by the audience is not easy. In his analysis of how Hollywood marketed Jackie Chan's action comedy to U.S. mainstream audiences, Steve Fore (1997) points out the main difficulty faced by the Hollywood studio was the deep-rooted cultural bias of U.S. audiences toward foreign films (p. 258). Chan's Chineseness gave the audience problems with finding a cultural proximity with his movie. Fore argues that the reason Chan's *Rumble in the Bronx* (1996) was finally well-accepted by U.S. audiences is because the distributor strengthened the cultural proximity redubbing into English, rescoring and reediting, and by emphasizing that the movie was set and produced in New York (p. 249). According to Fore's argument, the marketing of *Crouching Tiger, Hidden Dragon* to a U.S. mainstream audience was a mission impossible, because it is full of Chineseness, has an unknown cast, and needed subtitles to help the Western audiences understand the foreign language.

Sony Classics, the U.S. distributor of *Crouching Tiger, Hidden Dragon* took painstaking efforts to create a niche market for it. Its tactics included choosing to enter the film in the noncompetition screening at the Cannes Film Festival rather than risking competition because Sony Classics wanted this film to be "perceived outside the art-house ghetto." Furthermore there were many screenings for different target groups, such as graduates of a women's leadership institute, female athletes, karate fans, the artist community, and TV news anchors, in the hope that they would spread good impressions of the film through word-of-mouth. Sony also hired a 13-year-old boy to construct a website for this film to attract teen audiences (Lippman, 2001). However, the totally exotic movie-going experience may be the biggest selling point for *Crouching Tiger, Hidden Dragon*. Judging from the box office returns and highly acclaimed critiques (including the Academy Awards) garnered by *Crouching Tiger, Hidden Dragon*, it was very obvious that all these manoeuvres paid off.

All in all, the whole producing, promoting and marketing process of *Crouching Tiger, Hidden Dragon* can be examined in the context that Toby Miller et al. (2001) call Hollywood's "new international division of cultural labor" (NICL). The NICL, according to Miller et al., has developed a sophisticated system of surveillance, production, marketing and financing techniques to widen audiences, spread risk and ensure profit. This brief discussion of how and why *Crouching Tiger, Hidden Dragon* became such a huge success in the U.S. merely serves as a reminder of the complicated political economy behind the production and marketing of a non-Hollywood foreign film.[2]

ORIENTALISM OR THE ORIENTAL'S ORIENTALISM

Sometimes commercial and critical success in the international market can be the cultural original sin for a national cinema. Yet, in contrast to the works of Chinese Fifth-generation directors, such as Zhang Yimou's *Ju Dou* (1990), *Raise the Red Lantern* (1991), and Chen

Kaige's *Farewell My Concubine* (1993), Ang Lee's Mandarin-language productions rarely become the objects of criticism among Chinese/Taiwanese intellectuals. Again, this can be explained by Ang Lee's Chinese diaspora identity and his detachment from Chinese politics.

Ang Lee's films hardly refer to a substantial Chinese society: *Pushing Hands* and *The Wedding Banquet* are set in America and describe the lives of Chinese diaspora; *Crouching Tiger, Hidden Dragon* goes even further, set in an ancient and imagined China. The only exception is *Eat Drink Man Woman*. Yet, its setting in modern Taiwan only serves as a backdrop for the storyline; in fact, the family drama of *Eat Drink Man Woman* can hold true in any Chinese community, whether in Mainland China, Hong Kong or the Chinatown of New York City. It seems impossible to use political affiliation or a nation-state to categorize Ang Lee, and people can best pigeonhole him as a "Chinese director"—in a cultural sense.

The films directed by Zhang Yimou and Chen Kaige were seriously criticized as distortions of the "real China" because, first, they all specifically refer to the concrete China, the People's Republic of China or geographical Mainland China instead of Ang Lee's imaginary China. Second, according to Lu (1997b), Zhang and Chen inherited the traditional Chinese intellectual's role as a social critic, and they present their films as political/cultural critiques of the PRC government or Chinese society. The indignant indictment of the Fifth-generation directors' films as cultural sellouts of the Chinese nation in the international film market is basically constructed under the framework of the First/Third world dichotomy. In the Chinese intellectuals' eyes, China is unquestioningly categorized as a Third world country. So, the popularity of the Fifth-generation directors' films in the West "only reveals the fact that Third-World cinema is compelled to be part of a hegemonic, Orientalist discourse in order to be accepted by the West, which dominates the global cultural market" (Lu, 1997b, p. 128). On the contrary, Ang Lee's Chinese diaspora identity cannot be clearly mapped on this First/Third conflicting world framework; his ambiguous and marginalized position takes his works out of the focus in this West vs. Chinese cultural debate.

In this vein, it is meaningful to compare Ang Lee and Zhang Yimou, the two most popular *Chinese* directors in the international film market. Both of them are proficient at employing Orientalist aesthetics, although Zhang has a more critical attitude toward Chinese culture. While defending Zhang Yimou's films as not totally "selling Oriental exoticism to a Western audience" or "airing one's [Chinese] dirty laundry in public," Rey Chow argues that it is imprecise to criticize directors such as Zhang for producing a new kind of Orientalism, she says instead:

> [W]hat Zhang is producing is rather an exhibitionist self-display that contains, in
> its very excessive modes, a critique of the voyeurism of orientalism itself . . .
> this exhibitionism—what we may call the Oriental's orientalism. . . . In its
> self-subalternizing, self-exoticizing visual gestures, the Oriental's orientalism is
> first and foremost a demonstration—the display of a tactic.
>
> (1995, p. 170)

Chow's defense can also apply to Ang Lee. Even though not so defiant and controversial as Zhang's works, Ang Lee's Orientalist aesthetics still successfully transform a glossy "Chineseness" into a popular cross-cultural commodity, such as *The Wedding Banquet, Eat Drink Man Woman*, and *Crouching Tiger, Hidden Dragon*.

CULTURAL ARCADE AND CHINESE RESTAURANT: NATIONAL CINEMA IN GLOBALIZED CONSUMER CULTURE

Orientalism, which dominates the production and distribution of the international film market, has always been linked with cultural distortion and misrepresentation of Third world nations. When discussing globalization, quite a few scholars, such as Homi Bhabha (1997), Davis Morley and Kevin Robins (1995), have discussed the importance of cultural translation for local culture to gain a footing in the global cultural market. Rey Chow (1995) also sees national cinema in the postcolonial world as a special kind of cultural translation. Some critics of the national cinema presume that an *authentic* cultural text and the possibility of an undistorted intercultural translation exist. Orientalism presents an intended disfigurement and manipulation of the original cultural text to satisfy the Western gaze. For Western audiences Orientalism functions as a cultural logic to define their "self" in relation to the "other." In this vein, Orientalism is transformed into the criterion by which to judge a national/local cinema. If we say a film employs Orientalist aesthetics then we obviously imply that "it is a bad film," no matter how much pleasure it can bring to us.

Yet, as Chow argues, from the point of view of deconstruction, the authenticity and the perfect translation of a cultural text now become questionable. As Hall (1997) points out, in the globalization era, the dominant culture is *global mass culture* which "is dominated by television and by film, and by image, imagery, and styles of mass advertising" (p. 27). In other words, the main form of global mass culture is visionary. In the postmodern transnational and transcultural market, how to make the national/local culture visible is much more important than providing a questionable undistorted cultural representation. That is because in the postmodern global consumer culture, every national/local culture has to be transformed into a commodity and then it can be consumed by audiences through the mass media.

According to Mike Featherstone (1995), because of the fragmentation and disjuncture in global capitalism, "attention should be given to the mediations between the economy and culture by focusing on the activities of cultural specialists and intermediaries and the expanding audiences . . . for a new range of cultural goods." (p.2) Indeed, it does not matter that Ang Lee, Zhang Yimou, or James Schamus are exactly those "cultural specialists" or "intermediaries" who translate national/local cultural texts into popular commodities for the consumption of international audiences. However, in terms of cultural politics, are the sometimes conscious mistranslations which appear in their depiction of *China* really cultural sellouts or betrayal?

When defending the Chinese Fifth-generation directors' films against the accusation of Orientalism, Chow points out, according to the interpretations of Derrida and John Fletcher, that Benjamin emphasizes that a good translation, like an arcade or a passageway, can cast a light on the original text to make it shine more brilliantly; however, Chow argues that the arcade is also a commercial passageway where shop fronts display their commodities to attract the eyes of consumers (1995, pp. 200–201). Chow emphasizes that even contemporary Chinese cinemas employing Orientalist aesthetics still are the cultural translations of the globalization era. She argues "if translation is a form of betrayal, then the translators pay their debt by bringing fame to the ethnic culture. . . . It is in translation's faithlessness that 'China' survives and thrives" (1995, p. 202). This argument can also be used to defend Ang Lee's employing Orientalist aesthetics in *Crouching Tiger, Hidden Dragon* and all his other Mandarin-language productions.

In explaining his filmmaking strategies in Hollywood, Ang Lee takes a very pragmatic attitude toward the cultural politics of global mass culture. He uses the Chinese restaurant in the U.S. as a metaphor:

> I think . . . it is like running a Chinese restaurant business in the U.S.—the
> westerners begin Chinese food by trying Sweet and Sour Chicken. After a while,
> they will be able to taste more authentic Chinese food. The more Chinese
> restaurants we have here in the U.S., the easier we are able to find green onion
> and tofu in our nearby supermarket (as cited in Chung, 2000, p. 39).

Obviously, Ang Lee is very self-conscious about his employment of Orientalist aesthetics as a cultural tactic. The felicitous metaphor of the Chinese restaurant not only implies the commodity-nature of films, but also justifies his self-exoticization of Chineseness, or the selling of ethnic Chinese flavors, in his own works as a strategy to attract international audiences. Ang Lee's remarks imply Orientalist aesthetics might be the necessary evil for introducing more *authentic* Chinese films into the international film market. However, Ang Lee's hope might just be wishful thinking. Since there is no longer an *authentic* China existing in the globalized context, how could it be possible for Chinese film makers to produce any *authentic* Chinese film?

No matter whether you like *Crouching Tiger, Hidden Dragon* or not, no one can deny Ang Lee's accomplishments in transforming the Oriental gaze into a popular cultural product and, at the same time, his achievements in making "China" be seen by so many international audiences. It is still too early to predict whether the success of *Crouching Tiger, Hidden Dragon* is a contingency or really opens a gate for Asian talents to the international film market. However, the success of *Crouching Tiger, Hidden Dragon* has brought up some valuable questions in global cultural politics to be contemplated by cultural critics and all national cinema producers worldwide.

Notes

1   In terms of these questions, Ken-fang Lee provides a sophisticated interpretation in her article "Far Away, So Close: Cultural Translation in Ang Lee's *Crouching Tiger, Hidden Dragon*", in *Inter-Asia Cultural Studies*, Vol. 4, No. 2, pp. 281–295, 2003.
2   For full discussion of the production and marketing strategies of *Crouching Tiger, Hidden Dragon*, please see Wu & Chan (2003), Globalizing Chinese martial arts cinema: The global-local alliance and the production of *Crouching Tiger, Hidden Dragon*. Paper presented at the International Communication Association Annual Convention, May 23–27, 2003, San Diego, CA.

References

Allen, R. (1989). Bursting bubbles: "Soap opera," audiences, and the limits of genre. In E. Seiter, H. Borchers, G. Kreutzner, and E. M. Warth (Eds.), *Remote control: Television, audiences, and cultural power* (pp. 45–55). London: Routledge.

Anderson, B. (1983). *Imagined communities: Reflections on the orgin and spread of nationalism*. London: Verso.

Ang, I. (2000). Can one say no to Chineseness? Pushing the limits of the diasporic paradigm. In R. Chow (Ed.), *Modern Chinese literary and cultural studies in the age of theory: reimagining a field*. London: Duke University Press.

Berry, C. (1993). Taiwanese melodrama returns with a twist in *The Wedding Banquet*. *Cinemaya*, *21*, (Fall): 52–54.

Bhabha, H. K. (1997). "Fireflies caught in molasses:" Questions of cultural translation. In R. E. Krauss (Ed.). *October: The second decade, 1986–1996*. (pp. 211–223). Cambridge, MA: MIT Press.

Bordwell, D. (2000a). *Planet Hong Kong: Popular cinema and the art of entertainment*. Cambridge, MA: Harvard University Press.

—— (2000b). Richness through imperfection: King Hu and the glimpse. In P. Fu & D. Desser (Eds.), *The cinema of Hong Kong: History, arts, identity* (pp. 113–136). New York: Cambridge University Press.

Chen, K. H. (2000). Taiwanese new cinema. In J. Hill & P. C. Gibson (Eds.), *World cinema: Critical approaches* (pp. 173–177). London: Oxford University Press.

Chow, R. (1995). *Primitive passion: visuality, sexuality, ethnography and contemporary Chinese cinema.* New York: Columbia University Press.

Chow, R. (2000). Introduction: On Chineseness as a theoretical problem. In R. Chow (Ed.), *Modern Chinese literary and cultural studies in the age of theory: Reimagining a field.* (pp. 1–25). London: Duke University Press.

Chung, P. (2000). Asian filmmakers moving into Hollywood: Genre regulation and auteur aesthetics. *Asian Cinema, Spring/Summer*, 33–50.

Clifford, J. (1994). Diaspora. *Cultural anthropology 9 (3)*: 302–338.

Corliss, R. (2001, July 9). American best film director: Ang Lee. *Time*, Vol. 158, No. 1, 55.

Crouching Tiger, Hidden Dragon: A Portrait of the Ang Lee Film. (2000). New York: New Market Press.

Dariotis, W. M., & Fung, E. (1997). Breaking the soy sauce jar: Diaspora and displacement in the film of Ang Lee. In S. H. Lu (Ed.), *Transnational Chinese cinemas: identity, nationhood, gender* (pp.187–220). Honolulu: University of Hawaii Press.

Desser, D. (2000a). The kung fu craze: Hong Kong Cinema's first American reception. In P. Fu & D. Desser (Eds.), *The cinema of Hong Kong: History, arts, identity* (pp. 19–43). New York: Cambridge University Press.

—— (2000b). The martial arts film in the 1990s. In W. W. Dixon (ed.). *Film genre 2000: New critical essays* (pp. 77–109). Albany: State University of New York Press.

Dupont, J. (2000). Finding China. In *Crouching Tiger, Hidden Dragon: A portrait of the Ang Lee film* (p. 40). New York: New Market Press.

Featherstone, M. (1995). *Undoing culture: Globalization, postmodernism and identity.* London: Sage.

Fore, S. (1997). Jackie Chan and the cultural dynamics of global entertainment. In S. H. Lu (Ed.), *Transnational Chinese cinemas: identity, nationhood, gender* (pp. 239–262). Honolulu: University of Hawaii Press.

Hall, S. (1997). The local and the the global. In A. King (Ed.). *Culture, globalization and the world-system: Contemporary conditions for the representation of identity* (pp. 19–39). Minneapolis, MI: University of Minnesota Press.

Hardesty, M. (2001, May). Feature Nominees. *DGA Magazine, 26(1)*, 20–24.

Jameson, F. (1987). World literature in an age of multinational capitalism. In C. Koelb & V. Lokke (Eds.). *The current in criticism: Essays on the present and future of literary theory.* West Lafayette, ID: Purdue University Press.

Landler, M. (2001, February 27). Lee's Tiger, celebrated everywhere but at home. *The New York Times*, p. B1(N) p. E1(L).

Lee, A. (1999). Foreword. In J. Schamus (Ed.), *Ride with the devil.* (pp. ix–x). New York: Farber and Farber Limited.

—— (2000a). Foreword. In *Crouching Tiger, Hidden Dragon: A portrait of the Ang Lee film.* (p. 7). New York: New Market Press.

—— (2000b). Filmmaking. In *Crouching Tiger, Hidden Dragon: A portrait of the Ang Lee film.* (p. 116). New York: New Market Press.

—— (2000c). Fighting as a way of thinking and feeling. In *Crouching Tiger, Hidden Dragon: A portrait of the Ang Lee film* (p. 42). New York: New Market Press.

Lippman, J. (2001, January 20). Making Crouching Tiger: How Sony created a buzz that turned a Chinese martial-arts film into a box-office powerhouse. *The Wall Street Journal*, p. E5.

Lu, S. H. (1997a). Historical introduction: Chinese cinemas (1896–1996) and transnational film studies. In S. H. Lu (Ed.), *Transnational Chinese cinemas: identity, nationhood, gender* (pp. 1–31). Honolulu: University of Hawaii Press.

—— (1997b). National cinema, cultural critique, transnational capital: The films of Zhang Yimou. In S. H. Lu (Ed.), *Transnational Chinese cinemas: identity, nationhood, gender* (pp. 105–136). Honolulu: University of Hawaii Press.

Ma, S. (1996). Ang Lee's domestic tragicomedy: Immigrant nostalgia, exotic/ethnic tour, global market. *Journal of Popular Culture, 30 (1)*, 191–20.

Marchetti, G. (2000). *The Wedding Banquet:* Global Chinese cinema and the Asian American experience.

In D. Y. Hamamoto & S. Lin (Eds.). *Countervisions: Asian American film criticism* (pp. 275–297). Philadelphia: Temple University Press.

Miller, T., Govil, N., McMurria, J. & Maxwell, R. (2001). *Global Hollywood*. London: British Film Institute.

Morley, D. & Robins, R. (1995). *Spaces of identity: Global media, electronic landscapes and cultural boundaries*. London: Routledge.

Prashad, V. (2003). Bruce Lee and the anti-imperialism of Kung Fu: A polycultural adventure. *Positions*, *11 (1)*, 51–90.

Stokes, L. O. & Hoover, M. (1999). *City on fire: Hong Kong cinema*. London: Verso.

Teo, Stephen. (1997). *Hong Kong cinema: The extra dimensions*. London: British Film Institute.

Tu, W. M. (1994). Preface. In W. M. Tu (Ed.), *The living tree: The changing meaning of being Chinese today*. Stanford, CA: Stanford University Press.

Wu, H. & Chan, J. M. (2003). Globalizing Chinese martial arts cinema: The global-local alliance and the production of *Crouching Tiger, Hidden Dragon*. Paper presented at the International Communication Association Annual Convention, May 23–27, 2003, San Diego, CA.

Zhang, Y. (2002). *Screening China: Critical interventions, cinematic reconfigurations, and the transnational imaginary in contemporary Chinese cinema*. Center for Chinese Studies, University of Michigan Ann Arbor: Ann Arbor, MI.

In Chinese:

Chen, Bao-Xu, (1994). *Eat, Drink, Man, Woman: The screenplay and the shooting process*. Taipei: Yuan-Lui Publications.

Chapter 12

Ruth Zanker and Geoff Lealand

NEW ZEALAND AS MIDDLE EARTH: LOCAL AND GLOBAL POPULAR COMMUNICATION IN A SMALL NATION (2003)

RESEARCHERS ACROSS THE GLOBE are busily mapping how children use media, music, and associated merchandise in their everyday lives. Audience studies have flourished since the 1980s, when easy access to video recording and the proliferation of media channels enabled scholars to probe audience responses to texts and to closely observe children's culture. There is now considerable evidence about the creative ways that children these days mine popular communication for inspirational (and aspirational) "scripts," for the ongoing work of creating identity and claiming ownership.

In contrast, research on how producers and marketers shape the *local* cultural resources available for children in their playful (but serious) work of identity formation has been largely neglected. This is curious, in light of the fact that who gets to make television (and media in general) and how and where have long been the enduring concern of media democracy. Media policies in many countries share a desire to provide appropriate cultural range, diversity, and quality of media provision for local children. Media culture in smaller and poorer media markets with limited public funding are inevitably shaped by the media domination of affluent nations, but battles over local media production indicate the continuing political salience of local culture for many peripheral nations and the increasing slipperiness of that term during the 1990s (Goonasekera et al., 2000).

There are obvious barriers in the way of achieving access to the often commercially sensitive decision making of broadcasters, programmers, commissioners, producers, and marketers that prevent analysis of that decision making. But this work is important, if one is to grapple with the paradoxical global and local tugs within national cultures. New Zealand's physical distance from centers of global corporate power is of no significance in the eyes of New Zealand's children who, as elsewhere, embrace the latest fads and fashions. Media time and space have collapsed for children everywhere. In a far-flung country like New Zealand, sited at the capillary end of arterial capital flows, notions of shared interests by children in all capitalist cultural environments is greatly assisted, simply because marketing instrumentality can only ever manifest itself in the particularity of local children's media environments. Each child, whether viewing television in Ireland, San Jose, Vietnam, or Fiji, is now best conceptualized as being "at the end" of hybrid cultural flows.

New Zealand provides a valuable site in which to explore the industrial processes creating the postmodern cultural experiences of globalizing popular communication. Children in New Zealand respond as joyously to *Dragon Ball Z* and Britney Spears as do children in San Jose and Sheffield, and it is evident that the global can only be tracked in the ways it emerges in specific localities. However, it is often easier to discern emerging global patterns at the perceived "periphery" of corporate "power," possibly because global corporates believe there is less at stake in revealing data on local marketing strategies.

NEW ZEALAND AS MIDDLE EARTH

Nevertheless, New Zealand has suddenly become the center of global attention. In the early months of 2002, the citizens of New Zealand (3.8 million of them) were aglow with national pride, as the first film of the New Zealand-produced, New Line Cinema-financed trilogy *The Lord of the Rings* was creating box office records and gathering global awards. The director (Wellington-based Peter Jackson) was hailed as a national hero, his home city was temporarily renamed "Middle Earth," the Labour Government appointed a senior politician with the lofty title of the Minister in Charge of The Lord of the Rings, and tourists arrived in search of traces of Hobbiton or Mordor in the landscapes of New Zealand. With a generous injection of foreign capital and a local talent base, New Zealand could give the rest of the world a reason to pause and gaze on the remarkable cultural achievements of a tiny Pacific nation, sited at the very ends of the earth. As O'Hehir (2002) suggested in the prestigious British film magazine *Sight and Sound*:

> Perhaps the secret ingredient in Peter Jackson's extraordinary film interpretation of the first volume of J.R.R. Tolkien's *The Lord of the Rings* is New Zealand itself. (p. 50)

But in all things New Zealanders say and do, there is deep irony and ambiguity. New Zealand is constructed from a muddle and mixture of cultural borrowings, and some manifestations of public behavior must puzzle strangers, in a land where Christmas is celebrated in midsummer, with shops festooned with plastic holly and frosted with synthetic snow and a jolly Father Christmas is invited down chimneys, with Christmas roast dinners served up in summer heat. Amongst the enlightened, however, more appropriate *South Pacific* behavior is emerging; families now take picnics to the beach and the summer flowering pohutakawa tree is replacing holly berries and mistletoe. Other public ceremonies are shifting; Halloween is replacing Guy Fawkes Day in November, in a displacement of one cultural borrowing with another.

Contradictions and ambiguities are also found in *The Lord of the Rings*. It is the biggest, most profitable film ever made in New Zealand and has energized the local film industry. In terms of the norms of national cinema, however, it is *not* a New Zealand film. The male and female leads are British, American, and Australian; the narrative draws on the myths and legends of ancient Europe, and the giant U.S. media conglomerate AOL-Time Warner is at the end of the food chain.

Such are the contradictory spaces New Zealand inhabits; ever open to the world but also struggling to find its unique place in a globalized world of corporate economics and mass-distributed media. The search for cultural autonomy has not been helped by New Zealand's eagerness to remove all impediments in the way of free markets and unfettered membership of deregulated media. Throughout the 20th century, New Zealand imported or borrowed the best and the worst from international media producers (most particularly from the United States and Britain) but, in the past 15 years, it assisted the entry of imported media to quite unprecedented levels. In 1996, for example, the New Zealand media professionals group Screen Producers & Directors Association was able to claim:

> With ample justification New Zealand's broadcasting environment is now the most deregulated in the world. The regime which now operates is extremely permissive by world standards. (p. 6)

One thing is certain in New Zealand: Politicians will always fiddle with the structure of broadcasting, shaping it (television in particular) to fit the latest ideological fashion. Local content on television has always been expensive for New Zealand taxpayers, and programming has always been a hybrid mix of cheap local and hit imports. Generations of New Zealand children have grown up with fond memories of Disney, Saban, Nickelodeon, and the BBC, with a sprinkling of local favorites.

With the election of the Labour-Alliance Government in November 1999, the deregulated state-owned television network of Television New Zealand (TV ONE and Channel 2) was directed to turn away from commercial imperatives (maximizing profits, paying substantial and regular dividends to government coffers). It was required to return to clearer public service objectives, through compliance to a new Television New Zealand Charter, which included, among other provisions, that TVNZ will

- Provide shared experiences that contribute to a sense of citizenship and national identity.
- Feature programs that provide for the informational and entertainment needs of children and young people and allow for the participation of children and young people.

Such objectives may be clear to those who wrote the Charter, but how they might be realized and implemented remains a mystery to all others. These "others" include Television New Zealand and other broadcasters, policy makers and program funders, program makers, schedulers, advertisers, and, one suspects, the New Zealand viewing audience. The lack of clear objectives, together with the necessary industrial support to fulfill the Charter, is particularly marked in the area of children's and youth television, which has been swept by 2 or 3 decades of globalization, commercialism, and argument.

Children's and youth television illuminates, more than any other area, the dilemmas of contemporary *national* television. The perils and possibilities of funding, making, and scheduling television for young New Zealand audiences resemble the experiences of other countries but are further pounded and twisted by particular local forces. The tiny media market place, ruled by the ratings discourse, makes the local production of children's television in the "full-service BBC" a marginal endeavor. Local productions, no matter how cheap per hour (and early childhood programs have been made for $2000 NZ per half-hour episode; the NZ dollar currently hovers around 47 cents U.S.), are forced to compete with international hits that are the result of extensive market research and development and high production values. The noncommercial niche requirements of children are compounded by a cultural shift over the last 2 decades from an Anglo-Celtic cultural hegemony to new post-colonialist "Pacific" hybridity. Auckland is now the largest Polynesian city on Earth, and the cultural renaissance of indigenous Maori has been given political muscle from the mid-1980s decision to view the media as central to the cultural obligations under the Treaty of Waitangi (1840), signed between the British Crown and Maori tribes. The very sense of "New Zealand" itself has become an ongoing media project and public service television is largely defined by battles over what constitutes local culture. But these local marks (both icons and language) are a bar preventing producers from finding international customers and thus economies of scale, like the BBC (*Teletubbies*), ABC (*Bananas in Pajamas*), Nickelodeon (*Rugrats*), and CTW (*Sesame Street*).

But these intense production battles over representation in local media for the next generation compete for attention with other public issues. There have been, for example, regular moral panics about the harmful impact of both old (television) and new (Internet) media in children's lives. The impact of the media on children continues to be a staple news generator in media newsrooms on slow news days, and American effects research continues to be the source of evidence. Shows such as *Super Stars of Wrestling, Teenage Mutant Ninja Turtles, Mighty Morphin Power Rangers;* musicians such Marilyn Manson and Snoop Doggy Dog; and video games such as Doom and Terminator have all had their moment in the news.

Meanwhile, new consumer hits (*Pokemon* and *Harry Potter*) saturate the New Zealand markets faster than anywhere else on Earth, just as children's spending power is increasing. It is understandable that national commercial programmers compete for new hits at global trade shows, and those who market ice cream and candy vie for lucrative licensing rights. This market stampede, however, also creates parental anxiety that feeds, yet again, moral panics that blame television—this time for unhealthy eating habits and consumerism.

It is strange, given this, that there has been little scrutiny of how marketers and global conglomerates shape public spaces for children. There has been little scrutiny of the warping of American free speech arguments into a global corporate defense of "commercial free speech" across national boundaries. The freedom of transnationals to trade across boundaries increased massively during the 1990s, buttressed by the World Trade Organization's war on national tariffs and quotas and the interpretation of marketers and advertisers of free speech articles in a range of global conventions like the United Nations Covenant on Civil and Political Rights (Article 19) and the United Nations Convention of the Child (Article 13). Viewed from New Zealand in 2002, it appears that the United States is responsible for both exporting a problem (violent and scatological films and television programs, merchandising, and advertising) and for exporting the solutions (policy interventions, V-chip censorship, political rhetoric).

Recent global branding strategies and regional media footprints have seen cultural representation defined by market forces. What is missing is better informed explorations of local children's pleasures in global popular communication as they are played out in local media and the consequences for indigenous cultural production in a small nation.

CHILDREN AND POPULAR COMMUNICATION

Children's media culture, unlike youth culture, has been neglected by mainstream cultural scholars—in New Zealand and elsewhere. This is a pity, because children's pleasure in media consumption and the cultural meanings they take from media content lie at the heart of cultural reproduction. When funds permit, local research has been designed to ask a range of questions such as: "Where, with whom, and in what combinations do local children use media?", "What does popular communication mean to a range of children in New Zealand?", and "How does global and indigenous content interact in the 'work' of identity formation?"

A growing number of New Zealand research reports (Buckingham, 2000b; Lealand, 1995, 2001; Todd & Richardson, 2001; Walters & Zwaga, 2001; Zanker, 2001, 2002) point to the particular experiences of New Zealand children in respect to their engagement with and use of contemporary media. Even though the body of knowledge about New Zealand children is slight, it has given voice to their pleasures and informs policy debates for the first time. These studies contribute to a growing global body of cultural research (Buckingham, 2000a; Davies & Machin, 2000; Kinder, 1991; Lemish, Drotner, Liebes, & Stald, 1998; Mazzarella & Pecora, 1999; Pecora, 1999; Seiter, 1998). Researching the place of popular communication and media in children's lives enables us to determine what is universal about children's experiences of global popular communication and what is particular and local. Such research is important for understanding evolving childhoods and cultural globalization and how these are related to shifting relationships between adults and children. For example, it has proven useful to track how the shift from "mother at home" to "working mother" has accompanied a shift from age-specific constructs of childhood to the construct of the child who is "growing older younger" and of adults who remain eternally part of "extended youth." As adults consume children's cartoon icons and merchandise, so too children appear to increasingly choose adult popular communication over "age-appropriate" content. These changing habits are used to justify the shift from provision of public service content and regulation for "vulnerable" children to policies that enshrine parental responsibility and children as canny, knowing, sovereign consumers.

But there is a place for skepticism about forms of uncritical romanticism about children's consumer agency, contesting both post-structuralist constructs of the media-savvy child and the rhetoric of children's market. There are children who are very attuned to the ways and wiles of the media: there are many children who are not. Children can also be both media savvy and media naive, as a recent United Kingdom study by Day (2002) suggested:

> The youth of today are cynical, media-savvy, seen it all, done it all . . . who appreciate only the most achingly trendy adverts, TV shows and magazines, right? Wrong: that was so last generation. Today's youngsters don't "get" clever ads, are not in the least suspicious of commercials, don't know the difference between newspapers' political stances, or TV channels, and they don't mind admitting it.

The notion of media "savvy-ness" can indeed acknowledge the power and autonomy of children making their own judgments and constructing their understandings of the world. But it can also provide an excuse for laissez-faire marketing, wherein advertisers and marketers might argue that "anything goes" and there should be no limits on potentially exploitative practices because media-savvy children will filter out or reject that which offends them, or the hard sell.

There is further value in looking at such matters from the perspective of a small nation at the bottom of the world where issues of local cultural agency have continuing heat. Children appear to demonstrate their audience agency by flocking to heavily promoted global hits over low-cost and poorly promoted home-grown material. So what is the continuing justification for funding local children's productions? Does a child's right to *local* imaginative horizons under Article 17 of the United Nations Convention on Children's rights outweigh Article 13 that outlines the child's right to consumer sovereignty to shape local provision through exercise of audience agency?

DOING RESEARCH ON CHILDREN'S MEDIA IN A SMALL NATION

As has already been noted, New Zealand not only imports most of its popular communication but also most of its research "evidence." New Zealand politicians, educators, lobbyists, and marketers use imported research constructs of childhood to support a range of often conflicting cultural positions. It has become critical for us, as local cultural researchers, to interrogate these derivative, common-sense discourses of childhood as they keep circulating in the national media.

Globalism is not new for bit-players like New Zealand, which has always borrowed from the United States and Europe. New Zealanders have long had to think beyond the large nation binary of public service and commercial. The ragbag borrowings and mixes of the postmodern aesthetic are familiar to us. It is in the reversioning of local and global hybridity that local creative possibilities rest.

As two academics communicating across two small islands, we have chosen to wear many hats in the 15 years of sharing research interests in children's popular mediated culture. We are children's and media education advocates one day and parents grappling with our own children's willful ways the next day; one week, teachers of future media professionals and the next, critics of current media practice. Our interests straddle audience and policy research, advocacy for local children's production and media education for children, as well as media education for teachers, producers, and policy makers. By turning one's hand to both "pure" research and instrumental or policy research, one is constantly aware of the paradoxes and challenges that exist within the research field. One has the opportunity to investigate industry anxieties as well as question overseas theory in light of local data. One is kept alert to the provisional ways in which discursive power is forever shaping the cultural fields. The shift of the research lens from First World concerns and research questions to the different imperatives of a small nation enables scrutiny of assumptions made about globalizing processes, children's evolving public spaces, and the commodified popular communication by scholars in large, rich nations. The downside is that New Zealand public academics require thick skins and a high level of skepticism for received wisdom, and risk travel sores from long trips on cramped jets to join scholarly conferences that provide fellowship and refresh the parched soil of the theoretical imagination.

References

Buckingham, D. (2000a). *After the death of childhood: Growing up in the age of electronic media.* Cambridge. England: Polity.

Buckingham, D. (2000b). *The making of citizens: young people, news and politics.* London: Routledge.

Davies, M. M., & Machin, D. (2000). Children's demon TV—reality, freedom, panic: Children's discussion of "The Demon Headmaster." *Continuum: Journal of Media & Cultural Studies* 14, 37–50.

Day, J. (2002). Those crazy kids. *The Guardian.* February 11 Retrieved June 6, 2002. from http://media.guardian.co.uk/Print/0,3858,4353097,00.html

Goonasekera, A., Huang, C. Z., Eashwer, I., Guntarto, B., Bairaj-Ambigapathy, S., Dhungana, J., Lin, A., Chung, A., & Hanh, V. T. M. (2000). *Growing up with TV: Asian children's experience.* Singapore. Malaysia: Asian Media Information and Communication Centre.

Kinder, M. (1991). *Playing with power in movies, television and video games: From Muppet Babies to Teenage Mutant Ninja Turtles.* Berkeley: University of California Press.

Lealand, G. (1995). *Television and pre-schoolers: A longitudinal study.* Hamilton: University of Waikato.

Lealand, G. (2001). Some things change, some things stay the same: New Zealand children and media use. *Simile: Studies in Media and Information Literacy Education. 1, 1,* 1–9. Retrieved from http://www.utpjournals.com/jour.ihtml?/p=simile/issue 1/issue 1 toc.html

Lemish, D., Drotner, K., Liebes, E., & Stald, G. (1998). Global culture in practice: A look at children and adolescents in Denmark, France, Israel. *European Journal of Communication, 14,* 539–556.

Mazzarella, S., & Pecora, N. (1999). *Growing up girls: Popular culture and the construction of identity.* New York: Peter Lang.

O'Hehir, A. (2002). The Lord of the Rings: The Fellowship of the Rings [film review]. *Sight and Sound, 12*(2), 49–50.

Pecora, N. (1999). Children and television. *Communications Research Trends: A Quarterly Review of Communication Research*, *19*, 142.

Seiter, E. (1998). *Television and new media audiences*. Oxford, England: Oxford University Press.

Todd, S., & Richardson, D. (2001). New Zealand children talk about TV advertising. *Children's Issues*, *5*, 22–25.

Walters, R., & Zwaga, W. (2001). *The younger audience: Children and broadcasting in New Zealand*. Wellington, New Zealand: Dunmore.

Zanker, R. (2001). *What now? A New Zealand children's television production case study*. Unpublished doctoral dissertation. University of Waikato, Hamilton.

Zanker, R. (2002). Tracking the global in the local. In C. VanFeilitzen & U. Carlsson (Eds.). *Children and media violence yearbook 2002*. Sweden: Goteborg University. The UNESCO International Clearinghouse on Children and Violence on the Screen at Nordicom.

Chapter 13

Allen J. Scott

HOLLYWOOD AND THE WORLD: THE GEOGRAPHY OF MOTION-PICTURE DISTRIBUTION AND MARKETING[1] (2004)

INTRODUCTION

IN ONE SENSE, HOLLYWOOD IS A VERY specific place in Southern California, and, more to the point, a particular locale-bound nexus of production relationships and local labour market activities. In another sense, Hollywood is everywhere, and in its realization as a disembodied assortment of images and narratives, its presence is felt across the entire globe. These local and global manifestations of Hollywood are linked together by a complex machinery of distribution and marketing. In this manner, Hollywood's existence as a productive agglomeration is sustained, while the images and narratives it creates are dispersed to a far-flung and ever-expanding circle of consumers.

In the present paper, I focus mainly, though not exclusively, on one principal aspect of this problem, namely, first-run distribution of feature films to theatre audiences in the US and the rest of the world. There are, to be sure, other important channels of diffusion for Hollywood films involving broadcast or cable television, VHS (video home system) or DVD (digital videodisc), and more prospectively, the internet. At the same time, the theatrical exhibition of feature films is only one phase in a wider system of releasing windows and commercial exploitation that eventually fans out into extensive product franchises, including books, toys, games, records, clothing, theme park attractions, and so on (Wasko *et al.*, 1993; Wyatt, 1994). These alternative outlets will be alluded to from time to time as we proceed, but will remain largely in the background. Instead, priority will be given to questions of the all-important initial release, marketing, and distribution of films for theatrical exhibition. This emphasis is particularly pertinent given that the success or failure of these activities has significant impacts on the subsequent commercial performance of any film and its spin-off products.

THE US MOTION-PICTURE INDUSTRY: AN OVERVIEW

Majors and independents

At the outset, the US motion-picture industry can be identified in terms of a core group of companies constituting the so-called 'majors', together with a mass of smaller firms or 'independents'. Later, I shall introduce a third distinctive type of corporate entity, represented by subsidiaries owned by the majors.

The majors are Metro-Goldwyn-Mayer Inc, Paramount Pictures, Sony Pictures Entertainment, Twentieth Century Fox, Universal Studios, Walt Disney Co., Warner Brothers, and newcomer Dreamworks SKG, all of them headquartered in Hollywood. With the exception of Dreamworks, the majors are allied together in the Motion Picture Association of America (MPAA), a lobbying organization founded in 1922 that represents their interests worldwide. The majors all function as integrated production and distribution operations embedded within wider systems of corporate conglomeration focused on exploiting the multiple synergies running between the entertainment, media, and associated hardware sectors. Their hallmark product is the blockbuster film, as exemplified by the four top box-office champions ever, namely, *Titanic* (1997, $601 million total gross box-office), *Star Wars* (1977, $461 million), *E.T.* (1982, $431 million), and *Jurassic Park* (1993, $357 million). As I shall argue, the ability of the majors to operate on this particular market register is in large degree a reflection of the internal economies of scale that accrue to their distribution activities. All of the majors possess streamlined distribution infrastructures – rather like the early railroad and telegraph companies described by Chandler (1990) – through which the variable substantive content flows over wide territorial expanses. Until the late 1940s, the majors owned extensive theatre chains in addition to their production and distribution activities, but they were forced to divest themselves of these chains by the 1948 *Paramount* antitrust decree. The exhibition sector is thus largely independent today, though some significant re-integration of production, distribution and exhibition has been occurring since the early 1980s.

Although the majors dominate the motion-picture industry, they do not represent the totality of production and distribution activities. Independents also constitute an important element of the industry as a whole, and of the Hollywood complex in particular. Independents tend to be highly specialized in either production on the one side or distribution on the other, but cases where the two functions are vertically integrated are not uncommon. By and large, the independents deal in relatively small-budget films. Some independent production companies, however, work alongside the majors in various kinds of financing and distribution deals, thus enabling them to tap into the lucrative upper tier of the market. This tier is otherwise largely inaccessible to independents except for the occasional cases of small-budget films that unexpectedly become box-office successes.

Sectoral structures

According to the North American Industry Classification System (NAICS) that came into effect in 1997, the sectors making up the motion-picture industry can be described under four principal headings. These are:

- NAICS 5121101: Motion picture production, except for television.
- NAICS 5121201: Motion picture film exchanges (representing the distribution segment of the industry).

- NAICS 51213: Motion picture and video exhibition.
- NAICS 51219: Post-production and other motion-picture and video industries (representing the main providers of service inputs to production as a whole).

Data on receipts, establishments, and employment for these sectors in the US and Los Angeles County for the year 1997 are set forth in Table 13.1.[2] The data in Table 13.1 indicate clearly that Los Angeles is the dominant centre of the US motion-picture industry at large, except for exhibition, which, as we would expect, is widely diffused across the country. Los Angeles scores highly on total receipts and employment as a percentage of US totals, and all the more so because it is the home base of numerous large firms. However, it scores somewhat less impressively on its percentage of establishments, a circumstance that is due to the existence of many small firms serving miscellaneous audiovisual markets in other parts of the country. All sectors of the motion-picture industry in the US have grown significantly over the last decade or so, not only as a function of expanding domestic demand, but also of continued insistent penetration of foreign markets (Scott, 2002). Today, approximately 50 percent of all revenues earned in the industry come from exports, and since the early 1990s the domestic box-office has on average not even covered the majors' basic production costs.

In addition to its marked geographic agglomeration in Hollywood, the motion-picture industry shows signs of strong corporate concentration, as revealed by Table 13.2. The main production and distribution sectors (NAICS 5121101 and NAICS 5121201) are particularly given to this syndrome, with four-firm concentration ratios of 53.6 percent and 81.9 percent, respectively.[3] The notably high level of concentration in distribution points to this sector as the key organizational bottleneck in the industry as a whole.

FROM PRODUCTION TO DISTRIBUTION AND EXHIBITION

The Hollywood complex

In the aftermath of the *Paramount* decree of 1948 the motion-picture industry of Hollywood entered a long period of crisis and restructuring that was rendered even more intense because it was accompanied by a great expansion of television broadcasting and a consequent massive drain of audiences from motion-picture theatres. This period, which extended over much of the 1960s and 1970s, was marked by a transformation of the so-called old Hollywood, centred on the vertically integrated studio system, to a new Hollywood characterized by much more vertically disintegrated production processes and significant externalization of many of the detailed tasks of film-making (Blackstone and Bowman, 1999; Hozic, 2001; Storper and Christopherson, 1987). The basic motion-picture production complex of Hollywood today can be characterized as a dense constellation of many interdependent firms and workers, functioning together in a project-oriented work environment, along with a variety of institutional arrangements providing different sorts of coordinating services. The whole structure of agglomerated activity generates massive external economies of scale and scope providing a constant flow of competitive advantages to each individual firm (Scott, 2002; Storper and Christopherson, 1987).

More specifically, the kernel of the complex is constituted by shifting networks of specialized but complementary firms engaged in many different phases of film-making, with both the majors (dominantly) and independent production companies (vastly more numerous but with much less commercial leverage) as the central organizing agents. The production process itself is project-oriented in the sense that networks of firms and individuals

Table 13.1 Receipts and employment in the motion-picture industry, US and Los Angeles County, 1997

Sector	Receipts			Establishments			Employment		
	US (M$)	Los Angeles (M$)	LA as percent of US	US	Los Angeles	LA as percent of US	US	Los Angeles	LA as percent of US
NAICS 512110 (motion-picture production, except for television)	10,040	7,478	74.5	4,733	1,249	26.4	49,890	31,828	63.8
NAICS 512120 (Motion-Picture Film Exchanges)	9,211	5,366	58.3	477	165	34.6	7,744	3,488	45.0
NAICS 51213 (motion-picture and video exhibition)	7,597	685	9.0	6,358	364	5.7	125,041	9,752	7.8
NAICS 51219 (post-production and other motion-picture and video industries)	4,528	2,088	46.1	3,378	983	29.1	33,205	13,232	39.8

Source: US Department of Commerce, Bureau of the Census, *Economic Census*, 1997.

Table 13.2 Concentration ratios by largest firms in the US motion-picture industry

Sector	Four largest firms (%)	Eight largest firms (%)
NAICS 5121101 (motion-picture production, except for television)	53.6	60.6
NAICS 5121201 (motion-picture film exchanges)	81.9	91.4
NAICS 51213 (motion-picture and video exhibition)	30.7	51.0
NAICS 51219 (post-production and other motion-picture and video industries)	16.4	21.4

Source: US Department of Commerce, Bureau of the Census, *Economic Census*, 1997.

come together around particular joint tasks, only to fall apart as the tasks are completed, and to re-appear in some other shape as new projects are identified (DeFillippi and Arthur, 1998; Grabher, 2001). This kernel is complemented by an elaborate system of local labour markets in which an enormous diversity of skills and aptitudes is mobilized in the daily round of work. In keeping with the project-oriented structure of production, many of the workers caught up in the industry – even highly skilled and highly remunerated individuals – hold only temporary jobs or freelance engagements, and circulate with some frequency through the entire system. The whole agglomeration is underpinned by a tightly knit institutional fabric, comprising on the one side powerful trade organizations such as the MPAA, the Academy of Motion Picture Arts and Sciences (which organizes the annual Academy Awards), the Alliance of Motion Picture and Television Producers, the American Film Marketing Association (AFMA), and on the other side representatives of both professional and craft labour such as the Director's Guild, the Producers' Guild, the Screen Actors' Guild, the Writers' Guild, and the numerous specialized locals of IATSE (the International Alliance of Theatrical Stage Employees). Within the vortex of activity represented by the agglomeration as a whole, many-sided human interactions and exchanges of information occur at frequent intervals, and these forms of contact typically represent important sites of creativity and innovation (Scott, 2000).

These diverse elements of the Hollywood complex all contribute to its strong centripetal or agglomerative locational pull. They hold it together in geographic space as a dense and growing production machine based on endogenously created competitive advantages. Even if there is a growing trend to the actual shooting of Hollywood films at other locations (Monitor, 1999), the status of Hollywood as a pre-eminent focus of pre-and post-production work in the motion-picture industry remains for the present undiminished.

The organization and geography of motion-picture distribution

Just as the production system is organized around majors and independents, so distribution is similarly bifurcated. The majors focus on worldwide distribution of large-budget films, either through their own facilities, or in various kinds of agreements with distributors in other countries. Independent companies more typically take on responsibility for distribution over comparatively limited market territories, so that any one film may be distributed by a large number of different firms, both inside and outside the US. This type of arrangement means that production companies regularly face high transactions costs in working out distribution deals, but it also enables them to tap into multiple sources of finance. Independent distributors often take equity positions in the films they handle (Rosen and Hamilton, 1987).

The majors' stock in trade is the high-budget blockbuster film that calls not only for an elaborate production capacity, but equally for an extensive distributional infrastructure. In the case of the majors, these two sides of the business are always vertically integrated with one another. Nowadays, the majors' domestic distributional infrastructure is focussed on saturation theatrical openings across the country, and maximization of the box-office returns from the first weekend of exhibition. This strategy differs sharply from earlier distribution procedures geared to a staggered system of openings moving progressively from flagship theatres down the hierarchy of exhibition venues, and depending on word of mouth for publicity. The current strategy is especially well suited to the peculiarities of contemporary film markets where initial exhibition is the first stage in a chain of market windows for any given film, with strong effects on the film's subsequent performance throughout the chain (Litman and Ahn, 1998). There is some probability, too, that saturation openings will become more common in international markets in the not-too-distant future, not only as a commercial goal in its own right, but also as a way of pre-empting film piracy. With the shift-over in film formats from analog to digital, worldwide saturation openings will be increasingly feasible.

As we observed earlier in the discussion of Table 13.2, there is a marked degree of business concentration in the motion-picture distribution sector. However, this concentration is not so much an outcome of the physical effort needed to distribute films, for actually moving reels of film from point a to point b is a comparatively easy task. Concentration in the distribution side of the business is rather a function of the need to maintain continuous and extensive contact with large numbers of different theatre chains, and to coordinate placement of any one film in theatres across the country and the world according to a tight schedule of release dates. Levels of concentration are further boosted by the need to back up distribution, as such, with massive marketing campaigns, and, above all, to generate sufficient publicity nationally and locally for each film so that the opening weekend brings in significant threshold box-office returns. In order to secure these objectives, the majors all maintain branch offices in critical regional markets, thereby facilitating close and steady contact with theatre operators. Figure 13.1 displays the location of these branch offices in the US and Canada. All of them coincide with metropolitan areas in states or provinces where large numbers of theatre screens are to be found.

On the basis of information gathered in face-to-face interviews with representatives of distribution companies, we can characterize the interactions between these branch offices and the theatre chains with which they deal as a form of relational contracting. This signifies that both parties to any given transaction have long-term relations built on strong personal familiarity, in contradistinction to purely arms'-length dealings.[4]

Relational contracting between distributors and exhibitors is no doubt partially a substitute for vertical integration, for it permits collaborative programming of their interdependent activities over some fairly extended time horizon, without overt contravention of antitrust regulations. Even so, since the early 1980s, when the Justice Department under the Reagan administration adopted a more tolerant interpretation of the *Paramount* decision, some vertical re-integration between distribution and exhibition has been occurring (Blackstone and Bowman, 1999). The most visible case of this phenomenon involves the Sony Corporation which owns Loew's Cineplex, one of the largest theatre chains in the US, with 264 sites and 2,323 screens. The same search for vertical synergy is apparent in the majors' continuing quest for ownership (both directly and through their corporate umbrellas) of broadcast and cable television networks, as exemplified by Warner's direct

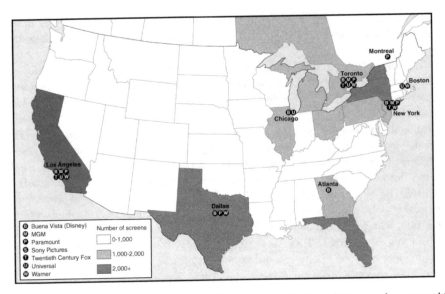

Figure 13.1 Offices of major Hollywood distribution companies in relation to the geographic incidence of theatre screens in the US and Canada.

interest in the Home Box Office Cable Network. Also, as home-video markets have soared upward over the 1990s, the majors have established specialized divisions to distribute films in both VHS and DVD formats.

Independent film distributors are mostly small in size and subject to especially erratic market swings. The largest independent distributor in the country currently is USA Films, which released 15 films in the year 2000 and earned just 1 percent of gross box-office receipts nationwide. Artisan Entertainment, Lion's Gate Films, Shooting Gallery, and Winstar Cinema, are a few of the many other independent distributors operating in the country today. According to data on motion-picture credits published by AMPAS (2001), some of the larger independent distributors in the US may deal with a dozen to a score of films a year, but the vast majority of independents handle no more than two or three. Independent distribution companies focus on films made by their own production arms or other independent producers, both American and foreign; they rarely or never deal with films produced by the majors. In a questionnaire survey of independent film production companies, carried out in Los Angeles over the summer of 2001, it was found that 27.7 percent of those respondents who had made a feature film in the previous year relied on the majors to get their films to market, while fully 72.3 percent relied on independent distributors.[5] It was evident, moreover, from the completed questionnaires that many respondents were making an unduly broad interpretation of the meaning of the term 'major' in this context. Film festivals are nowadays important venues in which independent producers and distributors come together to make deals with one another. On occasions, independent production companies will seek to distribute their own films, especially where these are directed to highly specialized audiences and the production company has an informed sense of the nature of the market, as in the case, say, of films that appeal to gays or certain ethnic groups. An increasing practice among independent producers is to make direct-to-video films and to dispense with theatrical exhibition altogether (Vogel, 1998).

Domestic motion-picture markets

As Table 13.3 indicates, gross domestic box office returns in the US motion-picture industry as a whole grew from $5,745 million in 1980 to $7,661 million in 2000 (in constant dollar terms). By far the greater share of these returns is accounted for by films released by the majors. In Table 13.4, aggregate box-office returns are broken down to show the portion earned by each of the major distributors at five-year intervals from 1980 to 2000. Buena Vista (the distribution arm of Disney) has tended to dominate the market over the last decade, but never by more than one or two percentage points. In fact, the data presented in Table 13.4 conform to a pattern of revolving leadership in which no one major remains at the head of the league for very long. MGM has clearly been a laggard over the last two decades, and this circumstance reflects its turbulent recent history of reorganizations and corporate takeovers. As it happens, the theatrical box-office is no longer the main source of the majors' revenues, although exhibition remains the key initial market window for any film as it moves through subsequent windows in video, television, in-flight entertainment, and so on. According to data published by Veronis Suhler (2001), home-video sales and rentals in the US (both VHS and DVD) amounted to $22,453 million in 2000, some three times larger than the total gross domestic box-office for that same year.

The historical pattern of annual releases of films in the US is presented in Figure 13.2. The figure shows the number of films released by the majors since 1945, and by independents since 1980. Over the crisis years, stretching from the 1950s to the 1970s, releases by the majors declined continually if erratically. These were years in which the majors were struggling to cope with rapidly shifting organizational and market trends, and to work out a viable new aesthetics and economics of popular cinema, leading eventually to the successful development of the high-concept blockbuster film as the industry's staple product. The data presented in Table 13.5 reveal a dramatic surge in the costs of producing and marketing films released by the majors between 1980 and 2000. In constant dollar terms these costs rose approximately threefold over this two-decade period. Marketing costs have on average run at just below half of production costs (negative costs), though in the case of specific highly promoted films the former can sometimes exceed the latter by a wide margin.

Figure 13.2 also demonstrates that the 1980s witnessed dramatic growth in the number of films released by independent distributors, a growth that occurred in response to the rise of diverse niche markets and the great expansion of ancillary markets in video and deregulated television broadcasting (Prince, 2000). This was a period in which the so-called minimajors (such as Cannon, Carolco, Miramax, Orion, or New Line) rose to prominence by capitalizing on these developments, though a number of the same firms have since vanished.

Table 13.3 Gross domestic box office, 1980–2000[a]

Year	Current M$	Constant M$	Majors' share
1980	2,749	5,745	91%
1985	3,749	6,000	77%
1990	5,022	6,617	80%
1995	5,494	6,208	86%
2000	7,661	7,661	83%

a Domestic box office includes receipts for both the USA and Canada.

Sources: Motion-Picture Association of America (http://www.mpaa.org/) and National Association of Theatre Owners, *Encyclopedia of Exhibition, 2001–2002.*

Table 13.4 Domestic theatrical film distribution, market shares of Hollywood majors, 1980–2000

Year	Market share (%)							
	Buena Vista/Disney	Columbia/Sony	Dreamworks	MGM	Paramount	20th C Fox	Universal	Warner
1980	4	14	–	7	16	16	20	14
1985	3	10	–	9	10	11	16	18
1990	16	5	–	3	15	14	14	13
1995	19	13	–	6	10	8	13	17
2000	15	9	10	1	11	10	15	12

Source: National Association of Theatre Owners, *Encyclopedia of Exhibition, 2001–2002.*

Table 13.5 Average negative and marketing costs, Hollywood majors, 1980–2000

Year	Millions of current dollars		Millions of constant dollars		Marketing costs as % of negative costs
	Negative cost[a]	Marketing costs[b]	Negative cost[a]	Marketing costs[b]	
1980	9.4	4.3	19.6	9.0	45.7
1985	16.8	6.5	26.9	10.4	38.7
1990	26.8	12.0	35.3	15.8	44.8
1995	36.4	17.7	41.1	20.0	48.6
2000	54.8	27.3	54.8	27.3	49.8

a Production costs, studio overhead and capitalized interest.
b Prints and advertising.
Source: Motion-Picture Association of America (http://www.mpaa.org/).

At this time, too, the majors began significantly to acquire or to create smaller affiliated production and distribution companies in order to exploit and shape some of the same market niches. The rising quantity and diversity of films on offer is reflected in the fact that whereas the number of theatre sites in the US has declined significantly over the last two decades, multiplex theatres (distinguished by their flexible arrangements for accommodating films with widely variable audience appeal) have increased greatly in number, with a concomitant expansion of the total number of screens available for exhibiting films. In 1980, according to NATO (2002), there were 17,675 screens in the country as a whole; in 1990 there were 23,814; and in 2000, there were 36,264 (at 6,979 sites, thus giving an average of 5.2 screens per theatre).

MARKET STRUCTURES AND THE DYNAMICS OF FILM RELEASING

Economic systems are shaped by both the production strategies of firms and the demand patterns of consumers. Out of this tense force-field of relations there emerges an

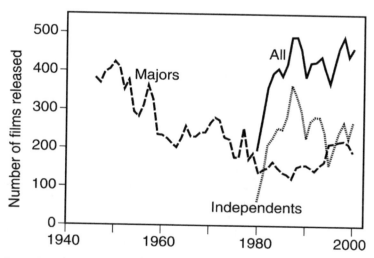

Figure 13.2 Number of new feature films released annually in the U.S. since 1945.

architecture of the market, which, in the motion-picture industry, is expressed in a particularly revealing manner by shifting structures of releasing activity over time, space, and delivery format.

Some determinants of releasing behaviour

The majors release films produced in-house as well as films produced with varying degrees of participation by independents (where for present purposes, independents include the majors' own subsidiaries). A first question, then, revolves around the changing origins of the films that flow through the majors' distribution systems. A data series pertinent to this question was constructed for the period 1980–2000 from listings of individual film credits given in the *Annual Index to Motion Picture Credits* published by the Academy of Motion Picture Arts and Sciences. The *Annual Index* provides information on the production and distribution companies involved in all films released in Los Angeles every year. From this information we can identify which films released by any major are produced with independent participation and which are not. Unfortunately, our source of information does not provide us with any clues about the precise nature of this participation in any given instance. In some cases, the major distributing the film exerts dominant control over the decisions of the independent producer(s). In other cases, the control is nominal. In yet other cases, as represented by so-called negative pickups, the distributor does not even know about the film until after it is completed. Despite the ambiguities involved, the outcome of this exercise appears to be fairly robust, and a strong (inverse) statistical association is observable in the two different types of films distributed by majors. The details are as follows.

Let y_t be the number of films made with independent participation and distributed in year t by any given major; let x_t be the corresponding number of films made in-house and distributed by the same major. These variables are de-trended by taking first differences ($\Delta y_t = y_t - y_{t-1}$, $\Delta x_t = x_t - x_{t-1}$), and simple linear regressions of the relationship between them are computed, for all majors individually and collectively, as laid out in Table 13.6. There is a marked negative relationship between the two variables across all regression equations. This suggests that the majors consistently substitute between films of type y and x in their distribution systems, so that when they distribute more of the latter, they distribute less of the former, and vice versa. The same finding implies that the majors are concerned to even out the flow of films through their distribution systems and to ensure that these systems

Table 13.6 Regression equations showing the relations between Δy_t and Δx_t, 1980–2000 (see text for definitions of variables)

Distributor	Constant value	Regression coefficient	Adjusted R^2
Columbia/Sony	0.24	−0.8741**	0.52
Disney/Buena Vista	0.56	−0.2448	−0.02
MGM	−0.12	−0.5250	0.09
Paramount	−0.18	−1.4172**	0.52
Twentieth-Century Fox	−0.09	−0.7292**	0.51
Universal	−0.07	−0.9216**	0.36
Warner	−0.07	−0.7481**	0.33
All majors	0.58	−0.8813**	0.50

** The double asterisk indicates significance level of 0.01 or better.

operate as close to optimal capacity as possible over time.[6] The regressions presented in Table 13.6 also point to important differences in production-*cum*-releasing strategies between the majors. Paramount is characterized by a much greater tendency to substitute between the two types of films than any other major, suggesting that it has developed a relatively flexible production–distribution strategy. In the case of Disney and its distribution arm, Buena Vista, the relation between the two sets of changes is unusually small and statistically insignificant, a circumstance that reveals Disney's much greater reliance on its own internal resources than the other majors.

A second and related question concerns temporal patterns of releasing in relation to general market conditions. Here, in addition to majors and independents, a third group of distribution companies is explicitly introduced, namely, subsidiaries of majors. The variables of interest in the present phase of the analysis are defined below:

I_t: Number of films released by independent distributors in year t.
S_t: Number of films released by majors' subsidiaries in year t.
M_t: Number of films released by major distributors in year t.
A_t: money spent on admissions to films in year t (in constant dollars).
i_t: the interest rate (federal funds, effective rate) in year t.

A series of regression equations was then computed linking the number of films distributed by these groups of companies to money spent on admissions and interest rates for each year from 1980 to 2000 (see Table 13.7). Notice that A_t enters these regressions with a time lag of one year. The signs on the coefficients of the independent variables in the regressions are all as expected. Thus, the number of films released by each of the three groups of distributors, and by all three in aggregate, is positively related to money spent at the box-office in the previous year, and negatively related to interest rates in the current year. Independent distributors are particularly sensitive to the former variable, possibly in part because they ride on the coattails of majors' successes. Releases by the subsidiaries of majors do not appear to be significantly related to either of the independent variables. The majors themselves (excluding their subsidiaries) are highly sensitive to interest rates in their releasing behaviour, a reflection, presumably, of their tendency also to cut back on production when rates are high. When we re-run the regression analysis using $I_t + S_t + M_t$ as the dependent

Table 13.7 Regression equations showing the effects of box-office returns and interest rates on temporal variations in films released by independents, majors' subsidiaries, and majors, 1980–2000 (see text for definitions of variables)

Dependent variable	Regression coefficients			
	Constant value	A_{t-1}	i_t	Adjusted R^2
I_t	−168.05	0.0577**	−2.1198	0.49
S_t	−52.16	0.0188	−3.7797	0.23
M_t	125.58	0.0010	−3.0057**	0.40
$I_t + S_t + M_t$	−94.66	0.0775**	−8.9052**	0.74

** The double asterisk indicates significance level of 0.01 or better.

Regressions based on data derived from the Academy of Motion Picture Arts and Sciences, *Annual Index to Motion Picture Credits*, and from the US Department of Commerce, Bureau of the Census, *Statistical Abstract of the United States*.

variable, both A_{t-1} and i_t emerge as having extremely significant effects, with an adjusted R^2 of 0.74. The regression coefficients in the latter model suggest, as we might anticipate, that the composite pattern of releasing is rather more volatile than it is in the case of independents, subsidiaries, or majors taken in isolation from one another.

A tripartite model?

Reference has frequently been made in all of the above to an essentially bipartite pattern of production–consumption relations in the motion-picture industry, revolving around the split between majors and independents. Only an occasional acknowledgment of a possibly distinctive role for the majors' subsidiaries has thus far been offered. In fact, since the early 1980s, and especially since the early 1990s, there has been a marked tendency for this group of companies to emerge as a peculiar domain of activity in its own right.

Today, every major has a larger or smaller stable of these subsidiaries, most of which act as quasi-independent production and distribution entities and possess a high degree of autonomy in their corporate decision-making. In this regard, the majors are coming increasingly to resemble the music majors that pioneered this form of corporate strategy (Negus, 1998; Scott, 1999). These subsidiaries function within a range of intermediate markets lying between those in which the majors proper operate and those in which the independents are typically ensconced. They also represent a sort of advance guard for the majors by reason of their more experimental approaches to the motion-picture business and their consequent ability to capture and shape emerging talent and trends. Among the more important subsidiaries with a substantial stake in distribution activity at the present time are Disney's Miramax, Sony Classics, Warner's New Line, MGM's Orion Pictures, Twentieth-Century's Fox Searchlight, Universal Focus and Paramount Classics.

Figure 13.3 provides some empirical details as to how the conjectured tripartite structure of US motion-picture production and markets is arranged. The figure shows frequency distributions of percentage box-office returns for films distributed by (a) independents, (b) majors' subsidiaries, and (c) majors (less subsidiaries). These percentage figures sum to 100 within each of the three types of distribution system. The x-axis of Figure 13.3 is drawn on a logarithmic scale in order to facilitate visual comparison of all the information available. What is immediately striking about the figure is the clear separation of each frequency distribution into lower, middle, and upper market segments. These three segments are sharply divided from one another in terms of the average box-office returns attributable to each. As Table 13.8 reveals, the average box office for independents was $3.8 million in the year 2000, for subsidiaries it was $14.3 million, and for majors $55.6 million.[7] A t-test indicates that these values are all different from one another at extremely high levels of statistical confidence. In the same year, the average number of films distributed by each type of firm was 2.0, 8.6, and 14.3, respectively, though there is much variance around these values. From these data it is apparent that the majors' subsidiaries (together with a few selected independents) are carving out a very definite middle-range market niche for themselves. Concomitantly, whenever any independent begins consistently to contest this same niche, it becomes a prime target for takeover by a major, as illustrated by Disney's purchase of Miramax in 1993 or Warner's acquisition of New Line by merger with Turner Broadcasting in 1995. Scrutiny of Figure 13.3 suggests that there is a fair degree of competition *within* each of the three niches, and more limited competition *between* them, but that the majors have a tight oligopolistic hold over the upper reaches of the market, strengthened by the strategic positioning of their subsidiaries in a sort of intermediate buffer zone. Data limitations mean that we cannot push this same analysis very far back in time. However, since

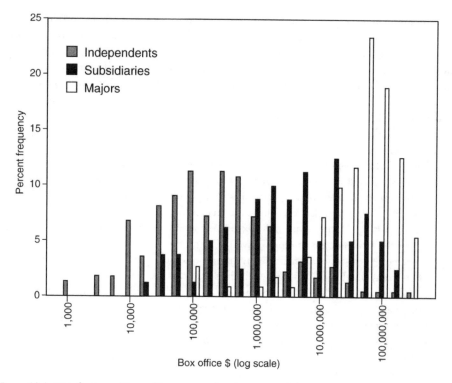

Figure 13.3 Distribution of box-office returns for domestic exhibition, 2000; releasing companies categorized by independents, subsidiaries of majors, and majors.

1991, the data show a strongly bifurcated market gradually giving way before trifurcation as the majors' subsidiaries expand in number and enlarge their lists of releases.

These remarks may be extended with the aid of a speculative model of hierarchical market relations in the motion-picture industry. The model is based on two key assumptions. The first is that we can identify different types of films in terms of the different market segments to which they appeal (e.g. low-budget films for limited audiences, middle-range films for wider but still selective audiences, blockbusters with sweeping popular appeal, and so on). Wyatt (1991) argues, for example, that high-concept blockbusters are a distinctive product deeply differentiated from other motion-picture products by their particular substance and packaging. The second assumption is that the expected gross box-office returns for a film of any given type bear a statistical relationship to the amount of money invested in the production and marketing of that film. Of course, other factors play a role in generating

Table 13.8 Breakdown of average box-office returns by types of releasing companies, 2000

Types of releasing companies	Number of films released	Average box-office ($000)	Percent of total box-office
Independents	221	3,752	10.2
Subsidiaries of majors	80	14,264	14.0
Majors	111	55,639	75.8

Source: Calculated from data in National Association of Theatre Owners, *Encyclopedia of Exhibition, 2001–2002.*

expected returns, such as the cast, the director, press reviews, and so on, but production and marketing budgets represent a primary element on which many other of these other factors themselves depend (cf. Daly, 1980; de Vany and Walls, 1997; Litman and Ahn, 1998; Robins, 1993). In this context, we need to note that the commercial performance of any single film is extremely unpredictable. An industry rule of thumb is that 7 or 8 out of every 10 films show a net loss, so that overall profitability in the industry is dependent on the other two or three films out of the 10 that actually earn money above and beyond their costs. It should be emphasized therefore that expected returns are represented here by expected *average* returns.

For the sake of simplicity, let us consider the case where just two market segments exist, one dominated by films with dense production values (and appealing to mass audiences), the other characterized by a proliferation of films with more meagre production values (and catering to relatively limited demands per film). For each type of market segment, i {i = 1, 2}, the expected box office for any given film will be an increasing function of the total amount of money invested in producing and marketing the same film. More specifically, the function can be identified as a logistic curve. This proposition follows from the strong likelihood that we will almost always observe low returns per dollar invested at low and high levels of investment (due to under- and over-investment, respectively, in production values), and relatively high returns at some intermediate point. The curve for any given segment is expected to be distinct from the curve for any other segment. Define C_i as the total production cost of a film serving market-segment i, and let its distribution and marketing cost be a simple proportion, α_i, of the same amount. Total investment in the film is thus $I_i = (1 + \alpha_i)C_i$ and its expected box-office earnings are $EBO_i = fi(\alpha_i, C_i)$. The problem that the producer–distributor must now face is to identify what particular market segment any planned film should be assigned to and then to find values of α_i and C_i that maximize $EBO_i - I_i$. A typical solution for this problem is shown in Figure 13.4, where for a film of type 1, a production cost of C^*_1 yields a profit-maximizing value of EBO^*_1, and for a film of type 2, a production cost of C^*_2 yields an optimal value of EBO^*_2. The lower panel of Figure 4 displays hypothetical frequency distributions of the occurrence of type 1 and type 2 films.

Depending on the dynamics of market supply and demand, various empirical expressions of this kind of logic are possible, ranging from a single, continuous frequency distribution of films relative to production costs, to a completely segmented pattern of frequencies. A tendency to the one extreme would be apt to occur if films could not be significantly differentiated from one another in terms of appropriate investment levels, i.e. where audience response is statistically unpredictable on the basis of production costs. A tendency to the other extreme would be more likely to occur where at least the top end of the market can be cornered by a select group of firms with strong internal economies of scale and the ability to mobilize significant resources. In this case, barriers to the entry of new competitors will be established, and these barriers will be accentuated as firms then hone their long-term competitive advantages in relation to that market segment. The market-cornering process, moreover, is reinforced in the motion-picture industry by the proclivity of the majors continually to raise the stakes as they gamble on ever more ambitious blockbuster films, thus making the entry of new competitors increasingly difficult. The remainder of the market may then converge around a single competitive norm at a lower average cost or price, or yet further cornering or quasi-cornering of selected segments may occur until the possibility of further partitioning is exhausted. Obviously, the number of different market segments that appear may vary from time, though it is likely to be small given finite markets, and equally, frequent overlap between the segments will tend to occur, as exemplified by cross-over films that start off in one segment and end up in another.

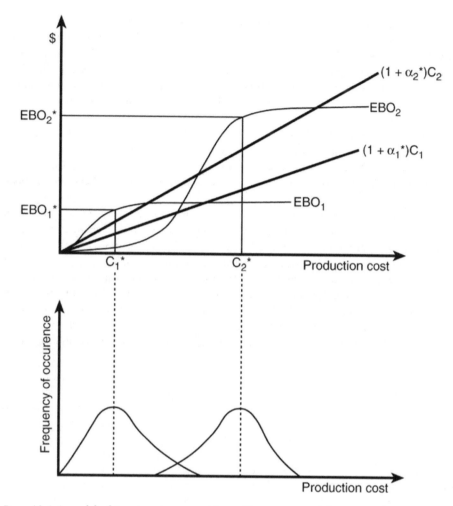

Figure 13.4 A model of investment, expected box-office returns, and frequency of occurrence for films of types 1 and 2.

This analysis proposes a mechanism whereby stable, differentiated market segments in the motion-picture industry might emerge, at least for a certain period of time. The model mirrors the earlier descriptive discussion of the layered structure of markets in the motion-picture industry. However, it represents only a first attempt at an explanatory schema, and plainly, considerable further refinement combined with rigorous empirical testing are essential before it can be taken to be anything much more than a speculative gesture.

TRADE AND GLOBALIZATION

Export markets

Right from the beginnings of Hollywood a century ago, American motion pictures have found ready markets in other countries. Since World War II, this export flow has expanded dramatically, and today the presence of Hollywood is felt virtually around the world (Hoskins *et al.*, 1997; Miller *et al.*, 2001; Wildman and Siwek, 1988).

Data on US film and tape rental exports to other countries between the years 1986 and 2001 are laid out in Table 13.9. The data refer to videotape rentals as well as motion-picture distribution overseas and they cover all US exports in these services. These rentals have grown with notable vigour over the last 15 years or so, and they now exceed the domestic box-office by a considerable margin. Whereas the gross domestic box office for motion pictures increased (in constant dollar terms) by 40.9 percent from $5,970 in 1986 to $8,413 million in 2001, exports of film and tape rentals over the same period increased by 452.8.0 percent from $1,683 million to $9,304 million. Table 13.9 informs us that by far the main importers of the products of Hollywood are the European countries. The UK, Germany, and the Netherlands alone account for 36.7 percent of all rental exports from the US. Japan and Canada, too, are major importers, as are Australia, Brazil and the Republic of Korea.

The majors maintain extensive distribution and marketing networks not only in North America, but also in other countries. Through their multinational operations the majors directly control distribution systems in all their principal foreign markets, as well as in many more secondary markets. United International Pictures, for example, is a joint venture of Universal and Paramount, which owns distribution facilities in as many as 37 different countries including the UK, France, Germany, the Netherlands, Australia and Japan, as well as in less lucrative territories like Hungary, Chile, Peru, the Philippines, and Thailand. Twentieth-Century Fox owns 21 foreign distribution facilities in an equally diverse set of countries. In countries where the majors do not actually own a distribution network

Table 13.9 US exports in the form of film and tape rentals; percentage values by destination

Destination	1986	1991	1996	2001
France	10.2	8.6	8.6	6.7
Germany	7.5	9.6	10.5	12.4
Italy	10.0	7.3	4.7	4.9
Netherlands	15.2	17.5	17.4	9.0
Spain	–	5.1	5.9	6.2
Sweden	–	1.8	1.4	1.2
UK	10.6	11.0	9.8	15.3
Europe	60.3	66.5	64.9	62.8
Australia	10.3	3.4	4.8	3.6
Japan	8.3	11.5	8.7	8.9
Republic of Korea	–	0.8	1.8	1.2
Taiwan	–	0.5	0.7	1.0
Asia and Pacific	22.1	18.3	19.3	17.1
Brazil	–	0.8	2.2	2.5
Canada	10.4	8.7	6.8	8.0
Mexico	1.3	0.9	1.3	2.6
Americas	17.9	12.5	13.0	16.9
South Africa	–	–	1.1	1.0
Africa	–	1.0	1.2	1.0
Middle East	–	0.5	0.8	1.1
World ($ millions, current)	1,071	1,962	4,982	9,304
World ($ millions, constant)	1,628	2,400	5,290	9,304

Source: US Bureau of Economic Analysis, *Survey of Current Business*.

totally

outright they often enter into joint ventures or long-term agreements with local companies in order to ensure distribution of their films. As indicated by Table 13.10, American films garner never less than half, and sometimes more than two-thirds of total box-office receipts in all their major markets. This phenomenon can be ascribed both to the unequalled ability of American multinational media corporations to disseminate the products of Hollywood across the globe, and their ability to make big-budget films that appeal powerfully to popular taste in many different cultures. In testimony to the latter remark, films that do well at the box office in the US invariably also do well abroad. Thus, the simple correlation between gross domestic box-office earnings and foreign box-office of 121 Hollywood films released in the year 2000 is 0.81, which is significant well beyond the 0.01 level.[8]

Strategic trade in Hollywood films

Strategic trade involves governmental support for export activities in circumstances where national interests are in some sense at stake (cf. Tyson, 1992). It comprises institutionalized market-opening practices whether for reasons of political influence or economic leverage (as in circumstances where extension of the market generates rents based on increasing returns effects within domestic production complexes).

Exports of motion-pictures from the US have long been a classic instance of this phenomenon, with federal bureaucracies continually pressing in various forums of trade negotiation for foreign governments to open their doors more widely to Hollywood films. Indeed, Hollywood has always received abundant help from the US State Department, the Commerce Department, and other agencies of federal government. At least since World War II, the interests of Hollywood and the aims of Washington have consistently coincided on the economic front even when there has been less accordance on the ideological front (Segrave, 1997). One particularly notable case of this convergence of interests occurred at the time of the Marshall Plan for Europe (1948–51) whose provisions linked levels of aid directly to recipients' willingness to accept imports of US motion pictures (Guback, 1969). These provisions were at once a boon to Hollywood, and, in theory at least, a means of ensuring that European minds would be appropriately fortified against pernicious left-wing political influences. More recently, as globalization has started to intensify, the US government has been aggressively promoting free-trade in goods and services (and

Table 13.10 Structure of selected national film markets, 2000

Country	Number of films produced	Total theatre entries (millions)	Total receipts ($ millions)	Domestic film industry share (percent)	US film industry share (percent)
Australia	31	82.2	401.0	8.0	87.5
France	204	165.5	821.3	28.9	58.3
Germany	75	152.5	463.5	9.4	81.9
Italy	103	103.4	258.1	17.5	69.5
Japan	282	135.4	1585.3	31.8	64.8
Spain	98	135.3	297.1	10.1	82.7
UK	90	142.5	941.2	19.6	75.3
US	460	1420.1	7661.0	96.1	—

Source: CNC Info, No. 283, 2002, Paris: Centre National de la Cinématographie.

cultural-products in particular) across the world, leading predictably to significant direct and indirect gains for Hollywood.

In the never-ending effort to ensure that the interests of Hollywood are promoted by the federal government in various forums of national and international deliberation, the MPAA plays a critical role as both industry mouthpiece and lobbying organization. Symptomatically, the Association has offices in Washington, DC, as well as in Southern California. The MPAA preaches an aggressive doctrine of free-trade, and it played a notably active role behind the scenes at the GATT negotiations in 1993 in the confrontation between the US and Europe (led by France) over trade in audiovisual products. Although the European position prevailed at that time by asserting a 'cultural exception' permitting each country to set up trade restriction according to its own cultural preferences, there is every likelihood, in the newly constituted WTO that succeeded GATT, that the US/MPAA position will eventually prevail. The MPAA is also the parent organization of the MPA (Motion Picture Association), formerly known as the MPEA (Motion Picture Export Association), established in 1946 as a legal cartel under the provisions of the Webb-Pomerane Export Trade Act.[9] Outside the US, the MPA has offices in Brussels, Rome, New Delhi, Rio de Janeiro, Singapore, Mexico City, Toronto, and Jakarta, and from these bases it carries out its basic mission of promoting exports of Hollywood motion pictures, protecting intellectual property rights, and advancing the goals of the industry generally in foreign markets.

Independent motion-picture distributors are represented by AFMA (the American Film Marketing Association), an active and influential organization founded 1981. AFMA's membership roster of over 170 firms is composed primarily of independent distributors and allied businesses based in Hollywood, but a large proportion is made up too of firms from other parts of the country and from abroad. Like the MPAA, AFMA is concerned to promote the interests of its members in regard to trade and public relations, with a special emphasis on issues of arbitration, piracy, marketing and tracking members' earnings from foreign sources. AFMA also promotes the American Film market, an annual event in Santa Monica representing the largest motion-picture trade event in the world, attracting over 7,000 people from over 70 different countries.

Globalization and the cultural economy

The steady globalization of Hollywood as an expression of both market forces and US government action on the international trade front, has, of course, engendered numerous clashes and disputes. Some of these reflect purely commercial differences of interest; some are focussed on cultural collisions of one sort or another; and some, perhaps the majority, are a complex mixture of the two. The official line of the MPAA and the US Department of Commerce is that international trade in cultural products should proceed in as open and as free a manner as possible, and should not be subject to any special restrictions. This line, however, overlooks the circumstance that unlike wheat or coal, cultural products are also intimately bound up with matters of selfhood, identity and consciousness. More generally, each individual's consumption of cultural products is replete with externalities for all other individuals in the same society. Politicized responses to the flow of cultural products from one society to another are therefore to be expected and need to be dealt with on their own terms. A rhetoric of market ideology inevitably misses the crucial point here. It might be plausibly argued that even within the US itself direct governmental engagement with the content of motion pictures has been averted only because of the formal and informal self-regulation of the industry, dating from the time of the promulgation of the Hays Code in 1930. In fact, governmental scrutiny of the motion-picture industry in the US has been frequent and usually intense, in episodes ranging from the House UnAmerican Activities Committee hearings in the late 1940s and early 1950s to recent congressional inquiries into the role of violence in films and television programs.

Given the appeal of Hollywood's entertainment products to mass audiences all over the world, the US will probably continue to maintain a strong lead as an exporter of motion pictures for the foreseeable future. There is evidence, however, that some important shifts may be in the offing. For one thing there has been a very significant rise in runaway production activities from Hollywood to cheaper locations in Canada, Mexico, and further afield. Hitherto, this phenomenon has not posed very much of a threat to the basic role of Hollywood as a centre of creativity and deal-making in the motion-picture industry, though there are signs that the outflow of capital and work may be helping to stimulate the rise of competitor film industries (for example in Toronto and Vancouver). At the same time, and independently of runaway activities from Hollywood, dynamic centres of audiovisual production in many different countries are now also beginning to contest and recontest global markets. Producers in places like London, Paris, Rome, Beijing, Hong Kong, Tokyo, Mexico City, Mumbai/Bollywood, Sydney, and so on, are all in various ways making efforts to improve their market performance and to compete internationally. Similarly, American media conglomerates are no longer the unchallenged champions of cultural globalization that they once were. With the rise of large multinational media corporations based in Europe and Japan, the global cultural landscape is becoming considerably more complex, and competitive pressures are mounting steadily. Some of these corporations are also acquiring significant stakes in American film, television, music, publishing and other cultural-products industries. For the moment, the Hollywood motion-picture industry remains unmatched in its commercial vigour and market reach. If the history of other formerly triumphant industrial agglomerations – from Manchester to Detroit – is any guide, however, the continued leadership of Hollywood is by no means automatically assured. In spite of Hollywood's acquired competitive advantages, it cannot be ultimately free from economic threats emanating from elsewhere, especially in view of the often unpredictable shifts in the structure of consumer preferences for motion-picture entertainment.

A FORWARD GLANCE

For almost a century, and especially since World War II, Hollywood has dominated national and international motion-picture markets. It has accomplished this record of success partly on the basis of the well-lubricated, large-scale production machine of Hollywood itself (with its unparalleled ability to cater to popular audiences), and partly on the basis of the industry's early perfection of its capacity to distribute films to mass markets across the nation and across the world.

With the advent of new electronic distribution technologies, Hollywood is again facing a major paradigm shift that may well have important impacts on the way it and its competitors do business in the future. These technologies will in all likelihood make it eventually possible to dispatch films directly and cheaply to the individual consumer. In this respect, we may perhaps derive some clues about the future of film markets from events in the television industry where deregulation and technological change have allowed programmes and distribution channels to proliferate over the last couple of decades (Brown, 1996; Staiger, 2000). On the one hand, then, consumers' choices will almost certainly continue to be shaped in significant ways by a limited number of firms with the resources to mount extravagant marketing campaigns, so that even if the audiences for blockbuster films stabilize or shrink (just as ratings for top television shows have tended to decline over the 1980s and 1990s) the phenomenon of high-revenue films at the top end of the market is likely to continue. On the other hand, the development of new delivery systems will in principle open up the market to more effective contestation by smaller independent film production and distribution companies (cf. Leyshon, 2001). Thus, the eventual attainment of film distribution by means of the internet will no doubt give rise to a great increase in the amount of cinematic material available to consumers, thereby widening the market and almost certainly making inroads on blockbuster audiences. Additionally, there are credible arguments for suggesting that foreign film industries might be re-entering the competitive foray, not only on the basis of revivified local production clusters, but also of enhanced distributional and marketing capacities aided by the rise of home-grown media conglomerates. Hollywood can never rest on its laurels.

Notes

1   [. . .]
2   These data are taken from the 1997 *Economic Census*. Unfortunately, data for the 2002 *Economic Census* are not yet available.
3   The n-firm concentration ratio in any given sector is the percentage of total receipts earned by the top n firms in that sector.
4   The complicated accounting relations that typically exist between motion-picture distributors and exhibitors are described in Cones (1997).
5   A total of 122 firms responded to the questionnaire. Of these, 55 had made a feature film in the previous year.
6   These remarks offer a somewhat more nuanced view of the relations between large and small firms than the one identified by Berger and Piore (1980) in terms of 'industrial duality'. In Berger and Piore's concept, large and small firms are functionally distinctive entities occupying distinctive market niches, the former serving a residuum of stable demands, the latter being relegated to a more unstable market spectrum. In the present instance, there is a zone of overlap in which large firms appear to use smaller firms as a means of ensuring synchronic stability of product flow.
7   Observe that the ratio of 14.3 to 3.8 is almost identical to the ratio of 55.6 to 14.3.
8   Data for this exercise were obtained from <http://www.worldwideboxoffice.com/>.
9   The same piece of legislation permits block-booking by American motion-picture distributors on foreign markets. This practice is expressly forbidden on domestic markets by antitrust legislation.

References

AMPAS (2001) *Annual Index to Motion Picture Credits (2000 Edition)*, Beverly Hills, CA.: The Academy of Motion Picture Arts and Sciences.

Berger, S. and Piore, M. J. (1980) *Dualism and Discontinuity in Industrial Societies*, Cambridge: Cambridge University Press.

Blackstone, E. A. and Bowman, G. W. (1999) 'Vertical integration in motion pictures', *Journal of Communication*, 49: 123–39.

Brown, L. (1996) 'Technology transforms', in L. S. Gray and R. L. Seeber (eds) *Under the Stars: Essays on Labor Relations in Arts and Entertainment*, Ithaca: Cornell University Press.

Chandler, A. D. (1990) *Scale and Scope: The Dynamics of Industrial Capitalism*, Cambridge, MA.: Belknap Press.

Cones, J. W. (1997) *The Feature Film Distribution Deal*, Carbondale and Edwardsville: Southern Illinois University Press.

Daly, D. A. (1980) *A Comparison of Exhibition and Distribution Patterns in Three Recent Feature Motion Pictures*, New York: Arno Press.

de Vany, A. and Walls, W. D. (1997) 'The market for motion pictures: rank, revenue, and survival', *Economic Inquiry*, 35: 783–97.

DeFillippi, R. J. and Arthur, M. B. (1998) 'Paradox in project-based enterprise: the case of film-making', *California Management Review*, 40: 125–39.

Grabher, G. (2001) 'Locating economic action: projects, networks, localities, institutions', *Environment and Planning A*, 33: 1329–31.

Guback, T. H. (1969) *The International Film Industry: Western Europe and America since 1945*, Bloomington: Indiana University Press.

Hoskins, C., McFadyen, S. and Finn, A. (1997) *Global Television and Film: An Introduction to the Economics of the Business*, Oxford: Clarendon Press.

Hozic, A. A. (2001) *Hollyworld: Space, Power and Fantasy in the American Economy*, Ithaca: Cornell University Press.

Leyshon, A. (2001) 'Time-space (and digital) compression: software formats, musical networks, and the reorganization of the music industry', *Environment and Planning A*, 33: 49–77.

Litman, B. and Ahn, H. (1998) 'Predicting financial success of motion pictures: the early 90s experience', in B. Litman (ed.) *The Motion-Picture Mega Industry*, Boston: Allyn and Bacon, pp. 172–97.

Miller, T., Govil, N., McMurria, J. and Maxwell, R. (2001) *Global Hollywood*, London: British Film Institute.

Monitor (1999) *US Runaway Film and Television Production Study Report*, Santa Monica: Monitor Company.

NATO (2002) *Encyclopedia of Exhibition, 2001–2002*, North Hollywood, CA: National Association of Theatre Owners.

Negus, K. (1998) 'Cultural production and the corporation: musical genres and the strategic management of creativity in the US recording industry', *Media, Culture and Society*, 20: 359–79.

Prince, S. (2000) *A New Pot of Gold: Hollywood under the Electronic Rainbow, 1980–1989*, New York: Charles Scribner's Sons.

Robins, J. A. (1993) 'Organization as strategy: restructuring production in the film industry', *Strategic Management Journal*, 14: 103–18.

Rosen, D. and Hamilton, P. (1987) *Off-Hollywood: The Making and Marketing of Independent Films*, New York: Grove Weidenfeld.

Scott, A. J. (1999) 'The US recorded music industry: on the relations between organization, location, and creativity in the cultural economy', *Environment and Planning A*, 31: 1965–84.

Scott, A. J. (2000) *The Cultural Economy of Cities: Essays on the Geography of Image-Producing Industries*, London: Sage.

Scott, A. J. (2002) 'A new map of Hollywood: the production and distribution of American motion pictures', *Regional Studies*, 36: 957–75.

Segrave, K. (1997) *American Films Abroad: Hollywood's Domination of the World's Movie Screens*, Jefferson, NC.: McFarland.

Staiger, J. (2000) *Blockbuster TV: Must-See Sitcoms in the Network Era*, New York: New York University Press.

Storper, M. and Christopherson, S. (1987) 'Flexible specialization and regional industrial agglomerations: the case of the US motion-picture industry', *Annals of the Association of American Geographers*, 77: 260–82.

Tyson, L. D. (1992) *Who's Bashing Whom? Trade Conflict in High-Technology Industries*, Washington, DC: Institute for International Economics.

Veronis Suhler (2001) *Communications Industry Forecast*, New York: Veronis Suhler Media Merchant Bank, 15th edition.

Vogel, H. L. (1998) *Entertainment Industry Economics: A Guide for Financial Analysis*, Cambridge: Cambridge University Press.

Wasko, J., Phillips, M. and Purdie, C. (1993) 'Hollywood meets Madison Avenue: the commercialization of US films', *Media, Culture and Society*, 15: 271–93.

Wildman, S. S. and Siwek, S. E. (1988) *International Trade in Films and Television*, Cambridge, MA: Ballinger.

Wildman, S. S. and Siwek, S. E. (1993) 'The economics of trade in recorded media products in a multilingual world: implications for national media policies', in E. M. Noam and J. C. Millonzi (eds) *The International Market in Film and Television Programs*, Norwood, NJ: Ablex Publishing, pp. 13–40.

Wyatt, J. (1991) 'High-concept, product differentiation, and the contemporary US film industry', in B. Austin (ed.) *Current Research in Film: Audiences, Economics and Law*, Norwood, NJ: Ablex, pp. 86–105.

Wyatt, J. (1994) *High Concept: Movies and Marketing in Hollywood*, Austin: University of Texas Press.

Chapter 14

Susan Christopherson

BEHIND THE SCENES: HOW TRANSNATIONAL FIRMS ARE CONSTRUCTING A NEW INTERNATIONAL DIVISION OF LABOR IN MEDIA WORK (2006)

INTRODUCTION

> Competition should flourish. It is citizens in each country who decide what movies they want to see, what TV programs they want to watch. This kind of competition stirs creative juices. It lifts the level of quality in the creative community. When a government tries to defy that truth, the future of its national industry is put to hazard.
>
> Jack Valenti, The Motion Picture Association of America[1]

PREDICTIONS THAT WORK IN FIELDS such as computer programming, architecture, and graphic design will be globally sourced have raised the specter of job losses among skilled workers in high wage economies. One of the most interesting cases tied to this controversy is that of so-called "runaway" motion picture and television production from the traditional center of entertainment media production in Los Angeles to non-US satellite production centers (Coe, 2000, 2001; Scott, 2005). Although runaway production is an old complaint in the entertainment media industries, the production location decisions of media entertainment firms since the mid-1990s look considerably different than those in the 1980s when a similar alarm was raised. Among the critical differences are: (1) the location of an expanded range of production activities in regions outside the "headquarters" location of Los Angeles; (2) the ability of transnational firms to access multiple, self-organized and networked pools of skilled labor in production locations outside Los Angeles; and (3) the expanded role of the sub-national state in reducing the overall production costs of transnational firms, including those attendant to their use of skilled labor pools.[2]

The current controversy provides an opportunity to consider how transnational firms use international out-sourcing to address their need for high-skilled and specialized labor in the production process.[3] This issue is of critical interest to the entertainment media industry labor force, which is composed of project-oriented workers who are concentrated in international territorial production complexes, and highly unionized. The increased power of transnational firms vis-à-vis these regionalized media labor forces has intensified pressure on the powerful media unions to reduce their wage demands, alter compensation packages, and loosen work rules across what are now multi-national production centers.

Transnational firms using skilled labor to produce creative or innovative products, face a particular set of problems. The first of these problems is labor supply – the continuous creation of a sufficiently large and skilled workforce, outside the historically sustaining framework of the firm. The second problem is control of the wage bargaining power of skilled workers in an unpredictable labor market. The third problem concerns firm needs to obtain flexible production conditions, governing hours of work and working conditions – what are generally called "work rules".

In looking at how these problems were solved in the 1980s and how they are solved in the early 2000s, we can see the impact of changes in both inter-regional, and inter- and intra-firm competition. Simply put, as regions have become more competitive with one another internationally, the transnational media corporations (TNCs) have taken steps to consolidate and concentrate their economic power. Conglomerate control of entertainment media distribution gateways has given them enhanced control over what is produced and how it is produced (Epstein, 2005). This control over both the production and distribution of core entertainment media, such as episodic (series) television and feature film, has increased TNC bargaining power vis-à-vis labor and regional governments.[4] In an inherently risky business, conglomeration (and its manifestation, concentrated power) has enabled TNCs to shift risk and the cost of sustaining a project-oriented creative workforce to the regional state.

At the regional scale, the rationale for taking on these burdens is that they will build industry capacity, create new well-paying jobs, and enable the region to compete in the global economy. Evidence from regions competing to host TNC media production suggests, however, that interregional competition primarily benefits the media conglomerates and may actually undermine the ability of regional complexes to develop comparative advantage in specialized segments of the industry.

Some of the reasons behind the change in the balance of power between transnational firms and the regions are well documented. They can be traced to an altered international trade environment in which TNCs move more easily across national borders, differentiating among various kinds of economies and the comparative advantages they provide (Kogut, 1984, 1985; Gereffi et al., 2005). At the same time, the devolution of national responsibility for social welfare and economic development to the regional scale has heightened tendencies toward "disorganized" or competitive capitalism, including at the regional scale (Brenner, 2005; Offe and Keane, 1984; Lash and Urry, 1987).

In addition, however, the changing power balance between TNCs and regions has been shaped by two other processes intimately connected with contemporary globalization: (1) the promulgation of an ideology of endogenous regional growth (Lovering, 2001; Martin and Sunley, 1997) and (2) changes in national regulatory regimes governing competition. Altered regulatory frameworks have resulted in concentrated economic power under the banner of creating globally competitive national champions.

In the US-based transnational entertainment media industries, the concentration of power has come about with changes in the policies that govern inter-firm competition. Of particular significance are: (1) the abrogation of the "Paramount decision" which limited ownership of distribution venues by media producers, and (2) the revocation of the regulations limiting production by the television networks (the so-called "financial syndication" rules). The past 20 years have witnessed horizontal integration across media industries (network and cable television, motion pictures) and vertical integration of production and distribution. In the highly concentrated media entertainment industry of the early 2000s the enhanced bargaining power of the entertainment TNCs has paved the way for new location strategies (Christopherson, 1996, 2002).

In what follows I examine how transnational media corporations have used political strategies to reshape market conditions and foster inter-regional competition and, ultimately, to reconstruct the international division of cultural labor (Miller et al., 2001). The goal of these strategies is not only to reduce labor costs but to control and reproduce a multi-regional creative workforce (Peck, 1992). As a first step I examine the interests of transnational firms with respect to innovative product production. I then look at the origins of the altered balance of power between media TNCs and regionalized labor, and its consequences for regional–territorial production complexes. Finally, I reflect on how the political strategies of media TNCs can add to our understanding of the fragmentation and out-sourcing of skilled work and of the particular character of contemporary globalization.

FIRM LABOR STRATEGIES IN INNOVATION-ORIENTED INDUSTRIES

In industries or industry segments where a premium is placed on control and exploitation of innovations, firms attempt to monopolize innovations, if only for a brief time, in order to maximize their profits until the product novelty wears off and the products become standardized. We see this "cycle of innovation", as (Galbraith, 2000) describes it, in a wide variety of products including new drugs as well as media products. Large transnational firms have particular advantages in monopolizing innovations because they can exert control over the distribution of innovative products (using the enforcement capacity of the state, for example) and extend the time–space of innovation exploitation (Krugman, 1990; Grossman and Helpman, 1991).

Innovation however, requires a skilled and creative workforce that is expensive to acquire and difficult to maintain. Some analysts of the new economy, including Galbraith, attribute the growing inequality in US labor markets to the increasing need for innovation and skills in an international division of labor in which US firms are at the short-term innovative end of the production spectrum. He asserts that, rather than higher returns to education, the need to pay more to maintain the innovative portion of the workforce is at the root of inequality, with firms continually squeezing less skilled, less innovative workers in order to support the firm's innovative capacity (Galbraith, 2000).

This is a compelling argument and in accord with theories about the bargaining power of creative workers in regional flexibly specialized industries. In concert with other theories about the knowledge economy, the creative economy and firm technical and innovative capacity, however, it assumes that firms have one spatial strategy: they identify regions with a good "business climate" and locate there. So, according to this view, firms in search of an innovative, skilled workforce identify regions that meet their needs (Florida, 2002; Reich, 1990; Friedman, 2005). They can seek out locations that appear to offer them cost advantages or the kind of labor force they need but if those input advantages do not materialize, or are affected by increased labor bargaining power, for example, the firm's only option is to de-camp.

A closer look at TNC location strategies reveals, however, that they relate to existing and potential production spaces in complex ways, devising methods to combine comparative advantage based on wage differentials with that rooted in territorially based agglomeration economies (Amiti, 2005; Gereffi et al., 2005; Storper, 1997). They not only respond to existing market and production conditions, they attempt to shape them – to increase profits and flexibility, and to reduce risks.

In this regard, Harrison's insights about the continued power of large corporations in shaping and re-shaping labor markets and regional production centers to meet their needs are prescient. His analysis emphasizes the compatibility of (industrial) concentration and decentralization and, most importantly, points to the sources of decentralized production centers:

> Rather than dwindling away, concentrated economic power is changing its shape, as the big firms create all manner of networks, alliances, short- and long-term financial and technology deals – with one another, with government at all levels, and with legions of generally (although not invariably) smaller firms who act as their suppliers and subcontractors. True, production is increasingly being decentralized, as managers try to enhance their flexibility (that is, hedge their bets) . . . But decentralization of production does not imply the end of unequal economic *power* among firms – let alone among the different classes of workers who are employed in the different segments of these networks.
>
> (Harrison, 1997, p. 9)

As Harrison anticipated and as the contemporary story of runaway production and out-sourcing in the media industries demonstrates, dominant transnational media conglomerates (as opposed to their network of suppliers) do not passively accept the limitations or high costs associated with regional production complexes. Nor are they passive with respect to the need to solve the key problems and costs associated with a creative labor force – labor force reproduction, wage control, and flexibility in production conditions. Instead, there is substantial evidence to demonstrate that transnational media conglomerates use their con-siderable political power to reconstruct the production environment, regionally, nationally, and internationally so as to increase both their profitability and their flexibility vis-à-vis product and labor markets. So, while all firms operate in a political–institutional con-text, the degree to which they can shape that context differs dramatically (Martinelli and Schoenberger, 1991). The shaping influence of the transnational firm is extensive, encompassing both the national and sub-national, that is, regional, state.

If TNCs are understood as market makers not just market takers, an explanation of their spatial strategies requires a political-economic rather than a purely economic analysis. For example, US-based transnational firms, including the media conglomerates, have con-siderable capacity to construct and reconstruct the conditions under which they produce innovative goods and services such as media products. This firm capacity arises from the size and scale of their operations but also from the governance regime that describes their legal obligations and prerogatives, and the extent and nature of their accountability (Hall and Soskice, 2001; Christopherson, 2002). Under US corporate governance "rules", firm accountability is narrowly defined, extending only to shareholders (and notably excluding employees or the public interest). And, large US-based transnational firms have unusual access to regulators and legislators at all levels of government because of the way elections are conducted and financed in the US (Gierzynski, 2000). Thus, large firms have considerable ability to influence the labor regulations under which they operate, the corporate governance rules to which they must adhere as well as their enforcement, and to shape public investments that may benefit their private purposes.[5] All of these capacities have implications for their exercise of power and coordinating capacity at the regional scale, both in the United States and in other investment sites.

To provide the basis for a broader discussion of how transnational media firms use political power and territorial strategies to reproduce and access regionalized supplies of skilled, innovative labor, I examine differences in the rhetoric and reality of "runaway production" in the 1980s and early 2000s. Once again, I focus on the key differences between the two periods: (1) the location of an expanded range of production activities in regional locations outside the "headquarters" location of Los Angeles, particularly in Canada; (2) the ability of transnational firms to access multiple, self-organized, and networked pools of skilled labor, and (3) the enhanced role of the sub-national, regional, state in reducing the overall production costs of transnational firms, including those attendant to their use of pools of skilled labor.

RUNAWAY PRODUCTION: THE EVOLUTION OF SPATIAL COMPETITION

As Allen Scott (2005) has demonstrated, the Los Angeles region has retained its position as the dominant pre-production, production, and post-production center for the media entertainment industries throughout the 20th and into the 21st centuries. That said, production activity outside Los Angeles has been an important factor in both the creative and economic calculus of producers – particularly since the 1970s. Both the geography of production and the factors driving it have changed, however, with the gradual emergence of a horizontally and vertically integrated media entertainment industry and new spatial investment strategies by the oligopoly of transnational firms that dominate the media entertainment industry.

IN THE 1980s . . .

As has already been suggested, runaway production is an old complaint in the media industries. Film crews have always left Los Angeles, the historically dominant production center, to shoot in exotic or less expensive locales. In the 1970s and especially in the 1980s, film shoots outside the Los Angeles region increased in conjunction with a rise in demand for media entertainment products. Demand was stimulated by the expansion of commercial television into global markets and the emergence of new domestic markets such as home video (Prince, 2000). During this period of market expansion, US national government-enforced market regulation fostered competition in distribution and production markets via anti-trust decisions and financial syndication rules (Epstein, 2005; Holt, 2001). A US Supreme Court decision in 1947 (known as The Paramount Decision)[6] forced the major motion picture studios to divest themselves of their distribution venue – in US movie theaters. Regulated competition curtailed the ability of the "Majors" (as the companies composing the oligopoly were known at the time), to distribute packages of films through a practice known as "block booking".[7]

In another key regulatory effort to encourage competition in the entertainment media industries, financial syndication rules, adopted in 1970, forced the, then three, commercial television networks to purchase prime time programming rather than produce it in-house. This led to the emergence of powerful independent mid-size production houses, primarily located in Los Angeles. In this regulatory environment, which shaped the media markets of the 1980s, overall differences in production strategies and product mix among the major film and television product producers decreased; at the same time, the creative differences among individual products accelerated. Maltby (1998, p. 31) describes this period as one in which "the post-Paramount attitude of regarding each production as a one-off event had reached a point where none of the majors any longer possessed a recognizable identity either in its personnel or its product." Uncertainty and higher risks in distribution markets and decentralized production across a wide spectrum of product suppliers fostered product differentiation. For a period, lasting no more than 20 years, the bargaining power of "independents", and their associated production networks, increased vis-à-vis the major studios.

Ultimately, the "majors" (Columbia Pictures, Warner Brothers, MGM, Twentieth Century Fox, Universal Studios, and Paramount Pictures) would use their political influence on regulation, and their ability to keep re-trying the Paramount decision in US courts to re-establish vertical and horizontal integration and their dominance over media production and distribution (Epstein, 2005; Holt, 2001). But, during this period – with a competitive market for media entertainment products and increasing demand, new markets, and a variety of product distributors, independent producers thrived (Christopherson and Storper, 1986).

Product differentiation also spurred technological change. Because of the application of television production methods and technology, filmmaking became more mobile and enhanced the independence of film crews from the studio and sound stage environment. Film crews were able to use these new technologies creatively to differentiate their products and to lower costs of shooting "on-location" to produce products that looked different because they were shot in Portland Maine or El Paso Texas rather than Los Angeles.

Producers took advantage of an expanding range of incentives provided by US cities and states to lure film crews to shoot their films outside California. The typical incentive package included inexpensive accommodations for film crews, tax breaks for using local businesses such as catering and construction, and easy permitting to use public spaces. States including Texas, Arizona, North Carolina, Florida, and Illinois vied for two or three films a year, knowing that there would be pay-offs beyond the short-term jobs created in restaurants, catering, and dry cleaning to serve the film crew. Because location was part of what distinguished products, such as "Deliverance" and "The Last Picture Show", place-based films were valuable as state promotional devices. Visibility in a film drew tourists and businesses to places far from Hollywood. These relatively modest incentives were part of community and state image marketing programs, intended to increase the media exposure of the state or city so as to attract tourists and long-term business investment.

The resulting increase in film shoots outside Los Angeles became an issue in the 1980s and was dubbed "runaway production" because the Majors were concerned about its impact on the utilization of their sound stages. The Majors were the most important promoters of runaway production as a policy issue at that time. Because of their large facilities, high overheads, and unionized workforce, they pushed for incentive packages by the state of California so as to keep as much production as possible in Los Angeles to fill up their sound stages and to use their equipment and services (Storper and Christopherson, 1985).

The media labor unions, overwhelmingly headquartered in Los Angeles, supported Major Studio appeals for incentives to stem runaway production (for example, providing free police or highway patrol protection to film crews, clean-up crews to mollify neighbor-hoods impacted by shooting, and easy permitting) because of what they saw as a need to support the regional industry, and because they preferred production close to their homes and families. They did not think, however, that their interests were directly threatened by shooting on-location. When working in LA, they were protected by "the 30 mile limit" (from La Cienega and Beverly Boulevards in Los Angeles) within which more restrictive work rules were enforced. Production outside this range triggered additional negotiated benefits. For the workforce, shooting on location meant inconvenient travel rather than job loss.

Because the locations where shooting occurred rarely could provide the skilled labor needed to make the film, the cinematographer, script supervisor, or grip went to Vermont or Texas to shoot scenes for a few days and then came home to the San Fernando Valley or

Santa Monica to spend his or her paycheck. Production outside LA did not entail job loss except for the less-skilled and non-unionized workers who provide transportation, catering, carpentry, and dry cleaning services to film crews on location (Christopherson and Storper, 1986; Storper and Christopherson, 1985).

With the exception of New York City, the skilled labor needed to shoot a film was not available in other locations. Key members of the production crew were hired in LA or New York because of their particular skills and connections within a production network. Although studio facilities existed in some other locations, such as Las Colinas in Texas, these were fragile operations because there was not sufficient work to sustain a skilled workforce in the region. In the rare case that a skilled production worker managed to capture enough experience through on-location shooting, he or she typically de-camped to Los Angeles in order to build a sustainable career (Christopherson and Storper, 1989).

In addition, pre-production, (the development of the product concept and origination of the production crew and financing), soundstage production, and post-production, the editing of the product and finishing for distribution, remained firmly rooted in Los Angeles. These activities were carried out by a skilled, specialized, regional labor force, which was highly unionized (Gray and Seeber, 1996). The competitive production environment fostered by the regulatory regime encouraged creativity and product differentiation and furthered the regionalization of production in Los Angeles despite high labor and transaction costs.

As a result, there was no credible inter-regional competition, including over labor cost. The frictions that existed between East Coast and West coast branches of media guilds or union locals were subdued by national collective agreements and by the dearth of regional competitors with substantial production capacity and a skilled workforce. Policies to stem "runaway" production were, in effect, indirect and rather ineffective strategies to increase demand for use of the fixed real estate (and sunk costs) represented by the major studio facilities in Los Angeles. In the 1980s, then, media producers used locations outside Los Angeles in limited ways primarily associated with product differentiation. They were dependent, one might even say captured, by their need to use the skilled and collectively organized Los Angeles, and (to a secondary extent) New York City media workforce. Finally, the state played a limited role. State film offices focused on making location shooting easier in order to encourage state tourism. While the state of California was more engaged in supporting the media entertainment industries because of their centrality to the economy, even in the case of California, support was limited to on-location production incentives.

IN THE EARLY 2000s . . .

According to evidence developed by the industry, US-based television and film production increased in the decade of the 1990s and has continued to expand into the 2000s (Monitor, 1999; State of California, Department of Employment, 2005). Los Angeles has maintained its dominant role in industry production during this period of expansion as evidenced by the region's ability to capture the majority share of new production. Both the number of productions and the dollar volume of total production in Los Angeles rose in California in the 1990s, with a 6.6% increase in total employment (California's Entertainment Work-force: Employment and Earnings (1991–2002), 2005). This continued growth took place, however, in a production and distribution environment very different from that which existed in the early 1980s: one in which a small number of media conglomerates have re-acquired ownership of entertainment media distribution channels: cable networks, commercial broadcast networks, DVD rentals, and theaters, and are now also able to legally produce their own products for those outlets.

Deregulation and lax enforcement of the market rules that structured competition in the 1970s and 1980s has led to a concentrated media entertainment industry in which a small number of firms control access to multiple distribution markets in film, broadcast and cable television, and DVD sales and rental. As one member of the Creative Coalition, a group of actors, writers, directors, and producers concerned with the effects of vertical integration on creativity, described the new market, "There are many voices but many fewer ventriloquists."

Six conglomerates – Viacom, Time Warner, NBC – Universal (owned by GE), Sony, Fox, and Disney overwhelmingly dominate the production and distribution of entertainment products in the US in the early 2000s. Together they control 98% of the programs that carry commercial advertising during prime time television (including commercial network and cable programming) and 96% of total US film rentals. They control 75% of commercial television in non-prime-time slots, 80% of subscribers to Pay TV, and 65% of advertising revenues in commercial radio (Epstein, 2005, p. 83). Although one might expect some competition within this oligopoly, inter-firm competition is dampened by both tacit and open cooperation among the conglomerates. The firms cooperate to influence regulatory policy (such as that compelling manufacturers of DVD players to implant a circuit that prevents playing movies from Europe in the United States) through their trade association and lobbying group, The Motion Picture Association of America (Epstein, 2005, p. 83). They have also formed alliances within the group of six to reduce their risks and to insure that they all have maximum access to global markets. One manifestation of this cooperation is co-financing of major products so that movies directed at a global audience are not released simultaneously (Epstein, 2005, p. 99; Goettler and Leslie, 2004).

According to Epstein (2005), the contemporary entertainment media firms are more accurately described as platforms, involved in extracting value from intellectual property. This property may be old (film libraries, ancient television series) or new, such as the popular "extreme home makeover" (a combination of soap opera, home renovation ideas, and venue for product placement revenues). The primary goal of the media merchants, then, is not production and distribution of products but identification of strategies to extract the maximum revenue from intellectual property. This orientation has implications for their interpretation of "creativity" and for how they think about the types of products they want to see produced and distributed and to whom. The intellectual property focus, in turn, affects producer prerogatives and production location decisions.

The early 2000s conglomerates are distinguishably different from their precursor distributors of television and film products in the 1970s and 1980s, in the scope and scale of their activities in production and distribution. While firm oligopolies dominated the distribution of entertainment products in key markets in the 1980s – the Major Studios in film, and the television networks in television series – their overall dominance of media entertainment markets was limited. They faced competition from each other as well as from smaller production firms and independent television stations and small film distributors who had increased in numbers and power in response to expanding global demand (Fabricant, 1992; Koch, 1990).

In the new era, the control of multiple end markets by the six media conglomerates has significantly increased their bargaining power with advertisers, producers, labor, and the regions in which the products they distribute are produced. While they present their operations as only loosely affiliated (describing them as "sister" firms), for accounting and regulatory purposes, they are, in fact, "virtually integrated" with important implications for what is produced and how it is produced (Christopherson, 1996, 2002).

Concentration has altered all aspects of the production and distribution of entertainment products, including the cost structure of production and the production process. At the heart of this restructuring is the ability of virtually integrated transnational media firms to use (or in industry jargon, to "repurpose") products – film, television series, or documentary – across their multiple distribution outlets. Repurposing multiplies the revenues that can be obtained from any one product. It also reduces the transaction and direct costs associated with product acquisition for downstream distribution venues, such as DVD rental and sale. In addition, it allows the bundling of television and film products for sale to ancillary markets such as in-flight entertainment. The control of multiple distribution markets by a handful of firms has spawned strategies to squeeze more profits out of products, both old and new, by multiplying the venues in which they can be distributed and increasing their value through cross-market advertising. Films produced by Universal are advertised on NBC, the conglomerate's broadcast television network, and hyped through its news and information programming. Theaters owned by the conglomerate advertise its other media products. Libraries of old television programs are mined to find anything that could attract an audience, fill cable hours, and attract even small advertising dollars.

Perhaps counter-intuitively, as the entertainment industry has concentrated, the cost of producing and distributing a feature film has increased dramatically (MPAA, 2005; Jones, 2002). Among the reasons for this increase are accounting rules for the industry, which were changed in 1981 as new distribution venues for entertainment products emerged (Fabricant, 1992). These rules permit the (now) conglomerate owners of multiple distribution venues to distribute the costs of marketing among theatrical release, network television, and cable and to rapidly write-off the cost of a product while at the same time increasing their bottom line (in current profits) by longer-term estimates of future revenues from these multiple outlets. This accounting strategy encourages the conglomerates to extract high advertising and marketing costs from their distribution outlets and raises the overall cost of marketing and advertising the product. This strategy, not coincidentally, raises barriers to entry from non-conglomerate controlled producers.

Media conglomerates are now able to limit the expensive, transaction-intensive process of competing for products from independent producers by producing products within their wholly owned subsidiaries. In the 1995–1996 US television season, the last in which broadcast networks were restricted from producing their own programming, the networks had at least partial ownership in under 20% of their new shows. In 2002, the television networks (and the media conglomerates of which they are a part) had increased that percentage to 77.5% (Manly, 2005).

THE RISE OF MEDIA CONGLOMERATE BARGAINING POWER WITH LABOR AND THE REGIONS

The restructuring of the media entertainment industry has demonstrably changed the bargaining relationship between capital and labor, even in the capital of industry production, Los Angeles.

Some of these changes in bargaining power can be traced to increasing demand for low-cost television programming to fill endless cable networks. Programs for cable networks are produced within small budgets and, frequently, by producers who use small, non-union crews. They rarely employ professional actors. The character of production for cable is significant because television production has outpaced film production in Los Angeles since the mid-1980s and much of the recent growth has been concentrated in low-cost production for cable television networks (Scott, 2004). The pattern of increasing production for cable television is even more pronounced in New York City because it hosts the cable network headquarters and because of the City's specialization in key industries contributing to cable programming, financial services and education. So, while the number of productions has increased in Los Angeles and New York, much of this increase is in low budget, non-unionized productions. The opportunities for employment in higher budget, unionized productions have been eroded by a decline in feature film production and in the proportion of scripted productions (such as dramatic series) for television.

Labor bargaining power has been further eroded by the expanded use of digital imaging in production and postproduction (Epstein, 2005). Although typically associated with innovation in production values, digital imaging is also employed to reduce labor and location costs.

Despite the decrease in labor's bargaining power, labor supply has increased faster than labor demand over the 1990s in Los Angeles and New York (EEI, 2005; Center for an Urban Future, 2005). This increase has been visible particularly in the "inclusive" guilds, such as the Screen Actors Guild, which has low barriers to membership. In both cities, analyses of employment document the presence of a workforce composed of a small core that is regularly employed and a large peripheral workforce that cannot derive a regular income from employment in the media industries (Gray et al., 2005).

The expansion of low budget production for cable, the growing labor pool, and slow growth in the more lucrative (for labor) production segments, such as feature film and broadcast network television series, explains why increased employment and production numbers in Los Angeles are combined with high levels of worker dissatisfaction and a sense of increased risk.

Hourly wages in the media industries remain high but reports from the unions indicate the work has become harder and less predictable than it was in the early 1990s. One common complaint is that producers attempting to cut costs will reduce shooting days by requiring overtime work from the production crew. While long working hours are legendary in the media entertainment industry, the boundaries that circumscribed abuse appear to have broken down as unions have lost power over industry practices and with an increase in the proportion of productions made on "shoe string" budgets.

While the number of marginal productions for television is increasing, producers of medium to high budget feature films have also been under pressure to cut costs. The pressure to reduce total expenses (emanating from rising star salaries and product marketing costs) has focused particularly on "below-the-line" or skilled craft labor costs because this work is perceived as less important in adding value to the product and acquiring necessary financing.

Although below-the-line or entertainment industry craft workers are most affected by the restructuring of the industry and the ability of entertainment conglomerates to squeeze producers in order to extract higher profits, the changes wrought by industry concentration affect even the most creative segments of the industry. According to one veteran film-maker: "in cable, residuals (payments for each showing of the product) for writers, actors, and directors are a percent of the producer's gross. But if that producer is a network who self-deals the rights to their cable company . . . there is no compensation for that. Suddenly you discover that the 11% or 12% gross residual among the three guilds that has been fought over for so many decades is virtually meaningless, as rights are simply self-dealt among related entities" (Hill, 2004, p. 20).

In response to these conditions, the media unions have focused on retaining the "good jobs", those still controlled by union contracts and in bigger, more lucrative and (in the case of television) longer-term projects. Medium budget ($20–$50 million) feature films and television series are at the core of the "good jobs" category. It is the unionized, higher budget segments of media production, those requiring sophisticated facilities and a skilled work-force, that are the object of intense inter-regional competition, both internationally and within the US.

VIRTUAL CONCENTRATION AND THE RISE OF
INTER-REGIONAL COMPETITION

The enhanced bargaining power of the conglomerates is directly reflected in the location of production activities. The decision regarding where to produce a film or a television program is, in the early 2000s, more likely to be rooted in a drive to secure product financing or reduce direct production costs, than in the desire for product differentiation that characterized the more competitive production and distribution environment of the 1970s and 1980s.

Since the late 1980s, production of media entertainment products for US and international markets has taken place outside the United States, particularly in Canada but also in the United Kingdom, Australia, and much more occasionally, in Eastern Europe. Once again, changes in the spatial location of production are being portrayed as "runaway production". The competitor to Los Angeles is no longer New York, as it was in the 1980s, however, but international production centers with sound stages, equipment companies, and, most importantly, less expensive and more "flexible" craft or below-the-line workers. By contrast with the 1980s, when runaway production referred to shooting on-location, since the mid-1990s, it has been soundstage production and post-production editing and special effects production, as well location shooting, that are taking place in international production "satellites", most particularly in Vancouver, Canada (Coe, 2000, 2001; Elmer and Gasher, 2005).

There have been other notable shifts in the runaway production discourse that reflect changes in the power relations among the media conglomerates, the producers who provide them with products, and the workforce. In this round of "runaway production" the major studios, now part of production and distribution conglomerates, are on the other side of the runaway production debate. They are supporting the "right" of producers to produce where they choose, including outside the US. And again by contrast with the controversy of the 1980s, US media unions are deeply engaged in the contemporary runaway production policy debates. Since the late 1990s, the Canadian government has been accused of unfair competition by US media unions, some media service firms and small non-conglomerate studios such as Raleigh in Los Angeles (FTAC, 2004; ITC).

At the heart of this charge is Canadian national and provincial provision of labor-based subsidies to US entertainment media conglomerates to encourage them not only to shoot on-location but also to use sound stages and post-production services in Canada. With a relative shift in the importance of factors driving production location decisions from product differentiation to production cost, producers were often required by their media conglomerate employers to move production to Canada to reduce costs or obtain financing via tax credits. While some "beauty shots" might be made in New York or Chicago where the film was actually set, the expensive sound stage work was transferred to lower cost facilities in Toronto and Vancouver. In Vancouver, the media entertainment firms leased sound stages so that they could be used by their contracted US-based producers, and established contractual relationships with "Canadian" production houses, such as Lions Gate Studio (which has its Executive Offices in Santa Monica, California) and post-production houses. The long-term rather than one-off project-based use of Vancouver as a satellite center is also indicated by the established presence of studio offices, such as that of Paramount, and industry associations, most prominently, The Association of Motion Picture and Television Producers (AMTPT), a US-based organization representing the Motion Picture Association of America member studios. All of these representatives of US-based conglomerate interests lobby Canadian officials to maintain and increase subsidies for foreign "service production".

The media conglomerates, along with some labor allies, such as The Directors' Guild, *support* the Canadian government's rationale for subsidies to what Canadians refer to as "service production", based in the "cultural exception", a provision of international trade law that allows governments to provide subsidies to encourage the production of media products that sustain cultural identity.

According to Bonnie Richardson, head of government relations at the Motion Picture Association of America, the trade association which represents the media conglomerates in the US and in Canada:

> Trade action against Canada "threatens to further sour US–Canada relations already strained by tariffs on Canadian lumber, as well as hurt efforts to dismantle barriers abroad to US movies . . . It's a 'dagger-to-the-heart' challenge to very sensitive cultural subsidies," said Richardson, whose group represents Hollywood Studios including the Walt Disney Co., Sony Corp.'s Sony Pictures and AOL Time Warner's Warner Brothers.
>
> (Pethel, 2002)

Despite the emphasis on the Vancouver–Los Angeles competition, the impact of TNC ability to ratchet-up its bargaining power with skilled labor and exercise a cost-based location strategy is most apparent in US production centers outside Los Angeles. These locations formerly benefited from location shooting for the purposes of product differentiation and have been the big losers in an environment in which cost (and state subsidies) trumps "look" in making location decisions.[8]

By the end of the 1990s, states such as Texas, North Carolina, Florida and Illinois, which had developed a small media industry base by providing technical assistance to film-makers shooting on-location, some studio facilities, and modest incentives, suffered dramatic declines in production shooting (Lee, 2002; Jones, 2002). The interpretation of this trend did not focus on firm strategies or on changes in what was produced and how it was produced, but rather on the ability of places and regions to supply the needs of a global industry. The increasing cost-based character of production location decisions was attributed to the rise of *international* competition based on the ability of regions in the US and abroad to provide both the physical and human infrastructure that supports the industry (Weinstein and Clower, 2000).

As a consequence, states and cities in the US were pressured by regional economic development coalitions, including local media industry unions, to find ways to "level the playing field", to move beyond the public service incentives they offered in the 1980s to provide direct subsidies, studio facilities, a skilled labor force, and production financing to media producers in order to keep them in the United States (Entertainment Industry Development Corporation, 2001; U.S. Department of Commerce, 2001; Jones, 2002; Monitor, 1999).

In the early 2000s, the most generous subsidies were provided by the ill-fated state of Louisiana, one of the poorest in the US. The Louisiana subsidies offset up to 17% of a film or television production budget and there were no caps on the amount of subsidies that the state provided to media conglomerates. In her state of the state address in January 2005, Louisiana's governor, Kathleen Babineaux Blanco said that Louisiana's $73 million dollar growth in tax revenues in 2004 would be unavailable for teacher raises because it would, instead, fund the (currently) $70 million film tax credit program (Webster, 2005). In Louisiana's program, investment tax credits are sold at a reduced rate to individuals and businesses, which use them to reduce their own tax liability. The cash goes directly to a conglomerate-owned production company. Twentieth Century Fox (owned by the conglomerate Fox News), and Disney are both users of the program (Miller et al., 2001). The tax credits are typically bought and used by professional business services, including the law firms representing the media conglomerates operating in Louisiana. A cottage industry has grown up around tax credit sales. One of the major firms in this new tax credit sales industry has established a non-profit organization to "unite the players in the state's entertainment industry (Miller et al., 2001) to lobby the state to maintain and increase the subsidies supporting the location of productions in Louisiana". Their goals are to obtain public capital to support the construction of a soundstage (Louisiana currently has one) and to monitor what other states are providing so that Louisiana can continue to match and exceed these bids (Miller et al., 2001). The state is also being encouraged to invest heavily in training programs to provide Louisiana with a skilled media entertainment workforce, which it currently lacks.

Some of the key actors lobbying for direct subsidies to transient production companies are similar to those who spurred location shooting incentives among states in the 1980s. Real estate interests, for example, play a critical political role in a growth coalition that stands to benefit from an increase in location shooting. At the same time, both the political arguments for supporting location shooting and the character of the support requested have changed significantly. In the 1980s, states invested modestly in film commissions and incentives to make it easier to shoot films (through eased permitting and location assistance) hoping to attract media attention and boost tourism. Incentives increased in the 1990s to include sales tax exemptions and waivers on hotel occupancy taxes, but since these incentives constituted a minuscule portion of the shooting budget, they had little impact on location decisions. In the new economic development environment regional growth coalitions (and their media industry allies) argue that, in a global marketplace in which all regions are competing for industries with good jobs, public capital plays a critical role in creating the conditions within which occasional film and television projects will be transformed into a stable and lucrative regional industry.

The scenario they lay out follows the well-worn path of stage theory. First, industry projects must be lured to a region by significant direct financial subsidies, demonstrating its good business climate. Second, the region is charged with developing and sustaining the infrastructure, including capital facilities and a skilled labor force, to sustain industry presence. With these investments, the regional industry eventually becomes self-sustaining and globally competitive and no longer requires subsidies. Canada is used as an exemplar of this process and its success is attributed to the initial stimulus of subsidies. An examination of how the "model" Canadian media industry has developed over time, however, suggests that development policies oriented toward providing subsidies, skilled labor services, and facilities to transnational corporations have uncertain and complex consequences even for high-skilled industries.

THE INTERSECTION OF REGIONALIZED LABOR AND FIRM STRATEGY: THE CANADIAN CASE

According to the US industry story, the movement of significant entertainment media production to Canada is attributable to the introduction of Canadian production tax subsidies in the 1990s (Jones, 2002; Monitor, 1999). The line of argument is that production costs rose in the 1990s and that media product producers looked for ways to reduce production crew and craft worker costs. They identified Canada as an alternative because Canadian labor-based production subsidies reduced crew costs. In 2003, for example, Canadian national subsidies to foreign producers, in the form of tax credits, were increased from 11%

to 16% of labor costs (CFTPA, 2003). Canadian national subsidies are enhanced by additional tax credits provided by Canadian provinces competing against each other to attract foreign production. The total tax credits available to US producers on payroll costs are as high as 44% (Blackwell, 2003). As a consequence, so the argument goes, production of television pilots, some series, and made-for-television movies began to take place in Canada (Jones, 2002; Monitor, 1999). Subsidies are given credit for attracting production away from US regions, including Los Angeles, and building a Canadian production industry that can compete with the US industry.

This case is then used to suggest that, to compete with Canada, the US must subsidize entertainment media production at the state and federal level to bring US labor costs in line with Canadian labor costs. Regional growth coalitions, including media labor unions and facilities owners or property developers, present states and cities with a trajectory of Canadian success. It begins with inter-regional competition via subsidies to attract transnational firm production with the lure of lower labor costs and ends with a successful free-standing capacity to compete in the global entertainment media industry (Monitor, 1999). A prominent New York economic development official tied the development of a successful and prototypical Canadian industry to the labor-based subsidies the Canadian government provided in the early 1990s. "Before those subsidies, producers were not interested in Canada". According to this supply-side explanation, the subsidies worked and "in a few years Canada had developed a competitive media industry" (Personal Interview, 2005).

This trajectory of Canadian success is contestable on a number of fronts. First it ignores the impact of the exchange rate differential. The value of the Canadian dollar lagged the US dollar throughout the 1990s and made the cost of producing in Canada relatively less expensive than in the United States. The cost savings did not occur across all categories of production expenditures, however. Studio and equipment rental services have remained roughly equivalent across North America (British Columbia Ministry of Economic Development, 2005) (in Canada, rising and falling depending on the value of the US dollar). Above-the-line labor costs, including the cost of directors and principal actors, are also not sensitive to exchange rate fluctuations. Only the cost of the "below-the-line" production crew is identified as susceptible to cost savings because of the exchange rate.

The savings from wage cost differentials produced by the exchange rate has obviously been important in the outsourcing of production to Canada. Trends in out-sourcing have generally tracked the exchange rate over the 1990s and into the 2000s (CFTPA, 2005). That it is not a sufficient explanation, however, is suggested by anomalies, particularly a 22% decrease in production from 1995 to 1996 and an increase of 12.5% from 1996 to 1997, all occurring under the same exchange rate (Droesch, 2004).

Because the cost savings could be achieved in only a portion of the total budget, the savings was most relevant in medium budget productions with high below-the-line crew costs for a unionized crew. Depending on firm strategies during a particular year, that cost saving could be more or less attractive. For example, a stronger emphasis on very low budget productions would tend to keep production in Los Angeles, where a large skilled non-union labor force is available at relatively low cost.

In the same way, the effect of tax subsidies can also be questioned as explaining outsourcing. Hollywood production in Vancouver predates the introduction of subsidies (in 1997), stretching back to the late 1980s and the establishment of Stephen J. Cannell productions in Vancouver. Out-sourcing does not emerge in conjunction with the subsidies. In addition and substantiating the weak link between outsourcing and subsidies, a recent econometric analysis of the impact of subsidies in British Columbia shows only a weak relationship between tax credits and production spending levels (British Columbia Ministry of Economic Development, 2005).

At base, while the exchange rate and subsidies have been important in expanding production, they would be ineffectual were it not for Canada's skilled media workforce. The presence of this workforce is the necessary condition underlying any US investment in Canada, whether short-term or long-term. However, the investments that constituted and continue to constitute this valuable labor supply are largely ignored in the policy research on out-sourcing.

The Canadian state has played an important role in developing and sustaining the regionalized media workforce in Canada, especially outside the national media center of Toronto. This role emerged because of the need to foster production of Canadian content programming.

The inability of Canadian independent film producers to make a dent in US dominated film distribution in Canada (Winseck, 2002) moved them to turn their attention to television, which was state-supported and regulated to promote an arena of Canadian content. In 1984, the Canadian Film Development Corporation became Telefilm Canada and since 1988 has invested more than $60 million annually in television programming. Government expenditures to support film and television production in Canada are significant, representing 10% of the total yearly budget for cultural activities (Montpool, 1998). This support focuses almost exclusively on television. In 2003, productions made with Canadian content received a 60% domestic tax subsidy on qualifying labor expenditures (Canadian Film and Television Production Association (CFTPA), 2003). The Canadian Television Fund has been important in encouraging regional production in the Canadian provinces and thus developing an industrial base throughout the country, including in Vancouver.

The Canadian media production workforce is trained to produce programming for television but these skills can be applied to feature film production for US-based media TNCs. The Canadian government supports training and mentorship programs administered by the CFTPA, which also works with Canadian producer–distributors to train Canadian media workers (CFTPA, 2005; Elmer and Gasher, 2005). In addition, both regional and national Canadian governments have invested in regional production facilities, such as Bridge Studio in Vancouver. Studio facilities not owned by a production company are rarely profitable, especially in a location such as British Columbia, which is dependent on foreign "service" production. So, public support for such studio facilities constitutes another potential subsidy to the transnational corporations locating production in Vancouver.

In fact, it could be argued that it is the weakness of the subsidized production complex in Vancouver that makes it a useful production site for Hollywood. By contrast with Toronto, where production investment is largely domestic, and Montreal, which has developed a distinctive regional industry based in Francophone productions, Vancouver's industry is highly dependent on government subsidies and the unpredictable strategies of US producers and the conglomerates who employ them. The very vulnerability of Vancouver drives requests for ever larger subsidies to US producers and pressure on the regional workforce to become more "flexible" in responding to the needs of foreign service production (Tysoe, 2004; Droesch, 2004).

Several conclusions emerge out of the Canadian story: First, while subsidies and exchange rates increased the propensity of US producers to use Canadian regions to reduce costs in particular types of productions, they did not build a sustainable industry in the key region in which the subsidy strategy was deployed, Vancouver. Second, the changing organization of production in the media entertainment industries allowed TNCs to utilize the investments that Canadian citizens made in developing regional production bases over a period of 50 years. Finally, the evidence from the Canadian "success story" suggests that inter-regional competition has increased the profits of transnational firms rather than building competitive regional industries.

The changes that have taken place in the capacities and strategies of media conglomerates since the deregulation of the industry also point to some key processes constructing a new international division of skilled labor.

A NEW INTERNATIONAL DIVISION OF SKILLED LABOR?

What can the case of media entertainment add to our understanding of the international out-sourcing of skilled work? At minimum, it raises some questions about the assumptions underlying prescriptions for clustering and agglomeration as a formula for regional economic development and competitiveness. The literature on regional production complexes has implicitly suggested that skilled labor has more bargaining power within these complexes. The case of the Los Angeles media workforce circa 2000 indicates, however, that firm dependence on regional production complexes will not necessarily limit out-sourcing if alternative regional labor forces are available and if political and economic strategies can be devised to use a similarly skilled regional labor force to reduce costs or provide labor flexibility.

In addition, evidence concerning the decreasing bargaining power of media labor in LA suggests that production can remain territorialized while, at the same time, labor conditions in the regional agglomeration deteriorate. The Los Angeles situation is certainly complex – not all segments of the workforce are affected by out-sourcing and different segments of the workforce are affected in different ways, some losing income, some being exposed to more risk. Overall, however, labor's bargaining power has weakened.

The case also suggests the importance of examining how TNCs devise ways to restructure the conditions under which they produce and distribute products. This restructuring can occur at various scales and take different political and economic forms. A key difference between the period of the 1980s when the Los Angeles media workforce felt reasonably secure despite employment in project-based work and the early 2000s when a larger portion of the workforce feels insecure, can be traced to the revised structure of the industry and the declining number of customers competing to distribute industry products and bargaining with the workforce. The ability of the conglomerates to decrease their risks at the distribution end has enabled them to seek out and invest in alternative regional production sites and to squeeze producers to look for financing and production cost reductions from regional states.

The story of how the location strategies of media production and distribution firms have changed between the 1980s and early 2000s also contains some valuable insights into the forces and processes shaping a new international division of *skilled* labor.

A literature on the new international division of labor stretching back to the 1970s, demonstrated that the ability of transnational firms to exploit comparative advantage in wage rates and labor power requires collaboration among transnational firms, a growth coalition including regional property developers, and a politically cooperative national and local state. Without modern infrastructure, transnational firms find it difficult and inefficient to take advantage of comparative differences in wage rates. The first enterprise industrial zones, distinctive enclaves in which the telecommunications and transportation infrastructure was made to order for transnational firms or their suppliers, were critical to the construction of a new international division of labor in low-skilled manufacturing. International competition among these manufacturing zones contributed to the ability of transnational firms to drive down wage rates while maintaining the logistical infrastructure to enable just-in-time production and distribution.

The out-sourcing of skilled work, especially that requiring innovation and creativity requires even more intensive use of state resources, not only in infrastructure but also in the provision of a skilled workforce. While it may be necessary to transnational investment, low cost labor is not sufficient even if that labor is skilled. Comparative advantage derives not just from an aggregation of lower-wage workers but also from the existence of the conditions that make it possible to exploit those low wages to extract increasing returns. This is particularly true in accessing a skilled workforce that needs to be creative in order to produce a product. If comparative advantage is not rooted solely in the presence of individual low-wage workers but depends on public investments and regulatory environments, we need to focus attention on how those regulatory environments and investment opportunities are politically constructed.

Notes

1   Jack Valenti Press Release, February 7, 2002. Available at: <http://www.mpaa.org/jack/2002/ 2002_02_07b.htm>.

2   This article draws on earlier research on runaway production and economic development policy (Christopherson and Storper, 1989; Storper and Christopherson, 1985). The current analysis draws on recent (2001–2004) interviews with union leaders, public officials, producers, studio owners, and industry lobbyists in New York, Washington, DC, and Los Angeles; policy reports on regional competition in media production in the US and Canada and analysis of secondary public employment data and proprietary data from unions and entertainment payroll companies.

3   Because it has come to focus on access to skilled labor, the policy debate over "runaway production" also provides an occasion to examine the contemporary labor question in the media industries. While the processes attendant to the vertical disintegration of production from the 1950s to the early 1980s have the subject of considerable examination and debate (cf. Aksoy and Robins, Blair and Rainnie, 2000; Christopherson and Storper, 1989; Storper and Christopherson, 1987; Hozic, 2001), the horizontally and vertically integrated production regime that began to emerge in the mid-1980s has received much less attention (Balio, 1998; Christopherson, 1996, 2002; Gomery, 1998; Scott, 2005). A consideration of labor issues and production politics has been particularly neglected in analysis of the new Hollywood that has emerged since the deregulation of the industry in the 1980s and 1990s. This is a major gap given the central role played by labor skills in media industries and the historical role that unions have played in organizing the industry (Christopherson and Storper, 1989).

4   Core industries products are more expensive to produce but have an extended life as profit-makers. They also compose a central component of income for the entertainment industry workforce. As project-based workers, they compose an income combining work from the core projects with that from lower budget and shorter profit-life vehicles. In some national economies there are measures to enforce accountability for claims on the public purse or to weigh and temper the costs of transnational firm agendas. In the US, however, firm influence on the political-economy is not tempered and so we see potential for firm influence in a clearer light. This being said, firms do attempt to rationalize their claims on the public purse and influence on regulation.

5   In some national economies there are measures to enforce accountability for claims on the public purse or to weigh and temper the costs of transnational firm agendas. In the US, however, firm influence on the political-economy is not tempered and so we see potential for firm influence in a clearer light. This being said, firms do attempt to rationalize their claims on the public purse and influence on regulation.

6   US versus Paramount, 1947.

7   Because the anti-trust provision did not extend outside the US, however, the major studios retained the ability to book films in Canadian theaters in package deals rather than individually. This effectively limited the development of an indigenous commercial film industry in that country (Winseck, 2002).

8   Independent film-makers continue to make films with the look and feel of particular places but these films are a very small segment of total film production and, if successful, serve the prestige needs of the media conglomerates rather than their profit goals.

References

Amiti, M., 2005. Location of vertically linked industries: agglomeration versus comparative advantage. *European Economic Review* 49 (4), 809–832.

Balio, T., 1998. A major presence in all the world's major markets: the globalization of Hollywood in the 1990s. In: Neale, S., Smith, M. (Eds.), *Contemporary Hollywood Cinema*. Routledge, London, pp. 58–73.

Blackwell, R., 2003. Canadian film industry worried. *Toronto Globe and Mail*, October 9 (Available at GlobeandMail.com).

Blair, H., Rainnie, A., 2000. Flexible films? *Media, Culture and Society* 22, 187–204.

Brenner, N., 2005. *New State Spaces, Urban Governance and the Rescaling of Statehood*. Oxford University Press, Oxford.

British Columbia Ministry of Economic Development, 2005. *Film and Television Industry Review*. The Ministry, Vancouver.

California's Entertainment Workforce: Employment and Earnings (1991–2002), 2005. The Entertainment Economy Institute and the PMR Group Inc. (December). EEI, Los Angeles.

California State Department of Employment Development, 2005. Biennial Report on the Motion Picture and Television Industry in California. Sacramento: State of California.

Canadian Film and Television Production Association, 2003. Producers applaud feds as they boost tax credit. Press release November 11. Available from: <www.cftpa.ca>.

Canadian Film and Television Production Association, 2005. Submission to the standing committee on finance pre-budget consultation. September 8. Available from: <www.cftpa.ca>.

Center for an Urban Future, 2005. Creative New York. Available from: <www.nycfuture.org>.

Christopherson, S., 1996. Industrial relations in an international industry, film production. In: Gray, L., Seeber, R. (Eds.), *Under the Stars, Industrial Relations in the Entertainment Media Industries*. Cornell University Press, Ithaca, pp. 86–112.

Christopherson, S., 2002. Project work in context: regulatory change and the new geography of media. *Environment and Planning* A 34, 2003–2015.

Christopherson, S., Storper, M., 1986. The city as studio; the world as backlot: the impact of vertical disintegration on the location of the motion picture industry. *Environment and Planning D: Society and Space* 4, 305–320.

Christopherson, S., Storper, M., 1989. The effects of flexible specialization on industrial politics and the labor market: the motion picture industry. *Industrial and Labor Relations Review* 42 (April), 331–347.

Coe, N.M., 2000. On location: American capital and the local labor market in the Vancouver film industry. *International Journal of Urban and Regional Research* 24, 79–91.

Coe, N.M., 2001. A hybrid agglomeration? The development of a satellite marshallian industrial district in Vancouver's film industry. *Urban Studies* 38, 1753–1775.

Droesch, A., 2004. Hollywood North: the impact of costs and demarcation rules on the runaway film industry. Unpublished manuscript. Stanford University, Stanford California 94305. Available from the author.

Elmer, G., Gasher, M., 2005. *Contracting Out Hollywood, Runaway Productions and Foreign Location Shooting*. Rowman & Littlefield, Toronto.

Entertainment Industry Development Corporation, 2001. MOW's—A Three Year Study. EIDC, Los Angeles.

Epstein, E.J., 2005. *The Big Picture, The New Logic of Money and Power in Hollywood*. Random House, New York.

Fabricant, G., 1992. Blitz hits small-studio pix. *The New York Times*, July 12, Section F, p. 7.

Film and Television Action Committee (FTAC), 2004. *We are Creating the Jobs Your Children want*. FTAC, Los Angeles.

Florida, R., 2002. *The Rise of the Creative Class*. Basic Books, New York.

Friedman, T.L., 2005. *The World is Flat*. Farrar, Strauss and Giroux, New York.

Galbraith, J., 2000. *Created Equal*. The University of Chicago Press, Chicago.

Gereffi, G., Humphrey, J., Sturgeon, T., 2005. The governance of global value chains. *Review of International Political Economy* 12 (1), 78–104.

Goettler, R., Leslie, P., 2004. Cofinancing to manage risk in the motion picture industry. Stanford University, Graduate School of Business, Stanford California, 94305. Available from the author.

Gierzynski, A., 2000. *Money Rules, Financing Elections in America*. West-view Press, Boulder.

Gomery, D., 1998. Hollywood corporate business practice and periodizing contemporary film history. In: Neale, S., Smith, M. (Eds.), *Contemporary Hollywood Cinema*. Routledge, London, pp. 47–57.

Gray, L., Seeber, R., 1996. *Under the Stars, Essays on Labor Relations in Arts and Entertainment*. Cornell University Press, Ithaca.

Gray, L., Figueroa, M., Richardson, D., 2005. Analysis of Employment Patterns in the Media Entertainment Industries. Cornell School of Industrial and Labor Relations, New York. Available from the authors.

Grossman, G.M., Helpman, E., 1991. *Innovation and Growth in the Global Economy*. MIT Press, Cambridge, MA.

Hall, P., Soskice, D., 2001. *Varieties of Capitalism*. Oxford University Press, New York.

Harrison, B., 1997. *Lean and Mean: The Resurrection of Corporate Power in an Age of Flexibility*, second ed. Temple University Press, Philadelphia.

Hill, L., 2004. Can media artists survive media consolidation? *The Journal of the Caucus of Television Producers, Writers and Directors* VVII, 17–21.

Holt, J., 2001. In deregulation we trust: the synergy of politics and industry in Reagan-Era Hollywood. *Film Quarterly* 55 (2), 22–29.

Hozic, A.A., 2001. *Hollyworld: Space, Power, and Fantasy in the American Economy*. Cornell University Press, Ithaca, NY.

Jones, M., 2002. Motion picture production in California. Report Requested by Assembly Member Dario Frommer, Chair of the Select Committee on the Future of California's Film Industry.

Koch, N., 1990. Action-packed expansion. *Channels* April 9, 20–28.

Kogut, B., 1984. Normative observations on the international value-added chain and strategic groups. *Journal of International Business Studies* 15 (2), 151–167.

Kogut, B., 1985. Designing global strategies: comparative and competitive value-added chains. *Sloan Management Review* Summer, 15–28.

Krugman, P., 1990. *Geography and Trade*. MIT Press, Cambridge, MA.

Lash, S., Urry, J., 1987. *The End of Organized Capitalism*. University of Wisconsin Press, Madison.

Lee, K., 2002. Remaking the geography of southern California's film and television industry. Paper presented at the Annual Meeting of the American Association of Geographers. March 19–23, Los Angeles.

Lovering, J., 2001. The coming regional crisis (and how to avoid it). *Regional Studies* 35, 349–354.

Maltby, R., 1998. 'Nobody Knows Everything': Post-classical historiographies and consolidated entertainment. In: Neale, S., Smith, M. (Eds.), *Contemporary Hollywood Cinema*. Routledge, New York, pp. 21–44.

Manly, L., 2005. Networks and the outside producer: can they co-exist? *New York Times*, June 20, C1, C7.

Martin, R., Sunley, P., 1997. The Post-Keynsian state and the space economy. In: Lee, R., Wiills, J. (Eds.), *Geographies of Economies*. London, pp. 278–289.

Martinelli, F., Schoenberger, E., 1991. Oligopoly is alive and well: notes for a broader discussion of flexible accumulation. In: Benko, G., Dunford, M. (Eds.), *Industrial Change and Regional Development*. Bellhaven, London, pp. 117–133.

Miller, T., Govil, N., McMurria, J., Maxwell, R., 2001. *Global Hollywood*. British Film Institute, London.

Monitor, 1999. US Runaway Film and Television Production Study Report. Commissioned by the Directors Guild of America and Screen Actors Guild. Monitor Company, Santa Monica, CA.

Montpool, T., 1998. Casting labour: the dynamics of Toronto's film and television production industry. Unpublished Master's thesis. Geography Department, University of Waterloo. Waterloo, Ontario, Canada.

Motion Picture Association of America (MPAA), 2005. US Entertainment Industry Market Statistic Report. MPAA, Los Angeles.

Offe, C., Keane, J. (Eds.), 1984. *Contradictions of the Welfare State*. MIT Press, Cambridge.

Peck, J., 1992. Labor and agglomeration: control and flexibility in local labor markets. *Economic Geography* 68 (4), 325–347.

Personal Interview, 2005. New York City Film and Television Office. New York, October.

Pethel, B., 2002. Canada's movie, TV subsidies under fire. *Toronto Star* (Ontario Edition), Entertainment Section, (July 4) 23.

Prince, S., 2000. *A New Pot of Gold: Hollywood Under the Electronic Rainbow*, 1980–1989. Charles Scribner's Sons, New York.

Reich, R.B., 1990. Who is us? *Harvard Business Review*, 1, January.

Scott, A.J., 2004. The other hollywood: the organizational and geographic bases of television-program production. *Media, Culture and Society* 26 (2), 183–205.

Scott, A.J., 2005. *On Hollywood: The Place, The Industry*. Princeton University Press, Princeton.

Storper, M., 1997. *The Regional World*. Guildford, New York.

Storper, M., Christopherson, S., 1985. The Changing Organization and Location of the Motion Picture Industry. Research Report R854, Graduate School of Architecture and Urban Planning, University of California, Los Angeles.

Storper, M., Christopherson, S., 1987. Flexible specialization and regional industrial agglomerations: the case of the US motion picture industry. *Annals of the Association of American Geographers* 77 (1), 104–117.

Tysoe, D., 2004. Report of the Industrial Inquiry Commission appointed by the provincial government of British Columbia. The Province of British Columbia, North Vancouver (March 4).

U.S. Department of Commerce, 2001. Report on Runaway Production. U.S. Department of Commerce, Washington.

Webster, R.A., 2005. *Proposed cap on tax credits would be harmful for LA's film industry*. New Orleans City Business (New Orleans, LA), (9 May).

Weinstein, B., Clower, T., 2000. Filmed entertainment and local economic development: Texas as a case study. *Economic Development Quarterly* 14 (4), 384–397.

Winseck, D., 2002. Netscapes of power: convergence, consolidation and power in the Canadian mediascape. *Media, Culture and Society* 24, 795–819.

PART 2

Text

INTRODUCTION

WHERE AND WHAT *is* a Hollywood film? Is it the original release print; or the director's cut; or the version on the DVD with commentary; or the gossip about the movie cultivated by publicists and promulgated across the airwaves and garden fences; or a pirated disc rented from a taxi stand? The analysis of textual properties and spectatorial processes is best supplemented by an account of *occasionality* that details the conditions under which a text is made, circulated, received, interpreted and criticized. Hollywood movies are not just signs to be read; they are not just coefficients of political and economic power; and they are not just industrial objects. Rather, they are all these things; they are hybrid monsters, coevally subject to rhetoric, status, and technology—to text, power, and science—all at once, but in contingent ways. We need a tripartite approach to analyzing Hollywood texts, viz. reconstruction of older interpretations; a focus on texts themselves via formal and stylistic analyses; and identification of how they are projected by their owners. Because films accrete and attenuate meanings as they rub up against, trope, and are troped by other texts and the social, we must consider all the shifts and shocks that characterize their existence as cultural commodities.

GENRE

Genres are types. In the Hollywood context, they refer to the interplay of repetition and difference, their organization and interpretation by producers, audiences, and critics. This can happen at the level of the movie studio, the exhibitor, the censor, or the reviewer. Each finds enough in common between texts to group them together, and enough that is different to make us want to experience more than one exemplar. This section is designed to show how genres and even media bleed into one another. Sarah Berry provides a general account of the idea of the genre in film studies, and Paul Kerr looks at the vexed question of perhaps the most-studied and -revered genre of all, the *film noir*. What and when was it? Should we understand it as a symbol of World War II's devastation of the male psyche and reversal of gender relations? Is it a symptom of a United States torn apart by cynicism, despair, and fear—the dark side of what is now referred to as "The Greatest Generation?" Or, more prosaically, was *film noir* an accommodation to the rhythms of a round-the-clock cycle of filmmaking that required economical use of such resources as people and lights? These studies in genre collectively ask what should be the balance between explanations of films that focus on their relationship to the social world and history versus their industrial origins as the product of work and capital.

PLEASURE

Pleasure addresses the vexed question of the fun we get from film. Is the medium in some way morally irresponsible for entertaining us through violence, for instance? The Papacy thinks so, as evidenced in the *Encyclical Letter* excerpted here, which urged priests to become amateur film critics in order to shepherd their flock. And what about the charge from more progressive quarters that Hollywood creates false consciousness, distracting people from the realities of the workaday world and its political economy by filling their lives with fantasies? That ongoing issue is engaged in a fascinating debate between Randy Rutsky and Justin Wyatt, on the one hand, who argue for the liberatory potential of fun through viewing, and Noel King, who asks us to look at this claim across its historical trajectory.

REPRESENTATION

Representation looks at the links between characters on screen and actual populations—what do we see when we look at images of women, of different races, of men, of the elderly, of the religious? What is Hollywood selling us, and how does that relate to the "real" world? The section includes Ed Guerrero looking at the African-American return to directorial prominence in the 1980s and 1990s via such figures as Spike Lee, and what that means given the issues swirling around how black folks are represented in US popular culture. Gina Escamilla, Angie L. Cradock, and Ichiro Kawachi use content analysis to establish patterns across screen texts of women smoking, putting us in a good position to assess the prevalence of such deadly product placement. Tania Modleski favors psychoanalysis to look at women on screen and the conflicts of sexuality that dominate their imaging. Chon Noriega considers the image of Latinos in Hollywood's classical era. Finally, Jack Shaheen examines the complexities of Hollywood's relationship to the Arabic world, a favored object of negative or romanticized imagery over eight decades.

Chapter 15

Sarah Berry

GENRE (2004)

> The books in a library must be arranged in one way or another. . . . Who can deny the
> necessity and the utility of such arrangements? But what should we say if some one
> began seriously to seek out the literary laws . . . of shelf A or shelf B, that is to say, of
> those altogether arbitrary groupings whose sole object was their practical utility?
>
> Benedetto Croce, *Aesthetic*

A CCORDING TO POPULAR USAGE, film genres are ways of grouping movies by style and story; a "genre film" is one that can be easily categorized with reference to a culturally familiar rubric. Genres offer prospective consumers a way to choose between films and help indicate the kind of audience for whom a particular movie was made. This emphasis on genres as means of popular market segmentation is, however, fairly recent. This chapter will offer a brief overview of how genres have been defined within film studies, beginning with post-war mythology and iconology studies and ending with contemporary debates about genres as broad discursive practices.

Western genre theory is often traced back to Aristotle's *Poetics* and its influence on eighteenth-century European classicism, when genres were seen as ideal types of artistic expression to be emulated and refined. Classical genres, however, quickly turned into academically defined rules governing style and content in the arts. With the nineteenth-century Romantic movement, many artists and writers came to see classical genres as an over-regulation of both representation and reception (Jameson 1981: 106; Buscombe 1995: 11). By the time of cinema's arrival in the 1890s, genres had become even more discredited through association with mass-market publishing, which displaced the Victorian "gentle reader" at the center of the publishing world (Wilson 1983: 41). As a result, genres were associated with popular culture and a "brand name system against which any authentic artistic expression must necessarily struggle" (Jameson 1981: 107).

Early film critics thus tended to see genre as something to be derided or overlooked, since Romantic and nascent modernist aesthetics defined art in terms of individual formative vision, not commercial or popular forms. Although individual critics and avant-garde groups like the surrealists admired slapstick comedy or Feuillade's detective serials, it was not until after World War II that film writers began to question the priority of authorship over genre in critical evaluation. Under the influence of the *Cahiers du cinéma*, mainstream film critics began to take genre films more seriously, but their praise of individual genre films still implied that such works transcended generic mediocrity thanks to their directors' personal vision. Andrew Sarris, for example, used the term "genre film" to describe works without distinction – although he occasionally described genre films as having "unexpected deposits of feeling" (cited in Alloway 1969: 11).

In 1969, however, British writer Lawrence Alloway argued for a radically different approach to film criticism. In his catalog for a screening of popular American crime films at the Museum of Modern Art, Alloway wrote:

> The proper point of departure for a film critic who is going to write about the movies is membership in the large audience for whom they are intended . . . the majority of film reviewers write as a hostile minority interested primarily in works that are above obsolescence. The emphasis in this book is on a description of popular movies, viewed in sets and cycles rather than as single entities. It is an approach that accepts obsolescence and in which judgments derive from the sympathetic consumption of a great many films. In terms of continuing themes and motifs, the obsolescence of single films is compensated for by the prolongation of ideas in film after film. (1969: 19)

Alloway's argument that genre films should be seen as part of "sets and cycles" has resonance today in relation to television studies and the recognition of how intertextuality and repetition structure individual television programs (cf. Browne 1987). Alloway's work offered a significant challenge to criticism that evaluated popular films solely in terms derived from more elite, individualized forms of cultural production. Instead, Alloway supported an approach based on the recurring "themes and motifs" of popular films, grouping them into loosely defined categories to be described and interpreted by genre critics.

1 PROBLEMS OF DEFINITION

Current debates on the status of film genres arise, in part, because of the different reasons for invoking them: film scholars tend to define genres for purposes of interpretation and critical analysis, while producers, publicists, and audiences may use them as descriptive tools. Genres are part of film production and reception around the world, and although many Hollywood genres are internationally recognized, they always have culturally specific meanings. The variety of contexts and uses for generic labels is important because it indicates the provisional nature of such categories. In practical terms, genres are vehicles for the circulation of films in industrial, critical, and popular discourses. As the culture industries rapidly expand their global reach, questions of the cross-cultural circulation of genres become increasingly central to an understanding of how cinematic meaning is constructed and "translated."

One might argue for a more limited, textual definition of genres by pointing out that generic conventions are not merely part of the circulation and reception of films, but are often inscribed as central aspects of film form and intelligibility. The film *Singin' in the Rain* (1952), for example, is not merely considered a musical by broad consensus; it also comments on and formally typifies the conventions of the "Hollywood musical." But generic meaning can never be inscribed within a single film – the repetition of genre motifs can only be experienced intertextually. Genre studies set out to define and codify such intertextual fields, and thereby create their own objects rather than simply discovering them. Certain formal or narrative patterns are seen as paradigmatic and thus serve, as Derrida suggests, to demarcate sameness and difference (Derrida 1980: 204). If we assume, however, that each film culture tends to generate some broadly agreed-upon generic categories, the question remains as to what significance they have. Are genres part of the dominant ideological bias of entertainment industries, functioning primarily to reconcile viewers to the status quo? Are they manifestations of the popular imagination, selected and repeated because of the viewing habits of sovereign film consumers? Are they simply stylistic and narrative patterns that engage viewers in pleasurable kinds of cognitive hypotheses and variations?

These questions have often been addressed by seeing genres as part of an interdependent relationship between audience, industry, text (Ryall, cited in Gledhill 1985: 58), although most genre studies tend to focus on one of these three sites of genre use. For example, audience reception studies tend to define genres as "reading practices": socio-discursive frameworks and "horizons of expectation" brought by viewers to each new film they see. In this sense, genres are social rather than textual constraints, allowing viewers to modify their generic frameworks and participate in the construction of meaning rather than simply "absorbing" it from the screen. For industry analysts, the ways that genres are used in relation to marketing strategies (advertising, merchandising, the star system, etc.) are seen to have a definitive influence on such reading practices. Lastly, texual and formal analysis in film studies tends to focus on the ways that narrative and stylistic conventions are "encoded" with genre-specific meanings. These aesthetic devices are seen to cue viewers to anticipate certain experiences (music or editing patterns that create suspense, for example, or the use of filters and sepia tones to indicate a period film). The history of such aesthetic codes is significant even when they are seen, ultimately, as dependent on larger discourses for their meaning (once we know we are watching a period film, for example, what kind of reading practices might come into play?). Ultimately, this circulation of meaning between audience, industry, and film text is irresolvable, but it is also central to any discussion of the significance of film genres.

2 EARLY GENRE STUDY: CLASSICISM AND MYTH

Early film genres were derived by the transposition of visual, narrative, and discursive patterns from older media onto cinematic forms. Early Japanese films, for example, not only adapted traditional storytelling and theatrical "content" for the screen, but they were also incorporated into theatrical productions, with films projected as backdrops for Kabuki and *shimpa* plays (Nolletti and Desser 1992: ix). In the US and Europe, early film categories were primarily derived from other popular forms such as melodrama, religious and occult spectacle, journalistic and pictorial photography, the Wild West show, the travel or scientific lecture, and the dime novel. In spite of this history of polyglot genre formation, the task of genre analysis in film studies has often been seen as one of clarifying the key qualities and limits of each genre. Like Aristotle's *Poetics*, such approaches imply that genres have highly specific qualities which, like art forms more generally, demonstrate their essence when developed into a classical or ideal form. David Bordwell has detailed the degree to which early film scholars adopted such developmental models of art, which proposed:

> a progressive development from simpler to more complex forms, treated according to that biological analogy of birth/childhood/maturity so common among art historians since Vasari. (1997: 9)

But Bordwell also notes that early film criticism adopted many tenets of aesthetic modernism, such as "the need for perpetual breaks with academicism" and a "radical' interrogation" of the medium (1997: 9). Early film critics thus tended to valorize individual works and see most genre films as formulaic products of a low-brow industry. Individual genre films were occasionally canonized, but it was not until the post-war reappraisal of Hollywood cinema by critics like André Bazin that the relationship between genre filmmaking and the Romantic/modernist model of artistic production was seriously explored.

The advent of genre criticism was marked by a shift in focus away from film's aesthetically "transformative" and medium-specific attributes toward a more sociological interest in relations between style, popular narrative, and myth. André Bazin's praise of the western, for example, centered on its representation of an imaginary past, and he described its formal motifs as "signs or symbols of its profound reality, namely the myth" (Bazin 1971b: 142). But Bazin also maintained the developmental assumptions and genre essentialism of traditional art history, seeing *Stagecoach* (1939), for example, in highly Platonic terms:

> *Stagecoach* is the ideal example of the maturity of a style brought to classic perfection. John Ford struck the ideal balance between social myth, historical reconstruction, psychological truth, and the traditional theme of the Western *mise-en-scène* . . . [it] is like a wheel, so perfectly made that it remains in equilibrium on its axis in any position. (Bazin 1971a: 149)

Post-war westerns, he argued, often abandoned this sense of the "profound reality" of the myth by becoming more self-conscious and thematically diverse (149).

This model of film genres' birth, evolution to a classical form, and inevitable decline is derived from art historians' periodization of stylistic movements into "experimental," "classical," and "baroque" phases. Although Bazin wrote that he did not claim to "explain everything by the famous law of successive aesthetic periods," such a teleology is implicit in his statement that "by 1938 or 1939 the talking film . . . had reached a level of classical perfection" due to the "maturing" of its dramatic and technical vocabulary (cited in Alloway 1969: 11). Thomas Schatz has cited art historian Henri Focillon's notion that the life-cycle morphology is "inherent in [art] forms themselves," although Schatz also draws on Russian formalist theory, which proposes that "as a genre gains popularity it loses its defamiliarizing role and moves inevitably into decadence, giving way to new forms" (Schatz 1981: 37; Gunning 1990: 87).

In early genre criticism, this genre morphology was frequently combined with a genre/ myth analogy, relating generic rise and fall in a mimetic relationship to changes in social consciousness. This audience-driven morphology assumes that film viewers either validate existing mythological forms or require that they undergo revision. John Cawelti has argued, for example, that following their phases of innovation and classicism, genres go through a period of revisionist "self-awareness on the part of both creators and audiences," resulting in the popularity of "parodic and satiric treatments," and the eventual formation of new genres (Cawelti 1979: 578). Although invoked by numerous film theorists, many have noted that this model of generic change relies on the degree to which commercial film genres "reflect" the collective sensibilities of a mass audience – a problematic thesis that will be explored in more detail below.

On the other hand, Steven Neale has argued that when seen in a larger historical context, the formalist approach to generic change can indicate the social dimensions of genre as a changing set of reading practices, rather than a fixed one. He notes that this requires equal attention to all three sites of generic meaning, however: audiences, industries, and texts. Citing Hans Robert Jauss, Neale argues that each new film seen by a particular viewer becomes part of the "founding and altering" of that viewer's horizon of generic expectations (Neale 1990: 57). Such an approach appeals to individual experience, since every film spectator has a personal viewing history and a set of cinematic associations and expectations; but how generic change is implemented remains unclear. Neale cites Jauss's suggestion that: "[s]uccessful genres . . . gradually lose their effective power through continual reproduction; they are forced to the periphery by new genres" (Neale 1990: 60). How a genre's "effective power" is determined, and how generic innovation is derived from reader responses remains unspecified, however; Neale concludes that the model "allows for a variety of factors" (61).

Earlier genre theorists often argued that, like myths, genres have an organic relation to social consciousness – an assumption that arises from traditional literary studies as well as art history. Post-Enlightenment models of literary history, following Kant and Hegel, described literary works as functioning to mirror a culture back to itself in a process of dialectical evolution toward cultural self-realization and -understanding (Corngold 1988: 139). The film/myth analogy applied this model of art as a form of cultural self-reflection to the more populist context of cinema. Significantly, this helped to dissolve film criticism's tendency to dismiss genre films as "formulaic" and thus unartistic: if the formulas themselves could be shown to be significant aspects of cultural selfawareness and evolution, they could be incorporated into "high-art" methods of articulating aesthetic value and meaning.

One disadvantage of this model, however, is that the search for the mythological essence of a particular genre is inevitably retrospective and elegiac. For if a genre is seen as a mythical form, how can the myth's essential meaning be defined unless it has already reached its "classical" phase of articulation? One can only interpret a set of films definitively by closing it off from new additions and thus locating its expressive acme in the past. It is not surprising, therefore, that the genre most easily characterized as mythological was the Hollywood western. By the mid-1950s, the western had enough canonical exemplars to be seen as having reached a "classical" peak in the 1930s and '40s, subsequently entering a period of "reinterpretation" and decline.

The American critic Robert Warshow was, along with Bazin, an early interpreter of film genre, and his book *Movie Chronicle: The Westerner* (1954) offered a comparative analysis of the heroes of Hollywood gangster films and westerns. Warshow points out that these "men with guns" represent a basic American fascination with violence, but he is more interested in the differences between the two types of hero and their relationship to violence. The gangster is, for example, a figure of "enterprise and success" whose frenetic career is nevertheless "a nightmare inversion of the values of ambition and opportunity." The western hero, on the other hand, is "the last gentleman," demonstrating such a restrained sense of purpose that he often "appears to be unemployed" (Warshow 1979: 471). His nobility is always somewhat anachronistic, as well as morally ambiguous, due to the fact that, "whatever his justifications, he is a killer of men." What makes the western compelling for Warshow is its "serious orientation to the problem of violence" and its ritualistic repetition of the "value" of violence under certain moral conditions. The fact that such heroic vigilantism is incompatible with the legal precepts of democracy simply adds to the western hero's mythical potency:

> What redeems him is that he no longer believes in this drama and nevertheless
> will continue to play his role perfectly: the pattern is all. (Warshow 1979: 480)

The consistency and purity of purpose that Warshow values in the western hero is also central to his definition of the "classical" western form. He writes, for example, that the western is "an art form for connoisseurs, where the spectator derives his pleasure from the appreciation of minor variations within the working out of a pre-established order" (1979:

480). Like Aristotle, Warshow is highly prescriptive in his definition of the genre's essence: he argues that westerns should avoid excesses of realism or stylization as well as the incorporation of any new motifs not present in the exemplary classical works. *The Virginian* (1929), for example, is "an archetypal Western movie" about the leader of a posse (Gary Cooper) who must oversee the lynching of his best friend for stealing cattle. But *The Ox-Bow Incident* (1943), which deals with the injustice and psychological implications of a lynching, is regarded as an "anti-Western" (Warshow 1979: 475). Purity of generic form is thus predicated on the anti-realist abstraction of its thematic content. Women, for example, represent "civilization" in the classic western, but in this capacity their role must remain marginal; Warshow complains that "in *The Gunfighter* the women and children are a little too much in evidence, threatening constantly to become a real focus of concern instead of simply part of the given framework" (Warshow 1979: 481; cf. Modleski 1997). Thus, while raising important issues about the representation of violent masculinity in American film, Warshow's work demonstrates the drawbacks of defining a genre's essential or "classical" qualities, which requires their abstraction from the socio-political and discursive contexts that organize their meaning.

The genre studies of Bazin, Warshow, and Alloway, together with the *Cahiers du cinéma* critics' valorization of mise-en-scène over script in regard to Hollywood film, allowed genres to be seen as expressive vocabularies rather than simply as constraints imposed by the film industry (cf. McArthur 1972). They were also compared positively by some scholars to classical traditions in the arts; in the mid-1970s, for example, Leo Braudy argued that by returning to pre-Romantic models of artistic production, genre films could be seen as "the equivalent of conscious reference to tradition in the other arts." The vision of the film auteur was seen as a process of "picking and choosing among possible conventions" in order to revivify classical forms. Braudy's ideal genre film is thus a "self-conscious mastery" of formal and narrative patterns that could raise genre films to the same level of expressivity as less generically coded films (Braudy 1979: 448). Jean-Loup Bourget has pointed out that genre auteurism reconciled "two apparently antagonistic approaches: the auteur theory, which claims that a film is the work of one creative individual, and the iconological approach, which assumes that a film is a sequence of images whose real meaning may well be unconscious on the part of its makers" (Bourget 1995: 51). As a result, Hollywood's conventionality could be seen, paradoxically, as the "reason for its creativity," forcing talented directors to transcend hackneyed plots through the "pure poetry" of visual elements (50).

3 ICONOLOGY AND GENRE STRUCTURALISM

In addition to the genre/myth analogy outlined by Bazin and Warshow, a primary influence on early genre studies was the work of art historian Erwin Panofsky (cf. Alloway 1969; McArthur 1972). His 1939 book *Studies in Iconology* concerned itself with the denotative and symbolic content of art, rather than its formal qualities. For Panofsky, the recognition of conventional meanings attached to images ("that a male figure with a knife represents St. Bartholomew, that a female figure with a peach in her hand is a personification of Veracity") constitutes iconographic analysis in a "narrow" sense. The deeper sense of iconographic meaning, however,

> is apprehended by ascertaining those underlying principles which reveal the basic attitude of a nation, a period, a class, a religious or philosophical persuasion.
>
> (Panofsky 1939: 7)

Works of art are thus directly mimetic of their *Zeitgeist*, and culture itself is seen as an expressive totality. The visual motifs found in a particular period and art form thus allow the art historian to:

> deal with the work of art as a symptom of something else which expresses itself in a countless variety of other symptoms, and . . . interpret its compositional and iconographical features as more particularized evidence of this "something else." (8)

Panofsky's iconology was useful to the study of film genre because it emphasized the visual motifs and symbolic language of art rather than individual authorship or mythic narrative. To some extent, it can be seen as a kind of visual content analysis, especially when iconology is applied to cinematic motifs without Panofsky's emphasis on interpretation. Alloway, for example, suggests that since "there is no body of literature" that defines the meaning of cinematic imagery, "it is necessary to derive the information from adequate samples of the films themselves" (Alloway 1969: 41). Alloway also rejects the notion that film iconology amounts to a kind of myth analysis, since he emphasizes the constant change and ephemerality of visual patterns in popular art (54). His application of iconology to film genres is thus more descriptive than interpretive. But Panofsky's own method presupposed that symbolic vocabularies reflected the essential concerns of a particular culture and period, which could be conceived as an organic essence manifesting itself consistently in all forms of expression. His work thus typifies E. H. Gombrich's critique of art history as "Hegelianism without metaphysics" (cited in Bordwell 1997: 44).

In "The Idea of Genre in the American Cinema," Ed Buscombe takes a position similar to Alloway's use of iconology, suggesting that generic visual conventions can be productively analyzed without assuming that they are part of a comprehensive thematic structure. For Buscombe, describing the western in terms of its mise-en-scène (the landscapes, towns, clothes, guns, horses, etc.) is not comprehensive or definitive of what westerns are about, but it is saying "something both intelligible and useful," namely that "the visual conventions provide a framework within which the story can be told" (Buscombe 1995: 15). Iconography is thus a palette of familiar motifs that can be recombined creatively (or ironically) in ways that provide both familiarity and variety. Buscombe's emphasis on familiarity and variation is reminiscent of Warshow's notion of the western as a genre for "connoisseurs," but without the nostalgia for a "pure" western form that had died out. A more thematic definition may nevertheless be implicit, since Buscombe notes that:

> the essential theme of *Guns in the Afternoon* (1962; U.S. title, *Ride the High Country*) is one that, while it could be put into other forms, is ideally suited to the one chosen. The film describes the situation of men who have outlived their time. Used to a world where issues were decided simply, on a test of strength, they now find this way of life threatened by complications and developments they do not understand. Since they cannot, or will not, adapt, all that remains to them is a tragic and bitter heroism. (24)

But the question of why this story is "ideally suited" to the western's iconographic language is not really addressed in Buscombe's descriptive paradigm. Definitions of genre based on loosely grouped sets of repeated motifs are thus open to shifting, intertextual, and historical meanings, but they often rely on implicitly mythological or auteur-based interpretations (Kitses and McArthur both combine iconographic genre analyses with auteur studies). What is lacking in most iconological analyses is a more historical approach to visual and thematic intertextuality, which might address the social semiotics of specific genre motifs for particular audiences.

Panofsky emphasized the art historian's search for "symptomatic" meanings, which must be inferred based on the totality of cultural production from any one period. The uptake of iconographic analysis in film studies, however, was equally informed by structural linguistics and anthropology. Structuralism assumes that the meanings attributed to signs within any symbolic language arise comparatively – they do not express a pre-existing cultural essence. No object or word can have meaning in a vacuum – its meaning must be derived by contrast with a different kind of meaning. Symbolic systems are thus structured by core tensions or differential values, and it is the task of the analyst to perceive those "deep structures." The difference between this model and Panofsky's is that a structuralist one sees forms of communication not as the expressions of a pre-existing social essence, but as systems of meaning that structure the social itself by encouraging certain forms of conceptualization and not others.

The structuralist genre studies of Jim Kitses (*Horizons West*, 1969), Will Wright (*Sixguns and Society*, 1975), and Thomas Schatz (*Hollywood Genres*, 1981) thus viewed genres as structures of differential meaning and as part of larger frameworks of difference between generic paradigms. Kitses, for example, begins his analysis of the Hollywood western by looking at the opposition proposed by Henry Nash Smith in *Virgin Land* between representations of the US West as garden and desert. Kitses defines this dichotomy as a core opposition between the wilderness and civilization, with additional oppositions aligned as sub-themes: tradition vs. change, restriction vs. freedom, community vs. individuality, etc. (Kitses 1969: 11). In addition to this thematic structure, Kitses sees the genre as drawing its meanings from frontier history, the chivalric codes of medieval romance, and pre-cinematic representations of the West. The core binary oppositions that structure the western film are thus seen to offer a certain socio-historical, narrative, and visual "language" for filmmakers to work within. For Kitses this structure has social significance because it is rooted in mythological and historical tensions, but it produces meaning dialectically by incorporating new approaches rather than evolving to a "classical" form and then dissipating.

Thomas Schatz's *Hollywood Genres* is explicitly informed by Lévi-Strauss's structuralist reading of myth. Schatz thus defines genres around sets of thematic binary oppositions, arguing that their narrative patterns work to temporarily resolve particular cultural tensions. However, as Lévi-Strauss suggests, such stories only provide a temporary resolution of these tensions and therefore must be told repeatedly in various ways. Schatz divides the major Hollywood genres into those that work to re-establish social order (westerns, crime and detective films) and those that work to establish social integration (the musical, comedy, and melodrama). Central to each of these genres is the social community they define, which consists of a set of character types who enact the conflicts inherent within that community. Often opposing value systems are mediated by an individual, or a romantic coupling signifies their integration. The resolution of these conflicts, according to Schatz, constitutes "the genre film's function as cultural ritual." Will Wright, in *Sixguns and Society*, made a similarly comprehensive analysis of the western, drawing on the work of Russian formalists such as Vladimir Propp and his analysis of narrative and character types in folktales. In this way, Wright analyzes not only the core conflicts that structure the western, but also the "character functions" that structure its plot patterns and offer "a conceptual response to the requirements of human action in a social situation" (Wright 1975: 17).

Both Schatz and Wright thus utilize analytical models drawn from earlier forms of narrative (myth and folktale) and apply them to the commercial cinema. The relatively close relations between producers and users of pre-industrial folkways are thus transposed to the capitalist marketplace for entertainment, which raises a number of problems. Schatz refers, for example, to generic change as the result of a "conversation" between filmmakers and audiences, whereby "the genre film reaffirms what the audience believes both on individual and on communal levels" (Schatz 1981: 38). On this point, he cites Leo Braudy's description of film audiences as agents of generic development: "change in genre occurs when the audience says 'that's too infantile a form of what we believe. Show us something more complicated' " (Schatz 1981: 38). Like Schatz, Will Wright proposes that the popularity of Hollywood film, measured in box-office dollars, stands as evidence of viewer demand for just such films and genres (Wright 1975: 12). Wright thus limits his study to films that grossed at least $4,000,000 on initial release.

Schatz and Wright, in other words, base their interpretation of Hollywood genres' social significance on the presumed existence of a feedback loop between audiences and film industries. This popularity, however, is measured in terms of attendance, just as television ratings are used in the US to argue that viewers get exactly what they want. This argument assumes that the market for entertainment works democratically, with each potential viewer having the financial power to "vote" by making consumer choices. The American film industry, however, has long controlled markets through vertical integration and anti-competitive distribution systems. To read profitability as a blanket endorsement of mainstream genres assumes a model of consumer sovereignty and "free market" competition inappropriate to highly monopolized media industries. In addition, as Steven Neale notes, it collapses the "multiplicity of reasons for consumer 'choices' " and varieties of viewing pleasure into a fictive unanimity of taste (Neale 1990: 64; cf. Jowett 1985).

Rick Altman has usefully summarized the differences between iconographic and structural approaches to genre in his essay "A Semantic/Syntactic Approach to Film Genre." Altman points out that these debates center on the classification of genres according to either broadly inclusive, iconographic definitions (a western is a film with cowboys and horses) or more interpretive definitions (a western is about historical tensions between American individualism and society). Altman notes that inclusive definitions, like Buscombe's and McArthur's, are descriptively useful but do not explain the social significance of genres. Interpretive definitions, such as Schatz's "genres of order/genres of integration" model, explain their social significance by simply excluding films that do not repeat those patterns found significant by the analyst. Altman calls inclusive definitions "semantic," since they describe the "building blocks" of genres; explanatory definitions are called "syntactic," since they describe the "structures" into which these elements are narratively presented. Altman proposes that these two definitional strategies are complementary, and that the full significance of film genre can only be understood by utilizing both approaches. He points out that:

> not all genre films relate to their genre in the same way or to the same extent. . . . In addition, a dual approach permits a far more accurate description of the numerous inter-generic connections typically suppressed by single-minded approaches . . . numerous films . . . innovate by combining the syntax of one genre with the semantics of another. (1995)

Such an approach indicates, for example, that the category of film noir is semantically distinctive (noir lighting, framing, and character types) but shares its syntactical patterns with larger categories like the thriller and detective film. It also facilitates analysis of how a film like *The Right Stuff* (1983), which is about astronauts, also uses many of the visual and characterological patterns of the western; or how *Blade Runner* (1982) combines a science-fiction narrative with film noir mise-en-scène.

4 GENRES AND IDEOLOGY

> In melodrama two themes are important: the triumph of moral virtue over
> villainy, and the consequent idealizing of the moral views assumed to be held by
> the audience. In the melodrama of the brutal thriller we come as close as it is
> normally possible for art to come to the pure self-righteousness of the lynching
> mob. We should have to say, then, that all forms of melodrama, the detective
> story in particular, were advance propaganda for the police state, in so far as
> that represents the regularizing of mob violence, if it were possible to take them
> seriously. But it seems not to be possible.
>
> Northrop Frye, *Anatomy of Criticism*

At roughly the same time that Schatz and Wright proposed a ritual significance for Hollywood
genres as expressions of collective imagination, the film journals *Cahiers du cinéma* and *Screen*
were arguing, instead, that Hollywood film imposed dominant ideological meanings on
audiences. In the 1980s, genre theory was thus marked by two very contradictory definitions
of genre – as social ritual and ideological tool. Robert Kapsis has described the ritual model
as a "reflection of society perspective," while the argument that genres are ideological is
referred to by Kapsis as the "production of culture perspective" (1991: 68–9). He offers a
critique of Wright, Schatz, and Cawelti's "reflection" approach based on his analysis of the
"interorganizational relationships" that dominate the American film industry's decision-
making processes, arguing that although historical audiences may exercise some influence
over general market trends, "the very existence of genre films and cycles is a product of the
film industry's attempt to overcome the problem of uncertainty, that is, of not knowing the
future tastes of the mass audience" (70).

For the most part, however, ideological readings of film genre have been based on
textual rather than industrial analysis. The 1970s and '80s genre debates in *Screen*, for
example, tended to see genre as a sub-set of the journal's broader ideological critique of
classical Hollywood narrative, since genres provided and regulated variety while still binding
the viewer to the cinematic institution as a whole in a position of textually inscribed
subjectivity. There were also those who argued for a more straightforward ideological
interpretation of genre. For example, in an article called "Genre Film and the Status Quo,"
Judith Hess Wright argued that, as products of the capitalist culture industry, genre films
"serve the interests of the ruling class by assisting in the maintenance of the status quo" (Hess
Wright 1995: 41). This, as Steven Neale pointed out, amounts to "reductivism, economism,
and cultural pessimism" (Neale 1990: 65). Such a position, like the "reflection of culture"
perspective, uses an overly simplified model of spectatorship, seeing only the influence of
industry over audience rather than the ritual theory's inverse schema. Text-based ideology
critique often assumes a degree of textual determinism, whereby viewers are more passive
than active in relation to cinematic meaning. However, in the 1980s, specific genres such as
melodrama and film noir were also seen as textual structures that manifested ideological
contradictions and thus invited viewers to negotiate or question the conventional resolutions
and patterns of Hollywood narrative.

In the case of melodrama, critical interest in the dynamic between auteurs and the
limits imposed by generic Hollywood scripts (in journals such as *Movie* and *Positif*) focussed
attention on the ability of filmmakers like Douglas Sirk, Nicholas Ray, Max Ophüls and
Vincente Minnelli to transform familiar melodramatic stories through mise-en-scène and the
"formal play of distanciation and irony" (Gledhill 1985: 73). Eventually, as Barbara Klinger
notes, "critics began to consider the relation of melodramatic form to ideology, without an
exclusive emphasis on the director as enabler of critique" (1994: 20). Christine Gledhill

states, for example, that, "through discovery of Sirk, a genre came into view" (cited in Klinger 1994: xii). For example, in 1978, when Laura Mulvey's "Notes on Sirk and Melodrama" was published in *Movie*, it took a somewhat critical view of Paul Willemen's earlier praise of Sirk for subverting the normatively conservative melodramatic form. Instead, Mulvey argued that the ideological tensions foregrounded in Sirk's films were "not produced by the exercise of a special authorial agency, but are a congenital feature of melodrama as a genre filled with ideological inconsistencies" (cited in Klinger 1994: 20).

The notion that genres can manifest "unconscious dynamics" which contradict the ideological values implied by their narratives suggests that they are both symptomatic and ideologically structured. Such an account rests on Althusser's notion of overdetermination, whereby texts are seen as sites of unconsciously conflicting structural forces. For example, one can argue that 1950s American melodrama "raised the contradictions inherent in bourgeois and patriarchal ideologies" (Klinger 1994: 22) or that American film noir exposed the misogyny of post-war angst over masculine self-determination. Such descriptions see the "subversive" genre as a particularly rich constellation of tensions within the dominant culture that structures mainstream filmmaking. Such readings, however, tend to rely on a definition of genres as loosely defined sets of expressive and narrative tropes. In his 1981 article "The 'Force-Field' of Melodrama," Stuart Cunningham argues that the inevitable problems of such textual definitions arise "only if melodrama is approached as an exclusively aesthetic category" (1981: 348). Instead, he proposes that melodrama be seen as a broader discursive category of "religious, moral, political, as well as aesthetic experience." Like Peter Brooks, Cunningham sees melodramatic discourse as a response to modernity and its shift from "the traditional Sacred and its representative institutions (Church and Monarch)" to a democratic society that must "propagate the new 'sacred' in purely ethical and personal terms" (Brooks 1976: 14–15; Cunningham 1981: 348). Melodrama thus becomes "the principal mode for uncovering, demonstrating, and making operative the essential moral universe in a post-sacred era." Cunningham argues that melodrama should be seen as a broadly discursive "mode, function, or effect," because its meaning is produced socially, historically, and "in a wide variety of media, narrative structures and aesthetic forms" (354).

If genres are seen as inter-media modes of discourse, then the problem of whether film industries or audiences are the source of generic meaning is displaced by the question of how film genres relate to other social, political, and aesthetic formations in particular historical contexts. This concept of genres as aspects of social discourse draws on a post-structuralist model of the ways texts take on meaning according to the epistemological and rhetorical modes to which they are linked. Discourses, in other words, are culturally specific frameworks of knowledge that determine what can be considered fiction, news, entertainment, obscenity, history, etc. From this perspective, it is not only a question of how genres work, but also what kind of "truth" they both presume and preclude. As Tony Bennett has argued, genres can thus be seen as socially rather than textually constituted:

> texts constitute sites around which the pre-eminently social affair of the struggle for the production of meaning is conducted, principally in the form of a series of bids and counter-bids to determine which system of inter-textual coordinates should be granted an effective social role in organising reading practices.
>
> (1990: 59–60)

In practice this approach is not incompatible with Altman's synthesis of semantic and syntactic genre analysis, but a discursive approach also requires attention to the historically particular cultural norms that govern both aesthetics and reception. Such an approach to genre does not disregard the importance of textual organization; it simply sees films as *sites* rather than *sources* of meaning. Their reception is thus primarily determined socio-culturally because of the ways that social discourses organize what sense viewers make of films' aesthetic and phenomenological effects.

5 FROM "GENRE" TO GENERIC READINGS

If genres are most productively seen as aspects of historically specific discourses, what are the implications for genre studies? One, as Barbara Klinger summarizes, is that the object of study shifts,

> from the text to the intertext – the network of discourses, social institutions, and historical conditions surrounding a work . . . Such contextual analysis hopes to reveal the intimate impact of discursive and social situations on cinematic meaning.
>
> (1997: 108)

Second, the transnational circulation of film genres becomes more clearly constituted as an arena for culturally specific, contextual research. As Mitsuhiro Yoshimoto argues with regard to melodrama,

> An examination of melodrama in the postwar Japanese cinema merely from a formal perspective does not lead to any significant conclusion; instead, we must place melodrama in a particular sociopolitical background of postwar Japan. Although various studies of what the melodramatic form of the Hollywood cinema signified in the 1950s' America are extremely significant, they cannot be a direct model.
>
> (1993: 101)

The hegemony of the American film industry has ensured that Hollywood genres are globally familiar; but their meanings in relation to localized generic structures are complex. For example, in his analysis of Hong Kong action film, Julian Stringer argues that while American genres are gender-coded as "male action or 'doing' genres (the Western, war films) and female 'suffering' genres (melodrama, the woman's film)", the Hong Kong action films of John Woo "collapse these two paradigms of masculinity into one. They combine simultaneously doing and suffering heroes" (1997: 29–30). Stringer concludes that Woo's work needs to be seen in relation to events such as the 1989 Tiananmen Square massacre and the 1997 handover of Hong Kong in order to see how:

> Hong Kong action cinema is somewhat unique in its crisis-ridden logic precisely because it cannot provide the system within which any new masculinity can be reconsolidated. (40)

Although the uneven global flow of media has made non-Western cinemas particularly marked by such genre hybridity due to the negotiation of Hollywood influence, hybridity is itself a hallmark of genre. Derrida even suggests that the tendency of critics to identify "mixed" generic objects simply confirms the fantasy that an "essential purity" of unmixed genres is possible (cited in Brunette and Wills 1989: 46). As Peter Brunette and David Wills conclude, "[g]enre is thus always indispensable and impossible at the same time" (49).

Historical research on "classical Hollywood" genres certainly supports a Bakhtinian or Kristevan model of texts as multi-vocal and citational; even in the studio era the use of genre categories was far from consistent, and usually involved mixed-genre descriptions. Similarly, film audiences have been found to utilize a wide variety of descriptive categories; for example, Richard Koszarski has described a 1923 poll of high school students that produced the following categories: "not true to life," "bad artistically," "immoral," and "brutality" (1990: 28–9). What is interesting is that these categories blur narrative, aesthetic, and ethical criteria, underscoring the regulatory aspect of genre classifications and their similarity to content ratings (the determination of who is allowed to see certain kinds of film). This raises the question of whether genre definition, as a social practice, can be separated from attempts to define the effects of film on audiences. Since the definition of concepts like "obscenity" ultimately rely on assumptions about what a text's effect will be on the typical viewer, how do assumptions about audiences underpin the definitions of categories like "romance" or "documentary"? Genre's relationship to fictive audiences is not limited to the targeting of particular markets as demographic and cultural types. As film theorists have pointed out, popular genre definitions are often made according to films' presumed effect: horror, suspense, "thrillers," "weepies," or "tear-jerkers" (cf. Williams 1995; Sobchack 1995). This practice of categorizing films according to their effects on particular kinds of viewers underscores the extent to which genres organize reading practices as much as they organize texts, by indicating to viewers what kinds of experiences to expect.

The instability of generic labels thus arises not only from the Bakhtinian "heteroglossia" of generic allusion that limits any attempt at film classification, but from the fact that genres function as tools for predicting and regulating the reception of texts. A text that cannot be located within some sort of genre is, for practical purposes, unreadable. What is important from an analytical standpoint, however, is that generic readings are not produced from a "virtual continuum of meaning containing all possible genres, but from a particular historical matrix supporting a handful of actual genres" (Hunter 1988: 219). The object of genre analysis should thus be the social constitution of their uses: the way they organize texts, identify them with certain modes of rhetoric and of discourse, and thus suggest the kind of reception and significance they should have.

6 CONCLUSION: THE POLITICS OF GENRE

> I take it . . . as one of the moments of "high seriousness" in the history of recent Marxist thought that when the aging Lukács felt the urgency of supporting Solzhenitsyn's denunciation of Stalinism but also of responding to the religious and antisocialist propaganda to which the latter lent his talent and the authority of his personal suffering, he did so by sitting down at his desk and producing a piece of genre criticism.
>
> Fredric Jameson, *The Political Unconscious*

It has been suggested that the confusion over film genre definition might be addressed by focussing on the more general categories of "narrative film, experimental/avant-garde film, and documentary" (Williams 1984: 121). This approach, modeled on traditional literary distinctions, would simply define westerns, melodramas, action films, etc., as narrative film sub-genres. As sensible as this may seem, it does not address the question of how genres function in relation to cinematic meaning: how, for example, do we differentiate between narrative fiction and documentary? In the United States, the 1980s and 1990s have seen a remarkable resurgence of popular interest in documentary film, indicated by the theatrical success of Errol Morris's *The Thin Blue Line* (1987), Michael Moore's *Roger and Me* (1989), Jennie Livingston's *Paris is Burning* (1991), and Michael Apted's *35 Up* (1991), among others. At the same time, the rise in the US of numerous television-based, hybrid formats has blurred the hypothetical line between documentary and fictional representation (verité-style programs like *Cops*, "infotainment" magazine formats such as *20/20, 48 Hours*, and *Dateline*, fact-based reenactment shows like *Emergency 911* and *America's Most Wanted*, and televised trials on Court TV) (cf. Corner 1995; Petley 1996; Bondebjerg 1996). Ironically, however, the 1990s has also seen the repeal of laws requiring television networks to air a minimum amount of public affairs programming. The notion that the television documentary functions, like the news, to provide viewers with information necessary for active citizenship has, in the US, been superseded by the documentary's ability to rate reasonably well as entertainment. Such a shift is not merely a textual one from, say, the civic exhortation of Edward Murrow's *Harvest of Shame* (1960) to the video-game images of US government-censored Gulf War coverage. It is an institutional and political one, based on a redefinition of the viewer as a consumer rather than a citizen.

Genres are socially organized sets of relations between texts that function to enable certain relations between texts and viewers. Because they organize the framework of expectations within which reading takes place, they help to enable the possibility of communication; the blurring of certain genres, therefore, can be seen as a political move to discourage certain forms of communication. For example, the 1934 US Federal Communications Act codified the notion that commercial broadcasters were responsible for producing programs in "the public interest"; the genres of television documentary, public affairs, and news were later defined as sites for the potential articulation of such public interests. But the potential viewer-use of these television genres has been increasingly limited since the deregulation policies of the Reagan-era Federal Communications Commission. American nonfiction television still shows the impact of Reagan's FCC Director Mark Fowler, who argued that "broadcasting is simply a business, and should be freed from myths . . . about service to the community" (cited in Kellner 1990: 92).

The loss of public financing for American documentary film due to attacks on the National Endowments for the Arts and Humanities has also had a direct effect on what kinds of discourse viewers can expect from nonfiction formats. The deregulation of television and the radical privatization of film funding thus constitute a more significant form of "genre revisionism" than any maverick auteur could provide. As Linda Williams has noted, contemporary documentary is marked by the postmodern recognition that the screen is less a "mirror with a memory" than a hall of mirrors. But, as she points out, epistemological reflexivity does not threaten the significance of documentary as a commitment to communicating "the 'truths' which matter in people's lives but which cannot be transparently represented" (Williams 1993: 13). With the loss of any generic (i.e. institutional and economic) protection for representations of "public interest," however, film and television viewers may become hard pressed to find any "truths" represented that run counter to the economic interests of corporate media owners and sponsors. Genre is thus about social as well as textual rules. Genres indicate what kind of communication will be facilitated in specific social formations, and it is in this regard that genre criticism can be a matter of "high seriousness."

References

Alloway, Lawrence. 1969. *Violent America: The Movies, 1946–1964*. Greenwich: New York Graphic Society and the Museum of Modern Art.

Altman, Rick. 1995. "A Semantic/Syntactic Approach to Film Genre." In *Film Genre Reader II*. Ed. Barry Keith Grant. Austin: University of Texas Press. 26–40.

Bazin, André. 1971a. "The Evolution of the Western." In *What is Cinema? Vol. 2*. Ed. and trans. Hugh Gray. Berkeley: University of California Press.

Bazin, André. 1971b. "The Western, or the American Film *Par Excellence*." In *What is Cinema? Vol. 2*. Ed. and trans. Hugh Gray. Berkeley: University of California Press.

Bennett, Tony. 1990. *Outside Literature*. London: Routledge.

Bondebjerg, Ib. 1996. "Public Discourse/Private Fascination: Hybridization in True-Life-Story Genres." *Media, Culture and Society* 18: 27–45.

Bordwell, David. 1997. *On the History of Film Style*. Cambridge: Harvard University Press.

Bourget, Jean-Loup. 1995. "Social Implications in the Hollywood Genres." In *Film Genre Reader II*. Ed. Barry Keith Grant. Austin: University of Texas Press. 50–8.

Braudy, Leo. 1979. "From *The World in a Frame*: Genre: The Conventions of Connection." In *Film Theory and Criticism: Introductory Readings*. 2nd edn. Ed. Gerald Mast and Marshall Cohen. New York: Oxford University Press. 443–68.

Brooks, Peter. 1976. *The Melodramatic Imagination: Balzac, Henry James, Melodrama, and the Mode of Excess*. New Haven: Yale University Press.

Browne, Nick. 1987. "The Political Economy of the Television (Super) Text." In *Television: The Critical View*. 4th edn. Ed. Horace Newcomb. Oxford: Oxford University Press. 585–99.

Brunette, Peter, and David Wills. 1989. *Screen/Play: Derrida and Film Theory*. Princeton: Princeton University Press.

Buscombe, Edward. 1995. "The Idea of Genre in the American Cinema." In *Film Genre Reader II*. Ed. Barry Keith Grant. Austin: University of Texas Press. 11–25.

Cawelti, John. 1979. "*Chinatown* and Generic Transformation in Recent American Films." In *Film Theory and Criticism: Introductory Readings*. 2nd edn. Ed. Gerald Mast and Marshall Cohen. New York: Oxford University Press. 559–79.

Corner, John. 1995. *Television Form and Public Address*. London: Edward Arnold. 20–31.

Corngold, Stanley. 1988. *Franz Kafka: The Necessity of Form*. Ithaca: Cornell University Press.

Croce, Benedetto. 1978 [1909, revised 1922]. *Aesthetic: As Science of Expression and General Linguistic*. Trans. Douglas Ainslie. Boston: Nonpareil Books.

Cunningham, Stuart. 1981. "The 'Force-Field' of Melodrama." *Quarterly Review of Film Studies* 6, 4 (Fall): 347–64.

Derrida, Jacques. 1980. "The Law of Genre." *Glyph* 7 (July): 202–29.

Frye, Northrop. 1957. *Anatomy of Criticism: Four Essays*. Princeton: Princeton University Press.

Gelman, Morrie. 1994. "Shop Around the Clock." *Emmy* 16, 3 (May–June): 30–3.

Gledhill, Christine. 1985. "Genre." In *The Cinema Book*. Ed. Pam Cook. New York: Panthcon Books.

Gunning, Tom. 1990. "Non-Continuity, Continuity, Discontinuity: A Theory of Genres in Early Films." In *Early Cinema: Space, Frame, Narrative*. Ed. Thomas Elsaesser. London: BFI Publishing.

Hess Wright, Judith. 1995. "Genre Films and the Status Quo." In *Film Genre Reader II*. Ed. Barry Keith Grant. Austin: University of Texas Press. 41–9.

Hunter, Ian. 1988. "Providence and Profit: Speculations in the Genre Market." *Southern Review* 22, 3: 211–23.

Jameson, Fredric. 1981. *The Political Unconscious: Narrative as a Socially Symbolic Act*. Ithaca: Cornell University Press.

Jowett, Garth S. 1985. "Giving Them What They Want: Movie Audience Research Before 1950." In *Current Research in Film: Audience, Economics, and Law, Vol. 1*. Ed. Bruce A. Austin. Norwood: Ablex Publishing Corporation.

Kapsis, Robert E. 1991. "Hollywood Genres and the Production of Culture Perspective." In *Current Research in Film: Audiences, Economics, and Law Vol. 5*. Ed. Bruce Austin. Norwood: Ablex Publishing Corporation. 68–85.

Kellner, Douglas. 1990. *Television and the Crisis of Democracy*. Boulder: Westview Press.

Kitses, Jim. 1969. *Horizons West: Anthony Mann, Budd Boetticher, Sam Peckinpah: Studies of Authorship within the Western*. Bloomington: Indiana University Press.

Klinger, Barbara. 1994. *Melodrama and Meaning: History, Culture, and the Films of Douglas Sirk*. Bloomington: Indiana University Press.

——. 1997. "Film History Terminable and Interminable: Recovering the Past in Reception Studies." *Screen* 38, 2 (Summer): 107–28.

Koszarski, Richard. 1990. *An Evening's Entertainment: The Age of the Silent Feature Picture, 1915–1928*. Vol. 3 of *History of the American Cinema*. General Ed. Charles Harpole. New York: Scribner's.

McArthur, Colin. 1972. *Underworld USA*. London: Secker and Warburg/BFI.

Modleski, Tania. 1997. "A Woman's Gotta Do . . . What a Man's Gotta Do? Cross-Dressing in the Western." *Signs: Journal of Women in Culture and Society* 22, 3: 519–44.

Neale, Steve. 1990. "Questions of Genre." *Screen* 31, 1 (Spring): 45–66.

Nolletti Jr., Arthur, and David Desser. 1992. "Introduction." In *Reframing Japanese Cinema: Authorship, Genre, History*. Bloomington: Indiana. University Press. ix–xviii.

Panofsky, Erwin. 1939. *Studies in Iconology: Humanistic Themes in the Art of the Renaissance*. New York: Harper and Row.

Petley, Julian. 1996. "Fact Plus Fiction Equals Friction." *Media, Culture and Society* 18: 11–25.

Ryall, Tom. 1978. *Teachers Study Guide No. 2: The Gangster Film*. London: BFI Education.

Schatz, Thomas. 1981. *Hollywood Genres: Formulas, Filmmaking, and the Studio System*. New York: Random House.

Sobchack, Vivian. 1995. " 'Surge and Splendor': A Phenomenology of the Hollywood Historical Epic." In *Film Genre Reader II*. Ed. Barry Keith Grant. Austin: University of Texas Press. 280–307.

Stringer, Julian. 1997. " 'Your Tender Smiles Give Me Strength': Paradigms of Masculinity in John Woo's *A Better Tomorrow* and *The Killer*." *Screen* 38, 1 (Spring): 25–41.

Warshow, Robert. 1979 [1964]. "Movie Chronicle: *The Westerner*." Rpt. in *Film Theory and Criticism: Introductory Readings*, 2nd edn. Ed. Gerald Mast and Marshall Cohen. New York: Oxford University Press. 469–87.

Williams, Alan. 1984. "Is a Radical Genre Criticism Possible?" *Quarterly Review of Film Studies* 9, 2 (Spring): 121–5.

Williams, Linda. 1993. "Mirrors Without Memories: Truth, History, and the New Documentary." *Film Quarterly* 46, 3 (Spring): 9–21.

Williams, Linda. 1995. "Film Bodies: Gender, Genre, and Excess." In *Film Genre Reader II*. Ed. Barry Keith Grant. Austin: University of Texas Press. 140–58.

Wilson, Christopher. 1983. "The Rhetoric of Consumption: Mass-Market Magazines and the Demise of the Gentle Reader, 1880–1920." In *The Culture of Consumption: Critical Essays in American History, 1880–1980*. Ed. Richard Wightman Fox and T. J. Jackson Lears. New York: Pantheon Books. 39–64.

Wright, Will. 1975. *Sixguns and Society: A Structural Study of the Western*. Berkeley: University of California Press.

Yoshimoto, Mitsuhiro. 1993. "Melodrama, Postmodernism, and Japanese Cinema." In *Melodrama and Asian Cinema*. Ed. Wimal Dissanayake. Cambridge: Cambridge University Press. 101–26.

Chapter 16

Paul Kerr

OUT OF WHAT PAST? NOTES ON THE B *FILM NOIR* (1986)

EVER SINCE THE PUBLICATION OF Borde and Chaumeton's pioneering *Panorama du Film Noir Américain* in 1955, there has been a continuing dispute about the genre's precise cultural sources and critical status.[1] In their attempts to provide *film noir* with a respectable pedigree, subsequent studies have cited not only cinematic but also socio-logical, psychological, philosophical, political, technological and aesthetic factors amongst its progenitors. What they have not done, however, is to relate these general – and generally untheorised – notions of 'influence' to the specific modes of production, both economic and ideological, upon which they were, presumably, exercised; in this case, those structures and strategies adopted by certain factions within the American film industry over a period of almost two decades. Instead, these archaeologists of the genre have excavated a wide range of 'ancestors' for *film noir* – the influx of German *émigrés* and the influence of expressionism; the influx of French *émigrés* and the influence of existentialism; Ernest Hemingway and the 'hard-boiled' school of writing; Edward Hopper and the 'ash can' school of painting; pre-war photo-journalism, wartime newsreels and post-war neorealism; the creators of *Kane* – Citizens Mankiewicz, Toland and Welles; the Wall Street crash and the rise of populism; the Second World War and the rise of fascism; the Cold War and the rise of McCarthyism. Finally, several critics have pointed, in passing, to a number of even less specific sources, such as general American fears about bureaucracy, the bomb and the big city, as well as one or two more substantial ones, including the industrialisation of the female work-force during the war and the escalating corporatism of American capital throughout the 1940s.[2] However pertinent some of these suggestions, attempts to establish a 'family tree' have usually revealed less about the formation of *film noir* in particular than about the poverty of film history in general. This article, therefore, is an attempt to refocus the debate on the specifically film-industrial determinants of the genre by concentrating on one important, industrially defined, fraction of it – the B *film noir*.

As I have indicated, most explanations have tended to credit either particular people (such as ex-employees of UFA and *Black Mask*) or events (the Depression and the war, for example) with the creation of – or, more accurately, a contribution to – *film noir*. Thus, in the first category, auteurists discuss the genre as if it were simply the chosen canvas of a few talented individuals, whether they were directors (Siodmak, Tourneur, Ulmer), writers

(Chandler, Mainwaring, Paxton) or cinematographers (Alton, Musuraca, Toland). Similarly, genre critics generally consider *film noir* either in terms of its function as social myth or, more simply, as no more than a symptom of social malaise.[3] Borde and Chaumeton begin their chapter on sources with an account of *film noir*'s literary and cinematic precursors, so endorsing an evolutionary model of film history, but they go on to propose a much more interesting industrial origin in Hollywood's 'synthesis of three types of films which at that time had developed such an autonomy that each studio had its own specialities from among them; the brutal and colourful gangster film, whose style carried over to other productions at Warner Bros; the horror film over which Universal acquired a near-monopoly; and the classic detective film of deduction which was shared by Fox and Metro-Goldwyn-Mayer.'[4] Having gone this far, though, Borde and Chaumeton fail to ask why such a synthesis should ever have taken place, if indeed it did. There are, I think, only two other theories which have been seriously put forward *vis-à-vis* the relationship between *film noir* and the film industry, both of which are equally untenable. The first argues that the genre was the cinema's unmediated reflection of an all-pervading postwar gloom and the second, that it was the expression of a community finally freed from its Depression duties as a dream factory by an audience that no longer needed cheering up.[5] In spite of their diametrically opposing views of postwar American 'morale', both theories employ a conception of Hollywood as monolithic, its products either entirely determined by American ideology or entirely autonomous of it.

Clearly, if we want to go on using the notion of 'determination' rather than relying on the dubious concept of 'derivation', it is necessary to approach the classic base/superstructure formulation with some caution. Indeed, Raymond Williams has remarked that

> . . . each term of the proposition has to be revalued in a particular direction. We have to revalue 'determination' towards the setting of limits and the exertion of pressure and away from a predicted, prefigured and controlled content. We have to revalue 'superstructure' towards a related range of cultural practices and away from a reflected, reproduced or specifically dependent content. And, crucially, we have to revalue 'the base' away from the notion of a fixed economic or technological abstraction, and towards the specific activities of men in real social and economic relationships, containing fundamental contradictions and variations and therefore always in a state of dynamic process.[6]

This article, then, taking its cue from the oft-cited specificity of *film noir* as a genre, will attempt to relate it not to the general American social formation (as some species of 'reflection'), nor to a monolithically conceived film industry, but rather to particular, relatively autonomous modes of film production, distribution and exhibition in a particular conjuncture. What follows, therefore, is an exploratory rather than an exhaustive analysis of the reciprocal relation which obtained between *film noir*'s primary determinants – the economic and the ideological. (The third determinant, at least in Althusserian terms, is that of the political, the effectivity of which with respect to the *film noir* would have to include the production code, the antitrust suits and the Hollywood blacklist. The political instance, for reasons of brevity, has here been subsumed within the other two categories.) This analysis attends in particular to the relatively autonomous and uneven development of the B *film noir*, a category constituted, I will argue, by a negotiated resistance to the realist aesthetic on the one hand and an accommodation to restricted expenditure on the other. Of course, none of these terms – relative autonomy, non-synchronicity, realism (not to mention *film noir* itself) – is unproblematic; their employment here, however, is a necessary condition of any discussion which hopes to account for the existence of a genre at different times and in different places with a number of different inflections. The crucial theoretical formulation here is that of 'determination' itself, since the identity of the infamous 'last instance' though classically considered to be the economic will actually fluctuate, at least in the short term. Thus, in the long term, Hollywood's ideological and economic aims are complementary: the reproduction of the conditions necessary for continued cinematic production and consumption – in other words, the perpetuation of the industry. In the short term, however, these determinants may be less compatible, and it is the shifting balance of relations between the two which accords Hollywood's 'superstructure' its relative autonomy from its economic 'base'. Furthermore, the economic or ideological space opened up for the American cinema in this way is in direct proportion to the urgency with which ideological or economic priorities in the industry are negotiated.

To take an example, Antony Easthope has argued that 'in the early Thirties Hollywood production was determined ideologically or even politically rather than economically'[7] but his argument, like so many others, hinges on a reading of American history in general and not that of the film industry. In fact, it seems equally plausible – if equally schematic – to suggest that Hollywood's product was dominantly determined economically only in periods of economic crisis in the industry (like the early 1930s when several studios were actually bankrupted by a combination of reduced receipts and excessive capitalisation), whilst in eras of relative economic stability but marked ideological and/or political unrest (like the mid-1940s, when receipts rose to a new high but both international and industrial relations were of crucial importance) that product would have tended to be, primarily at least, ideologically determined. In modification of this latter formulation, however, it is necessary to add that low-budget and blockbuster film-making, neither of which was really established across the industry until the latter half of the 1930s – having their origins in precisely those economic conditions outlined above – might have been more vulnerable to economic imperatives ('masking' and 'flaunting' their respective production values) than the admittedly slightly hypothetical 'mid-budgeted' mainstream A products of the studios at that time. This privileging of the economic imperative on the B film, in a period of film history which was otherwise primarily ideologically determinate (at least until about 1947), might begin to account for the presence of several aesthetically (and therefore ideologically) unorthodox practices within the B *film noir*.

TOWARDS A DEFINITION

Before a discussion of such suggestions can legitimately begin, however, some kind of critical consensus about these 'practices' and the period in which they were pursued is needed. The authors of the *Panorama* focus their own analysis on those films produced between 1941 and 1953 but more recent critics have broadened these bounds somewhat to include films made from the beginning of the 1940s (and sometimes even earlier) until the end of the following decade. If we employ the more elastic of these estimates and allow an additional – and admittedly arbitrary – margin at the beginning of the period, we may be able to reconstruct at least some of the industrial determinants of the genre. Furthermore, several critics have tried to demonstrate that *film noir* comprises a number of distinct stages. Paul Schrader, for example, has outlined 'three broad phases' for the genre: the first lasting until about 1946 and characterised by couples like Bogart and Bacall and 'classy' studio directors like Curtiz; the second spanning the immediate postwar years, when shooting began to move out of the studios and into the streets; and the third and final phase in which both characters and conventions alike were subject to extraordinary permutations. Perhaps film history will ultimately explain the industrial underpinnings of such 'sub-generic' shifts as well as the primary determinants and eventual demise of the wider genre itself.[8] Until then, whether the period of *film noir* production is relatively easily agreed upon or not, the volume of that production is decidely more difficult to ascertain. This is due, to some degree at least, to the primacy of the economic and relative autonomy of the ideological instances of the *film noir*. Equally important is its controversial status as a genre at all, since it is usually defined in terms of its style rather than – as most genres are – in relation to content, character, setting and plot. Further difficulties derive from its relative inaccessibility as an object of study: retrospectives are all too rare and there are still no book-length analyses of the genre in English – even the *Panorama* remains untranslated. *Film noir*, therefore, has still not received its due in terms of either critical or archival attention.

Despite such difficulties, it still remains possible to offer at least an outline of the genre's defining characteristics.[9] Primarily, *film noir* has been associated with a propensity for low key lighting, a convention which was in direct opposition to the cinematographic orthodoxy of the previous decade. In the 1930s the dominant lighting style, known as high key, had been characterised by a contrast ratio of approximately 4:1 between the light value of the key lamp on the one hand and the filler on the other. *Noir*, with a considerably higher range of contrasts, is thus a *chiaroscuro* style, its low key effects often undiffused by either lens gauzes or lamp glasses – as they certainly would have been in conventional high key style. Instead, *noir* sets are often only half or quarter lit, with the important exception of those brief sequences in the '*blanc*' (that is, 'normal') world which are sometimes employed as a framing device at the beginning and end of the narrative. Otherwise, shooting tends to be either day-for-night or night-for-night and the main action has a habit of occurring in shadowy rooms, dingy offices, overlush apartments and rainwashed streets. In such settings both actors and decor are often partially obscured by the foregrounding of oblique objects – shutters and banisters, for instance, casting horizontal or vertical grids of light and dark across faces and furniture. Meanwhile, the arrangement of space within the frame is often equally irregular, both in regard to its occupation by actors and props as well as to the width and depth of focus. This can lead to a 'discomposition' of the image (and consequent disorientation of the spectator) in terms of the neo-classical conventions of composition generally used and, indeed, reinforced by Hollywood. These kinds of disorientation can be accentuated by the use of 'perversely' low and high camera angles (a perversity defined entirely in relation to contemporary realist criteria) and the virtual elimination of those other staples of realism, the establishing long shot and the personalising close-up. In fact, the latter is often used ironically in the *film noir* in soft focus treatment of male villainy (signifying feminine decadence) whilst women, the conventional 'objects' of such attention, are often photographed in harsh, unflattering and undiffused light with wide angle distorting lenses. Such an emphasis on unconventional camera angles and lighting set-ups, however, is often achieved at the (literal) expense of camera movement and classical editing. A number of other realist conventions, including the shot-reverse-shot alternation of points of view and the 180 degree rule, are also occasionally infringed by the *film noir*.[10] Finally, there is a great deal of reliance on such fragmented narrative structures as the flashback, which lend an additional sense of inevitability to the plot and helplessness to the characters. Hitherto, most definitions of the genre have more or less rested at this point, tending to ignore that plot and those characters. One recent critic, however, has assembled what he calls a 'rudimentary working prototype' of characteristic content for *film noir* along the following lines:

> Either because he is fated to do so by chance, or because he has been hired for a
> job specifically associated with her, a man whose experience of life has left

him sanguine and often bitter meets a not-innocent woman of similar outlook to whom he is sexually and fatally attracted. Through this attraction, either because the woman induces him to it or because it is the natural result of their relationship, the man comes to cheat, attempt to murder or actually murder a second man to whom the woman is unhappily or unwillingly attached (generally he is her husband or lover), an act which brings about the sometimes metaphoric but usually literal destruction of the woman, the man to whom she is attached and frequently the protagonist himself.[11]

This schematic summary of *film noir* will have to suffice for our purposes here, if only as a result of the extremely tentative account of the genre's determination outlined below.

THE COMING OF THE B FEATURE

The B film was launched as an attempt by a number of independent exhibitors to lure audiences back into their theatres at a time of acute economic crisis in the industry. Along with the double bill these independents had already – by the beginning of the 1930s – introduced lotteries, live acts, quizzes, free gifts and several other gimmicks in order to build up bigger audiences and, at the same time, keep those patrons already had in their seats a little longer, so boosting both box-office takings and confectionery sales whilst relegitimising admission prices. The double bill, however, had the additional – and, as it proved, crucial – advantage of enabling independent exhibitors to accommodate their programme policies to the majors' monopolistic distribution practices (such as blind selling and block booking) and allowing them to exhibit a more independent product at the same time. Of the 23,000 theatres operating in the United States in 1930, the five majors (MGM, RKO, Fox, Warners and Paramount) either owned or controlled some 3,000 – most of that number being among the biggest and best situated of the first-run theatres; these 3,000 theatres, though comprising less than 14 per cent of the total number then in operation, accounted for nearly 70 per cent of the entire industry's box-office takings that year. This left the independents with some 20,000 theatres in which to screen what were either second-run or independent films. By the end of 1931 the double bill, which had originated in New England, had spread its influence on programme policy right across the country, establishing itself as at least a part of that policy in one-eighth of the theatres then in operation. In 1935, the last of the majors to adopt double bills in their theatres – MGM and RKO – announced their decision to screen two features in all but two of their theatres. By 1947, the fraction of cinemas advertising double bills had risen to nearly two-thirds. In normal circumstances, of course, any such increase in the volume of films in exhibition would have led to a similar increase in the volume of film production but this was not the case. Overproduction by the majors since the advent of sound had accumulated an enormous backlog of as yet unreleased material. It was not, therefore, until this reservoir of ready-made second features had been exhausted that it became necessary to set up an entirely new mode of film production – the B unit.

While those units within the vertically integrated majors virtually monopolised the independent exhibition outlets a number of B studios established to meet the same demand were compelled to rely on the so-called States Rights system, whereby studios sold distribution rights to film franchises on a territorial basis. Lacking theatre chains of their own, several independent production companies were forced to farm out their product to a relatively unknown market. Monogram and Republic did eventually set up small exchanges of their own in a few cities and their main rival, PRC, even acquired some theatres of its own in the 1940s but the distinction between such venues and those owned by the majors should not be forgotten. Certainly, the producers of the B films themselves would have been acutely aware of the kind of cinemas in which the bulk of their products would have been seen and this may have been as influential a factor in B film production as the picture palaces undoubtedly were for the As. Mae D. Huettig,[12] for instance, has described how Los Angeles's eleven first-run theatres exhibited 405 films in the year 1939/40 of which only five were the product of independent companies, all but one of that five being shown at the bottom of a double bill. Wherever such double bills were programmed, however, few exhibitors could afford the rentals of two top quality (i.e. top price) products at the same time. The double bill, therefore, was a combination of one relatively expensive A film and one relatively inexpensive B, the former generally deriving from the major studios and costing, throughout the 1940s, upwards of $700,000 and the latter being produced by low budget units at the same studios as well as by several B studios, at anything less than about $400,000.[13] In general, the A feature's rental was based on a percentage of box-office takings whilst the Bs played for a fixed or flat rental and were thus not so reliant on audience attendance figures at all – at least, not in the short term. In the long term, however, these B units would be compelled to carve out identifiable and distinctive styles for themselves in order to differentiate their product – within generic constraints – for the benefit of audiences in general and exhibitors in particular.

In most cases the B *film noir* would have been produced – like all Bs – on a fixed budget which would itself have been calculated in relation to fixed rentals. In illustrating the effects such economies exercised on these Bs I have restricted reference, as far as possible, to one large integrated company, RKO, and one small independent company, PRC.[14] At the beginning of the decade the budgets of RKO's most important production unit in the B sector were approximately $150,000 per picture; at PRC, several years later, most units were working with less than two-thirds of that amount. To take two examples: Val Lewton's films at RKO had tight, twenty-one-day schedules whilst Edgar G. Ulmer's at PRC were often brought in after only six days and nights. (To achieve this remarkable shooting speed nightwork was almost inevitable and Ulmer's unit used to mount as many as eighty different camera set-ups a day.) Props, sets and costumes were kept to a minimum, except on those occasions when they could be borrowed from more expensive productions, as Lewton borrowed a staircase from *The Magnificent Ambersons* for his first feature, *The Cat People*. Nick Grinde, a veteran of B units in the 1940s, has described how a producer would resist charges of plagiarism on the grounds that 'the way he will shoot it no-one will recognise it for the same set. He'll have his director pick new angles and redress the foreground . . . [and] . . . will even agree to shoot at night . . .'[15]

Night shooting, of course, was an obvious and often unavoidable strategy for getting films in on short schedules as well as fully exploiting fixed assets and economising on rentals. (It also suited those employees who sought to avoid IATSE overtime bans.) Mark Robson, an editor and later director in Lewton's unit, has recalled that 'the streets we had in *The Seventh Victim*, for instance, were studio streets and the less light we put on them the better they looked.'[16] Similarly, expensive special effects and spectacular action sequences were generally avoided unless stock footage could be borrowed from other films. This 'borrowing' became known as the 'montage' and involved the use of 'a series of quick cuts of film'. As Grinde has explained,

> You can't shoot a first-rate crime wave on short dough, so you borrow or buy about twenty pieces of thrilling moments from twenty forgotten pictures. A fleeing limousine skids into a street-car, a pedestrian is socked over the head in an alley, a newspaper office is wrecked by hoodlums, a woman screams, a

couple of mugs are slapping a little merchant into seeing things their way. And so on until we end up on a really big explosion.[17]

Not all such 'thrilling moments' were 'borrowed' from 'forgotten pictures', however. Fritz Lang, for example, has noted that footage from *You Only Live Once* (UA 1937), including a classic bank robbery sequence, found its way into *Dillinger* (Monogram 1945).[18]

The exploitation of borrowed footage and furniture was only really possible as long as films were still being shot inside the studios. Until the middle of the 1940s location shooting was extremely rare and even independents like Monogram and PRC had their own studio facilities. As fixed and variable costs began to escalate at the end of the war, however, production units were encouraged to go out on location and this practice was extended by the prolonged studio strikes of 1945–47. In 1946, the abolition of block booking encouraged the appearance of a number of small studio-less independent production companies and these also contributed to the 'street' rather than 'studio' look in the latter half of the decade. Constraints at both the production and distribution ends of the industry meant that the running length of Bs fluctuated between about fifty-five and seventy-five minutes; raw footage was expensive, audiences had only limited amounts of time and of course, exhibitors were keen to screen their double bills as many times a day as possible. In 1943 the government reduced basic allotments of raw film stock to the studios by 25 per cent and once again it was the B units which were hardest hit. Consequently 'montages' became even more common. Casts and crews on contract to B units were kept at a manageable minimum, so prohibiting plots with long cast lists, crowd scenes and complicated camera or lighting set-ups. Similarly, overworked script departments often produced unpolished and occasionally incoherent scripts. (Film titles were pretested with audiences before stories or scripts were even considered.) Despite such drawbacks, however, the B units, throughout the 1940s and as late as the mid-1950s, employed the same basic equipment as their big budget rivals, including Mitchell or Bell and Howell cameras, Mole Richardson lighting units, Moviola editing gear and RCA or Western Electric sound systems. Such economies as B units practised, therefore, were not related to fixed assets like rents and salaries but to variable costs like sets, scripts, footage, casual labour and, crucially, power.

RKO's production of *noir* Bs seems to have been inaugurated in 1940 with the release of Boris Ingster's extraordinary *Stranger On The Third Floor*. The studio had emerged from receivership at the end of the previous decade – a period of some prosperity for the other majors – to make only minimal profits of $18,604 in 1938 and $228,608 in 1939. In 1940 the studio lost almost half a million dollars and began to augment its low budget policy with B series like *The Saint* and *The Falcon*. It was not until 1942, however, when RKO plunged more than two million dollars into debt that the trend towards the B *film noir* became really evident. In that year, George Schaefer was fired as president and replaced by his deputy, Ned Depinet, who immediately appointed Charles M. Koerner – from RKO Theatres Inc. – as vice-president in charge of production. It was at this point that Val Lewton was brought to the studio to set up his own B unit. Within the limitations I have outlined, as well as the generic constraints of having to work in the 'horror' category, Lewton's unit, and others like it, were accorded a degree of autonomy which would never have been sanctioned for more expensive studio productions.[19] At PRC the situation was rather different. The company had been formed in March 1940 by the creditors of its predecessor, the Producers' Distributing Corporation, and with the cooperation of the Pathé Laboratories. The new Producers' Releasing Corporation had five separate production units and the Fine Arts Studio (formerly Grand National). At first the emphasis was on comedy and westerns; PRC produced forty-four films, mostly in these genres, in the 1941/42 season. By 1942, however, PRC had acquired twenty-three films exchanges and with the replacement of

George Batchelor by Leon Fromkess as production head, there was an increased diversification of product. While most units concentrated on comedies and musicals, others began to
turn out cut-rate westerns and crime thrillers. It was also in 1942 that Edgar G. Ulmer
began work for the studio. Allowed only about 15,000 feet per picture, Ulmer's unit, like
Lewton's, economised with stock footage (as in *Girls in Chains* PRC 1943) and minimal casts
and sets (as in *Detour* PRC 1946).

Artistic ingenuity in the face of economic intransigence is one critical commonplace
about the B *film noir* (and about people like Lewton and Ulmer in particular). Against this, I
have suggested that a number of *noir* characteristics can at least be associated with – if not
directly attributed to – economic and therefore technological constraints. The paucity
of 'production values' (sets, stars and so forth) may even have encouraged low budget
production units to compensate with complicated plots and convoluted atmosphere. Realist
denotation would thus have been de-emphasised in favour of expressionist connotation (in
The Cat People RKO 1942, for example). This 'connotative' quality might also owe something
to the influence of the Hays Office, which meant that 'unspeakable' subjects could only be
suggested – *Under Age* (Columbia 1941), although concerned with the criminal exploitation
of young girls, could never actually illustrate that exploitation. Similarly, compressed shooting schedules, overworked script editors and general cost cutting procedures could well
have contributed to what we now call *film noir*. Nevertheless, an analysis of *film noir* as
nothing more than an attempt to make a stylistic virtue out of economic necessity – the
equation, at its crudest, of low budgets with low key lighting – is inadequate: budgetary
constraints and the relative autonomy of many B units in comparison with As were a
necessary but by no means sufficient condition for its formation. It was, I have suggested,
constituted not only by accommodation to restricted expenditure but also by resistance to
the realist aesthetic – like the B film generally, it was determined not only economically but
also ideologically. For instance, the double bill was not simply the result of combining any
two films, one A and one B, but often depended on a number of quite complex contrasts.
The Saint in New York, for example, was billed with *Gold Diggers in Paris*, *Blind Alibi* with
Holiday. According to Frank Ricketson Jr, the tendency of both distributors and exhibitors
was to ensure that

> Heavy drama is blended with sparkling comedy. A virile action picture is mated
> with a sophisticated society play. An all-star production is matched with a light
> situation comedy of no-star value. An adventure story is contrasted with a
> musical production.[20]

Initially, of course, B films had been little more than low budget versions of profitable A
releases but as the industry was rationalised after the Depression this imitative trend was
partially replaced by another differentiation. Thus, while early Bs had tended to remain in
the least expensive of successful genres – westerns, situation comedies, melodramas,
thrillers and horror films – the exhibitors themselves began to exert a moderating influence
(by means of intercompany promotions like Koerner's within the integrated companies; by
means of advertisements in the trade papers among the independents). By the end of the
1930s, therefore, double bills were beginning to contrast the staple A genres of that decade
– gangster films, biopics, musicals, screwball comedies, mysteries and westerns – with a
number of Poverty Row hybrids, mixtures of melodrama and mystery, gangster and private
eye, screwball comedy and thriller (and, later, 'documentary' and drama). In part, of course,
this hybrid quality is explicable in terms of studio insecurities about marketing their
B products; nevertheless, the curiously cross-generic quality of the *film noir* is perhaps a
vestige of its origins as a kind of 'oppositional' cinematic mode. Low key lighting styles, for

example, were not only more economic than their high key alternatives, they were also dramatically and radically distinct from them.

STYLISTIC GENERATION

In considering the concept of stylistic differentiation it is useful, at this point, to introduce the work of the Birmingham Centre for Contemporary Cultural Studies on "the process of stylistic generation".[21] Although specifically addressed to the "styles" adopted by such subcultural groups as Teds, punks and Rastas, this work seems to me to be applicable, with some reservations, to the style of the B *film noir*. Whether or not one can legitimately describe Poverty Row as a subculture is clearly a matter for serious debate but, until we have some kind of social history of Hollywood, a final decision on the matter is premature. Lacking such knowledge, it remains striking how appropriate some of the Birmingham conclusions are for the present study. In their analysis the authors make admittedly eclectic use of Lévi-Strauss's concept of bricolage; but whereas Lévi-Strauss is concerned with situations and cultures where a single myth is dominant, John Clarke concentrates on the 'genesis of "unofficial" styles, where the stylistic core (if there is one) can be located in the expression of a partly negotiated opposition to the values of a wider society.'[22] (I will return to the notion of 'negotiated opposition' later.) Clarke proposes a two-tiered theory of stylistic generation, the first axiom of which states that the generation of subcultural styles involves differential selection from within the matrix of the existent and the second, that one of the main functions of a distinctive subcultural style is to define the boundaries of group membership as against other groups. I hope that the pertinence of these two axioms (the first 'economic', the second 'ideological') to the group which I have designated the B *film noir* will become apparent. Clarke even goes on to discuss the process whereby such subcultural styles are assimilated into/recuperated by the dominant culture; a process which Raymond Williams refers to as 'incorporation'. The defusion and dilution of the B *film noir*'s unorthodox visual style within the aesthetic of the A film clearly fits this kind of pattern, with the most economically secure studios at that time – MGM, Fox and Paramount – tending to produce not only fewer films in the genre than their competitors but also more lavish ones like *The Postman Always Rings Twice, Laura* and *Double Indemnity*. Furthermore, it was Fox who were to launch and lead the break-away police procedural strand at the end of the 1940s, a strand which emanated from and to a certain extent replaced that studio's location-based *March of Time* series.[23]

Meanwhile, the monopoly structure of the industry – which had been initially, if indirectly, responsible for the B phenomenon – was being challenged. In May 1935 the Supreme Court voted to revoke Roosevelt's National Industrial Recovery Act (under which *A Code Of Fair Competition For The Motion Picture Industry* had more or less condoned the industry's monopoly practices) on the grounds that it was unconstitutional. Opposition to motion picture monopolies was mounting, not only among the independent companies but also in the courts and even in Congress itself. Finally, in July 1938, the Department of Justice filed an Anti-Trust suit against the majors, United States versus Paramount Pictures Inc. *et al.*, so launching a case which was to reach the Supreme Court a decade later. In the suit the majors were accused of separate infringements of Anti-Trust legislation but, in November 1940, the case was apparently abandoned; in fact it was merely being adjourned for the duration of hostilities, the government being unwilling to provoke Hollywood at a time when the communications media were of such crucial importance. The suit was settled out of court with the signing of a modest Consent Decree, the provisions of which included an agreement by the majors to 'modify' their use of block booking, to eliminate blind selling and to refrain from 'unnecessary' theatrical expansion. Most important of all the Decree's requirements, however, was the majors' agreement to withdraw from the package selling procedures which had compelled independent exhibitors to screen shorts, re-issues, serial westerns and newsreels with their main features. The last provision expanded the market for low budget production almost overnight. Whereas at the end of the 1930s there had been very few independent companies, by 1946 (the year in which block booking was finally abolished) there were more than forty. The Anti-Trust Commission never entirely dropped their case against Hollywood, however, and finally, in 1948, the five fully integrated companies were instructed to divest themselves of their theatrical holdings. Paramount was the first to obey this ruling, divorcing its exhibition arm from the production/distribution end of its business in late 1949. RKO followed in 1950, 20th Century-Fox in 1952, Warner Bros. in 1953 and MGM in 1959. Rather ironically, the divorce meant the demise of many independent studios which had thrived on providing films for the bottom half of the bill; quite simply, low budget productions could no longer be guaranteed fixed rentals in exhibition. Consequently, one of the first casualties of divorcement was the double bill. The majors cancelled their B productions and the independents were forced to choose between closure and absorption. In 1949 PRC was absorbed by Rank and transformed into Eagle Lion; the following year it ceased production altogether and merged with United Artists. In 1953 Monogram became Allied Artists Pictures Corporation and began to operate an increasingly important television subsidiary. Republic, whose staple product had always been westerns and serials, was finally sold to CBS in 1959 and became that network's Television City studio.

It was thus between the first filing of the Anti-Trust suit in 1938 and the final act of divorcement in 1959 that the B *film noir* flourished. Obviously, however, the trend towards media conglomerates and away from simple monopolies was by no means the only 'political' determinant on cinematic modes in that period, a period which witnessed American entry into the war, the rise of McCarthyism and a series of jurisdictional disputes in the labour unions.[24] During the Second World War the international market for American films shrank drastically and the domestic market expanded to take its place. By 1941, the cinemas of continental Europe, where the majors had earned more than a quarter of their entire box office in 1936, were no longer open to American distributors. Even in Britain, where most cinemas remained open throughout the war and where attendance actually rose from a weekly average of nineteen million in 1939 to more than thirty million in 1945, the Hollywood majors were unable to maintain even prewar profits. The introduction of currency restrictions severely limited the amount that American distributors could remove from the country; thus, only half their former revenues – some $17,500,000 – were withdrawn in 1940 and only $12,900,000 in 1941. Meanwhile, however, American domestic rentals soared from $193,000,000 in 1939 to $332,000,000 in 1946. By the end of the war, average weekly attendance in the US was back at about 90,000,000, its prewar peak. As the majors' profits rose, the volume of their production actually fell: having released some 400 films in 1939 the big eight companies released only 250 in 1946, the balance being made up by a flush of new B companies. This geographically – but not economically – reduced constituency may have afforded Hollywood the opportunity to take a closer look at contemporary and specifically American phenomena without relying on the 'comfortable' distance provided by classic genres like the western or the musical. That 'closer look' (at, for instance, urban crime, the family and the rise of corporations) could, furthermore, because of the national specificity of its audience and as a result of the 'dialectic' of its consumption (within the double bill), employ a less orthodox aesthetic than would previously have been likely.

The aesthetic orthodoxy of the American cinema in the 1940s and 1950s was realism and so it is necessary to relate cinematic realism to the *film noir*. Colin MacCabe has suggested its two primary conditions:

(1)   The classic realist text cannot deal with the real as contradictory.
(2)   In a reciprocal movement the classic realist text ensures the position of the subject in a relation of dominant specularity.

These two conditions, the repression of contradiction and the construction of spectatorial omniscience, are negotiated through a hierarchy of narrative discourses:

> Through the knowledge we gain from the narrative we can split the discourses of the various characters from their situation and compare what is said in these discourses with what has been revealed to us through narration. The camera shows us what happens – it tells the truth against which we can measure the discourses.[25]

Elsewhere MacCabe has restated this notion quite clearly: 'classical realism . . . involves the homogenisation of different discourses by their relation to one dominant discourse – assured of its domination by the security and transparency of its image.'[26]

It is this very 'transparency' which *film noir* refuses; indeed, Sylvia Harvey has noted that 'One way of looking at the plot of the typical film noir is to see it as a struggle between different voices for control over the telling of the story.' From that perspective, *film noir* represents a fissure in the aesthetic and ideological fabric of realism. Thus,

> Despite the presence of most of the conventions of the dominant methods of film making and storytelling, the impetus towards the resolution of the plot, the diffusion of tension, the circularity of a narrative that resolves all the problems it encounters, the successful completion of the individual's quest, these methods do not, in the end, create the most significant contours of the cultural map of film noir. The defining contours of this group of films are the product of that which is abnormal and dissonant.[27]

Gill Davies, on the other hand, has suggested that such 'dissonance' can quite comfortably be contained by the 'weight' of generic convention.

> The disturbing effect of mystery or suspense is balanced by confidence in the inevitability of the genre. Character types, stock settings and the repetition of familiar plot devices assure the reader that a harmonious resolution will take place. This narrative pattern pretends to challenge the reader, creates superficial disorientation, while maintaining total narrative control. Our knowledge of the genre (supported, in the cinema, with the reappearance of certain actors and actresses in familiar roles) takes us through a baffling narrative with the confidence that all problems will ultimately be solved.[28]

In terms of *film noir*, however, I would argue that the 'surplus' of realist devices catalogued by Harvey and Davies indicates an attempt to hold in balance traditional generic elements with unorthodox aesthetic practices that constantly undermine them. *Film noir* can thus be seen as the negotiation of an 'oppositional space' within and against realist cinematic practice; this trend could only be effectively disarmed by the introduction of a number of stock devices derived from other genres (such as melodrama or the detective story). It is not an object of this article, though, to gauge the degree to which that resistance was or was not successful. Rather, its task is to begin to establish those historically contemporaneous strands of realism – Technicolor, television and the A film – against which any such resistance would necessarily have defined itself.

TELEVISION AND TECHNICOLOR

In 1947 there were only 14,000 television receivers in the United States; two years later that number had risen to a million. By 1950 there were four million and by 1954 thirty-two million. In the face of such swiftly escalating opposition and as a consequence of the impending demise of the double bill (in the aftermath of the Anti-Trust decision), several of the smaller studios began renting theatrical films for television exhibition and even producing tele-films of their own. Thus, in 1949, Columbia formed a subsidiary, Screen Gems, to produce new films for and release old films to the new medium. In 1955, the first of the five majors, Warner Bros., was persuaded to produce a weekly ABC TV series, to be called *Warner Brothers Presents*, based on three of that studio's successful 1940s features: *King's Row* (1941), *Casablanca* (1944) and *Cheyenne* (1947). It is perhaps worth pointing out that *Cheyenne* was the only one which lacked elements of the *'noir'* style and also the only one to enjoy a mass audience; indeed, it was ultimately 'spun off' into a seven-year series of its own while the other two 'thirds' of the slot were quietly discontinued. In December of 1955 RKO withdrew from film production altogether and sold its film library to a television programming syndicate; two years later, the old RKO studio itself was in the hands of Desilu, an independent television production company owned by ex-RKO contract player Lucille Ball and her husband Desi Arnaz. In fact, Lucille Ball's comedy series *I Love Lucy* had been the first 'filmed' (as opposed to live) series on American television; it was only dislodged from its place at the top of the ratings by another filmed series, *Dragnet*. The latter, characterised by high key lighting, sparse shadowless sets and procedural plots, was to provide a model for television crime fiction for more than two decades. It is particularly ironic, therefore, to note that *Dragnet* derived from a 1948 B *film noir* produced by Eagle Lion, *He Walked By Night*, a film which contains what is perhaps the most dramatically *chiaroscuro* scene ever shot in Hollywood. In 1954 Warner Bros. released a cinematic spin-off from the series, again called *Dragnet*, but this time without a trace of the stylistic virtuosity which had characterised its cinematic grandparent. (The fact that this film proved unsuccessful at the box office, far from invalidating my thesis about the relationship between television and the *film noir*, actually corroborates my account of the different 'spaces' occupied by the discourse of realism in television and the cinema.) Very simply, the low contrast range of television receivers meant that any high contrast cinematic features (like *films noirs*) were inherently unsuitable for tele-cine reproduction.

If *film noir* was determined to any degree by an initial desire to differentiate B cinematic product from that of television (as A product was differentiated by colour, production values, 3D, wide screens and epic or 'adult' themes), as, too, its ultimate demise relates to capitulation to the requirements of tele-cine, that 'difference' can also be seen as a response to the advent of colour. The first full-length Technicolor feature, *Becky Sharp*, was released in 1935 (by RKO), and its director, Rouben Mamoulian – one of the few professionals in favour of colour at that time – has described in some detail the aesthetic consensus into which the new process was inserted:

> For more than twenty years, cinematographers have varied the key of lighting
> in photographing black-and-white pictures to make the visual impression

enhance the emotional mood of the action. We have become accustomed to a definite language of lighting: low key effects, with sombre, heavy shadows express a sombrely dramatic mood; high key effects, with brilliant lighting and sparkling definition, suggest a lighter mood; harsh contrasts with velvety shadows and strong highlights strike a melodramatic note. Today we have color – a new medium, basically different in many ways from any dramatic medium previously known . . . Is it not logical, therefore, to feel that it is incumbent upon all of us, as film craftsmen, to seek to evolve a photodramatic language of color analogous with the language of light with which we are all so familiar?[29]

Mamoulian's implicit appeal to a 'logic of the form' might well have impressed some of the 'creative' workers associated with A film productions but it is unlikely to have been heard sympathetically among employees of the Bs. Indeed, the advent of colour actually exacerbated the situation he had outlined: the Technicolor process demanded 'high key effects, with brilliant lighting and sparkling definition' as a very condition of its existence. It is, therefore, hardly surprising that a cinema of 'low key effects, with sombre heavy shadows' flourished in counterpart to it. Furthermore, the films actually employing Technicolor were often characterised by exotic locations, lavish sets, elaborate costumes and spectacular action sequences (generally of the musical or swashbuckling variety) and so fell into an expanding group of 'colour-specific' genres – westerns, musicals, epics, historical dramas, etcetera – leaving melodramas, thrillers, and horror films to the lower budgets of black and white. Finally, in 1939 the really decisive blow for the industrial endorsement of colour was struck by the unprecedented success of *Gone With The Wind*. However, wartime economic and technological restraint frustrated much further movement to colour for several years – as it also postponed the rise of television – and perhaps the very 'dormancy' of the Technicolor phenomenon in those years encouraged people engaged in and/or committed to black and white to continue to experiment. If the war years saw no great increase in Technicolor features (from eighteen in 1939 to twenty-nine in 1945), the postwar period witnessed a rapid acceleration of colour production; in 1949 *Variety* confidently predicted that 30 per cent of all forthcoming features would be in colour and on 15 July 1952 *Film Daily* announced that well over 75 per cent of features in production were shooting in colour.

At the other end of the colour quality spectrum, but perhaps equally influential on the *film noir*, was the development of a number of low budget, two-colour processes. In 1939, the first of these, Cinecolor, became available and the following year the first full-length Cinecolor feature – Monogram's *The Gentleman From Arizona* – was released. Costing only 25 per cent more than black and white stock and considerably less than Technicolor and with the additional advantage of overnight rushes, Cinecolor (and other 'primitive chromatic' processes like it – Vitacolor, Anscocolor, Trucolor) naturally appealed to and was rapidly adopted by certain genres at the low budget end of the industry. By 1959, Allied Artists, Columbia, Eagle Lion, Film Classics, MGM, Monogram, Paramount, 20th Century-Fox, United Artists and Universal had all made some use of the process. Meanwhile, on the A front, Technicolor did have its disadvantages. For instance, because of the prism block between the back element of the lens and the film gates, neither wide angle lenses nor those with very long focal lengths could be accommodated by the new three strip cameras. Indeed, even the introduction of faster (black and white and colour) negative stock in 1938 was unable to produce any depth of focus without wide angle lenses and, for Technicolor, faster film stock necessitated stronger floodlighting throughout the late 1930s, the 1940s and into the 1950s; floodlighting which in turn made for a flatter image and a marked lack of contrast. For black and white, on the other hand, the introduction of faster film stock allowed a decrease in lighting levels and aperture openings commensurate with previously impractical *chiaroscuro* effects. Single source lighting became steadily more feasible and was attractively economic – cheap on both power and labour. Similarly, night for night shooting, which generally involved the payment of prohibitive overtime rates, was particularly applicable to B units which paid set rates for all hours worked.

Apart from colour, perhaps the most important technological development in the late 1930s was the introduction of a new range of Fresnel lenses which, for the first time, made it possible to place large diameter lenses close to a powerful light source without loss of focus. Consequently, spotlights began to replace floodlights for key light functions. While colour stock still needed diffused high key lighting, the new fast black and white stock opened the way for smaller lighting units – such as Babys or Krieg Lilliputs – which permitted lower lighting levels. In 1940, small spotlights with Fresnel lenses and 150- or 300-watt tungsten incandescent bulbs began to outmode heavier, less mobile Carbon Arc lamps. The combination of swinging keys, lightweight spots and mobile military cameras made unorthodox angles possible but involved the erection of previously unnecessary set ceilings. It was for precisely this reason that Sid Hickox, Howard Hawks's cameraman on *To Have And Have Not* (1944),

> had a problem with his set ceilings: in wanting to hang the incandescent lights low, he had to remove most of the ceilings, but the camera shooting from the floor would reveal the lights themselves. So he set up ready-made three quarter ceilings of butter muslin, just sufficiently dark to conceal the incandescents massed behind them, with the other incandescents only a fraction beyond the range of vision.[30]

There were also important developments in camera production in this period. The Mitchell BNC – produced in 1934 but not used in Hollywood until 1938 – enabled synch-sound shooting with lenses of 25 mm widths for the first time. The only new 35 mm camera introduced in the 1940s in any quantity was the Cunningham Combat Camera, a lightweight (13 lb) affair which allowed cinematographers to move more easily whilst filming and to set up in what would previously have been inaccessible positions. Even more appropriate for hand-held and high or low angle shooting, however, was the Arriflex, which was captured from German military cameramen. (The subjective camera opening sequence of Delmer Davies's *Dark Passage* in 1947, inspired by the previous year's *Lady In The Lake*, was shot with a hand-held Arriflex.) In 1940 the first practical anti-reflective coatings became available, coming into general cinematic currency after their use in *Citizen Kane*. These micro-thin coatings, known as Vard Opticoats, together with twin-arc broadside lamps which were also developed for Technicolor, minimised light loss at the surface of the lens (through reflection or refraction) and at the same time accelerated shutter speeds and facilitated the use of good wide-angle lenses – though once again only with black and white. So-called Tolandesque deep focus was therefore only technologically possible from 1938 when the new fast 1232 Super XX Panchromatic Stock could be combined with Duarc light, 25 mm wide-angle lenses and considerably reduced apertures. Wide-angle lenses were extensively used thereafter until they were somewhat anachronised by the advent of wide screens in 1953 and the accommodation to television standards later in that decade. In the same way, the use of deep focus photography continued until it was necessarily abated by Hollywood's brief romance with 3D which lasted from 1952 until 1954. The first CinemaScope murder mystery – Nunnally Johnson's *Black Widow* (1954) – suffered from its screen size just as much as those 3D thrillers released at the same time – *I, The Jury* (1953) and *Dial M For Murder* (1954), all of which illustrate precisely how such processes militated against projects which might, only a few months earlier, have been *films noir*.[31]

This line of argument should not, however, be mistaken for a covert reintroduction of the tenets of technological determinism.[32] Indeed, these various 'innovations' were all either side effects of the (profoundly ideological) desire for ever-increasing degrees of verisimilitude (Technicolor, Deep Focus) or were determined by a negotiated differentiation from and resistance to that realism (exemplified by the A film, by television and by Technicolor itself) in accordance with economic constraints. I would like, finally, to suggest that it was, specifically, the absorption of a colour aesthetic within realism which generated the space which *film noir* was to occupy. Indeed, just as the advent of radio in 1924 had provoked a cinematic trend away from realism until it was reversed in 1927 with the coming of sound to the cinema, so while colour originally signified 'fantasy' and was first appropriated by 'fantastic' genres, it too was soon recuperated within the realist aesthetic. Compare, for instance, the realist status of black and white sequences in *The Wizard Of Oz* (1939) and *If* (1969). The period of this transition, the period in which the equation between black and white on the one hand and realism on the other was at its most fragile, was thus the period from the late 1930s – when television, Technicolor and the double bill were first operating – to the late 1950s, when television and colour had established themselves, both economically and ideologically, as powerful lobbies in the industry, and the double bill had virtually disappeared. That period, of something less than twenty years, saw the conjunction of a primarily economically determined mode of production, known as B film-making, with what were primarily ideologically defined modes of 'difference', known as the *film noir*. Specific conjunctures such as this – of economic constraints, institutional structures, technological developments, political, legal and labour relations – are central to any history of film; they represent the industrial conditions in which certain representational modes, certain generic codes come into existence. This is not to argue that cinema is somehow innocent of extra-industrial determinants but simply to insist that Hollywood has a (so far unspecified) relative autonomy within the wider American social formation, however theoretically unsatisfactory that 'relativity' remains. The point of this article, therefore, has been to map out an influential fraction of that Hollywood terrain and, as part of that process, to challenge the conceptual catch-all of 'mediation' with the concrete specificities of industrial history.

Notes

1   Raymond Borde and Etienne Chaumeton, *Panorama du Film Noir Américain* (Paris: Les Editions de Minuit, 1955). I use the term 'genre' in this article where others have opted for 'subgenre', 'series', 'cycle', 'style', 'period', 'movement', etc. For a recent discussion of critical notions of (and approaches to) *film noir*, see James Damico 'Film noir: a modest proposal' in *Film Reader* no. 3, 1978.

2   In an article on 'Woman's place: the absent family of film noir' (in E. Ann Kaplan, *Women In Film Noir* (London: British Film Institute, 1978) p. 26), Sylvia Harvey has described how 'the increasing size of corporations, the growth of monopolies and the accelerated elimination of small businesses' all contributed to an atmosphere in which it was 'increasingly hard for even the petit bourgeoisie to continue to believe in certain dominant myths. Foremost among these was the dream of equality of opportunity in business and of the God-given right of every man to be his own boss. Increasingly, the petit bourgeoisie were forced into selling their labour and working for the big companies, instead of running their own business and working for themselves.' Other genres have been analysed in this way: for example, Will Wright's *Sixguns and Society* (Berkeley: University of California Press, 1975) treats the development of the Western as a (generically coded) reflection of the development of American capital.

3   This is not to deny the possible efficacy of such approaches, but rather to insist on their being predicated on the sort of industrial analysis attempted here.

4   Borde and Chaumeton's chapter on 'The sources of film noir', translated in *Film Reader*, no. 3, p. 63.

5   An example of the first is Paul Schrader, 'Notes on film noir' in *Film Comment*, vol. 8, no. 1, Spring 1972, p. 11; of the second, Raymond Durgnat, 'Paint it black: the family tree of film noir' in *Cinema*, nos. 6–7, August 1970.

6   Raymond Williams, 'Base and superstructure in Marxist cultural theory', in *New Left Review*, no. 82, November–December 1973.

7   Antony Easthope, 'Todorov, genre theory and TV detectives', mimeo, 1978, p. 4.

8   The poverty of film history already referred to is less material than conceptual. For a useful contribution to the historical debate see Edward Buscombe's 'A new approach to film history', published with other papers from the Purdue University Conference in the 1977 *Film Studies Annual*.

9   Much of the stylistic detail in this outline is indebted to J. A. Place and L. S. Peterson, 'Some visual motifs of film noir' in *Film Comment*, vol. 10, no. 1, January–February 1974.

10   For further examples of such infringements see Stuart Marshall, '*Lady in the Lake*: identification and the drives', in *Film Form*, vol. 1, nos. 1–2, 1977; Stephen Heath, 'Film and system: terms of analysis', in *Screen*, vol. 16, nos. 1–2, Spring/Summer 1975; Kristin Thompson, 'The duplicitous text: an analysis of *Stage Fright*', in *Film Reader*, no. 2, 1977; and idem, 'Closure within a dream: point-of-view in *Laura*', in *Film Reader*, no. 3, 1978.

11   Damico, 'Film noir: a modest proposal'.

12   Mae D. Heuttig, *Economic Control of the Motion Picture Industry* (Philadelphia: University of Pennsylvania Press, 1944).

13   These figures are, of course, approximate – several of the smallest B companies actually produced films on budgets of less than $100,000 – but they do at least indicate the degree of economic difference between the various 'modes'.

14   Producers' Releasing Corporation: for information on this see Todd McCarthy and Charles Flynn (eds), *Kings of the Bs* (New York: Dutton, 1975); Don Miller, *B Movies* (New York: Curtis Books, 1973); idem, 'Eagle-Lion: the violent years', in *Focus on Film*, no. 31, November 1978.

15   Nick Grinde, 'Pictures for peanuts', in *The Penguin Film Review*, no. 1, August 1946 (reprinted London: Scolar Press, 1977, pp. 46–7).

16   Mark Robson, interviewed in *The Velvet Light Trap*, no. 10, Fall 1973.

17   Grinde, 'Pictures for peanuts', p. 44.

18   Peter Bogdanovich, *Fritz Lang in America* (London: Studio Vista, 1967).

19   For information on the Lewton unit see Joel Siegel, *Val Lewton, The Reality of Terror* (London: Secker & Warburg/BFI, 1972). For further detail on RKO see the special issue (no. 10) of *The Velvet Light Trap*. On production in general see Gene Fernett, *Poverty Row* (Satellite Beach, Florida: Coral Reef, 1973).

20   Frank Ricketson Jr, *The Management of Motion Picture Theatres* (New York: McGraw-Hill, 1938), pp. 82–3.

21   Stuart Hall and Tony Jefferson (eds), *Resistance Through Rituals: Cultural Studies*, nos. 7–8, Summer 1975; reprinted London: Hutchinson, 1976.

22   John Clarke, 'Style', in ibid., pp. 175–92.

23   Fox's *March of Time* series lasted from 1934 until 1953 and its photo-journalistic aesthetic carried over into that studio's 'documentary' fictions in the late 1940s. Similarly, MGM's series of shorts, *Crime Does Not Pay*, which ran from 1935 until 1948, also complemented Metro's own output in that genre.

24   For one account of the effect of these pressures on the cinema see Keith Kelly and Clay Steinman, '*Crossfire*: a dialectical attack', in *Film Reader* no. 3.

25   Colin MacCabe, 'Realism and the cinema: notes on some Brechtian theses', *Screen*, vol. 15, no. 2, Summer 1974, pp. 10–12.

26   Colin MacCabe, 'Theory and film: principles of realism and pleasure', *Screen*, vol. 17, no. 3, Autumn 1976, p. 12.

27   Sylvia Harvey, 'Woman's place', p. 22.

28   Gill Davies, 'Teaching about narrative', *Screen Education*, no. 29, Winter 1978/79, p. 62.

29   Rouben Mamoulian, 'Controlling color for dramatic effect', in *The American Cinematographers*, June 1941, collected in Richard Koszarski (ed.), *Hollywood Directors 1941–1976* (New York: Oxford University Press, 1976) p. 15.

30   Charles Higham, *Warner Brothers* (New York: Charles Scribner's Sons, 1975) p. 157.
31   The major sources of technological history drawn on here are Barry Salt, 'Film style and technology in the thirties', in *Film Quarterly*, vol. 30, no. 1, Fall 1976 and 'Film style and technology in the forties', in *Film Quarterly*, vol. 31, no. 1, Fall 1977; and James Limbacher, *Four Aspects of the Film* (New York: Brussel & Brussel, 1968).
32   See, in this respect, Patrick Ogle 'Technological and aesthetic influence upon the development of deep focus cinematography in the United States' and Christopher Williams's critique of that article's elision of notions of ideology and economy. Both are anthologised in *Screen Reader*, 1 (London: SEFT, 1977).

Chapter 17

_____

Pius XII

MIRANDA PRORSUS: ENCYCLICAL LETTER ON MOTION PICTURES, RADIO AND TELEVISION (1957)

INTRODUCTION

THOSE VERY REMARKABLE TECHNICAL inventions which are the boast of the men of our generation, though they spring from human intelligence and industry, are nevertheless the gifts of God, Our Creator, from Whom all good gifts proceed: "for He has not only brought forth creatures, but sustains and fosters them once created".[1] Of these inventions, some increase and multiply the strength and power of men; others improve their conditions of life; while others — and these particularly concern the mind — reach the mass of the people themselves, either directly or through the pictures and sounds they produce, and convey to them in a form easy to understand, the news, thoughts and usages of every nation, and by these means provide, as it were, food for the mind especially during the hours of rest and recreation.

With regard to this last type of invention, in our own age the greatest impetus has been received by the arts connected with Motion Pictures, Radio and Television.

REASONS FOR THE CHURCH'S INTEREST

From the time when these arts first came into use, the Church welcomed them, not only with great joy, but also with a motherly care and watchfulness, having in mind to protect Her children from every danger, as they set out on this new path of progress.

This watchful care springs from the mission She has received from the Divine Saviour Himself; for, as is clear to all, these new forms of art exercise very great influence on the manner of thinking and acting of individuals and of every group of men.

There is, in addition, another reason why the Church considers a matter of this kind to be particularly Her concern: Hers is the duty, and for a much stronger reason than all others can claim, of announcing a message to every man: this is the message of eternal salvation; a message unrivalled in its richness and power, a message, *in fine*, which all men of every race and every age must accept and embrace, according to the saying of the Apostle of the Gentiles: "To me, the least of all the saints, is given this grace, to preach among the gentiles the unsearchable riches of Christ, and to enlighten all men that they may see what is the mystery which hath been hidden from eternity in God, who created all things".[2]

PREVIOUS PAPAL UTTERANCES

It is therefore not surprising that they who exercise the supreme authority of the Church, have treated of this important matter with the intention of providing for the eternal salvation of those who are "not redeemed with corruptible things of gold and silver . . . but with the precious blood of Christ, as of a lamb unspotted and undefiled";[3] and they have weighed carefully all the questions with which Motion Pictures, Radio, and Television today confront Christians.

More than twenty years have passed since Our predecessor of happy memory, Pius XI, making use of "the remarkable invention of Marconi", issued the first message by Radio "to all nations and to every creature".[4]

A few years later, this same predecessor of Ours sent to the Hierarchy of the United States of America that memorable Encyclical Letter entitled *Vigilanti Cura*.[5] In that letter, while giving wise principles concerning films, adapted to existing needs, he said this: "Here is a matter for which immediate provision is absolutely necessary: we must ensure that all progress made, by God's favour, both in human knowledge and in technical skill, shall in practice so serve God's glory, the salvation of souls and the extension of Christ's kingdom, that we all, as the Church bids us pray, may so pass through temporal goods that we may not lose what is eternal."[6]

And We Ourselves, in the course of Our Supreme Pontificate, have often, when opportunity offered, dealt with this same question, giving appropriate directives not only to Bishops, but also to various branches of Catholic Action and to Christian educators. And, further, We have gladly admitted to Our presense those whose special profession it is to practise the art of the Motion Pictures or Radio or Television. To these, after We have made clear Our admiration for the notable progress they have achieved in those arts, We have pointed out the obligations by which each is bound; and at the same time, beside the great merit they have won, We set out the dangers into which they can easily fall, and the high ideals which ought to enlighten their minds and direct their wills.

We have also, as you know, taken steps to set up in the Roman Curia a special Commission,[7] whose task it is to make careful study of the various questions connected with Motion Pictures, Radio and Television which touch on the Catholic Faith and Christian morals. From this Commission, Bishops and all other interested parties can expect to obtain appropriate directives.

Very often We Ourselves have made use of the modern remarkable inventions by which We can unite the worldwide flock with its Supreme Pastor, so that Our voice, passing in sure and safe flight over the expanse of sea and land and even over the troubled emotions of souls, may reach men's minds with a healing influence, in accordance with the demands of the task of the supreme apostolate, confided to Us and today extended almost without limit.[8]

RESULTS OF THE PAPAL TEACHING

We are not a little comforted since We know that the addresses on this subject, both Our own and those of Our late predecessor of happy memory, Pius XI, have had considerable influence in directing the arts of Motion Pictures, Radio and Television to the task of recalling men to the pursuit of the perfection of their individual souls, and thus, to the promotion of God's glory.

For, by your diligent and watchful care, Venerable Brethren, the initiative was given to works by which an apostolate on these lines was not only encouraged in individual dioceses and nations, but also embraced whole peoples by means of united efforts and plans.

Not a few statesmen as well as those who are engaged in the professions or in business, and most of those, Catholic and non-Catholic alike, who attend shows of this kind, gave evidence of their sane thinking on this important matter; and, at the cost of trouble and even material loss, made efforts that not only the dangerous evils should be avoided, but that the sacred commandments of God should be obeyed and the dignity of the human person kept safe.

Yet We must, alas, repeat that sentence of the Apostle of the Gentiles: "Not all obey the Gospel";[9] for, in this matter, there are not wanting those who neither understand nor recognise the teaching function of the Church; some even oppose it by every possible means. They are, as you know, those who are moved by an inordinate desire for gain; or, deceived by errors, they do not have a balanced view on human dignity and freedom; or finally, they give full acceptance to a false opinion about the real meaning of art.

Though the manner of acting of these men fills Our mind with grief, yet We cannot fail in Our duty and turn aside from the right path; We hope that there will be said likewise of Us, those words which His enemies used of Our Divine Redeemer: "We know that thou art a true speaker, and teachest the way of God in truth, neither carest thou for any man".[10]

REASONS FOR THIS LETTER

Just as very great advantages can arise from the wonderful advances which have been made in our day, in technical knowledge concerning Motion Pictures, Radio and Television, so too can very great dangers.

For these new possessions and new instruments which are within almost everyone's grasp, introduce a most powerful influence into men's minds, both because they can flood them with light, raise them to nobility, adorn them with beauty, and because they can disfigure them by dimming their lustre, dishonour them by a process of corruption, and make them subject to uncontrolled passions, according as the subjects presented to the senses in these shows are praiseworthy or reprehensible.[11]

In the past century, advancing technical skill in the field of business frequently had this result: machines, which ought to serve men, when brought into use, rather reduced them to a state of slavery and caused grievous harm. Likewise today, unless the mounting development of technical skill, applied to the diffusion of pictures, sounds and ideas, is subjected to the sweet yoke of the law of Christ,[12] it can be the source of countless evils, which appear to be all the more serious, because not only material forces but also the mind are unhappily enslaved, and man's inventions are, to that extent, deprived of those advantages which, in the design of God's Providence, ought to be their primary purpose.[13]

Consequently, since We, as a father, have daily pondered with ever greater anxiety, the essential nature of this problem and have considered the salutary benefits – so far as films are concerned – which have resulted during more than two decades from the Encyclical Letter

Vigilanti cura, yielding to the petitions of the Bishops and those laymen who make a study of these arts, We wish by this letter to give directives and instructions with regard to both sound broadcasting and television.

Therefore, after We have made earnest prayer to God, and sought the help of His Virgin Mother, We address you, Venerable Brethren, whose wise pastoral care is well known to Us, with a view not only to setting forth clearly the Christian doctrine in this matter, but to undertaking suitable plans and initiatives. And so, with all the force at Our command, We desire to impress upon you how the flock, committed to the care of each one, should be protected against any errors and harm from whatever source, which the use of the arts under discussion can introduce – with serious risk – to the practices of Christian life.

1. GENERAL INSTRUCTION

Publicising Christian doctrine

We are aware that each of these three arts of the Motion Pictures, Radio and Television, in fostering the development of mind and spirit, sets its own special problems to be solved in the field not only of the arts, but of technology and economics. But before We deal with the particular questions affecting each, We think it right to outline briefly the principles which concern the diffusion to the greatest possible extent, of the benefits which are destined both for human society in general and for individual citizens.

The "good seed"

Since God is the supreme Good, He at all times pours out His gifts on men who are objects of His special loving care. Of these gifts, some are to assist the material life on earth, but others concern the spirit; and, clearly, the former are subject to the latter in much the same way as the body should be subject to the soul with which, before God can communicate Himself by the beatific vision, He is united by faith and charity which "is poured forth in our hearts by the Holy Ghost who is given to us".[14]

And further, since He longs to see in man the image of His own perfection,[15] He even wills him to be made a sharer in this supreme generosity, and has linked him with His own activity as the proclaimer of those good tidings, making him become their donor and dispenser to his brethren and to the whole human race. From the beginning of time, it has been man's natural and normal tendency to share with others the treasures of his mind by means of symbols whereby he daily tried to develop a more perfect means of expressing his material problems. Thus, from the drawings and inscriptions of the most ancient times down to the latest technical devices, all instruments of human communication inevitably have as their aim the lofty purpose of revealing men as in some way the assistants of God.

Hence, in order that the plan of God's Providence may be put more surely and fruitfully into effect, by virtue of Our Apostolic authority, We constituted, in an Apostolic Letter[16] "the Archangel Gabriel, who brought to the human race the long-desired news of man's Redemption, heavenly patron" of those arts by which men can employ electrical forces to transcribe words at very great speed to others at a distance, can hold converse from places widely apart, send messages by wireless, and view pictures of objects and events brought before them as if they were immediate spectators, though they are, in fact, far away.[17] For, when We made choice of this heavenly patron, it was Our intention that all employed in these arts might fully understand the nobility of the task entrusted to them, for into their hands have been placed these useful instruments by which the priceless treasures of God may be spread among men like good seed which bring forth fruits of truth and goodness.

"Evil seed"

For as We consider those honourable and lofty purposes to which this technical skill should be directed, the question presents itself: why do these same arts sometimes become the means, and, as it were, the paths leading to evil? "Whence then hath it cockle?"[18]

All evil, of course, which is opposed to right moral principles, cannot have its origin in God, Who is complete and absolute Good; nor does it come from the techniques themselves, which are His precious gifts. It can be only from the fact that man, endowed as he is with free will, can abuse those gifts, namely, by committing and multiplying evil, and thus associating himself with God's enemy, the prince of darkness: "An enemy hath done this".[19] Consequently true human liberty demands that we use, and share with others, all these resources which can contribute to the strengthening and perfecting of our nature.

True freedom of communication

But since the Church is the teacher of the doctrine which leads to salvation, and has all that is necessary for the attainment of holiness, She is exercising an inviolable right when She teaches what has been committed to Her by divine command. It ought to be the duty of all public officials to recognise this sacred right, with the result that She should be given ready access to those arts by which She may spread truth and virtue.

Indeed, all true and active sons of the Church, since they recognise the priceless gift of the Redemption, are bidden to ensure, to the extent of their power, that the Church may use these technical discoveries in so far as they may assist the sanctification of souls.

Yet when We assert and claim these rights for the Church, it is not Our desire to deny to the State the right of spreading by the same means, that news and those teachings which are really necessary or useful for the common good of human society.

And further, let it be permitted even to individual citizens – due regard being paid to actual circumstances and the safeguarding of principles which promote the common good – to contribute according to their capacity to the enriching and development of their own and others' intellectual and spiritual culture.

Errors concerning freedom of communication

Contrary, however, to Christian teaching and the principal end of these arts is the will and intention of those who desire to use these inventions exclusively for the advancement and propagation of political measures or to achieve economic ends, and who treat Our noble aim as if it were a mere business transaction.

In like manner, approval cannot be given to the false principles of those who assert and claim freedom to depict and propagate *anything at all*, even though there has been established beyond dispute in these past years both the kind and the extent of the damage to both bodies and souls which has had its source in these principles. There is no question here of the true liberty of which We have spoken above, but rather of an uncontrolled freedom, which disregards all precautions, of communicating with others anything at all, even though it be contrary to sound morals and can result in serious danger to souls.

The Church encourages and supports everything which truly concerns a fuller enrichment of the mind – for She is the patron and fostermother of human knowledge and the noble arts; therefore She cannot permit the violation of those principles and laws which direct and govern man in his path to God, his final end. Let no one, then, be surprised if, in this matter, where many reservations are necessary, the Church acts with due thought and discretion, according to that saying of the Apostle: "But prove all things: hold fast that which is good. From all appearance of evil refrain yourselves".[20]

Those, therefore, are certainly to be blamed who openly declare that public communication of matters which impede, or are directly opposed to, principles of morality, should be encouraged and carried out so long as the method is in accord with the laws of the liberal or technical arts. In a short discourse, on the occasion of the fifth centenary of the death of Fra Angelico, We recalled to the minds of Our hearers that "it is true that an explicitly moral or religious function is not demanded of art as art"; but "if artistic expression gives publicity to false, empty and confused forms, – those not in harmony with the Creator's design; if, rather than lifting mind and heart to noble sentiments, it stirs the baser passions, it might, perhaps, find welcome among some people, but only by nature of its novelty, a quality not always of value and with but slight content of that reality which is possessed by every type of human expression. But such an art would degrade itself, denying its primary and essential element: it would not be universal and perennial as is the human spirit to which it is addressed".[21]

Competence of public authority and of the entertainment industry

Beyond all doubt, public administrators are strictly bound to be watchful over these modern arts also: nor should they look on this matter from a merely political standpoint, but also from that of public morals, the sure foundation of which rests on the Natural Law, which, inspired testimony assures us, is written in our hearts.[22]

It cannot be asserted that this watchful care of the State's officials is an unfair limitation on the liberty of individual citizens, for it is concerned with, not the private citizen as such, but rather the whole of human society with whom these arts are being shared.

"We are well aware", as We have already said on another occasion, "that there is a widespread opinion among men of our time who are unreasonably intolerant of the intervention of public authority, that censorship is to be preferred which comes directly from the Industry itself";[23] but though the persons professionally engaged in these arts can, in a praiseworthy manner, support the action of public officials and render ineffective the evils which can easily damage true morality, yet those rules and safeguards which issue from the former ought in no way to be opposed to the serious duty of the latter.

Hence, both Our late predecessor and We Ourselves readily praised those who, in accordance with the task committed to them in this sphere, published suitable safeguards and rules without in any way prejudicing what belongs to the competence of public authority. For We think that, then only can these new arts make their proper and natural contribution to the right fashioning of the minds of those who use them, if the Church, the State, and those engaged in these professions, pooling their resources in an orderly way, cooperate with each other to secure the desired end; if the opposite happens, i. e. if these arts, without set laws or any moral safeguards, embark on a downward and uninhibited path, they will certainly restrict the people's true development and weaken their morals.

Sight and sound communication

Among the various technical arts which transmit the ideas of men, those occupy a special place today, as We said, which communicate as widely as possible news of all kinds to ears and eyes by means of sounds and pictures.

This manner of spreading pictures and sounds, so far as the spirit is concerned, is supremely adapted to the nature of men, as Aquinas says: "But it is natural to man to come to things of the understanding through things of sense; for all our knowledge has its origin in a sense".[24] Indeed, the sense of sight, as being more noble and more honourable than other senses, more easily leads to a knowledge of spiritual things.[25]

Therefore, the three chief technical methods of telecommunication, i. e. those of the Motion Pictures, Radio and Television, deal not only with men's recreation and leisure – though many who "listen-in" and view, seek this alone, – but especially with the propagation of those subjects which, while aiding both mental culture and spiritual growth, can powerfully contribute to the right training and shaping of the civil society of our times.

Much more easily than by printed books, these technical arts can assuredly provide opportunities for men to meet and unite in common effort; and, since this purpose is essentially connected with the advancement of the civilization of all peoples, the Catholic Church – which, by the charge committed to it, embraces the whole human race – desires to turn it to the extension and furthering of benefits worthy of the name.

Indeed, this should be the first aim of the arts of the Motion Pictures, Radio and Television: to serve truth and virtue.

In the service of truth and virtue

Let them be at the service of truth in such a way that the bonds between peoples may become yet closer; that they may have a more respectful understanding of each other; that they may assist each other in any crisis: that, finally, there may be real cooperative effort between the State officials and the individual citizens.

To be at the service of the truth demands not only that all refrain from error, from lies, from deceit of all kinds, but also that they shun everything that can encourage a manner of living and acting which is false, imperfect, or harmful to another party.

But above all, let the truths, handed down by God's revelation, be held sacred and inviolable. Rather, why should not these noble arts strive particularly to this end, that they spread the teaching of God and of His Son, Jesus Christ, "and instil into minds that Christian truth which alone can provide the strength from above to the mass of men, aided by which they may be able with calmness and courage, to overcome the crises and endure the severe trials of the age in which we now live?"[26]

Moreover, these new arts should not only serve the truth, but also the perfecting of human life and morals. Let them make an active contribution to this in the three ways We are now going to write about: namely, in the news published, in the instruction imparted, in the shows presented.

News

News of any event, even if nothing but the bare fact is related, has yet an aspect of its own which concerns morality in some way. "This aspect, affecting human morals, must never be neglected; for news of any kind provokes a mental judgment and influences the will. The news-reader who worthily fulfils his task, should crush no one by his words, but try rather to understand and explain as best he can, the disasters reported and the crimes committed. To explain is not necessarily to excuse; but it is to suggest the beginning of a remedy, and consequently, to perform a task at once positive and constructive".[27]

Instruction

What We have just written has doubtless more force when it is a question of imparting instructions; documentary films, radio broadcasts, and television for schools provide ideas and open up new possibilities here, not only with regard to those who are still young, but also with regard to those of mature years. Yet every precaution must be taken that the instructions given are in no way contrary to the Church's teaching and its sacred rights, or impede or frustrate the proper duty of educating the young within the home circle.

Similarly, it is to be hoped that these new arts of publicity, whether exercised by private citizens or controlled by rulers of states, will not spread doctrines while suppressing all mention of God's name and taking no account of His divine law.

However, We are fully aware, alas, that in some nations amid which atheistic Communism is rampant, these methods of telecommunication are directed in the schools to root out all religious ideas from the mind. Indeed, anyone who considers this situation calmly and without prejudice, cannot fail to see that the consciences of children and youths, deprived of divine truth, are being oppressed in a new and subtle way, since they are unable to learn that truth revealed by God, which, as our Redeemer declared, makes us free; and that by this cunning method a new attack is being made on religion.[28]

But We earnestly desire, Venerable Brethren, that these technical instruments, by which eyes and ears are easily and pleasantly attracted to events happening far away, should be employed to a particular end, namely, to provide men with a broader cultural background in the knowledge necessary for the fulfilment of their duties, and above all, in Christian principles. If these principles are neglected, there can be no progress worthy of the name, even in merely human matters.[29] We desire, therefore, to pay due tribute of praise to all those who, whether by films or sound broadcasting or television shows, direct their efforts towards this most honourable goal.

Shows

Further, it must be noted that, apart from the published news and the instructions delivered, these new arts can contribute considerably towards the true good of men by shows as well.

The progammes have generally something which has reference not only to entertaining men and giving them news, but also to the training of their minds. With complete justice, then, Our predecessor of happy memory, Pius XI, called the film theatres the "schools of events";[30] for they can be called schools in this sense, that the dramatic plot is joined with scenes in which the vivid pictures which are portrayed by the moving light, are synchronised with sounds of voices and music in a most fascinating manner, with the result that they reach not only the intelligence and other faculties, but the whole man, and, in some way, link him to themselves, and seem to sweep him into a participation in the plot presented.

Although the arts of the Motion Pictures, Radio and Television include, in some fashion, various types of spectacle already long in use, yet each expresses a new product, and thus a new kind of spectacle which is aimed not at a few chosen spectators, but at vast throngs of men, who differ among themselves in age, way of life and culture.

Mass education

In order, then, that, in such conditions, shows of this kind may be able to pursue their proper object, it is essential that the minds and inclinations of the spectators be rightly trained and educated, so that they may not only understand the form proper to each of the arts, but also be guided, especially in this matter, by a right conscience. Thus they will be enabled to practise mature consideration and judgment on the various items which the film or television screen puts before them, and not, as very frequently happens, be lured and arbitrarily swept away by the power of their attraction.

If there is lacking this mental training and formation, enlightened by Christian teaching, then neither reasonable pleasures which "everyone readily admits are necessary for all who are involved in the business and troubles of life", nor the progress of mental development can be kept safe.[31]

The sound policy of Catholics who have encouraged, especially in recent years, the need to educate the spectators in this way, is most praiseworthy; and several plans have been launched which aim at making both youths and grown-ups willing to examine adequately and competently the benefits and the dangers of these shows, and give a balanced decision on them. This, however, should not provide an excuse for attending shows which are contrary to right morals; rather, it ought to lead to pointing out and choosing those only which are in accord with the Church's commandments on the grounds of religion and of the moral law, and which follow the instructions issued by the ecclesiastical Offices in this matter.

Provided these plans, in accordance with Our hopes, correspond to pedagogical principles and right rules of mental development, We not only give them Our approval, but also heartily commend them; and thus We desire them to be introduced into every type of school, Catholic Action groups, and parish societies.

Right training and education of the spectators in this fashion will ensure, on the one hand, a lessening of the dangers which can threaten harm to morals; and, on the other hand, permit Christians, through the new knowledge they acquire, to raise their minds to a contemplation of heavenly truths.

While speaking on this point, We desire to praise in a particular manner those preachers of the divine word who make right use also of the means provided by Motion Pictures, Radio and Television to this end. They are aware that they are in duty bound to preserve the integrity of morals of those peoples to whom they minister and lead towards the path of truth; and thus they share with them the genuinely salutary benefits and inventions which our times have introduced. We therefore desire that those who wield authority, either in Church or State, should in a special way support the activity and enterprise of these preachers.

Entertainments for youth

Yet it must be noticed that, in exercising control in this matter, the right training and education of the spectators, of which We have spoken, is not in itself sufficient. Each of the shows must be suited and adapted to the degree of intelligence of each age, the strength of their emotional and imaginative response, and the condition of their morals.

This, indeed, assumes a very great importance because sound radio and television shows, since they easily penetrate right into the domestic circle, threaten to undermine the protective barriers by which the education of the young must be kept safe and sound until such time as advancing age gives the necessary strength to enable them to overcome the buffetings of the world. For this reason, three years ago, We wrote thus to the Bishops of

Italy: "Should we not shudder if we reflect attentively that by means of television shows, even within home surroundings all can inhale that poisoned air of "materialistic" doctrines which diffuse notions of empty pleasures and desires of all kinds, in the same way as they did over and over again in cinema halls?"[32]

We are aware of the initiatives which have been encouraged not only by public authorities but also by private groups who are engaged in the education of youth; We mean those undertakings and plans by which they make every possible effort to withdraw young people from those shows which are unsuited to their age, though they are too often being attended, with resulting serious harm. Whatever is being done in this praiseworthy cause, We heartily approve; yet it must be noticed that, even more than the physiological and psychological disturbances which can arise therefrom, those dangers must be guarded against which affect the morals of youth, and which, unless turned aside and forbidden in due season, can greatly contribute to the damage and overthrow of human society itself.

Concerning this matter, We make a father's appeal to the young so dear to Us, trusting that – since it is a question of entertainment in which their innocence can be exposed to danger – they will be outstanding for their Christian restraint and prudence. It is their grave obligation to check and control that natural and unrestrained eagerness to see and hear *anything*; and they must keep their mind free from immodest and earthly pleasures and direct it to higher things.

The work of the church – national offices

Since the Church knows well that, from these new arts which directly affect the eye and ear, very many benefits as well as very many evils and dangers can arise, according as men make use of them, She desires to perform her duty in this matter also – in so far as it concerns directly, not culture in general, but religion in particular and the direction and control of morals.[33]

With a view to carrying out this task more fittingly and easily, Our predecessor of immortal memory, Pius XI, declared and proclaimed that "it is absolutely essential for Bishops to set up a permanent National Office of supervision whose business it would be to encourage decent films, but to give to others a recognised classification, and then to publish their judgment and make it known to priests and faithful";[34] and that it was necessary, he added, that all Catholic initiative with regard to the Motion Pictures be directed to an honourable end.

In several countries, the Bishops, with these directives before their eyes, decided to set up Offices of this kind not only for matters connected with Motion Pictures, but also for Radio and Television.

As We consider, then, the spiritual advantages which can spring from these technical arts, together with the need to protect the integrity of Christian morals which such entertainments can easily endanger, We desire that, in every country, if the Offices referred to do not already exist, they be established without delay; these are to be entrusted to men skilled in the use of these arts, with some priest, chosen by the Bishops, as adviser.

Moreover, Venerable Brethren, We urge that in each country, these Offices dealing with Motion Pictures, or Radio or Television should depend on one and the same Committee, or at least, act in close cooperation. At the same time, We urge the faithful, particularly those who are vigorous members of Catholic Action, to be suitably instructed so that they may perceive the need to give willingly to these Offices their united and effective support.

And since there are a number of questions on this subject not capable of easy explanation and solution in individual countries, it will certainly be very useful if the National

Offices of each country unite into an International Association to which this Holy See, after due consideration, will be able to give approval.

We have no doubt, Venerable Brethren, that you will produce fruitful and salutary results from what you will do, at some cost in toil and inconvenience, to obey these directives. But the result will be more easily and aptly attained if the particular rules, which We are going to set out in the course of this Encyclical Letter with regard to the Motion Pictures, Radio and Television separately considered, are carefully put into practice.

2. MOTION PICTURES

Motion Pictures, which came into existence some sixty years ago, must today be numbered among the most important means by which the ideas and discoveries of our times can be made known. Concerning their various processes and their power of attraction, We have, when occasion offered, already spoken.[35] Out of this growth, particularly in the case of films which reproduce a definite story expressed in a vivid manner by pictures and sounds, there has also sprung up a great industry in which not only craftsmen, labourers and technicians, but also financial groups unite their activities; for private individuals cannot easily carry through such an extensive and complex operation. Hence, in order that the cinema may remain a worthy instrument by which men can be guided towards salvation, raised to higher things, and become really better, it is absolutely necessary for each of those groups just referred to, exercising a true sense of responsibility, to cooperate readily with each other to produce and distribute films which can win approval.[36]

To all those who practise vigilance and act intelligently concerning film shows, We have already more than once made clear the seriousness of the subject, while exhorting them to produce, in particular, the kind of "ideal film" which can certainly contribute to a well balanced education.[37]

Do you, Venerable Brethren, take a special interest in seeing that, through the individual National Offices, which must be subject to your authority, and about which We have written above, there shall be imparted to the various classes of interested citizens information on the matters to be viewed, – the advice and the directives by which, in accordance with the different times and circumstances, this most noble art, which can so much help the good of souls, may be as far as possible advanced.

Film classification

For this purpose, "let tables or lists be composed and printed in a definite arrangement, in which films distributed will, as frequently as possible, be listed so as to come to the notice of all";[38] and let this be done by a Committee of reliable men, which will depend on each of your National Offices. These men, of course, should be outstanding for their doctrine and practical prudence since they have to pass judgment on each film according to the rules of Christian morality.

We most earnestly exhort the members of this Committee to devote in a suitable manner to these topics, deep and prolonged study and devout prayer; for they have to deal with a most important matter which is closely bound up with the Christian concept of life, and consequently, they must have a sound knowledge of that power which is exerted by the cinema, and which varies according to the different circumstances of the spectators.

As often as they have to judge the moral aspect of a cinema programme, they should attentively revise within themselves those directives already many times given by Us, as occasion offered; and particularly when We spoke of the "ideal film", of the points which concern religion, and at the same time of representation of evil deeds: it should never ignore or be opposed to human dignity, to the modesty of the home surroundings, to holiness of life, to the Church of Jesus Christ, to human and civil types of association.

Moreover, let them remember that the task allowed to them of classifying and passing judgment on each film programme, aims especially at giving clear and appropriate guidance to public opinion, with the intention of leading all to value highly the rules and principles of morality, without which the right development of minds and true civilization become meaningless terms. Unquestionably, therefore, one must repudiate the manner of acting of those who, from excessive indulgence, admit films which, for all their technical brilliance, nevertheless offend right morals; or, though they appear on the surface to conform to the moral laws, yet contain something which is contrary to the Catholic Faith.

But if they have clearly and publicly indicated which films can be seen by all, by the young, by adults; and those, on the other hand, which are a moral danger to the spectators; and finally, those which are entirely bad and harmful, then each will be able to attend those films only, from which "they will come out with minds happier, freer and better";[39] and they will be able to avoid those which can be harmful to them, and doubly so, of course, when they will have been a means of gain for traffickers in evil things, and given bad example to others.

Repeating the timely instructions which Our predecessor of happy memory, Pius XI, published in his Encyclical Letter, entitled *Vigilanti Cura*,[40] We earnestly desire that Christians be not only warned with care, as frequently as possible, on this topic, but that they fulfil the grave obligation of acquainting themselves with the decisions issued by Ecclesiastical Authority on matters connected with Motion Pictures, and of faithfully obeying them. The Bishops, if they deem it appropriate, will be able to set aside a special day each year devoted to this matter, on which the faithful will be carefully instructed concerning their duty, particularly with regard to Film shows, and urged to offer earnest prayers to God about the same.

To make it easy for all to be familiar with these decisions and to obey them, these directives, together with a short commentary on them, must be published at some suitable time, and distributed as widely as possible.

Film criticism

To this end, Catholic Film critics can have much influence; they ought to set the moral issue of the plots in its proper light, defending those judgments which will act as a safeguard against falling into so-called "relative morality", or the overthrow of that right order in which the lesser issues yield place to the more important.

Quite wrong, therefore, is the action of writers in daily papers and in reviews, claiming to be Catholic, if, when dealing with shows of this kind, they do not instruct their readers concerning the moral position to be adopted.

Theatre managers

There is a duty of conscience binding the spectators who, each time they buy a ticket of admission, – as it were casting a vote – make choice of good or bad motion pictures; a similar duty, and even more so, binds those who manage movie theatres or distribute the films.

We are well aware of the magnitude of the difficulties which today confront those engaged in the Motion Picture industry because of – in addition to other considerations – the great increase in the use of television. Yet, even when confronted by these difficult circumstances, they must remember that they are forbidden in conscience to present film programmes which are contrary to the Faith and sound morals, or to enter into contracts by which they are forced to present shows of this kind. But since in many countries, men engaged in this industry have bound themselves not to exhibit, for any consideration, film programmes which might be harmful or evil, We trust that the excellent initiative will spread to all parts of the world, and that no catholic in cinema management will hesitate to follow such sane and salutary proposals.

We must also utter a vigorous warning against the display of commercial posters which ensnare or give scandal, even though, as sometimes happens, such publicity refers to decent films. "Who can say what harm is wrought in minds, especially of the young, by these pictures, what base thoughts and impure pleasures are aroused, how much they contribute to the corruption of public morals with consequent damage to the well-being of the State itself?"[41]

Catholic halls

Consequently, in cinema halls subject to ecclesiastical authority, since there have to be provided for the faithful, and particularly for the young, shows which are suitable to upright training and in keeping with the surroundings, it is clear that only those films may be exhibited which are entirely beyond reproach.

Let the Bishops, keeping a watchful eye on these halls, – including those of exempt religious, – to which the public has access, warn all ecclesiastics on whom the responsibility falls, to observe faithfully and exactly the rules laid down in these matters, and let them not be too much taken up with their personal advantage if they wish to play their part in this ministry which the Holy See considers of the highest importance. We especially advise those who control these Catholic halls, to group themselves together – as, with Our full approval and consent, has been done in a number of places – the more effectively to put into practice the recommendations of the respective National Offices, and support common advantages and policies.

Film distributors

The counsel which We have given to theatre managers We wish to apply also to the distributors who, since they sometimes contribute financially to the making of the actual films, have obviously a greater opportunity and, consequently, are bound by a more serious obligation, of giving their support to reputable films. For distribution cannot be in any sense reckoned as a technical function of the business, since films – as We have often stated – are not only to be regarded as articles for sale, but also, and this is more important, to be considered as food for the mind and, as it were, a means of spiritual and moral training for the ordinary people. So distributors and hirers share to the same degree in merit and responsibility according as something good or evil results from the screen.

Actors

Since, therefore, there is question of bringing the Motion Picture industry into line with sounder policies, that is no slight responsibility which rests on the actors; they, indeed, remembering their dignity as human beings and as experienced artists, should know that they are not permitted to lend their talents to parts in plays, or to be connected with the making of films, which are contrary to sound morals. But an actor, having gained a famous name by his talent and skill, ought to use that renown which he has justly won in such a way that he inspires the mind of the public with noble sentiments; in particular, he should remember to give a notable example of virtue to others in his private life. When addressing professional actors on one occasion in the past, We made this assertion: "Everyone can see that, in the presence of a throng of people listening open-mouthed to your words, applauding and shouting, your own feelings are stirred and filled with a certain joy and exaltation".[42] But if it can be said that someone is fully justified in feeling these emotions, yet it does not follow that Christian actors may accept from their audience expressions of praise which savour of a type of idolatry, since, in this case also, Our Saviour's words apply: "So let your light shine before men, that they may see your good works, and glorify your Father Who is in heaven".[43]

Producers and directors

But the heaviest responsibility – though for a different reason – falls on the directors and producers. The awareness of this burden is not an obstacle to noble undertakings, but rather ought to strengthen the minds of those who, endowed with good will, are influential by reason of their money or natural talent in the production of films. In addition, it often happens that film producers and directors meet a serious difficulty when the circumstances and demands of their art come into contact with the precepts of religion and the moral law. In that case, before the film is printed, or while it is being produced, some competent advice should be sought and a sound plan adopted to provide for both the spiritual good of the spectators and the perfection of the work itself. Let these men not hesitate to consult the local established Catholic Motion Pictures Office, which will readily come to their assistance by delegating some qualified ecclesiastical adviser to look after the business, should this be necessary, and so long as due precautions are observed.

And the result of this confidence which they place in the Church, will not be a lessening of their authority or popularity; "for the Faith, until the end of time, will be the bulwark of the human person"[44] and in the production of the works themselves, the human person will be enriched and perfected in the light of Christian teaching and correct moral principles.

Nevertheless, ecclesiastics are not permitted to offer their cooperation to film directors without the express consent of their superiors, since, obviously, to give sound advice in this matter, special excellence in the art and a more than ordinary training are essential, and a decision on these cannot be left to the whim of individuals.

We therefore give a fatherly warning to Catholic film directors and producers, not to permit films to be made which are opposed to the Faith or Christian morals; but if, – which God forbid – this should happen, it is the duty of the Bishops to admonish them, and, if necessary, to impose appropriate sanctions.

But We are convinced that, to bring the Motion Pictures to the heights of the "ideal film", nothing is more effective than for those engaged in film production to act in conformity with the commandments of Christian law.

Let those responsible for making films approach the sources from which all the highest gifts flow, let them master the Gospel teaching, and make themselves familiar with the Church's traditional doctrine on the certainties of life, on happiness and virtue, on sorrow and sin, on body and soul, on social problems and human desires; they will then obtain new and excellent plots which they may adopt, and they will feel themselves inspired by a fresh enthusiasm to produce works of lasting value.

Those initiatives and practices, therefore, must be encouraged and extended by which their spiritual life is nourished, and given strength and development; but particular attention must here be paid to the Christian training of those young people who are planning to enter the cinema world professionally.

To conclude these instructions with regard to the Motion Pictures, We urge State officials not on any account to lend support to the production or making available of films of a low type, but, by establishing suitable regulations, to lend their aid to the providing of decent film programmes which can be commended, particularly when they are intended for youth. When such large sums are being spent on public education, let them direct their attention to this also: that reasonable assistance be given to this matter, which is essentially a part of education.

But since in certain countries, and also in international festivals, prizes are established and rightly awarded to those films which are recommended for their educative and spiritual value, We trust that all good and prudent men, following Our counsels, will strive to ensure that the applause and approval of the general public will not be wanting, as a prize for really worthwhile films.

3. RADIO

No less carefully do We desire to express to you, Venerable Brethren, the anxiety which besets Us with regard to that other means of communication which was introduced at the same period as the cinema: We refer to Radio.

Though it is not endowed to anything like the same extent with scenic properties and other advantages of time and place, as is the cinema industry, sound radio has yet other advantages, not all of which have yet been exploited.

For, as We said to the members and directors of a broadcasting company, "this method of communication is such that it is, as it were, detached from and unrestricted by conditions of place and time which block or delay all other methods of communication between men. On a kind of winged flight much swifter than sound waves, with the speed of light, it passes in a moment over all frontiers, and delivers the news committed to it".[45]

Brought to almost complete perfection by new inventions, wireless telegraphy brings outstanding advantages to technical processes, since, by means of a ray, pilotless machines may be directed to a determined place. But We rightly think that the most excellent function which falls to Radio is this: to enlighten and instruct men, and to direct their minds and hearts towards higher and spiritual things.

But there is in men, though they may be within their own homes, a deep desire to listen to other men, to obtain knowledge of events happening far away, and to share in aspects of the social and cultural life of others.

Hence it is not remarkable that a very large number of houses have, within a short period of time, been equipped with receiving sets, by which, as it were through secret windows opening on to the world, contact is made night and day with the active life of men of different civilizations, languages and races. This is brought about by the countless wireless programmes which cover news, interviews, talks, and items conveying useful and pleasant information derived from public events, the arts, singing, and orchestral music.

For as We said recently, "how great is the advantage enjoyed, how great the responsibility laid on men of the present day, and how great the changes from times gone by when instruction in truth, commandments of brotherly love, promises of everlasting happiness, came slowly to men through the Apostles, treading the rough paths of that former age; whereas, in our day, the divine message can be conveyed to tens and hundreds of thousands of men at one and the some time".[46]

It befits Catholics, then, to make use of this privilege of our day, and to draw extensively from the rich fund of doctrine, recreation, art and also of the divine Word, which sound broadcasting brings to them, since they can thus increase and widen their range of interests.

Everyone knows what a great contribution good radio programmes can make to sound education; yet from the use of this instrument there arises an obligation in conscience as in the other technical arts, since it can be employed to achieve good or evil. Those words, then, written in Scripture, can be applied to the art of Radio: "By it we bless God and the Father; and by it we curse men, who are made after the likeness of God. Out of the same mouth proceed blessing and cursing".[47]

Duty of the listener

The first duty of the radio listener is that of choosing carefully and deliberately from the programmes offered; these must not be permitted to enter the home indiscriminately, but access should be given them on the same principles as are observed in a deliberate and prudent invitation to a friend. A person would act wrongly if he made no selection in introducing friends into his home. So radio programmes which are given entrance there, must be such as encourage truth and goodness, and do not draw members of the family away from the fulfilment of their duty, whether to individuals or to society; they should be such as strengthen them to carry out these duties properly, and, in the case of children and youths, cause no harm, but rather assist and extend the salutary control of parents and teachers.

Let the Catholic Offices for Radio set up in each country, making use of Catholic daily papers and reviews, endeavour to inform the faithful beforehand on the nature and value of the programmes. It will not always be possible to give such advance notice; and often, these will only be summary views, where the content of the programme cannot be known easily beforehand.

Parish priests should warn their flocks that they are forbidden by divine law to listen to radio programmes which are dangerous to their Faith or morals, and they should exhort those engaged in the training of youth, to be on the watch and to instill religious principles with regard to the use of radio sets installed in the home.

Moreover, it is the duty of the Bishops to call on the faithful to refrain from listening to stations which are known to broadcast a defence of matter formally opposed to the Catholic Faith.

Another duty which binds listeners, is to make known to the directors of the programmes their wishes and justifiable criticism. This obligation arises clearly from the nature of sound radio, which is such that a wholly one-sided policy may come into existence, namely, that directed by the speaker to the listener. Although those systems of surveying public opinion, which are increasing in these days, to find out the degree of interest aroused in the listeners by each programme, are doubtless useful to those who direct the programmes, yet it can happen that popular appreciation, more or less vigorously expressed, can be attributed to trivial or transient causes, or to enthusiasms with no rational basis, so that a judgment of this kind cannot be taken as a sure guide for action.

That being the case, radio listeners ought to rouse themselves to obtain a well-balanced opinion among the general public, by which, while observing proper methods, these programmes are – according to their merits-approved, supported, rebuked, thus bringing it about that the art of Radio, considered as a method of education, "may serve the truth, good morals, justice and love".[48]

To bring about this effect is the task of all Catholic societies which are zealous for securing the good of Christians in this matter. But in those countries where local circumstances suggest it, groups of listeners or viewers can be organized for this purpose, under the supervision of the National Motion Pictures, Radio and Television Offices established in each country.

Finally, let listeners to the Radio be aware that they are obliged to encourage reputable programmes, and particularly those by which the mind is directed towards God. In this age in particular, when false and pernicious doctrines are being spread over the air, when, by deliberate "jamming", a kind of aerial "iron curtain" is being created with the express purpose of preventing the entry of truth which would overthrow the empire of atheistic materialism, in this age, We say, when hundreds of thousands of the human race are still looking for the dawning light of the Gospel message, when the sick and others likewise handicapped look forward anxiously to taking part in some manner in the prayers and the ceremonies of the Mass of the Christian community, should not the faithful, especially those who make daily use of the advantages of the Radio, show themselves eager to encourage programmes of this kind?

Religious programmes

We are fully aware of the effort already made in some countries, and now being made, to increase the Catholic programmes from Radio stations. Many, from among both clergy and laity, have been in the front of the fight, and by vigorous exertions, have secured for religious radio programmes a place befitting divine worship, which is more important than all human affairs taken together.

But in the meantime, while We ponder to what extent Radio can assist the work of the sacred ministry, and while We are moved strongly by the command of our Divine Redeemer, "Going into the whole world, preach the Gospel to every creature",[49] We feel We must exhort you paternally, Venerable Brethren, to strive – according to the need and resources of your respective localities – to increase in number and make more effective programmes dealing with Catholic affairs.

Since a properly dignified presentation of liturgical ceremonies, of the truths of the Catholic Faith, and of events connected with the Church, by means of Radio, obviously demands considerable talent and skill, it is essential that both priests and laymen who are selected for so important an activity should be well trained in suitable methods.

This end would clearly be assisted if, in countries where Catholics employ the latest radio equipment and have day-to-day experience, appropriate study and training courses could be arranged, by means of which learners from other countries also could acquire that skill which is indispensable if radio religious programmes are to attain the best artistic and technical standards.

It will be the function of the National Offices to encourage the various types of religious programmes within their territory and to organize and coordinate them with each other; they will, in addition, offer their cooperation, as far as possible, to the directors of the other Radio stations, due care being observed that nothing creeps into these transmissions contrary to sound morals.

With regard to ecclesiastics, including exempt religious, who are engaged in Radio or Television stations, it will be the Bishops' duty to impart suitable directives, the carrying out of which will be committed to the various National Offices.

Catholic radio stations

We should like particularly to speak words of encouragement to Catholic radio stations. We are fully aware of the almost countless difficulties which have to be faced in this sphere; yet We trust that this apostolic work which We value so highly, will be pursued by them with energy and with mutual collaboration.

For Our part, We have arranged for the extension and perfecting of the Vatican Radio Station which has done excellent work for the Church, the salutary activity of which, as We declared to the Catholics of Holland who contributed to it so generously, has well responded to "the ardent desires and the vital needs of the whole Catholic world".[50]

Programme responsibility

Moreover, We desire to extend Our thanks to all upright directors and producers of radio programmes for their fair assessment of the needs of the Church to which many of them have borne testimony, either by freely assigning a suitable time for the propagation of God's Word, or by supplying the necessary equipment. By this way of acting, they are certainly sharing in the special reward of apostolic work, even though it is being carried out over the air, according to Our Lord's promise: "Who receives a prophet in the name of a prophet, will receive the reward of a prophet".[51]

In these days, technical excellence in radio programmes requires that they be in conformity to the true principles of the art; hence their authors and those engaged in preparing and producing them must be equipped with sound doctrine and a well-stored mind. Consequently, We earnestly invite them also, as We did the members of the Motion Picture industry, to make full use of that superabundance of material from the storehouse of Christian civilization. Finally, let the bishops remind State officials that it is part of their duty to exercise appropriate diligence in safeguarding the transmission of programmes relating to the Catholic Church, and that special consideration should be given to holy days and to the daily spiritual needs of Christians.

4. TELEVISION

It remains, Venerable Brethren, to speak briefly to you about Television, which, in the course of Our Pontificate, has in some nations taken tremendous steps forward, and in others is gradually coming into use.

The ever growing development of this art, which beyond all doubt is an event of great importance in human history, has been followed by Us with lively interest and high hopes, but also with serious anxiety; and while on the one hand, We have, from the beginning, praised its potentialities for good and the new advantages springing therefrom, We have also, on the other hand, foreseen and pointed out the dangers, and the excesses of those who misuse it.

There are many characteristics common to both Television and Motion Pictures, for in both, pictures of the movement and the excitement of life are presented to the eye; often, too, Television material is derived from existing films. Moreover, Television shares, in a sense, in the nature and special power of sound broadcasting, for it is directed towards men in their own homes rather than in theatres.

We consider it superfluous in this place to repeat the warnings with regard to film and radio programmes, which We have already given concerning the obligations binding, in this matter, on spectators, listeners, producers and State officials.

Nor need We again refer to the care and diligence which must be observed in the correct preparation and encouragement of the different types of religious programmes.

Catholic programmes

It is well known to Us with what deep interest vast numbers of spectators gaze at television programmes of Catholic events.[52] It is obvious, of course, – as We declared a few years ago – that to be present at Mass portrayed by Television is not the same as being actually present at the Divine Sacrifice, as is of obligation on holy days. However, from religious ceremonies, as seen on Television, valuable fruits for the strengthening of the Faith and the renewal of fervour can be obtained by all those who, for some reason, are unable to be actually present; consequently, We are convinced that We may wholeheartedly commend programmes of this kind.

In each country, it will be for the Bishops to judge of the suitability of televised religious programmes, and commit their execution to the established Office, which, of course, as in similar matters, will be active and alert to publish information, to instruct the minds of the audience, and to organize and coordinate everything in a manner in keeping with Christian morals.

Special problems on television

But Television, besides the common element which it shares with the other two inventions for spreading information, of which We have already spoken, has a power and efficacy of its own. For, by the art of Television, it is possible for the spectators to grasp by the eye and the ear, events happening far away at the very moment at which they are taking place, and thus to be drawn on, as it were, to take an active part in them; and this sense of immediacy is increased very much by the home surroundings.

This special power which Television enjoys, of giving pleasure within the family circle, is to be reckoned of very great importance, since it can contribute a great deal to the religious life, the intellectual development and the habits of those who make up the family; of the sons, especially, whom the more modern invention will certainly influence and captivate. But if that saying, "a little leaven corrupteth the whole mass"[53] corresponds at all to the truth, and if physical growth in youths can be prevented, by some infectious germ, from reaching full maturity, much more can some base element of education steal its way into the fibres of the religious life, and check the due shaping of morals. Everyone knows well that, very often, children can avoid the transient attack of a disease outside their own home, but cannot escape it when it lurks within the home itself.

It is wrong to introduce risk in any form into the sanctity of home surroundings; the Church, therefore, as her right and duty demand, has always striven with all her force to prevent these sacred portals suffering violence, under any pretext, from evil television shows.

Since Television certainly has this among other advantages, that both old and young can easily remain at home, it can have considerable influence in strengthening the bonds of loyalty and love within the family circle, provided the screen displays nothing which is contrary to those same virtues of loyalty and chaste love.

There are, however, some who completely deny that, at least at the present time, these lofty demands can be put into practice. For they repeatedly assert that the contract made with the spectators in no way permits any part of the time allotted to television to be left unoccupied; further, that they are forced by the necessity of always having a variety of programmes ready to hand, to put on shows sometimes which were originally intended only for the public theatre; and finally, that television is an affair not just for the young but for grown-ups as well. We admit that in this matter difficulties readily occur; nevertheless, their solution should not be postponed to some future date, for the practice of this art, hitherto not controlled by the reins of prudent counsel, has already inflicted serious harm on individuals and on human society; the extent of this damage up to the present time can be gauged only with difficulty.

But in order that the unravelling of these difficulties may advance side by side with the increasing use of Television in each country, the most urgent efforts should be devoted to the preparation of the different shows, ensuring that they correspond to ethical and psychological requirements as well as to the technical aspects of Television.

For this reason We paternally exhort Catholics, well-qualified by their learning, sound doctrine and knowledge of the arts, – and in particular clerics, and members of Religious Orders and Congregations – to turn their attention to this new art and give their active cooperation, so that whatever benefits the past and true progress have contributed to the mind's development, may be also employed in full measure to the advantage of Television.

In addition, it is essential that producers of television films take care not only to preserve intact religious and honourable principles, but also to be on special guard against the danger which the young may perhaps fall into, if they are present at shows intended for grown-ups. With regard to similar performances which are put on in cinemas and theatres, in order to preserve the common good, appropriate precautions have been deliberately taken in almost all civilized countries, with the object of keeping young people away from immoral entertainments. But it is common knowledge that television – and with greater reason – needs the benefits and safeguards of alert vigilance. It is praiseworthy that, in some countries, items forbidden to the young are excluded from the television programmes; but if it happens that certain places admit such, then, at least, definite precautions are absolutely essential.

It is useless for anyone to suppose that excellent principles and an upright conscience on the part of those engaged in these arts are sufficient either to ensure that nothing but good flows from the small white screen, or to remove all that is evil. In this matter, then, prudence and watchful care are especially demanded of those who make use of television. Due moderation in its use, prudence in admitting the children to viewing according to their different ages, a balanced judgment based on what has been seen before, and finally, exclusion of children from what are in any sense improper spectacles: all these are the duties which weigh heavily on parents and on all engaged in education.

We do not overlook the fact that the directives We have just given in the last section, can sometimes produce serious difficulties and considerable inconveniences; for the awareness of their role as educators will often demand that parents give clear example to their offspring, and also bid them deny themselves – not without some personal sacrifice – some programmes they would like to see. But who thinks the burden on parents is too heavy when the supreme good of the children is at stake?

This being so, – as We declared in a letter to the Italian Bishops – "it is a most pressing need that the conscience of Catholics with regard to television should be formed by the sound principles of the Christian religion";[54] the more so, in order that this kind of art may not be at the service of error or the squares of vice, but may prove to be rather a help "to educate and train men, and recall them to their higher state".[55]

CONCLUSION

To the clergy

We cannot conclude this Letter, Venerable Brethren, without recalling to your mind the importance of the function committed to the priest for encouraging and mastering the inventions which affect communication, not only in other spheres of the apostolate, but especially in this essential work of the Church.

He ought to have a sound knowledge of all questions which confront the souls of Christians with regard to Motion Pictures, Radio and Television. As We said in a discourse to those taking part in a Study Week for the bringing up to date of pastoral practice in Italy at the present time, "The priest with 'the care of souls' can and must know what modern science, art and technique assert whenever they touch on the end of man and his moral and religious life".[56] Let him learn to use these aids correctly as often as, in the prudent judgment of ecclesiastical authority, the nature of the ministry entrusted to him and the need of assisting an increasing number of souls demand it. Finally, if these arts are employed by the priest to advantage, his prudence, self-control and sense of responsibility will shine out as an example to all Christians.

SUMMING UP

We decided to lay before you, Venerable Brethren, Our thoughts and anxieties, which you, of course, also share, concerning the grave dangers which can beset Christian Faith and morals if the powerful inventions of Motion Pictures, Radio and Television are perverted by men to evil uses.

We have not, however, passed over the benefits and advantages which these modern instruments can bring. To this end, with the precepts of the Christian Faith and Natural Law to enlighten Us, We have explained the principles which must guide and regulate both the action of the directors of the means of publicity, and the conscience of those who use them. And for the same reason, namely, that the gifts of Divine Providence may secure the good of souls, We have paternally exhorted you not only to exercise a watchful care, but also to use positive action and authority. For it is the function of those National Offices, which on this occasion also We have commended to you, not only to preserve and defend, but, more especially, to direct, organize and assist the many educational projects which have been begun in many countries, so that by means of this difficult and extensive province of the arts, the Christian ideas may be ever more widely spread.

But since We have firm confidence in the ultimate triumph of God's cause, We do not doubt that these precepts and instructions of Ours – which We entrust for due execution to the Pontifical Commission for Motion Pictures, Radio and Television – can rouse new enthusiasm for the apostolate in this sphere, which promises such a plenteous and fruitful harvest.

Relying on this hope, which Our well-founded knowledge of your pastoral zeal very much strengthens, We impart with all Our heart, as a pledge of heavenly graces, the Apostolic Benediction on you, Venerable Brethren, as well as on the clergy and people committed to your care and in particular on those who work actively to bring our desires and instructions to fulfilment.

From St Peter's, Rome, the eighth day of September, the feast of Our Lady's Nativity 1957, the nineteenth year of Our Pontificate.

Notes

1   S. IOAN. CHRYS., *De consubstantiali, contra Anomoeos*: P.G., 48, 810.

2   *Ephes*. III, 8–9.

3   *I Petr*. I, 18–19.

4   Radiophonicum nuntium *Qui arcano*, d. 12 Februarii, a. 1931: A. A. S., vol. XXIII, 1931, pag. 65.

5   Epist. Enc. *Vigilanti cura*, d. 29 Iunii, a. 1936: A. A. S., vol. XXVIII, 1936, pag. 249 sq.

6   *Ibid*. pag. 251.

7   Cfr. A. A. S., d. 16 Decembris, a. 1954, vol. XLVI, 1964, pag. 783–784.

8   Cfr. Sermo ad catholicos Hollandiae, d. 19 Maii, a. 1950 habitus: *Discorsi e Radiomessaggi di S. S. Pio XII*, vol. XII, pag. 75.

9   *Rom*. X, 16.

10   Matth. XXII, 16.

11   Cfr. Sermo ad cultores cinematographicae artis ex Italia Romae congregatos, d. 21 Iunii, a. 1955: A. A S., vol. XLVII, 1955, pag. 504.

12   Cfr. Matth., XI, 30.

13   Cfr. Sermo ad radiophonicae artis cultorum coetum, d. 5 Maii, a. 1950 ex omnibus Nationibus Romae habitum: *Discorsi e Radiomessaggi* di S. S. Pio XII, vol. XII, pag. 54.

14   *Rom*. V, 5.

15   Cfr. Matth. V, 48.

16   Litt. Apost. d. 12 Ianuarii, a. 1951: A. A. S., vol XLV, 1952, pag. 216–217.

17   *Ibid*. pag. 216.

18   Matth. XIII, 27.

19   Matth. XIII, 28.

20   I *Thess*. V, 21–22.

21   Cfr. Sermo, quinto exeunte saeculo ab Angelici obitu, in Aedibus Vaticanis habitus d. 20 Aprilis, a. 1955: A. A. S., vol. XLVII, 1955, pag. 291–292; Litt. Enc. *Musicae Sacrae*, d. 25 Decembris, a 1955: A. A. S., vol. XLVIII, 1956, pag. 10.

22   Cfr. Rom. II, 15.

23   Sermo ad cultores artis cinematographicae ex Italia Romae congregatos, d. 21 Iunii, a. l955: A. A. S., vol. XLVII, 1955, pag. 505.

24   S. THOM., *Summ. Theol.*, I. q. 1, a. 9.

25   Cfr. *Ibid*. I, q. 67, a. 1.

26   Sermo ad sodales Radiophonicae Societatis Italiae, d. 3 Decembris, a. 1944 habitus: *Discorsi e Radiomessaggi* di S. S. Pio XII, vol. VI, pag. 209.

27   Sermo ad Nationum Societatis Consilium publicis ordinandis nuntiis, d. 24 Aprilis, a. 1956 habitus: *Discorsi e Radiomessaggi* di S. S. Pio XII, vol. XVIII, pag. 137.

28   Cfr. Ioan. VIII, 32.

29   Cfr. Nuntius radiophonicus ad christifideles Columbianae Reipublicae, d. 11 Aprilis, a. 1953 habitus, cum Statio Radiophonica Sutacentiae inaugurabatur: A. A. S., vol. XLV, 1953, pag. 294.

30   Ep Enc. *Vigilanti cura*, d. 29 Iunii, a. 1936: A. A. S., vol. XXVIII, 1936, pag. 255.

31   Ep. Enc. *Vigilanti cura*: ibid. pag. 254.

32   Cfr. Adhortatio de televisione, d. 1 Ianuarii, a. 1954: A. A. S., vol. XLIV, a. 1964, pag. 21.

33   Cfr. Sermo ad moderatores, docentes, et cultores Consociationis ex omnibus Nationibus Institutorum Archaeologiae, Historiae, et Artis Historiae, d. 9 Martii, a. 1956, habita: A. A. S., vol XLVIII, 1966, pag. 212.

34   Ep. Enc. *Vigilanti cura*, d. 29 Iunii, a. 1936: A. A. S., vol. XXVIII, 1936, pag. 261.

35   Cfr. Sermo ad cinematographicae artis cultores ex Italia Romae congregatos, d. 21 Iunii, a. 1955, A. A. S., vol. XLVII, 1955, pag. 501–502.

36   Cfr. Sermo ad cinematographicae artis cultores, d. 28 Octobris, a. 1955, Romae congregatos: A. A. S., vol. XLVII, 1955, pag. 817.

37   Cfr. Sermones d. 21 Iunii et 28 Octobris, a. 1955 habiti: *ibid.*, pag. 502, 505 et 816 sq.

38   Ep. Enc. *Vigilanti cura*, d. 29 Iunii, a. 1936: A. A. S., vol. XXVIII, 1936, pag. 260–261.

39   Cfr. Sermo ad cultores cinematographicae artis ex Italia Romae congregatos, d. 21 Iunii, a. 1955: A. A. S., vol. XLVII, 1955, pag. 512.

40   Ep. Enc. *Vigilanti cura*, d. 29 Iunii a. l936: A. A. S., vol. XXVIII, 1936, pag. 260.

41   Cfr. Pii XII sermo ad Urbis Parochos sacrosque per Quadragesimae tempus Oratores die 5 Martii 1957 habitus: vide diarium *L'Osservatore Romano*, 6 Martii 1957.

42   Cfr. Sermo de arte scaenica d. 26 Augusti, a. 1945 habitus: *Discorsi e Radiomessaggi di S. S. Pio XII*, vol. VII, pag. 157.

43   Matth. V, 16.

44   Cfr. Epist. Pii XII ad christifideles Germaniae, ob conventum a "Katholikentag" appellatum, Berolinum congregatos die 10 Augusti, a. 1952: A. A. S., vol. XLIV, 1952, pag. 725.

45   Cfr. Sermo d. 3 Decembris, a. 1944 habitus: *Discorsi e Radiomessaggi* di S. S. Pio XII, vol. VI, pag. 209.

46   Cfr. Nuntius radiophonicus ad eos qui interfuerunt tertio generali conventui de communicationibus inter cives et nationes, sexagesimo volvente anno a radiotelegraphia inventa, Genuae habito: A. A. S. vol. XLVII, 1955, pag. 736.

47   Iac. III, 9–10.

48   Cfr. Sermo Pii XII d. 3 Octobris, a. 1917 quinquagesimo expleto anno ab arte radiophonica inventa habitus: *Discorsi e Radiomessaggi di S. S. Pio* XII, vol. IX, pag. 267.

49   Marc. XVI, 15.

50   Cfr. Sermo ad Hollandiae catholicos, d. 19 Maii, a. 1950 habitus: *Discorsi e Radiomessaggi di S. S. Pio XII*, vol. XII, pag. 75.

51   Matth. X, 41.

52   Cfr. Sermo ad radiophonicae artis cultores conventum ex omnibus Nationibus participantes: d. 5 Maii, a. 1950; *Discorsi e Radiomessaggi di S S. Pio* XII, vol. XII, pag. 75.

53   *Gal.* V, 9.

54   Cfr. Adhortatio Apostolica, de televisione, d. 1 Ianuarii. a. 1954: A.A.S., vol. XLVI, 1954, pag. 23.

55   Cfr. Sermo de gravi televisionis momento, d. 21 Octobris, a. 1955: A. A. S., vol. XLVII, 1955, pag. 777.

56   Cfr. Sermo d. 14 Septembris, a. I956 habitus: A. A. S. vol. XLVIII, 1956, pag. 707.

Chapter 18

R. L. Rutsky and Justin Wyatt

SERIOUS PLEASURES: CINEMATIC PLEASURE AND THE NOTION OF FUN (1990)

ACADEMIC PLEASURES: SADISM AND THE DISCIPLINES OF KNOWLEDGE

ACADEMIC FILM CRITICISM, LIKE academic discourse in general, can rarely be described as fun. This is not to say that film criticism does not have its rewards, its pleasures, but they are, for the most part, relatively sober ones. Such pleasures are not excessive; they are not the pleasures of sensation. They are pleasures that presume a purpose: intellectual or moral pleasures. They are, in other words, *serious pleasures*.

But if academic film criticism has always been serious about its own pleasures, it has also had a certain difficulty in theorizing a pleasure that was not "serious." For pleasure to enter into academic discourse, it was necessary for it to be transformed into a topic appropriate to academia; it had to be made serious. Indeed, within academic film theory, the very use of the term "pleasure" has served to promote this seriousness. It is significant that film theory speaks of a discourse of pleasure, as opposed to a discourse of, for instance, "distraction," "entertainment," or "fun."

This repression of the "non-serious" aspects of pleasure, of a discourse of fun, is not, of course, a total exclusion. Notions of distraction, diversion, and entertainment have appeared with regularity in the academic discourse on cinematic pleasure. Yet, within that discourse, they are almost invariably positioned as negative terms. They are often figured as decadent—betrayals of truth, morally corrupt, politically incorrect—or, at best, as escapist or trivial. Indeed, it seems that the vast majority of the academic "discourse on pleasure" has been calculated to distinguish between these "corrupt" pleasures and more acceptable, "serious" pleasures.

This distinction between "good" and "bad" pleasures has lain at the heart of academic discourse from its very beginnings. For it was, after all, in the very first Academy (Plato's) that the first exclusion of the "merely pleasurable" took place:

> There is an ancient quarrel between philosophy and poetry. . . . Notwithstanding this, let us assure the poetry that aims at pleasure, and the art of imitation, that if she will only prove her title to exist in a well-ordered state we shall be

> delighted to receive her—we are very conscious of her charms; but it would
> not be right on that account to betray the truth . . . let [poetry's defenders]
> show not only that she is pleasant but also useful to states and human life, and
> we will listen in a kindly spirit; for we shall surely be gainers if this can be
> proved, that there is a use in poetry as well as a delight.[1]

It is certainly not insignificant that poetry is figured here as female, as a seductress who, through sensual "charms," might lead one to "betray" the lawful spouse Truth. There is, in fact, considerable evidence that this marriage of the philosopher to Truth is a homosexual liaison, but, in Plato's figuration the exclusion of the "feminine" pleasures of poetry from the realm of philosophy, from the Academy, is not based simply on the fact that their gender is wrong, but on the fact that they are "wanton." They must, therefore, be "domesticated," given a "lawful" husband: only to the extent that they can be "married" to the ideal state's principles of rationality and utility can these pleasures be admitted to the Republic/ Academy.

Plato, in fact, applies this same strategy of domestication in order to regulate sexual relations in the ideal state; such wanton pleasures must be subjected to the rule of a legislated matrimony, determined according to the same principles of rationality and utility that apply to the breeding of animals (Book V, Sect. 458–59). Yet Plato consistently associates such pleasures and desires, even when they occur in men, with femininity.[2] Indeed, it is precisely this "licentiousness," this capacity for wanton pleasures and desires, that determines women as inferior in comparison to the "temperance" and "self-mastery" of a masculine reason, one that develops as "the beard begins to grow." It becomes clear, therefore, that the kind of marital relations Plato has in mind are essentially male homosexual. Only to the extent that women become the same as men, only to the extent that they control their desires and subject their pleasures to the laws of reason and utility, can they enter into union with the State, with the Academy.[3] Thus it is that those pleasures that remain "feminine," that refuse to take vows to a masculine law of Truth—that is, that refuse to become serious— must be excluded from academia.

This double gesture has continued to define academia ever since; through it, academia constitutes itself as, in Michel de Certeau's phrase, "the realm of the serious (*le sérieux*)" and excludes those pleasures that it deems not to serve a rational, serious purpose.[4] This gesture is nowhere more obvious than in film criticism, whose academic legitimacy has always been based on the distinction between serious pleasures and mere diversion (the repeated attempts to separate "high" from "mass" culture, art from "mere" commodity). Indeed, auteurist film criticism seems to have been designed precisely to "redeem" the pleasures of certain commercial films and to give them the status of a "serious" topic—that is, the status of art. The history of academic film theory could, in fact, easily be written as a series of attempts to establish systematic criteria for distinguishing serious pleasures. As Sylvia Harvey has noted, much of post-'68 film theory was founded on what Fredric Jameson has called an "aesthetic of political modernism," in which pleasure—at least serious, politically acceptable pleasure—could only be derived from a critique of formal conventions.[5] But, as Harvey has also noted, such a position tended to validate only unpopular, experimental forms. It was, in other words, elitist.[6] Even when film theory tried to consider popular, commercial films, those films—and their pleasures—ended up being classified according to criteria founded on the "aesthetic of political modernism."

One of the earliest and most influential of these formulations, by Jean-Louis Comolli and Jean Narboni in the *Cahiers du cinéma*, outlined a classificatory system in which commercial films fell into two categories: "films which are imbued through and through with the dominant ideology" and "films which seem at first sight to belong firmly within the ideology

. . . but which turn out to be so only in an ambiguous manner." Although pleasure is not an explicit issue in this article, Comolli and Narboni's comments on the two categories offer some insight on this topic. The films of the first category contain nothing that "jars against the ideology . . . they are very reassuring for audiences." In the second category, "an internal criticism is taking place which cracks the film apart at the seams . . . it is splitting under an internal tension which is simply not there in an ideologically innocuous film."[7] This privileging of the serious and "difficult" pleasures of "criticism" over the too easy pleasures of "reassurance" is, in many ways, symptomatic of academic film theory's attitude toward pleasure.

There are undoubtedly many other examples that might be cited here, from the neo-formalism of Bordwell and Thompson to the formal/ideological critique of various Marxist critics, to the textual analyses of Bellour, Heath, and others. In all, the more "difficult," more "enlightening" pleasures of non-narrative form and formal experimentation are affirmed over reassuring, conventional pleasures, pleasures frequently associated with commercial or mass culture. These "difficult" pleasures are often thought to require a certain (critical) distance, an "alienation" that allows the spectator the space to think about, to consciously examine, what was "too close," too familiar, too obvious to come to consciousness (usually, conventional bourgeois ideology). But then, it is hardly surprising that academic film theory would favor these kind of pleasures, for they are, after all, the very pleasures on which academic discourse is based: the pleasures of analysis and critique.

Laura Mulvey's influential article, "Visual Pleasure and Narrative Cinema," offers a particularly useful example of film theory's privileging of critical pleasures. Mulvey argues that classical narrative films place the male spectator in a position of power from which he may draw pleasure both from identification with an active male protagonist and from objectifying the passive female body. Cinematic pleasure is therefore a form of sadism, defusing the (castration) threat posed by the female body and reassuring the male spectator of his dominant position. Against this reassuring pleasure which upholds the conventional ideology of male dominance, Mulvey takes a position of critical anti-pleasure. Only an oppositional or avant-garde film practice, she argues, can "free the look of the camera . . . and the look of the audience" and therefore "destroy" the "satisfaction, pleasure and privilege" of traditional narrative film.[8] Thus, Mulvey, although she has modified her position somewhat in later articles and interviews, maintains the basic distinction of political modernism —between serious critique and conventional pleasure.

But there is also an obvious similarity between the gesture by which Mulvey excludes pleasure, or at least a certain type of pleasure, and Plato's exclusion of the pleasures of Poetry from the ordered state. For Plato the only legitimate pleasures are those based on the pursuit of transcendental truth, while for political modernism, pleasure can only be legitimated on the basis of a historical and material truth (i.e., if it opposes or "critiques" the historical and material inequities of capitalism, imperialism, racism, sexism, etc.). Yet in both cases, legitimate, serious pleasures, if they exist, must be "domesticated"; they must remain subordinated to, in the service of, an external standard of judgment, a *truth* that, whether idealist or materialist, is always rational. Those pleasures that do not serve rational truth, that have no rational purpose, can only be conceived by academic discourse as either trivial diversions or treacherous seductions. Indeed, the pleasures of "mere" entertainment or diversion are generally cast as a reassuring but false surface that covers over the dangerous, irrational pleasures of a libidinal, capitalist, or patriarchal economy. Such pleasures, whether they are figured as masculine or feminine, are considered illegitimate and are therefore to be analyzed, critiqued, exposed.

The pleasures of rational critique, then, are the pleasures of self-legitimation. Yet defining oneself, one's discourse, and one's pleasures as "serious" can only take place by excluding other discourses, other pleasures. When, for example, Mulvey criticizes the pleasure of classical narrative cinema as sadistic, she overlooks how her own discourse replicates that same structure of sadistic pleasure, privileging itself (and those who "identify" with it) as occupying the position of knowledge/power. Mulvey's gesture here typifies the operation of rational critique: it attributes abuses of power to irrationality while "rationalizing" its own position of power. Rational discourse can, in fact, only legitimate itself on the presumption of a privileged position, a position of knowledge. Its authority to speak, to make judgments, in other words, its power, is predicated on the assumption that one has a certain *mastery* of *knowledge*, a certain *expertise*. But this presumption of knowledge also assumes that one knows more than others; otherwise, everyone would have equal authority to speak. And the notion of expertise, on which academic disciplines and discourse are founded, loses its validity if everyone is an expert. The pleasures of rational critique, then, are always sadistic; they assume a position of authority, of power, *over* others.

In academic discourse, this privileging of critical pleasures is often presented as masochistic: one submits oneself to the service of Truth. In these terms, Truth might be represented as a kind of black-leather goddess, or god, depending on one's tastes. But this version of truth is largely a myth, a myth that legitimizes the academic/philosopher's own position of knowledge and power, of mastery. The academic is rarely a humble servant of knowledge, he or she is the authority, the one who sees what others cannot, the one who knows more and better. Thus furnished with the whip and chains of "expertise," the academic is free to practice the bondage of definition and categorization, to flay falsity and to punish the "misbehaviors" of errant thinkers. Seen in this light, the term "academic discipline" takes on new meaning, as do the tactics of inclusion and exclusion by which such "disciplines" are practiced.

MASOCHISM AND THE DISCOURSE OF RADICAL PLEASURE

Yet for all its "discipline," academic discourse is not immune to the "seductive charms" of those pleasures it has excluded. It is worth noting that these pleasures have—from Plato's representation of Poetry as a seductress to Nietzsche's opposition of women and (rational) truth—frequently been figured as feminine. Nietzsche, in fact, defines femininity precisely in terms of its resistance to "seriousness": "From the beginning, nothing has been more alien, repugnant, and hostile to woman than truth—her great art is the lie, her highest concern is mere appearance and beauty. Let us men confess it: we honor and love precisely *this* art and *this* instinct in woman—we who have a hard time and for our relief like to associate with beings under whose hands, eyes, and tender follies our seriousness, our gravity and profundity almost appear to us like folly."[9] For Nietzsche, then, femininity is figured in terms of a pleasure that lacks depth and seriousness, a pleasure of "mere appearance," a superficial pleasure. Yet such pleasures, which might be spoken of today as the pleasures of the signifier, are not necessarily trivial. Unbound by serious purpose or truth, they come to be represented as wild, unpredictable, and dangerous, as promising a pleasure that is without limits, an "other" pleasure that lies beyond the bounds of rational meaning or expression. It is often seen as a pleasure of transgression, of rebellion, a radical pleasure. And it is precisely the "otherness" of this radical pleasure, its status as the "beyond" of rational truth, that has allowed it to achieve its peculiar appeal.

Perhaps even more than trivial pleasures, this radical pleasure has traditionally been linked to femininity. This linkage seems to have been based on the notion that women, more emotional, more intuitive, and more elemental than men, are closer to the basic drives and forces of life, and hence to pleasure, than any man, or at least any *rational* man, can be. Thus,

Nietzsche can suggest that woman's nature "is more 'natural' than man's" and speak of "her uneducability and inner wildness, the incomprehensibility, scope, and movement of her desires and virtues."[10] This "naturalness," which, as Nietzsche notes, evokes both fear of and pity for "this dangerous and beautiful cat 'woman,' " seems to imply a lack of conscious, rational control and openness or receptivity to the irrational forces of life and the unconscious. This openness has, particularly in religious and artistic discourses, almost invariably been figured as "feminine."[11] Both the artist and the devotee give themselves over to, allow themselves to be used by, a force greater than themselves: God, the Muses, the Spirit, the Sublime. The pleasure of this process is, as Lacan's discussion of Bernini's statue of St. Theresa makes clear, eminently sexual:[12] *jouissance*, ecstasy, rapture—it is a pleasure of abandonment, of allowing oneself to be dominated, mastered by a force beyond one's control or understanding. In other words, radical pleasure is thoroughly masochistic.[13]

In film theory, Gaylyn Studlar's "Masochism and the Perverse Pleasures of the Cinema," reformulates the question of cinematic pleasure in terms of masochistic pleasure.[14] Working from Deleuze's *Masochism: An Interpretation of Coldness and Cruelty*, Studlar suggests that the cinematic screen resembles a dream screen through which the spectator "regresses to a similar state of orality as the masochist." Masochism in this sense is not simply reciprocal to sadism but a manifestation of an earlier, more primary phenomenon in which the scopic drive and the image are predominant. The cinematic spectator draws pleasure not from an identification with an active, controlling, male protagonist (for Mulvey, a sadistic pleasure), but from those on-screen images that cannot be controlled, that dominate the spectator. Sadistic pleasure is based on the spectator/subject's control over the image/object, a control achieved through the narrative. Masochistic pleasure relies on the loss of that control, on the image/object's dominance over the narrative. In sadistic pleasure, the narrative places the spectator in a position of knowledge and power. In masochistic pleasure, the spectator faces an image that is "other," that cannot be made the subject of knowledge and controlled.

For Studlar—as for Deleuze—masochistic pleasure is connected to the maternal image. Yet Studlar is careful to define her terms such that the mother is not simply the reverse of the male: "Within masochism, the mother is not defined as lack nor as 'phallic' in respect to a simple transference of the male's symbol of power." The mother, as the "active nurturer, first source of love and object of desire, first environment and agent of control"[15] is the source of masochistic pleasure. Cinematic images thus draw their force (and their pleasure) from that primary image of a controlling force, the image of the mother. Because the image of the mother and the masochistic pleasure associated with it are basic to both male and female, Studlar hopes to define spectatorial positions (and pleasures) that are not exclusively male.

In exploring the role of masochistic pleasure and the image within cinema, Studlar's work represents a welcome attempt within film theory to open a space for a pleasure that is neither analytical nor ideologically complicit. Yet in defining masochistic pleasure in terms of a primary maternal image, as outside of rational knowledge and truth, Studlar repeats the Platonic (and essentialist) gesture of connecting "femininity" to irrational pleasure, of defining "the feminine" as outside of rational discourse.[16] The opposition between rational truth and radical pleasure remains, with only a reversal of the privileged terms, the privileged gender. In this case, masochistic pleasure becomes an "other Truth," a "maternal Truth." Masochistic pleasure, in other words, becomes *serious*.[17]

Masochistic pleasure, however, is simply one of a number of terms (*jouissance*, the sublime, the Dionysian, desire, etc.) through which a reversal of the opposition rational knowledge/radical pleasure has operated. When these terms are affirmed, they are generally characterized as wilder and more exciting, more basic and vital, than the rather stolid solemnity of rational knowledge. Under these circumstances, rational knowledge is often represented as a kind of death, a stasis that seeks to bind and taxonomize the wild, creative energies of life. This type of characterization perhaps explains why those cases where radical pleasure becomes a major part of academic discourse frequently seem closer to the arts than to academia: dada and surrealism, Artaud, Nietzsche, Bataille, Deleuze, late Barthes, etc. Yet despite its grounding in the metaphors of freedom, creativity, and force, so long as radical pleasure is simply the privileged term in an opposition with rational discourse, it remains *serious*. In privileging its "otherness" from rational discourse, radical pleasure simply reverses the terms of the opposition: danger, chaos, violence, passion, etc. become, not disruptive, destructive forces, but the correlates of a liberatory, revolutionary creativity. Yet despite the shift of privileged terms, the structure of hierarchy, legitimacy, and exclusion remains the same as in the rational discourse. Radical pleasure simply takes its outcast status, its danger, its force, and yes, its "femininity," as the foundation for its legitimacy; it makes its otherness the basis for its seriousness.

BEYOND THE PLEASURE PRINCIPLE: THEORIZING/HAVING FUN

The reversals and reappropriations of the opposition between rational knowledge and radical pleasure have underlain western thought since Plato. Indeed, despite the precedence generally accorded to it in western thought, rational discourse often seems to need the force that radical pleasure carries in order to avoid becoming too static, too boring, too serious. Thus, the "divorce" of radical pleasure from rational knowledge frequently seems to be temporary, a "trial separation" designed to add some spice to the relationship. For once the "divorce" has taken place, rational discourse and radical pleasure often find a way to "remarry." In Marxist discourse, for instance, the exclusion of bourgeois pleasures takes place on the grounds of their lack of seriousness, their failure to serve any positive function. These pleasures, in fact, are often represented in the terms of a femininity of which Madame Bovary still stands as the model: domestic, conventionally bourgeois, trivial, and dull. The "force" of radical pleasure can then be represented by a term such as "revolution," which is characterized as a release of repressed forces and pleasures, freed from the bonds of bourgeois conventions. Here, a rational discourse reappropriates to itself a notion of radical force/pleasure, giving it a "serious," rational purpose (the overthrow of capitalism, the building of a socialist utopia). Thus, however pronounced the separation between rational discourse and radical pleasure may seem, however "final" their divorce, the relationship is complicitous; one cannot exist without the other.

It seems, therefore, that however "pleasure" has been constituted, it has always been implicated in an oppositional structure that can only be described as sado-masochistic. Whether one draws pleasure from a position of mastery or from being mastered by some greater force, pleasure operates on the basis of hierarchy, of power. And it is precisely this basis in power that makes pleasure serious. For power is always serious: it always implies an exclusion, a hierarchy, a privileging *over* something or someone. And serious pleasure is always based on power.

But then, perhaps we are taking our pleasure a bit too seriously? It is, after all, rather difficult in an academic discourse to avoid the pleasures of seriousness, as this article all too amply demonstrates. Indeed, to divorce ourselves from serious pleasure would immediately involve us in another marriage with it, the very gesture of exclusion reinscribing us in its hierarchical structure. Once again, the radical pleasure of abandoning seriousness becomes a serious pleasure. Yet, if it is impossible to abandon serious pleasure completely, there are degrees of involvement. If academic discourse has defined itself within the oscillation between the seriousness of rational pleasure and the seriousness of radical pleasure, always excluding as trivial those pleasures that it sees as merely reassuring, conventional, or easy, not every discourse has taken itself so seriously. Yet when an academic discourse such as film theory presumes to analyze the pleasures of such a discourse, it can only do so in terms of seriousness. And while the analysis of films in terms of sadistic and masochistic pleasures can account for a great deal of cinematic pleasure, such an analysis always excludes the trivial pleasures of those films that do not take themselves very seriously, those pleasures that we might describe as *fun*.

In this sense, fun should be distinguished from pleasure, or at least, from the serious pleasures of rationality and radicality. For, while fun is pleasurable, its pleasure is not the sadistic pleasure of rational knowledge and authority nor the masochistic pleasure of radical abandon and fascination. Fun, in other words, is not *based* on hierarchy, on power; it is never *entirely* serious. And yet, fun is not simply the opposite of seriousness either. It is not an absolute relativism that would deny the possibility of ever taking a position, of ever being critical or serious. Indeed, in a certain way, fun is always critical: it always involves a deflation or leveling of pretentiousness, of the overly serious. Fun, in other words, makes fun of that which takes itself *too* seriously, of that which cannot laugh at itself. In its essence, then, fun is parodic, ironic. Fun's ironic position must, however, be distinguished both from that sadistic irony that degrades and excludes others in order to justify its own position of dominance, and from that critical distantiation through which serious, rational critique legitimates its position of knowledge.

This distinction requires that "fun" be redefined somewhat. If fun is not the same as serious pleasure, the term cannot be used, as it sometimes is in common usage, to designate certain pleasures that are based on power. And indeed, who would argue that "killing someone for fun," or "the fun of fascism," or any of those varieties of "fun" based on sexism, racism, etc., are not perversions of the word? These are clearly serious, sado-masochistic pleasures that must be distinguished from the sense in which "fun" is used here. The "fun" of, for instance, a sexist film is similarly a species of sadistic pleasure; it degrades women in order to place men in a position of power. The pleasure of a film that is fun is not based on this kind of hierarchy, but on the deflation of pretension and seriousness, including its own. Fun, in other words, is not ironic in the sense that supposes an essential superiority to its object. While it takes a position of distance or autonomy that is necessary to any irony, it also acknowledges its commonality with its object. Its ironies, then, always include a note of self-irony. Its critiques, unlike those of academia, are always provisional, contingent; they are based on a relational rather than an external ground. Thus, any discourse where the differential in seriousness between what it includes and what it excludes becomes too great, any discourse that comes to take itself, its knowledge, or its power too seriously, will become liable to the "critique" of fun. In other words, fun tends to "level" those hierarchical structures on which seriousness is legitimated, to bring both the "heights" of mastery and the "abyss" of abandon to the "surface."

Thus, while serious pleasure always depends on a notion of vision that either penetrates and masters or involves and fascinates, the viewing of fun might be described as obvious or *superficial*. Unlike the penetrating gaze of sadistic pleasure or the fascinating look of the radical other, the viewing of fun cannot be figured in terms of depth. It slides over the surface of a text like a passing glance, never staying fixed for long, never "anchoring" itself in the depths of meaning, character identification or imagistic fascination. If one were to try to figure this viewing, it would not be represented in terms of dreams, hypnosis, or fetishism; it would not be a "gaze" or "look," or "stare" but a rather sheepish glance that passes between a text and its audience and punctuates itself with a mark that acknowledges its own lack of vision, that is, with a self-ironic wink.[18] In other words, fun, unlike serious pleasure, does not take itself *too* seriously.

Film theory has generally given a very limited consideration to fun and to films that are fun: in a few cases, these kind of films have been appropriated as serious texts, usually on the basis of some version of "auteurism" or, occasionally, as subversive of the dominant ideology. More often, such films have been condemned as "products" that hide their support of the dominant ideology behind the veneer of "entertainment" or "spectacle." Perhaps even more often, however, films that are seen as "merely fun" have been ignored as uninteresting or unworthy of analysis. And indeed, one of the characteristics of fun films seems to be that they do not easily admit to in-depth analysis and critique; they are too shallow, too obvious. Moreover, it has been difficult for film theory to explain the pleasure of these films except in the broadest of brushstrokes (in essence, the arguments almost always fall back on the notion of "reassuring" pleasures).

But perhaps it would be better if we looked at an example of a film whose pleasure film theory seems unable to account for: a film that both *is* and *is about* fun.

PARODIES OF PLEASURE, PRINCIPLES OF FUN

Even the title of John Hughes's film, *Ferris Bueller's Day Off*, implies a sense of frivolity, of a lack of purpose. Indeed, this is a film about "taking off" from "purposeful" work (school) for a day of leisure, as the poster for the film makes clear. (It shows a relaxed Ferris, hands clasped behind his head, with the catch-phrase "Leisure Rules.") The purpose of the day off: to have fun. This is, of course, the purpose of the film too. It makes no pretensions to art, and its moral statements are limited to the proposition that, rather than submitting oneself to the often sadistic dictates of seriousness, dictates that are frequently officious and authoritarian, one should learn to "take the day off" and "have some fun."

In fact, the whole story of the film is centered around the question of having fun. Those characters who oppose fun (Dean of Students Ed Rooney, Cameron's parents) are clearly figured as sadistic: they attempt to impose their "rules," their power, on others. On the other hand are those (masochistic) characters who seem unable to have fun (Cameron, Ferris's sister Jeannie). In the course of the day off, however, these characters learn to "lighten up," to have some fun instead of worrying about "conforming to" or "living up to" the standards of others. Thus, fun seems not only to rebel against the imposition of the dictates of seriousness and authority but to provide a space for a sense of self-worth that is not entirely determined by external standards. To at least some extent, then, fun is an autonomous space.

Yet for traditional academic film theory, a film like *Ferris Bueller* tends to be automatically suspect. Indeed, the very fact of a film's popularity often becomes the grounds for the complaint that it is complicit with the dominant ideology; no film, the argument goes, can be popular without supporting that ideology; the pleasures of mass culture, in other words, must be reassuring pleasures that support the racism, sexism, and class oppression of bourgeois ideology. By this argument, then, the pleasures of mass culture are always sadistic.

Rather, however, than launching a critique that, in analyzing how this position replicates the structure of "sadistic pleasure," would itself reduplicate that same structure, let us simply see what happens when we apply the notion of sadistic pleasure to a textual analysis of the chase scene from *Ferris Bueller*.

In this scene, Ferris is racing to make it home before his parents. The sequence begins with Ferris's near collision with the car carrying his mother and his sister Jeannie. The long look that Jeannie and Ferris exchange—emphasized by the alternation of extreme close-ups—establishes the importance, not only in this sequence but throughout the film, of the questions of seeing/not seeing and being seen/not being seen. For, as Jeannie is well aware,

Ferris's pursuit of leisure (his "day off"), his ability to "get away with things," and indeed his whole status as an almost mythic figure are based on the ability to avoid detection (and punishment), to not be seen. Thus, the castrating hostility of Jeannie's glare in these close-ups represents her desire to "expose" Ferris to the same gaze to which she is subjected, that of her parents and Dean Rooney, that is, to the gaze of the Law. For it is by escaping that gaze that Ferris has achieved, in her eyes, his unfair position of dominance in the Bueller house-hold and in life in general. The race that follows is predicated on the question of whether Ferris will be "caught" by this gaze.

But if Ferris's leisure, his pleasure, is based on his avoidance of the gaze, his situation can be taken as representative of the position of the male spectator in general. It is only by escaping the gaze that one can achieve the spectatorial position necessary for cinematic pleasure, the position of the voyeur. Thus, through his identification with Ferris, the male spectator finds confirmation of his own pleasure in looking without being looked at. Yet for the male spectator to enjoy this pleasure, the castrating gaze of the woman (Jeannie), which would "expose" the male position of dominance and destroy the sadistic pleasure inherent in it, must be contained, tamed. When, therefore, at the end of the chase sequence, Ferris is in fact "caught" by Dean Rooney, Jeannie's initial look is reversed: as she rescues Ferris from Rooney, her glance is punctuated by a smiling wink. The castration threat represented by her gaze is transferred to its "proper object": Dean of Students Rooney, a move that is once again signaled by extreme closeups. In these shots, it is Rooney—the representative of the Law—who is objectified and castrated: his eyes bulge blindly, his mouth loses the power of articulate speech. Through this displacement, the threat to Ferris's (and the male specta-tor's) dominant position is resolved; the sadistic pleasure of the male look is safely preserved from exposure to the gaze.

For those who have not seen *Ferris Bueller*, of course, this "analysis" may seem entirely reasonable. For most of those who have, it will probably seem like a parody. Indeed, parody generally seems to be the result when "serious" theories of cinematic pleasure are applied to films that are fun. This is not to say, however, that the preceding critique is simply a misreading; like all parodies, it bears a certain likeness to its object. And who would deny that some elements of *Ferris Bueller* are sexist, or that it is possible to derive a certain sadistic pleasure from the identification with its protagonist? While granting the "seriousness" of these sorts of questions, however, we must also question the extent to which such a reading accounts for the pleasures of a film like *Ferris Bueller*.

The previous reading, while noting that the film's pleasure depends in large part on "not being seen," conflates this situation with voyeuristic pleasure, with "seeing." Yet while it is true that the pleasure of the voyeur depends on not being seen, remaining unseen does not necessarily make one a voyeur. Indeed, unlike many teen films, *Ferris Bueller* is not explicitly voyeuristic: women's bodies are not generally displayed for the male gaze. It could be argued, in fact, that the film works to discredit the voyeuristic, sadistic gaze. For it is by avoiding the gaze of the Law (of parents, of institutions) that leisure and fun are possible. Cameron and Jeannie have internalized this notion of surveillance: as Jeannie says when asked why she doesn't do the things Ferris does, "Because I'll get caught." The events of the "day off" allow Cameron and Jeannie to "see" that they need not fear this gaze. In this case, therefore, not being seen does not lead to the sadistic pleasures of voyeurism, but allows the space for that position of autonomy necessary to fun.

It is true, however, that the character of Ferris is able, in Mulvey's phrase, to "make things happen and control events better than the subject/spectator" (*VPNC*, 12). Indeed, Ferris does seem to serve as an active "ideal ego" with whom the male spectator can identify. Yet this identification does not seem to follow the pattern described by Mulvey: as much as Ferris advances the plot, he also interrupts it, exhibiting himself both in performance and in direct addresses to the audience.[19] Thus, not only is the narrative flow interrupted, but the audience's voyeuristic position and its identification with the character are undercut. The "imaginary" status of "the character as ideal ego" is clearly recognized, a recognition reinforced by such devices as the series of jokes built around the impossibly growing concern for Ferris's supposed illness and by the fantastic nature of his exploits (e.g., his performance at the parade). This type of identification is exemplary of fun. It ironizes both the audience's position of control, of voyeurism, and Ferris's position as "the bearer of the look of the spectator" (*VPNC*, 12). Yet, as previously noted, the self-ironic stance of fun should not, despite certain resemblances, simply be equated with critical "distantiation"; if fun is not a matter of identification-in-depth, neither is it simply a matter of "distance," of the exclusion of identification. In fun, as we have noted, identification is shallow, superficial. It is not, in other words, serious.

Yet if the superficiality of fun does not allow enough depth for the sadistic pleasures of serious character identification nor enough distance for the sadistic pleasure of serious critique, neither does it allow enough space for the masochistic pleasures of image identification. In films that are fun, the spectators do not find themselves fascinated, drawn in by the images on the screen. Rather, the viewing of fun seems best described by Walter Benjamin's famous phrase: "reception in a state of distraction." The images, often drawn from popular culture, do not generally carry the auratic force of the radically other; they are not mysterious, but obvious. Indeed, fun seems to result not so much from the images themselves but from a playful recombination that has little respect for either the seriousness of rationality or the fascination of the other. And just as the distracted reception of film was, for Benjamin, linked to the principles of montage, fun describes the pleasures of a mass culture that has generalized those principles, that has become a pastiche of images. The hyperabundance of disconnected images in such a pastiche tends to level the seriousness of conscious rationality and unconscious fascination; it can only be viewed distractedly, superficially, as fun.

From the point of view of political modernism, of course, fun has generally been seen as another term for the easy, trivial or reassuring pleasures of mass culture, pleasures that "cover over" a serious ideological complicity, a false consciousness. Political modernism tends to see fun as a seduction, as a dangerous but attractive lie that either hides the betrayal of rational Truth or leads to its abandonment. It is precisely this attitude that has caused academic film theory, and academic discourse in general, such difficulty in dealing with mass cultural pleasures. With its basis in political modernism, film theory has tended to affirm only those critical pleasures that oppose or subvert the deceptive triviality of conventional pleasures. And indeed, even those theories that have affirmed a masochistic or radical pleasure have tended to separate such a pleasure from the trivial, conventional pleasures of mass culture, to present it as radically other, as serious. In a sense, then, these tendencies may be seen as the two halves of the aesthetic of political modernism: both define themselves in opposition to conventional, bourgeois ideology and pleasures, which each conveniently attributes to the other.

Yet as recent theory has begun to note, the exclusion of the pleasures of mass culture from academic discourse may well ignore the fact that many people seem to find a kind of empowerment or autonomy in such pleasures.[20] Fun, we would like to suggest, may be one way of theorizing a mass cultural pleasure that is not *simply* ideologically complicit. And although not all mass cultural pleasures are fun, fun has generally been linked to mass culture, and especially to American mass culture. Indeed, fun seems to be a particularly American concept, which the dominance of our culture industry has capitalized on and exported worldwide. It seems arguable, in fact, that the very premise of mass culture—and thus, of American film—is precisely to have fun—although all too often at someone else's expense. And yet, in a large way, the fun of American films has not simply been a means of asserting dominance—it has been at least as much a way of leveling pretension and privilege, of poking fun at those in a position of power and authority. Consider, for instance, how frequently policemen and bankers tend to be the butt of the joke in early films. And while there is a sometimes disturbing and sadistic violence to the humor of some of these films, that violence generally works as a leveling agent, undercutting any position of authority. It is also worth noting how the great silent comics, while making fun of their own characters, manage to assert an inimitable autonomy that levels the privilege and power of their antagonists. This element of fun seems central not only to many Hollywood films, but to much of American humor. In fact, in this sense, fun might actually be considered democratic.

Critics of bourgeois ideology, of course, will claim that such "fun" (like the democracy of capitalism) is merely a cover for the inequities of power and wealth that capitalism or patriarchy maintain, or that it is a form of escapism that ignores real and serious problems. As an example, they might well cite the way that entertainment or fun is privileged over social consciousness in a film like *Sullivan's Travels*. And there is an undeniable truth to such claims. But is there not also a pleasure, a fun, to *Sullivan's Travels* that exceeds such an account? Are the masses really so ignorant that they simply "buy the lie" of easy, reassuring pleasures? Are the critics really in such a superior position that they can "see through" this false consciousness? Academic discourse has often bemoaned the anti-intellectualism of mass culture, but that has never stopped it from assuming its superiority to mass culture. Academic discourse seems, in fact, to have always seen the notion of mass cultural fun as a threat to its seriousness, to its legitimacy. Thus, cultural critics have tended to repeat the Platonic and Nietzschean gestures; they exclude fun in order to legitimate their own (superior) position of knowledge and power. And there can be little doubt that the insistence of many cultural critics on their own seriousness has contributed to an anti-intellectualism that characterizes them as pretentious at best, and at worst as fanatics. In either case, the characterization seems based on the idea that "they don't know how to have fun," an idea that suggests that "having fun" is based on the ability to place onself in a non-hierarchical position, a position that is liable to fun.

Thus, to introduce fun into academic discourse is to change the way that discourse positions itself. And without unreservedly affirming the stance of either *Sullivan's Travels* or *Ferris Bueller*, we would like to suggest that they, and mass culture in general, can provide certain examples for such a repositioning. In *Ferris Bueller*, as we have noted, fun serves as an autonomous space that resists, and in fact levels, the presumed superiority of seriousness. In taking this position, the film in fact adopts a commonly assumed stance in American humor: a stance that from its rambunctious to its gently ironic modes, from the "ring-tailed roarer" to Will Rogers, rebels against the domineering laws of seriousness and pokes fun at formality and pretension. It does so, however, without hierarchizing its own position, without taking itself too seriously. Fun does not, however, position itself as external to seriousness (however much serious discourse tries to exclude it); it is not the negation of seriousness; it does not mean that "nothing should be taken seriously." Fun is, rather, the limit of seriousness, the space where seriousness begins to make fun of itself. The position of fun, therefore, is neither amoral nor apolitical. It does not exclude taking a position on particular issues, nor does it disallow a critique of the abuses or inequities of power. Indeed, *Sullivan's Travels*, in its way, is quite critical of the capitalist social system. Yet it does not fetishize its own position of critique; it does not position itself simply as serious, but recognizes its own liability to fun.

Thus, there is no such thing as a *pure* discourse of fun, or of seriousness. Yet to say that all discourse contains both fun and seriousness is not to say that all discourses are equal. One need only compare the fun of *His Girl Friday* to the fun of *Citizen Kane* ("I think it might be fun to run a newspaper") or the seriousness of John Waters's *Hairspray* to the seriousness of *The Blackboard Jungle*. There will, of course, be disagreements about the extent to which a particular text is fun: is, for example, *Two or Three Things I Know About Her* fun or pretentiously over-serious? What about *Scorpio Rising*? *All That Heaven Allows*? As must be obvious, then, fun (or seriousness) always depends in large part on the eye of the beholder. A film may be viewed as either fun or serious depending on the extent to which it is seen to level the hierarchies of seriousness—without placing itself or its audience in a position of superiority. Fun is not an objective, purely textual phenomenon. Yet while an audience's reading of a text may vary considerably, there are limits to such readings: some texts are, quite simply, more given to fun than others. And as we all are well aware, not everything is equally fun. Nor, we might add with an eye toward academic film theory, are all discourses equally disposed to fun.

Perhaps because film theory has only relatively recently entered academic discourse and is still in the process of legitimating itself institutionally, and perhaps also because of the strong commercial and entertainment aspects of film ("the film industry," "the entertainment business"), film theory seems to have remained somewhat insecure about its place in academia. Because of this insecurity, academic film theory often seems to bend over backwards in its attempts to distinguish what is serious about its field from what is not. Yet in a world where audiences are increasingly familiar with a large variety of mass cultural forms, where images are continually reformulated and recontextualized, where pastiche, collage and montage techniques, self-irony and self-parody, kitsch, camp and the whole range of what has generally been described under the heading of "postmodernism" are so prominent, the seriousness of film theory risks becoming a quite unintended parody of itself. Perhaps it is time that film theory realized that in such a world, the best models for cinematic pleasure are not the serious pleasures of political modernism, of critical/avant-garde theory/art, but precisely those mass cultural discourses that it has sought to critique and exclude. In other words, what we are suggesting is that mass culture serve not just as a subject matter for film theory and academic discourse, but as a theoretical, discursive model. For it is in the playfulness of mass culture, in its leveling montage of images, words, and ideas, in its non-rational associations, puns, and figures, that we can find a theoretical model for a discourse of fun. And while this essay tends to argue for such a discourse rather than demonstrate it, the reasons for this approach are perhaps obvious: could such a discourse be published within an academic context, and if it were, would it not be simply in order to exclude it once again as a negative term? For a discourse of fun will certainly seem scandalous to some; they will, in a kind of curious ritual, dance around the holy edifice of critique and chant time-worn phrases; they will invoke the ghosts of Horkheimer and Adorno and utter dire prophecies; they will curse the ever increasing encroachment of the religion of commodification and pledge to defend to the death the ivory tower of critical theory, the monolith of academic discourse. And while such an overblown rhetorical flourish as this metaphor cannot, by the rules of rational discourse, be taken too seriously, it can still serve to suggest a rather "serious" point—that in excluding fun, in excluding mass culture, academic discourse has only succeeded in excluding itself.

Notes

1   Plato, *The Dialogues of Plato*, Book X, Sect. 607b–c, trans. Benjamin Jowett (Oxford: Oxford University Press, 1953).

2   See, for example, his distinction in *The Symposium* between the common and the heavenly Aphrodite, which, in equating masculinity with maturity and rationality, serves as a justification for male love (as opposed to the "indiscriminate" sensual love associated with women and boys): "The Love who is

the son of the common Aphrodite is essentially common, and has no discrimination, being such as the meaner sort of men feel, and is apt to be of women as well as of youths, and of the body rather than of the soul. . . . The goddess who is his mother is far younger, and she was born of the union of the male and female, and partakes of both sexes. But the son of the heavenly Aphrodite is sprung from a mother in whose birth the female has no part, but she is from the male only; this is that love which is of youths only, and the goddess being older has nothing of wantonness. Those who are inspired by this love turn to the male, and delight in him who is the more valiant and intelligent nature. . . . For they love not boys, but intelligent beings whose reason is beginning to be developed, much about the time at which their beards begin to grow" (Sect. 180d–181e).

3   For a thorough discussion of this gesture in Plato, see Luce Irigaray's *Speculum of the Other Woman*, trans. Gillian Gill (Ithaca: Cornell University Press, 1985), especially "On the Index of Plato's Works: Woman," 152–59, and "Plato's *Hystera*," 243–364.

4   Michel de Certeau, *Heterologies: Discourse on the Other*, trans. Brian Massumi (Minneapolis: University of Minnesota Press, 1986), 12–13.

5   Sylvia Harvey, *May '68 and Film Culture* (London: British Film Institute Publishing, 1980), 81; the citation is from Fredric Jameson, "Reflections in Conclusion," *Aesthetics and Politics* (London: New Left Books, 1977), 196–213.

6   This is not to say that experimental forms are necessarily elitist, nor that all of modernist art was elitist.

7   Jean-Louis Comolli and Jean Narboni, "Cinema/Ideology/Criticism, Part I," *Screen* 12, no. 1 (Spring 1971): 2–11. (Translated from an article originally printed in *Cahiers du cinéma*, No. 216 [Oct.-Nov. 1969]).

8   Laura Mulvey, "Visual Pleasure and Narrative Cinema," *Screen* 16, no. 3 (Autumn 1975): 6–18. Further references to this article will be included in the text as *VPNC*.

9   Friedrich Nietzsche, *Beyond Good and Evil*, trans. Walter Kaufmann (New York: Vintage, 1966), 169.

10   Ibid.

11   See Irigaray, "*La Mystèrique*," in *Speculum of the Other Woman*, 191–202.

12   "You have only to go and look at Bernini's statue in Rome to understand immediately that she's coming, there is no doubt about it." Lacan, "God and the *Jouissance* of The Woman," in *Feminine Sexuality: Jacques Lacan and the école freudienne*, trans. Jacqueline Rose (New York & London: Norton, 1982), 147.

13   Irigaray notes the conjunction of "woman" with an unlimited, radical pleasure that has strong masochistic elements: "*How strange is the economy of this specula(riza)tion of woman, who . . . calls for the dart which, while piercing through her body, will with the same stroke tear out her entails [sic]. Thus 'God' will prove to have been her best lover since he separates her from herself only by that space of her jouissance where she finds Him/herself. To infinity perhaps, but in the serenity of the spacing that is thus projected by/in her pleasure. At present that pleasure is still hemmed in by representations—however metaphysical—and by prescriptions—still ethically onto-theological—which determined it (and her) and thus limit their extension. And if she does not feel raped by God, even in her fantasies of rape, this is because He never restricts her orgasm, even if it is hysterical. Since He understands all its violence*" ("*La Mystèrique*," 201).

     The masochistic aspect of the *sublime* seems to have been acknowledged by Burke: "Whatever is fitted in any sort to excite the ideas of pain, and danger, that is to say, whatever is in any sort terrible, or is conversant with terrible objects, or operates in a manner analogous to terror, is a source of the sublime." Kant, somewhat more subtly, suggests that a sublime state of mind must be based not simply on "fear and apprehension," but on "a voluntary subjection of [one]self" to the object regarded as sublime. Edmund Burke, *A Philosophical Enquiry into the Origin of our Ideas of the Sublime and Beautiful*, ed. J. T. Boulton (London: Routledge and Kegan Paul, 1958), 39. Immanuel Kant, *Critique of Judgment*, trans. J. H. Bernard (New York: Hafner Press, 1951), 99–103.

14   Gaylyn Studlar, "Masochism and the Perverse Pleasures of the Cinema," in *Movies and Methods Vol. II*, ed. Bill Nichols (Berkeley: University of California Press, 1985), 602–21.

15   Ibid., 608, 609.

16   For a view of how this mystification has been connected both to mass culture and to modernist/avant-gardist writings, see Andreas Huyssen, "Mass Culture as Women: Modernism's Other," in *After the Great Divide* (Bloomington: Indiana University Press, 1986), 44–62. See also Teresa de Lauretis's critique of philosophical "feminization" (in which she refers admiringly to Mulvey's essay), "The Violence of Rhetoric: Considerations on Representation and Gender," in *Technologies of Gender* (Bloomington: Indiana University Press, 1987), 31–50.

17   In this regard, consider Studlar's examples, the films of Josef von Sternberg, which are clearly part of the canon of "serious" film studies.

18   Of course, not all winks are self-ironic. In fact, a wink often serves as an invitation to join in certain sadistic forms of humor.

19   Cf. Mulvey: "Man is reluctant to gaze at his exhibitionist like" (12).

20   See, for example, the work of Tania Modleski and Dana Polan, especially their essays in *Studies in Entertainment*, ed. Tania Modleski (Bloomington: Indiana University Press, 1986).

Chapter 19

Noel King

LOST IN THE FUNHOUSE: A RESPONSE TO R. L. RUTSKY AND JUSTIN WYATT (1992)

> The ritual of the Ph.D. has to do at once with the authorisation of interpretative credentials and with the transmission—but also the controlled transformation—of a disciplinary structure.
>
> —John Frow[1]

IN THEIR PROVOCATIVE ATTEMPT TO establish themselves as the masculinist Cyndi Laupers of film criticism (*boys* who just wanna have fun) R. L. Rutsky and Justin Wyatt produce a piece of writing which reaches beyond the specific domain of film studies and into the broader field of cultural criticism.[2] In particular their article connects with debates concerning popular culture and its unpopular academic critical discussion, corresponding quite closely to some recent comments from Simon Frith. Frith characterised the peculiar dilemma of the popular culture critic in the following way: "Isn't the very act of 'intellectualising' the popular (a close reading of *The Cosby Show* or *Batman* or Madonna) a move away from it, a form of misreading?"[3] Frith went on to conclude that the domain of popular culture, far from constituting a significant political site, more closely resembled a fantasy land where "the fantasies are those projected onto it by (male) intellectuals themselves: intellectuals longing, daring, fearing to transgress: intellectuals wondering what it would be *not to be an intellectual*" (235).

These comments seem quite close to the things Rutsky and Wyatt are saying in their article insofar as they repeat a familiar assessment of the relation of "academic discourse" to "popular culture." Although their article moves from Plato to Laura Mulvey, from Comolli/Narboni to Deleuze and Studlar, and although their eventual example is *Ferris Bueller's Day Off*, the general drift of their argument, together with some of the particular terms they come to privilege, connects closely with the discussion of popular culture offered by writers such as Roland Barthes, Dick Hebdige, and Iain Chambers.[4]

For Rutsky and Wyatt "academic film criticism" as a subset of "academic discourse in general" has "pleasures that presume a purpose: intellectual or moral pleasures." They are, in other words, "*serious pleasures*" (3) as opposed to being pleasures of sensation and excess. Here we can note the exemplary opposition between a criticism instrumentalised by its subordination to purposes and a criticism given over to the ecstasy of immediate contemplation. The double-bind of academic film criticism is said to reside in its obligation to be "serious about its own pleasure" and in its having extreme difficulty in "theorizing a pleasure that was not 'serious' " (3). The academic legitimacy of film criticism is said to be based on "the distinction between serious pleasures and mere diversion" to such an extent that "the history of academic film theory could . . . easily be written as a series of attempts to establish systematic criteria for distinguishing serious pleasures" (4). Rutsky and Wyatt then cite a number of baleful tendencies within the field of academic film criticism, from the marauding influence of "an aesthetic of political modernism" through to the (presumably "Althusserian") moment of film criticism found to be persisting in the writing of Comolli/ Narboni. This moment is characterised in the following way: "a privileging of the 'serious' and 'difficult' pleasures of 'criticism' over the too easy pleasures of reassurance is, in many ways, symptomatic of academic film theory's attitude towards pleasure" (5).

In the kinds of films it chooses to discuss, academic film discourse is alleged to favour the very pleasures on which its *own* discourse is based, the pleasures of "analysis and critique" (5). This is another version of mimetic criticism whereby film criticism comes to "resemble," say, a Straub-Huillet film or a Godard film (from the late sixties and early seventies). In an effort to deduce political consequences from what is essentially an aesthetic failing, Rutsky and Wyatt then outline a series of forms of (film) critical discourse whose claims to "expertise" and "a certain mastery of knowledge" (6) result in an assertion of the *sadistic* pleasures of rational critique. These are pleasures that "assume a position of authority, of power, *over* others" (6). They depict the academic as a stern figure of Authority, "the one who knows more and better" (6) and from this observation they move to a scene somewhere between *Venus in Furs* and *The Story of O:* "Thus furnished with the whip and chains of 'expertise', the academic is free to practice the bondage of definition and categorization, to flay falsity and to punish the 'misbehaviors' of errant thinkers" (6–7). Their attempt to make no claims on the text, to ask nothing of it that it does not ask of and for itself, leads Rutsky and Wyatt to reject the theme of "radical pleasure." Apparently, in being opposed to "rational discourses" this term too would fall under the sign of the serious: "the radical pleasure of abandoning seriousness becomes a serious pleasure" (10). And even when the writing of Gaylyn Studlar is opposed to that of Laura Mulvey, such a move from sadistic to masochistic pleasures can't help with "the trivial pleasures of those films that do not take themselves very seriously, those pleasures that we might describe as *fun*" (10). Although this overlooks the fact that, in terms of economic calculation, fun films clearly take themselves *very* seriously, Rutsky and Wyatt are more concerned to situate their concept of "fun" outside "the sadistic pleasure of rational knowledge and authority" (10) (e.g., Mulvey's account of "visual pleasure"), and outside "the masochistic pleasure of radical abandon and fascination" (10) (e.g., Studlar's writing). "Fun," we learn, "is *not* based on hierarchy, on power: it is never *entirely* serious" (10). This ludic, elusive concept of "fun" is "always critical: it always involves a deflation or leveling of pretentiousness, of the overly serious. Fun . . . makes fun of that which takes itself *too* seriously, of that which cannot laugh at itself. In its essence . . . fun is parodic, ironic" (10). "Fun" is democratic, demotic, never degrading or excluding other critical positions. "Fun" is radically populist: "The pleasure of a film that is fun is not based on hierarchy, but on the deflation of pretension and seriousness, including its own" (10–11). Always self-ironic, always acknowledging a commonality with its subject, the critiques practiced by "fun," "unlike those of academia, are always provisional, contingent" (11). "Fun" is the great leveler, a kind of Robin Hood of critical discourse: "Thus any discourse where the differential in seriousness between what it includes and what it excludes becomes too great, any discourse that comes to take itself, its knowledge, or its power, too seriously, will become liable to the 'critique' of fun" (11). Rutsky and Wyatt offer a description of the visual-metaphorical status of "fun" and counterpose it to that of "serious pleasure." While the latter "depends on a notion of vision that either penetrates and masters or involves and fascinates, the viewing of fun might be described as obvious or *superficial*" (11). Consequently, "the viewing of fun cannot be figured in terms of depth. It slides over the surface of a text like a passing glance, never staying fixed for long, never 'anchoring' itself in the depths of meaning" (11). The "sheepish glance," the "self-ironic wink" of fun "does not take itself *too* seriously" (11) and wouldn't dream of trying to redeem popular cinema by way of an isolating, evaluative auteurist gaze or through a (depth-reading) revelation of subversions of dominant ideologies. The message is clear. Even pleasure can be instrumentalised by the heavy hand of reason. Even the happiest of critics might be happy for a reason and hence not truly happy. Here we are approaching the point where the most sophisticated critical response will be the pure laughter of those who don't write criticism for scholarly journals. But surely this would be both too much to hope for and too little: too much because such laughter is meant to excoriate and humiliate those who are incapable of it and so it must be written or publicised; too little because we need to know from what sources such fun derives its ethical force.

In their valorising of a superficial, passing glance, Rutsky and Wyatt align themselves with Iain Chambers's comments on popular cultural texts and the kinds of analysis appropriate for them.[5] In the introduction to his *Popular Culture*, Chambers refers to an "official culture," a culture "preserved in art galleries, museums and university courses," a culture that "demands cultivated tastes and a formally imparted knowledge" (12). This culture "demands moments of attention that are separated from the run of daily life" (12). Popular culture, on the other hand, "mobilises the tactile, the incidental, the transitory, the expendable, the visceral. It does not involve an abstract aesthetic research amongst privileged objects of attention, but invokes mobile orders of sense, taste and desire" (12). Rather than cast a "contemplative stare" that adopts "the authority of the academic mind that seeks to explain an experience that is rarely personal" (13), Chambers opts for "an informal knowledge of the everyday, based on the sensory, the immediate, the pleasurable, the concrete" (13). Rather than be "appropriated through the apparatus of contemplation," popular culture is better approached through Walter Benjamin's notion of "distracted reception" (12).

Meaghan Morris has indicated some of the critical limitations and unwitting self-ironies attaching to projects that conceive of themselves in this way.[6] Insofar as some sort of appeal is made to the category of "the popular," the popular culture critic ends up turning "the people" into "the textually delegated, allegorical emblem of the critic's own activity" (23). Morris refers to the "play of *identification* between the knowing subject of cultural studies, and a collective subject, 'the people' " (22–23). In a situation where "the people" are "both a source of authority for a text and a figure of its own critical activity" (23) then "the populist enterprise is not only circular but . . . narcissistic in structure" (23). Morris calls writing of this kind "antiacademic pop-theory" (24) and claims that within it "a stylistic enactment of 'the popular' as *essentially* distracted, scanning the surface and short on attention span performs a retrieval, at the level of *enunciative* practice, of the thesis of 'cultural dopes' " (24).

There seem to be a number of overlaps between Chambers's remarks on how best to constitute popular culture as an object of analysis and Rutsky and Wyatt's version of the inevitably solemnising tendencies of academic film criticism. In each case the implication seems to be that descriptions of *popular* popular cultural texts calls for a form of discourse that somehow could, on its own enunciative terms, embody the essential elements of the thing it is describing. The drive to render energy, pulsions, feelings, sensations, velocities, volatilities demands an intensely affective, performative mode of writing, one more likely to effect a kind of *mimetic capture* of the essence of the object, or at least better able to convey some of its most encapsulating details. In part this demand derives from the belief that there *is* an immediate, spontaneous affective dimension, an intense *thrill*, bound up with the experience of watching a film and that to interpose a dry, stolid, critical language between this experience and its description, is to alienate, distort, *mis*describe.

When Rutsky and Wyatt shift their discussion onto films that seem "too obvious and shallow for in-depth analysis" (11) they take as their example a film "whose pleasure film theory seems unable to account for: a film that *is* and *is about* fun" (11). The film is *Ferris Bueller's Day Off*, whose very title "implies a sense of frivolity, of a lack of purpose" and which proves to be a film about "taking off from 'purposeful' work (school) for a day of leisure" (11). The purpose of the day is to have fun and this is "of course the purpose of the film too. It makes no pretensions to art" (12) and its moral statements are taken to be limited to saying that one should refuse seriousness in order to have some fun. Again we can see here the presence of a powerful strategy derived from the regime of aesthetic exegesis. A reading of a text that thematises the aesthetic is offered as evidence of the latter's validity. But you don't prove psychoanalysis is true by undergoing it, only that it exists and has therapeutic effects.

One unusual feature of Rutsky and Wyatt's description is that it ignores any discussion of genre and sub-genre: no real mention is made of comedic form or the teenpic. They choose to describe as "sadistic" those figures in the film who are opposed to fun (Ed Rooney, Cameron's parents) but an equally plausible account would see them as versions of a quite ancient comic persona: the figure of Rule and Authority who blocks the energies and growths of the Young and whose destiny is to be evaded, denounced, and gulled. (Indeed in their article, "academic film criticism"—unified into a boring, lumbering monolith—is cast in the role of Ed Rooney, Dean of Students). And equally "the day off" could be taken to correspond to the notion of "carnival" in comedy, that strictly limited period of licence in which the usual social order is reversed or upset, etc. Further, it seems a bit misleading to say that the film's moral statements are limited to suggesting that we all should have fun. Like many teenpics, *Ferris Bueller's Day Off* moralises heavily about the relation of middle-class and/or rich kids to their parents, and a number of discourses of therapy invade these films at particular moments, much as they do television programs from *Family Ties* through to *thirtysomething*. But Rutsky and Wyatt are excluded from such readings by the routine profundity of their own exegetical strategem.

For Rutsky and Wyatt "fun" becomes "an autonomous space" (12) and for the critic who can embrace it, "having fun" means being able "to place oneself in a non-hierarchical position" (16). Throughout their article "fun" seems analogous to the more traditional notion of "aesthetic play" and becomes the principal means by which individuals can use films as devices for calling *themselves* into question. For all its desire to be seen to be escaping the constraints of conventional academic film-critical discourse, Rutsky and Wyatt's writing can be seen to constitute a specific social–ethical activity, one that establishes a link between the ethical style of an individual (here the film popular culture critic) and the way this individual (in this case) watches films. The films thereby become the occasion for the critic to concern himself with himself, although *any* other cultural artifact (a novel, a tv program) *could* be used in precisely this way, could also become the means for an individual to call himself into question as one who requires some further work of self-stylisation, self-cultivation.[7] For Rutsky and Wyatt this further process of (late-twentieth century) self-fashioning occurs by way of the figure of "fun," and to refuse the injunction to "fun" would be to demonstrate a failure in the area of self-stylisation. It would be to show oneself as too serious, rational, in control, too out of touch with the senses (and "the people"), too much the unself-reflexive egghead. The paradox contained in all this, though, is that even the evangelists for fun could be equally eggheaded and ham-fisted in their attempts to cultivate an appropriate lightness of being (insofar as they treat these qualities as the "other" of the serious and the rational). This is to say that the very way in which "fun" is defended or promoted might betray the embarrassing and deforming presence of an underlying earnestness. The fact that "fun" can be approached only with the lightest of touches, can be addressed only by way of the most refined of intellectual instruments, reveals its power as a device of ethical self-problematisation.[8]

But as Wittgenstein might have said, fun too has its conditions. Rather than ask what it is that escapes established academic discourse and conventional moral purposes, and answer "fun!," we could instead ask under what conditions certain individuals (say a doctoral candidate and a recent Ph.D.) come to treat the intellect as necessarily and inevitably stereotyping? Rather than accept the proposition that "fun" is what always escapes the high-seriousness of a stolid, alienating, academic discourse, we might instead ask under what conditions, in what specific circumstances "fun" can be taken from a hedonistic playground in order to perform its (solemn) task of lightening the intellectual load? To do this would be to insist that the writing of Rutsky and Wyatt constitutes a quite sophisticated ethical–rhetorical exercise, one precisely enabled by a range of education, reading, and research. At the bottom of the first page of their article we learn of their respective academically certified statuses and on the inside back cover of the journal we find some other writing that indicates the passage their article would have followed before bursting into print and urging academic film criticism to adopt the category of "fun." First, "only members of the Society for Cinema Studies may submit essays to *Cinema Journal*"; secondly, "after a prescreening, articles are anonymously refereed by at least two specialist readers, one of whom is a member of the journal's editorial board"; and finally "to be considered for publication, manuscripts shall be no longer than 7,500 words, should follow the format specified by *The Chicago Manual of Style* (13th edition) and should be double spaced." One strategy available to Rutsky and Wyatt would have been to have included these instructions (cut-up style) in the body of their text as a means of indicating some quite practical, first-instance examples of the *expertise* and *mastery* their *own* critical discourse needed to exhibit in order to have its appeal to the notion of "fun" heard at all. For after all, *which* social group is likely to worry about being too intellectual or about being intellectual in the wrong way? Who, other than intellectuals, has access to these ethical exercises and instruments of such intense introspection, this array of techniques that *constitutes* the capacity for such a heightened self-consciousness and self-concern?

Remarks of this kind should indicate that the defence of "fun," "pleasure," "shallowness," "surface," is a version of what Ian Hunter has called "ethical athleticism":[9] constituting a specific intellectual exercise, an activity which has at its center a rule which says "read films by way of the category of fun." The critical practice of Rutsky and Wyatt is a self-distinguishing one to the extent that it seeks to set itself apart from a leaden intellectualism by displaying a nimbleness of response that barely disturbs the surface of a film whose very popularity signifies its delicate, recessive character. Such a practice of self-distinction is quite routine for a post-Romantic criticism in which the authority of judgment derives from the aesthetic style and standing of the critical persona. It becomes quite literally an occasion for the critic to "engage in a specific public staging of the self."[10] For example it only becomes possible to say that a film like *Ferris Bueller's Day Off* contains, in a thematic form, the dialectic of fun and seriousness, spontaneity and Law, when you demonstrate this by performing an allegorical reading (much as Rutsky and Wyatt perform a hermeneutic reading of the film's "surface" in order to demonstrate "the truth of fun").

At the bottom of their call for a thoroughly self-reflexive critical practice lies a particular irony. Many of the intellectually trained *do* indeed watch teenpics for "fun" in the sense of "after work," "without writing articles about them" and "without using the concept of fun as a means of self-interrogation." So we have a tribe of the intellectually trained watching films for fun. Does this mean that theoretical funsters such as Rutsky and Wyatt are the anthropologists of this tribe? Perhaps, but as soon as the anthropologists of the fun-ritual transcribe it, they necessarily put it to a new use and I'm suggesting here that it is being put to use in a practice of aesthetic self-stylisation. To say this is not to say that watching fun films for fun is ineffable or untheorisable, rather it is to say that "not too much can be made of it without making it into something else"[11]—such as an article in *Cinema Journal*.

Notes

1   John Frow, "Discipline and Discipleship," *Textual Practice* 2, no. 3 (1988): 318. Frow's description continues: "In its usual form it is organised as a passage from an undergraduate community to post-graduate loneliness; a breaking down of ego; and the acquisition of a specialised lore through a difficult and intense relation to a supervisor. The ordeal of candidature is a mad process in its assignment of a structural role to insecurity. It challenges the candidate's sense of worth, provoking a trauma of loss as one of its central knowledge-producing mechanisms, one which is often cruelly prolonged or repeated."

2   R. L. Rutsky and Justin Wyatt, "Serious Pleasures: Cinematic Pleasure and the Notion of Fun," *Cinema Journal* 30, no. 1 (1990): 3–19 (subsequent references included in the text).

3   Simon Frith, "Review Article," *Screen* 31, no. 2 (1990): 232 (subsequent references included in the text).

4   Roland Barthes, *Mythologies* (London: Paladin, 1972), especially 156–59; Dick Hebdige, *Subculture: The Meaning of Style* (London: Methuen, 1979), 139–40; Iain Chambers, *Popular Culture* (London: Methuen, 1986), 12–13. Also see Terry Eagleton, "Preface" to *The Function of Criticism* (London: Verso, 1984).

5   Chambers, *Popular Culture*. Subsequent references included in the text.

6   Meaghan Morris, "Banality in Cultural Studies," in *Logics of Television*, ed. Patricia Mellencamp (London: British Film Institute, 1990), 14–43. Subsequent references included in the text.

7   See Ian Hunter, "Criticism as a Way of Life," *Typereader* no. 4 (1990): 5–21.

8   Many of the following comments are derived from Ian Hunter's work in progress on "Aesthetics as a Practice of Self-Stylisation."

9   Ian Hunter, *Culture and Government* (London: Macmillan, 1988).

10   See Ian Hunter, "Learning the Literature Lesson: The Limits of the Aesthetic Personality," in *Towards a Critical Sociology of Reading Pedagogy*, eds. A. Luke and C. D. Baker (Amsterdam: John Benjamin, 1991).

11   Ian Hunter, in conversation.

Chapter 20

R. L. Rutsky and Justin Wyatt

THROWING SHADE IN THE KINGDOM: REPLY TO NOEL KING (1992)

O N RECEIVING NOEL KING'S COMMENTARY on our recent article on "fun," we at first imagined writing a monograph-length response, à la Derrida in his debate with John Searle, or at least a lengthy essay patterned after Stephen Heath's response to Noël Carroll. Upon consultation with the editorial staff of *Cinema Journal*, however, we learned that a response of that length was perhaps not appropriate. With regret that *Cinema Journal* does not find this "debate" to be of sufficient importance to devote an entire issue (at a minimum) to it, we have downscaled our ambitions somewhat.

TOP 8 RESPONSES TO PROFESSOR KING

(8) Presenting credentials to the court

Professor King seems terribly concerned with questions of academic authority and credentialing. He begins his commentary with a quotation on "the ritual of the Ph.D." and later manages to work in a parenthetical reference to our credential status – "(say a doctoral candidate and a recent Ph.D.)" – at the time that the original article was published. He returns to this point shortly thereafter, noting that "at the bottom of the first page of their article we learn of their respective academically certified statuses." He then goes on to observe that "on the inside back cover of the journal we find some other writing which indicates the passage their article would have followed before bursting into print. . . . First, 'only members of the Society for Cinema Studies may submit essays to *Cinema Journal*'; secondly, 'after a prescreening, articles are anonymously refereed by at least two specialist readers, one of whom is a member of the Journal's editorial board,' " etc. If we understand him correctly, Professor King wishes to point out our complicity in the structures of academic authorization. He even goes so far as to suggest that we might have included the above instructions, "cut-up style," in our article. We very much like this suggestion (although we should perhaps also include a citation from one of those anonymous reader's reports, which found that our article did not "respect the highest standards of research and argument"). We are, however, somewhat surprised that we would be perceived as denying our own complicity in academic discourse and its authority structures. Indeed, we would have thought that this complicity was fairly obvious, not only given the context that Professor King cites, but our explicit statement, which he does not cite, that our essay "tends to argue for [a discourse of fun] rather than demonstrate it" and that the reasons for such an approach are precisely those "standards" that govern publication in an "academic context."

(7) The man who would be King

The attempt to account for the fun paper along the lines of establishing a "reputation" in academia could be tossed right back into Professor King's court. How else to establish a reputation than to offer a critical dialogue in an international journal? (Which we, as recent Ph.D.s, are only too happy to continue [ad infinitum]).

(6) The boundaries of the kingdom

Throughout his essay, Professor King argues that we have attempted to position the notion of fun (and ourselves) as outside the boundaries of academic or intellectual discourse, as that which "escapes" seriousness. In fact, we argued that "Fun does not . . . position itself as external to seriousness . . . it is not the negation of seriousness." While we did note that serious discourse has often tended to exclude the notion of fun, our point was that this exclusion is neither necessary nor advisable. Indeed, it seems that Professor King has a much stronger sense than we do of an "inevitable" division between the "solemnizing tendencies" of academic discourse and a discourse of fun. By his account, in fact, it would seem that the very moment an academic begins to speak of fun, fun ceases to exist. Yet while this account may be a reasonably accurate description of a historical tendency, it is not, we would at least like to believe, an essential truth.

(5) Pleasures of the King

In Professor King's dialectics, it is not simply fun that is opposed to academic or intellectual discourse. Fun is also equated with "the popular" and with what Professor King refers to as "aesthetic self-stylisation." The basis for this conflation at first mystified us, especially given that we had not even used the terms "the popular" (much less "the people") or "aesthetic" to refer to fun. We eventually realized, however, that Professor King's argument seemed to be directed less at our work than at that of Iain Chambers. For we had certainly never claimed that fun was in some essential way related to popularity or that we, as "theorists of fun," were in any sense representative of "the people" (indeed, we would argue strenuously against such an idea). Similarly, Professor King's figuration of fun in terms of an "aesthetic" of "the sensory, the immediate, the pleasurable" seems to draw more on Chambers's description of popular culture than on our description of fun. There may be "an immediate, spontaneous affective dimension, an intense thrill, bound up with the experience of watching a film," but such an experience seems, to us, less a matter of fun than what we described as a notion of "radical pleasure," a pleasure that indeed often defines itself as an "immediate, spontaneous aesthetic experience" opposed to rational discourse. The extent to which Professor King ignores the section of our essay devoted to "radical pleasure" gives an indication of the degree to which his argument is based precisely upon the opposition between the seriousness of rational knowledge and (still serious) "anti-seriousness" of radical pleasure.

(4) All the King's men

If the notion of fun merely exists as an attempt at "aesthetic self-stylisation," Professor King's commentary clearly falls prey to the same claim. According to Professor King, the "fun" piece places us in a well defined academic "region": "The general drift of their argument, together with some of the particular terms they come to privilege, connects closely with the discussions of popular culture offered by writers such as Roland Barthes, Dick Hebdige, and Iain Chambers." While we thank Professor King for comparing two recent Ph.D.s to the likes of Barthes, Hebdige, and Chambers, we have to wonder about Professor King's own reliance on Ian Hunter as a touchstone. Does King merely want to belong to a different "gang of thieves"? The attempt to "label" fun by attaching it to the work of popular culture theorists can be interpreted as an attempt to dismiss fun by assimilating it into mainstream academic discourse. This kind of strategy, as we attempted to show, places the author in a (kingly) position of knowledge.

(3) Performing for the court

While Laura Mulvey invokes films by Hitchcock (e.g., *Rear Window*, *Marnie* and *Vertigo*) to illustrate her argument on scopophilia and narrative pleasure, films which are obviously structured just around looking, sadism, and power, our use of *Ferris Bueller's Day Off*, on the other hand, is not, as Professor King suggests, simply a thematization of the concept of fun ("A reading of a text which thematises the aesthetic is offered as evidence of the latter's validity"). Our article attempts to mime the form of fun. It attempts, in fact, to perform fun. If this is what Professor King means by self-stylization, then we gladly accept the characterization. Indeed, the use of *Ferris Bueller's Day Off* does not offer a mimetic representation, but rather a mime of the performance aspects of the film.

(2) The King's new clothes

Professor King accuses us of "aesthetic self-stylisation," but self-stylization occurs inevitably as a factor in the process of writing. Indeed, the response by Professor King, or any written discourse, inevitably ends up stylizing the author (whether as a "theoretical funster" or as a "serious academic"). For our part, we tend to be less interested in Professor King's self-stylization than in his re-stylization of us. Consider his description of us as "the masculin- ist Cyndi Laupers of film criticism (boys who just wanna have fun)," the "Robin Hoods" of critical "discourse" or as "evangelists for fun." While we like the idea of being simultaneously Cyndi Lauper, Robin Hood, and Jimmy Swaggart, we have to wonder how Professor King can, in all seriousness, reconcile these disparate "styles" with his own notion of academic discourse. It seems that Professor King has (despite himself) fallen prey to fun.

(1) Giving the King his due

After being subjected to a particularly vicious attack by an opposing speaker, Marcel Duchamp was asked what he thought of the speech. Duchamp replied that "it was perhaps insufficiently lighthearted." We would have liked to have been in a position to use Duchamp's line as a reply to Professor King. We find, however, that in good conscience, and in good fun, we cannot. First, Professor King's commentary is hardly a vicious attack;

indeed, it would be difficult to call it an attack at all. Second, if Professor King is to some degree guilty of "insufficient lightheartedness," it is certainly to a lesser extent than the majority of serious academic discourse. Finally, we too, as participants in academic discourse, cannot escape this charge. Yet to acknowledge this is not to accede to Professor King's division of academic discourse and fun. The serious self-stylization of academia need not exclude other stylizations through which people throw shade and have fun.

2C REPRESENTATION

Chapter 21

Ed Guerrero

A CIRCUS OF DREAMS AND LIES: THE BLACK FILM WAVE AT MIDDLE AGE (1998)

T**HE CIRCUS PROVES TO BE A USEFUL** and poetic metaphor for black "progress" in the film industry since the end of the civil rights movement. With Jesse Jackson and other social critics and activists once again protesting Hollywood's exclusion of African Americans,[1] that effort toward progress seems to have come full circle to the issues at the frustrated beginnings of African American open mass resistance to white supremacy in the 1950s and 1960s. In spite of some measured progress evinced by a sprinkling of new black actors, directors, and producers, and because of very few changes in Hollywood's executive offices, the 1990s' black film wave has hit an interesting, stalemated, plateau, one that belies its auspicious take-off in the mid-1980s. Then, young, insurgent filmmakers like Spike Lee with *She's Gotta Have It* (1986), Robert Townsend with *Hollywood Shuffle* (1987), and Julie Dash with *Daughters of the Dust* (1991), all playing variations on the theme of "guerrilla financing," helped crack the discriminatory insider networks and investment ceilings that kept African Americans shut out of the production end of the movie business after the collapse of the Blaxploitation period in the mid-1970s. While varied discussions and definitions of "black cinema" and its much debated independent and mainstream tendencies will always be important issues, this essay will primarily focus on the tangled workings of *race* in Hollywood and those feature films made by or about black people that enjoy a popular commercial audience. As well, I will rummage through and unpack some of the symptomatic expressions of *blackness* and *whiteness* on the big screen.

With the new black movie boom now slouching toward middle age, one can expect the industry to release twenty or so black-cast, black-focused, or black-directed mainstream films a year. Beyond the industry's persistent color problems, its hackneyed short-term, profit-focused scenarios and stereotypes, the potential for a fully developed black cinema, featuring an interesting range of new films and directions, cultural trends, and rising star personas, still lingers, albeit as a long shot. For one thing, the 1990s' black film wave has been amplified and sustained by the emergence of a new generation of black film scholars and critics who have defined and shaped black cinema's circus maximus.[2] But also, black films and filmmakers are enjoying an expanded audience, a heterogeneous mix of crossover, youth, and art-house moviegoers.

It is this variety of expressions, activities, and innovative directions in black filmmaking and its critical discourse that stands out as the most promising development in popular black cinema production and consumption to date. However, as with all circuses – cinematic, metaphoric, or otherwise – we must contend with a downside. As Federico Fellini so recurrently and brilliantly revealed in his work, the circus and cinema are closely related cultural forms. Both are built on the suspension of disbelief and rely on large doses of spectacle. Both forms also mask a certain hard reality with the veil of aesthetic pleasure, illusion, and trickery. In the case of Hollywood's ongoing, lucrative flirtation with the sign of *blackness*, the tricks have been habitual and predictable as the film industry persists in skewing its representations of African Americans while containing much of black film production within the limitations of its most profitable and expedient marketing strategies and narrative formulas.

Accordingly, then, the most important circumstance informing the production of all *blackness* on the big screen, and the primary hoax or illusion in the American collective psyche, continues to be the social construction and contestation of *race* and how we as a nation negotiate our turbulent, multivalent racial definitions and power relations. The symptoms of our delusional and troubled racial condition endure, from the sensational Susan Smith double murder case with its traditional evocation of the black bogeyman,[3] to the acrimonious black/white split in public opinion over the verdict in the O.J. Simpson murder case, to the emancipatory upsurge of 1996's Million Man March, to a wave of black church burnings throughout the South, or the rise of militant militias across the land. Feeding the tense racial climate in the mid-1990s, the affirmative action backlash metastasized with the passage of California's anti-immigrant Proposition 187. Also by mid-decade, there arose a racially polarized national electorate, accompanied in print by the pseudo-scientific claims of black intellectual and genetic inferiority in *The Bell Curve* or the laughable assertion in *The End of Racism* that white supremacy and racism are no longer social maligancies.[4]

"The Devil's greatest trick was to convince the world that he doesn't exist," goes the most memorable line in the hit film noir thriller *The Usual Suspects* (1995). And so it goes when confronting the elusive, resilient demon of racism. In a pattern that has endured at least since the end of World War II, *race* continues to smolder unconsciously in the social psyche and then, with dismal regularity, leap into public focus and media exploitation with the revelation of some racial crime or competition over shrinking resources. Ralph Ellison's trope of "invisibility," which, really, maps the dialectic of visibility/invisibility, in part explains this phenomenon. Blacks are highly visible in society as suspects, victims, or noble exceptions to the rule, while simultaneously they are invisible when it comes to the recognition of their individuality, their basic humanity and rights. Unfortunately, the cycle has degenerated into vulgar, reflexive habit that begins with a state of racial denial that passes for the social norm. This so-called normative state is disrupted by some racial issue or "incident," followed by feigned shock and innocence, then anger, then repression and a return to a primal and uneasy state of collective denial. It should come as no surprise, then, that with the end of the Cold War, a nation that has defined and unified itself with the threat of an external, foreign enemy for more than fifty years now increasingly finds *race*, in all of its themes, coded forms, and endless variations, such a charged and divisive issue.

Consequently, our chronic racial condition multiply informs how we play out *blackness*, from the most evident stereotypes to the most encrypted racial arguments and assumptions in commercial cinema and the media. Making the point in a perhaps unconscious way, the hit noir comedy *Get Shorty* (1995) depicts the exclusion and marginality that Hollywood routinely inflicts on African Americans in its portrayal of two underworld figures, John

Travolta as a mob loan collector and Delroy Lindo as an upper-level black L.A. drug dealer, who are competing to turn a hot film script into a movie. As the plot unfolds, the Lindo character is eliminated while the Travolta character prevails and goes on to produce the film. Besides Hollywood's usual death wish for Lindo as a stereotypical black loser, what *Get Shorty* reveals about the inner workings of the film industry is exactly how and why African Americans are excluded from its highest decision-making levels. Using a series of clever deceptions, mixed with some intensive networking, Chili Palmer (Travolta), manages to sign a big-name star, Michael Weir (Danny DeVito), to his script and move it into production. Thus, *Get Shorty* explores the same Hollywood business culture that made Robert Altman's *The Player* (1992) and the art-house film *Swimming with Sharks* (1995) so potently satirical. All of these films self-reflexively depict how the executive levels of the movie industry work as a "relationship business."[5] Whatever superficial liberal concessions Hollywood makes to racial equality on TV talk shows, or in its award ceremonies, when it comes to greenlighting film scripts, building stars' careers, or investing large amounts of capital for short-term profit, moviemaking is an overwhelmingly white male insider's game. And unfortunately, at the highest levels in the movie industry, *blackness* bears little "relationship" to "business."

In one sense, contemporary Hollywood has broken with its openly white supremacist origins. Mostly gone are the obvious caricatures: the stern Mammies, bug-eyed Sambos, grunting Tontos, and pidgin-speaking Charlie Chans of the past. Yet, off the screen in the executive suites, when it comes to money and power, control over decision-making in production and distribution remains firmly a white monopoly. But then again, one also could argue that crude racial slander has outlived its usefulness and been supplanted by the more insidious and potent subtleties of racial coding, implication, symbolism, and co-optation. It is in this more subtle sense that Hollywood's racial ideology remains intact and almost thoroughly pervades the content of its films. Take, for instance, the sustained racial allegory in the science fiction hit *Stargate* (1994), which deploys a recuperative strategy[6] that subtly undermines the popular black claim to African American origins in classical Egyptian civilization by portraying the Sun God Ra (Jaye Davidson) as the epitome of black, decadent, hermaphroditic evil. In one of the more fantastic rationalizations of the history of slavery, an expedition of white-led earthlings shows up on an alien planet to destroy Ra and liberate an enslaved population from this wicked black slavemaster deity.

Some of the conflicting ideological tensions between mainstream and black independent perspectives become clear when one contrasts Hollywood's *Stargate* with the independent, black-cast *Space Is the Place* (1972). Exactly inverting *Stargate*'s perspective, in *Space Is the Place* jazz musician Sun Ra, playing the Sun God Ra, comes to planet Earth to liberate its population with the blues-jazz harmonies of his advanced musical technology. But clearly, blues and jazz as the mark of *blackness* in mainstream cinema will, mostly, continue to be the locus of an exotic, oppositional pathology or evil, as drug- and alcohol-addicted geniuses stumble through tired master narratives under the care of white buddies, as in *Round Midnight* (1986) or *Bird* (1988). Or as with the otherwise innovative animated feature *The Nightmare Before Christmas* (1993), in which, yet again, the epitome of primordial evil looms as a jive-talking blues-jazz spook, the "Boogey-woogey Man."

Blackness has always been in vogue in the mainstream culture industry, but it has been relentlessly framed and controlled by an overdetermining sense of white hegemony. Consequently, the biracial buddy formula has found ample expression in the 1990s, continuing to be dominant cinema's most standard and profitable strategy for representing African Americans on the commercial screen.[7] Among the rising black talent of the decade, Samuel L. Jackson, Morgan Freeman, Angela Bassett, Denzel Washington, Will Smith, Laurence Fishburne, and Wesley Snipes have all found themselves in the protective custody of buddy movies that achieved varying degrees of commercial success. The box-office hit *Pulp Fiction*

(1995), starring crime partners John Travolta and Samuel L. Jackson, marked one of the revealing, ironic variations on the buddy theme, with Jackson's character and performance carrying much of the film. Articulating that transgressive sense of outlaw blackness that Hollywood finds so alluring, Jackson plays an L.A. hit man who by the end of the flick goes through a profound inner transformation.

The ironics of *Pulp Fiction* are at least twofold, the first irony dealing with the way the script exploits and fetishizes the word "nigger," liberally and gratuitously invoking it throughout the dialogue. Here, one of the grand absurdities of American identity applies. For everyone fantasizes about being black in a hip, cultural sense, even to the point of using "niggah" in the familiar, insider way that some black people do. However, no one wants to live the social disadvantage and inequality of actually *being* a nigger, as only black people are forced to do in America. This is the great hidden energy that animates the Jackson and Travolta performances, the painfully tangled, historic interplay between the black man and his white buddy, from Jim and Huck Finn, to Rocky and Apollo Creed, on into infinity. *Pulp Fiction*'s second irony is more important, simply because it is about Hollywood power relations—that is to say, how the political economy of stardom works when it comes to *race*. Samuel Jackson was the dramatic force and moral center of the film, but it was John Travolta's career that was revived by the film and took off. With credit to his talent and effort, Travolta has moved, once again, into the adoring, national spotlight, to star in a series of popular films including *Get Shorty, Phenomenon* (1996), and *Broken Arrow* (1996). Conversely, the equally talented and persevering Jackson has moved laterally through the endless purgatory of yet another biracial buddy movie, *Die Hard with a Vengeance* (1995), the supporting lead in *A Time to Kill* (1996), and the lead in the pedestrian, black-made comedy *The Great White Hype* (1996).[8] Morgan Freeman also exemplifies how the buddy system traps and contains black talent, as he moved from *Driving Miss Daisy* (1989), to prison buddy of Tim Robbins in *The Shawshank Redemption* (1994), to driving Mr. Brad Pitt in his star vehicle, the complex psychological thriller *Seven* (1995).

By far the most interesting buddy variation of the 1990s has to be *Strange Days* (1995), a film so thematically radical and creative in terms of race, gender, and romance that it is inevitably located in an uncomfortably, near authoritarian, future Los Angeles. *Strange Days* ends on a powerful note of love and miscegenation between the black female and white male leads, Angela Bassett and Ralph Fiennes. In part because it premiered at the moment of the O. J. Simpson verdict and held its disturbing focus on *race*, the moviegoing audience stayed away from the film. On the other hand, *Money Train* (1995), starring buddies (in this case, foster brothers) Wesley Snipes and Woody Harelson, extended the crossover refrain of conscience liberalism that the pair struck in *White Men Can't Jump* (1992) and made out at the box office. With the grand success of Will Smith and Jeff Goldblum bonding to fight alien *otherness* in the megahit *Independence Day* (1996), or Arnold Schwarzenegger rescuing Vanessa Williams in *Eraser* (1996), it is a safe bet that the biracial buddy formula in all of its variations is destined for a long run in Hollywood.

In contrast to the endless ways that dominant cinema subordinates and plays *blackness* in its films, it would be productive here to mention some of the ways that Hollywood constructs the naturalized, privileged sign of *whiteness*. It is easy enough to realize that in a long trajectory of historical contexts, representations, and films, *blackness* has been trapped in expressions of the primitive, the physical body, violence, and eros, while *whiteness* has been associated with civilization and the refinements and gifts of the mind and intellect.[9] Certainly the films *Powder* (1995), about a Caucasian albino gifted with psychic powers, and *Phenomenon* (1996), about an average white guy who is suddenly anointed with the gift of superintelligence continue this traditional black-body, white-mind binary. But perhaps most interesting for this discussion we should explore how one of the leading, box-office hits of the 1995–96 season constructs the naturalized, sovereign sign of *whiteness*. In spite of all its cutting-edge technology, the computer-animated blockbuster *Toy Story* (1995) follows a traditional strategy of omitting *blackness* from its simulacral world, underscoring one of the most powerful but subtle ways that *whiteness* is naturalized and revered.[10] Yet if there are no black subjects in the film per se, because no film can ever completely escape the *race* context of the society whose values it mediates, *Toy Story*, at least by analogy, recognizes the pain of a "double consciousness" in the way that Buzz Lightyear must come to realize that he is not human, but rather "just a toy."

Toy Story's characters and scenes are rendered in the clean, flawless, "look" of new toys, pristine images completely free of anchoring in material reality. What is most interesting about this visual style is the crisp, untanned white-pink skin, and standardized middle-America voices of the leading characters,[11] who in complexion, sound, and appearance come to represent a purely simulated, primally innocent *cyber-whiteness*, suggesting the possibility of some future homogeneous, psychic state free of the social tensions of constantly taking into account a sense of an oppositional *blackness*. With complete demographic heterogeneity encroaching on the social horizon, such a world can exist only in the total constructedness of cyber-animation. Yet, however innocent their makers allege animation to be, its ideological effects are pervasive. Cartoons and animated features most deeply influence the habits and perceptions of Hollywood's youngest and therefore longest-term consumers: children. And *Toy Story*, with its idealized white world, like *Home Alone* (1990) before it, turned out to be one of Hollywood's biggest blockbusters.

There is, however, some good news in all of this. Because the moviegoing audience is vast, heterogeneous, and fragmented along many lines—including the abiding differences of class, race, gender, education, religion—and because consumer tastes and trends are perpetually agitated and shifting as a result of the way the market economy functions, no studio executive can predict exactly which big entertainment investments, no matter how calculated or formulaic, will be box-office winners. So Hollywood's domination of commercial cinema can never be seamless or absolute. Also contributing to the insecure, sometimes contradictory nature of Hollywood's hegemony, black filmmaking and black participation in mainstream cinema tend to evoke a variety of oppositional currents, resistant practices, and insurgent moments against the norms and conventions of the dominant cinema system. Generally speaking, these currents of opposition arise simply because black filmmaking mediates the experiences of a marginalized, oppressed people. Thus, narratives about blacks or the black world tend to be set in more desperate, contested circumstances, or they tend to voice resistant social critiques, often in new, emergent vocabularies and cultural styles.

In response to the challenge of an oppositional black creative discourse, one of the most subtle and powerful features of the dominant cinema system has been its ability not so much to eradicate independent and countercultural impulses, but rather to co-opt and contain them. Hollywood has been highly proficient at buying up and then marketing the signs of *blackness*, emptied of their social and political meanings. In the entertainment and movie businesses, the interplay of resistance and co-optation is a continual push-pull dynamic. This, in part, explains the commercial success of films like Ice Cube's ribald, insider black comedy *Friday* (1995), or the music phenomenon of gangsta rappers decrying the desperate realities of ghetto life to their audience, which is in large part white youth safely tucked away in the suburbs. (As rapper Dr. Dre succinctly puts it: "We're marketing black culture to white people.")[12] Under these complex conditions, then, black-focused filmmakers are struggling to maintain a diverse middle-market niche by drawing the attention and limited investment of industry executives and the mixed patronage of a sizable consumer audience.

Thus, a key factor informing low-budget to mid-budget black filmmaking aimed at popular circulation comes down to the need to increasingly innovate and diversify the subject matter and the genres of black-focused product. The exploration of a shifting range of ideas and subjects in anticipation of an ever-restless moviegoing audience's boredom with worn-out styles and genres is foremost an economic necessity. But, since black people are themselves a diversely heterogeneous social formation that cannot adequately be defined by any one style, class, or identity, this is also a cultural imperative. So as the end of the decade, century, and millennium approaches, the most obvious genre to exhaust itself is the ghetto-action-gangsta flick. After reaching the zenith of box-office success with *Boyz N the Hood* (1992), and a sort of perfection of representational violence in the Hughes brothers' hit *Menace II Society* (1993), or a more socially conscious tone in the Oliver Stone-sponsored *South Central* (1994), or Spike Lee's *Clockers* (1995), or a range of expression in a dozen or so genre fillers like *Trespass* (1992), *Sugar Hill* (1994), and *New Jersey Drive* (1995), the popularity of these films has dwindled. The best of these movies manifest signs of a more sophisticated noir style, which I will return to. But reminiscent of the collapse of the Blaxploitation boom, critics and audience members, black and white alike, once again have tired of seeing African American life narrowly portrayed in terms of ghetto violence, adventure, and pathology.[13]

On the horizon, the fresh, imaginative work of filmmakers such as Rusty Cundieff, David Johnson, Darnell Martin, Leslie Harris, and Carl Franklin suggests creative directions and solutions to stylistic dead ends and genre traps like the homeboy-ghetto-action flick. Such new impulses in black cinema frequently show up in low-budget or independent features that do not always enjoy success at the box office. Often, these films find their largest audience on the second bounce, at the video store. Such has been the case with Rusty Cundieff's relentlessly funny and cutting satire of the rap, hip-hop music business, *Fear of a Black Hat* (1994), which was made for less than $1 million. Taking up the mock documentary style of *This Is Spinal Tap!* (1984) with its critique of heavy metal bands, *Fear of a Black Hat* follows the escapades of "Niggaz with Hats" in a brilliant parody of the cultural politics and style of the rap group N.W.A. *Fear of a Black Hat* outdoes the more expensive, Nelson George-produced rap comedy *CB4* (1993), which suffers from being too close to the material it is trying to satirize to be more than erratically funny. By contrast, what makes director-star Cundieff's humor so potent is his ability, as rap star "Ice Cold," to mock the way that some rappers deftly gloss over or excuse their blatant misogyny or violence with the most ludicrous rationalizations. Ice Cold, for instance, glibly tries to explain why the group's hit, "Booty Juice," is uplifting for women, or that their *Kill Whitey* album has no social implications but refers specifically to a former manager named Whitey. Unfortunately, both *CB4* and *Fear of a Black Hat* slept at the box office, in part because of the speed at which rap culture evolves. By the time they were released, their object of parody, the swiftly mutating rap scene, had moved light years past either film's gags and allusions. However, Cundieff's humor and his mocking style with its distinct political edge and subversive currents suggest a potent new direction in the development of black comedy.

Cundieff refined his talent for casting his work in specific political or social contexts without lapsing into editorial propaganda in his second feature, the Spike Lee-produced *Tales from the Hood* (1995). Working in an unevenly explored genre for black filmmaking, the horror flick, and taking off on the style of the *Tales from the Crypt* films and TV series, *Tales from the Hood* consists of a round of stories told to three homeboys by a spooky mortician. If, as critics Michael Ryan and Douglas Kellner, among others, argue,[14] the great dread in the horror film is the return of those repressed energies in the form of the monster that society cannot openly deal with, then the monsters that animate *Tales from the Hood* are markedly political and express the great terrors of African American life: police brutality, lynching, racism, the catastrophic effects of social inequality. In one of the most original and stunning sequences in the horror genre, a gothic scientist (Rosaland Cash) tries to deprogram the violent rage of a black youth by exposing him to a sustained, gruesome photo montage of real lynchings, thus replaying the long historical nightmare of genocidal violence inflicted upon black people. This brutal vignette clearly makes the point that the homicidal rage that young black men inflict on each other merely carries on the work of more traditional racist forces in the society.

Tales ends with that perfect register of cultural humor and irony that marks the insider perspective of a black filmmaker with an ear for the subtle nuances of 'hood vernacular. By the end of the round of tales, predictably, the three young gang-bangers realize that they are actually dead and that their host, played brilliantly by Clarence Williams III, is not a mortician at all, but really the Devil. In a close-up, the undertaker's face morphs into that of Satan, who articulates his deep mastery of worldly wickedness by turning the homeboys' obscene argot back on them, as he announces their fate. In a controlled sardonic voice, the Devil closes the film with the line "Welcome to Hell, *motherfuckers*," as the camera pulls back on the homeboys dancing in a whirlwind of flames. It is exactly this kind of sly counter-current linguistic detail that distinguishes *Tales from the Hood* from the comparatively more mainstream black horror flick, the Wes Craven-directed star vehicle for Eddie Murphy and Angela Bassett, *Vampire in Brooklyn* (1995).

Another low-budget, Spike Lee-produced feature that mediates complex expressions of opposition to the Hollywood norm is *Drop Squad* (1994), directed by David Johnson. Following up on the concerns of a string of early 1990s black-made, or black-focused, mainstream films like *Jungle Fever, Livin' Large*, and *Strictly Business* that explore the contradictions and anxieties of black middle-class identity and "buppie" assimilation into white business culture, *Drop Squad* pushes these identity issues a step further by questioning what constitutes a stable, "authentic" *black* self and who gets to determine precisely what that "self" might be. Adopting the atmospherics of a movie about the French Resistance during World War II, *Drop Squad* depicts the clandestine operations of an underground black organization that abducts and deprograms sellout "buppies." When Bruford Jamison, Jr. (Eriq La Salle), is kidnapped, or "dropped," the dauntingly complex problem of black identity formation in the heterogeneous post-Black Nationalist 1990s is rigorously interrogated and satirized.

Drop Squad assumes an open or unfinalized stance on nineties' black identity in that Bruford's deprogramming ends on a painful, ambiguous note. While Bruford's neoconservative, Uncle Tom consciousness is the source of the film's funniest moments and best satire, in the Drop Squad's frustrated attempts to deprogram him, their tactics turn increasingly violent and fascistic. Bruford comes to see the error of his buppie ways, but he justifiably feels injured and wronged by the deprogramming process itself. Finally, the Drop Squad's two leaders—Rocky (Vondie Curtis-Hall) and Garvey (Ving Rhames) – are forced to recognize that the moment for 1960s-style shock therapy and consciousness-raising has passed. They split over tactics and decide to fulfill the mission of salvaging black identity and culture by going their separate ways. Contrary to the dominant Hollywood style that provides pat solutions to an assenting consumer audience, *Drop Squad* dares to leave the audience with more questions and uncertainties than answers. The film's ending is open and unresolved, quite simply because black social identity in the mid-1990s itself is diverse, in process, and so unresolved.

Also drawing upon dissident perspectives or modes of expression, Mario Van Peebles's *Panther*, and the Hughes brothers' *Dead Presidents* (both 1995) exemplify that curious mix of oppositional tendencies with grudging concessions to mainstream Hollywood style often found in popularly consumed black films. In that it offers a creative, revisionist reading of history, Van Peebles's *Panther* fits well into the trajectory of political works by more established directors: Spike Lee with *Malcolm X* (1992), Oliver Stone with *JFK* (1991) and *Nixon* (1995), or Costa-Gavras with *Missing* (1982). In the case of *Panther*, its relevance as black, oppositional cinema was confirmed by how instantly and vehemently the film was attacked by the right wing of the media, and how quickly it disappeared from theater circulation after its release.[15] Set in Oakland, *Panther* sympathetically depicts the founding of the Black Panther Party in 1966 and explores the grievances of the black community, the police terror, ghettoization, and social injustice that brought the party into being. *Panther* ends, à la Hollywood, with both a climactic shootout (with nefarious, government-controlled drug dealers) and a sentimental denouement in which a stoplight that the community had agitated for in the beginning of the film is finally installed. Following up on an idea raised by Spike Lee's *Malcolm X*, perhaps, *Panther*'s most significant contribution to black cinema will be to suggest that one can tell a politically focused story from a collective black point of view in the style of the heroic, individualistic, Hollywood action-adventure narrative.

With historical hindsight, *Panther* stops at a prudent historical moment in that the film ends with Huey Newton at the height of his powers, before his decline and eclipse in the seventies and eighties. The Hughes brothers' second film, *Dead Presidents* (1995), is located in the same politicized, Vietnam era as *Panther*, and it deals with many of the same injustices, discontents, and tensions. *Dead Presidents*, the title alluding to those faces on paper money, tells the coming-of-age story of a black youth, Anthony (Lorenz Tate), as he journeys from a working-class background in the Bronx, through Vietnam combat, and back to the old neighborhood and the economic and social dead end that dominant society has carefully prepared for so many of its returning black veterans. Anthony's pent-up frustrations culminate in one of the most visually fantastic heists in recent cinema. If *Dead Presidents* is canonized for nothing else, it will be for the brilliantly imagined image of black bandits in whiteface stealing the government's worn-out, about-to-be-burned money, or for the close-up shots of the faces on that money burning in the film's opening credit sequence.

The politics of *Dead Presidents* can be found in the way that the film subtly charts the slow economic and social decline inflicted on the black community after the formal, legal gains of the civil rights movement, as well as the resulting epistemic break between black generations. Youth that once settled disputes with fisticuffs now ice each other with guns. Brothers that would have held down steady jobs or gone to college now stand idle and junked-out on ghetto street corners. Yet, however ambitious their intentions, Allen and Albert Hughes have created a rambling, panoramic narrative that tries to cover and say too much—from the Bronx to Vietnam and back again. This is the film's minor weakness, but it is also the filmmakers' great strength, the fact that the Hughes brothers are willing to experiment with form, to push the material beyond normative boundaries of what would have routinely been edited down by the dominant film industry to an apolitical, adventure-caper flick.

To date, the most glaring example of Hollywood's cultural hegemony, and the way its system of discrimination intensifies according to the number of excluded categories one fits into, has to be the token to nonexistent participation of black women in mainstream filmmaking. If black male filmmakers have been marginalized, even with the "new black movie boom" producing, at most, a dozen or so new black male directors, then black women are, to employ the phrase of legal scholar Derrick Bell, the "faces at the bottom of the well."[16] Since Julie Dash's breakthrough with *Daughters of the Dust* (1991), only two black women, Leslie Harris and Darnell Martin, have each managed to make and release one mainstream theatrical feature film. This is not to say that many other black women have not made outstanding feature films, including the late Kathleen Collins's *Losing Ground* (1982), Ayoka Chinzera's *Alma's Rainbow* (1992), and Camille Billops's *KKK Botique Ain't Just Rednecks* (1993). A number of varied explanations—from black women's narratives being too "soft" and not conforming to Hollywood marketing formulas or genres, to black women not being able to "fit in" and negotiate in what is overwhelmingly a male business—have surfaced to account for the lack of black women's films in theatrical distribution.[17] As a result, the major share of black women's feature filmmaking has been declared "independent" and channeled into the relatively more obscure circuit of museums, universities, and film festivals.

Contesting the inertia and exclusionary games of the industry, then, Leslie Harris's gender-focused *Just Another Girl on the I.R.T.* (1993), takes an unsentimental look at the enormous difficulty of making one's way out of the lower-class/working-class projects, especially if one is black, female, and young. *Just Another Girl* opens with a precocious high school student, Chantel (Ariyan Johnson), telling the audience of her plans to skip her senior year and go directly to college and then medical school so that she can become a doctor. The painful irony of Chantel's words becomes clear as the film contrasts her ambitions with the limitations imposed by her cramped, impoverished environment. Things are further complicated when she hits one of life's speed bumps. In that accidental teenage manner that afflicts so many urban youth, she becomes pregnant and has to put her imagined future on hold.

Leslie Harris's directorial touch is subtly intelligent and noneditorial; it points out that talk is cheap, and it is always a struggle to make one's dreams tangible. Related to gender, it is interesting to note that *Just Another Girl* was released at the same time as *Menace II Society*, and that while both films focused on the same generational and locational politics, they performed very differently at the box office. *Menace*, which was made for New Line Cinema for $2.5 million, was released to more screens and better press coverage and went on to become a hit, grossing $30 million, while *Just Another Girl*, made for $500,000, did modestly well at the box office and went into the comparable obscurity of "film society" screenings and the shelf in the video store.[18] While it would be reductive to argue that these two differently financed, made, and positioned dramatic features should have performed at the same box-office level, it is worth noting that their gender and genre orientations had much to do with how they were marketed and consumed.

Darnell Martin's *I Like It Like That* (1994), mediating many of the same gender concerns as *Just Another Girl*, explores the rigors and complications of pursuing one's ambitions and dreams in spite of the barriers set so relentlessly against lower-class black/Latino women. Lisette (Lauren Velez) struggles to realize a business career in the record industry and feed her three children, while her rakish husband languishes in jail for petty theft. Besides depicting the usual hassles and limitations of the 'hood' environment, Martin's film brilliantly articulates the concept of *mestizaje* (cross-cultural hybridity and heterogeneity). Bringing to life a creative mix of tensions and dialogue that shifts between the tragic and comic, Lisette is biracial black, her husband is Latino, and her brother is a transvestite. At one hilarious point, Lisette's mother-in-law (Rita Moreno), who considers her family to be of "pure Castilian blood," sarcastically comments while dressing her grandchildren, "I don't know how to comb nappy hair." Martin's talent resides in her ability to handle a fast-paced, character-focused drama with moments of comedic punctuation. Her work was backed by Columbia Pictures with a $5.5 million budget, and the film had modest box-office success.[19] Wisely, both Leslie Harris and Darnell Martin have confronted one of the main problems contributing to the underdevelopment of black women filmmakers. Both have managed to sustain their momentum in the business by quickly moving on to their next projects, with Martin working on a horror movie about a mixed race family called *Listening to the Dead*, and Harris working on a feature about a black woman executive in the music industry called *Royalties, Rhythm and Blues*.

The issue of black women's film and filmmaking has been further highlighted, and complicated, by the release of the mega-hit screen adaptation of Terry McMillan's novel, *Waiting to Exhale* (1996). Although directed by a black man, Forest Whitaker, in many ways *Waiting to Exhale* fulfills the promise and aspirations set in motion by earlier films made about, or by black women, especially the mainstream *The Color Purple* (1985) and the independent *Daughters of the Dust*. Black women went to see *Waiting to Exhale*, en masse, held discussion groups and parties after shows, and sparked an ongoing dialog-debate in the media. *Waiting to Exhale*'s enthusiastic reception has evinced how, as black film critic Jacqueline Bobo argues in her work, black women are accustomed to "reading through the text" as in the case of *The Color Purple*, in order to extract their own resistant, countercurrent meanings.[20] Accordingly, because so few mainstream features are made from a woman's point of view, let alone a black woman's, over the years, tremendous, pent-up demand to see their subjectivities on the big screen has steadily built up among black women as a segmented audience. These issues, partly, account for the film's success among black women, and the film's crossing over to women in general.

Like many other successful, black feature films from Blaxploitation on, *Waiting to Exhale* became a major hit as much for its music, featuring women singers from Whitney Houston to Aretha Franklin and Patti LaBelle, as for its gendered subjectivity and the appeal of its stars, Whitney Houston, Angela Bassett, Wesley Snipes, and Gregory Hines. Consequently, *Waiting to Exhale*'s thematic, dramatic soundtrack has gone platinum as a CD. Add a phenomenal $45 million gross in the first seventeen days of exhibition on a production cost of a mere $15 million, and profits running at $70 million for an overall profit-to-cost ratio of 5-to-1 after twelve weeks, and one has every studio VIP's fantasy of a hit black film. There is, of course, another, more critical take on all of this. *Waiting to Exhale* is every studio mogul's dream because black films are held to an unequal standard compared to commercial films made by white male filmmakers. In 1997 the average cost of a mainstream white film was about $30 million, with the industry demanding a profit-to-cost ratio of 3-to-1. At the same time, the cost of a black feature was held well under $20 million, while executives used a much higher profit-to-cost ratio, 5-to-1, in order to consider a black film a success. When it comes to Hollywood economics, the system is markedly skewed. When one considers the meager capital that Hollywood puts into black films, it becomes clear that the bottom of white people's expectations forms the sky of black people's aspirations, as in so many other areas of American life.

Beyond those black men who were critical of what they perceived as their routine devaluation in yet another dominant cinema vehicle, *Waiting to Exhale*'s phenomenal success has sparked a lively critical debate. While many women writers have praised the film throughout the media, other women, black and white, have been insightfully critical. In an episodic, soap-opera narrative style that carries considerable gender appeal, *Waiting to Exhale* follows the romantic misadventures, entanglements, and triumphs of four successfully career-oriented, middle-class black "girl-friends." The film celebrates the idea that black women can find true love and "exhale." These women, as well, form deep, insightful relationships among themselves without the domination and validation of men. Critic Karen DeWitt rightly observes in a *New York Times* article that *Waiting to Exhale* has tapped into the tremendous pent-up demand of black women for their equitable representation in cinema, and that the film's instincts about black women's issues and lives have been more than confirmed by the fervent way it has been consumed by them. DeWitt, along with studio executives, notes that black women found the film a realistic portrayal of their concerns as well as entertaining. But curiously, she goes on to say that the film "has nothing to do with racism, interactions with whites, or ghetto life," and that while black men have their Million Man March, *Waiting to Exhale* "becomes the female equivalent."[21]

Immediately after DeWitt's survey of the positive social impacts of *Waiting to Exhale*, black writer and social critic bell hooks responded in a *New York Times* op-ed piece wryly titled "Save Your Breath, Sisters." In her essay, hooks notes that the film is practically empty of any feminist consciousness or politics. Moreover, hooks comments on Hollywood's co-optative strategies, saying that "no doubt it helps crossover appeal to set up a stereotypically racist and sexist conflict between white women and black women competing to see who will win the man in the end." As for the comparison of *Waiting to Exhale* to the Million Man March, hooks perceptively cautions black women that "we are being told and we are telling ourselves that black men need political action and black women need a movie."[22] While the desire of black women to see themselves honestly depicted on the big screen is palpable and valid, one must always remember that, here, the situation is intensely ironic. For Hollywood, through its relentless discrimination against black women, has created this "desire" in the first place.

Co-optation is Hollywood's strongest suit. So once again, as was done with *Lady Sings the Blues* (1972) and *Mahogany* (1972), the film industry has colonized the very desire that it is responsible for inflicting on black women, and then it has sold it back to them as packaged "entertainment." In her *Sight and Sound* review, critic Amanda Lipman puts it most eloquently, saying that *Waiting to Exhale* "raises difficult, thorny issues, then strangles them with the velvet glove of liberalism."[23] The true and direct expression of black women's subjectivities in commercial cinema is going to have to emerge out of the political consciousness and filmmaking of, first, black women, but also black people as a collectivity, beyond the ideological filters and games of Hollywood's co-optative liberalism. Put simply, the real promise of black women's filmmaking resides in the work and imaginations of black women directors themselves, perhaps always working against the grain of Hollywood.

Another interesting development now under way in popular black cinema has to do with the subtle genre shift away from the hood action flick and toward an emerging black-made, or black-focused, film noir genre. Certainly African Americans have been well-acquainted with the noir world since their arrival in America. W. E. B. Du Bois's notion of "double consciousness," literally having to think and see "double," within the constraints of an oppressive, racist system, that is, having to read the official version as well as its corrupt underside, has been a primary black survival tool as well as a motive force in much of black cultural production. If the classic style of film noir depicts the decaying urban world of crime and violence fed by corrupt, indifferent social institutions, then, from the resistance and protest of the slave narratives, through the crime fiction of Richard Wright, Chester Himes, and Donald Goines, or the ghetto action of Blaxploitation, or the gangsta poetics of Snoop Doggy Dogg and Coolio, black people have honed and perfected a wicked, penetrating vision of America's noir world that can only be described as the funkier side of noir.

The principal difference between the noir world of dominant cinema and the funky noir world of African Americans resides in the difference between the perception of crime as the act of a deviant individual and crime as survival, as the informal resistance of a subject people against a racially unjust system. When a white person turns to crime, he or she turns against a system that is designed to defend and support dominant white society. Conversely, while black people are fully aware that they are disproportionately the victims of crime and want criminals held accountable for their acts, most blacks, including those leading "the life" as they call the funky noir experience, also view crime more in a socioeconomic context.[24] They feel that they have been trapped by a racist system that was set against them from the beginning. "I know it's rough, but it's the only game the Man left us to play," as Eddie tells Priest in *Superfly* (1972). In the noir world, whites feel that they have failed the system, while, conversely, blacks feel that the system has failed them.[25] This sense of funky noir accounts for an implicit yearning for racial justice in many films or the ambivalent endings that negate or expose the hypocrisy of the system. It is not surprising, then, that one can see the persistent developing momentum of this funky noir genre over a long trajectory of black films from *Shaft* (1971) and *Superfly* on through *A Rage in Harlem* (1991), *Deep Cover* and *One False Move* (both 1992), *Menace II Society* (1993), to *Devil in a Blue Dress*, *New Jeresy Drive*, and *Clockers* (all 1995).

The case of *Devil in a Blue Dress* proves instructive in exploring the funky noir style and, more importantly, in demonstrating how the success of a black film is always, in some way, defined and overdetermined by the social construction and contestation of *race*. Directed by Carl Franklin and adapted by him from Walter Mosley's successful novel, *Devil in a Blue Dress* follows the adventures of part-time detective Easy Rawlins (Denzel Washington) as he tracks the whereabouts of mystery lady Daphnie Monet (Jennifer Beals), who is known to occasionally stray from the white world in search of the forbidden pleasures of soul food, jazz, and "dark meat." The funkier side of noir reveals itself in *Devil in a Blue Dress*'s subtle cultural details and gestures, its racial ironies, its character sketches and impressions, as Rawlins follows Monet through the soul food cafés, juke joints, and smoky bars of L.A.'s black world, circa 1948.

Marking a funky noir detail, instead of the cheap suit favored by the typical film noir detective, Rawlins wears casual clothes that suggest his predicament as a laid-off aircraft worker. Just as the cheap suit marks the social distance between the white private eye and his wealthy clientele, Rawlins's attire, slacks with an undershirt, signify his black, working-class status and his powerlessness relative to the forces he is up against. With mortgage payments due on his modest house, Rawlins is an ordinary brother trying to unravel a mystery while being acutely aware that he is meddling in the corrupt business of powerful, contending white forces: the city government's ruling elite, the police department, and organized crime. Denzel Washington's characterization shows that he understands the psychology and appeal of Easy Rawlins, a black man painfully squeezed by every conceivable power relation and economic circumstance of a racially unjust society. He plays Rawlins with social vulnerability and caution mixed with an underlying toughness that gradually builds into a cunning, assertive rage against injustice. "They thought I was some kinda new fool . . . and I guess I was," Rawlins says, recognizing the doubleness and danger of his situation.

The principal, tangled mystery of *Devil in a Blue Dress* is caught up in a nagging question: how could a film based on a hit novel, directed by an outstanding filmmaker, a film generally praised by critics and featuring the star power of Denzel Washington, be such a flop with the mass audience? The answer to the mystery of *Devil* at the box office alludes to the answer to the central mystery of the film's narrative. The key to both mysteries is found in the multiple expressions of that enduring social construct, the great American obsession and catastrophe: *race*. The persistent irony driving all of Mosley's novels, and certainly Franklin's film, has to do with the many ways that Easy Rawlins's double consciousness as a black man empowers him as an occasional private eye. The fact that he is on this case at all is because he is black and can move and detect things in those circles and in that world forever closed to whites. The ultimate joke of *Devil* is that double consciousness facilitates double vision. Rawlins can see deeply into both black and white worlds and find out what powerful whites want to know, but also what they do not want to know, or at least what they want to deny or hide.

As the plot evolves, we find out that the elusive Daphnie Monet is engaged to one of L.A.'s leading mayoral candidates, Todd Carter (Terry Kinney). In an attempt to protect herself in a counter-blackmail scheme, Daphnie disappears into the black world where Rawlins finds her. Then, in a spectacular gunfight, he rescues her from the gangsters who originally retained him. At this point the mystery of the *Devil in a Blue Dress* is revealed: Daphnie is not white at all, but rather a "tragic mulatto" passing for white. Miscegenation being the potent, socially charged act that it was in 1948 (and still is), Daphnie's upcoming marriage into one of the city's elite families definitely can never happen. In a final act of double consciousness, confirming his true powers as a black private eye, Rawlins functions as go-between, negotiating the breakup of the miscegenational liaison. For his trouble, Rawlins receives a generous settlement for all concerned, as the rich white man, Carter, retreats back across the color line into his world. All is happily resolved as noir becomes a bright L.A. morning, the foreboding ghetto turning into the African American community.

As for that other mystery, *Devil in a Blue Dress*, like *Strange Days*, had the misfortune to be released at the time of the O. J. Simpson verdict. And that, in my opinion, was the kiss of death at the box office: guilt by association. The film clearly did not cross over. Racial divisions and tensions were running high, and angry, post-verdict whites were in no mood for a tour of L.A.'s black world, 1948, 1999, or otherwise. But *Devil* also failed to attract the youth audience, black or white, and this group accounts for much of the black film market. While black cinema's audience is restless for new experimentation, genres, and narratives, and the 'hood-homebody-action flick is brain-dead, filmgoing youth did not make the leap to consuming this excellent cinematic translation of a brilliant novel. This lack of response has much to do with contemporary youth's focus on electronic rather than print culture. But the film's disappointing box office also relates to the difference in social visions between now and the time of the film, 1948, between an inherent contemporary pessimism, as opposed to the basic optimism of post-World War II America. *Devil* ends on exactly the right historical note, but a note perhaps strange to the contemporary audience. Easy Rawlins, the homeowner, walks down the sunny, modest street of his friendly community, as superficial order—and separation between the races—for the moment, at least, is restored.

Our discussion concludes at an interesting social moment that exemplifies so many of the issues and problems related to the way in which the film industry deals with the sign of *blackness:* the annual Academy Award ceremonies. While the 1996 event was produced by Quincy Jones, hosted by Whoopi Goldberg, and featured walk-ons by a number of black celebrities, it was protested from the sidewalk outside the auditorium by Jesse Jackson and roundly denounced in *People* for its complete "blackout" of African American nominations to its award categories. Beyond the pertinent issue of why black people should even seek validation from such a racially corrupt institution, or the utter banality of the year's event (with a film about a pig contending for best picture), we should note the disparity between appearance and reality. For Hollywood is always the circus of dreams and lies as it exploits the image of *blackness*, while relentlessly keeping African Americans and other people of color marginalized and locked out of its mode of production and executive process, and therefore out of the largest share of its power and profits. In other words, the reality of Hollywood's racism resides in the disparity between Quincy, Whoopi, et al. as images on the stage, and the dismal figures for black participation in the film industry's guilds and unions, figures that have not changed since the late 1960s.[26]

On a final, cautiously optimistic note, I will speculate that there is still room for expansion in the shaky, but ongoing, black film wave. The display of Eddie Murphy's talents in his comeback hit, *The Nutty Professor* (1996), or the release of the prolific Spike Lee's *Girl 6* (1996) are relevant here. And certainly there have always been a few courageous innovations in the way that Hollywood reads *race*, like Robert De Niro's excellent *A Bronx Tale* (1993) or the Harry Belafonte and John Travolta acting collaboration, *White Man's Burden* (1995). But cause for whatever limited hope there is pales against the cultural apartheid expressed in Hollywood's images, films, and genres, or the racist and sexist employment practices structuring all levels of the industry. Rather, because the moviegoing audience is a perpetually shifting social formation that is increasing in its heterogeneity, and a fair number of "blockbuster" investments regularly fail, and because black people overconsume film in proportion to their numbers, the industry has committed itself to making a steady quantity of small-to-medium-budget black features as insurance against white, big picture flops.[27] Beyond the great industry motivator of greed for ever larger profit margins that, for now at least, will keep open a narrow window of opportunity allowing low-to-mid budget black films to survive and, hopefully, gain an increasing portion of the diversifying consumer audience, one must always keep in mind, when considering whether or not Hollywood can change, that the industry's racial attitudes cannot be separated from the broader social context of America's racial condition. In a way, then, it all comes back to the resistance practices and oppositional currents of black filmmakers, critics, and the potential for an evolving social consciousness of the audience. For if Hollywood can never free itself from, or change, the dictates and images of American racial protocol, then black filmmaking, in all of its many aspects is destined to struggle against, represent, and mediate the fundamental condition of black people in America.

Notes

1   Pam Lambert, "Hollywood Blackout," *People*, March 18, 1996, pp. 42–52.
2   Kevin Hagopian. "Black Cinema Studies: Shadows and Acts," *Journal of Communication* 45 (Summer 1995): 177–85. Some of the influential new authors and works mapping the emergent area of black cinema are James Snead, *White Screens, Black Images*; Ed Guerrero, *Framing Blackness*; Manthia Diawara, ed., *Black American Cinema*; Mark Reid, *Redefining Black Film*; Jesse Rhines, *Black Film, White Money*; Nelson George, *Blackface*; Thomas Cripps, *Making Movies Black*; and Ella Shohat and Robert Stam, *Unthinking Eurocentrism*.
3   Don Terry, "Woman's False Charge Revives Hurt for Blacks," *New York Times*, November 6, 1994, pp. 12, 32; Kevin A. Ross and Bruce Levitt, "Drowning Case Embitters U.S. Race Relations," *New York Times*, November 11, 1994, pp. A18, A30.
4   Tom Wicker, *Tragic Failure: Racial Integration in America* (New York: William Morrow, 1996); Derrick Bell, *Gospel Choirs: Psalms of Survival for an Alien Land Called Home* (New York: Basic Books, 1996); Earl Ofari Hutchinson, *Beyond O.J.* (Los Angeles: Middle Passage Press, 1996).
5   Dennis Greene, "Tragically Hip," *Cineaste* 20 (October 1994): 28–29.
6   Guerrero, *Framing Blackness: The African American Image in Film* (Philadelphia: Temple University Press, 1993), pp. 113–17.
7   Ed Guerrero, "The Black Image in Protective Custody: Hollywood's Biracial Buddy Films of the Eighties," in *Black American Cinema*, ed. Manthia Diawara (New York: Routledge, 1993), pp. 237–46.
8   Ellen Holly, "Waiting for a Black Heathcliff," *New York Times*, March 26, 1996, p. A19. Holly makes the insightful observation that Hollywood puts most black male actors' careers on hold, deploying them as character actors until they are safely past their youth and prime. Consequently, black men cannot become the high-voltage sexualized movie stars that white men can.
9   Shohat and Stam, chap. 4, "Tropes of Empire," *Unthinking Eurocentrism: Multiculturalism and the Media* (New York: Routledge, 1994); Richard Dyer, *Heavenly Bodies: Film Stars and Society* (New York: St. Martin's Press, 1986), pp. 67–139.
10 Shohat and Stam, *Unthinking Eurocentrism*, pp. 223–30; Snead, *White Screens/Black Images* (New York: Routledge, 1994), pp. 6–7.
11 It is relevant to note here that the voices of the two lead toys were provided by white comedy stars Tom Hanks and Tim Allen, in contrast to the distinctly *black voice* of Levi Stubbs in *Little Shop of Horrors* (1986). See Guerrero, *Framing Blackness*, pp. 56, 118.
12 John Leland, "Rap and Race," *Newsweek*, June 29, 1992, p. 48.
13 Bernard Weinraub, "Black Film Makers Are Looking Beyond Ghetto Violence," *New York Times*, September 11, 1995, pp. C11, C14; Guerrero, chap. 3. "The Rise and Fall of Blaxploitation," in *Framing Blackness*.
14 Douglas Kellner and Michael Ryan, *Camera Politica* (Bloomington. Indiana University Press, 1990), p. 169; Michael Paul Rogin, *Ronald Reagan, the Movie, and Other Episodes in Political Demonology* (Berkeley: University of California Press, 1987), p. 237.
15 "*Panther:* An Interview with Mario Van Peebles," *Tikkun* 10, (July–August 1995): 20–24, 78.
16 Derrick Bell, *Faces at the Bottom of the Well* (New York: Basic Books, 1992).
17 Rhines, *Black Film, White Money* (New Brunswick, N.J.: Rutgers University Press, 1996), pp. 125–42.
18 Amy Taubin, "Girl in the Hood," *Sight and Sound*, August 1993, pp. 16–17.
19 Jan Hoffman, "Mom Always Said, Don't Take the First $2 Million Offer," *New York Times*, October 9, 1994, p. 28H.

20   Jacqueline Bobo, *Black Women as Cultural Readers* (New York: Columbia University Press, 1995).

21   Karen DeWitt, "For Black Women a Movie Stirs Breathless Excitement," *New York Times*, December 31, 1995, pp. 1, 25.

22   bell hooks, "Save Your Breath, Sisters," *New York Times*, January 7, 1996, p. E19.

23   Amanda Lipman, *"Waiting to Exhale," Sight and Sound*, February 1996, p. 56.

24   Andrew Hacker, chap. 11, "Crime: The Role Race Plays," in *Two Nations: Black and White, Separate, Hostile, Unequal* (New York: Charles Scribner's Sons, 1992); Wicker, chap. 9, "Throwing Away the Key," *Tragic Failure*.

25   Manthia Diawara, "Noir by Noirs: Toward a New Realism in Black Cinema," *African American Review*, Winter 1993, pp. 525–38. Also see H. Bruce Franklin, *Prison Literature in America: The Victim as Criminal and Artist* (New York: Oxford University Press, 1989), p. xv.

26   In one instance black representation has actually declined since the late 1960s when black membership in Hollywood's craft unions stood at barely 6 percent. Today, Local 44, which includes set decorators and property masters, has less than 2 percent black membership. Compare the numbers in Dan Knapp, "An Assessment of the Status of Hollywood Blacks," *Los Angeles Times*, September 28, 1969; "Black Craftsmen's Talents Untapped on Entertainment Scene," *Los Angeles Times*, October 5, 1969; Pam Lambert, "Hollywood Blackout," *People*, March 18, 1996, pp. 42–52.

27   Rhines, *Black Film, White Money*, p. 216; Bernard Weinraub, "Dismay Over Big-Budget Flops," *New York Times*, October 17, 1995, pp. C13, C18.

Chapter 22

G. Escamilla, A. L. Cradock and I. Kawachi

WOMEN AND SMOKING IN HOLLYWOOD MOVIES: A CONTENT ANALYSIS (2000)

ACCORDING TO THE CENTERS FOR DISEASE Control and Prevention, over one third (34.7%) of female high school students in a national survey reported smoking at least 1 cigarette in the previous month, up 10% since 1993 and 32% since 1991.[1] Cigarette smoking is initiated primarily in adolescence. Among adult regular smokers, 71% reported having formed the habit before the age of 18 years.[2]

Television and popular films have contributed to the allure of smoking. A recent study found that young adults smoked in about 75% of music videos.[3] Although tobacco industry documents suggest that manufacturers have not engaged in deliberate product placement in Hollywood movies since the late 1980s,[4] recent evidence indicates that smoking continues to be depicted at very high levels. Moreover, the gap between the prevalence of tobacco use in movies and in actual life has steadily widened through the 1990s.[5] A recent analysis of G-rated children's animated films found that more than two thirds featured tobacco or alcohol use in story plots, with no clear reference made to the adverse health consequences associated with these substances.[6]

Popular film actresses are likely to be role models for young women and adolescent girls. The way that movie stars portray cigarette smoking on the screen may influence young girls' attitudes toward the habit. In this study, we analyzed the portrayal of smoking by 10 leading Hollywood actresses.

METHODS

Selection of actresses

We selected 10 leading Hollywood actresses by surveying the 1997 issues of 5 popular magazines that had the highest readership among women aged 18 to 24 years, according to *Simmons Study of Media and Markets*.[7] Magazine titles from the "Special Interest" and "Women's Magazines" categories were selected if the editorial descriptions taken from *Bacon's Magazine Directory*[8] included 1 or more of the following key words or phrases: entertainment, contemporary or current, Hollywood, celebrity, film or movie, personality profiles, women in their 20s, or young women. All issues for the period January 1997 through December 1997 were obtained for the magazines *Cosmopolitan, Glamour, Vogue, Vanity Fair,* and *Rolling Stone.* Each issue was analyzed for the appearance of female film stars. Advertisements were excluded, and the search was limited to women whose careers are primarily in film. The number of magazine appearances was tallied for each actress, and the 10 actresses with the greatest number of appearances were selected.

Selection of films

A list of films starring each selected actress was generated from the Web site www.tvguide.com. This Web site, maintained by TV Guide Entertainment Network, provides information on the cast, credits, and reviews for some 35 000 movies. Five titles released between 1993 and 1997 were randomly selected for each of the 10 actresses. We excluded period dramas as well as movies in which the actresses did not play a lead or major supporting role. The title, year of release, rating (R, NC-17, PG, PG-13, G), and genre of each film were recorded.

Content analysis

We followed the analytic approach described by Hazan et al.[9] Each film was divided into 5-minute intervals. The occurrence of smoking episodes in each interval was recorded on a coding sheet. We recorded both actual and implied smoking behavior (e.g., holding or smoking a lit or unlit tobacco product); the presence of cigarettes or other smoking paraphernalia (e.g., cigars, matches, and ashtrays); and environmental messages, including "no smoking" signs, tobacco advertising, and tobacco merchandise. Additionally, we recorded smoker characteristics (e.g., gender; whether lead, supporting, or other character); location (i.e., outdoors or in a bar, restaurant, home, or car); the social context of the event (i.e., smoking alone or with others and whether consideration was shown to nonsmokers). We also noted verbal and nonverbal tobacco messages (i.e., positive or negative consequences of smoking behavior and discussion about tobacco products, including positive, negative, or mixed reference to tobacco use). To establish interrater reliability, 5 films (10% of total sample) were randomly selected and independently rated by graduate student coders (G. Escamilla and A. L. Cradock). The coders had 99% agreement on all of the parameters examined regarding the depiction of smoking.

After viewing each film, the coders also completed a qualitative assessment of smoking themes and behaviors, addressing contextual issues such as the emotional valence attached to the smoking behavior and the significance of smoking for the character portrayed. All statistical analyses were performed with Stata.[10]

RESULTS

The 50 films, representing approximately 96 hours of footage, were broken down into 1116 5-minute intervals (excluding introductions and credits). Of these, 317 (28.4%) of the intervals depicted smoking behavior (Table 22.1). Cigarettes were the most common tobacco product shown (23.9%). Over half of the smoking episodes (58.7%) occurred in the presence of others who were not smoking.

Table 22.1 Depiction of smoking behavior and paraphernalia, smoking context, and location of smoking behaviors in 50 Hollywood movies

	No. of 5-Min Intervals	Total 5-Min Movie Intervals, % (n = 1116)	Intervals Containing Smoking Behavior, % (n = 317)
Smoking behavior and paraphernalia			
Smoking (actual or implied) behavior	317	28.4	. . .
Cigarettes	267	23.9	. . .
Cigarette packs	64	5.7	. . .
Matches/lighter	108	9.7	. . .
Cigars, pipes, or smokeless tobacco	71	6.4	. . .
Ashtray	105	9.4	. . .
Social context of smoking behavior[a]			
Alone	46	. . .	14.5
With others (nonsmokers)	186	. . .	58.7
With others, including smokers and nonsmokers	71	. . .	22.4
Consideration shown to nonsmokers	5	. . .	1.6
Location of smoking behavior[b]			
Bar/lounge	25	. . .	7.9
Home/apartment	84	. . .	26.5
Restaurant	28	. . .	8.8
Car	40	. . .	12.6
Outside	103	. . .	32.5
Other location	69	. . .	21.8

a A total of 4.4% of intervals depicted incidental smoking by characters other than the lead/supporting actors.

b Percentages total more than 100 as smoking may have occurred in more than one context in the same interval.

As Table 22.2 indicates, smoking was significantly more likely to be depicted in R-rated or unrated films than in PG/PG-13-rated films ($P < .001$). Although the percentage of lead actors or supporting actors shown smoking was similar for men and women (38% and 42%, respectively), sex differences were apparent according to the film's rating. Males in lead or supporting roles were 2.5 times more likely to be shown smoking in R-rated/unrated movies than in PG/PG-13-rated films ($P < .001$). By contrast, the portrayal of smoking by a

Table 22.2 Odds ratios (ORs) and 95% confidence intervals (95% CIs) for the occurrence of smoking behavior in R-rated/unrated movies

	OR[a]	95% CI
Overall smoking behavior	1.62	1.20–2.14
Smoking by male lead or supporting actor	2.48	1.55–3.97
Smoking by female lead or supporting actor	1.23	0.88–1.86

a Referent is PG/PG-13 movies.

female lead or supporting character was not significantly different according to the movie's rating; that is, female actresses were *equally likely* to light up in movies aimed at juvenile audiences as in those aimed at mature audiences.

Smoking was also more likely to be depicted in the movies starring younger actresses. The mean age of the 10 actresses was 29.3 years (range=21–40 years). When we categorized actresses according to quartiles by age, movies starring actresses in the youngest quartile featured 3.6 times as many intervals depicting smoking as did movies starring actresses in the oldest age group (95% confidence interval [95% CI] = 2.4, 5.4).

Negative messages regarding tobacco product use (e.g., depictions of the consequences of the use of tobacco products, such as coughing or grimacing at the smell of smoke) were more common than positive messages (30 vs 23) among the 50 films viewed. However, only 9 of 22 messages in PG/PG-13 films depicted smoking in a negative light, compared with 21 of 31 messages in R-rated/unrated films; that is, movies aimed at young audiences were *less* likely (odds ratio = 0.33; 95% CI = 0.11, 1.01) to carry negative messages associated with tobacco use than were movies made for mature audiences.

In a qualitative analysis of the social context of smoking, sex differences were detected in the themes associated with tobacco use. Women were likely to be portrayed using tobacco products to control their emotions, to manifest power and sex appeal, to enhance their body image or self-image, to control weight, or to give themselves a sense of comfort and companionship. Men were more likely to be depicted using tobacco products to reinforce their masculine identity; to portray a character with power, prestige, or significant authority; to show male bonding; or to signify their status as a "protector" (the last 3 themes were associated with cigar smoking).

DISCUSSION

The results of this study raise concerns about exposure to smoking in popular movies. According to social learning theory, by paying attention to the behaviors of a person who possesses the qualities, skills, and capacities one hopes to achieve, a young observer learns to model these behaviors.[11] Among third- through sixth-grade students who had smoked, having role models who smoked was more common, and having beliefs about the adverse consequences of smoking was less common, than among their peers who never smoked.[12]

The prevalence of smoking by both female (42%) and male (38%) lead or supporting actors was substantially higher than the national smoking prevalence for females (24.3%) and males (29.2%) aged 18 to 44.[13] This discrepancy is significant, given that adolescents who overestimate smoking prevalence among young people and adults are more likely to become smokers themselves. In the films viewed, over half of the smoking episodes occurred in the presence of others who were not smoking, and in fewer than 2% of the intervals was consideration shown to nonsmokers (e.g., smoker leaves the room or asks permission to smoke). The depiction of smoking in Hollywood would thus appear to reinforce smoking as an acceptable and normative behavior in society. While most young people older than 18 years are able to acknowledge that on-screen smoking is part of a movie role, this may be more difficult for younger females aged 12 to 17 years, among whom smoking initiation is taking place.

Our qualitative analysis of smoking identified several themes related to smoking. One of the most prominent themes was using smoking to control emotion, which was specific to female characters and occurred during times of stress or difficulty, when the character was trying to regain or establish control, to repress or deny emotion, or to exit a negative or threatening situation.

Important limitations of this study should be noted. First, the sampling of magazine titles was limited to those with the highest readership among women aged 18 to 24 years. On the other hand, given the content and focus of the magazines, it is highly likely that they are widely read by adolescent girls. Surveying the issues of only 5 magazines may have biased our sample of actresses. However, a recent study on the influence of movie stars on adolescent smoking identified 6 of the 10 actresses in our sample as being the "most favorite" among girls.[14] Given that African American and Latina women have become targets for tobacco advertisements, it would also be informative to survey movies starring actresses of different racial/ethnic backgrounds. Future studies need to be extended to popular male actors as well. Finally, replication of our findings through the use of raters who are unaware of the hypotheses would be desirable, since the smoking-related themes emerging from our qualitative analyses may have been biased.

Our findings, in conjunction with those of others,[14] suggest the need for the development of policies—such as the adoption of a voluntary code of ethics by the entertainment industry—to eliminate the depiction of smoking in ways that appeal to adolescent audiences.

References

1. Centers for Disease Control and Prevention. Tobacco use among high school students—United States, 1997. *MMWR Morb Mortal Wkly Rep*. 1998;47:229–233.
2. *Preventing Tobacco Use Among Young People: A Report of the Surgeon General*. Atlanta, Ga: National Center for Chronic Disease Prevention and Health Promotion, Office on Smoking and Health; 1994.
3. DuRant RH, Rome ES, Rich M, Allred E, Emans SJ, Woods ER. Tobacco and alcohol use behaviors portrayed in music videos: a content analysis. *Am J Public Health*. 1997;87:1131–1135.
4. http://www.philipmorris.com/getallimg.asp. DOC_ID = 2025863645/3659. Accessed July 1998.
5. Stockwell TF, Glantz SA. Tobacco use is increasing in popular films. *Tob Control*. 1997;6: 282–284.
6. Goldstein AO, Sobel RA, Newman GR. Tobacco and alcohol use in G-rated children's animated films. *JAMA*. 1999;281:1131–1136.
7. Simmons Market Research Bureau. *Simmons Study of Media and Markets, M1*. New York, NY: Simmons Market Research Bureau; 1994: 0162–0163.
8. *Bacon's Magazine Directory: Directory of Magazines and Newsletters*. Chicago, Ill: Bacon's Information Inc; 1988.
9. Hazan AR, Lipton HL, Glantz S. Popular films do not reflect current tobacco use. *Am J Public Health*. 1994;84:998–1000.
10. *Stata Statistical Software: Release 5.0*. College Station, Tex: Stata Corporation; 1997.
11. Greaves L. *Mixed Messages: Women, Tobacco and the Media*. Ottawa, Ontario: Health Canada; 1996.
12. Greenlund KJ, Johnson CC, Webber LS, Berenson GS. Cigarette smoking attitudes and first use among third- through sixth-grade students: the Bogalusa Heart Study. *Am J Public Health*. 1997;87:1345–1348.
13. Centers for Disease Control and Prevention. Cigarette smoking among adults—United States, 1995. *MMWR Morb Mortal Wkly Rep*. 1997;46:1217–1220.
14. Distefan JM, Gilpin EA, Sargent JD, Pierce JP. Do movie stars encourage adolescents to start smoking? Evidence from California. *Prev Med*. 1999;28:1–11.

Chapter 23

Tania Modleski

A ROSE IS A ROSE? REAL WOMEN AND A LOST WAR (1998)

IF THERE EVER WAS A PURELY MASCULINE genre, it is surely the war film.[1] That women in the genre represent a threat to the male warrior is revealed in a timeworn convention: a soldier who displays a photograph of his girlfriend, wife, or family is doomed to die by the end of the film. The convention is so well-known that it is parodied in *Hot Shots* (1991), a spoof of the very popular film *Top Gun* (1986). Playing off the nicknaming of fighter pilots, one of the early scenes in *Hot Shots* shows the hero's sidekick slamming a locker door on which is taped a family photo. He then introduces himself to the hero as "Dead Meat."

Feminist critics of the war film, most notably Susan Jeffords, have convincingly argued that the genre is not only *for* men but plays a crucial role in the masculinizing process so necessary to the creation of warriors. Through spectacle (bombs bursting in air) and sound (usually heavy rock), pro-war fantasies like *Top Gun* mobilize the kind of aggression essential to the functioning of men as killing machines. So, too, often enough, do antiwar films. Indeed, it is frequently noted that films like *Platoon* (1986) not only do not effectively protest war but actually participate in and extend it, to the point where the spectator him- or herself becomes the target of the warrior-filmmaker's assault. As Gilbert Adair, in a thoughtful critique of *Platoon*, puts it: "It is surely time that film-makers learned that the meticulously detailed aping of an atrocity *is* an atrocity; that the hyper-realistic depiction of an obscenity cannot avoid being contaminated with that obscenity; and that the unmediated representation of violence constitutes in itself an act of violence against the spectator."[2] Moreover, just as it is the goal of war to crush opposing viewpoints and violently secure the opposing side's assent to the conquerer's truth, films like *Platoon* "bully" us into "craven submission," as Adair puts it, by pointing "an accusatory finger" and asking, " 'How do you know what it was like unless you've been there?' " (p. 169).[3] Such questions are often literally addressed to women in the Vietnam films: "Who the hell are you to judge him?" the uncle, a vet (Bruce Willis), rebukes his niece (Emily Lloyd) in Norman Jewison's *In Country* (1989) when she expresses dismay at the racist remarks she finds in the diary that her father kept before being killed in the war. Thus, since "being there" has so far been out of the question for women (who are prohibited from combat), their authority on any issue related to war is discredited from the outset, and insofar as they may be inclined to question or oppose war (except in and on the terms granted them by men), they find themselves consigned to the ranks of the always-already defeated.[4]

Given the extent to which war has been an exclusive masculine preserve, it is not surprising to find the critics themselves desiring generic purity, expressing discomfort when bits of "feminine discourse"—for example, melodrama and the love story—are used for non-ironic purposes, thereby "contaminating" the war film. One of the earliest films about the Vietnam War, *Coming Home* (1978), which David James condemns because it "rewrite[s] the invasion of Vietnam as erotic melodrama," is a case in point.[5] While commentators like John Hellman have found much to praise in other films' rewriting of the invasion in terms of *male* genres—the western (*The Deerhunter*, 1978) and the detective genre (*Apocalypse Now*, 1979)—*Coming Home*'s incorporation of female genres provokes derision.[6] Of course, *Coming Home* is not really about the "invasion" of Vietnam but about its aftermath, and thus it is situated in a tradition of films about veterans' adjustment to civilian life. Nevertheless, critics have faulted it for not focusing more on "the problems of returning veterans than on the clichéd love story."

Coming Home is about a disabled veteran, Luke (Jon Voigt), returning to civilian life and meeting a woman named Sally (Jane Fonda) who is married to a Marine serving in Vietnam and whose consciousness about the war is raised when she serves as a volunteer in a VA hospital. This consciousness receives a gigantic boost when Sally makes love with Luke, who brings her to climax orally, giving her her first orgasm. Critics have struggled to understand this scene in symbolic terms. Jason Katzman writes, "[*Coming Home*] uses the love story as a metaphor for the impotence of an entire country in understanding Vietnam. . . . Sally's ability to reach an orgasm with Luke where she could never before with her husband Bob (Bruce Dern), is one of the more widely discussed symbols."[7]

It is not clear to me what exactly the woman's orgasm is a symbol *of*; but it is clear that the event was less satisfying to some male critics than it was to *her*. Albert Auster and Leonard Quart express uneasiness about this plot element, but they do not really specify the source of their discomfort. "Unfortunately," they write, "Sally's transformation seems unconvincing and mechanical, especially in the emphasis it places on her achieving orgasm . . . while making love to Luke."[8]

Suppose, however, we take the orgasm to be an end in itself, rather than a symbol or a metaphor for something else. Suppose, in fact, that one of the problems with Vietnam War films in particular is their relentless exploitation of experiences and events for the sole significance that they have to the soldiers who fought rather than to the men's loved ones, allies, or enemies. I suspect that the critics' discomfort stems from the vividness with which the film demonstrates the point that men's losses may be a gain for women. Kaja Silverman has identified a similar theme in *The Best Years of Our Lives*, William Wyler's 1946 film about men returning from World War II and attempting to adjust to civilian life. Silverman heralds the film as a kind of feminist milestone in the history of what she calls "libidinal politics," since at this moment of "historical trauma," in which men came back from war mutilated both psychically and physically, non-phallic forms of male sexuality presumably emerged.[9]

One might argue that from the point of view of women on the home-front, *Coming Home* is even more important in this regard. Unlike *The Best Years of Our Lives*, in which the women must find satisfaction in an eroticized maternal relation to their men, *Coming Home*, based on a story by a woman, Nancy Dowd, was made at a time when feminists were vociferously proclaiming the myth of the vaginal orgasm and agitating for the requisite attention to be paid to the clitoris. Women were hardly passive beneficiaries of the historical vicissitudes of male sexuality (and male warmongering) but were actively demanding and sometimes winning their sexual rights. However attenuated the film's politics are in other respects (and these politics are indeed feeble in some regards),[10] it is important not to overlook the film's significant place in the ongoing struggles over sexual politics.

To see how far women have been forced to retreat from this position of sexual advantage, we need only briefly compare *Coming Home* to a film on the same subject made a dozen years later. In Oliver Stone's *Born on the Fourth of July* (1989), a fictionalized version of the story of Ron Kovic, a war hero, who is obsessed about his dysfunctional penis; the Kovic character reaches a low point when he goes to Mexico and spends days and nights whoring, gambling, and boozing with other disabled veterans. Going to bed with a whore, Kovic appears to bring her to climax through manual stimulation; but in contrast to *Coming Home*, which focuses on the woman's tears of joy and passion, in this film we see *the man* crying out of self-pity for his lost potency. (*In Country* also contains a scene in which a vet is impotent with the young heroine, who is kind and understanding. Nowhere is there a hint that his hard-on might not be the sine qua non of *her* sexual pleasure, for the question of her sexual pleasure is not even on the horizon.) In a brief subsequent scene in *Born on the Fourth of July*, the camera assumes the hero's point of view as he wheels himself around a whorehouse in which various Mexican women beckon him with lewd remarks. Racism and misogyny combine in a scene meant to demonstrate the depths of degradation to which the hero has sunk. Here we see an example of the commonplace phenomenon in Vietnam films in which exploited people (in this instance, the prostitutes) are further exploited by the films themselves for the symbolic value that they hold for the hero. Thus do the films perpetuate the social and cultural insensitivity that led to America's involvement in the war and the atrocities committed there.

The film *Casualties of War* (1989) presents an even more extreme example of this phenomenon. In this film, as Pat Aufderheide argues, the rape and murder of a Vietnamese peasant girl by American soldiers signify "the collapse of a moral framework for the men who kill her. The spectacular agony of her death is intended to stir not the audience's righteous anger at the grunts . . . but empathy for the ordinary fighting men who have been turned into beasts by their tour of duty."[11]

Equally extreme and still more bizarre is a scene in *Born on the Fourth of July* in which Kovic and another vet quarrel over which of them has killed more babies. The implication is that the superior person is the one who has killed the most babies since he has to carry a greater burden of guilt![12]

It is eminently clear from *Born on the Fourth of July* that historical trauma does not necessarily result in a progressive politics—"libidinal" or otherwise. Nor is the phallus necessarily relinquished by men who have suffered from such trauma. As Tony Williams has shrewdly observed, the trip to Mexico allows Kovic to "confront his dark side . . ., confess his sins to the family of the man he shot, and gain the phallus (if not the penis) by speaking at the 1984 Democratic convention before an audience mainly composed of silent . . . and admiring, autograph seeking women."[13] Earlier in the film, when Kovic is released from the hospital, he goes to see his girlfriend from high school days. She, however, is so caught up in antiwar activities that she is unable to connect with him. As Kovic wheels through her college campus, he declares his love for her, and the camera focuses on her walking beside him but looking away, in the direction of a group of activists about to hold a meeting. The proper role for a woman in the antiwar movement, the film makes clear, is that of silent supporter of male protestors, not independent actor. The feminism that grew up partly in response to this attitude is, needless to say, nowhere evident in the film.

In addition to *Coming Home*, one other film is noteworthy not only for its incorporation of a love story, but, most importantly, for the emphasis it places on the effects of the war and the war's aftermath on women's subjectivity. In *Jacknife* (1989) Ed Harris plays Dave, a pent-up alcoholic vet whose antisocial attitudes and behavior are ruining the life of his school-teacher sister (Kathy Baker) with whom he resides.[14] A friend called Megs, played by Robert De Niro, comes to visit and attempts to break Dave out of his shell, and in the process Megs falls in love with Dave's sister. Dave violently opposes the relationship and (often unconsciously) works to sabotage it. One night when his sister and Megs are at the prom (she is there as a chaperone, but clearly they are both attempting to capture something lost in their youth), Dave comes to the high school and smashes a glass trophy case. After he runs off, his sister attempts to go on with the evening as if nothing had happened, while Megs is understandably distracted and distraught. Astonishingly, the film does not demonize the woman for resenting the way her brother's trauma has circumscribed her life. Indeed, it shows that the brother needs to accept a certain amount of responsibility for casting a pall on her existence. At the end, we see him in group therapy coming to terms with the fact that he betrayed Megs one time in battle and coming to terms as well with what he sees as his own cowardice. It hardly seems necessary to point out how seldom issues relating to inglorious combat behavior get raised in Vietnam films.

Rick Berg, a combat veteran, has written in an influential essay, "Losing Vietnam," that "the vet can begin to overcome his alienation" only when he recognizes that Vietnam's "consequences range throughout a community."[15] While, for the most part, Berg's concern is with issues of class, *Jacknife* has the merit of focusing on the vet's recognition of the way that the war affects the relations between the sexes. *Jacknife* is certainly not without many of the problems characteristic of films about post-Vietnam life. It never, of course, even alludes to the feminism that arose from anti-war activity; on the contrary, the sister is cast in stereotypically spinsterish terms ("I know what I am," she says, not, however, voicing the dreaded term), and to her the goal of a life of her own is having a husband and family. The ending of the film is especially problematic in suggesting that somehow the union of Megs and Dave's sister will allow the two to capture the lost innocence of their high school days. Nevertheless, if the film accomplished nothing more than granting Baker the line, "Don't you want a point of view?" when her brother says he won't take her, a woman, fishing with his friend, it would have done more than almost any other Vietnam film in granting a woman an independent subjectivity and hinting at the possibility that she can be the maker and not just the bearer of meaning.[16]

The ending of *Jacknife*, with its nostalgic promise of a return to innocence, is characteristic of the genre. "Return" is a constant motif in Vietnam films, as many critics have noted. In the Rambo-type films there is one heroic man's return to Vietnam so that he can "win the war this time." For all its apparent liberalism, the same concern is detectable in *Born on the Fourth of July*. Ron's activism at the end of the film is *explicitly* associated with warfare: turned out of the Republican convention that the veterans have stormed, Ron uses militarist language in instructing his men to return and "take the hall." Not only is Kovic thus positioned as a victorious warrior, a man who wins the war against the war, but in taking the hall he reverses another ignominious defeat—that is, a wrestling match he lost in high school, to the tremendous disappointment of his mother and girlfriend.

The notion of return is also present in the constant process of "metaphorization" that occurs in these films, which as we have seen make everything and everyone (raped women, murdered babies, etc.) refer back to and stand in for the American soldier (or veteran) and his plight. Difference and otherness are recognized only to the extent that they are seen to signify something about the American male. Some feminists have identified metaphor, which reduces differences to versions of sameness, as basic to Western "phallocentric" thought; in making this point, they draw on the paradigmatic Freudian scenario whereby the male reads the female body in terms of his own standard—the penis, which the female body is judged to be lacking.[17] Now, given the crisis in America's "phallic" authority that opened up with the loss of the war, and given the occasionally literal severing of the penis from the phallus that symbolizes it, it is not surprising to see metaphorical operations such as those described move into high gear in representations of Vietnam. Thinking again of the coming in *Coming Home*, we can see why a feminist would appreciate the sex scene in that film, might prize its brief acknowledgment of feminine difference, and want to insist that sometimes a clitoris is just a clitoris, and a woman's orgasm simply that.

This preamble is designed to put in relief the achievement of Nancy Savoca's understated, small-budget film *Dogfight* (1991) since it is easily lost in the midst of the loud, frantic, spectacular representations with which we have been bombarded by so many male directors of Vietnam films. *Dogfight* is a film about a group of marines about to be shipped overseas (they do not know it, but they are destined for Vietnam). The group members set up a "dogfight," a dance, to which each of the marines is supposed to bring an ugly date. The man who finds the ugliest woman is the winner and receives a cash prize. One of the four men, Eddie (River Phoenix), is unsuccessful at convincing the women he encounters to go out with him; more or less giving up on the attempt, he goes into a diner and meets Rose (Lili Taylor, padded up a bit for the role), a waitress whose mother owns the diner and who, when he first sees her, is picking a folk tune on her guitar. He invites her to the dance, and excited about the prospect of going to a party and escaping for a time her humdrum life, she accepts. One of the interesting aspects of this setup is that the spectator is not sure whether or not Eddie really considers Rose to be "dogfight" material, a question that the film never clears up. During the evening Rose discovers the purpose of the dogfight, slugs Eddie, and leaves in a rage. Remorseful, Eddie goes to the apartment over the diner and gets Rose to agree to go out with him for the night. Scenes of their evening out together, which is sweetly romantic, despite their arguments (Rose is clearly a budding peacenik), are intercut with scenes of Eddie's three friends spending their last night in the States brawling with sailors, watching pornography in a theater, being fellated by a prostitute, who does each of them in turn in the theater, chewing gum in between bouts, and getting tattoos of bees on their arms (each has a last name beginning with "B") to mark their loyalty to one another. Eddie and Rose sleep together, and then he runs to meet his bus. After a very brief battle scene set in Vietnam, Eddie returns, wounded, to San Francisco, and the film very movingly presents us with the point of view of a man who sees an entirely different world from the one he left. Flower children fill the street, and one walks by and softly asks, "Hey, man, did you kill any babies over there?" For all the preoccupation of films like *Born on the Fourth of July* with soldiers' readjustment to civilian life, in my view no scene in any other movie captures more vividly their estrangement and confusion. Eddie goes into the diner that Rose now runs and encounters a more mature woman; as they look at each other, they are at a loss for words, and in a mournful ending they embrace.

I want to argue against the grain of the voluminous criticism on Vietnam War movies and to propose that it is precisely because the film is a love story and gives us a woman's perspective on war and the warrior mentality that it is less compromising in its opposition to war than the films in that most paradoxical of genres, the antiwar war film. The antiwar sentiment is present not only in *Dogfight*'s narrative but is conveyed at the level of style: much of the film's subversiveness lies in the peacefulness and restraint of its pacing, rhythms, and soundtrack. There is a sweetness in the encounter between the boy and girl that is genuinely moving. But it must be said that this film is less sentimental than most Vietnam films, which Andrew Martin has convincingly shown to be, for the most part, male melodramas.[18] To measure the gap between the sentimentality of some of these films and *Dogfight*'s uncompromising view of the cruelties of which people are capable and which, after all, have some bearing on our desire or at least our willingness to make war, we need only compare one event that is featured prominently in Vietnam films with a very different one in Savoca's film. I refer to, respectively, the high school prom and the dogfight—the dogfight being an event for which it is difficult to muster up the same sort of nostalgia inspired by the prom.

The eponymous event of the dogfight may be seen as the antithesis of the prom scenes in both *Jacknife* and *Born on the Fourth of July*, both of which nourish us in the dangerous illusion of a time of lost innocence and unimpaired relations between the sexes. In *Born on the Fourth of July*, Ron Kovic, on the eve of his departure for military service, runs through a storm in his old clothes and arrives soaked at the prom to dance with his starry-eyed girlfriend. In *Dogfight*, of course, the "dance" is the cruel event of the dogfight itself (staged again on the eve of the men's departure for overseas, and as it turns out, for Vietnam). Rose finds out about the dogfight in a scene that takes place in the ladies' room. Standing in front of a mirror, one of the girls, Marcy, who has gone toothless to the affair and earned the prize for her date, tells Rose about the rules of the contest while putting her teeth back in. "The thing that gets me," says Marcy, "is how great they think they are. Did you ever see such a pack of pukes in your life?" Rose is, naturally, appalled and marches out to Eddie and punches him, confronting him directly with his cruelty and lack of feelings for others. In this regard, the script, written by a former marine, Bob Comfort, has the infinite merit of focusing on the anger and humiliation of the object rather than the sad plight of the subject of the cruelty.

Yet in creating Rose, who in the original script was supposed to be overweight, Comfort intended to make the woman serve as a "metaphor" for the marine, her unacceptable looks symbolizing his "outsider status."[19] Comfort has publicly expressed his unhappiness with Savoca's changes in his script, and one can only speculate that his feeling of dispossession— his sense of dis-Comfort, as it were—stemmed from Savoca's resistance to turning the heroine into a metaphor, a reflection of the hero. According to Savoca, in the original script Rose "was more of a catalyst for change," and, she says, "this bored me and Lili to tears." They resolved to make the character "someone in her own right." Importantly, however, the transformation in the female character does not occur at the *expense* of the male character (almost a primal fear of men when women make art); on the contrary, Savoca maintains, "as her IQ comes up, so does his. Because rather than reacting to a thing, he's reacting to a complicated person. Something happens between two people and not just between this guy and his revelation." Savoca continues:

> We decided that the first thing to do was give her a passion—so that regardless of what she looks like there's something going on within herself. And that something is music. . . . He becomes attracted to her because she has a love in her that goes beyond their small world and the rigid narrow existence he's used to living—and not because one day she takes out the ribbon in her hair and, oh my god, she's stunning.[20]

In view of the narcissistic self-referentiality of many male-directed Vietnam films, which repeatedly and utterly disqualify women as authorities in matters of war and peace (we recall Ron Kovic's girlfriend being judged harshly by the film *Born on the Fourth of July* for turning away from Kovic and toward the antiwar demonstrators), we can perhaps appreciate Savoca's audacity in having her heroine's aspirations and values point a way out of the trap in which the soldier finds himself. Indeed, we might say that, by extension, just as Eddie is required to treat Rose as a person with an independent subjectivity who has the potential for giving him a glimpse of more expansive horizons, so too does Savoca's encounter with Comfort's text strengthen it while respecting and underscoring its powerful indictment of a society that devours young working-class men and spits them out.

Rose is a young girl who dreams of changing the world, of possibly joining the civil rights movement in the South or engaging in some other form of social activism; she also aspires to be a folksinger, and during their date she argues with Eddie throughout the evening about the most effective means of changing the world. He, of course, has opted for guns; she for guitars. That the aspirations and values of the heroine are expressed in her love of folk music is particularly appropriate. Vietnam was, as more than one critic has noted, America's rock-and-roll war, and many of the films about the war are edited to the super-charged rhythms of the Rolling Stones and similar groups; even if the lyrics of many of these songs are intended to make an ironic or critical comment on the war, the music itself often serves to pump up the testosterone level, working viscerally against the antiwar sentiments supposedly being conveyed.[21] Such music, as David James has argued, is always at least ambivalent.[22] In this regard, then, we might compare the nihilistic song by the Stones, "Paint It Black," that ends Stanley Kubrick's antiwar, antimilitary film, *Full Metal Jacket* (1987), with the Malvina Reynolds' song that Rose haltingly sings sitting at a piano in a nearly deserted café as Eddie looks on: "The grass is gone / the boy disappears / and rain keeps falling like helpless tears."

Eddie and his friends do disappear, and only Eddie returns. When he comes back to San Francisco, the world has changed drastically, and he is viewed with disdain and suspicion by the flower children milling around in the street. Eddie, wearing his uniform, limps into a bar across the street from Rose's café. When the bartender sees Eddie's tattoo, he shows him his: a girl who jiggles and performs a "belly dance" on his protruding gut. Eddie asks about Rose, describing her as kind of chubby; the bartender responds, "She ain't no prize," and one of the men chimes in, "yeah, like you're really something, eh, Carl?" At one point the bartender asks Eddie if he served in Vietnam. When Eddie responds in the affirmative, the bartender, clearly at a loss for words, says, "Yeah, bummer," and walks away. "No charge on that," says the owner of the bar when Eddie gets a second drink. "Thank you," Eddie replies. "Thank *you*," says the man quietly, but he cannot look Eddie in the eye.

As I have said, these few moments convey the pathos and isolation of the returning veteran more eloquently than a thousand bombastic moments in an Oliver Stone movie. They strike a note of pure loss, prolonged through the final shots when Eddie goes across the street to see Rose, and she too seems not to know what to say or do. They embrace, though this is clearly not the embrace of two people destined to live happily ever after; it is an act of mutual consolation over all the sorrow and loss that has occurred in the intervening years, including the severing of their slender connection, which of course cannot ever be reforged. Warner Bros., encouraged by a preview audience's positive response to the first part of the movie ("Rah, rah, dogfight,"), exerted intense pressure on Savoca to change the ending to make it more upbeat. Finally, an exasperated Savoca asked sardonically, "Do you want us to change the ending so we win the war?"—apparently not realizing that that was *exactly* what Hollywood wanted and what, over the last decade or so, it has gotten from movie directors all too happy to oblige.

Dogfight, in a certain sense, may be seen as the second in a two-part series that Savoca filmed on relations between the sexes. Her brilliant film debut was a movie that gained a cult following among women. Drawing on some techniques of documentary, her first film, *True Love* (1989), is a dystopian "wedding comedy" that focuses on the rituals leading up to the big day. Donna and Mikey, the engaged couple, battle over whether or not Donna will get to go out with Mikey after his bachelor party. Throughout the film, Savoca cuts between the group of guys (Mikey and his friends) and the group of girls (Donna and hers), showing us two worlds that are so separate that their inhabitants might as well live on separate planets. "Sometimes she says things to me and I don't understand what the fuck she's talkin' about," says Mikey at one point. As the boys party on throughout the night, getting drunker and drunker (while the camera gets wilder and wilder, positioned, for example, as the ready bank teller machine and the jukebox, capturing Mikey in unflattering close-up as he leans down and pushes the buttons), the girls just hang out, waiting, talking of marriage, home decorating, etc. Although at one point they go to watch male strippers, it is clear they do so defiantly, in order to prove their ability to have the same kind of fun as the boys—thereby, of course, proving the opposite. The climax of the movie occurs during the wedding itself when Mikey proposes to his friends that they go out for a while on the wedding night. He begs Donna to let him go with the boys for just an hour or two, and she runs crying into the ladies' room, where she is followed first by her friends and then by Mikey. (Savoca adds a wonderful touch when she has a mother drag her protesting little son into the ladies' room; glancing at Mikey, she says, "See, this boy is in here, too.") The film ends inconclusively, though one senses that the two will go on with married life, living it as happily, or rather as unhappily, as most.

True Love documents better than any film I have ever seen the asymmetries of life as it is generally lived by the two sexes in modern America. It submits to a trenchant analysis the relations among men that are glorified and idealized by the overwhelming majority of Hollywood films. Dogfight continues in this vein, alternating scenes of the developing relation between Eddie and Rose with scenes of Eddie's friends out on the town boozing and whoring. From wedding to war and home again, Savoca's films, taken together, cover the same territory as Michael Cimino's lengthy and controversial Vietnam film The Deer Hunter, and they may be read as a rewriting of that film in feminist terms.

Roughly the first third of The Deer Hunter depicts a wedding that takes place in a highly sex-segregated working-class community of Russian-Americans, just as True Love is situated in a working-class Italian-American section of the Bronx. In an excellent analysis of The Deer Hunter, Susan Jeffords has shown that the wedding sets up the basic conflict of the film, which is most clearly played out by the character of Nicky, who is killed off by the film precisely because his loyalties are divided between the world associated with women (sex, marriage, domesticity) and his affiliation with men (specifically one man, Michael, played by Robert De Niro). Jeffords writes, "One must either live all of the points of the code ['discipline, endurance, purity'] or not attempt it at all . . ., but not attempt and fail; one must fulfill either the masculine or the feminine, but not both."[23] Of course, these two options are not equally valued by the film (for the character who chooses the feminine comes home a paraplegic); rather, its primary emotional investment is in the relations among men, in particular, the relations between Nick and Michael, whose friendship is highly idealized by Cimino. Jeffords goes so far as to claim that "Vietnam is . . . not the subject of The Deer Hunter but merely the occasion for announcing the primacy of the bonds between men."[24]

While many Vietnam films, most notably perhaps Full Metal Jacket, have exposed the misogynistic aspects of military life, none of them focuses as unwaveringly as Dogfight on the more unappealing aspects of the male bonding that is part and parcel of the misogyny— the dirty jokes, the lies about sexual prowess, the animal behavior and brawling, the humili- ation of those further down the pecking order, and so on. Soldiers who fought in Vietnam were, after all, just boys out of high school (a fact we are inclined to forget when a thirty- something Robert De Niro is the star). Dogfight goes very far indeed in contravening one of the most basic assumptions of Hollywood war films in regard to women and male bonding, suggesting not that men must give up ties to women and families in order to survive, but that the unthinking loyalty to the all-male group (marines vs. "squid shit," for example), an ideal promoted by military life and by much of our civilian culture as well, is what threatens their survival. The point may seem obvious, but it is never made in Hollywood films.

To emphasize the irrationality of these bonds, the film includes a discussion at the dogfight in which the boys explain to the girls how it is that their surnames all begin with the same initial. One of the four explains that they had to line up by alphabetical order when they were in infantry training. Rose conversationally concludes, "So you got to be friends by standing in line?" There is an awkward pause, and then Marcy, the toothless girl, guffaws loudly. The guys call themselves the four B's, and the film makes much of the ritual in which they get themselves tattooed with bees on their arms—all except Eddie, who is with Rose. When Eddie rejoins the group the morning after sleeping with Rose, he tells Burzon that he has learned from Rose that Burzon "fixed" the dogfight. Burzon, in turn, tells Eddie that when he was getting his tattoo he saw him with Rose—and not with the gorgeous officer's wife Eddie has lied about. In a rare moment of honesty between men, Eddie asks his friend Burzon, "How'd we get to be so full of shit like this?—such idiots?" All these lies are "bullshit," Eddie says. Burzon replies:

> Let me tell you something about bullshit. It's everywhere. You hit me with a little, and I buy it. I hit you with a little, you buy it. That doesn't make us idiots. It's what makes us buddies. We buy what the Corps hands out, and that's what makes us Marines. And the Corps' buying all the bullshit from President Kennedy and President Kennedy's buying all the bullshit from everybody in the U.S. of Fuckin' A and that's what makes us Americans.

"It's still bullshit," Eddie insists. "Right, and we're in it up to our goddam lips, Buddy. . . . I don't know if I'm making sense, but [here he rolls up his sleeve to show the bee tattoos], this makes a hell of a lot of sense to me. There's no bullshit in this." At this point, one of the four "bees" farts loudly; the guys all start laughing and joking again about the officer's wife. In a chilling gesture Eddie tears up the address that Rose has given him and throws the pieces out the window of the bus, where they are scattered to the wind. The act of renouncing association with women would help in the logic of most war films to secure the man's safety, which as I noted at the outset is endangered whenever men keep mementos of their attachments at home.

In *Dogfight* the outcome is very different. The film devotes about one minute of screen time to depicting the men in combat, thereby avoiding the contradictions involved when films "rely on combat sequences for their antiwar message." In this brief scene we see the four young men sitting around playing cards, and one of them brings up a joke, "What did the ghost say to the bee? 'Boo, bee.'" As two of the four "bees" laugh at a dumb pun that condenses various themes of the film male bonding (as in the four bees), the degradation of women (the crude reference to "booby" as part of female anatomy), and death (the ghost)—a mortar round falls into their midst and apparently kills Eddie's friends. It might be said that, at the fantasmatic level, Eddie is allowed to survive *because* his loyalties were at least temporarily divided between the male group and a woman—the very reason, in Jeffords's argument, that Nick in *The Deer Hunter* must be killed off.

In Savoca's *True Love*, the heroine, Donna, resents the all-male group but recognizes its primacy. The night before the wedding, Donna takes Mikey aside and cuts both their hands to intermingle their blood—like "blood brothers," she explains. The acknowledgment of the primacy of male bonds, along with the yearning to become a member of the privileged male group, is characteristic of representations of Vietnam created by women. In her discussion of Bobbie Ann Mason's *In Country*, for instance, Jeffords shows how the heroine longs to have the same kind of understanding of war that men have and how finally the novel confirms "collectivity as a function of the masculine bond."[25] When Sam/Samantha, who is named after her father, goes to the Vietnam War Memorial, she is able to touch her own name and symbolically become part of the collectivity from which she has felt excluded. In *Dogfight*, however, the woman stands for a higher form of collectivity—higher than the military swarm, exemplified by the four bees—and her vision of a better world achievable through artistic endeavor and political activism (*not* through any essentialized categories such as feminine nurturance) is presented by the film as admirable, if vague and a bit naïvely idealistic.

On the film's horizon is a faint glimpse, barely discernible, of another kind of collectivity. Taking place on the eve of a feminist revolt that would gain momentum in the seventies, *Dogfight* reminds us, most particularly in the casting of feminist folksinger Holly Near as the mother of a heroine who believes in the power of music to change the world, of a time when *women* would bond together in lesbian separatist spaces, preeminent of which was the woman's music festival. Additionally, in locating Rose and her mother in a place called "Rose's Coffee Shop," which is handed down from mother to daughter, beginning with Rose's grandmother, the film privileges matrilineality and presages the alternative economies that feminists would be attempting to devise.

The fullness of that story, though, is left to another time, another film. For Savoca and her husband, screenwriter Richard Guay, with whom she works closely, the principal concern is the relation, or more accurately nonrelation, between the sexes.[26] One finds a fairly persistent pessimism in Savoca's work about the possibilities for meaningful union between male and female. But the connection between Rose and Eddie when it does occur is luminescent. The physical part of the relationship begins after Rose has sung for Eddie in the café. He takes her to a musical arcade where they put money in all the machines and dance to a cacophony of music box tunes. Then, as the music winds down, it is as if the raucous soundtrack of every Vietnam film ever made were being stilled, the rhythm cranked down, and a temporary truce called in the hostilities between men and women. In place of the noisy soundtrack, there is the sound of two people awkwardly embracing, fumbling to get their arms right, breathing unevenly in excitement and surprise at the intense pleasures of newly awakening sexuality.

When Eddie goes to Rose's bedroom, they begin kissing as we hear a Malvina Reynolds song playing on Rose's phonograph; then Rose goes into her closet "to change." Eddie whisks out of his clothes and stops when he remembers to go through his wallet to find a condom. He slips it under the bib of Rose's teddy bear and quickly gets into the bed. Rose comes out wearing a long flannel nightgown, and Eddie is dazzled: "You look good, you look real good." The process in which Rose goes from (possibly) being perceived as dogfight material to being looked upon as a vision of loveliness is complete and entirely believable, without the film's ever stopping to make a point of it. As if responding to the commentators who have criticized Vietnam representations for seldom acknowledging that warriors are just boys, the film in this scene touchingly evokes precisely the liminal space between childhood and adulthood so crucial to the future of humanity (its end—in war: its beginning—in sex).

Because the movie is about teenagers, Warner Bros thought it should be marketed as a teen comedy—the ghetto to which so many women directors are relegated in Hollywood. Such a confusion might seem laughable on the face of it, but the fact that the movie is as much about a teenage *girl* as it is about boys makes it especially vulnerable to being judged trivial. Nor is *Dogfight* alone in being patronized because of its protagonist. In an article entitled "Men, Women, and Vietnam," Milton J. Bates writes of Bobbie Ann Mason's novel *In Country:* "Mason, having elected to tell her story from a teenage girl's point of view, cannot realistically venture a more mature critique of the War or sexual roles. Why inflict such a handicap on one's narrative?"[27] One might as well say that *Huckleberry Finn* is handicapped by having a young boy as its protagonist and that consequently Mark Twain cannot venture a mature critique of American society or slavery. I am arguing, however, that having a teenage girl as (co)protagonist enables Savoca a unique vantage point from which to advance an important critique of the war mentality and especially of war narratives—a critique, in part, of their exclusive emphasis *on the white male soldier's point of view*.

During a discussion of the sex scene in class, one of my students remarked that this was the first time in the movies she had seen a man ask a woman if it was okay to proceed in his sexual "advances." It is in such small details that the subversive nature of women's popular cinema often lies. This detail might be dismissed as another instance in which "the invasion is rewritten as erotic melodrama." But I would counter that in being anti-invasion on a very minute scale, the film points to the existence of other subjectivities and other desires besides those of the white male hero. In so saying, I do not, I hope, commit the same error I lamented in mainstream representations of Vietnam and implicitly offer Rose as a metaphor for Asia. I do, however, mean to suggest that in the film one man takes a crucial *step* toward recognizing otherness in the variety of forms it takes; the movie thus prepares the ground for the emergence of an antiwar sensibility, even though it does not go the entire distance.

Dogfight itself respects the integrity and independence of its viewers, and it never bludgeons them with a moral; rather than beginning by condemning the men for their barbarous treatment of women, for example, the film depicts the staging of the dogfight in such a way that the point of the men's search for ugly women, which may initially strike us as somewhat amusing, only gradually becomes clear. We tend to be identified with Eddie until Rose learns about the dogfight, and then we find ourselves implicated in his lack of sensitivity and his propensity for cruelty. This development, along with the film's somber finale, angered audiences who wanted the comfort of a happy and predictable ending: boy loses war but at least wins girl (the boo-bee prize).

The preview audience's anger at the film's ending is certainly understandable. The war itself seemed to many Americans to have had the wrong ending, and rather than mourning its loss they have fallen victim to a widespread melancholia in which they cling to the lost object rather than let it go.[28] According to Sigmund Freud, when people are unable to mourn a loss and put it behind them, they internalize it; preserving it within themselves, they become inconsolable. Turning inward, they appear narcissistic. This malady is what Freud calls "melancholia."[29] Having denied loss, denied the fact of having lost the war, America internalized the war and cannot seem to move beyond the question of what this loss has meant to itself, much less what it has meant to others who also were affected. *Dogfight* points to the necessity of moving beyond narcissism and coming to terms with the losses that incurred in being vanquished—the necessity, then, of mourning.

And in mourning, who better than women to lead the way? In her important study, *The Gendering of Melancholia*, Juliana Schiesari, following and reassessing Freud, discusses mourning as a social ritual that has generally been performed by women. Melancholia, by contrast, is a category by which a solitary male elevates and glorifies his losses (a comrade; a lover; a war) into "signifiers of cultural superiority."[30] A literary critic, Schiesari is speaking primarily of poets and other creative writers who through masterful elegiac displays put their own exquisite sensibilities forward for us to admire, offering themselves as objects to be pitied for the losses they have sustained, and—in some cases—hoping to acquire immortality through having created for posterity a work that supposedly acknowledges death. For our purposes, Oliver Stone, who cannot seem to stop making movies about Vietnam, might be seen as an example of the inconsolable melancholiac. A quintessentially melancholic scene would be the one in *Born on the Fourth of July* in which we are asked to focus on *Kovic*'s pain and guilt when he has to talk to the parents of a dead buddy. Schiesari concludes that mourning is a social ritual which "accommodates the imagination to reality," while melancholia accommodates reality to the imagination. In her capacity as mourner, too, then, woman stands for the collectivity over male individualism.

Doing the work of mourning, accommodating the imagination to reality, *Dogfight* confronts us with both the reality of our losses and, concomitantly, with the real—as opposed to figural—status of woman. The struggle to establish this reality by asserting a female vision and female authority was waged at several levels of the film's production and reception. First, in order to make the female character of equal importance to the male, Savoca had to take on scriptwriter Comfort, who was displeased at some of her revisions. Second, many of the changes were decided on during the filming and were worked out collectively between cast and crew, most particularly between Savoca and Taylor. Finally, after preview audiences responded unfavorably to the film's ending, Savoca refused to comply with Warners' attempts to get her to change it. She conceded that Warners had the authority to do what they liked with the film, but she demanded that her name be taken off the project if the ending was reshot. Warner Bros. executives called River Phoenix and Lili Taylor, but both refused to reshoot the ending without Savoca. Savoca believes that neither she nor Taylor counted for much with the studio, but she thinks that Phoenix's refusal to reshoot forced Warners' decision to stop pursuing the issue (whereupon, according to Savoca, the project was dumped "into the toilet"). I like to think that Phoenix's role taught him something about resisting the orders of a male power structure and the desirability of sometimes deferring to the vision of a woman—in this case, Nancy Savoca, who elicited from him one of the finest performances of his tragically short life. Fittingly, Phoenix ended up being eloquently memorialized in a work that asserts the legitimacy of female authority.

Notes

1   [. . .]
2   Gilbert Adair, *Hollywood's Vietnam: From "The Green Berets" to "Full Metal Jacket"* (London: Heinemann, 1989), p. 159.
3   Ibid., p. 169.
4   See my chapter, "A Father Is Being Beaten," in *Feminism Without Women* (New York: Routledge, 1991), pp. 61–75.
5   David James, "Rock and Roll in Representations of the Invasion of Vietnam," *Representations* 29 (Winter, 1990): 91.
6   See John Hellman, *American Myth and the Legacy of Vietnam* (New York: Columbia University Press, 1986).
7   Jason Katzman, "From Outcast to Cliché: How Film Shaped, Warped and Developed the Image of the Vietnam Veteran," *Journal of American Culture* 16, no. 1 (1993): 12.
8   Albert Auster and Leonard Quart, *How the War Was Remembered: Hollywood and Vietnam* (New York: Praeger, 1988).
9   Kaja Silverman, *Male Subjectivity at the Margins* (New York: Routledge, 1992), pp. 52–121.
10   As David James reminds us, though, *Coming Home*'s "unequivocal assertion that the invasion is *wrong* distinguishes it from all other films made in Hollywood." See James, "Rock and Roll," p. 90.
11   Pat Aufderheide, "Good Soldiers," in *Seeing Through the Movies*, ed. Mark Crispin Miller (New York: Pantheon, 1990), p. 88.
12   One might be tempted to read the scene as satiric; yet the entire film presents its hero and its subject with such hysterical immediacy and apparent overidentification that it lacks the distance necessary for a satiric commentary.
13   Tony Williams, "Narrative Patterns and Mythic Trajectories in Mid-1980s Vietnam Movies," in *Inventing Vietnam: The War in Film and Television*, ed. Michael Anderegg (Philadelphia: Temple University Press, 1991), p. 129.
14   This film also has been criticized for involving a "love story," which, writes Katzman, "digressed from the film's more interesting element, which was Dave's healing process." "From Outcast to Cliché," p. 21.

15   Rick Berg, "Losing Vietnam: Covering the War in an Age of Technology," in *From Hanoi to Hollywood: The Vietnam War in American Film*, ed. Linda Dittmar and Gene Michaud (New Brunswick, N.J.: Rutgers University Press, 1990), p. 65.

16   These are Laura Mulvey's terms in "Visual Pleasure and Narrative Cinema," in *Movies and Methods*, vol. 2, ed. Bill Nichols (Berkeley: University of California Press, 1985), p. 305.

17   See ibid.

18   Andrew Martin, *Reception of War: Vietnam and American Culture* (Norman: University of Oklahoma Press, 1993).

19   Quoted in Julie Lew, "After *True Love* There Comes the *Dogfight*," *New York Times*, July 22, 1990, p. H20.

20   All quotations are from an interview I conducted with Nancy Savoca on November 30, 1994.

21   In addition to James's "Rock and Roll," see David James, "The Vietnam War and American Music," in *The Vietnam War and American Culture*, ed. John Carlos Rowe and Rick Berg (New York: Columbia University Press, 1991), and Douglas W. Reitinger, "Paint It Black: Rock Music and Vietnam War Film," *Journal of American Culture* 15, no. 3 (1992): 53–59.

22   James, "Rock and Roll."

23   Susan Jeffords, *The Remasculinization of America: Gender and the Vietnam War* (Bloomington: Indiana University Press, 1989), p. 95.

24   Ibid., p. 99.

25   Ibid., p. 62.

26   Savoca's third film moves into different terrain, with mixed results. Savoca tries her hand at magical realism in *Household Saints* (1993), a story of three generations of Italian women. The granddaughter, played by Taylor, has visions of Jesus and ultimately dies. The film leaves an explanation for the visions (whether they result from madness or mysticism) unresolved.

27   Milton J. Bates, "Men, Women and Vietnam," in *America Rediscovered: Critical Essays on Literature and Film of the Vietnam War*, ed. Owen Gilman, Jr., and Lorrie Smith (New York: Garland, 1990), p. 29.

28   J. Hoberman speaks of the war's "bummer of a finale that's left us with a compulsion to remake, if not history, then at least the movie." See Hoberman, "America Dearest," *American Film* 13 (May 1988): 41.

29   Sigmund Freud, "Mourning and Melancholia," in *The Standard Edition of the Complete Psychological Works of Sigmund Freud*, vol. 17, trans. James Strachey (London: Hogarth, 1974).

30   Juliana Schiesari, *The Gendering of Melancholia: Feminism, Psychoanalysis, and the Symbolics of Loss in Renaissance Literature* (Ithaca, N.Y.: Cornell University Press, 1992), p. 62.

Chapter 24

Chon Noriega

CITIZEN CHICANO: THE TRIALS AND TITILLATIONS OF ETHNICITY IN THE AMERICAN CINEMA, 1935–1962 (1991)

BETWEEN 1935 AND 1962, AT LEAST TEN social-problem films addressed the issue of the "place" of the Mexican American in the United States.[1] With the exception of two gang-exploitation films—*Boulevard Nights* and *Walk Proud* (both 1979)—these remained the only feature-length films to be "about" Mexican Americans or Chicanos until the emergence of Chicano-produced feature films in the late 1970s.

These films were produced at a significant moment in the development of an American as well as an ethnic-American national identity. In these social-problem films, the political, socioeconomic, and psychological issues related to race and ethnicity operate at the manifest level of the narrative rather than as the "political unconscious." In the end, these films must still resolve these social contradictions and situate the Mexican American within normative gender roles, social spaces, and institutional parameters.

Before I turn to the films themselves, it is necessary to sketch in the contours of the period between the Depression and the election of John F. Kennedy, a period Chicano scholars have identified as the Mexican-American Generation.[2] Within Chicano historiography, the period is framed on either side by the border conflict era (1848–1929) and the Chicano Movement (1963–75).

It is between 1929 and 1941, as Richard Garcia argues, that the "Mexican-American mind" emerged. By 1930, border conflict had dismantled the remnants of the old Mexican political and economic system. Mexicanos, including a new wave of immigrants, had provided cheap labor for the agricultural and industrial transformation of the midwest and southwest, particularly during World War I and the 1920s. In the 1930s, the simultaneous rise of a middle class with its own organizations, such as the League of United Latin American Citizens, and a sharp decline in immigration fostered a "new zeitgeist of Mexican-Americanism, . . . a cohesive collective cluster of ideas that permeated the extensive Mexican communities throughout the Southwest."[3]

Participation in World War II provided additional cause for patriotic Americanism, as well as a liberal reformist politics aimed at securing the rights of citizenship. Between 1930 and 1963, Mexican Americans, while still raised in the cultures of both Mexico and the United States, felt that "political accommodation and assimilation were the only path toward equal status in a racist society."[4]

The progressive nature of the Mexican-American political stance becomes apparent when we consider the concurrent national policies and actions toward Mexican Americans and Mexicans. In fact, the Mexican-American Generation starts at the same moment in which the United States, between 1929 and 1934, "repatriated" some 400,000 Mexicans, including Mexican Americans and legal immigrants, in order to cut welfare payments during the Depression.[5] Under these pressures, immigration in the 1930s dropped to less than 5 percent of the peak level set in the 1920s.[6]

In 1942, with U.S. entry into World War II, repatriation contributed to a labor short-age. In addition to the 400,000 "Mexicans" deported, upward of 500,000 Mexican-American men had enlisted or been drafted into service, while 120,000 Japanese Americans had been interned as "security risks." As a result, the Bracero Program was negotiated with Mexico, which agreed to provide the United States with unskilled laborers on a short-term basis in order to harvest its labor-intensive crops. In what would become a "ratchet effect," the increased migration under the Bracero Program gave rise to a neonativism, so that Operation Wetback was implemented in order to locate and deport "illegal aliens" or "wetbacks." Between 1952 and 1956, some 2.9 million Mexicans and Mexican Americans were deported. Once again, these actions threatened the cheap agricultural labor force, and Congress extended the Bracero Program, which continued until 1964.[7]

Under both repatriation and Operation Wetback, a significant number of Mexican Americans (including U.S.-born children of immigrants) were deported, while the Bracero Program brought in an unskilled, foreign work force intended to return to Mexico. The denial of citizenship operated along both class and political lines as a means to return industrial-sector jobs to Anglo-Americans, support agribusiness, and deport Mexican-American political activists and labor leaders.[8] It is within this context that Mexican-American organizations advocated assimilation and integration, and—in the late 1950s—moved into national politics.[9]

In contrast to the politics (or denial) of Mexican-American citizenship, schools—often segregated—and the YMCA, among other social institutions, sought to assimilate Mexican-American youths to the "American way of life."[10] But, "[u]ntil the advent of the Sleepy Lagoon case [in Los Angeles, 1942]," Mauricio Mazón notes, "Mexican-American youth had not been the focus of either widespread police or journalistic investigation."[11] The incident, on August 1, 1942, in which a Mexican-American youth was found dead after a party (perhaps run over by a hit-and-run driver), resulted in the arrest and conviction of twenty-two Mexican-American youths for criminal conspiracy, assault, and murder. The next summer, in an event reported extensively in the press as a military offensive, Anglo service-men in "taxicab brigades" entered the barrio in search of pachucos or zoot-suiters. The servicemen, in what Mazón calls a "ritual of role reversal," stripped the Mexican-American youths of their zoot suits and shaved their hair, "aggressively mimicking and reenacting their own experience in basic training."[12] On October 4, 1944, two years after the Sleepy Lagoon case, the convictions were reversed on appeal for lack of evidence, and the judge was cited for bias and violation of the defendants' constitutional rights.[13]

Despite the court reversal and the psychological rationale for the zoot-suit riots, the institutional response to these events—press coverage, popular culture, police and FBI investigations—established both the inherent "criminality" of Mexican-American youths and the role of the state as surrogate "parent."[14] The trial also maintained the need for an "external guiding intelligence"—whether Nazi, sinarquista, or Communist—since "Mexicans" were understood to be at once prone to violence and yet unable to defend themselves. In this manner, the Sleepy Lagoon Defense Committee—which included Hollywood activists such as Orson Welles, Anthony Quinn, and Rita Hayworth (the latter two of Mexican descent)—was viewed as a foreign-inspired conspiracy rather than as "one of the more enduring coalitions between Mexicans, Jews, Blacks, and Anglos in American history."[15]

Between 1934 and 1968, the Production Code Administration (PCA), or Hays Office, served as the self-regulatory, institutional link between Hollywood films and the moral and political status quo. Prior censorship gave the PCA a significant role in shaping film texts, from initial treatment to final shooting script to final cut. The withholding of the PCA seal of approval could severely limit a completed film's distribution.[16] While the PCA did not mandate film production, it did define and monitor the outer limits of ideological expression and, in conjunction with the House Un-American Activities Committee (HUAC), ensured an almost nonexistent distribution for two of the more progressive (and the only independent) films about Mexican Americans: *Salt of the Earth*, based on a recent, successful miners strike in New Mexico, and *The Lawless*, about the bigotry and mass hysteria of a small town toward a Mexican-American youth falsely accused of murder and attempted rape.[17]

In its evaluation of social-problem films about Mexican Americans, the PCA often based its changes on the anticipated reaction of the Mexican government and people. PCA director Joseph Breen's letter to Dore Schary, producer of *My Man and I*, is typical: "We would like to urge that you get proper technical advice from the Mexican angle to make certain that there are not details in the script that might be offensive to that nation."[18] In *My Man and I*, Mexican-born Chu Chu Ramirez (Ricardo Montalban) has just become an American citizen, whereupon he encounters anti-Mexican slurs and actions that test his patriotic optimism. In all other films, phrases such as "you Mexican jerk!," "damn Mexicans," and "greaser fighter" were flagged by the PCA and removed.[19] In April 1955, Breen's replacement, Geoffrey Shurlock, went so far as to flag "one aspect of *Giant* which has nothing to do with the Code": errors in the Spanish-language dialogue. In particular, he pointed to the phrases "Bien venudo" and "Perdonome," and cited the film's "rather touchy subject matter" as an impetus for correcting the errors.[20] While *Giant* is often remembered as, among other things, James Dean's last film, its plot centers on racist Texan patriarch Bick Benedict (Rock Hudson) and his relationship with his "Mexican" laborers and daughter-in-law.

But despite the fact that these films depicted Mexican Americans *qua* social problem, from the start the PCA positioned the central issue, or "touchy subject matter," as a "racial question" or "race distinction" that existed on an international level, between Mexico and the United States. In a letter to Jack Warner, Breen raised numerous objections to the script for *Bordertown*, including the fact that "Mexicans [sic] are constantly referred to as 'greasers' and other derogatory names." In *Bordertown*, Johnny Ramirez (Paul Muni) is a violent Mexican American who heads to a Mexican bordertown in order to get rich as a prohibition-era casino manager. Breen, later in his letter, placed the issue of "Mexican" representation in context:

> It presents Johnny, although an American, as a Mexican and in such a role that he becomes a murderer, gambler and crook, always trying to "go American." The whole story raises very vividly the race distinction between Mexicans and Americans, which is bound to be offensive to our Southern neighbors.[21]

One month later, Breen acknowledged Warner's assurances that the final script would not elicit Mexican protest.[22] The concern was a legitimate one for the industry, insofar as international distribution generated profits and Mexico and other Latin American countries had in the past banned studios that produced derogatory films.[23] But, in the repeated references to "our neighbors to the South," the PCA also revealed the influence of F.D.R.'s Good Neighbor Policy, whose sentiments were expressed in one of the code's twelve "particular applications": "The history, institutions, prominent people and citizenry of other nations shall be represented fairly."

The advent of World War II reinvigorated the Good Neighbor Policy and its impact on film production. In April 1941, the PCA hired a bilingual Latin American affairs expert, Addison Durland. Also, the federal Office for Coordination of Inter-American Affairs established a motion picture section, charged with the "basic job of spreading the gospel of the Americas' common stake in this struggle."[24] Together, these two agencies monitored Hollywood films and provided "technical assistance" in order to protect both international alliances and markets.[25] In the process, the representation of Mexican Americans was measured against an "external guiding intelligence," Mexico, rather than the Mexican-American community.

Likewise, the censors invoked the communist threat when the films' critique of domestic "social problems" suggested that discrimination had either institutional or popular (hence democratic) underpinnings. In a letter to Luigi Luraschi about *The Lawless*, Breen made these ideological limits clear:

> . . . certain it is that the story itself is a shocking indictment of America and its people, and, indeed, is a sad commentary on "democracy at work," which the enemies of our system of government like to point to. The shocking manner in which the several gross injustices are heaped upon the head of the confused, but innocent, young American of Mexican extraction, and the willingness of so many of the people in your story to be a part of, and to endorse, these injustices, is, we think, a damning portrayal of our American social system.
>
> The overall effect of a story of this kind made into a motion picture would be, we think, a very definite disservice to this country of ours, and to its institutions and its ideals. Our apprehensions about it is [sic] very deep. . . .[26]

In response to the script for *The Ring*, Breen warned: "We feel that it would not be good to infer that the police discriminate against these boys because of their nationality."[27] In *The Ring*, Tomás "Tommy Kansas" Cantanios (Lalo Rios) tries—and fails—to make it out of the East L.A. barrio as a professional boxer. While Tomás blames the "Anglos" for the limited opportunities and discrimination that he faces, in the final film version it is a police officer who makes sure that "the boys," including Tomás, are served at an all-white diner.

In the most unusual instance, PCA censors threatened to withhold the seal of approval for *Trial*, an anticommunist courtroom drama that also deals with discrimination against a Mexican-American youth falsely accused of rape. The film is able to combine these two themes, since the youth's lawyer is revealed to be a communist organizer using the case to stir up "race hatred." The script was seen as "a subtly Communist vehicle" since, in the words of the PCA, it seemed to present a "plea" against "guilt by association" and an investigating committee run by "an obnoxious Senator," while it also sought "kindness" for former, repentent communists.[28] Despite the rather obvious allusion to Senator Joseph McCarthy, the film was granted a seal of approval, even though, as censors noted, only the plea against "guilt by association" was dropped.[29] In part, the approval marked the steady decline of McCarthy's influence since the Senate had "condemned" him a year earlier, in 1954. But, as I will demonstrate later, "guilt by association" provided a conceptual and "actual" link between the communist threat, Mexican Americans, and juvenile delinquency. In *Trial*, which bears remarkable similarities to the Sleepy Lagoon case, "guilt by association" enables the narrative to resolve the inherent legal contradictions.

As with Mexican-American representation, the PCA based its censorship of material that criticized social institutions on the potential for "public hue and cry." This time, however, it was an American rather than a Mexican public. That—as Shurlock made explicit—the mere "likelihood" of public protests would lead the PCA to withhold the seal of approval[30] suggests that the popular appeal, like the communist threat, provided a convenient facade for the status quo which the code's "General Principles" upheld. In this way, the PCA diffused the challenge that the Mexican-American experience presented to American society and institutions, bifurcating it into Mexican and American components. Each component expressed, no doubt, the "enlightened" values of the time. Mexican Americans could not be called "greasers" or portrayed in a negative or inauthentic manner. Nor could social institutions be ridiculed or natural and human laws violated. And, as the censorship correspondence reveals, the PCA observed a strict concern for the social and moral impact of film, often in the name of the people. The PCA's overall strategy, however, engaged the same politics of citizenship found in the state courts and federal immigration policies, a politics of denial. On the one hand, control over Mexican-American representation was "repatriated" as a *Mexican* issue; while, on the other hand, the "racial question" or social problem was defined within institutional parameters as an *American* one.

The social-problem films operated within these ideological limits, enforced by PCA censorship. Given the nature of the social problem (broadly speaking, American citizenship), however, the narratives had to define the internal-external paradigm as a domestic rather than international one. As Arthur Pettit argues, American popular fiction and, later, film function to "localize" Mexican Americans to a specific geographical space: the southwest.[31] But, if we apply his concept more broadly, feature films "about" and "with" Mexican-American characters also "localize" or delimit them to certain genres: western-conquest, social-problem, and exploitation films. In this way, the film discourse on Mexican Americans is itself "localized" to violence (and sex), with the narrative constructed toward a judgment that determines the appropriate place for the Mexican-American character. Thus the films reinforce, in the words of Homi K. Bhabha, the "space of identification" or "fixity" for the Other, for the Mexican American.[32] It is important to note, however, that these films must give expression in one form or another to the social contradictions, ambiguities, and contestation that are the historical basis for "fixity" or "localized" discourse.

While an in-depth analysis of how these narratives situate the Mexican-American subject is well beyond the scope of this paper, I want to offer an initial elaboration on the scheme presented above with respect to genre, action, judgment, and social placement.[33] In the first instance, the social-problem films fall into three major genres: romantic melodrama (*Right Cross, My Man and I, A Medal for Benny*); courtroom drama/juvenile delinquent (*The Lawless, Trial*, and, as a precursor, *Bordertown*); and boxing film (*The Ring, Right Cross, Requiem for a Heavyweight*). *Right Cross* is almost identical to *The Ring*, except that it adds romantic melodrama to the plot and resolution. In addition, *Giant* can be classified as a modern western, while, in theme, *Giant* and *Salt of the Earth* combine if not conflate labor, racial, and gender issues.

While in general these genres provide for diverse courses of action, each of the above films has an act of violence as the "inciting incident," the incident the narrative attempts to resolve.[34] In the boxing films, of course, the inciting incident has to do with the Mexican-American boxer's temper and anger, which are shown to have been the result of an ethnic paranoia about the "gringo conspiracy." In addition, fist fights also start at least two other films: *Bordertown* and *The Lawless*. In *A Medal for Benny*, the "inciting incident" occurs off-camera but frames the entire narrative as the nature and impact of Benny Martín's absence unfolds. Martín had been a violent and criminal youth "run out of town" by the local judge, whereupon he enlisted in the service, killing "more than a hundred Japs" before he himself is killed. Beyond violence between men, often between Mexican American and Anglo American, nearly half of the films are based upon an accusation of interracial rape and/or crime of passion: *Bordertown, My Man and I, The Lawless*, and *Trial*. Thus, as the narratives explore Mexican-American citizenship with all good and earnest intent, they do so through the textual filter of the Mexican-bandit stereotype, the "greaser" who threatens to "shoot the cowboy" and "rape his woman."

The "greaser" is a product of American thought and popular culture since the 1820s, when Anglo Americans first settled in Texas, then the northernmost state of Mexico.[35] The "greaser" would continue to appear in dime westerns and, in the 1910s, in silent films. In numerous films, from *Licking the Greasers* (1910) to *Guns and Greasers* (1918), the Mexican bandit threatened death and rape, while the Anglo-American hero often ended up with a "greaser" wife, as in *Broncho Billy's Mexican Wife* (1915). These films represent an expression of the border-conflict period, anticipating the more direct and "enlightened" treatment of Mexican-American citizenship of the social-problem films. While the "greaser" was always Mexican, often he lived north of the border. And, in the treatment of the concurrent Mexican Revolution, these films initiated, indirectly, the immigration narrative,[36] with Mexican women as the sanctioned border crossers. In this manner, the "greaser" genre resolved the southwest's political unconscious, which returns or reemerges under the impetus of increased Mexican immigration and, in 1912, statehood for Arizona and New Mexico (exceptional for its Mexican majority). In addition to miscegenation with Mexican women, the films sometimes presented a redeemed or "noble greaser" who would protect Anglo Americans from other "greasers." It is in these two resolutions that we see the first Mexican-American or Chicano characters in the American cinema: for to be a "noble greaser" was to be a double outcast, neither Mexican nor American; while to be Broncho Billy's or Shorty Hamilton's (*Licking the Greasers*) or Dick Henshaw's (*Aztec Treasure*, 1914) wife meant assimilation, with neither economic power nor the right to vote.

The social-problem films did attempt to transcend the stereotypical representations of the "greaser" genre. In particular, the films produced in the 1950s reflect a significant liberal impulse from within Hollywood, one often poised against the HUAC investigations. These include: King Brothers Productions (*The Ring*), which regularly hired blacklisted personnel under pseudonyms; MGM's Dore Schary, producer of *My Man and I, Right Cross*, and *Trial*, who attempted to mediate or mitigate HUAC decrees; and Herbert Biberman (*Salt of the Earth*), one of the "Hollywood Ten"; and blacklisted director Joseph Losey (*The Lawless*).[37] The nature of these changes, however, was a matter of degree rather than of kind: rape and murder now became a false accusation of rape and murder. While the false accusation allowed the films to play upon and expose racist expectations, it did little to expand the discourse on Mexican Americans beyond them. Thus the violent inciting incident leads to a comparable climax: judgment. In most films, judgment is the result of either a fist fight— *Right Cross, The Ring, Giant*, and *Requiem for a Heavyweight*—or a court decision—*Bordertown, The Lawless, My Man and I*, and *Trial*. In all cases, the Mexican-American protagonist loses the physical fight but wins the legal battle.[38]

In a broad sense, these two judgments or resolutions—fight and trial—mark a crucial boundary within the domain of discourse on the Mexican American, one that I have already shown to have circulated within immigration, legal, and censorship institutions: *Mexican* psychological deficiencies and *American* institutional activism. In *Right Cross* and *The Ring*, the fight ends the protagonist's career, causing his considerable anger at Anglo-American society to dissipate. These characters are revealed to have shadowboxed and to have destroyed, not a racist society, but the demons within themselves. Likewise, the young men in *Bordertown* and *A Medal for Benny* are shown to have misdirected their inherent violence toward "making it" under American capitalism and are redirected toward more acceptable and distant areas: helping one's people in the barrio or fighting for one's country overseas. While the films that are resolved in the courtroom affirm Mexican-American virtue, the fact that the narratives are predicated on Mexican-American violence, even if by false accusation, restricts the judgment. After all, it is the Mexican American on trial, and not the racist individuals or society that put him there. At the same time, the trials reaffirm the activist role of the legal system and state, often with lynch mobs as the alternative, so that racism must, in effect, be worked out through the passing of judgment upon the Mexican-American protagonist. What interests me here, however, is how in both instances the judgment functions to situate the Mexican-American characters within a social matrix of assimilation, within either barrio segregation or, in a few instances, racial integration.

For the most part, the social-problem films return the protagonist to the barrio, where he belongs. The Mexican American's efforts to enter the professional mainstream (*Bordertown*) or achieve economic parity (*A Medal for Benny, The Ring, Salt of the Earth*) are sanctioned only within the confines and reduced scale of the barrio. In *Bordertown*, Johnny Ramirez fails both as a lawyer and, having been disbarred for violent behavior, as a border-town casino manager. In the end, he returns to the barrio, "Back where I belong . . . with my own people," framed between his *padre* and mother, between church and home, the barrio's two more traditional (read: conservative) institutions.[39] Even that, however, may not have been enough closure within the Mexican-American Generation, as the *New York Times* reviewer made clear: "The Mexican's [*sic*] feeble confessional . . . is an unconvincing and inconsistent denouement for the career of such a vigorous rebel against the *established order*."[40] Subsequent films would achieve closure through national, rather than barrio, institutions: the press, military, legal system, and, in *Salt of the Earth*, labor union.

In *A Medal for Benny* and *The Lawless*, discrimination is identified as the product of small-town provincialism. In particular, the films contrast the town's business leaders and police with more benevolent national institutions: the military in *A Medal for Benny* and the free press in *The Lawless*. Ultimately, however, this conflict is a red herring, insofar as the towns' social hierarchies remain unchallenged. The conflict is not over federalism but over the "space of identification" for the Mexican American. In *A Medal for Benny*, Joe Morales (Arturo De Cordova) at first identifies himself with the economic opportunism of the town's chamber of commerce, which intends to exploit Benny Martín's heroism. When the general and military come to town, Martín's father, Charley (J. Carroll Naish), is "given" a nice house rather than have him represent the town from his barrio shack. Likewise, earlier in the film Morales "borrows" Charley's rent money in order to invest in a boat and, when it sinks, "borrows" even more in order to purchase an expressive dress for Benny's girlfriend, Lolita Sierra (Dorothy Lamour). When Charley refuses to play along, the general, to the surprise of the town leaders, insists on going to the barrio to present the medal, since "a lot of fine Americans come out of shacks." Whereas the town leaders, in full police escort, had earlier descended upon the barrio in order to retrieve Charley, the general arrives with a full military parade in order to salute the contribution Charley made from within the barrio. At this point, Morales's identification shifts from economic opportunism (business/town) to national service (military/barrio), and he enlists, a move that rewards him with Benny's girlfriend, when and if he returns to the barrio.

The placement within an institutional paradigm, however, continued to center on the construction of an actual or symbolic family. The parentless Morales, in effect, replaces Benny Martín for Charley and Lolita, this time "run out of town" by the military rather than the police. As the "better" son, he will be allowed to return to the barrio.[41] In *The Lawless* and *Trial*, each of the accused, fatherless Mexican-American youths acquires an Anglo-American, institutional father figure who defends him. The journalist in *The Lawless* saves Paul Rodriguez (Lalo Rios) from a lynch mob, and later uses the press to initiate a defense committee. At one point, Rodriguez tells the journalist that he reminds him of his older brother, who died in the war.[42] While the film depicts a barrio newspaper run by a woman,

Sunny Garcia (Gail Russell), it is the Anglo-American journalist whose commitment and sacrifice (his press is destroyed) will save Rodriguez. And, in fact, the journalist character functions on two levels to further displace the notion that a barrio journalist could have defended the community: through an incipient romantic relationship with Garcia, and, at the end, when he commandeers her press in order to "say all the things *I've* left unsaid."[43]

In *Trial*, the paternal connection is made even more explicit in the lawyer's half-hearted insistence that Angel Chavez (Rafael Campos) behave like his client and not his son. Throughout the trial, Chavez asks questions so that he, too, can become a lawyer. These questions provide a clever exposition device that allows the film to describe "due process" and "guilt by association," with Chavez complicit, if not eager, in the way these lead to his own conviction and death sentence.

Chavez is accused of murder when he is caught at an all-white beach with his white girlfriend dead at his feet. She had just recovered from rheumatic fever, and the excitement of "making love" (kissing) resulted in a heart attack. In the course of the trial, Chavez's lawyer discovers that his own boss is a communist and is using the case to raise funds, stir up racial hatred, and martyr Chavez for the party. In the end, the jury finds Chavez guilty of murder, punishable by death. Chavez's lawyer, however, exposes his boss's affiliations and intentions to the judge, and offers an alternative judgment since Chavez is a minor.[44]

Rather than apply the letter of the Felony Murder Act, he suggests that the judge *also* apply the letter of the Juvenile Defenders Act (normally for "trivial offenses"), which allows for an "indeterminate sentence." Thus, he argues, "through its own technicalities," the law can correct its own errors. The prosecution agrees with the defense's "most ingenious theory of law," and admits that he was "sure that Angel Chavez was technically guilty . . . [but] . . . that his guilt was only technical." In essence, the two lawyers agree that Chavez is, in fact, innocent of murder, but uphold the conviction and the "harsh rules of law" that secured it. In these two references to legal "technicalities," *Trial* suggests that the law is an arbitrary construct, not rooted in a moral absolute. What does hold the legal system together, then, is the notion of "guilt by association": that in his sexual and political mis-associations, Chavez merits some form of punishment. (Meanwhile, the racist townspeople "have learned an awful lot" as mere *spectators*.) Thus the judge sentences Chavez to the State Industrial School for an indeterminate period of time, "until the principal determines that your release will serve your own best interests and those of society." In perhaps the most visceral way, the law(yer) becomes Chavez's father, and metes out the "justice" he claims the reformed townspeople now desire: his socialization by the state into the working class.

In an apparent (and isolated) shift in this dynamic, two Ricardo Montalban films—*My Man and I* and *Right Cross*—end with his character's marriage to an Anglo-American blonde. For perhaps the first time in the American cinema, the sanctioned miscegenation between Mexican and American involved a Mexican-American male. Upon closer examination, how-ever, these films do not result in the Mexican American's integration into the so-called "dominant white culture." Nor do they punish and exile the Anglo-American woman to the barrio. While the Mexican American is repeatedly identified in the United States as a "racial" minority, black-and-white race dynamics at some point fail to hold. In part, Montalban's status as a second-generation Latin Lover (itself a step removed from "Mexican") and light skin color place him in the color line's gray zone. After all, while the PCA prohibited miscegenation, it defined it as sex between the *black* and *white* races. Even more crucial, while the women in both films are blondes, neither represents the dominant culture. In *My Man and I*, Shelley Winters, Hollywood's "bad girl," portrays a low-class alcoholic down on her luck; while in *Right Cross*, June Allyson, Hollywood's "girl next door," portrays an ethnic-Catholic Irish American long before it was thought one could become president. Thus the Mexican-American character can, through assimilation and miscegenation, leave the barrio behind, but still be emplaced within class and ethnic boundaries. In *Right Cross*, the Irish are shown to be the same short-tempered, devout, dispossessed, yet nostalgic nationalists as the Mexican-American characters, who—in most films—state how their ancestors once controlled the town, county, or zinc mine. Chu Chu Ramirez, in *My Man and I*, evinces the same self-sacrifice toward Winters's character that the Mexican Americans in other films do toward the barrio or war effort. In fact, his ceaseless optimism as a newly naturalized citizen reforms all the other low-life and redneck white characters, in particular Mr. and Mrs. Ames, despite the couple's various attempts to seduce, cheat, injure, and frame him for attempted murder.

While the script for *My Man and I* led Breen to recommend to MGM producer Dore Schary that he "get proper technical advice from the Mexican angle,"[45] the end product raises questions about the narrative function of Mexican-American representation in the social-problem films. On a manifest level, the social contradictions about Mexican-American citizenship are resolved, with the Mexican-American Generation repatriated, segregated, and institutionalized in the name of assimilation, the same ideal the Mexican-American Generation incorporated into its own, reformist political discourse. But in its representation of the Mexican American, most social-problem films were more concerned with not offending Mexico than with presenting an "authentic" ethnic-American portrayal. In *My Man and I*, *A Medal for Benny*, and *Bordertown*, the Mexican-American characters speak a pidgin English devoid of definite articles and pronouns, even though the Spanish language makes even greater use of these modifiers than does English. But perhaps the most telling sign is that every film presents Spanish-language dialogue *without* subtitles. In these respects, *Giant* is an exception: the production files reveal considerable research into authentic "Mexican" costume and villages, even though these scenes, unlike in the other films, are marginal. And while Shurlock cites errors in the Spanish-language dialogue, *Giant* alone uses that dialogue, again unsubtitled, to establish two levels of signification. Bick Benedict speaks fluent Spanish to order about his "Mexican" employees, while his new, East Coast wife does the unthinkable and asks for their names and about their health, in English. In the other films, when the characters speak Spanish, it is not supposed to function as a speech act that signifies within or has an impact upon the narrative but exists instead as an empty code for ethnicity. In short, there is no need for subtitles because nothing is said.

It is here that the narrative function of emplacement becomes visible, in the recognition of the de facto "mainstream," monolingual audience for these films. These were not, after all, the equivalent of the Hollywood "race" films. The oft-praised *Salt of the Earth* was no exception: it spoke more to the ex-Hollywood production team's blacklisting than to the New Mexico *hispano* community, which it portrays as *mexicano* with an even more improbable neoindigenous nationalism.[46] Thus the social-problem films situated the Mexican-American character for a largely Anglo-American audience. For a narrative articulation of this process, recall the townspeople *qua* spectators in *Trial*. But the significance of the audience is perhaps most evident in the relationship between sanctioned miscegenation and genre. Briefly, the two films in which Ricardo Montalban marries a blonde woman are romantic melodramas: in other words, women's films. The print ads for both films feature Montalban, without shirt, embracing the female lead. For *Right Cross*, one caption reads, "Girls!!! Would you do what June Allyson did? Have you ever loved a man so much that you'd pursue him no matter what?"[47] Perhaps more than anything, these ads construct a "space of identification" for the post–World War II working-class woman. Thus the placement of the Mexican-American protagonist within normative social or institutional parameters likewise places the female audience identified with the female lead/star. That identification is constructed in opposition to the married seductresses in *My Man and I* and *Bordertown* (classified at the time as a melodrama), who serve as the real evil forces in the films. In *Bordertown*, the single socialite who plays with Ramirez, calling him "savage," is also punished (with death) for her willful transgression of class *and* racial boundaries.

In *Giant*, like earlier westerns and "greaser" films, it is the Anglo-American man who marries the Mexican woman. It is in the western, a male-identified genre, that the Anglo-American protagonist can cross racial *and* class boundaries and take, in both cases, a step down. In the 1950s variant on American patriarchal society, after all, it is the man who determines/provides economic and class status as well as family name. *Giant*, however, provides a subtle turn on these conventions. It is not the hero, Bick Benedict, but his effeminate son, Jordan (Dennis Hopper), who marries the submissive mestiza Juana (Elsa Cardenas). Furthermore, their nearly equitable relationship produces the logical outcome that the "greaser" films point toward but can in no way envision: a mestizo-Anglo infant (and his Anglo cousin), depicted in wide-screen close-up. It is a rare moment in the American cinema on ethnicity, one that stops the narrative cold, with both hope and uncertainty.

With the exception of *Salt of the Earth* and *Giant*, the social-problem films "about" Mexican Americans center on a "Mexican" male protagonist and his place or role within American society. In contrast, *Salt of the Earth* and *Giant* employ a protofeminist critique in order to reorient class and racial hierarchies. *Giant*, however, does so on both corporeal and symbolic levels, with "miscegenation" between east (Leslie [Elizabeth Taylor]) and west (Bick) and, in the next generation, north (Jordan) and south (Juana). In this sense, the film embodies, or finds affinities with, the Latin American concept of *mestizaje*, which, in post-World War War II thought, offered mestizo racial mixture as the solution to ideologies of racial purity.[48] In its familial construction of a new American culture—eastern liberalism, western capitalism, and Mexican Americanism—*Giant* also anticipates the cultural redefinition of *mestizaje* by Chicano and Anglo-American border artists.[49]

But, as I have argued, the role of women has often been the "political unconscious" in the social-problem films, so that Anglo-American and Mexican-American women become complicit in the placement of the Mexican-American protagonist within an appropriate class-defined, Protestant work ethic. In *A Medal for Benny* and *The Ring*, it is the "traditional" Mexican-American girlfriend who leads the protagonist back to the barrio, where—one way or another—he will support her. In this way, the female spectator, to the extent that she identifies with the female lead, unwittingly places herself alongside the Mexican-American male, becoming the mechanism that will keep him (and, by extension, her) within a marginal social context.

It is here, in the trials and titillations of Mexican-American citizenship, that the gender, "racial," and political discourses come together. To date, film critics and theorists who research the period between 1930 and 1960 have examined these discourses in relative isolation from each other. This is particularly so with respect to the representation of the Mexican American. To imply that the HUAC investigations, social-problem films, classical Hollywood style, and PCA censorship were distinctly *American* issues, and yet give little or no voice to the Mexican-American presence, is to engage and perpetuate the period's politics of denial toward the Mexican-American Generation.

It is perhaps worthwhile, then, to end with a word about Chicano Cinema, an alternative film practice that developed in the late 1960s within the overall project of the Chicano civil rights movement. During the movement, these filmmakers documented the concurrent social protests. In the postmovement period, but especially under the historical amnesia of the Reagan era, Chicano directors initiated a historical revisionism of the Mexican-American Generation. In feature films (*Zoot Suit* [1981], *La Bamba* [1987], *Break of Dawn* [1988]), documentaries (*Ballad of an Unsung Hero* [1983], *The Lemon Grove Incident* [1985]), and short dramas (*Distant Water* [1990]), filmmakers researched and reclaimed lost moments in American history.

In the initial development of Chicano Cinema as a cohesive or collective movement, writer/director/producer Jesús Salvador Treviño and others researched the unwritten history of Mexican-American and Chicano representation. *Salt of the Earth* was identified as a precursor; and when the Chicano Cinema Coalition organized in 1978, *Citizen Kane* (1945) was one of the first films its members screened and studied. Thus "classical" and Chicano-themed films became part of the filmmakers' self-conscious frame of reference. And, in fact, one can argue that the first two Chicano feature films draw upon the Hollywood social-problem film, but do so in order to invert its usual ideological thrust. *Raices de sangre* (Mexico, 1977, d. Jesús Treviño), for example, retells *Bordertown*, shifting the moral point of view from the Anglo-American to the Chicano community, thereby transforming the earlier film's enlightened segregationism into a radical separatism. In both films, the protagonist, a bordertown lawyer, reforms when he comes around to the film's moral point of view, eschews violence, and returns to the barrio. *Only Once in a Lifetime* (1978, d. Alejandro Grattan), on the other hand, uses the social-problem "drama-comedy," a hybrid used in *A Medal for Benny* and somewhat typical of American social-problem films in the 1970s. Again, the protagonist returns to the barrio, but, as in *Raices de sangre*, with an activist intent designed to confront American society on a collective rather than individual level.

In that subtle yet significant shift, these two Chicano-produced feature films initiated a counterdiscourse on Mexican-American citizenship, one that stressed a cultural nationalist, rather than assimilationist, identity, or found traces of it in historical dramas of resistance such as *Zoot Suit* and *Break of Dawn*. For its part, Hollywood responded as it had in the past, when Mexico protested the silent "greaser" films: it simply stopped producing films "about" Mexican Americans or Chicanos. Taken together, the silent "greaser" films, the social-problem films about Mexican Americans, and the Chicano-produced feature films constitute the American cinema's explicit discourse on Chicano citizenship. Throughout the eighty years of that discourse, Hollywood has engaged—through outright stereotype, "enlightened" segregationism, and now silence—in a politics of denial. In the period between 1930 and 1960, often with the intervention of PCA censors, these films attempted to mediate Mexican-American demands for assimilation and the rights of citizenship, and resituate them around other issues related to national politics, juvenile delinquency, and changes in class-based gender roles. It is little wonder, then, that the post-Mexican-American Generation, or Chicanos, would reject "political accommodation and assimilation," and stress instead a politics of cultural difference.

Notes

1   These films are: *Bordertown* (1935), *A Medal for Benny* (1945), *The Lawless* (1950), *Right Cross* (1950), *My Man and I* (1952), *The Ring* (1952), *Salt of the Earth* (1954), *Trial* (1955), *Giant* (1956), and *Requiem for a Heavyweight* (1962).

2   See Carlos Muñoz, Jr., "From Segregation to Melting Pot Democracy: The Mexican-American Generation," in *Youth, Identity, Power: The Chicano Movement* (London: Verso, 1989), pp. 19–46; and Mario T. Garcia, *Mexican Americans: Leadership, Ideology and Identity, 1930–1960* (New Haven: Yale University Press, 1989).

3   Richard A. Garcia, "The Mexican American Mind: A Product of the 1930s," in *History, Culture, and Society: Chicago Studies in the 1980s* (Ypsilanti, Mich.: Bilingual Press/Editorial Bilingüe, 1983), pp. 67–93.

4   Muñoz, "From Segregation," p. 49. In a similar argument, Richard A. Garcia defines Mexican-Americanism as a dualistic identity: "Mexican in culture and American in ideas and ideology" ("The Mexican American Mind," p. 84). For an account of Mexican-American response and attitudes toward Mexican immigration in this period, see Garcia, *Mexican Americans*; and John R. Chávez, *The*

Lost Land: The Chicano Image of the Southwest (Albuquerque: University of New Mexico Press, 1984), pp. 85–106.

5   For an extensive historical account, see Abraham Hoffman, *Unwanted Mexican-Americans in the Great Depression* (Tucson: University of Arizona Press, 1974); and Mercedes Carreras de Velasco, *Los Mexicanos que devolvió la crisis, 1929–1932* (Mexico: Secretaria de Relaciones Exteriores, 1974).

6   Mexican immigration: 1901–10, 49,642; 1911–20, 219,004; 1921–30, 459,298; 1931–40, 22,319; 1941–50, 60,589; 1951–60, 299,811; and 1961–70, 453,937. Source: U.S. Department of Justice, *1976 Annual Report: Immigration and Naturalization Service* (Washington, D.C.: U.S. Government Printing Office, 1976), pp. 86–88; cited in Howard M. Bahr et al., *American Ethnicity* (Lexington, Mass.: D.C. Heath, 1979), p. 56.

7   For an extensive historical account, see Juan Ramon Garcia, *Operation Wetback: The Mass Deportation of Mexican Undocumented Workers in 1954* (Westport, Conn.: Greenwood Press, 1980).

8   The later political deportations fell under the rubric of the McCarran–Walter Act (U.S. Immigration and Nationality Act) of 1952. See Garcia, *Operation Wetback*, p. 198. For an earlier account, see Patricia Morgan, *Shame of a Nation: A Documented Story of Police-State Terror Against Mexican-Americans in the U.S.A.* (Los Angeles: Los Angeles Committee for Protection of the Foreign Born, 1954), in particular, pp. 38–39.

9   Muñoz, *Youth, Identity, Power*, pp. 50–51.

10   *Ibid.*, p. 20–31.

11   Mauricio Mazón, *The Zoot-Suit Riots: The Psychology of Symbolic Annihilation* (Austin: University of Texas Press, 1984), p. 20.

12   *Ibid.*, pp. 86–87, 92.

13   Rodolfo Acuña, *Occupied America: A History of the Chicanos*, 3rd ed. (New York: Harper & Row, 1988), pp. 253–259.

14   Two significant institutional responses were the California Youth Authority and the Los Angeles Youth Project. As the director of the latter program acknowledged, "The 'zoot-suit' riots brought matters to a head" (quoted in Mazón, *Zoot-Suit Riots*, p. 101).

15   Mazón, *Zoot-Suit Riots*, pp. 23, 27.

16   The PCA began to lose power in the mid-1950s with the advent of television and the dismantling of the studio system under the "consent decrees" (which required the studios to divest themselves of distribution and exhibition holdings by 1953). Most of the social-problem films, however, were produced in the period before these changes had a significant impact on PCA censorship.

17   For an account of the rise and development of the PCA, see Marvin N. Olasky, "The Failure of Movie Industry Public Relations, 1921–1934," *Journal of Popular Film & Television* 12 (Winter 1984–85): 163–170; and Gregory D. Black, "Hollywood Censored: The Production Code Administration and the Hollywood Film Industry, 1930–1940," *Film History* 3 (1989): 167–189. While the PCA monitored some 20,000 films between 1934 and 1968, film criticism of these films often overlooks, as Lea Jacobs argues, how "censorship functioned at the level of representation, as a set of rules which governed the production of meaning" (Lea Jacobs, "Industry Self-Regulation and the Problem of Textual Determination," *The Velvet Light Trap* no. 23 [Spring 1989]: 4–15). In " 'Something's Missing Here!'—Homosexuality and Film Reviews During the Production Code Era, 1934–1962," I examine the code's censorship of homosexual depictions and the reception of film reviewers: *Cinema Journal* 30 (Fall 1990): 20–41. For two recent case studies on film censorship, see Gerald Gardner, *The Censorship Papers: Movie Censorship Letters from the Hays Office, 1934 to 1968* (New York: Dodd, Mead, 1987) and Leonard J. Leff and Jerold L. Simmons, *The Dame in the Kimono: Hollywood, Censorship, and the Production Code from the 1920s to the 1960s* (New York: Grove Weidenfeld, 1990). Both books reprint "The Motion Picture Production Code." On *Salt of the Earth*, see Michael Wilson and Deborah Silverton Rosenfelt, *Salt of the Earth* (New York: Feminist Press, 1978).

18   Joseph Breen, letter to Dory Schary, M-G-M, 9 July 1952. MPAA Production Code Administration case files: *My Man and I* (1951). The Margaret Herrick Library. Beverly Hills, California.

19   These particular phrases are taken from an initial script of *The Ring*. See Joseph Breen, letter to Franklin King, King Bros. Productions, 19 November 1951. MPAA Production Code Administration case files: *The Ring* (1951). The Margaret Herrick Library. Beverly Hills, California.

20   As cited in Finlay McDermid, memo to George Stevens and Henry Ginsberg, 13 April 1955. Warner Brothers Archives. Production Files: *Giant* (1956). Box #403. School of Cinema-Television. University of Southern California. Los Angeles, California.

21   Joseph Breen, letter to Jack Warner, Warner Brothers, 10 July 1934. Warner Brothers Archives,

Production Files: *Bordertown* (1935). B-29. School; of Cinema-Television. University of Southern California. Los Angeles, California.

22   Joseph Breen, letter to Jack Warner, Warner Brothers, 10 August 1934. Warner Brothers Archives. Production Files: *Bordertown* (1935). B-29. School of Cinema-Television. University of Southern California. Los Angeles, California.

23   See Allen L. Woll, *The Latin Image in American Film* (Los Angeles: UCLA Latin American Center Publications, 1977), pp. 16–22; and Helen Delpar, "Goodbye to the 'Greaser': Mexico, the MPPDA, and Derogatory Films, 1922–1926," *Journal of Popular Film & Television* 12 (1984): 34–41.

24   John Hay Whitney, Director of the Motion Pictures Section, as quoted in Woll, *Latin Image in American Film*, p. 54.

25   See Woll, *Latin Image in American Film*, ch. 4, "Hollywood's Good Neighbor Policy," pp. 53–75.

26   Joseph Breen, letter to Luigi Luraschi, Paramount Pictures, 5 October 1949. MPAA Production Code Administration case files: *The Lawless* (1949). The Margaret Herrick Library. Beverly Hills, California.

27   Joseph Breen, letter to Franklin King, 19 November 1951, cited above.

28   J.A.V. [Jack A. Vizzard], "Memo for the Files," 30 March 1955. MPAA Production Code Administration case files: *Trial* (1955). The Margaret Herrick Library. Beverly Hills, California.

29   *Ibid.*, and "Analysis of Film Content" form [same citation], which gives June 10, 1955, as date of approval.

30   Geoffrey Shurlock, letter to Dore Schary, M-G-M, 30 March 1955. MPAA Production Code Administration case files: *Trial* (1955). The Margaret Herrick Library. Beverly Hills, California.

31   Arthur G. Pettit, *Images of the Mexican American in Fiction and Film* (College Station: Texas A&M University Press, 1980), p. xv.

32   Homi K. Bhabha, "The Other Question. . . .," *Screen* 24 (November–December 1983): 18–36.

33   Charles Ramirez-Berg provides an in-depth analysis of *Bordertown*, which he argues established the ideological and narrative features for subsequent social-problem films about Mexican Americans. He places these films within a larger generic group he calls the "assimilation narrative" ("*Bordertown*, the Assimilation Narrative and the Chicano Social Problem Film," in Chon Noriega, ed., *Chicanos and Film: Essays on Chicano Representation and Resistance* [New York: Garland Publishing, forthcoming]). I am indebted to Charles Ramirez-Berg for our numerous discussions of these films.

34   In my discussion, I rely upon the concepts of practitioner-oriented script analysts for "classic" story structure. For an initial application of these concepts to recent Chicano-produced and -themed feature films, see Mario Barrera, "Story Structure in Latino Films," in Noriega, *Chicanos and Film*.

35   Arnoldo De León, *They Called Them Greasers: Anglo Attitudes Toward Mexicans in Texas, 1821–1900* (Austin: University of Texas Press, 1983).

36   For a comparative genre analysis of Mexican immigration films, see David R. Maciel, "Braceros, Mojados, and Alambristas: Mexican Immigration to the United States in Contemporary Cinema," *Hispanic Journal of Behavioral Sciences* 8 (1986): 369–385.

37   Victor S. Navasky, *Naming Names* (New York: Viking Press, 1980), pp. xxi, 83–84, 155–156, 337.

38   In *Giant*, Bick Benedict (Rock Hudson) also loses the climactic fist fight, when he at last "does the right thing" and defends his Mexican daughter-in-law.

39   Here *padre* refers to a priest, but its other meaning, father, is also significant in terms of how the ending situates Ramirez within the barrio by way of a symbolic, institutional family.

40   Emphasis mine. Andre Seenwald, "The Strand Reopens With *Bordertown*, a Picturesque Melodrama With Paul Muni and Bette Davis," *New York Times*, Jan. 24, 1935, p. 22. The reviewer may have also objected to the fact that Ramirez uses his ill-gotten wealth to endow a barrio law school.

41   Better because his opportunism tends more toward capitalism than outright robbery, although this, too, is corrected, and his future as a laborer accepted. With respect to the overall message, *A Medal for Benny* was one of many wartime "racial unity" films that were released as enlistment propaganda. The initial treatment for the film was completed March 16, 1943, and the final film released April 9, 1945.

42   Although Rodriguez's father is alive, his "defeatist withdrawal" allows the journalist to assume a father-like big-brother role. I use Peter Roffman and Jim Purdy's apt phrase in *The Hollywood Social Problem Film: Madness, Despair, and Politics from the Depression to the Fifties* (Bloomington: Indiana University Press, 1981), p. 255.

43   Emphasis added. The last scene depicts Garcia showing the journalist how to line-o-type and set the press, an act that identifies her as more skilled laborer than professional.

44   In an example of the limits of Latino representation in Hollywood, the judge, who is chosen for the

case because he is "Negro" and cannot be accused of racism against Chavez, is played by Puerto Rican actor Juano Hernandez.

45   See note 18.

46   Likewise, Deborah Rosenfelt's introduction to the book *Salt of the Earth* (cited above) glosses over the powerful and not-so-uplifting women's experience that emerges in her interviews with Virginia Chacon, and which the film highly romanticizes into a "feel good" message.

47   M-G-M Press Book: *My Man and I* and *Right Cross*. School of Cinema-Television. University of Southern California. Los Angeles, California.

48   For the definitive expression of this concept, see José Vasconcelos, *La raza cósmica* (México, D.F.: Espasa-Calpe Mexicana, 1948).

49   In particular, I refer to the Border Arts Workshop/Taller de Arte Frontierzo (BAW/TAF) in San Diego/Tijuana, whose members included Isaac Artenstein, David Avalos, Phillip and Amy Brookman, Emily Hicks, and Guillermo Gómez-Peña. See, for example, the BAW/TAF publication *Broken Line/La Linea Quebrade* (San Diego); Guillermo Gomez-Peña and Jeff Kelley, eds., *The Border Art Workshop: A Documentation of Five Years of Interdisciplinary Art Projects Dealing with U.S.-Mexico Border Issues, 1984– 1989* (New York: Artists Space/La Jolla: Museum of Contemporary Art, 1989); and Guillermo Gomez-Peña, "The Multicultural Paradigm: An Open Letter to the National Arts Community," *High Performance*, September 1989, pp. 18–27.

Chapter 25

Jack Shaheen

REEL BAD ARABS: HOW HOLLYWOOD VILIFIES A PEOPLE (2003)

INTRODUCTION

Al tikrar biallem il hmar (By repetition even the donkey learns).

THIS ARAB PROVERB ENCAPSULATES how effective repetition can be when it comes to education: how we learn by repeating an exercise over and over again until we can respond almost reflexively. A small child uses repetition to master numbers and letters of the alphabet. Older students use repetition to memorize historical dates and algebraic formulas.

For more than a century Hollywood, too, has used repetition as a teaching tool, tutoring movie audiences by repeating over and over, in film after film, insidious images of the Arab people. I ask the reader to study in these pages the persistence of this defamation, from earlier times to the present day, and to consider how these slanderous stereotypes have affected honest discourse and public policy.

GENESIS

In [my book *Reel Bad Arabs*], I document and discuss virtually every feature that Hollywood has ever made—more than 900 films, the vast majority of which portray Arabs by distorting at every turn what most Arab men, women, and children are really like. In gathering the evidence for this book, I was driven by the need to expose an injustice: cinema's systematic, pervasive, and unapologetic degradation and dehumanization of a people.

When colleagues ask whether today's reel Arabs are more stereotypical than yester-year's, I can't say the celluloid Arab has changed. That is the problem. He is what he has always been—the cultural "other." Seen through Hollywood's distorted lenses, Arabs look different and threatening. Projected along racial and religious lines, the stereotypes are deeply ingrained in American cinema. From 1896 until today, filmmakers have collectively indicted all Arabs as Public Enemy #1—brutal, heartless, uncivilized religious fanatics and money-mad cultural "others" bent on terrorizing civilized Westerners, especially Christians and Jews. Much has happened since 1896—women's suffrage, the Great Depression, the civil rights movement, two world wars, the Korean, Vietnam, and Gulf wars, and the collapse of the Soviet Union. Throughout it all, Hollywood's caricature of the Arab has prowled the silver screen. He is there to this day—repulsive and unrepresentative as ever.

What is an Arab? In countless films, Hollywood alleges the answer: Arabs are brute murderers, sleazy rapists, religious fanatics, oil-rich dimwits, and abusers of women. "They [the Arabs] all look alike to me," quips the American heroine in the movie *The Sheik Steps Out* (1937). "All Arabs look alike to me," admits the protagonist in *Commando* (1968). Decades later, nothing had changed. Quips the U.S. Ambassador in *Hostage* (1986), "I can't tell one [Arab] from another. Wrapped in those bed sheets they all look the same to me." In Hollywood's films, they certainly do.

Pause and visualize the reel Arab. What do you see? Black beard, headdress, dark sunglasses. In the background—a limousine, harem maidens, oil wells, camels. Or perhaps he is brandishing an automatic weapon, crazy hate in his eyes and Allah on his lips. Can you see him?

Think about it. When was the last time you saw a movie depicting an Arab or an American of Arab heritage as a regular guy? Perhaps a man who works ten hours a day, comes home to a loving wife and family, plays soccer with his kids, and prays with family members at his respective mosque or church. He's the kind of guy you'd like to have as your next door neighbor, because—well, maybe because he's a bit like you.

But would you want to share your country, much less your street, with any of Hollywood's Arabs? Would you want your kids playing with him and his family, your teenagers dating them? Would you enjoy sharing your neighborhood with fabulously wealthy and vile oil sheikhs with an eye for Western blondes and arms deals and intent on world domination, or with crazed terrorists, airplane hijackers, or camel-riding bedouins?

REAL ARABS

Who exactly are the Arabs of the Middle East? When I use the term "Arab," I refer to the 265 million people who reside in, and the many more millions around the world who are from, the 22 Arab states.[1] The Arabs have made many contributions to our civilization. To name a few, Arab and Persian physicians and scientists inspired European thinkers like Leonardo da Vinci. The Arabs invented algebra and the concept of zero. Numerous English words—algebra, chemistry, coffee, and others—have Arab roots. Arab intellectuals made it feasible for Western scholars to develop and practice advanced educational systems.

In astronomy Arabs used astrolabes for navigation, star maps, celestial globes, and the concept of the center of gravity. In geography, they pioneered the use of latitude and longitude. They invented the water clock; their architecture inspired the Gothic style in Europe. In agriculture, they introduced oranges, dates, sugar, and cotton, and pioneered water works and irrigation. And, they developed a tradition of legal learning, of secular literature and scientific and philosophical thought, in which the Jews also played an important part.

There exists a mixed ethnicity in the Arab world—from 5000 BC to the present. The Scots, Greeks, British, French, Romans, English, and others have occupied the area. Not surprisingly, some Arabs have dark hair, dark eyes, and olive complexions. Others boast freckles, red hair, and blue eyes.

Geographically, the Arab world is one-and-a-half times as large as the United States, stretching from the Strait of Hormuz to the Rock of Gibraltar. It's the point where Asia, Europe, and Africa come together. The region gave the world three major religions, a language, and an alphabet.

In most Arab countries today, 70 percent of the population is under age 30. Most share a common language, cultural heritage, history, and religion (Islam). Though the vast majority of them are Muslims, about 15 million Arab Christians (including Chaldean, Coptic, Eastern Orthodox, Episcopalian, Roman Catholic, Melkite, Maronite, and Protestant), reside there as well.

. . . Their dress is traditional and Western. The majority are peaceful, not violent; poor, not rich; most do not dwell in desert tents; none are surrounded by harem maidens; most have never seen an oil well or mounted a camel. Not one travels via "magic carpets." Their lifestyles defy stereotyping.

. . . Through immigration, conversion, and birth, . . . Muslims are America's fastest growing religious group; about 500,000 reside in the greater Los Angeles area. America's six to eight million Muslims frequent more than 2,000 mosques, Islamic centers, and schools. They include immigrants from more than 60 nations, as well as African-Americans. In fact, most of the world's 1.1 billion Muslims are Indonesian, Indian, or Malaysian. Only 12 percent of the world's Muslims are Arab. Yet, moviemakers ignore this reality, depicting Arabs and Muslims as one and the same people. Repeatedly, they falsely project all Arabs as Muslims and all Muslims as Arabs. As a result, viewers, too, tend to link the same attributes to both peoples.

. . . Hollywood's past omission of "everyday" African-Americans, American Indians, and Latinos unduly affected the lives of these minorities. The same holds true with the industry's near total absence of regular Arab-Americans. Regular Mideast Arabs, too, are invisible on silver screens. Asks Jay Stone, "Where are the movie Arabs and Muslims who are just ordinary people?"[2]

Why is it important for the average American to know and care about the Arab stereotype? It is critical because dislike of "the stranger," which the Greeks knew as xeno-phobia, forewarns that when one ethnic, racial, or religious group is vilified, innocent people suffer. History reminds us that the cinema's hateful Arab stereotypes are reminiscent of abuses in earlier times. Not so long ago—and sometimes still—Asians, American Indians, blacks, and Jews were vilified.

Ponder the consequences. In February 1942, more than 100,000 Americans of Japanese descent were displaced from their homes and interred in camps; for decades blacks were denied basic civil rights, robbed of their property, and lynched; American Indians, too, were displaced and slaughtered; and in Europe, six million Jews perished in the Holocaust.

This is what happens when people are dehumanized.

Mythology in any society is significant. And, Hollywood's celluloid mythology domin-ates the culture. No doubt about it, Hollywood's renditions of Arabs frame stereotypes in viewers' minds. The problem is peculiarly American. Because of the vast American cultural reach via television and film—we are the world's leading exporter of screen images—the all-pervasive Arab stereotype has much more of a negative impact on viewers today than it did thirty or forty years ago.

Nowadays, Hollywood's motion pictures reach nearly everyone. Cinematic illusions are created, nurtured, and distributed worldwide, reaching viewers in more than 100 countries, from Iceland to Thailand. Arab images have an effect not only on international audiences, but on international movie makers as well. No sooner do contemporary features leave the movie theaters than they are available in video stores and transmitted onto TV screens. Thanks to technological advances, old silent and sound movies impugning Arabs, some of which were produced before I was born, are repeatedly broadcast on cable television and beamed directly into the home.

Check your local guides and you will see that since the mid-1980s, appearing each week on TV screens, are fifteen to twenty recycled movies projecting Arabs as dehumanized caricatures: *The Sheik* (1921), *The Mummy* (1932), *Cairo* (1942), *The Steel Lady* (1953), *Exodus* (1960), *The Black Stallion* (1979), *Protocol* (1984), *The Delta Force* (1986), *Ernest in the Army* (1997), and *Rules of Engagement* (2000). Watching yesteryear's stereotypical Arabs on TV screens is an unnerving experience, especially when pondering the influence celluloid images have on adults and our youth.

. . . Arabs, like Jews, are Semites, so it is perhaps not too surprising that Hollywood's image of hook-nosed, robed Arabs parallels the image of Jews in Nazi-inspired movies such as *Robert and Bertram* (1939), *Die Rothschilds Aktien von Waterloo* (1940), *Der Ewige Jude* (1940), and *Jud Süss* (1940). Once upon a cinematic time, screen Jews boasted exaggerated nostrils and dressed differently—in yarmulkes and dark robes—than the films' protagonists. In the past, Jews were projected as the "other"—depraved and predatory money-grubbers who seek world domination, worship a different God, and kill innocents. Nazi propaganda also presented the lecherous Jew slinking in the shadows, scheming to snare the blonde Aryan virgin.

Yesterday's Shylocks resemble today's hook-nosed sheikhs, arousing fear of the "other." Reflects William Greider, "Jews were despised as exemplars of modernism," while today's "Arabs are depicted as carriers of primitivism—[both] threatening to upset our cozy modern world with their strange habits and desires."[3]

. . . Because of Hollywood's heightened cultural awareness, producers try not to demean most racial and ethnic groups. They know it is morally irresponsible to repeatedly bombard viewers with a regular stream of lurid, unyielding, and unrepentant portraits of a people. The relation is one of cause and effect. Powerful collages of hurtful images serve to deepen suspicions and hatreds. Jerry Mander observes, screen images "can cause people to do what they might otherwise never [have] thought to do."[4]

One can certainly make the case that movie land's pernicious Arab images are sometimes reflected in the attitudes and actions of journalists and government officials. Consider the aftermath of the 19 April 1995 bombing of the federal building in Oklahoma City. Though no American of Arab descent was involved, they were instantly targeted as suspects. Speculative reporting, combined with decades of harmful stereotyping, resulted in more than 300 hate crimes against them.[5]

A BASIS FOR UNDERSTANDING

. . . [I have reviewed] more than 900 feature films displaying Arab characters. Regrettably, in all these I uncovered only a handful of heroic Arabs; they surface in a few 1980s and 1990s scenarios. In *Lion of the Desert* (1981), righteous Arabs bring down invading fascists. Humane Palestinians surface in *Hanna K* (1983) and *The Seventh Coin* (1992). In *Robin Hood, Prince of Thieves* (1991), a devout Muslim who "fights better than twenty English knights," helps Robin Hood get the better of the evil Sheriff of Nottingham. In *The 13th Warrior* (1999), an Arab Muslim scholar befriends Nordic warriors, helping them defeat primitive cavemen. And in *Three Kings* (1999), a movie celebrating our commonalities and differences, we view Arabs as regular folks, with affections and aspirations. This anti-war movie humanizes the Iraqis, a people who for too long have been projected as evil caricatures.

Most of the time I found moviemakers saturating the marketplace with all sorts of Arab villains. Producers collectively impugned Arabs in every type of movie you can imagine, targeting adults in well-known and high-budgeted movies such as *Exodus* (1960), *Black Sunday* (1977), *Ishtar* (1987), and *The Siege* (1998); and reaching out to teenagers with financially successful schlock movies such as *Five Weeks in a Balloon* (1962), *Things Are Tough All Over* (1982), *Sahara* (1983), and *Operation Condor* (1997). One constant factor dominates all the films: Derogatory stereotypes are omnipresent, reaching youngsters, baby boomers, and older folk.

I am not saying an Arab should never be portrayed as the villain. What I am saying is that almost all Hollywood depictions of Arabs are bad ones. This is a grave injustice. Repetitious and negative images of the reel Arab literally sustain adverse portraits across generations. The fact is that for more than a century producers have tarred an entire group of people with the same sinister brush.

VILLAINS

. . . Beginning with *Imar the Servitor* (1914), up to and including *The Mummy Returns* (2001), a synergy of images equates Arabs from Syria to the Sudan with quintessential evil. In hundreds of movies "evil" Arabs stalk the screen. We see them assaulting just about every imaginable foe—Americans, Europeans, Israelis, legionnaires, Africans, fellow Arabs, even—for heaven's sake—Hercules and Samson.

Scores of comedies present Arabs as buffoons, stumbling all over themselves. Some of our best known and most popular stars mock Arabs: Will Rogers in *Business and Pleasure* (1931); Laurel and Hardy in *Beau Hunks* (1931); Bob Hope and Bing Crosby in *Road to Morocco* (1942); the Marx Brothers in *A Night in Casablanca* (1946); Abbott and Costello in *Abbott and Costello in the Foreign Legion* (1950); the Bowery Boys in *Bowery to Bagdad* (1955); Jerry Lewis in *The Sad Sack* (1957); Phil Silvers in *Follow That Camel* (1967); Marty Feldman in *The Last Remake of Beau Geste* (1977); Harvey Korman in *Americathon* (1979); Bugs Bunny in *1001 Rabbit Tales* (1982); Dustin Hoffman and Warren Beatty in *Ishtar* (1987); Pauly Shore in *In the Army Now* (1994); and Jim Varney in *Ernest in the Army* (1997).

Some protagonists even refer to Arabs as "dogs" and "monkeys." As a result, those viewers laughing at bumbling reel Arabs leave movie theaters with a sense of solidarity, united by their shared distance from these peoples of ridicule.

In dramas, especially, Hollywood's stars contest and vanquish reel Arabs. See Emory Johnson in *The Gift Girl* (1917); Gary Cooper in *Beau Sabreur* (1928); John Wayne in *I Cover the War* (1937); Burt Lancaster in *Ten Tall Men* (1951); Dean Martin in *The Ambushers* (1967); Michael Caine in *Ashanti* (1979); Sean Connery in *Never Say Never Again* (1983); Harrison Ford in *Frantic* (1988); Kurt Russell in *Executive Decision* (1996); and Brendan Fraser in *The Mummy* (1999).

Perhaps in an attempt to further legitimize the stereotype, as well as to attract more viewers, in the mid-1980s studios presented notable African-American actors facing off against, and ultimately destroying, reel Arabs. Among them, Eddie Murphy, Louis Gossett Jr., Robert Guillaume, Samuel Jackson, Denzel Washington, and Shaquille O'Neal.[6]

In the Disney movie *Kazaam* (1996), O'Neal pummels three Arab Muslims who covet "all the money in the world." Four years later, director William Friedkin has actor Samuel Jackson exploiting jingoistic prejudice and religious bigotry in *Rules of Engagement* (2000). The effects of ethnic exploitation are especially obvious in scenes revealing egregious, false images of Yemeni children as assassins and enemies of the United States.

To my knowledge, no Hollywood WWI, WWII, or Korean War movie has ever shown America's fighting forces slaughtering children. Yet, near the conclusion of *Rules of Engagement*, US marines open fire on the Yemenis, shooting 83 men, women, and children. During the scene, viewers rose to their feet, clapped and cheered. Boasts director Friedkin, "I've seen audiences stand up and applaud the film throughout the United States."[7] Some viewers applaud Marines gunning down Arabs in war dramas not necessarily because of cultural insensitivity, but because for more than 100 years Hollywood has singled out the Arab as our enemy. Over a period of time, a steady stream of bigoted images does, in fact, tarnish our judgment of a people and their culture.

Rules of Engagement not only reinforces historically damaging stereotypes, but promotes a dangerously generalized portrayal of Arabs as rabidly anti-American. Equally troubling to this honorably discharged US Army veteran is that *Rules of Engagement*'s credits thank for their assistance the Department of Defense (DOD) and the US Marine Corps. More than fourteen feature films, all of which show Americans killing Arabs, credit the DOD for providing needed equipment, personnel, and technical assistance. Sadly, the Pentagon seems to condone these Arab-bashing ventures, as evidenced in *True Lies* (1994), *Executive Decision* (1996), and *Freedom Strike* (1998).

On November 30, 2000, Hollywood luminaries attended a star-studded dinner hosted by Defense Secretary William Cohen in honor of Motion Picture Association President Jack Valenti, for which the Pentagon paid the bill—$295,000. Called on to explain why the DOD personnel were fraternizing with imagemakers at an elaborate Beverly Hills gathering, spokesman Kenneth Bacon said: "If we can have television shows and movies that show the excitement and importance of military life, they can help generate a favorable atmosphere for recruiting."

The DOD has sometimes shown concern when other peoples have been tarnished on film. For example, in the late 1950s, DOD officials were reluctant to cooperate with moviemakers attempting to advance Japanese stereotypes. When *The Bridge over the River Kwai* (1957) was being filmed, Donald Baruch, head of the DOD's Motion Picture Production Office, cautioned producers not to overemphasize Japanese terror and torture, advising:

> In our ever-increasing responsibility for maintaining a mutual friendship and respect among the people of foreign lands, the use of disparaging terms to identify ethnic, national or religious groups is inimical to our national interest, particularly in motion pictures sanctioned by Government cooperation.[8]

Arabs are almost always easy targets in war movies. From as early as 1912, decades prior to the 1991 Gulf War, dozens of films presented allied agents and military forces— American, British, French, and more recently Israeli—obliterating Arabs. In the World War I drama *The Lost Patrol* (1934), a brave British sergeant (Victor McLaglen) guns down "sneaky Arabs, those dirty, filthy swine." An American newsreel cameraman (John Wayne) helps wipe out a "horde of [Arab] tribesmen" in *I Cover the War* (1937).

In *Sirocco* (1951), the first Hollywood feature film projecting Arabs as terrorists, Syrian "fanatics" assail French soldiers and American arms dealer Harry Smith (Humphrey Bogart). *The Lost Command* (1966) shows French Colonel Raspeguy's (Anthony Quinn) soldiers killing Algerians. And, Israelis gun down sneaky bedouins in two made-in-Israel films, *Sinai Guerrillas* (1960) and *Sinai Commandos* (1968).

Arabs trying to rape, kill, or abduct fair-complexioned Western heroines is a common theme, dominating scenarios from *Captured by Bedouins* (1912), to *The Pelican Brief* (1993). In *Brief*, an Arab hit man tries to assassinate the protagonist, played by Julia Roberts. In *Captured*, desert bandits kidnap a fair American maiden, but she is eventually rescued by a British officer. As for her bedouin abductors, they are gunned down by rescuing US Cavalry troops.

Arabs enslave and abuse Africans in about ten films, including *A Daughter of the Congo* (1930), *Drums of Africa* (1963), and *Ashanti* (1979). Noted African-American filmmaker Oscar Micheaux, who made "race movies" from 1919 to 1948, also advanced the Arab-as-abductor theme in his *Daughter of the Congo*. Though Micheaux's movies contested Hollywood's Jim Crow stereotypes of blacks, *A Daughter of the Congo* depicts lecherous Arab slavers abducting and holding hostage a lovely Mulatto woman and her maid. The maiden is eventually rescued by the heroic African-American officers of the 10th US Cavalry. Anti-Christian Arabs appear in dozens of films. When the US military officer in *Another Dawn* (1937) is asked why Arabs despise Westerners, he barks: "It's a good Moslem hatred of Christians." Islam is also portrayed as a violent faith in *Legion of the Doomed* (1959). Here, an Arab is told, "Kill him before he kills you." Affirms the Arab as he plunges a knife into his foe's gut, "You speak the words of Allah." And, in *The Castilian* (1963), Spanish Christians triumph over Arab Muslim zealots. How? By releasing scores of squealing pigs! Terrified of the pigs, the reel Arabs retreat.

Arabs invade the United States and terrorize innocents in *Golden Hands of Kurigal* (1949), *Terror Squad* (1988), *True Lies* (1994), and *The Siege* (1998). *The Siege* is especially alarming. In it, Arab immigrants methodically lay waste to Manhattan. Assisted by Arab-American auto mechanics, university students, and a college teacher, they blow up the city's FBI building, kill scores of government agents, blast theatergoers, and detonate a bomb in a crowded bus.

. . . Oily Arabs and robed thugs intent on acquiring nuclear weapons surface in roughly ten films. See *Fort Algiers* (1958) and *Frantic* (1988).

At least a dozen made-in-Israel and Golan-Globus movies, such as *Eagles Attack at Dawn* (1970), *Iron Eagle* (1986), and *Chain of Command* (1993), show Americans and/or Israelis crushing evil-minded Arabs, many of whom are portrayed by Israeli actors.

More than 30 French Foreign Legion movies, virtually a sub-genre of boy's-own-adventure films, show civilized legionnaires obliterating backward desert bedouin. These legion formula films cover a span of more than 80 years, from *The Unknown* (1915) to *Legionnaire* (1998). Scenarios display courageous, outnumbered legionnaires battling against, and ultimately overcoming, unruly Arabs. Even Porky Pig as a legionnaire and his camel join in the melee, beating up bedouins in the animated cartoon, *Little Beau Porky* (1936).

. . . Observes William Greider of the *Washington Post*, "Much of what Westerners 'learned' about Arabs sounds similar to what nineteenth-century Americans 'discovered' about Indians on this continent . . . acceptable villains make our troubles so manageable." In the past, imagemakers punctuated "anti-human qualities in these strange people," American Indians. They projected them as savages, not thinking like us, "not sharing our aspirations." Once one has concluded that Indians thrive on violence, disorder, and stealth, it becomes easier to accept rather than challenge "irrational" portraits. Today, says Greider, "The Arab stereotypes created by British and French colonialism are still very much with us."[9]

Film producers, broadcast journalists, and military leaders echo Greider's Arab-as-Indian analogy. Seeing marauding desert Arabs approach, the American protagonist in the war movie *The Steel Lady* (1953) quips, "This is bandit area, worse than Arizona Apache." In talking up his film *Iron Eagle* (1986), producer Ron Samuels gushed: Showing an American teen hijacking a jet and wiping out scores of Arabs "was just the kind of story I'd been looking for. . . . It reminded me of the old John Wayne westerns."

SHEIKHS

The word "sheikh" means, literally, a wise elderly person, the head of the family, but you would not know that from watching any of Hollywood's "sheikh" features, more than 160 scenarios, including the Kinetoscope short *Sheik Hadj Tahar Hadj Cherif* (1894) and the Selig Company's *The Power of the Sultan* (1907)—the first movie to be filmed in Los Angeles. Throughout the Arab world, to show respect, people address Muslim religious leaders as sheikhs.

Moviemakers, however, attach a completely different meaning to the word. As Matthew

Sweet points out, "The cinematic Arab has never been an attractive figure . . . in the 1920s he was a swarthy Sheik, wiggling his eyebrows and chasing the [Western] heroine around a tiled courtyard. After the 1973 oil crisis . . . producers revitalized the image of the fabulously wealthy and slothful sheikh, only this time he was getting rich at the expense of red-blooded Americans; he became an inscrutable bully—a Ray-Ban-ed variation of the stereotypes of the Jewish money lender."[10]

Instead of presenting sheikhs as elderly men of wisdom, screenwriters offer romantic melodramas portraying them as stooges-in-sheets, slovenly, hook-nosed potentates intent on capturing pale-faced blondes for their harems. Imitating the stereotypical behavior of their lecherous predecessors—the "bestial" Asian, the black "buck," and the "lascivious" Latino—slovenly Arabs move to swiftly and violently deflower Western maidens. Explains Edward Said, "The perverted sheikh can often be seen snarling at the captured Western hero and blonde girl . . . [and saying] 'My men are going to kill you, but they like to amuse themselves before.' "[11]

Early silent films, such as *The Unfaithful Odalisque* (1903), *The Arab* (1915), and *The Sheik* (1921), all present bearded, robed Arab rulers as one collective stereotypical lecherous cur. In *The Unfaithful Odalisque*, the sheikh not only admonishes his harem maiden, he directs a Nubian slave to lash her with a cat-o'-nine-tails. In *The Sheik* (1921), Sheikh Ahmed (Valentino) glares at Diana, the kidnapped British lovely and boasts: "When an Arab sees a woman he wants, he takes her!"

Flash forward 33 years. Affirms the sheikh in *The Adventures of Hajji Baba* (1954): "Give her to me or I'll take her!"

Moving to kidnap and/or seduce the Western heroine, clumsy moneyed sheikhs fall all over themselves in more than 60 silent and sound movies, ranging from *The Fire and the Sword* (1914) to *Protocol* (1984). Sheikhs disregard Arab women, preferring instead to ravish just one Western woman.

But Hollywood's silent movies did not dare show Western women bedding sheikhs. Why? Because America's movie censors objected to love scenes between Westerners and Arabs. Even producers experiencing desert mirages dared not imagine such unions.

Some viewers perceived Valentino's *The Sheik* (1921) to be an exception to the rule. Not true. Valentino's Sheikh Ahmed, who vanquishes Diana, the Western heroine in the movie, is actually a European, not an Arab. This helps explain why the European lover-boy dressed in Arab garb was viewed so positively by his essentially female audience. Note the dialogue, revealing Ahmed to be a European:

Diana, the heroine: "His [Ahmed's] hand is so large for an Arab."
Ahmed's French friend: "He is not an Arab. His father was an Englishman, his mother a Spaniard."

Other desert scenarios followed suit, allowing the hero and heroine to make love, but only after revealing they were actually Western Christians!

In Europe, it was otherwise. As early as 1922, a few European movies such as *The Sheikh's Wife* (1922) countered fixed themes, showing Western heroines embracing dashing Arab sheikhs.

Both good and evil sheikhs battle each other in about 60 Arabian Nights fantasies, animated and non-animated. A plethora of unsavory characters, wicked viziers, slimy slavers, irreverent magicians, and shady merchants contest courageous princes, princesses, lamp genies, and folk heroes such as Ali Baba, Sinbad, Aladdin and, on occasion, the benevolent caliph. You can see some of them in the four *Kismet* fantasies (1920, 1930, 1944, 1955), *Prisoners of the Casbah* (1955), and *Aladdin* (1992).

Even animated cartoon characters thump Arabs. My childhood hero, Bugs Bunny, clobbers nasty Arabs in *1001 Rabbit Tales* (1982). Bugs trounces an ugly genie, a dense sheikh, and the ruler's spoiled son. My other cartoon hero, Popeye, also trounces Arabs. In the early 1930s, Fleischer Studios' lengthy Popeye cartoons presented Arab folk heroes as rogues, not as champions. Popeye clobbers, not befriends, Ali Baba and Sinbad in *Popeye the Sailor Meets Ali Baba's Forty Thieves*, and *Popeye the Sailor Meets Sinbad the Sailor*.

Beginning in the mid-1970s, fresh directors also projected Arab leaders through warped prisms. Emulating their predecessors' stereotypes they, too, displayed Western heroines fending off over-sexed desert sheikhs. Yet, there are dramatic differences in sheikh images. Once-upon-a-time Arabian Nights movies, such as *Ali Baba Goes to Town* (1937) and *Aladdin and His Lamp* (1952), show indolent sheikhs lounging on thrones. But, contemporary films present oily, militant, ostentatious sheikhs reclining in Rolls Royces, aspiring to buy up chunks of America.

Today's films present anti-Christian, anti-Jewish Arab potentates perched atop missile bases, armed with nuclear weapons, plenty of oil, and oodles of cash. Using Islam to justify violence, today's reel mega-rich hedonists pose a much greater threat to the West, to Israel, and to fellow Arabs than did their predecessors. You can catch a few of their kind in *Rollover* (1981), *Wrong Is Right* (1982), *The Jewel of the Nile* (1985), and *American Ninja 4: The Annihilation* (1991).

Scantily clad harem maidens attend sheikhs in more than 30 scenarios. The rulers shrug off some, torture others, and enslave the rest. Enslaving international beauties in the X-rated movie, *Ilsa: Harem Keeper of the Oil Sheikhs* (1976), is a depraved Arab ruler and his cohort—Ilsa, the "She-Wolf of the S.S." Depraved sheikhs also subjugate dwarfs and Africans; see *Utz* (1992) and *Slavers* (1977).

Often, producers falsify geopolitical realities. During WWII many Arab nations actively supported the Allies. Moroccan, Tunisian, and Algerian soldiers, for example, fought along-side French troops in North Africa, Italy, and France. Also, Jordanian and Libyan troops assisted members of the British armed services. And, late in the conflict, Egypt, Saudi Arabia, and Iraq declared war on Germany.[12]

Yet, most movies fail to show Arabs fighting alongside the good guys. Instead, bur-noosed pro-Nazi potentates, some belonging to the "Arabian Gestapo," appear in more than ten sheikh movies; see, for example, *A Yank in Libya* (1942), *Action in Arabia* (1944), and *The Steel Lady* (1953). As early as 1943, about fifty years before the Gulf War, *Adventure in Iraq* (1943) depicts the US Air Force bombing the pro-German Iraqi ruler's "devil-worshiper" minions into oblivion.

From the start, protagonists ranging from Samson to 007 have battled burnoosed chieftains. Flashback to the 1900s. Two 1918 films, *Tarzan of the Apes* and *Bound in Morocco*, show Tarzan and Douglas Fairbanks, respectively, trouncing shifty sheikhs.

Cut to the 1940s. Abbott and Costello, Bing Crosby, and Bob Hope follow suit by belittling Arabs in *Lost in a Harem* (1944) and *Road to Morocco* (1942).

Advance to the 1950s. The Bowery Boys and Tab Hunter thrash robed rulers in *Looking for Danger* (1957) and *The Steel Lady* (1953), respectively.

Flash forward to the 1960s and the 1970s. Elvis Presley, Pat Boone, and Jerry Lewis deride Arabs in: *Harum Scarum* (1965), *The Perils of Pauline* (1967), and *Don't Raise the Bridge, Lower the River* (1968). Other stars bashing sheikhs were Ron Ely in *Slavers* (1977), Michael Douglas in *The Jewel of the Nile* (1985), Cheech and Chong in *Things Are Tough All Over* (1982), and Eddie Murphy in *Best Defense* (1984). And I almost forgot—Burt Braverman drubs two of movie land's ugliest sheikhs in *Hollywood Hot Tubs 2: Educating Crystal* (1990).

The movies of the 1980s are especially offensive. They display insolent desert sheikhs with thick accents threatening to rape and/or enslave starlets: Brooke Shields in *Sahara*

(1983), Goldie Hawn in *Protocol* (1984), Bo Derek in *Bolero* (1984), and Kim Basinger in *Never Say Never Again* (1983).

Finally, five made-in-Israel films lambast sheikhs. Particularly degrading is Golan and Globus' *Paradise* (1981). A combination of Western teenagers and chimpanzees finish off the "jackal," a Christian-hating bedouin chieftain, and his cohorts.

MAIDENS

Arab women, meanwhile, are humiliated, demonized, and eroticized in more than 50 feature films.

Half-Arab heroines as well as mute enslaved Arab women appear in about sixteen features, ranging from foreign legion films to Arabian Nights fantasies. "The Arabian Nights never end," writes William Zinsser. "It is a place where young slave girls lie about on soft couches, stretching their slender legs, ready to do a good turn for any handsome stranger who stumbles into the room. Amid all this décolletage sits the jolly old Caliph, miraculously cool to the wondrous sights around him, puffing his water pipe. . . . This is history at its best."[13]

Stereotypical idiosyncrasies abound, linking the Arab woman to several regularly repeated "B" images:

1. They appear as bosomy bellydancers leering out from diaphanous veils, or as disposable "knick-knacks," scantily-clad harem maidens with bare midriffs, closeted in the palace's women's quarters.
2. Background shots show them as Beasts of Burden, carrying jugs on their heads. Some are "so fat, no one would touch them."
3. In films such as *The Sheltering Sky* (1990) they appear as shapeless Bundles of Black, a homogeneous sea of covered women trekking silently behind their unshaven mates.
4. Beginning in 1917 with Fox's silent *Cleopatra*, starring Theda Bara, studios labeled Arab women "serpents" and "vampires." Subsequently, the word "vamp," a derivation of that word, was added to English dictionaries. Advancing the vampire image are movies such as *Saadia* (1953) and *Beast of Morocco* (1966). Both display Arab women as Black magic vamps, or enchantresses "possessed of devils."
5. In *The Leopard Woman* (1920) and *Nighthawks* (1981) they are bombers intent on killing Westerners.

When those dark-complexioned femmes fatales move to woo the American/British hero, they are often disappointed. The majority of movies, such as *Outpost in Morocco* (1949), posit that an Arab woman in love with a Western hero must die.

A few films allow Arab maidens to embrace Western males. In *A Café in Cairo* (1925) and *Arabesque* (1966), actresses Priscilla Dean and Sophia Loren appear as bright and lovely Arab women. Only after the women ridicule and reject Arab suitors, does the scenario allow them to fall into the arms of Western protagonists.

Regrettably, just a handful of movies—*Anna Ascends* (1922), *Princess Tam Tam* (1935), *Bagdad* (1949), *Flame of Araby* (1951), and *Flight from Ashiya* (1964), present brave and compassionate Arab women, genuine heroines. There are also admirable queens and princesses in several Cleopatra films and Arabian fantasy tales.

. . . Taken together, her mute on-screen non-behavior and black-cloaked costume serve to alienate the Arab woman from her international sisters, and vice versa. Not only do the reel Arab women never speak, but they are never in the work place, functioning as doctors, computer specialists, school teachers, print and broadcast journalists, or as successful, well-rounded electric or domestic engineers. Movies don't show charitable Arab women such as those who belong to the Mosaic Foundation, which donates millions to American hospitals. Points out Camelia Anwar Sadat, Syria and Egypt gave women the right to vote as early as Europe did—and much earlier than Switzerland. Today, women make up nearly one-third of the Egyptian parliament. You would never guess from Hollywood's portrayal of Arab women that they are as diverse and talented as any others. Hollywood has not yet imagined a woman as interesting as Ivonne Abdel-Baki, the daughter of Lebanese immigrants and Ecuador's ambassador to Washington. Abdel-Baki, a specialist in conflict resolution, graduated from Harvard University's Kennedy School of Government and is fluent in five languages. Or De' Al-Mohammed, the University of Missouri's blind fencing star.[14] And many, many more.

EGYPTIANS

. . . Egyptian caricatures appear in more than 100 films, from mummy tales to legends of pharaohs and queens to contemporary scenarios. Reel Egyptians routinely descend upon Westerners, Israelis, and fellow Egyptians. Interspersed throughout the movies are souk swindlers as well as begging children scratching for baksheesh. An ever-constant theme shows devious Egyptians moving to defile Western women; see Cecil B. DeMille's *Made for Love* (1926) and *Sphinx* (1981).

Steven Spielberg's films *Raiders of the Lost Ark* (1981), *Young Sherlock Holmes* (1986), and *Indiana Jones and the Last Crusade* (1989) merit special attention, as do Golan-Globus' 1960s scenarios, made-in-Israel: *Cairo Operation* (1965) and *Trunk to Cairo* (1965). The producers paint Egyptians as nuclear-crazed and pro-Nazi. Their scenarios are particularly objectionable given the real-life heroics of the Arab Brotherhood of Freedom, a group of brave Egyptians who sided with the Allies during World War II.

Imagemakers are not so harsh with Queen Cleopatra. Beginning with Helen Gardner's *Cleopatra* (1912), Hollywood enlisted stars such as Ava Gardner, Theda Bara, Vivien Leigh, Sophia Loren, Claudette Colbert, and Elizabeth Taylor to portray Egypt's seductive queen. Approximately fifteen movies show Egypt's queen, encircled by stereotypical maidens, pining over Roman leaders. Only four movies display Egyptian queens romancing Egyptians. The majority display Egyptian royals feuding with fellow Egyptians as well as Rome's soldiers.

A few movies, such as Cecil B. DeMille's *The Ten Commandments* (1923) and DreamWorks' Jeffrey Katzenberg's *The Prince of Egypt* (1998), feature Egyptian rogues trying to crush heroic Israelites. I found the animated *Prince of Egypt* to be less offensive than DeMille's scenarios. Though Katzenberg's movie displays plenty of Egyptian villains, *Prince of Egypt* offers more humane, balanced portraits than do DeMille's 1923 and 1956 versions of *The Ten Commandments*. DeMille's 1923 film shows Egyptian guards beating "the dogs of Israel" and Pharaoh's ten-year-old son whipping Moses.

From the start, moviemakers linked Egypt with the undead. In Georges Méliès's film *The Monster* (1903), the camera reveals a bearded Egyptian magician removing a skeleton from its casket. Presto! He transforms the bony thing into a lovely maiden. But, not for long. The cunning magician changes the woman back into a skeleton.

Say "Egypt" and producers think "Mummies" and "Money." Beginning with Vitagraph's *The Egyptian Mummy* (1914) and *Dust of Egypt* (1915), Hollywood presented about 26 mummy films. In order to spook viewers, cinematographers placed gauze over the camera's lens, creating chilling, dreamlike, and exotic moods. Topping the list is Universal's *The Mummy* (1932). Due to a fine screenplay and Boris Karloff's performance as the mummy

Imhotep, this classic stands the test of time as the mummy film. Other popular mummy movies are *The Mummy's Hand* (1940), *The Mummy's Tomb* (1942), and *The Mummy's Revenge* (1973).

Mummy plots are relatively simple: Revived mummies and their caretaker "priests" contest Western archaeologists. In most scenarios, the ambitious gravediggers ignore tomb curses. So of course they suffer the consequences for daring to reawaken Egypt's sleeping royals. Meanwhile, the Westerners dupe ignorant, superstitious, and two-timing Egyptians.

Once fully revived, the bandages-with-eyes mummy lusts after the archaeologist's fair-skinned daughter. And, the mummy crushes panicked Egyptian workers and all crypt violators—"infidels," "unbelievers," and "heretics." Occasionally, movies like *The Awakening* (1980) pump up the action by offering decomposed horrors; also in this one, a queen's evil spirit so contaminates the Western heroine, she kills her father.

Obviously, there's more to the state of Egypt, the most heavily populated of all Arab countries, than pyramids and curses. Egypt is comprised of a people who take pride in their culture and their long and honorable history. Moving to modernize its economy and to improve the living standards of its population, Egypt now boasts more than fourteen state universities. The likes of scholarly students or noted Egyptian archeologists, men like the celebrated Kamal El Malakh, are absent from movie screens.

Nor do screenwriters present scenarios patterned after Egypt's renowned journalists and authors, like Rose El-Yousef and Nobel Laureate Naguib Mahfouz. Egyptians, like most other Arabs, are deeply religious and are noted for their warm hospitality. In villages and throughout cosmopolitan cities like Cairo and Alexandria, *Ahlan wa Sahlan* (Welcome, this is your home) is spoken as often as "good morning."

PALESTINIANS

. . . Observed Mark Twain, "We are all ignorant, just about different things." When it comes to the Middle East, many Americans are ignorant about the history and plight of the Palestinian people. One reason is that moviegoers may mistakenly believe reel Palestinians, those ugly make-believe film "terrorists," are real Palestinians. Should this be true, then what must viewers think of Palestinians after exiting movie theaters?

To assume viewers acquire some true knowledge of Palestinians after watching the 45 Palestinian fiction films that I discuss here is both dangerous and misleading. It's the same as thinking that you could acquire accurate knowledge of Africans by watching Tarzan movies, or that you would know all about Americans after watching movies about serial killers.

More than half of the Palestinian movies were released in the 1980s and 1990s; nineteen from 1983–1989; nine from 1990–1998. Absent from Hollywood's Israeli-Palestinian movies are human dramas revealing Palestinians as normal folk—computer specialists, domestic engineers, farmers, teachers, and artists. Never do movies present Palestinians as innocent victims and Israelis as brutal oppressors. No movie shows Israeli soldiers and settlers uprooting olive orchards, gunning down Palestinian civilians in Palestinian cities. No movie shows Palestinian families struggling to survive under occupation, living in refugee camps, striving to have their own country and passports stating "Palestine." Disturbingly, only two scenarios present Palestinian families.

. . . One year after the state of Israel was born, the film, *Sword of the Desert* (1949), presented Palestine according to the popular Zionist slogan, as a land without a people—even though the vast majority of people living in Palestine at the time were, in fact, Palestinians. This myth—no-Palestinians-reside-in-Palestine—is also served up in *Cast a Giant Shadow* (1966) and *Judith* (1966).

A decade after *Sword of the Desert* Paul Newman declared war on the Palestinians in *Exodus* (1960). Hollywood's heroes followed suit. In *Prisoner in the Middle* (1974), David Janssen links up with Israeli forces; together they gun down Palestinian nuclear terrorists. Films from the 1980s such as *The Delta Force* (1986) and *Wanted: Dead or Alive* (1987) present Lee Marvin, Chuck Norris, and Rutger Hauer blasting Palestinians in the Mideast and in Los Angeles. In the 1990s, Charlie Sheen and Kurt Russell obliterate Palestinians in Lebanon and aboard a passenger jet, in *Navy SEALs* (1990) and *Executive Decision* (1996).

In *Ministry of Vengeance* (1989) filmmakers dishonor Palestinians and American military chaplains as well. In lieu of presenting the chaplain, a Vietnam veteran, as a devout, non-violent man, the minister exterminates Palestinians. The minister's parishioners approve of the killings, applauding him.

Seven films, including *True Lies* (1994) and *Wanted Dead or Alive* (1987), project the Palestinian as a nerve-gassing nuclear terrorist. In more than eleven movies, including *Half-Moon Street* (1986) *Terror in Beverly Hills* (1988), and *Appointment with Death* (1988), Palestinian evildoers injure and physically threaten Western women and children.

The reader should pay special attention to *Black Sunday* (1977), Hollywood's first major movie showing Palestinians terrorizing and killing Americans on US soil. Telecast annually the week of Super Bowl Sunday, the movie presents Dahlia, a Palestinian terrorist, and her cohort Fasil. They aim to massacre 80,000 Super Bowl spectators, including the American President, a Jimmy Carter look-alike.

Dictating numerous Palestinian-as-terrorist scenarios is the Israeli connection. More than half (28) of the Palestinian movies were filmed in Israel. Nearly all of the made-in-Israel films, especially the seven Cannon movies, display violent, sex-crazed Palestinian "bastards [and] animals" contesting Westerners, Israelis, and fellow Arabs.

I believe Cannon's poisonous scenarios are not accidental, but rather propaganda disguised as entertainment. Even in the early 1900s studio moguls knew that motion pictures could serve propagandists. Following WWI, Adolph Zukor, the head of Paramount Pictures affirmed this film-as-propaganda fact, saying fiction films should no longer be viewed as simply "entertainment and amusement." The war years, he said, "register[ed] indisputably the fact that as an avenue of propaganda, as a channel for conveying thought and opinion, the movies are unequaled by any form of communication."[15]

WHY THE STEREOTYPE?

. . . Ask a film industry executive, director, or writer whether it is ethical to perpetuate ethnic or racial stereotypes and you can expect a quick negative response. How then, to explain that since 1970, these very same individuals produced, directed, and scripted more than 350 films portraying Arabs as insidious cultural "others"?

Either filmmakers are perpetuating the stereotype unknowingly, and would immediately disassociate themselves from such activities were they to realize the implications of their actions, or they are doing so knowingly and will only stop when sufficient pressure is brought to bear on them.

It is difficult to imagine that screenwriters who draft scenes of fat, lecherous sheikhs ogling Western blondes, or crazed Arab terrorists threatening to blow up America with nuclear weapons, are not precisely aware of what they are doing. But we sometimes forget that one of the elements that makes stereotyping so powerful, and so hard to eliminate, is that it is self-perpetuating. Filmmakers grew up watching Western heroes crush hundreds of reel "bad" Arabs. Some naturally repeat the stereotype without realizing that, in so doing, they are innocently joining the ranks of the stereotypes' creators.

Huge inroads have been made toward the elimination of many racial and ethnic stereotypes from the movie screen, but Hollywood's stereotype of Arabs remains unabated. Over the last three decades stereotypical portraits have actually increased in number and virulence.

The Arab stereotype's extraordinary longevity is the result, I believe, of a collection of factors. For starters, consider print and broadcast "if it bleeds it leads" news reports. Like most Americans, creators of popular culture (including novelists, cartoonists, and filmmakers), form their opinions of a people, in part, based on what they read in print, hear on the radio, and see on television. Like the rest of us, they are inundated and influenced by a continuous flow of "seen one, seen 'em all" headlines and sound bites.

. . . The image began to intensify in the late 1940s when the state of Israel was founded on Palestinian land. From that preemptive point on—through the Arab-Israeli wars of 1948, 1967, and 1973, the hijacking of planes, the disruptive 1973 Arab oil embargo, along with the rise of Libya's Muammar Qaddafi and Iran's Ayatollah Khomeini—shot after shot delivered the relentless drum beat that all Arabs were and are Public Enemy No. 1.

Right through the 1980s, the 1990s, and into the twenty-first century, this "bad people" image prevailed, especially during the Palestinian intifada and the Israeli invasion of Lebanon. In 1980, the rabid followers of Iran's Ayatollah Khomeini held 52 Americans hostage at the US Embassy in Teheran for 444 days. Nightly, TV cameras blazoned across the planet Khomeini's supporters chanting "Death to America!" and calling our country "the Great Satan" as they burned our flag and, in effigy, Uncle Sam himself.

At the height of the Iranian hostage crisis anti-Arab feelings intensified, as 70 percent of Americans wrongly identified Iran as an Arab country. Even today, most Americans think of Iranians as Arabs. In fact, Iranians are Persians, another people altogether.

. . . It got worse in the 1990s. Two major events, the Iraqi invasion of Kuwait that led to the Gulf War, and the bombing of New York City's World Trade Center, combined to create misguided mindset, leading some Americans to believe all Arabs are terrorists and that Arabs do not value human life as much as we do. As a result, some of us began even perceiving our fellow Americans of Arab descent as clones of Iraq's Saddam Hussein and the terrorist Osama bin Laden. Well, I think you get the picture.

. . . Not only do these violent news images of extremists reinforce and exacerbate already prevalent stereotypes, but they serve as both a source and excuse for continued Arab-bashing by those filmmakers eager to exploit the issue. In particular, the news programs are used by some producers and directors to deny they are actually engaged in stereotyping. "We're not stereotyping," they object. "Just look at your television set. Those are real Arabs."

Such responses are disingenuous and dishonest. As we know, news reports by their very nature cover extraordinary events. We should not expect reporters to inundate the airwaves with the lives of ordinary Arabs. But filmmakers have a moral obligation not to advance the news media's sins of omission and commission, not to tar an entire group of people on the basis of the crimes and the alleged crimes of a few.

. . . Why would anyone take part in the denigration of a people knowingly? I think one answer is the Arab-Israeli conflict. Though the majority of moviemakers are fair-minded professionals, there are some who, in the interests of pursuing their own political or personal agenda, are willing to perpetuate hate. These individuals may be expected to continue to indict Arabs on movie screens for as long as unjust images are tolerated.

New York Times columnist Maureen Dowd offers another answer: "[S]tereotypes are not only offensive [but] they are also comforting. They . . . exempt people from any further mental or emotional effort. They wrap life in the arch toastiness of fairy tale and myth. They make complicated understandings unnecessary."[16] Convenient stereotypes make everyone's job easier. Rather than having to pen a good joke, the writer inserts a stumbling, bumbling sheikh. Looking for a villain? Toss in an Arab terrorist—we all know what they look like from watching movies and TV. No thought required. As for the audience? Well, it also makes some of us feel better to see ourselves as superior to someone else. If one is no longer allowed to feel superior to Asians, Jews, Latinos, or blacks, at least we can feel superior to those wretched Arabs.

. . . Certainly, the Department of Defense's rubber-stamping of motion pictures that lambaste Arabs plays a role. The fact is, the government has a history of playing a role in what movies do and don't get made. As early as 1917, the federal government not only acknowledged the power of film to influence political thought, it took on the wrongful role of censor. As soon as the United States declared war on Germany, the government declared that no Hollywood movie could arouse prejudice against friendly nations. The 1917 film *The Spirit of '76* reveals heroic American revolutionaries such as Patrick Henry and Paul Revere. But, some frames show British soldiers committing acts of atrocities. As England was our World War I ally, the government protested; a judge declared producer Robert Goldstein's movie advanced anti-British sentiments. Calling the film "potent German propaganda,"[17] the judge sentenced Goldstein to prison.

Greed, too, is an incentive. Bash-the-Arab movies make money. Thus, some producers exploit the stereotype for profit.

. . . The absence of vibrant film criticism is another cause. A much-needed recourse against harmful Arab images would be more vigorous criticism emanating from industry executives and movie critics. I recall, still, Bosley Crowther's *New York Times* review of *Adventure in Sahara* (1938). Instead of criticizing stereotypes, Crowther advanced them, writing: "We know the desert is no picnic and you can't trust an Arab very far."

Another factor is silence. No significant element of public opinion has yet to oppose the stereotype; even scholars and government officials are mum. New York's Andrew Cuomo, for example, is running for governor of New York, a state where many Americans of Arab heritage reside. Cuomo is "very interested in the topic of discrimination" and stereotyping; he is alert to the fact that there is "a robust hunger for vulgar stereotypes in popular culture." Imagemakers, he says, are "still stereotyping Italian-Americans, Irish-Americans, African-Americans, Indian-Americans and American Jews."[18] Yet, Cuomo fails to mention coarse stereotypes of Arab-Americans. If we are ever to illuminate our common humanity, our nation's leaders must challenge all hateful stereotypes. Teachers need to move forward and incorporate, at long last, discussions of Arab caricatures in schools, colleges, military, and government classrooms.

Ethnic stereotypes do not die off on their own, but are hunted down and terminated by those whom the stereotypes victimize. Other groups, African-Americans, Asian-Americans and Jewish-Americans, have acted aggressively against discriminatory portraits. Arab-Americans as a group, however, have been slow to mobilize and, as a result, their protests are rarely heard in Hollywood and even when heard, are heard too faintly to get the offenders to back off.

Another reason is lack of presence. With the exception of a few movies, *Party Girl* (1995) and *A Perfect Murder* (1998), Arab-Americans are invisible on movie screens. One reason, simply put, is that there are not many Arab-Americans involved in the film industry; not one is a famous Hollywood celebrity.

What does their absence have to do with contesting stereotypes? Well, one answer is that movie stars have clout. Consider how Brad Pitt altered the scenario, *The Devil's Own* (1996). After reading the initial script, Pitt protested, telling the studio the screenplay made him "uneasy" because it was loaded with stereotypes—"full of leprechaun jokes and green beer." The dialogue, he argued, unfairly painted his character as a stereotypical Irish "bad" guy. Explains Pitt, "I had the responsibility to represent somewhat these [Irish] people whose lives have been shattered. It would have been an injustice to Hollywood-ize it." Unless changes were made to humanize the Irish people, especially his character, Pitt "threatened to walk." The studio acquiesced, bringing in another writer to make the necessary changes.

Also, when it comes to studio moguls, not one Arab-American belongs to the media elite. The community boasts no communication giants comparable to Disney's Michael Eisner, DreamWorks' Jeffrey Katzenberg, Fox's Rupert Murdoch, or Time-Warner's Ted Turner.

The lack of an Arab-American presence impacts the stereotype in another way. The industry has a dearth of those men and women who would be the most naturally inclined to strive for accurate and balanced portrayals of Arabs. But a number of high-level Arab Americans in the industry over the course of time would rectify the situation. It's difficult to demean people and their heritage when they're standing in front of you, especially if those persons are your bosses.

. . . Regrettably, America's Arabs do not yet have an organized and active lobby in Los Angeles. To bring about fundamental changes in how motion pictures project Arabs, a systematic lobbying effort is needed. Though the Arab-American and Muslim-American presence is steadily growing in number and visibility in the United States, only a few Arab-Americans meet with and discuss the stereotype with filmmakers. When dialogue does occur, some discriminatory portraits are altered. Declares a February 3, 2001, Council on American-Islamic Relations (CAIR) fax: "The villains in Paramount's upcoming film, *The Sum of All Fears*, were changed to European neo-Nazis." CAIR officials acknowledged Paramount for this important change, as Tom Clancy's book, on which the movie is based, presents Arab Muslims detonating a nuclear device at the Super Bowl in Denver. In a letter to CAIR, the film's director, Phil Alden Robinson, wrote: "I hope you will be reassured that I have no intention of portraying negative images of Arabs or Muslims."

Ongoing informal and formal meetings with movie executives are essential. Such sessions enable community members to more readily explain to producers the negative effects misperceptions of Arabs have on their children as well as on American public opinion and policy. Also, Arab-Americans need to reach out and expand their concerns with well-established ethnic and minority lobbying groups—with Asians, blacks, Jews, Latinos, gays and lesbians, and others.

POSITIVES

To see is to make possible new ways of seeing. . . . I have tried to be uncompromisingly truthful, and to expose the Hollywood stereotype of Arabs for all to see. While it is true that most filmmakers have vilified the Arab, others have not. Some contested harmful stereotypes, displaying positive images—that is, casting an Arab as a regular person.

In memorable well-written movies, ranging from the Arabian nights fantasy *The Thief of Bagdad* (1924), to the World War II drama *Sahara* (1943), producers present Arabs not as a threateningly different people but as "regular" folks, even as heroes. In *Sahara*, to save his American friends, a courageous Arab soldier sacrifices his life.

Note this father and son exchange from the film *Earthbound* (1980):

Son: "Why do they [the police] hate us, so?"
Father: "I guess because we're different."
Son: "Just because somebody's different doesn't mean they have to hate 'em. It's stupid."
Father: "It's been stupid for a long time."

At first, I had difficulty uncovering "regular" and admirable Arab characters—it was like trying to find an oasis in the desert. Yet, I discovered more than 50 motion pictures sans Arab villains, five percent of the total number reviewed here. Refreshingly, the movies debunk stale images, humanizing Arabs.

As for those Arabian Nights fantasies of yesteryear, only a few viziers, magicians, or other scalawags lie in ambush. Mostly fabulous Arabs appear in *The Desert Song* (1929), *Ali Baba and the Forty Thieves* (1944), *Son of Sinbad* (1955), and *Aladdin and His Magic Lamp* (1969). The movies present viewers with brave and moral protagonists: Aladdin, Ali Baba, and Sinbad. Emulating the deeds of Robin Hood and his men of Sherwood Forest, Arabs liberate the poor from the rich, and free the oppressed from corrupt rulers.

Worth noting is the presence of glittering Arabs in non-fantasy movies. A heroic Egyptian princess appears in the movie serial, *Chandu the Magician* (1932). A courageous Egyptian innkeeper assists British troops in *Five Graves to Cairo* (1943). *Gambit* (1966) displays a compassionate Arab entrepreneur. In *King Richard and the Crusaders* (1954), Saladin surfaces as a dignified, more humane leader than his counterpart, Richard.

Some independent Israeli filmmakers, notably those whose movies were financed by the Fund for the Promotion of Israeli Quality Films, allow viewers to empathize with Palestinians, presenting three-dimensional portraits. To their credit, producers of *Beyond the Walls* (1984) and *Cup Final* (1992) contest the self-promotional history and Palestinian stereotypes spun out by most other filmmakers. Both movies show the Palestinian and the Israeli protagonist bonding; the two men are projected as soul-mates, innocent victims of the Arab-Israeli conflict.

Notes

1   The 22 Arab states are Algeria, Bahrain, Chad, Comoros, Djibouti, Egypt, Iraq, Jordan, Lebanon, Libya, Mauritania, Morocco, Oman, Palestine, Qatar, Saudi Arabia, Somalia, Sudan, Syria, Tunisia, United Arab Emirates, and Yemen.
2   Jay Stone, *Ottawa Citizen* 16 March 1996.
3   William Greider, "Against the Grain," *Washington Post* 15 July 1979: 4E.
4   Jerry Mander, *Four Arguments for the Elimination of Television* (New York: William Morrow, 1978).
5   See ADC, "The Anti-Discrimination Hate Crimes," (Washington, DC, 1996).
6   For movies featuring African-American actors destroying reel Arabs, see *Best Defense* (1984), *Iron Eagle* (1986), *The Delta Force* (1986), *Wanted: Dead or Alive* (1987), *Firewalker* (1986), *Kazaam* (1996), *The Siege* (1998), and *Rules of Engagement* (2000).
7   Matthew Sweet, "Movie Targets: Arabs Are the Latest People to Suffer the Racial Stereotyping of Hollywood," *The Independent* 30 July 2000.
8   Lawrence Suid, *Sailing on the Silver Screen: Hollywood and the U.S. Navy* (Annapolis, MD: Naval Institute Press, 1996): 151.
9   Greider 1E.
10   Sweet.
11   Edward W. Said, *Orientalism* (New York: Pantheon, 1978): 125.
12   I.C.B. Dear and M.R.D. Foot, eds., *The Oxford Companion to World War II* (Oxford: Oxford University Press, 1995).
13   William Zinsser, "In Search of Lawrence of Arabia," *Esquire* June 1961: 72.
14   "Fencing by Ear," *Missou* Fall 1997: 11.
15   Adolph Zukor, "Most Important Events of the Year," *Wid's Year Book* 1918. For more on Palestinian portraits, see my essay "Screen Images of Palestinians in the 1980s," *Beyond the Stars, Volume 1: Stock Characters in American Film*, ed. Paul Loukides and Linda K. Fuller (Bowling Green, OH: Bowling Green State University Press, 1990).
16   Mareen Dowd, "Cuomos vs. Sopranos," *New York Times* 22 April 2001.
17   *Censored!*, documentary, American Movie Classics, 7 December 1999.
18   Dowd.

PART 3

Circulation

INTRODUCTION

HOW DO HOLLYWOOD FILMS COME TO US—how do they get to where we are, and *vice versa*? And how do we make sense of them? What is the role of the state in all this? And how does globalization complicate or facilitate the story? Film distribution covers everything from promotional material through to the literal travel of the text across space and time, whether by bicycle or satellite. It is the most profitable part of Hollywood, because its costs and risks are relatively low, but it remains the least-understood segment of the business. Audiences, by contrast, are seemingly never in the shadows—their uptake and disposal of film texts is the key to both anxieties and pleasures surrounding the industry's reputation. And the state? We are conventionally told today that two models govern the economics of cinema. The first is *laissez-faire*, represented by Bollywood, Hong Kong and, *primus inter pares*, Hollywood. The second is *dirigisme*, represented by Western Europe and most of the global South. Let's look at the binary oppositions that supposedly sustain this distinction:

LAISSEZ-FAIRE *FILM INDUSTRY*	DIRIGISTE *FILM INDUSTRY*
No state investment in training, production, distribution or exhibition	Major state subvention of training and production, minimal or no support for distribution and exhibition
No governmental censorship or governmental censorship	Governmental censorship
Copyright protection	Copyright protection
Monopoly restrictions	Monopoly restrictions
Export orientation	Import substitution

LAISSEZ-FAIRE *FILM INDUSTRY*	DIRIGISTE *FILM INDUSTRY*
Market model	Mixed-economy model
Ideology of pleasure before nation	Ideology of nation before pleasure
Governmental anxiety over the impact of film sex and violence on the population	Governmental anxiety over the impact of imported film on the population

They have some items in common, such as the role of the state in policing property, but their fundamental missions seem incompatible. Yet they actually bleed into one another. The reality is more like this:

HOLLYWOOD FILM INDUSTRY	*NATIONAL FILM INDUSTRY*
Massive state investment in training via film schools and production commissions, major diplomatic negotiations over distribution and exhibition arrangements	Major state subvention of training and production, minimal or no support for distribution and exhibition
Industry censorship	Governmental censorship
Copyright protection as a key service to capital along with anti-piracy deals	Copyright protection
Monopoly restrictions minimized to permit cross-ownership and unprecedented domestic concentration and international oligopoly	Monopoly restrictions
Export orientation aided by plenipotentiaries, equal reliance on local audience	Import substitution, some export to cognate language groups
Market model, mixed-economy practice	Mixed-economy model
Ideology of pleasure, nation and export of *Américanité*	Ideology of nation, pleasure and job creation
Governmental anxiety over the impact of film sex and violence on the population	Governmental anxiety over the impact of imported film on the population, as alibi for *bourgeois* subvention

The role of the state is a powerful influence both domestically and internationally.

In **Distribution**, Jeff Himpele's ethnographic eye discloses the difference between watching Hollywood in one part of Bolivian society by contrast with another. He finds that the viewing experiences are structured in dominance: they privilege the wealthy and powerful in terms of the quality of venues and prints. Martine Danan explains how US movies are promoted in France—the art of selling through cross-cultural communication; and Suman Basuroy, Subimal Chatterjee, and S. Abraham Ravid ask about how significant press reviews are in the success of films with audiences.

Audiences again offer multiple methods of analysis. Drawing on her own experiences and related fieldwork, JoEllen Shively comes up with surprising findings about how Native

Americans interpret their representation in Westerns. Philippe Meers examines the opinions of young people—the audience Hollywood most prizes, and Francis L. F. Lee applies economic methods to comprehend the performance of Hollywood in Hong Kong.

Government starts with legal concerns, specifically the role of publicity rights in celebrity images via Rosemary J. Coombe's feminist account. Then Thomas H. Guback uses political economy to consider the hidden nature of state subsidies, and Kelly Gates turns our attention to copyright—once an obscure concern but now on the lips of teenagers across the world.

Globalization features Tom O'Regan looking at the conditions of cultural exchange in a general way, while Scott R. Olson argues that Hollywood globalized due to a mixture of managerial finesse and fitness plus narrative transparency. Bill Grantham finishes the volume with a bravura historical study of Hollywood's connections to France.

By the time you have finished reading the *Reader*, you will have made your way through a fascinating, crisis-laden, but enduring labyrinth—Hollywood yesterday and today.

3A DISTRIBUTION

Chapter 26

Jeffrey D. Himpele

FILM DISTRIBUTION AS MEDIA: MAPPING DIFFERENCE IN THE BOLIVIAN CINEMASCAPE (1996)

THE TRAVELS AND TRANSMUTATIONS OF DRACULA [1]

O N JANUARY 1, 1993 *BRAM STOKER'S DRACULA* (Sony-Tristar) debuted in La Paz at the Cinema Monje Campero, the spacious single-screen theater located on the Prado, a wide promenade that runs along and, like a seam, splits the bottom center of the steep urbanized canyon. Facing the Prado's wide sidewalks and central manicured garden set in the center of traffic are expensive hotels, art and shopping galleries, airline offices, ethnic restaurants (Italian, Chinese, U.S.), bookstores, and a state university. This area of the city, known also as the "Centro," is the stage of national cultural events as well as protest marches. Most viewers who saw *Dracula* at the Monje Campero are professionals, bureaucrats and entrepreneurs, and their families, who work in nearby official retail, government and service businesses and live in apartment buildings here or in homes in the elite tree-lined neighborhoods of the Southern Zone below the main canyon of the city. *Dracula* stayed at the Monje Campero for seven weeks, one of the longest running film exhibitions in La Paz.

Dracula then moved across the Prado a half of a mile and more than twenty stories higher in urban elevation to the Cinema Monumental Roby (hereafter Cine Roby, as people call it), a large *cine popular* (popular cinema) on the Plaza Garita de Lima. The Garita is a center of the city for the popular classes of Aymara immigrants (*cholos*) and their families. [2] In the streets surrounding the plaza, they operate the growing markets as merchants of imported official and contraband goods and agricultural produce. People eat their meals, gossip, watch their children, and organize syndicates and popular protests in the markets surrounding the plaza. Many vendors who work in this zone descend from homes many blocks higher to work for prosperous Aymara entrepreneurs who live here. As a popular cultural center, people organize and rehearse dance fraternities for elaborate festival parades and hold parties for days afterwards in the many social halls up the street and further up the canyon from the Cine Roby.

By late-January, *Dracula* had already appeared in the markets surrounding the Garita, reproduced many times over as a pirated videocassette with poor technical quality. After a short stay at the Cine Roby, the official *Dracula* film returned below to the Centro to a cinema on the Plaza Murillo, the well-manicured cede of the state government surrounded by blocks of glitzy shops and offices. Then Dracula ascended and traveled among several small theaters in the popular neighborhoods across and above the Prado. Now with each stop Dracula climbed the wall of the city canyon away from the Centro as pirated video copies also continued to proliferate and circulate. Months later, in August, *Dracula* returned to Cine Roby for another week. By this time, Dracula's circulation had left tell-tale marks on film and the videotapes. The images and the soundtrack that were noticeably scratched and filled with static could tell of where he had been, where he was, for how long he had been traveling, and how far this *Dracula* was from the original copy.

Dracula, and *Dracula*, reproduce and circulate multiple copies of themselves to move simultaneously across times and spaces, seemingly as they wish. To do so, and to survive, they need the circulatory material of others—blood and money—and Dracula and *Dracula* acquire it by hypnotizing and tempting as they make their marked extractions. As if embodying these universal currencies too, the key for both *Dracula* and Dracula is to become a different character in each locale and tell different tales in their appearances. As with the degrading copies, such tales derive from Dracula's travels. In the course of debuts and exhibitions in La Paz, *Dracula* descended in the urban social hierarchy and appeared to audiences in immigrant indigenous neighborhoods with later access to "new" releases. *Dracula's* movement across the city's screens of this wide and steep canyon maps out and distributes the dominating social discourse in which social rank and indigenous identity correspond inversely with the sharp gradations in altitude.

It is because *Dracula*, like most films that arrive in La Paz, marks, separates, connects, and ranks human differences through its distribution, that I explore film "itineraries" in this article. I use the term itinerary to fuse time and space in order to trace the tempo of travel and the routes of their debuts. We could think of such itineraries as "spatializing practices" that, as Michel de Certeau writes ". . . traverse and organize places; they select them and link them together . . ." (de Certeau 1984: 115) to narrate difference. For such tales to be told as films tour the city, a social imaginary, or social field, for the narrative actions must also be cleared, as de Certeau would say, ". . . which serves as their base and their theater" (*ibid*: 124). From this dialectic between tour and map (*ibid*. 118–22), between film distribution and its maps, film distributors and audiences open subject positions for themselves and others in social narratives.

One such story made from *Dracula's* itinerary was told to me at the Cine Esmeralda, a *cine popular* a few blocks from the Cine Roby. José, a recent Peruvian immigrant to La Paz who is the manager of Cine Esmeralda, was explaining to me that *Dracula* had done very well all around Lima, Peru, but the film's poor performance here was due to the "uniqueness" of his clientele:

> *Dracula* had a [waiting] line when it debuted at Monje Campero [in the La Paz Centro]. It is a good film. It had good recommendations. But not here in the Cine Esmeralda. It is for a type of people from the lower parts of the city. But the people here, they go in to see the film, and they do not understand the conflict, they leave. They do not understand. Here we showed *Dracula* only a week. Here the people are very unique . . . Bring to this cinema a 'Van Damme' and the people come. Or *'las chinas'* [martial arts films] and the people will come also. Before we could show anything oriental, but the taste of the people is changing. Now it's variable. So we are showing different types, one for

kids, terror, and an action film. You have to know the parameters of the people
to show what they like in the zone.

Since *Dracula*'s stopping points and lengths of stay are discriminate, in José's description, I will analyze here how ". . . to know the parameters of the people . . ." is a crucial
practice for film exhibitors and distributors. What social fields do they define, and for
whom? While many recent studies of commodities, art, and artifacts circulating through
various cultural contexts emphasize, quite valuably, how consumers create meaning with
them, these analyses do not allow circulation to bear on difference until the point of
reception or criticism. How does the circulation itself distribute difference by dispersing
audiences? How do their distribution itineraries mark, separate, and organize the relations
between people and places and what stories are told about them?

When *Dracula* arrived in Bolivia in 1993 it was more than a week after its debut in
Buenos Aires, Argentina. Most often, a single copy of a film arrives to La Paz, Bolivia several
months after debuts in the United States and larger Latin American markets such as Chile
and Argentina. Like many of the copies of films that appear in South America, the film is a
refurbished U.S. domestic print with Spanish subtitles added after playing there; or it may
come directly from a larger Spanish-speaking country, if the print is not too worn by its use.
Films are part of the traffic to poorer states of a wider field of commodities designed and
used in richer contexts.[3] Among items in a clothing store in central La Paz or in unofficial
markets are pieces from last year's unsold J. Crew clothing line, for example, with the
brand-name clipped out. Similarly, most cars in La Paz are imported used cars; buses are
depreciated machines from Brazil and other Latin American countries. In La Paz, where
many in the popular classes conserve the newness of items by keeping their labels, do not
appreciate the worn-out style of clothing, or talk nostalgically about older commodities,
people cynically remark that the old used airplanes of the military's passenger service which
have crashed were donated by the United States "as if they were a gift."

Unlike the value of some other objects in circulation, circulating films lose their value in
exchange. Their ticket prices drop as they are transferred to each new appearance in the
hand-me-down transit of films to and within La Paz cinemas until distribution has inserted
too many marks to make them attractive for trade. Thus, like all current Hollywood releases
here, in three years when it is unusable and the contract is up, *Dracula* is burned and melted
to death in the deal with the distributor from Hollywood. But, of course, we know that
Dracula never dies and that *Dracula* will reappear elsewhere.

FLASHBACK TO THE SITES AND SIGHTS OF FILM DISTRIBUTION

Before discussing the distributors themselves, in this section I provide further historical
contextualization of this cinemascape.[4] A brief view of the history of film exhibition in La
Paz shows that the spatialization of cinemas and the timing of debuts corresponds to the
historical modes of distributing difference, in which, for example, entrenched colonial race
and class hierarchies meant that Aymaras and Quechuas and their families were for long
tacitly prohibited from entering the Center of the city. From the beginning of permanent
cinema exhibitions in La Paz in the 1910s, cinema audiences were disseminated to two sides
of the city: laboring and merchant *mestizos* and indigenous immigrant *cholos* from higher
neighborhoods toward a theater on the western side of the canyon, and Westernized creole-
mestizo professionals and bureaucrats from the lowest residential zones to theaters in the
Centro. This spatial distribution of social hierarchy also extended to the international level
during the intensification of U.S. film distribution in the late 1910s. U.S. film distributors

considered Latin American audiences to be composed of 'the very poor or uneducated' and they sent to this market used, scratched and incomplete film prints (in Usabel 1982: 12–13).

At the same time, however, the Latin American bourgeoisie would attempt to create and mark its status by appearing to collapse space and time by seeing (and being seen at) the first national debuts of globally-distributed films. Having the earliest access to the newest merchandise from Europe and films from Hollywood allowed them to appear as if they were participating in an international bourgeois class on the basis of contemporary consumption. In early twentieth-century Buenos Aires, for example, a U.S. consul noted that audiences wanted to see each new film, "at the same time that it is being shown in the large cities of the world." To meet that demand, underground pirating networks formed to sell copies of films, many of which were of poor quality. Because such degradation was a tell-tale sign of wear and use, and not of a contemporaneous debut, the pirated films had no market with bourgeois audiences and they were exhibited in cheaper working-class neighborhood cinemas (Usabel *ibid*).

If before the transformation to commercial narrative cinema in the 1920s, the visual exhibition of the machinery itself was a cinematic attraction (Gunning 1986), then the spectacle extended to the theaters, audiences and urban zones in La Paz. The architecture of the exhibition site also served as a means of encircling social class by designating its patrons' social status. The early cinemas in the Centro were built as large public spaces with ornate and spacious lobbies that denoted and sold images of white urban wealth and status and attending the cinema became a prestige event for the emerging professional classes. After the early 1920s, according to distributors with whom I spoke, the country of origin had become the local standard of quality for films, with new Hollywood films at the top and European and Latin American films following. This nationality, as seen on theater billboards, was the identifying emblem of the movie theaters. Along with its cinemas, the Centro emerged as the official commercial center for Western luxury. White bourgeois consumer culture has since been displayed by the clothing, for example, from famous U.S. and European designers and labels in store windows.

Following the nationalist revolutionary 1950s, many Aymaras and their families were forced to immigrate to peripheral neighborhoods in La Paz as they lost land in the privatization of haciendas from which they were "liberated" from debt-bondage. As a sign of the liberal expansion of market-mediated social relations, "Indians" were also renamed with a class term, as *campesinos*, or rural peasants. As nationalist *mestizaje* (cultural mixing) dominated official political rhetoric, Aymaras were also to be allowed into the Centro, but audiences continued to disperse themselves to cinemas on either side of the entrenched colonially-derived dichotomies.[5] As the city continued to grow in the 1960s and 1970s,[6] white bourgeois and military families poured into the lower and warmer tree-lined Southern Zone while *cholo* immigrant families were displaced by Westernized-mestizo families to move further from the Centro and upward on the steep canyon wall to new and further "peripheral zones." These poor neighborhoods of the city now extend up to the canyon brow. During these decades, some theaters in the Centro closed and theater construction expanded in the relatively lower established commercial immigrant neighborhoods around Cine Roby, such as Tejar, Ch'jini, and Gran Poder, where some Aymara *chola/o* merchant entrepreneurs were achieving economic prosperity that rivaled the Western middle classes.

These Aymara merchant classes have displayed their urban success materially in ostentatious parades during religious festivals by using images of their own native rural past to simultaneously embody and displace rural indigenous culture. In daily life, clothing in La Paz is still a central local practice of identifying oneself as urban or rural born and it identifies class status while displaying ethnic pride. Expensive clothing also distinguished achieved urban status as women used urban cash to buy wide and heavy layered *pollera* skirts and bowler hats to display indigenous native identity, and men dressed in Western-style suits sometimes worn over or beneath rural indigenous clothing. In contrast with the cheaper single-layer Western clothing, this self-display of the emerging Aymara middle class still results in *chola/o* women and men being racially separated as "Indians" by people in white middle classes who are antagonized by the prosperous bourgeoisie flaunting their native indigenous culture.

In the expanding *cholo* neighborhoods, *cines populares* were built as smaller and architecturally indistinct buildings. Many *cines populares* do not show films at night because it is too cold, while Centro theaters are now advertised as heated. The seats in *cines populares* are smaller and harder, putting viewers into a position which registers the social site and class of exhibition onto one's *trasero* (behind) and knees, if tall enough. And during exhibitions, the clothing of the audiences and the degree of tell-tale audio-visual scratches and static register one's social location in global distribution circuits.

In the 1970s and early 1980s, a combination of the political and economic crises in the Argentine and Mexican film industries, Bolivian hyper-inflation and political instability, and the introduction of private television programming on multiple private channels, created a 50% drop in movie theater attendance. These factors also created a vacuum on the screens that was filled by films issued by the capital-rich U.S. producer-distributors who had survived global political economic changes of the 1970s with blockbuster investments and a renewed blitz in global distribution. Since the mid-1970s, the percentage of U.S. films exhibited in theaters in Bolivia has increased from under 50% (Susz 1985: 149–161) to more than 77% in the 1990s (Cinemateca Boliviana).[7] The balance is made up of used martial arts films and used B-grade action, horror, and pornographic films from the U.S. and Brazil that circulate in popular cinemas and in some older smaller Centro theaters. Thus, while the categories that separated audiences seemed to be blurring after the 1970s, cinemas were identified by the genres of U.S. films they showed instead of the country of origin or language of their films. As Andres, manager of Cine 6 de Agosto, explained to me,

> each cinema is exclusively characterized by types of films. For example, Cine Monje Campero is characterized by action. Cine Universo by action, Cine 6 de Agosto by comedy, suspense and terror, at Cine 16 de Julio, finer films.

It appears that some popular cinemas are diverging from this model. Now, they show two or three films and combine in a single day martial arts, B-action, and reprises of a variety of major U.S. action, terror, comedy films, all for one price in order attract more customers.

Currently, there are twenty-six official film theaters in La Paz. Each has one screen and during an advertised period the six large cinemas in the Centro still exhibit one film, usually the first-run of films from "the majors" (the transnational producer-distributors) during three daily projection times. In my observation, only the Monje Campero has been permitted by distributors to keep films for up to seven or eight weeks if they are successful. Although the single copy of a film may travel throughout the city, it debuts in the Centro and when it arrives to the *cines populares*, it is usually for one-week periods.[8] The cut in movie-going in La Paz has continued because of the introduction of private television in the early 1980s, home videocassettes, and escalating prolonged unemployment among the lower classes.

VIDEOCASSETTES: A NEW SPECTACLE, AGAIN?

Videotape exhibition of film follows similar patterns of socio-spatial encirclement, but it also challenges them. In white elite neighborhoods "Errol's" is a chain of Chilean video stores that rents official releases of movies for 5 bolivianos (5bs. = $1US) per film. They arrive here delayed after pirated copies. "Errol's" stores are designed in the decor of video chain stores in most of the United States, including computerized rental and inventory systems. Part of the prestige of being a customer at Errol's is the display of status by carrying the plastic yellow and red "Errol's" bag.

In the working class and immigrant altitudes of the city canyon there are several "video bars," small restaurants that rent videotapes and show them for about twelve U.S. cents. In many official and unofficial commercial parts of the city, vendors on the street and in small neighborhood video stores called "video clubs" sell and rent pirated copies of official subtitled U.S. films that usually come through Chile. Another group of viewers, many of them unemployed, sees films for free where televisions are on display in the city Centro and unofficial market-places. According to research by the Cinemateca Boliviana, video and television are how most people in the popular classes in La Paz watch films (Ramiro Cabellero Hoyos, Carranza and Barragán 1991). Official distributors, theater-owners and official video cassette stores say that videotapes and video machines shared among families and friends are *the* major challenge to their businesses. In this neo-liberal context of increasing unemployment, urban migration and government lay-offs, and an expanding informal market, however, criminalizing video piracy is controversial and difficult to execute.

Sometimes sold on the street in the Centro itself before their corresponding films appear in theaters, pirated films on tape usually cost 5 bolivianos (5bs.) for a cassette recorded with two or three films, or 25bs. to purchase a used tape. Pirated videocassettes reverse the usual itineraries of film distribution in cinemas, but the correlation between the comfort and prestige value of the exhibition site remains. Even the itineraries of pirated copies (which are copies of copies of copies—a process of electronic signal distribution and magnetic marking) leave accumulating smeared imagery and distorted sound and unstable images that tell tales about where they have come from.

In sum, the location of cinemas, the genre of films they show, their price and the timing (or delay) of their debuts correspond and separate social and cultural differences among film and video audiences. Throughout the cinemascape, the decor, comfort and prestige of the exhibition site and its image-quality drop as urban altitude rises. Prices for access to video and cinema exhibitions rise with and stand for spheres of social hierarchy.

DISTRIBUTORS OF DIFFERENCE

If the maps of urban identity are made by the direction and timing of film traffic, then their itineraries, the selections of films, their international and urban paths, and their specific exhibition sites are made by people positioned as their travel agents—film distributors. As commercial agencies, distributors-exhibitors look across the local maps of difference to create itineraries for films based on what they know formally and informally about audiences and what audiences want to see. Their social imagination of the city clears the space for the traffic of cultural and financial flows across globally discontinuous spaces.

SOCIAL MAPS AS FINANCIAL BARRIERS

Carlos Alvarez has worked in film distribution in Latin America for thirty years. He worked in the offices of Fox in Peru and Ecuador until the 1970s and has owned an independent distributor, Cine Internacional, since 1982. His map of cinema distribution-exhibition in

La Paz is a social imaginary of difference and an argument that people have to see films in their own social spaces:

> It is known that the people of the Centro do not go to the neighborhood cinemas because of their location and that the popular classes do not come to the Centro. The Centro has a public from neighborhoods like Sopocachi, all of the Zona Sur, Obrajes, Calacoto. Another level. The upper middle-class. The people over here [he points out and upward], they are catalogued like '*popula-cho*,' the masses, public that is part *campesino* [rural peasant]. So the films shown here in the Centro, the nominees and prize-winners are of a different type—finer. They are for a more refined taste. The others have their cines *populares* and go there. Now they have their own 'advantages.' Here they show only one film in the Centro. In the *cines populares* they show triple, double, or continuous. The people want quantity. They can see two or three for one price that does not exceed sixty cents of a dollar. And they are happy. . . .
> . . . This barrier between one public and another has always existed. Always existed. On the Montes Avenue, an extension of the Prado, there is the Cine Mexico, that showed only Mexican films fifty-two weeks a year. Double. They showed two films. If they put the same films in other theaters, nobody went. Or very few went people to that cinema. . . . The people do not mix here in the Centro. It's rare. It's very marked, Señor.

Alvarez is among another five or so independent distributors who buy copies of used older (more than three years old) Hollywood films, B-movies, and independent material for $2,000 to $3,000 and circulate them in the secondary and tertiary cinemas around the country.

Two other national distributors, López Films and ZW Films, have exclusive rights to distribute new Hollywood releases and each has arrangements with specific producer-distributors, the U.S.-based majors, to keep a commission of each films' local income.[9] During the first week of exhibition, distributors remit up to 60% of the gross earnings to the U.S. producer-distributors; then their commission slides to 40% over the following two to three years. Local distributors also divide their commission with the theaters in a sliding scale from 60%–40% to a 40%–60% split. Because the producers-distributors in the United States may set a quota for the first weeks of exhibition in order to pay off their own investment loans quickly to pay less interest, it is important to debut films where they will do best commercially in a short amount of time. So that profit can be maximized from the earliest audiences, theaters have urban identities; that is, distributors and exhibitors must create spaces—such as the Centro—where money is concentrated and the prices can be conventionally higher. This is a system of urban social spaces that distributors must create and protect, as distributor Manuel López implies:

> Logically, we put the best films in the best cinemas. For example, Cine Monje Campero always has well-chosen material. Why? Because they [the viewers] are demanding, too. And because it is the best cinema in Bolivia commercially and because it's among the best-equipped cinemas . . . If a cinema is number one, we have to try to take care of that cinema. If it specializes in a certain type of material, then we try to give it to them successively. . . .

As intermediaries between producers and consumers who are unable to control the conditions of their own institutional reproduction (Ang 1991), they employ their social

imagination to obtain some certainty. In creating, or distributing, social spaces, film distributors here ascribe "barriers" between audiences about whom they are fundamentally
uncertain as they try to bridge the market gap in which they themselves operate. As Ien Ang
has written, media institutions see consumers as objects to be conquered and known in a
one-way model of mass communication, but as they "desperately seek" (to hold/control/
know) audiences, they "freeze" audiences into taxonomic categories based on their current
formal and informal knowledge of local difference. In La Paz, distributors in this situation
map onto the cinemascape the "barriers" of local social discourses.

As if signaling the uncertainties of film distribution, however, one *cine popular* manager
could not explain why film genres are associated with specific neighborhoods:

> If we show a film from Monje Campero here, it does not work because every
> theater has its public. Monje Campero does not show '*las chinas*' [martial arts].
> And in the cinemas around here—Madrid, Imperio—they like pure *chinas*.
> Pure action. Below, they like the social films . . . The truth is that I have no idea
> why they like it. But in these zones they like these films.

For other distributor-exhibitors, there are no social differences among audiences for
their material. At Cine Murillo, only a few blocks up from the Centro, pornography is
usually shown. The managers there told me, "Here there is no class distinction. People who
like these films come here from all social classes." In discussions about cinema exhibition
sites and their audiences, people in La Paz suggested to me that these managers are guarding
their business from being degraded by association with "the lower classes who go there." Yet
in contrast with these two readings of attendance there, I observed mostly male middle-class
bureaucrats and young men attending that theater. Despite the blurring of classes in discourse about the theater, it is gender difference that is dispersed.

More certain about the divisions in the cinemascape perhaps, the president of the
successful distribution company which handled 75% of the new films in 1990, Manuel López
of López Films, explained to me how cultural divisions intrinsically separate the audiences:

> The peasants feel forced to come to city because the style of life is better,
> relatively. They want to wear shoes. They want to dress like urban people . . . If
> he had potable water, if he had gas to cook with, access to electricity, his
> television, the peasant would not come. We would not have the invasion, the
> migration of peasants to the city.

López sees assimilation as natural because of the attractiveness of urban comforts and,
as he also explained to me, because the government will not redistribute money in the
countryside. Here in the city, he said, rural immigrants have no time to go to the cinema and
must spend all of their time selling, ". . . some little thing. Besides they have a 'super-special'
mentality." López went on to subvert the linear narrative of urban acculturation because
rural and urban native culture determine capacity for urban life:

> Let's say this country arrives at a moment of fantasy, that it would have money
> to get everything in the world it wants. First, the peasant does not take care of
> things. Never is he going to care for things because he is not used to that. If you
> give him a refrigerator, he'll have it until he breaks it and if he does, he is not
> going to be able to fix it. It's complicated. It would be a little difficult.

Alvarez's map of social barriers and López's views on assimilation follow a local Paceño model for "cataloguing" and ranking people in the city's definitions of cultural difference and hierarchy. Do U.S. film producers who do about half of their distribution outside the United States depend on these local distributors and their local social knowledge of audiences in order to distribute films?[10] The situation is not easily dichotomized. While the itineraries of films within the city may be made by local distributors, choices about what films will travel to Bolivia are often made elsewhere. Z. Willi of ZW Films, López's counterpart in distributing new releases from the major producer-distributors, explained,

> In my case, I depend on the Panama office [of United International Pictures, which distributes Metro-Goldwyn, Paramount, Universal, and United Artists]. That is because Panama distributes to Venezuela, Central America and Bolivia. So they choose and say, 'Take this.' And many times I see the list of some of the films available that I have not received. [If I ask for something from it] 'It's not worth it,' they say, 'Because it has not done well, the film has done poorly. You will not do anything.'

Yet challenging the Hollywood-centered trickle-down narrative of film dispersion, film distributor and owner of popular Cine Universo, W. Guerra, told me that his Cine Universo debuted the 1993 action/sci-fi film *The Fortress* before its U.S. debut. Occasionally, he explained, U.S. distributors send films in advance to Bolivia and to other countries as a marketing test, a sign of the fundamental uncertainties about audiences inherent in the multinational distribution. As I will show later, however, both distributors interpreting the challenges of video piracy as well as audiences reading the itinerary of films to Bolivia emplot themselves in narratives about national development and modernity.

DISTRIBUTORS OF U.S. CULTURAL EXPANSION, OR IMPROVEMENTS IN FILM GENRES AND AUDIENCE TASTE?

The social discourse of distributors perpetuates sales for a virtual global monopoly in film distribution for the Hollywood majors, on the one hand, and separates local audiences on the other. I asked distributors if they thought that U.S. films alienated people from their own culture, as Leftist filmmakers in Bolivia had argued forcibly for years. Unsurprisingly, no distributor claimed to be the agent of U.S. expansionism. Manuel López and Z. Willi pointed out that some films had spurred "superficial" fads in dancing, hair style and clothing for short periods. López said that rap music was briefly popular among youth who traveled to the United States and knew its dances and among some children who saw *Ninja Turtles* films. Salsa, he said was introduced in Bolivia in the film *Salsa*, but the dance is still not generally very popular here. Willi pointed out that people often say, "the foreign is always better," but in terms of cultural alienation, he said:

> Not necessarily from the United States, but across our own borders. No. I do not see the U.S. films as alienating. But I see it in Mexican films, for example . . . If you see the TV series *Chavo del Ocho* and you hear the people here say, 'You are in the right!' or '*chavos*,' then people are changing how they speak. That is alienating! [He laughs.] Because it is changing how people speak.

As the smaller popular cinemas add more Hollywood reprises to their programming, special effects are replacing what independent distributor Carlos Alvarez called "the spectacular material" of martial arts and B-movie violence with blockbuster films. For Alvarez, the effect of the higher investments in the exhibitionary aspect of cinema since the 1970s has been that Hollywood films have become more "universal":

> The American films are more assimilable, I would say, here in Bolivia. They are assimilated more. The public apprehends them faster. That is why the films are more successful.

Z. Willi explained the increase in Hollywood films in "two aspects": the crisis in Mexican cinema and the over-saturation of Mexican films that appeared on the private TV channels that opened and began transmitting in the early 1980s. As a result, he said, the cinemas have had to use Hollywood films to compete with and distinguish their programming from television. Willi reasoned that people also will get bored with that material because of its increasing circulation in the cinemas and on TV. In his reading of the shift to Hollywood films, however, he also sees a change in peoples' motives:

> What do they look for in cinema? A very small amount of people go looking to do an analysis of the film. The majority go for a distraction. We live in a country that has a lot going on, more problems. So to go to think in the cinema is not agreeable. So the majority looks for something agreeable, to relax for a moment, to reduce and get rid of stress. For at least a moment.

Willi argued that the quality and distraction that audiences now look for is found in commercial Hollywood films: "For me American cinema is its technique, its focus on some things, with a lot of technique. That is, very well made." The American version of a story of the survivors of a plane crash in the Andes was much better made than its Mexican version, he said. He believes audiences are captured by the technical quality and special effects of Hollywood cinema. ". . . By using modern equipment and computers they can do anything, effects that are incredible."

Similarly, instead of seeing the visual qualities of Hollywood films as a sign of finance capital or as a result of transnational political economic structures, Manuel López observed the increased distribution of Hollywood films among popular cinemas as a concurrent change in the mentality of audiences:

> Until fifteen-twenty years ago, Bolivia was a market where the Mexican films worked very well because the public was accustomed to it. The mentality has been changing slowly . . . I think there is a change because the people are getting used to seeing a certain type of film. The quality of American cinema is always better than the Mexican cinema. As one gets accustomed to American cinema, one leaves the other. Why? Because the other has no quality, the other has had all the same actors. It does not have much innovation. There is any type of film that one wants to see. As one North American has told me, [in English] 'The people are so smart.' The public is very awake now.

López also said that 'the smarter public' now can choose to see a film

> . . . it can laugh at. They are not going to see a film that is ambiguous, where you have to think after seeing the film. You leave and you cannot understand some things . . . like European films.

Each of the distributors perpetuated the hegemonic definition of cinema as diversionary entertainment, rather than defining it as a medium for social analysis and critique as film-makers in Bolivia have. In fact, distributors said that Bolivian films are not exhibited because there is no money to sustain an industry.

Distributors' images of audiences' tastes also addressed the replacement of Spanish-speaking films with English-speaking and Spanish-subtitled films. The audiences, some distributors pointed out, are more literate than before and are now accustomed to reading Spanish subtitles. Carlos Alvarez observed that,

> I understand that the public has accustomed itself to subtitling, to the 'subtitles' of the films. The people do not know how to speak it, they do not know how to read it fluently, but they are accustomed to the English phonetics. It is the actor that talks in English, in fact. Many people do not need to look at the words. It's enough that the actor is American and English to be preferred. I have distributed a mountain of Russian films, but under one condition, that they are dubbed in English. Dubbed and then subtitled. So the Russian, spoken in Russian and translated [subtitled] does not work.

Whereas people in white upper and middle classes read subtitles and watch dramatic narratives and character dilemmas, many people in the immigrant and popular classes told me they read very little of the subtitles, and most popular discourse about films is about their exhibitionary rather than narrative qualities. Interestingly, my research suggests that this is the center of discourse about local popular spectacles as well (Himpele 1995). Because of their visual narratives and special effects, people explained to me, action films are the most popular, interesting, and worth paying to see in a cinema. I found that action films are the most popular in video stores across the city as well. The manager of one official video store in white middle class Sopocachi told me that violent and action films were very popular in La Paz because they countered the lives of audiences:

> Clearly people prefer the films with violence and action. It is because there is not much violence in Bolivia. The streets are tranquil, unlike those of Mexico and the United States, for example. There are protest marches and other incidents here, but it is generally a peaceful place.

Though he mentions popular protest, his view of urban audiences does not associate violent films with unruly and potentially threatening immigrant masses lining the canyon walls above. He uses action films to define a peaceful city ("La Paz") by contrast, yet he excludes from his social imaginary issues of the structural and domestic violence and cultural marginalization among tens of thousands of immigrants who live and operate in unofficial markets. Further, whites and several mestizos also frequently characterized the "Aymara psychology" among the popular classes as "closed" or "inexpressive" (thus incapable of self-representation), despite the visible popular protest marches and festivals that move through the Centro displaying ethnic pride. It is as if the popular classes who see the same— even more of—action, terror, and martial arts films cannot be incited by them because of an innate passive psychology.

VIDEO PIRACY AND COUNTER-ITINERARIES

Fears of popular uprisings, structural uncertainty among immigrants, and the uncertainties of distributors, however, can be unraveled in the controversy over pirated videos descending the urban canyon walls in itineraries that continually upset the staggered class correspondences of early access to newly-released films. Offering the fastest access to film debuts to the popular classes, a pirated film is often available on videotape unofficially in the street markets within a couple of weeks of, or before, its national debut in a theater in the city Centro or as an official video copy.

"The same day that the films debut in Puerto Rico, with Spanish subtitles or dubbed in Spanish, or if they debut in Miami or in California also in Spanish, the first pirated copy exists twenty-four hours later. These come through Panama," Walter Guerra explained to me. This is an enormous problem for official distributors and filmmakers who have argued that tying it to the issue of copyright would also be a legal basis for directing money toward national film production. A law against contraband videotapes and unofficial businesses was recently passed, but instead of resulting in a "video crackdown" (Hamilton 1993), it is not being fully executed as the informal market and prolonged unemployment expand together in a precarious neoliberal political economic environment. I recall hearing that one state minister was reported to say that it is better to have an informal market filling the sidewalks than to have the people in the jungle training to be guerrillas.

Guerra went on to tell me, "The unemployed who sell the videos are also operating in a free market like we are, but they must do it legally." He explained that he has contacted the Motion Picture Association of America for help with the piracy problem in Bolivia, but he is caught in the middle. Commenting on his position as he countered the decentralized challenges of video piracy, he sarcastically tapped the discourse of modern development when he told me that he suggested to them,

> If you sell us the official videos for less, with the same laws of the market-place we can make the piraters leave. But the response is 'No.' But they are the great geniuses. We are underdeveloped. They know what they are doing . . .

FILM DISTRIBUTION AS MEDIA

In La Paz film debuts are classificatory moments. Each time the same film debuts, it is a unique event since each debut occurs in a theater with a new sector of the urban movie-attending audience. As a film moves through cinemas on its itinerary, it separates sites of exhibition to which audiences disperse themselves and connects them in a narrative that emplots difference and the hierarchical organization of local terms of class, cultural identity, and urban space. People in the city used such narratives of film distribution—but not of video-cassettes—to describe social and cultural hierarchies. For example, as Reynaldo, a twenty-three year-old university student, defined the "popular classes":

> It does not refer to the general public, but to the lower middle class and poor people . . . They are from zones higher up in the city and further from the Centro. The peripheral zones. People who work in the streets. These are people who do not go to the cinema, for example, because they do not have the money. You will see these people at cinemas like Cine Mexico, where they show Mexican films; Cine Centro; or Cine Murillo. They are 3bs. and some show two films for the one price. There are all types of films shown: action, comedy, martial arts. I do not know why so many people like them. Eventually the big movies go there. First, they debut at a cinema like Monje Campero, then they go to a smaller cheaper cinema.

Marcos, fifty, a professional engineer who lives in the Centro, used cinema locations to encircle the psychology of immigrant classes:

> The people from peripheral zones that go to the neighborhood cinemas go because they have less self-esteem, they are humble people [*gente humilde*]. Those cinemas are cheaper and not as nice as the others . . . On Sunday's they are filled with the *cholitas* [young Aymara women domestic employees] who have Sundays off.

And Andrea, a thirty-two year-old teacher who lives in a higher popular neighborhood, used cinema spectatorship to define white elite culture:

> I had a friend at the University from Calacoto [in the elite Southern Zone]. She always used clothing styles that she saw in movies. During a movie she would say, "Look at that outfit," and then go have the same thing made. The Southern Zone is another world. People down there—probably because of their economic position—are oriented toward the foreign. Clothing, music, film and a way of life—going to the supermarket, for example. You will not see them playing folklore music. It really has to do with where you are born. They have the attitude that they are better than the rest and do not associate with us. All the classes up here have more in common here than any of us do with them—the same music, ways of dressing, and ways of thinking.

People also use their positions within film itineraries to create national subject positions. "Bolivia will always be the child of the United States," say some people reading the delayed debuts of films, other commodities, and their currency's exchange value as signs of their country's international status. "Bolivia is always *atrasado* ('behind')," others say. It is as if contemporaneously having the newest available commodities defines the "Modern."

The distributors who are "timekeepers" (Wilk 1994) of this modernity use staggered debuts to deny coevalness and rank separate social groups.[11] As gatekeepers to circulating commodities, distributors distribute local differences by composing a series of sights and sites—like narrative cinema's internal succession of inter-cutting scenes—to form a media containing potent narrative schemes. Reading this temporal and spatial field (what I have called itineraries) spectators insert themselves as subjects when they decide, or feel it is decided for them, which films to see and where to see them. Thus, if film distribution is such a media, what media theories can we use to understand it?

DISTRIBUTION AS CINEMA APPARATUS

Analyzing media signification, scholars have recently argued for the consideration of exhibition and reception as social history (Allen 1979; Allen 1990), cross-culturally (Hahn 1990), including the architecture of the exhibition space (Herzog 1984). Other work on spectatorship has emphasized the relationships between spectators who negotiate meanings within textual "horizons of expectation" (Jauss 1982) or who decode narrative structures and characters according to the pretexts of multiple and shifting identities they bring to viewing (Hall 1993; Mayne 1993). Ethnographic work has shown how people form self-identities as well as those of their alters by mimicking and appropriating cinematographic images, constructions of cultural differences, and schemes of alterity (Lutz and Collins 1993; Martínez 1992).

These theories of media signification are important for understanding the mutual relations of version and subversion in which media-texts embed audiences and audiences use and imagine the people and places in media texts. To hold these processes in tension, Judith Mayne (1993: 78), for example, supports the idea of an uncollapsable gap separating the subjects imagined by the media industry and real viewers. These supposed "gaps," I show, are inhabited by film distributors who, according to their knowledge of audiences, profit nevertheless by dividing and dispersing film-goers into ranked groups of viewers with staggered access to the debuts of films within the field of available films.

Approaches that emphasize viewer–text–context relations, then, have overlooked film distribution as a mediator and as an agent in media signification. Distribution is not a passive conduit merely linking the sites of production and consumption of film. It separates and connects differences among viewers in the social field. Following Arjun Appadurai's (1991) point that media's "de-territorialized imaginary" has a place in global social practices, I also ask what films enter into this circulation? How do they get to specific audiences? Transnational media does not "travel" autonomously; so who decides film itineraries? How does transnational circulation itself enter into the social imaginary? Is not the accumulating wear and tear left on *Dracula* inscribed into the text to define the meaning of the film and the identities of audiences who see it?[12]

In writing about the itineraries of film distribution and posing distribution as one form of media agency, I am using something other than monolithic apparatus analysis. Yet to understand the distribution of difference through the itineraries of film distribution, the perspective of apparatus theory is also suggestive. Just as the movements of a film/video camera as it reframes new subjects are typically edited out, we have edited the signification of film distribution out of our analyses.

Apparatus theory, as a moment in cinema theory,[13] explained films as the powerful institutional agents of a cinematic apparatus that forms the subjectivity of film-goers through a process of interpellation, or constituting viewers as subjects (Althusser 1986). Audiences positioned by narrative schemes and cinematic spaces share or identify with characters and the points of view of the camera (e.g., Baudry 1975; Metz 1982), editing, and by extension, the ideological apparatus of the capitalist industry. Understanding this "suturing" or stitching of the audiences into the narrative film has roots in Lacanian theory as a practice of signification that creates meaning and identity through negations (see Heath 1981). Such negations in film include the shot/reverse-shot sequence that alternates between presence/absence and self/other in order to stitch together the subjective viewpoints in the filmic narrative.

Films move similarly in their distribution itineraries in La Paz. In reading the cinemascape here, distributors and audiences use and form perceptions of selves and others in a social field of distinct audiences imagined to be frozen in their cultural spaces and always alternately present or absent as films travel between specific social sites of film exhibition. With shot/reverse-shot in mind, let us now take a closer look at the sequence in *Dracula*'s itinerary of appearances in La Paz. Descent in social status and rise in urban topography is the cumulative tale of the itinerary, as mentioned earlier, but the initial alternation from the Cinema Monje Campero in the Centro, to the popular Cine Roby, back to the elite Plaza Murillo, and then on to small cinemas in popular immigrant neighborhoods stitches together a narrative of alternating difference and an alternative to the modernist one of linear assimilation and core–periphery relations.

Though mapped in cultural and racial terms, this distribution is also driven by commercial interests that reveal a prosperous Aymara cholo-mestizo bourgeoisie. This alternation maps the city as a space of mutual antagonisms, rather than neat oppositions, between parallel Western and Aymara middle classes (Himpele 1995). This polycentric tale of cultural dispersion in the city, however, is obstructed by the dominant linear trickle-down narratives and models of single class ladders, with their social evolutionary subtexts, that are usually evoked in the narratives of film distribution. The dispersion and reproduction of videotapes also suggests similar polycentric narratives.[14] Working in the edited "gap" between production–consumption, between here–there, and between self–other, I question how self–other relations exist not as a dialectic, but in the means and media of the dispersion of one from the other and the circulations between them (Himpele 1995).

DISTRIBUTING DIFFERENCE

If the agency of distribution has been edited out in media signification, it also is absent in understanding the politics of difference. In a transnational field defined by hybrid cultures and circulations, James Clifford argues with an implicit theory of discourse that "self–other relations are matters of power and rhetoric rather than of essence" (1988: 14). Akhil Gupta and James Ferguson (1992: 16) argue for looking "beyond culture" toward "difference-producing set of relations." Like others who have also adapted Michel Foucault's (1978) use of *discours*[15] for post-orientalist studies of the production of subjectivities and representations, their approaches leave distribution itself in a passive position.

In his works, filled with spatializing metaphors, Foucault was of course very interested in dispersal. He showed that discursive and non-discursive disciplinary practices have been disseminated throughout modern society and infinitesimally multiply sites of power and resistance. Without a single origin/center, power relations are diffused between the organized and enclosed sites of power he writes about. "Power," Foucault said, "is deployed *through* distributions" (1980: 77, my emphasis), leaving distribution to be the passive instrument of productive strategies and tactics created and practiced, seemingly industrially, elsewhere. Recalling the theater manager José who pointed out that, "You have to know the parameters of the people," I argue for the study of the discourses about and practice of distribution as active sites of power/knowledge, rather than as neutral conduits for the dissemination of subjects and representations produced and consumed elsewhere. What I am demonstrating here, to modify the provocative phrase from Gupta and Ferguson, is the analysis of *difference-distributing sets of relations*.

THE TRANSNATIONAL DISTRIBUTION APPARATUS: INVISIBLE OR VISIBLE? DISCIPLINE OR SPECTACLE?

A transnational difference-distributing set of relations forms an apparatus that disperses the sites of production and consumption and has grown to powerful proportions because of their techniques for extracting circulatory material—money—from them. The buildings in the center of La Paz are the visible "bridge-heads" of global financial and commodity currents, while the distributors inside anonymously peripheralize (immigrant zones sometimes are called "gente *periférica*") indigenous immigrants and their families and popular audiences into the surrounding canyon walls, distributing them into microsites of consumption. Quite vividly, the Centro set at the bottom of the canyon could appear as a panopticon, an oft-used metaphor for a differentiating and disciplinary apparatus, as Foucault described it: "Instead of bending all its subjects into a single uniform mass, it separates, analyses, differentiates, carries its procedures of decomposition to the point of necessary and sufficient single units" (1979: 170). From behind the scenes of their discriminating media spectacles, the distributors discussed above disperse narrative cuts and negations as they glance up at the canyon walls of people surrounding them.

Seen as a spectacle instead, the twenty-plus-story high-rise buildings clustered in the Centro along the bottom of the canyon, however, are also a constant exhibition of state and Western bourgeois power. In La Paz, invisible flows of finance are exhibited as theater architecture, itineraries of films through these sites, and the self-displays of social class by spectators who make visible popular immigrant and Western middle class identities, and the social antagonisms between them. Further enhancing the visibility and the agency of the distribution apparatus is the annual film festival in Bolivia for which prizes are awarded to the distributors who imported the winning films.

The itineraries of film distribution form a media simultaneously embodying exhibitionary forms of power and anonymous economizing agencies that execute them; powerful agencies coexist, blur, and depend on each other, as if two sides of a coin, each side as valuable and formative as the other.[16] Consider the concentration of wealth we see and do not see in the very first scene in the current exhibition of *Dracula* (who, of course, does not die). Though the image appears flat to viewers, it is composed of multiple electronic layers of crisp cloud images in front of which a white unicorn buoyantly bounds toward us. The electronically-superimposed text reads:

TRI-STAR PICTURES HOME VIDEO

Tri-Star, a sibling company of Columbia Pictures, *Dracula*'s producer, was in charge of *Dracula*'s distribution. Their parent company is SONY.[17]

DISPLACING THE APPARATUS

If film itineraries issue from an apparatus that distributes difference, then dispersion is also a context where social struggles for representation take place. Though too complex to fully describe here, one such site is the citywide festival parade for the Lord of Great Power (The *Gran Poder*, a church parish in a prosperous Aymaracholo neighborhood near Cine Roby). The popular classes who participate in the parade are effectively agents in film distribution as they divert money away from the cinema industry.

During the 1994 event, I saw the popular Cine Imperio open behind the crowd of people lining the street to watch the twelve-hour parade. "It is worth opening for the few people we get," said the manager to me, "People in this neighborhood save all year to dance in the *Gran Poder*, so it takes money from us all year." The parade is a measure and means of social status and ethnic pride for rural immigrants and is part of the local "culture industry,"[18] of festivals that displaces the flow of films designed in richer contexts (Himpele 1995). Further, as the thousands of immigrant dancers descend from the popular Cine Roby and past the Cine Monje Campero in the Centro, they distribute difference by ostentatiously putting their multiple identities into relief against the changing audiences as they descend into the Centro. They pluralize the uni-centric map of cultural dispersion. Near the end of the parade's itinerary, the thousands of dancers must circulate back to their neighborhoods to finish the festival. There they continue with a street party after the parade. One of the dancers, an older and prosperous merchant woman named Elena, told me:

> We Bolivians are very *folklorista* with our music and dancing . . . Not everyone dances. Some people prefer to watch. The rich do not dance. Only us poor. They prefer to build skyscrapers than to dance. The rich do not dance because they rather would buy cars and travel. But they cannot take that with them when they die, can they? But I can take with me the joy I have when I am

dancing. I am dancing for the Lord of Great Power. He watches me and he knows what I am doing for him. With faith. That I can have when I die. One cannot have cars and skyscrapers.

Elena tore down the spectacle of the Centro with her own spectacle of excess. Furthermore, she also brings us to subject positions in tension with those available to the media of film distribution. Viewed from the popular neighborhoods above, the Centro is humbled. From up above, the concentration of buildings in the bottom center appears miniature, suggesting a peripheral status for the white Western well-to-do and of cinema culture.

Seen from the neighborhoods in the canyon high above the Cine Monje Campero and the skyscrapers, the visible "gaze" of centers of government and commodity importers and the media monopoly are reduced to a "glance" (cf. Orlove 1991). To use the panopticon model to define the transnational distribution apparatus here would assume a central vantage point that can constantly see and monitor all. If transnational ". . . capitalism is becoming more tightly organized through dispersal" (Harvey 1989: 159), my analysis also reveals what gets squeezed out from its tightening and widening grasp. Given the fundamental uncertainties of media institutions in the market "gap" in which they work (Ang 1991), distributor-producers can only guess at the activities of consumers here because they cannot see them directly nor constantly (cf. Rofel 1992). With social maps and narratives of difference, distributors inhabit and mediate this space between powerful stereotypes and peoples' own complex activities, motives, and self-representations.

Notes

1   [. . .]
2   If the term "popular classes" appears to reduce a sociocultural complexity to a homogeneous mass of people, this article is about how people with diverse ethnic, gender, age, and economic subject positions are separated and attributed with a common identity as "the masses." People in La Paz also use the terms "class" and "popular" to position and define themselves as urban non-elites. More broadly, "popular culture" in Latin America does not refer to an authentic culture but a cultural zone where they appropriate, trade, articulate, alter, limit, and mediate culture and identity, often in ironic exchanges with elites (Himpele 1995).
3   Ulf Hannerz (1992) imagines this transnational transit as an "urban swirl." He calls the international traffic of used and out-of-fashion commodities "cultural dumping" and argues that the concept is only useful if we study the consumers' creative uses of the second-hand material. Here, I would argue that the concept is useful if we consider the stories that "dumping" itself tells. Further, I do not want to reduce the sort of traffic I am talking about here to a North–South divide in the flow of used goods.
4   Elsewhere (Himpele 1995: Chapter 2; n.d.a.), I elaborate a social history of film distribution-exhibition in La Paz, showing how urban space and the itineraries of film distribution-exhibition have been entwined in the multiple agencies of transnational cinema and consumer culture, the local history of filmmaking, and local cultural politics. Since the 1910s, capital has been directed to building theaters for exhibiting films from Europe and the United States and not toward local cinema production (Himpele n.d.a.) Since the 1920s, Bolivian film production has been episodic at best due to heavy censorship and very little state support, with the exception of the 1950s (Himpele n.d.b.) This is also due to its displacement by local popular culture (mentioned below and discussed fully in Himpele 1995).
5   During the 1950s, the state supported documentary filmmaking that promoted mestizo nationalism and development; these films were often placed before features from Hollywood, suggesting that a national modernization process would lead to the US consumer lifestyle (Himpele n.d.b.).
6   In these two decades, many of the socially committed Bolivian films produced by Jorge Sanjinés and Grupo Ukamau were immediately government-censored. It is notable too that the Western bourgeoisie did not attend their film *Ukamau* when it debuted in 1966 (it was censored days

later) because "it was in Aymara and showed only Indios." White audiences only wanted to see the film after it traveled to Europe and was marked with recognition at Cannes when its director, Jorge Sanjinés, won the Cannes Prize for best young director (Sanjinés, in Mesa Gisbert 1979: 145).

7   It is important to recognize that the percentage of films shown does not take into account the cumulative screen time of films. Films from Europe and elsewhere in Latin America are almost exclusively shown at the Cinemateca Boliviana, a semi-private national film archive and "art" film theater, or other white cultural venues and may only be shown twice. Films from Hollywood in the commercial cinemas may be exhibited two or three times a day for up to three years.

8   In 1940s New York City, there was a similar "run-zone-clearance" program (Allen and Gomery 1985). Films debuted at first-run theaters owned by the Hollywood studios and their tickets were sold at top-price. Later runs of films in locally-owned smaller movie houses could only sell cheaper ticket prices.

9   During and after the hyper-inflationary early 1980s, half of the twelve distributors in Bolivia closed, as did several cinemas near the Centro. López, ZW, and other independents were consolidated from other companies in the aftermath of that period.

10   If in La Paz, institutional uncertainty is rendered in social discourses of difference, what of the context of mass media in the United States? Clint Wilson and Félix Gutierrez (1985) write that market segmentation, as a divide-and-conquer consumerist approach by U.S. media institutions, is a response to the continued growth of racial diversity, technological change, and continued segmentation of audiences by advertisers. This will mean an overall growth in minority media and a media diversity, they say, as if signaling an end to the "melting pot" ideology in a world of articulated identity politics and advanced communication technologies. They argue,

> The audience of masses was essential to the media because advertisers demanded that they attract a large and somewhat undifferentiated audience . . . But now with audience segmentation, the approach of the media to their audience is the opposite. The media now look for differences and ways to reinforce them (231).
>
> As a result of tailoring products among a racially segmented public, the authors envision U.S. society as one being divided by the same media that once created a common world view (234).

11   Richard Wilk also touches on the cultural politics of access to media delivery systems and the discursive practices of manipulating and defining media distribution paths. His recent article in this journal (1994) on Belize discusses how until satellite delivery, the delay of television programming (in "colonial time") bolstered the bourgeois class and its ideological definition of the country as culturally dependent—an ideology that keeps them positioned as the merchants of circulating media.

12   In this La Paz cinemascape, I re-address Walter Benjamin's (1968) work on the reproduction of art, Jean Baudrillard's (1988) on media simulations, and Michael Taussig's (1993) study of mimesis and alterity with these questions: Does mechanically-reproduced art lose something other than its aura as it travels? Can we only read the endless copies in the media as a simulacrum that challenges our notions of authenticity? And how do the perpetual copies in mimesis that distinguish themselves as same-but-different lead us to refocus on the social processes of differentiation? Here, I look in-between the multiple identical copies of a capitalist media at how the social process of distribution inserts itself and leaves marks of alterity on copies.

13   The concept of a narrative apparatus of cinema follows work in the 1970s by film scholars concerning positive effects of film texts and cinema institutions (see, for example, Rosen 1986) in order to move beyond analyses of the "false" ideologies inherent in film content and style.

14   It also prevents us from seeing how cinema is displaced (not replaced) by local popular culture (Himpele 1995).

15   It is striking that some theorists concerned with the dissemination of difference (e.g., Jacques Derrida) and the dispersal of power (e.g., Michel Foucault) share national space with the origin of mass media distribution of scale. From France, Charles Pathé created the first international film distribution company with world-wide offices; it was the largest firm until World War I. Before then, colportage in 18th century France was a similarly a literary enterprise of 3,000 peddlers who distributed 20 million copies a year (Martín-Barbero 1993/1987: 102–3). As Jesús Martín-Barbero writes, these distributors were cultural mediators between the upper and lower classes as they circulated culture between them.

16   In an article that explores the practices of power in the nineteenth century "exhibitionary complex,"
      Tony Bennett (1994) argues that exhibitions are "generalizing in their focus" because they do not
      render the public visible to invisible and individualizing disciplinary power, but exhibitions render
      power publicly visible. Such "permanent display of power/knowledge," Bennett argues (133) ". . .
      placed people behind it, inveigled [the public] into complicity with it rather than cowed into
      submission with it" (130). He argues that exhibition entails a visual code that does not serve to
      "atomize and disperse the crowd, but to regulate it, and to do so by making it visible to itself, by
      making the crowd the ultimate spectacle" (131–2).
           In another work that also complicates the quick association of bureaucratic modernity with an
      invisible disciplinary apparatus, Lisa Rofel (1992) looks at visibility and power in the management of
      a factory in China. She also shows that an invisible disciplinary apparatus collides and coexists with
      prior spatial practices based on "the metaphysics of display" that executes power.
17   Like Coca-Cola, the name "SONY" is its own attraction and its own authority. It appears in multiple
      sites at home among consumers, in the office, and among professional media producers-exhibitors.
      As theater-owner on display or behind the scenes, this media corporation financier makes a spectacle
      of distribution and the sites for extracting capital.
18   Such festival events are part of the local "culture industry" and, like cinema in other places (including
      the Southern Zone of the city), they are a topic of everyday conversation and controversy and the basis
      of a significant year-round economy of production and merchandising that includes the tourist market.
      These cultural events also entail a political economy of access and a cultural discourse of status.

References

Allen, Robert C.
    1983 Motion Picture Exhibition in Manhattan. In *Film Before Griffith*. J.L. Fell, ed. pp. 162–175.
    Berkeley: University of California Press.
    1990 From Exhibition to Reception: Reflections on the Audience in Film History. *Screen* 31(4):
    347–356.
Allen, Robert C. and Douglas Gomery
    1985 *Film History: Theory and Practice*. New York: Alfred A. Knopf.
Althusser, Louis
    1986 Ideology and Ideological State Apparatuses (Notes Toward an Investigation). In *Video
    Culture: A Critical Investigation*. J.G. Hanhardt, ed. pp. 56–95: Gibbs M. Smith, Inc., Peregrine
    Smith Books, in association with Visual Studies Workshop Press.
Ang, Ien
    1991 *Desperately Seeking the Audience*. London and New York: Routledge.
Appadurai, Arjun
    1991 Global Ethnoscapes: Notes and Queries for a Transnational Anthropology. In *Recapturing
    Anthropology: Working in the Present*. R.G. Fox, ed. pp. 191–210. Santa Fe: School of American
    Research Press.
Baudrillard, Jean
    1988 Simulacra and Simulations. In *Jean Baudrillard: Selected Writings*. M. Poster, ed. Pp. 166–184.
    Stanford: Stanford University Press.
Baudry, Jean-Louis
    1975 Ideological Effects of the Basic Cinema Apparatus. *Film Quarterly* 28(1):39–47.
Benjamin, Walter
    1968 Art in the Age of Mechanical Reproduction. In *Illuminations*. H. Arendt, ed. Pp. 217–251.
    New York: Schocken Books.
Bennett, Tony
    1994 The Exhibitionary Complex. In *Culture/Power/History*, N. Dirks, G. Eley and S. Ortner,
    eds. Pp. 123–154. Princeton: Princeton University Press.
Clifford, James
    1988 *The Predicament of Culture: Twentieth-Century Ethnography, Literature, and Art*. Cambridge, MA
    and London: Harvard University Press.
de Certeau, Michel
    1984 *The Practice of Everyday Life*. Berkeley: University of California Press.

Foucault, Michel
    1978 *The History of Sexuality, Volume I: An Introduction*. New York: Vintage Press.
    1979 *Discipline and Punish: The Birth of the Prison*. New York: Vintage.
    1980 Questions of Geography. In *Power/Knowledge: Selected Interviews and Other Writings, 1972–1977*. C. Gordon, ed. Pp. 63–77. New York: Pantheon Books.
Gunning, Tom
    1986 The Cinema of Attraction: Early Film, Its Spectator and the Avant-Garde. *Wide Angle* 8(3–4):63–70.
Gupta, Akhil, and James Ferguson
    1992 Beyond 'Culture': Space, Identity, and the Politics of Difference. *Cultural Anthropology* 7(1):6–23.
Hahn, Elizabeth
    1994 The Tongan Tradition of Going to the Movies. *Visual Anthropology Review* 10(1):103–111.
Hall, Stuart
    1993 Encoding and Decoding. In *The Cultural Studies Reader*. S. During, ed. Pp. 90–103. London and New York: Routledge.
Hamilton, Annette
    1993 Video Crackdown, or The Sacrificial Pirate: Censorship and Cultural Consequences in Thailand. *Public Culture* 5(3):515–531.
Hannerz, Ulf
    1992 *Cultural Complexity: Studies in the Social Organization of Meaning*. New York: Columbia.
Harvey, David
    1989 *The Condition of Postmodernity: An Enquiry into the Origins of Cultural Change*. Cambridge, MA and Oxford: Basil Blackwell Ltd.
Heath, Stephen
    1981 *Questions of Cinema*. Bloomington: Indiana University Press.
Herzog, Charlotte
    1984 The Archaeology of Cinema Architecture: The Origins of the Movie Theater. *Quarterly Review of Film Studies* 9(1):11–32.
Himpele, Jeffrey D.
    1995 Distributing Difference: The Distribution and Displacement of Media, Spectacle, and Identity in La Paz, Bolivia. Ph.D. dissertation, Princeton University.
    n.d.a Silent Shouts and Silent Eras: Conditions for Cinema in Bolivia. Manuscript.
    n.d.b Cinematics for a Modern Bolivian State: Revolutionary Realities and Jorge Ruiz. Manuscript.
Jauss, Hans Robert
    1982 *Toward an Aesthetic of Reception*. Timothy Bahti, transl. Minneapolis: University of Minnesota Press.
Lutz, Catherine A., and Jane L. Collins
    1993 *Reading National Geographic*. Chicago and London: University of Chicago Press.
Martín-Barbero, Jesús
    1993/1987 *Communication, Culture and Hegemony: From the Media to Mediations*. Elizabeth Fox and Robert A. White, transl. London: Sage Publications.
Martínez, Wilton
    1992 Who Constructs Anthropological Knowledge? Toward a Theory of Ethnographic Film Spectatorship. In *Film as Ethnography*. P.I. Crawford and D. Turton, eds. Pp. 131–164. Manchester: Manchester University Press.
Mayne, Judith
    1993 *Cinema and Spectatorship*. New York and London: Routledge.
Mesa Gisbert, Carlos, et. al., eds.
    1979 *Cine Boliviano: Del Realizador al Critico*. La Paz: Editorial Gisbert.
Metz, Christian
    1982 *The Imaginary Signifier: Psychoanalysis and Cinema*. C. Britton, A. Williams, A Guzetti, transl. Bloomington: Indiana University Press.
Orlove, Benjamin
    1991 Mapping Reeds and Reading Maps: The Politics of Representation in Lake Titicaca. *American Ethnologist* 18(2):3–38.

Ramiro Cabellero Hoyos, J., Freddy Carranza, and Sandra Cárdenas Barragán
    1991 *La difusión cinematográfica en La Paz y El Alto. Propuesta de un programa cognitivo de investigación.*
    Cinemateca Boliviana research report.
Rofel, Lisa
    1992 Rethinking Modernity: Space and Factory Discipline in China. *Cultural Anthropology*
    7(1):93–114.
Rosen, Phillip, ed.
    1986 *Narrative, Apparatus, Ideology.* New York: Columbia University Press.
Susz, Pedro
    1985 *La Pantalla Ajena: El Cine que Vimos, 1975–1984.* La Paz: Editorial Gisbert.
Taussig, Michael
    1993 *Mimesis and Alterity: A Particular History of the Senses.* New York and London: Routledge.
Usabel, Suzanne
    1982 *The High Noon of American Films in Latin America.* Ann Arbor: UMI Research Press.
Wilk, Richard
    1994 Colonial Time and TV Time: Television and Temporality in Belize. *Visual Anthropology*
    Review 10(1):94–102.
Wilson, Clint C., and Felix Gutierrez
    1985 *Minorities and Media: Diversity and the End of Mass Communication.* Beverly Hills: Sage
    Publications.

Chapter 27

Martine Danan

MARKETING THE HOLLYWOOD
BLOCKBUSTER IN FRANCE (1995)

THE MARKETING OF HIGH-BUDGET films in our current "image society" or mass media age has emerged as a complex operation designed to predict the public's reactions and, above all, to influence the reception of blockbusters in such a way as to widen their appeal with the largest possible cross section of the population worldwide. As the major U.S. film companies (the Majors) have become integral parts of whole empires built around the integrated leisure and communication industries, they have embraced more systematic and scientific marketing strategies to transform superproductions into colossal, global, media events. But paradoxically, global strategies cannot be deployed without taking into account cultural differences that defy scientific methodology. The case of France may be particularly illuminating regarding the complex interplay of cultural and scientific economic factors involved in the successful international marketing of Hollywood films. France has a strong national filmgoing tradition and a relatively healthy domestic film industry. However, the appeal of U.S. films (i.e., of a few Hollywood blockbusters) has dramatically increased in France since the late 1980s. The growing popularity of American films may be attributed to four key elements: the close interaction of global and local marketing campaigns; the search for new advertising and publicity techniques to circumvent national legislative restrictions; the reliance on scientific marketing research to address local preferences; and the coordination of management decisions between the U.S. headquarters and local subsidiaries. Yet, those four factors are in themselves a scientific oversimplification that does not fully account for the unpredictability of cultural reactions that can make or break a film shown in another country.

COORDINATING GLOBAL AND LOCAL MEDIA EVENTS

The recent restructuring of the Majors within huge integrated entertainment and media empires (such as the 1989 Time-Warner merger) has given unprecedented importance to the blockbuster phenomenon. As cinema is once again a profitable business within the new multimedia environment, the highly integrated media empires, which are in the information-communication business, are willing to invest in the soaring production and marketing costs required by the competitive film industry.[1] Only the most powerful companies can risk investing heavily in the production and international promotion of super-productions, from which they can expect to derive related benefits if they succeed (through profits from spin-off merchandise, videocassettes, books, music, and so on) or absorb the losses if they fail.

However, rising costs and stakes, combined with the relative decline of domestic theatrical earnings, have made U.S. film companies increasingly dependent on foreign and especially European revenues.[2] More than ever the global market is influencing production decisions about mainstream movies, which may be the first and most crucial marketing decision facing studio executives. Because an increasing number of movies are currently grossing more from foreign box-office revenues than domestic ones, many producers must decide whether or not to go ahead with a project on the basis of its potential foreign sales. Casting is frequently the result of the promotional potential of a movie star abroad. For instance, a major consideration in Paramount's decision to cast Sean Connery as Harrison Ford's father in *Indiana Jones and the Last Crusade* (1989) was the fact that Connery, known for his portrayal of James Bond, was extremely popular in Europe and other parts of the world.[3]

Moreover, as a result of the emphasis on globalization, the release and promotion of American films in the home and foreign markets have become closely interrelated. American audiences are huge test markets for the world at large because any film with a budget over $12 million is almost certain to be released in foreign theaters, unless it is a disaster in the domestic market.[4] And success at the American box office becomes a "selling tool" in itself in other parts of the world because "[c]ontemporary international audiences are plugged into what's hot on American marquees," especially when a film has "a high-profile release in America."[5] One way film companies derive the greatest benefits from the impact of an American release and create media events on an international scale is through fast, high-visibility, foreign releases. If a film is successful in the United States, it is now not uncommon to release it worldwide within a few weeks (as soon as dubbed and subtitled versions are available), whereas, formerly, American films were released abroad at least six months after their releases in the United States (so that the American prints could be reused overseas).[6] Furthermore, as in the United States, American studios now tend to saturate foreign markets with prints in order to capitalize on the impact of a new release. It is not uncommon for a blockbuster to be distributed abroad with over 2,000 prints. In France alone, a major American blockbuster can be released with as many as 500 prints (compared to an average 150 prints for national distribution by French companies), at a cost of nearly $1 million solely in prints.[7]

In some cases, however, studios deliberately choose to postpone the foreign release of films and adopt a more cautious strategy. In particular, they tend to do so with films that they consider more difficult to market or that did not meet with the expected success at home. Columbia's *Hero*, which did poorly for its U.S. release in October 1992, started appearing in other countries only six months later. The time lapse gave the studio time to examine its mistakes and design a new marketing campaign that advertised the film as a satire rather than a straight comedy, and to change its name to *Accidental Hero*.[8] In addition, it may be advisable to delay the foreign opening of a film in order to adjust to specific national environments. Summer, for example, is known to be a slow movie-going period in France, whereas October is usually the best month. Distributors also take into account their competitors' distribution plans abroad to avoid overcrowding the market. According to its French distributor, the success of *The Mask* in France was largely due to its positioning; it was the only comedy during a time that the public was assailed by massive publicity for several other American blockbusters.[9]

Attracting the public's attention is indeed the key to success. To do so, marketing executives have to decide on general strategies and oversee complex international campaigns that rely as much on actual advertising as on well-orchestrated publicity (that is, unpaid advertising). As far as publicity is concerned, the marketing of new films greatly depends on the media coverage generated by movie stars in the United States as well as abroad. Movie companies enlist the help of publicists who provide the press with selective glamorous information about their stars.[10] The stars, in turn, often become studio ambassadors, who willingly discuss their new films with the press and provide details about new or upcoming releases through information media ranging from magazines to television shows. The goal of the publicity and extensive press coverage is to pique the curiosity of overinformed consumers. By striving to get press coverage of movies that are still in production, and by multiplying the information channels featuring new films and their stars, studios attempt to heighten the audience's expectations and curiosity to the point of driving them to the theater.

In France, the audience's increased interest in mundane details is reflected by the appearance in the 1980s of a number of glossy, illustrated fan magazines such as *Première* and *Studio*, in which superficial coverage and photo spreads play a much greater role than film reviews. However, even more important is the publicity generated by television programs featuring movies, film festivals, and star appearances. France's "proud cinematic tradition" has created an important "film culture" as well as independent-minded spectators who like to think of themselves as informed film critics.[11] Film clips from new releases are often shown as newsworthy events during mainstream daily reporting; twice a week, during prime time, in a program that successfully encourages moviegoing, the pay channel Canal Plus shows trailers of films being released.[12] Television coverage of films and movie stars is at its highest during prestigious French-based international film festivals, in particular the famous Cannes Film Festival (the number-one film festival in Europe) and the American film festival in Deauville highlighting new U.S. features. Because they generate extensive media coverage, these festivals act as a springboard for the promotion of new movies in France, and have a spillover effect for the rest of Europe and even the United States. Created in 1946 as a major art event, the Cannes festival has evolved, in the words of a *Variety* journalist, "into a frenzied international media circus . . . [which] is accelerating the release of Croisette-hyped pics in France and the rest of Europe," and Deauville "has become a focal point for French and European media."[13]

Film studios are also realizing the increasing importance of systematically tapping the appeal of American movie stars in France. Popular stars like Robert De Niro, Robin Williams, Dustin Hoffman, and Arnold Schwarzenegger have already made special appearances at French film festivals for several years to help promote the films in which they starred. However, in the last few years, the practice of perfunctory star appearances abroad in television programs, together with press conferences, has become much more institutionalized with some studios. Until the late 1980s, for example, Columbia TriStar organized only two yearly tours of the main foreign markets (mostly France, England, and Japan), during which famous stars could promote their most promising new releases. In 1992, in contrast, stars from soon-to-be-released pictures were systematically flown to Paris to give television interviews and hold press conferences, to which journalists from other European countries were invited.[14]

Because of France's special interest in film directors, who are perceived as auteurs (a perception that goes back to the prestige of film culture and film art), film directors also are often invited to make public appearances. The director of *Malcolm X* (1992), Spike Lee, was taken to France twice by the film's marketing team before the movie was released. To get the press to "write what you want it to write about the film," French journalists were invited to New York to meet Malcolm X's widow and Denzel Washington, the star of the film.[15] As another example, France is the only country where Woody Allen allows his name to be associated with the film title on a poster because he feels that French filmgoers respect directors.[16] But in spite of the seemingly more cultural nature of France's interest in directors, the hoped-for outcome of all the intense publicity is simply to create media events that outdo earlier ones.

ADAPTING TO THE FRENCH LEGISLATIVE ENVIRONMENT

Although American studio executives and Hollywood-based advertising agencies design worldwide advertising campaigns, they are forced to adapt to local legislative restrictions and find a number of new venues for their French campaigns. In France—in contrast to the United States (where 90 percent of the major film companies' advertising budgets is spent on television commercials), and unlike most other European countries—legislation prohibits the use of television commercials for film advertising.[17] Consequently, advertising films in France relies heavily on the use of billboards or posters, in strategic locations in city streets and in the Paris subway.[18]

Consequently, a good share of a French advertising campaign may be devoted to posters. At Columbia TriStar, for example, a low-budget campaign that relies exclusively on posters may cost 400,000 francs (approximately $72,000). A Woody Allen movie, likely to attract a faithful group of discriminating moviegoers, still requires a fairly low marketing budget (around one million francs or $180,000). On the other extreme, the marketing of a block-buster like *Terminator 2*, requires millions of francs for radio and newspaper ads in addition to posters. *Terminator 2* cost six million francs (over $1 million), which broke the former advertising-cost record in France—over five million francs for the 1989 launching of *Indiana Jones and the Last Crusade*, released by UIP (in charge of distributing and marketing Universal and Paramount films in France). But even UIP's expenses did not compare with the extravagant fifteen million-franc campaign (about $3 million) spent by Warner for the promotion of *Batman* the same year.[19] Overall, the average budget for the French advertising of a U.S. film likely to be popular, without ranking it among the top superproductions, is between three and four million francs (between $500,000 and $700,000), as was the case for *The Silence of the Lambs* (1990) or *Malcolm X* (for each of which posters alone cost about $200,000).[20] Such campaign budgets, which are based on a production's estimated appeal with the local audience, usually must be approved by the parent company in the United States.

The poster chosen for the French campaign may depart from the American poster or the rest of the international campaign to render a film more explicitly (as no television commercials provide background information about the film's storyline). For example, the American poster for *Drop Zone*, a skydiving action film, shows the main character's face under actor Wesley Snipes's name, which is displayed in big letters. The French poster was changed to a picture of a character jumping from a plane, and Snipes's name, unknown in France, is given a much less prominent place.[21] In addition to the plot, a French poster often needs to highlight the mood or key images a film is built upon, and it often reflects a more cerebral approach than an American poster. For Oliver Stone's political thriller *Salvador*, for example, the French distributor suggested the portrayal of the three main characters with their hands up to suggest revolt, thus emphasizing the political aspect of the movie.[22] The American poster for *Frankenstein* was a greenish, sinister image that evoked a morgue. In contrast, French advertisers from Columbia chose violent colors and lightning bolts to combine the ideas of electricity with life and joy and included a direct reference to Mary Shelley, whose story cultivated French viewers were likely to know.[23]

French film posters also commonly display a series of logos of other national and local media (such as radio stations or magazines) that are partners in the promotion of a movie. This form of media partnership is not restricted to actual advertising; it has also recently expanded to non-conventional publicity, in particular to screening programs, that is, private VIP screenings organized in agreement between an American distributor and special clients for public relations purposes. The clients invite important personalities or their own clients (publicists, advertisers) to the screening; outside of Paris, they may invite their readers or listeners. The companies that sponsor the screenings benefit from the prestige of offering a special event to their patrons. In exchange for the event, the sponsor offers free publicity space to the film company, which in turn derives direct promotional benefits from the deal. Furthermore, spectators, who usually feel flattered to be invited to a private screening, are likely to react positively to the movie and initiate a word-of-mouth campaign, which often plays an essential role in France. This approach is particularly crucial for films that are not based on obvious concepts to market. For example, *Forrest Gump* (1994), staging a simpleton, was of no particular interest to the French audience, which tends to value cleverness. Therefore, UIP, *Forrest Gump*'s European distributor, had to rely on a large-scale, important screening program to foster the movie's image and visibility.[24]

Since the late 1980s, other forms of creative partnerships between the major film companies and various companies intent on promoting their own products have flourished in order to launch U.S. films in the French market. Partnerships include an agreement between a film company and a restaurant chain, which may offer a movie ticket with the purchase of a meal.[25] A company may also supply American distributors with the prizes they increasingly give out in competitions aimed at promoting a new film. (Terminator scooters, for example, were donated by a toy company.) Furthermore, Columbia initiated the practice of having competitions that viewers could enter by dialing a special telephone number or an access code to the Minitel (France's nationwide home-computer system). The paying calls both brought attention to a new release and provided a source of revenue.[26] Thus, France's ban on television film commercials has forced distributors to take advertising and, above all, publicity to new creative heights.

MODERN MARKETING RESEARCH FOR A NON-HOMOGENEOUS PUBLIC

Adapting to foreign environments is but one instance of the complexities that now face marketing executives in charge of vast global campaigns. Not surprisingly, the marketing departments of the major studios are currently the fastest growing departments, and the international marketing divisions of these companies are no exception.[27] However, the most profound transformation of American marketing is not quantitative but qualitative as American film marketing techniques become more dependent on scientific market research. It is not rare for executives who have been with a company for years to be suddenly replaced with younger "Harvard MBA" types who approach the marketing of films more scientifically than "cinema people." Whereas traditional studio managers stress that marketing research, even in the hands of "number-oriented technicians," can only indicate probable pitfalls but cannot foresee the public's unpredictable reactions, the younger, business-oriented executives feel confident that U.S. marketers have superior ability to reach the targeted audiences.[28]

Modern marketing techniques in the United States no longer simply rely on research bearing on the movie itself (such as concept testing and sneak previews, which measure an audience's reactions to film content and concepts before a company delivers the "final cut," with modified scenes and endings).[29] Today, the bulk of marketing research consists of designing a coherent strategy that best targets the expected audiences of a film.[30] Marketing research, based on sophisticated audience tracking surveys, examines the public's receptiveness to advertising themes, trailers, posters, and other promotional materials, and helps devise effective campaigns geared toward a film's potential audiences. Such campaigns must adapt to each individual film and target various groups of spectators, highlighting some aspects of the film and hiding others. For example, MarketCast, a research firm founded by social scientist film buffs, claims that movie preferences can swing by from 10 percent to 60 percent if the way a movie is described is changed. Consequently, the firm compiles 108 descriptions of one movie, then tests the descriptions by doing a telephone survey of "avid" moviegoers (who see 24 or more pictures a year, usually shortly after their release, and who become the catalysts for word-of-mouth advertising).[31]

The following examples will illustrate companies' attempts to alter the perception of their movies in an effort to reach broader audiences. Fearing that *Dances with Wolves* (1990) would be perceived as a Hollywood western, Orion targeted an upscale, adult audience with an aggressive campaign that portrayed the film as a serious "epic" with a documentary-like depiction of Native American life.[32] In the case of the controversial *Malcolm X*, the movie's domestic distributor, Warner Brothers, hired Universal World Group, one of the largest advertising firms owned by blacks, to market the film to black customers. In addition, Warner Brothers prepared trailers that portrayed Malcolm as a political moderate to allay the fears of whites who may associate Malcolm with militant violence.[33] Advertising campaigns must evolve quickly with the public's reactions once the film is released. For example, the initial print campaign for Disney's *Who Framed Roger Rabbit* (1988) sought to appeal to sophisticated filmgoers who might not be attracted to the idea of a cartoon, while media coverage and merchandising tie-ins focused on the animation. But when the studio found that most adult viewers reacted favorably to the cartoon characters, it immediately changed the direction of its print campaign and incorporated cartoon artwork in the ads.[34] In short, a new-movie advertisement campaign resembles a political campaign, adapting to fast-changing events and seeking the "one-time vote," the ticket bought by the moviegoer.[35]

Similarly, the marketing of American films abroad must assess and address the ways in which the foreign public differs culturally from the American public. Not all studio executives agree on the best approach to design a localized marketing campaign, but they admit that an undifferentiated worldwide approach is not always best. In fact, it is estimated that movie campaigns are modified for international release about 50 percent of the time, in order to highlight some aspects and downplay others. For example, for the international marketing of *A League of Their Own* (1992)—which is based on elements of American culture (an American women's baseball team) that do not have great significance abroad—Columbia's marketers "spent months trying to take baseball out of the campaign for a movie that is fundamentally about baseball" (without very successful results).[36]

More generally speaking, understanding cultural specificities is crucial for the marketing of films that depart from the adventure or visual spectacle superproductions with scarce dialogue. Traditional American box-office champions, such as *Indiana Jones*, *Terminator* and its sequel, or *Jurassic Park*, are considered to have "universal" appeal and can rely on simple marketing concepts. But surprisingly, these recent "cosmic" films have been overtaken at the French box office by films that go beyond the universal formulas. In particular, more French spectators saw *Dances with Wolves* and *Dead Poets Society* (over 7 million and 6.5 million spectators, respectively) than *Indiana Jones and the Last Crusade*, *Terminator 2*, and *Jurassic Park* (6.2 million and less than 6 million spectators for the last two).[37] Yet to build their appeal with a foreign audience, films relying on less standardized formulas need innovative marketing campaigns that have been adapted to specific national contexts with the assistance of foreign marketing teams. However, there are no set norms as to the proper way to ensure the financial success of such films, especially in a foreign cultural environment, and each company is still seeking the best strategy to maximize its chances for the greatest returns. As a consequence of this uncertainty, most companies avoid candid discussions about their marketing strategies and claim the right to proprietary secrecy in this domain.[38]

One artful approach that film companies could apply to the marketing of some movies is to play on a mythical image of the United States in France. Although specific portrayals of life in "Mid-America" may be of no special interest to a foreign audience, the French public is sensitive to a certain vision of America, one largely created by past Hollywood films seen by generations of filmgoers. The campaign for *Dances with Wolves*, for example, played on the mythical and wild open spaces of the American West in the French imagination. This sense of wonder struck such a chord with the French public that, at one point, its distributor decided to no longer interfere with the "miracle" and stopped advertising the film.[39] However, in spite of their indisputable liking for American images, French audiences tend to think of themselves as critical of U.S. culture and politics. Therefore, films that evoke American culture, yet appear critical of it, have particular appeal for the French audience. For instance, *Accidental Hero*, which satirized American media and the gullibility of Americans while claiming to portray universal values, met with greater success in France than in the United States.[40] For the poster advertising *Malcolm X*, the French distributor suggested adding to the image of Malcolm a burning U.S. flag within the X, therefore suggesting rebellion against the American establishment. However, the campaign was also careful to educate the French public about the role of the black leader in the United States in the late 1950s and early 1960s, because Malcolm X was not known to the average French moviegoer.[41]

The educational dimension of films is in fact a venue that film publicists may choose to explore for the promotion of movies considered to have some substance. Because cinema has been taken traditionally as a serious art form among the French elite, another nontraditional marketing technique for films worthy of a serious audience consists of appealing to high school teachers. Distributors may place posters on high school walls and, above all, provide educators with pedagogical material for classroom use.[42] Films such as *Schindler's List* and *Philadelphia* were selected as worthy springboards for profound reflection by their distributors, who provided free pamphlets describing the films' plots and the significance of the themes. The publications even included citations and questions that could serve as topics for written assignments. For example, the following subheadings, listed under the heading "Suggested Reflections," appeared in the pamphlet on *Philadelphia*: "Illness and the Cinema," "The Struggle Over Dignity," "Illness and Exclusion," and "Ignorance and Fear." Under such headings, topics such as the following were suggested: " 'Ignorance is the ferment of fear,' Jonathan Demme asserted. How do you analyze this assertion?" or "It's difficult to deal sensitively with AIDS and illness in movies. What do you think of the manner in which cinema, in general, has represented these topics?"

Such innovative marketing techniques, therefore, are based on the local marketers' knowledge of consumption patterns among various French audiences (in spite of the absence of tracking surveys or sneak previews in France). But to target different audiences, French marketing teams are faced with an even more crucial decision: determining the appropriate translation method and more specifically, the optimal proportion of dubbed versus subtitled copies. Dubbed versions usually are intended for the mainstream public, while subtitled versions tend to be associated with art films and geared to spectators at a higher socioeducational level.[43] *Dead Poets Society*, (1989) did well in its subtitled version, according to Warner Brothers' sales manager in Paris.[44] As *Dead Poets Society*, reaching 2.5 million spectators in five weeks, became a real social phenomenon, it gave rise to a heated debate in all the high schools in the French National Education system. Many prints, mostly dubbed, were then added to the original distribution plan (from a total of 93 prints to 200 prints by the third week).[45] According to Steve Rubin, general manager of Warner Brothers, France, the success of the dubbed version outside of Paris meant that the movie was "broadening the depths of its audience base" and also reaching more occasional viewers.[46]

Similarly, because of Spike Lee's reputation as an auteur, an upscale French audience was the original target for the launching of *Malcolm X*. For the opening week, 10 out of 15 theaters in Paris were showing the film in its subtitled version. However, unlike former movies by Lee, the French-dubbed version did better than the subtitled one because the film unexpectedly attracted a large immigrant public who came to Paris from the working-class suburbs to see it—in spite of the fact that few were familiar with Malcolm X before hearing about the film. To capitalize on the popular audience, which usually refuses to see a film subtitled, the marketing campaign had to be quickly adjusted and more dubbed prints than subtitled ones made available.[47]

A DELICATE BALANCE BETWEEN THE LOCAL AND THE GLOBAL

Thorough knowledge of products and consumers is clearly a prerequisite for success in foreign markets, and most U.S. marketing executives usually work closely with their foreign subsidiaries' counterparts or with local distributors for independent releases.[48] A delicate balance must be achieved between centralized decisions originating from the U.S. head-quarters and decisions taken at the local level. The American company usually provides the worldwide marketing plan and material for a film's marketing campaign; it also draws upon the results of the American campaign. The foreign team may suggest ways to improve the campaign for the local market, and the modifications must in turn be approved by the parent company.

However, management styles and degrees of cooperation greatly differ from one major film company to another, as there appears to be no industrywide standard for the degree of initiative granted to local subsidiaries. For example, the 1992 annual report of Sony Corporation, the parent company of Columbia TriStar Pictures, pointed out the corporation's intent to "actively promote localization in various of its overseas operations," in particular marketing, and work in closer cooperation with the local communities.[49] In fact, unlike other major U.S. film companies, Columbia does not have a single British coordination center for its largest European markets (France, Germany, and Italy). Furthermore, if a foreign team fights for its autonomy and makes suggestions that prove to be particularly successful—as the French one did in the past—Columbia tends to reward it by giving it greater power of decision. As a result of such flexibility, half the posters used recently in France by Columbia had been designed by its French team.[50] Such a degree of autonomy at Columbia may reflect a Japanese management style or simply a general manager's personal philosophy, since the head of international marketing in Los Angeles, who is British, may be more sensitive to differences among European audiences than most of his American counterparts. On the other hand, Fox International, in a cost-cutting effort, recently let go 150 employees in its international operation and has opted for more centralized control.[51]

For most major film companies, however, there appears to be a trend toward greater centralization and standardization, especially when merchandising is involved. Since the release of *Jurassic Park* in the early 1990s, in particular, emphasis on merchandising has reached new heights for UIP, and the internationalization of products (toys, games, and so on)—released under their American names all over the world—is imposing new constraints upon foreign marketing managers. As a direct result of the added emphasis placed on merchandising, some foreign teams have lost much of the initiative they enjoyed and are forced to adhere to marketing decisions made in London for the whole European market.

One direct consequence of the decreased autonomy of some national marketing teams is greater standardization in the use of posters. The change is particularly noticeable at UIP because until the early 1990s its French team had the option to design its own poster, in addition to a choice between the American poster or one designed in London for the European market. Today, UIP in France is no longer allowed to propose its own poster, unless the film is a failure in the United States (as in the case of *Drop Zone*, mentioned above). Overall at UIP, American posters have been kept in 70 percent of the cases—when the film was reasonably successful; in the remaining 30 percent of the cases, the London European headquarters decided for all the countries under its jurisdiction whether to use the American poster or to adapt it.[52]

Another concrete consequence of reduced autonomy at the national level is the increasing number of film titles that remain untranslated, especially when tie-ins and merchandising are at stake. Marketers working in France for UIP, under orders from the London office, even convinced the French publisher Laffont to change the title of the book *Parc jurassique* to its English title (although the book already had been printed). Overall, UIP released about one-third of its films in 1993 and 1994 under their English titles for the French market, occasionally against the recommendation of the French team.[53] For example, UIP's headquarters insisted that the English title *The Flintstones* be kept (also for global merchandising reasons), in spite of warnings by the French marketing team that the title was a liability with the French public. French marketers claimed that French people would refuse to see a movie whose title they could not easily pronounce; they also stressed that the English name failed to capitalize on characters which had been popular on French television under their French names. The movie was indeed a failure in France and was finally re-released under its French title, *La famille Pierrafeu*.

The trend toward a more frequent use of English titles goes beyond merchandising considerations, however. Companies also hope to capitalize on the attraction the English language has for younger, educated viewers. Warner Brothers, for example, is now releasing up to 50 percent of its movies with their English titles in France primarily for this reason, according to its general manager.[54] And even at Columbia, where managers seem more attuned to cultural differences, more films are released in France with their English titles, especially when the title is easily pronounceable or has a certain recognizable "music" to it: *Only You* and *I Like It Like That*, for example, kept their English titles.[55] But in the process of anglicizing titles, marketers may run the risk of appealing only to the urban elite and lose access to the broader, more diverse French public who have probably contributed to the huge successes of *Danse avec les loups* and *Le cercle des poètes disparus* (the French titles of *Dances with Wolves* and *Dead Poets Society*).

CONCLUSION

Promoters are taking unprecedented care with the costly promotion of American blockbusters in the hope of transforming them into commodities with global appeal. Marketing research and thorough knowledge of national cultural identities can help draw attention to the commodities, better target differentiated foreign audiences, and adapt marketing campaigns to the changing cultural aspirations of the international public. Such strategies also require coordination of efforts both at the American and local levels, as was shown in the case of France. Occasionally, however, conflicts may arise between a more homogenized marketing approach drawing directly on global campaigns and the need to adapt to the specificity of a foreign public's responses. Film industry specialists are still divided about the best way to resolve such conflicting approaches, in part because in recent years marketing practices have evolved so quickly that the results are still inconclusive. Some studios feel that they are nearing the single, dream market in which the glamour of Hollywood films can supplant cultural identities, as foreign publics appear increasingly sensitive to the prestige of American movies, stars, and even language. Others still stress that even "scientific" marketing research cannot always succeed in erasing cultural differences or predicting the best way to circumvent them because the business of selling moving images remains largely linked to the public's unpredictable reactions. For example, by reacting favorably to *Jurassic Park*, in spite of its English title, and rejecting *The Flintstones*, the French public gave marketers mixed signals about the importance of taking French culture into account. The jury is still out, therefore, on the extent to which Hollywood needs to cater to cultural preferences and national identities in the age of increasing globalization.

Notes

1   Charles-Albert Michalet, *Le drole de drama du cinéma mondial* (Paris: La Découverte, 1987) 42, 44.

2   Nicholas Garnham, *Capitalism and Communication: Global Culture and The Economics of Information* (London: Sage, 1990) 205–09.

3   Richard W. Stevenson, "Hollywood Takes to the Global Stage," *New York Times* 16 Apr. 1989, sec. 3: 1.

4   "Global Prices for US Theatrical Films," *Variety* 6 May 1991: C122.

5   Richard Gold, "Major Studios Speed up Their Foreign Openings to Synch with US Push," *Variety* 22 Aug. 1990: 96.

6   "This Summer's Hot Overseas Releases," *Variety* 22 Aug. 1990: 1, 96.

7   For example, Columbia released 481 prints in France for *Terminator 2* according to Patrick Laurence (sales manager, Columbia TriStar Films France), personal interview, 6 Feb. 1992; CNC info 233 (1991): 20–21; Ralph Alexander (vice president of sales and distribution, Columbia TriStar Film Distributors International), personal interview, 14 Apr. 1993.

8   Thomas R. King, "Open Wide," *Wall Street Journal* 26 Mar. 1993: R13.

9   Paul Rassain, AMLF chief executive of marketing, telephone interview, 27 Dec. 1994.

10 Mark Crispin Miller, "Introduction: The Big Picture," *Seeing Through Movies*, ed. Mark Crispin Miller (New York: Pantheon, 1990) 8.

11 Gold 96.

12 René: Bonnell, *La vingt-cinquième image: une économie de l'audiovisuel* (Paris: Gallimard/FEMIS, 1989) 94–95.

13 Don Groves, "Europe Preps in Varying Ways for Summer U.S. Hits' Arrivals," *Variety* 19 Oct. 1988: 16; Andrew Milner (senior vice president of international theatrical sales, The Samuel Goldwyn Company), personal interview, 7 Apr. 1993; Richard Gold, "Major Studios" 96.

14 Mimi Burri (vice president, international marketing, Columbia TriStar Film Distributors International), personal interview, 8 Apr. 1993.

15 Joel Coler (Joel Coler and Friends, International Marketing Consultants), personal interview, 8 Apr. 1993.

16 Burri.

17 Steve Rubin, general manager of Warner Brothers France, telephone conversation, 4 Jan. 1995.

18 Burri.

19 "UIP Top Paris Distrib. in '89; AMLF Leads Indies with No. 1 French Pic.," *Variety* 22 Oct. 1989: 381; Burri.

20 Burri; Coler.

21 Caroline Decriem, director of public relations for Lumière (publicity agency for UIP), personal interview, 27 Dec. 1994.

22 Maureen Burke, "Hollywood's New Hype," *Stills* Nov. 1986: 82, 84.

23 Bruno Chatelain, director of publicity, Columbia TriStar France, personal interview, 4 Jan. 1995.

24 Decriem.

25 Chatelain.

26 Chatelain.

27   Vincent Bleuse (management associate, Columbia Pictures Marketing Department), personal interview, 8 Apr. 1993.

28   Coler; David Gross, vice president of marketing and distribution at Twentieth Century Fox International Corporation, personal interview, 14 Apr. 1993.

29   Richard Gold, "Modern Movie Mix: Money, Method, and Moxie," *Variety* 13 June 1990: 47; Randall Rothenberg, "Advertising: Movie Promoters Adopting Modern Marketing Skills," *New York Times* 23 Feb. 1990: D16; Lawrence Cohn, "Test Marketing: A Tried-and-True Formula for Finding an Audience," *Variety* 4 Apr. 1990: 8; Faye Brookman, "With Big Bux at Stake, They Do Their Homework," *Variety* 13 June 1990: 45.

30   Brookman 45.

31   "Movies by the numbers," *Variety* 13 June 1990: 45.

32   Greg Evans, "Orion Creates Epic Pitch for 'Dances with Wolves,' " *Variety* 5 Nov. 1990: 97.

33   Mark Whitaker et al., "Malcolm X," *Newsweek* 16 Nov. 1992: 68.

34   Richard Gold, "Marketers Do Heated Battle for B.O." *Variety* 17 Aug. 1988: 18.

35   Rothenberg, "Advertising" D16. In this comparison with politics, Rothenberg was citing Mike Kaiser, the creative director of Seiniger Advertising—one of the leading agencies for Hollywood advertising.

36   Burke 82; Thomas R. King, "Local Lures," *Wall Street Journal* 26 Mar. 1993: R13.

37   CNC Info 246 29; CNC Info 251 27. To better measure the remarkable success of the films mentioned, only 52 films out of all the French and foreign films released in France between 1956 and 1992 achieved an admission level of over 6 million spectators.

38   Gold, "Modern" 47. During my research in the Los Angeles area, a number of film marketing executives refused to discuss their companies' strategies: Several executives at Warner Brothers declined to be interviewed for various reasons: the senior vice president of International Marketing, Buena Vista Pictures, declared that it was a company-wide policy never to discuss its marketing decisions (Kevin Hyson, telephone interview, 29 Mar. 1993). National Research Group, a specialized film marketing research company (Ed Lambek, telephone interview, 8 April 1993) also stated that marketing information was strictly confidential because it was paid for by the client.

39   Rassain.

40   Burri.

41   Coler.

42   Decriem.

43   For a more detailed analysis of the French public's attitude toward dubbing and subtitling, see Martine Danan, *From Nationalism to Globalization: France's Challenges to Hollywood's Hegemony* (thèse de doctorat, Michigan Technological University, 1994) chap. 4.

44   Chenard.

45   Bruce Alderman, " 'Poets' Knocks Them Dead at French Boxoffice," *Variety* 7 Feb. 1990: 19. *Dead Poets Society* was entitled to a unique three-page spread in *L'Express* (2 Mar. 1990) to discuss the social significance of the film. Even teachers and administrators from prestigous Parisian high schools participated in the debate by stating their pedagogical philosophy in interviews or articles sent to mainstream magazines like *L'Express* or *Le Nouvel Observateur*: See, for example, Marie-Laure de Léotard's interview of Paul Deheuvels (principal), "Un discours de plaisir et de jouissance," *L'Express* 2 Mar. 1990: 33; Suzanne Juillard-Agié: (teacher), "La passion d'enseigner," *Le Nouvel Observateur* 25 Jan. 1990: 105.

46   Tony Crawley, "Native fill in Francais for U.S. Players" *Variety* 2 May 1990: 110; Alderman 19.

47   Christian Simenc, "Qui va voir '*Malcolm X?*' " *Le Monde* 12 Mar. 1993.

48   Milner; Bleuse.

49   Sony Corporation, Annual Report to Stockholders, 31 Mar. 1992: 6.

50   Chatelain.

51   Judy Brennan and Don Groves, " 'Shadow' Deal Leaves Distribs. in the Dark," *Variety* 24 May 1993: 65.

52   Decriem.

53   Decriem.

54   Rubin.

55   Chatelain.

Chapter 28

Suman Basuroy, Subimal Chatterjee and S. Abraham Ravid

"HOW CRITICAL ARE CRITICAL REVIEWS?" THE BOX OFFICE EFFECTS OF FILM CRITICS, STAR POWER, AND BUDGETS (2003)

CRITICS PLAY A SIGNIFICANT ROLE in consumers' decisions in many industries (Austin 1983; Cameron 1995; Caves 2000; Einhorn and Koelb 1982; Eliashberg and Shugan 1997; Goh and Ederington 1993; Greco 1997; Holbrook 1999; Vogel 2001; Walker 1995). For example, investors closely follow the opinion of financial analysts before deciding which stocks to buy or sell, as the markets evidenced when an adverse Lehman Brothers report sunk Amazon.com's stock price by 19% in one day (*Business-Week* 2000). Readers often defer to literary reviews before deciding on a book to buy (Caves 2000; Greco 1997); for example, rave reviews of *Interpreter of Maladies*, a short-story collection by the then relatively unknown Jhumpa Lahiri, made the book a *New York Times* bestseller (*New York Times* 1999). Diners routinely refer to reviews in newspapers and dining guides such as *ZagatSurvey* to help select restaurants (Shaw 2000).

However, the role of critics may be most prominent in the film industry (Eliashberg and Shugan 1997; Holbrook 1999; West and Broniarczyk 1998). More than one-third of Americans actively seek the advice of film critics (*The Wall Street Journal* 2001), and approximately one of every three filmgoers say they choose films because of favorable reviews. Realizing the importance of reviews to films' box office success, studios often strategically manage the review process by excerpting positive reviews in their advertising and delaying or forgoing advance screenings if they anticipate bad reviews (*The Wall Street Journal* 2001). The desire for good reviews can go even further, thus prompting studios to engage in deceptive practices, as when Sony Pictures Entertainment invented the critic David Manning to pump several films, such as *A Knight's Tale* and *The Animal*, in print advertisements (*Boston Globe* 2001).

In this article, we investigate three issues related to the effects of film critics on box office success. The first issue is critics' role in affecting box office performance. Critics have two potential roles: influencers, if they actively influence the decisions of consumers in the early weeks of a run, and predictors, if they merely predict consumers' decisions. Eliashberg and Shugan (1997), who were the first to define and test these concepts, find that critics correctly predict box office performance but do not influence it. Our results are mixed. On the one hand, we find that both positive and negative reviews are correlated with weekly box office revenue over an eight-week period, thus showing that critics can both influence and predict outcomes. On the other hand, we find that the impact of negative reviews (but not positive reviews) on box office revenue declines over time, a finding that is more consistent with critics' role as influencers.

The second issue we address is whether positive and negative reviews have comparable effects on box office performance. Our interest in such valence effects stems from two reasons; the first is based on studio strategy and the second is rooted in theory. First, although we might expect the impact of critical reviews to be strongest in the early weeks of a run and to fall over time as studio buzz from new releases takes over, studios that understand the importance of positive reviews are likely to adopt tactics to leverage good reviews and counter bad reviews (e.g., selectively quote good reviews in advertisements). Intuitively, therefore, we expect the effects of positive reviews to increase over time and the effects of negative reviews to decrease over time. Second, we expect negative reviews to hurt box office performance more than positive reviews help box office performance. This expectation is based on research on negativity bias in impression formation (Skowronski and Carlston 1989) and on loss aversion in scanner-panel data (Hardie, Johnson, and Fader 1993). We find that the negative impact of bad reviews is significantly greater than the positive impact of good reviews on box office revenue, but only in the first week of a film's run (when studios, presumably, have not had time to leverage good reviews and/or counter bad reviews).

The third part of our investigation involves examining how star power and budgets might moderate the impact of critical reviews on box office performance. We chose these two moderators because we believe that examining their effects on box office revenue in conjunction with critical reviews might provide a partial economic rationale for two puzzling decisions in the film industry that have been pointed out in previous works. The first puzzle is why studios are persistent in pursuing famous stars when stars' effects on box office revenue are difficult to demonstrate (De Vany and Walls 1999; Litman and Ahn 1998; Ravid 1999). The second puzzle is why, at a time when big budgets seem to contribute little to returns (John, Ravid, and Sunder 2002; Ravid 1999), the average budget for a Hollywood movie has steadily increased over the years. Our results show that though star power and big budgets seem to do little for films that receive predominantly positive reviews, they are positively correlated with box office performance for films that receive predominantly negative reviews. In other words, star power and big budgets appear to blunt the impact of negative reviews and thus may be sensible investments for the film studios. In the next section, we explore the current literature and formulate our key hypotheses. We then describe the data and empirical results. Finally, we discuss the managerial implications for marketing theory and practice.

THEORY AND HYPOTHESES

Critics: their functions and impact

In recent years, scholars have expressed much interest in understanding critics' role in markets for creative goods, such as films, theater productions, books, and music (Cameron 1995; Caves 2000). Critics can serve many functions. According to Cameron (1995), critics provide advertising and information (e.g., reviews of new films, books, and music provide valuable information), create reputations (e.g., critics often spot rising stars), construct a consumption experience (e.g., reviews are fun to read by themselves), and influence preference (e.g., reviews may validate consumers' self-image or promote consumption based on snob appeal). In the domain of films, Austin (1983) suggests that critics help the public make a film choice, understand the film content, reinforce previously held opinions of the film, and communicate in social settings (e.g., when consumers have read a review, they can intelligently discuss a film with friends). However, despite a general agreement that critics play a role, it is not clear whether the views of critics necessarily go hand in hand with audience behavior. For example, Austin (1983) argues that film attendance is greater if the public agrees with the critics' evaluations of films than if the two opinions differ. Holbrook (1999) shows that in the case of films, ordinary consumers and professional critics emphasize different criteria when forming their tastes.

Many empirical studies have examined the relationship between critical reviews and box office performance (De Silva 1998; Jedidi, Krider, and Weinberg 1998; Litman 1983; Litman and Ahn 1998; Litman and Kohl 1989; Prag and Casavant 1994; Ravid 1999; Sochay 1994; Wallace, Seigerman, and Holbrook 1993). Litman (1983) finds that each additional star rating (five stars represent a "masterpiece" and one star represents a "poor" film) has a significant, positive impact on the film's theater rentals. Litman and Kohl's (1989) subsequent study and other studies by Litman and Ahn (1998), Wallace, Seigerman, and Holbrook (1993), Sochay (1994), and Prag and Casavant (1994) all find the same impact. However, Ravid (1999) tested the impact of positive reviews on domestic revenue, video revenue, international revenue, and total revenue but did not find any significant effect.

Critics as influencers or predictors

Although the previously mentioned studies investigate the impact of critical reviews on a film's performance, they do not describe the process through which critics might affect box office revenue. Eliashberg and Shugan (1997) are the first to propose and test two different roles of critics: influencer and predictor. An influencer, or opinion leader, is a person who is regarded by a group or by other people as having expertise or knowledge on a particular subject (Assael 1984; Weiman 1991). Operationally, if an influencer voices an opinion, people should follow that opinion. Therefore, we expect an influencer to have the most effect in the early stages of a film's run, before word of mouth has a chance to spread. In contrast, a predictor can use either formal techniques (e.g., statistical inference) or informal methods to predict the success or failure of a product correctly. In the case of a film, a predictor is expected to call the entire run (i.e., predict whether the film will do well) or, in the extreme case, correctly predict every week of the film's run.

Ex ante, there are reasons to believe that critics may influence the public's decision of whether to see a film. Critics often are invited to an early screening of the film and then write reviews before the film opens to the public. Therefore, not only do they have more information than the public does in the early stages of a film's run, but they also are the only source of information at that time. For example, Litman (1983) seems to refer to the influencer role in his argument that critical reviews should be important to the popularity of films (1) in the early weeks before word of mouth can take over and (2) if the reviews are favorable. However, Litman was unable to test this hypothesis directly because his dependent variable is cumulative box office revenue. To better assess causation, Wyatt and Badger (1984) designed experiments using positive, mixed, and negative reviews and found audience interest to be compatible with the direction of the review. However, because their study is based on experiments, they do not use box office returns as the dependent variable.

390 S. BASUROY, S. CHATTERJEE AND S. ABRAHAM RAVID

Inferring critics' roles from weekly correlation data

In our research, we follow Eliashberg and Shugan's (1997) procedure. We study the correlation of both positive and negative reviews with weekly box office revenue. However, even with weekly box office data, we argue that it is not easy to distinguish between critics as influencers and as predictors. We illustrate this point by considering three different examples of correlation between weekly box office revenue and critical reviews.

For the first example, suppose that critical reviews are correlated with the box office revenue of the first few weeks but not with the film's entire run. A case in point is the film *Almost Famous*, which received excellent reviews (of 47 total reviews reported by *Variety*, 35 were positive and only 2 were negative) and had a good opening week ($2.4 million on 131 screens, or $18,320 revenue per screen) but ultimately did not do considerably well (grossing only $32 million in about six months). This outcome is consistent with the interpretation that critics influenced the early run but did not correctly predict the entire run. Another interpretation is that critics correctly predicted the early run without necessarily influencing the public's decision but did not predict the film's entire run.

For the second example, suppose that critical reviews are correlated not with a film's box office revenue in the first few weeks but with the box office revenue of the total run. The films *Thelma and Louise* and *Blown Away* appear to fit this pattern. *Thelma and Louise* received excellent reviews and had only moderate first-weekend revenue ($4 million), but it eventually became a hit ($43 million; Eliashberg and Shugan 1997, p. 72). In contrast, *Blown Away* opened successfully ($10.3 million) despite bad reviews but ultimately did not do well. In the first case, critics correctly forecasted the film's successful run (despite a bad opening); in the second case, critics correctly forecasted the film's unsuccessful run (despite a good opening). In both examples, the performance in the early weeks countered critical reviews. Our interpretation is that critics did not influence the early run but were able to predict the ultimate box office run correctly. Eliashberg and Shugan (1997) find precisely such a pattern (i.e., critical reviews are not correlated with the box office revenue of early weeks but are significantly correlated with the box office revenue of later weeks and with cumulative returns during the run); they conclude that critics are predictors, not influencers.

For the third example, suppose that critical reviews are correlated with weekly box office revenue for the first several weeks (i.e., not just the first week or two) and with the entire run. Consider the films *3000 Miles to Graceland* (a box office failure) and *The Lord of the Rings: The Fellowship of the Ring* (a box office success). Critics trashed *3000 Miles to Graceland* (of 34 reviews, 30 were negative), it had a dismal opening weekend ($7.16 million on 2545 screens, or $3,000 per screen), and it bombed at the box office ($15.74 million earned in slightly more than eight weeks). *The Lord of the Rings: The Fellowship of the Ring* opened to great reviews (of 20 reviews, 16 were positive and 0 were negative), had a successful opening week ($66.1 million on 3359 screens, or approximately $19,000 per screen), and grossed $313 million. In both cases, critics either influenced the film's opening and correctly predicted its eventual fate or correctly predicted the weekly performance over a longer period and its ultimate fate.

These three examples demonstrate that it is not easy to distinguish critics' different roles (i.e., influencer, predictor, or influencer and predictor) on the basis of weekly box office revenue. Broadly speaking, if critics influence only a film's box office run, we expect them to have the greatest impact on early box office revenue (perhaps in the first week or two). In contrast, if critics predict only a film's ultimate fate, we expect their views to be correlated with the later weeks and the entire run, not necessarily with the early weeks. Finally, if critics influence and predict a film's fate or correctly predict every week of a film's run, we expect reviews to be correlated with the success or failure of the film in the early and later weeks and with the entire run. The following hypotheses summarize the possible links among critics' roles and box office revenue:

> H1: If critics are influencers, critical reviews are correlated with box office revenue in the first few weeks only, not with box office revenue in the later weeks or with the entire run.
>
> H2: If critics are predictors, critical reviews are correlated with box office revenue in the later weeks and the entire run, not necessarily with box office revenue in previous weeks.
>
> H3: If critics are both influencers and predictors or play an expanded predictor role, critical reviews are correlated with box office revenue in the early and later weeks and with the entire run.

Inferring critics' roles from the time pattern of weekly correlation

Several scholars have argued that if critics are influencers, they should exert the greatest impact in the first week or two of a film's run because little or no word-of-mouth information is yet available. Thereafter, the impact of reviews should diminish with each passing week as information from other sources becomes available (e.g., people who have already seen the film convey their opinions, more people see the film) and as word of mouth begins to dominate (Eliashberg and Shugan 1997; Litman 1983). However, the issue is not clear-cut: If word of mouth agrees with critics often enough, a decline may be undetectable, but if critics are perfect predictors, such a decline cannot be expected. In other words, if there is a decline in the impact of critical reviews over time, it is consistent with the influencer perspective. Thus:

> H4: If critics are influencers, the correlation of critical reviews with box office revenue declines with time.

Valence of reviews: negativity bias

Researchers consistently have found differential impacts of positive and negative information (controlled for magnitude) on consumer behavior. For example, in the domain of risky choice, Kahneman and Tversky (1979) find that utility or value functions are asymmetric with respect to gains and losses. A loss of $1 provides more dissatisfaction (negative utility) than the gain of $1 provides satisfaction (positive utility), a phenomenon that the authors call "loss aversion." The authors also extend this finding to multiattribute settings (Tversky and Kahneman 1991). A similar finding in the domain of impression formation is the negativity bias, or the tendency of negative information to have a greater impact than positive information (for a review, see Skowronski and Carlston 1989).

On the basis of these ideas, we surmise that negative reviews hurt (i.e., negatively affect) box office performance more than positive reviews help (i.e., positively affect) box office performance. Two studies lend further support to this idea. First, Yamaguchi (1978) proposes that consumers tend to accept negative opinions (e.g., a critic's negative review) more easily than they accept positive opinions (e.g., a critic's positive review). Second, recent research suggests that the negativity bias operates in affective processing as early as the initial categorization of information into valence classes (e.g., the film is "good" or "bad"; Ito et al. 1998). Thus, we propose the following:

H5: Negative reviews hurt box office revenue more than positive reviews help box office revenue.

Moderators of critical reviews: stars and budgets

Are there any factors that moderate the impact of critical reviews on box office performance? We argue that two key candidates are star power and budget. We believe that examining the effects of these two moderators on box office revenue in conjunction with critical reviews may provide a partial economic rationale for the two previously mentioned puzzling film industry decisions about pursuing stars and making big-budget films. In the following paragraphs, we elaborate on this issue by examining the literature on star power and film budgets.

Star power has received considerable attention in the literature (De Silva 1998; De Vany and Walls 1999; Holbrook 1999; Levin, Levin, and Heath 1997; Litman 1983; Litman and Ahn 1998; Litman and Kohl 1989; Neelamegham and Chintagunta 1999; Prag and Casavant 1994; Ravid 1999; Smith and Smith 1986; Sochay 1994; Wallace, Seigerman, and Holbrook 1993). Hollywood seems to favor films with stars (e.g., award-winning actors and directors), and it is almost axiomatic that stars are key to a film's success. However, empirical results of star power on box office performance have produced conflicting evidence. Litman and Kohl (1989) and Sochay (1994) find that stars' presence in a film's cast has a significant effect on that film's revenue. Similarly, Wallace, Seigerman, and Holbrook (1993, p. 23) conclude that "certain movie stars do make [a] demonstrable difference to the market success of the films in which they appear." In contrast, Litman (1983) finds no significant relationship between a star's presence in a film and box office rentals. Smith and Smith (1986) find that winning an award had a negative effect on a film's fate in the 1960s but a positive effect in the 1970s. Similarly, Prag and Casavant (1994) find that star power positively affects a film's financial success in some samples but not in others. De Silva (1998) finds that stars are an important factor in the public's attendance decisions but are not significant predictors of financial success, a finding that is documented in subsequent studies as well (De Vany and Walls 1999; Litman and Ahn 1998; Ravid 1999).

Film production budgets also have received significant attention in the literature on motion picture economics (Litman 1983; Litman and Ahn 1998; Litman and Kohl 1989; Prag and Casavant 1994; Ravid 1999).[1] In 2000, the average cost of making a feature film was $54.8 million (see Motion Picture Association of America [MPAA] 2002). Big budgets translate into lavish sets and costumes, expensive digital manipulations, and special effects such as those seen in the films *Jurassic Park* ($63 million budget, released in 1993) and *Titanic* ($200 million budget, released in 1997). Ravid (1999) and John, Ravid, and Sunder (2002) show that though big budgets are correlated with higher revenue, they are not correlated with returns. If anything, low-budget films appear to have higher returns. What, then, do big budgets do for a film? Litman (1983) argues that big budgets reflect higher quality and greater box office popularity. Similarly, Litman and Ahn (1998, p. 182) suggest that "studios feel safer with big budget films." In this sense, big budgets can serve as an insurance policy (Ravid and Basuroy 2003).

Although the effects of star power and budgets on box office returns may be ambiguous at best, the question remains as to whether these two variables act jointly with critical reviews, as we believe they do, to affect box office performance. For example, suppose that a film receives more positive than negative reviews. If the film starts its run in a positive light, other positive dimensions, such as stars and big budgets, may not enhance its box office success. However, consider a film that receives more negative than positive reviews. In this case, stars and big budgets may help the film by blunting some effects of negative reviews. Levin, Levin, and Heath (1997) suggest that popular stars provide the public with a decision heuristic (e.g., attend the film with the stars) that may be strong enough to blunt any negative critic effect. Conversely, as Levin, Levin, and Heath explain (p. 177), when a film receives more positive than negative reviews, it is "less in need of the additional boost provided by a trusted star." Similarly, Litman and Ahn (1998) suggest that budgets should increase a film's entertainment value and thus its probability of box office success, which consequently compensates for other negative traits, such as bad reviews. On the basis of these arguments, we propose the following:

> H6: For films that receive more negative than positive reviews, star power and big budgets positively affect box office performance; however, for films that receive more positive than negative reviews, star power and big budgets do not affect box office performance.

METHODOLOGY

Data and variables

Our data include a random sample of 200 films released between late 1991 and early 1993; most of our data are identified in Ravid's (1999) study. We first pared down the sample because of various missing data for 175 films. We gathered our data from two sources: Baseline in California (http://www.baseline.hollywood.com) and *Variety* magazine. Although some studies have focused on more successful films, such as the top 50 or the top 100 in *Variety* lists (De Vany and Walls 1997; Litman and Ahn 1998; Smith and Smith 1986), our study contains a random sample of the films (both successes and failures). Our sample contains 156 MPAA-affiliated films and 19 foreign productions, and it covers approximately one-third of all MPAA-affiliated films released between 1991 and 1993 (475 MPAA-affiliated films were released between 1991 and 1993; see Vogel 2001, Table 3.2). In our sample, 3.2% of the films are rated G; 14.7%, PG; 26.3%, PG-13; and 55.7%, R. This distribution closely matches the distribution of all films released between 1991 and 1993 (1.5%, G; 15.8%, PG; 22.1%, PG13; and 60.7%, R; see Creative Multimedia 1997).

Weekly domestic revenue

Every week, *Variety* reports the weekly domestic revenue for each film. These figures served as our dependent variables. Most studies cited thus far do not use weekly data (see, e.g., De Vany and Walls 1999; Litman and Ahn 1998; Ravid 1999). Given our focus and our procedure, the use of weekly data is critical.

Valence of reviews

Variety lists reviews for the first weekend in which a film opens in major cities (i.e., New York; Los Angeles; Washington, D.C.; and Chicago). To be consistent with Eliashberg and Shugan's (1997) study, we collected the number of reviews from all these cities. *Variety* classifies reviews as "pro" (positive), "con" (negative), and "mixed." For the review classification, each reviewer is called and asked how he or she rated a particular film: positive, negative, or mixed. We used these classifications to establish measures of critical review assessment similar to those Eliashberg and Shugan use. Unlike Ravid's (1999) study and consistent with that of Eliashberg and Shugan, our study includes the total number of reviews (TOTNUM) from all four cities. For each film, POSNUM (NEGNUM) is the number of positive (negative) reviews a film received, and POSRATIO (NEGRATIO) is the number of positive (negative) reviews divided by the number of total reviews.

Star power

For star power, we used the proxies that Ravid (1999) and Litman and Ahn (1998) suggest. For each film, Baseline provided a list of the director and up to eight cast members. For our first definition of *star*, we identified all cast members who had won a Best Actor or Best Actress Academy Award (Oscar) in prior years (i.e., before the release of the film being studied). We created the dummy variable WONAWARD, which denotes films in which at least one actor or the director won an Academy Award in previous years. Based on this measure, 26 of the 175 films in our sample have star power (i.e., WONAWARD = 1). For our second measure, we created the dummy variable TOP10, which has a value of 1 if any member of the cast or the director participated in a top-ten grossing film in previous years (Litman and Ahn 1998). Based on this measure, 17 of the 175 films in our sample possess star power (i.e., TOP10 = 1). For our third and fourth measures, we collected award nominations for Best Actor, Best Actress, and Best Directing for each film in the sample and defined two variables, NOMAWARD and RECOGNITION. The first variable, NOMAWARD, receives a value of 1 if one of the actors or the director was previously nominated for an award. The NOMAWARD measure increases the number of films with star power to 76 of 175. The second variable, RECOGNITION, measures recognition value. For each of the 76 films in the NOMAWARD category, we summed the total number of awards and the total number of nominations, which effectively creates a weight of 1 for each nomination and doubles the weight of an actual award to 2 (e.g., if an actor was nominated twice for an award, RECOGNITION is 2; if the actor also won an award in one of these cases, the value increases to 3). We thus assigned each of the 76 films a numerical value, which ranged from a maximum of 15 (for *Cape Fear*, directed by Martin Scorsese and starring Robert De Niro, Nick Nolte, Jessica Lange, and Juliette Lewis) to 0 for films with no nominations (e.g., *Curly Sue*).

Budgets

Baseline provided the budget (BUDGET) of each film; the trade term for budget is "negative cost," or production costs (Litman and Ahn 1998; Prag and Casavant 1994; Ravid 1999). The budget does not include gross participation, which is ex post share of participants in gross revenue, advertising and distribution costs, or guaranteed compensation, which is a guaranteed amount paid out of revenue if revenue exceeds the amount.

Other control variables

We used several control variables. Each week, *Variety* reports the number of screens on which a film was shown that week. Eliashberg and Shugan (1997) and Elberse and Eliashberg (2002) find that the number of screens is a significant predictor of box office revenue. Thus, we used SCREEN as a control variable. Another worthwhile variable reflects whether a film is a sequel (Litman and Kohl 1989; Prag and Casavant 1994; Ravid 1999). The SEQUEL variable receives a value of 1 if the movie is a sequel and a value of 0 otherwise. There are 11 sequels in our sample. The industry considers MPAA ratings an important issue (Litman 1983; Litman and Ahn 1989; Ravid 1999; Sochay 1994). In our analysis, we coded ratings using dummy variables; for example, a dummy variable G has a value of 1 if the film is rated G and a value of 0 otherwise. Some films are not rated for various reasons; those films have a value of 0. Finally, our last control variable is release date (RELEASE). In some studies (Litman 1983; Litman and Ahn 1998; Litman and Kohl 1989; Sochay 1994), release dates are used as dummy variables, following the logic that a high-attendance-period release (e.g., Christmas) attracts greater audiences and a lower-attendance-period (e.g., early December) release is bad for revenue. However, because there are several peaks and troughs in attendance throughout the year, we used information from Vogel's (2001, Figure 2.4) study to produce a more sophisticated measure of seasonality. Vogel constructs a graph that depicts normalized weekly attendance over the year (based on 1969–84 data) and assigns a value between 0 and 1 for each date in the year (Christmas attendance is 1 and early December attendance is .37; these are high and low points of the year, respectively). We matched each release date with the graph and assigned the RELEASE variable to account for seasonal fluctuations.

RESULTS

Table 28.1 reports the correlation matrix for the key variables of interest. The ratio of positive reviews, POSRATIO, is negatively correlated with the ratio of negative reviews, NEGRATIO; that is, not many films received several negative and positive reviews at the same time. The most expensive film in the sample cost $70 million (*Batman Returns*) and is the film that has the highest first-week box office revenue ($69.31 million), opening to the maximum number of screens nationwide (3700). In our sample, the average number of first-week screens is 749, the average first-week box office return is $5.43 million, and the average number of reviews received is 34 (43% positive, 31% negative). Using a sample of 56 films, Eliashberg and Shugan (1997, p. 47) reported 47% positive reviews and 25% negative reviews. In our sample, *Beauty and the Beast* had the highest revenue per screen ($117,812 per screen, for two screens) and the highest total revenue ($426 million).

The role of critics

H_1–H_4 address critics' role as influencers, predictors, or both. To test the hypotheses, we ran three sets of tests. First, we replicated Eliashberg and Shugan's (1997) model by running separate regressions for each of the eight weeks; we included only three predictors (POSRATIO or NEGRATIO, SCREEN, and TOTNUM). In the second test, we expanded Eliashberg and Shugan's framework by including our control variables in the weekly regressions. In the third test, we ran time-series cross-section regression that combined both cross-sectional and longitudinal data in one regression, specifically to control for unobserved heterogeneity.

The replications of Eliashberg and Shugan's (1997) results are reported in Tables 28.2 and 28.3. The coefficients of both positive and negative reviews are significant at .01 for each of the eight weeks, and they seem to support H_3. Critics both influence and predict box office revenue, or they predict consistently across all weeks.

Table 28.1 Variables and correlations

	BUDGET	RELEASE	POSRATIO	NEGRATIO	TOTNUM	POSNUM	NEGNUM	WONAWARD
BUDGET Mean = 15.68 S.D. = 13.90	1.00							
RELEASE Mean = .63 S.D. = .16	.004	1.00						
POSRATIO Mean = .43 S.D. = .24	−.131	.017	1.00					
NEGRATIO Mean = .31 S.D. = .22	.042	−.068	−.886	1.00				
TOTNUM Mean = 34.22 S.D. = 17.46	.605	.150	.252	−.341	1.00			
POSNUM Mean = 15.81 S.D. = 12.03	.283	.056	.740	−.704	.760	1.00		
NEGNUM Mean = 9.23 S.D. = 7.06	.498	.124	−.579	.556	.448	−.179	1.00	
WONAWARD Mean = .15 S.D. = .36	.358	.077	.126	−.139	.430	.379	.169	1.00

Notes: S.D. = standard deviation.

Table 28.2 Replication of Eliashberg and Shugan's (1997) regression results with percentage of positive reviews

Week	R² (Adjusted R²)	POSRATIO Unstandardized Coefficient (Standardized Coefficient)	POSRATIO t-Statistic (p-Value)	TOTNUM Unstandardized Coefficient (Standardized Coefficient)	TOTNUM t-Statistic (p-Value)	SCREEN Unstandardized Coefficient (Standardized Coefficient)	SCREEN t-Statistic (p-Value)	F-Ratio (p-Value)
1 (n = 162)	.7268 (.7217)	5.114 (.14017)	2.96 (.0036)	.037 (.07176)	1.49 (.1394)	.00890 (.85073)	17.49 (<.0001)	141.03 (<.0001)
2 (n = 154)	.7229 (.7174)	4.02465 (.15252)	3.15 (.0020)	.0498 (.13428)	2.70 (.0076)	.00593 (.81576)	16.22 (<.0001)	131.32 (<.0001)
3 (n = 145)	.6542 (.6469)	3.2968 (.15427)	2.79 (.0060)	.03661 (.12538)	.2.17 (.0315)	.00451 (.77171)	13.23 (<.0001)	89.56 (<.0001)
4 (n = 139)	.7174 (.7111)	2.15975 (.14426)	2.91 (.0042)	.01495 (.07051)	1.32 (.1891)	.00361 (.82838)	1.32 (.1891)	115.07 (<.0001)
5 (n = 137)	.7325 (.7265)	1.709 (.14897)	3.14 (.0021)	.00566 (.03552)	.69 (.4927)	.00302 (.84327)	16.72 (<.0001)	122.33 (<.0001)
6 (n = 132)	.7079 (.7011)	1.58248 (.15050)	3.06 (.0027)	−.00147 (−.01003)	−.19 (.8502)	.00299 (.84839)	16.15 (<.0001)	104.22 (<.0001)
7 (n = 130)	.5763 (.5663)	2.28437 (.20870)	3.56 (.0005)	−.00396 (−.02546)	−.41 (.6858)	.00299 (.76491)	12.13 (<.0001)	57.59 (<.0001)
8 (n = 122)	.7013 (.6938)	1.20016 (.16071)	3.17 (.0019)	−.00551 (−.05212)	−.95 (.3432)	.00262 (.8577)	15.62 (<.0001)	93.14 (<.0001)

Notes: Dependent variable is weekly revenue. Method is separate regressions for each week.

Table 28.3 Replication of Eliashberg and Shugan's (1997) regression results with percentage of negative reviews

Week	R^2 (Adjusted R^2)	NEGRATIO Unstandardized Coefficient (Standardized Coefficient)	t-Statistic (p-Value)	TOTNUM Unstandardized Coefficient (Standardized Coefficient)	t-Statistic (p-Value)	SCREEN Unstandardized Coefficient (Standardized Coefficient)	t-Statistic (p-Value)	F-Ratio (p-Value)
1 (n = 162)	.7290 (.7239)	−6.05792 (−.1525)	−3.18 (.0018)	.0285 (.05479)	1.10 (.2738)	.00888 (.84904)	17.80 (<.0001)	142.58 (<.0001)
2 (n = 154)	.7273 (.7219)	−5.10837 (−.17391)	−3.53 (.0005)	.04204 (.11328)	2.22 (.0276)	.00598 (.82294)	16.51 (<.0001)	134.26 (<.0001)
3 (n = 145)	.6518 (.6444)	−3.39389 (−.14618)	−2.59 (.0105)	.03451 (.11819)	1.98 (.0496)	.00447 (.76423)	13.16 (<.0001)	88.59 (<.0001)
4 (n = 139)	.7118 (.7054)	−1.97242 (−.12094)	−2.38 (.0187)	.01486 (.07007)	1.26 (.2090)	.00355 (.81431)	15.37 (<.0001)	111.95 (<.0001)
5 (n = 137)	.7298 (.7237)	−1.78567 (−.14178)	−2.89 (.0044)	.00418 (.02621)	.49 (.6252)	.003 (.83882)	16.60 (<.0001)	120.63 (<.0001)
6 (n = 132)	.7065 (.6997)	−1.73476 (−.14911)	−2.95 (.0038)	−.00368 (−.02515)	−.46 (.6465)	.00299 (.84649)	16.10 (<.0001)	103.52 (<.0001)
7 (n = 130)	.5564 (.5500)	−2.10310 (−.1672)	−2.76 (.0066)	−.00606 (−.03903)	−.60 (.5503)	.00296 (.7576)	11.79 (<.0001)	53.97 (<.0001)
8 (n = 122)	.6945 (.6868)	−1.20867 (−.13982)	−2.68 (.0083)	−.00704 (−.06662)	−1.18 (.2408)	.00261 (.85507)	15.39 (<.0001)	90.20 (<.0001)

Notes: Dependent variable is weekly revenue. Method is separate regressions for each week.

We added the control variables to the regressions. Tables 28.4 and 28.5 report the results of this set of regressions.[2] The results confirm what is evident in Tables 28.2 and 28.3: The critical reviews, both positive and negative, remain significant for every week. For the first four weeks, SCREEN appears to have the most significant impact on revenue, followed by BUDGET and POSRATIO (NEGRATIO). After four weeks, BUDGET becomes insignificant, and critical reviews become the second most important factor after screens. In general, the R^2 and adjusted R^2 are greater than those in Tables 28.2 and 28.3, suggesting an enhanced explanatory power of the added variables.

For the third test, we ran time-series cross-section regressions (see Table 28.6; Baltagi 1995; Hsiao 1986, p. 52).[3] In this equation, the variable SCREEN varies across films and across time; the other predictors and control variables vary across films but not across time. We also created a new variable, WEEK, which has a value between 1 and 8 and thus varies across time but not across films. In this regression, we added an interaction term (POSRATIO × WEEK or NEGRATIO × WEEK) to assess the declining impact of critical reviews over time. The results support H_3 and partially support H_4. The coefficient of positive and negative reviews remains highly significant ($\beta_{positive} = 3.32$, $p < .001$; $\beta_{negative} = -5.11$, $p < .001$), pointing to the dual role of critics (H_3). However, the interaction term is not significant for positive reviews, but it is significant for negative reviews, suggesting a declining impact of negative reviews over time, which is partially consistent with critics' role as influencers.

These results are somewhat different from Eliashberg and Shugan's (1997) findings (i.e., critics are only predictors) and Ravid's (1999) results (i.e., there is no effect of positive reviews). There are several reasons our results differ from those of Eliashberg and Shugan. First, although they included only those films that had a minimum eight-week run, our sample includes films that ran for less than eight weeks as well. We did so to accommodate films with short box office runs. Second, the size of our data set is three times as large as that of Eliashberg and Shugan (175 films versus 56). Third, our data set covers a longer period (late 1991 to early 1993) than their data set, which only covers films released between 1991 and early 1992. Fourth, we selected the films in our data set completely at random, whereas Eliashberg and Shugan, as they note, were more restrictive. Similarly, our results may differ from those of Ravid because we included reviews from all cities reported in *Variety*, not only New York, and we used weekly revenue data rather than the entire revenue stream.

Negative versus positive reviews

H_5 predicts that negative reviews should have a disproportionately greater negative impact on box office reviews than the positive impact of positive reviews. Because the percentages of positive and negative reviews are highly correlated (see Table 28.1; $r = -.88$), they cannot be put into the same model. Instead, we used the number of positive (POSNUM) and negative (NEGNUM) reviews, because they are not correlated with each other (see Table 28.1; $r = .17$), and thus both variables can be put into the same regression model. We expected the coefficient of NEGNUM to be negative, and thus there may be some evidence for negativity bias if $|\beta_{NEGNUM}|$ is greater than $|\beta_{POSNUM}|$. Table 28.7 reports the results of our time-series cross-section regression.

Because we found that negative reviews, but not positive reviews, diminish in impact over time. A stronger test for the negativity bias should then focus on the early weeks (the first week in particular) when the studios have not had the opportunity to engage in damage control. As we expected, the negativity bias is strongly supported in the first week. Although β_{NEGNUM} is negative and significant $\beta_{NEGNUM} = -.209$, $t = -3.42$, $p < .0001$), $\beta_{POSNUM} = .052$,

Table 28.4 Effect of critical reviews on box office revenue: weekly regression results with percentage of positive reviews and other control variables

Week	Constant	WONAWARD	G	PG	PG-13	R	TOTNUM	RELEASE	SEQUEL	BUDGET	POSRATIO	SCREEN	R^2	Adjusted R^2	F-Ratio
1 (n = 162)	-6.59*	.255	-5.101**	-.857	-.445	-.1210	-.032	3.035	5.223*	.1763*	6.796*	.007*	.791	.776	51.92*
		(.0106)	(-.109)	(-.035)	(-.0218)	(.0067)	(.0609)	(.0545)	(.149)	(.278)	(.186)	(.938)			
2 (n = 154)	-4.50*	.927	-1.38	.05574	-.634	-.186	.009	.549	1.889***	.097*	4.670*	.005*	.757	.738	40.44*
		(.0547)	(.0428)	(.0032)	(-.043)	(-.015)	(.026)	(.014)	(.078)	(.217)	(.177)	(.697)			
3 (n = 145)	-2.416	.966	-.310	1.485	-1.042	-.059	-.003	-.914	.228	.105*	3.590*	.0035*	.728	.706	32.64*
		(.075)	(-.013)	(.109)	(-.093)	(-.006)	(-.011)	(-.030)	(.012)	(.310)	(.168)	(.601)			
4 (n = 139)	-1.92	.521	-.360	1.204	-.515	.438	-.005	-.159	-.716	.039**	2.424*	.003*	.758	.738	36.51*
		(.058)	(-.019)	(.127)	(-.065)	(.0634)	(-.024)	(-.007)	(-.054)	(.164)	(.162)	(.753)			
5 (n = 137)	-1.929**	.776**	-.727	.603	-.101	.3575	-.008	1.084	-.578	.005	1.867*	.003*	.768	.748	37.97*
		(.114)	(-.051)	(.085)	(-.017)	(.068)	(-.055)	(.067)	(.057)	(.027)	(.163)	(.866)			
6 (n = 132)	-1.413	.564***	.228	.202	.132	.191	-.006	.744	-.718	-.008	1.416**	.003*	.727	.702	29.30*
		(.091)	(.018)	(.031)	(.024)	(.040)	(-.044)	(.050)	(-.075)	(-.050)	(.135)	(.892)			
7 (n = 130)	-1.608	.477	2.265***	.134	.248	.286	.00011	.285	-.874	-.0109	1.792*	.003*	.614	.578	17.19*
		(.076)	(.176)	(.020)	(.045)	(.057)	(.0007)	(.018)	(-.084)	(-.065)	(.163)	(.766)			
8 (n = 122)	-.937	.511**	.359	-.135	.072	.081	-.004	.678	-.219	-.018***	.867**	.003*	.733	.706	27.65*
		(.118)	(.042)	(-.029)	(.018)	(.023)	(-.037)	(.064)	(-.032)	(-.152)	(.116)	(.921)			

* $p < .01$.

** $p < .05$.

*** $p < .1$.

Notes: Dependent variable is weekly revenue; method is separate regressions for each week. Standardized betas are reported in parentheses.

Table 28.5 Effect of critical reviews on box office revenue: weekly regression results with percentage of negative reviews and other control variables

Week	Constant	WONAWARD	G	PG	PG-13	R	TOTNUM	RELEASE	SEQUEL	BUDGET	NEGRATIO	SCREEN	R^2	Adjusted R^2	F-Ratio
1 (n = 162)	-.390	.381 (.016)	-5.415** (-.116)	-1.234 (-.051)	-1.055 (-.051)	-.612 (-.034)	-.036 (-.069)	2.543 (.046)	4.938* (.141)	.172* (.271)	-7.173* (-.181)	.007* (.689)	.789	.774	51.50*
2 (n = 154)	.019	1.106 (.065)	-1.742 (-.054)	-.360 (-.020)	-1.115 (-.075)	-.623 (-.050)	.04 (.011)	.215 (.005)	1.655 (.068)	.091* (.205)	-5.476* (-.186)	.005* (.710)	.759	.741	41.06*
3 (n = 145)	.822	1.097 (-.0855)	-.441 (-.0181)	1.215 (.0899)	-1.380 (-.123)	-.330 (-.034)	-.004 (-.011)	-1.266 (-.0416)	.0998 (.005)	.0996* (.292)	-3.573* (-.154)	.004* (.602)	.726	.703	32.21*
4 (n = 139)	.185	.5999 (.066)	-.229 (-.012)	1.083 (.114)	-.698 (-.089)	.281 (.040)	-.005 (-.024)	-.363 (-.017)	-.802 (-.060)	.038** (.157)	-2.310* (-.142)	.003* (.740)	.754	.733	35.73*
5 (n = 137)	-.280	.838 (.123)	-.619 (-.044)	.538 (.076)	-.213 (-.035)	.273 (.052)	-.010 (-.063)	.942 (.058)	-.669 (-.066)	.004 (.021)	-1.952* (-.155)	.003* (.862)	.767	.746	37.64*
6 (n = 132)	-.0526	.604*** (.097)	.255 (.020)	.119 (.017)	.020 (.004)	.094 (.019)	-.008 (-.058)	.625 (.042)	-.826 (-.086)	-.008 (-.0513)	-1.607* (-.138)	.003* (.891)	.728	.704	29.48*
7 (n = 130)	.056	.513 (.082)	2.30 (.173)	-.084 (-.013)	-.018 (-.0033)	.055 (.011)	.00029 (.002)	.133 (.0087)	-.988 (-.096)	-.013 (-.082)	-1.645** (-.1308)	.0029* (.764)	.607	.571	16.72*
8 (n = 122)	-.133	.524 (.122)	.348 (.040)	-.226 (-.0488)	-.043 (-.011)	-.015 (-.004)	-.004 (-.039)	.616 (.058)	-.280 (-.040)	-.018** (-.163)	-.840*** (-.097)	.0028* (.921)	.729	.703	27.27*

* $p < .01$.
** $p < .05$.
*** $p < .1$.

Notes: Dependent variable is weekly revenue; method is separate regressions for each week. Standardized betas are reported in parentheses.

Table 28.6 Effect of critical reviews on box office revenue (Fuller-Battese estimations)

Variable	Using Percentage of Positive Reviews			Using Percentage of Negative Reviews		
	Coefficient	t-Value	Significance (p-Value)	Coefficient	t-Value	Significance (p-Value)
Constant	−1.42	−.98	.33	2.14	1.33	.18
WONAWARD	.58	1.46	.14	.69	1.59	.11
G	−1.18	−1.07	.28	−1.46	−1.19	.23
PG	.102	.10	.91	−.33	−.31	.75
PG-13	−.042	−.04	.96	−.48	−.46	.64
R	.22	.24	.81	−.16	−.16	.86
TOTNUM	−.006	−.52	.60	−.007	−.59	.55
RELEASE	1.02	1.21	.22	.77	.82	.41
SEQUEL	.73	1.30	.20	.55	.89	.37
BUDGET	.032	2.24	.02	.023	1.47	.14
POSRATIO	3.321	3.33	.00			
NEGRATIO				−5.11	−4.41	.00
SCREEN	.005	22.06	.00	.005	21.79	.00
WEEK	−.436	−2.23	.02	−.55	−2.38	.01
POSRATIO × WEEK	−.023	−.14	.89			
NEGRATIO × WEEK				.42	2.17	.03
R^2		.47			.43	
Hausman test for random effects	M = 1.00		.60	M = 2.00		.36

Notes: Dependent variable is weekly revenue; method is time-series cross-section regression. N = 159.

$t = 1.60$, p = not significant), and their difference ($|\beta_{NEGNUM}| - |\beta_{POSNUM}|$) is significant ($F_{1,151} = 3.76$, $p < .05$).

Separate weekly regressions on the subsequent weeks (Week 2 onward) did not produce a significant difference between the two coefficients. The combined data for the first two weeks show evidence of negativity bias (Table 28.7).

It is possible that the negativity bias is confounded by perceived reviewer credibility. When consumers read a positive review, they may believe that the reviewers have a studio bias. In contrast, they may perceive a negative review as more likely to be independent of studio influence. To separate the effects of credibility from negativity bias, we ran an analysis that included only the reviews of two presumably universally credible critics: Gene Siskel and Roger Ebert.[4] We were only able to locate their joint reviews for 72 films from our data set; of these films, 32 received two thumbs up, 10 received two thumbs down, and 23 received one thumb up. We coded three dummy variables: TWOUP (two thumbs up), TWODOWN (two thumbs down), and UP&DOWN (one thumb up). In the regressions, we used two of the dummy variables: TWOUP and TWODOWN. The results confirmed our previous findings. The coefficient of TWODOWN is significantly greater than that of TWOUP in both the first week ($\beta_{TWODOWN} = -6.51$, $\beta_{TWOUP} = .32$; $F_{1,57} = 4.95$, $p < .03$) and the entire eight-week run ($\beta_{TWODOWN} = -2.28$, ($\beta_{TWOUP} = .42$; $F_{1,501} = 3.46$, $p < .06$).

Table 28.7 Tests for negativity bias

	Fuller-Battese Estimation		Week 1 Regression		Week 1 + Week 2 Regression	
Constant	.53	(.38)	−2.94	(−1.34)	−2.47	(−1.56)
WONAWARD	.55	(1.39)	.08	(.07)	.41	(.56)
G	−1.65	(−1.50)	−6.21	(−2.46)*	−4.43	(−2.47)*
PG	−.58	(−.62)	−2.09	(−1.00)	−1.39	(−.93)
PG-13	−.71	(−.78)	−1.50	(−.74)	−1.45	(.99)
R	−.46	(−.51)	−1.22	(−.63)	−1.13	(−.81)
RELEASE	1.10	(1.31)	3.55	(1.70)***	2.45	(1.67)***
SEQUEL	.64	(1.14)	4.85	(3.37)*	3.45	(3.51)*
BUDGET	.03	(2.17)**	.18	(5.05)*	.15	(5.76)*
β_{POSNUM}	.032	(2.34)**	.052	(1.60)	.055	(2.40)*
β_{NEGNUM}	−.056	(−2.29)**	−.209	(−3.42)*	−.148	(−3.49)*
SCREEN	.005	(22.70)*	.007	(12.82)*	.006	(15.46)*
WEEK	−.446	(−2.33)*	—		—	
F-value for $\mid \beta_{NEGNUM} \mid$ − $\mid \beta_{POSNUM} \mid$	.54, N.S.		3.76*		2.71***	
N	159		162		317	
R^2	.471		.798		.736	

* $p < .01$.

** $p < .05$.

*** $p < .1$.

Notes: Dependent variable is weekly revenue; methods are time-series cross-section regression and weekly regressions (Week 1 and Week 1 + Week 2). The t-values are reported in parentheses. N.S. = not significant.

Star power, budgets, and critical reviews

H6 predicts that star power and big budgets can help films that receive more negative than positive reviews but do little for films that receive more positive than negative reviews. Because we made separate predictions for the two groups of films (POSNUM − NEGNUM ≤ 0 and POSNUM − NEGNUM > 0), we split the data into two groups. The first group contains 97 films for which the number of negative reviews is greater than or equal to that of positive reviews, and the second group contains the remaining 62 films for which the number of positive reviews exceeds that of negative reviews. We ran time-series cross-section regressions separately for the two groups. Table 28.8 presents the results.

Table 28.8 shows that when negative reviews outnumber positive reviews, the effect of star power on box office returns approaches statistical significance when measured with WONAWARD (β = 1.117, t = 1.56, p = .12) and is statistically significant in the case of RECOGNITION (β = .224, t = 2.09, p < .05). In each case, BUDGET has a positive, significant effect as well. However, when positive reviews outnumber negative reviews, neither the budget nor any definition of star power has any significant impact on a film's box office revenue. The results imply that star power and budget may act as countervailing forces against negative reviews but do little for films that receive more positive than negative reviews.

Table 28.8 Effects of star power and budget on box office revenue

Variable	When POSNUM − NEGNUM ≤ 0 (i.e., Negative Reviews Outnumber Positive Reviews) (n = 62)		When POSNUM − NEGNUM > 0 (i.e., Positive Reviews Outnumber Negative Reviews) (n = 97)	
	Star Power Is WONAWARD	Star Power Is RECOGNITION	Star Power Is WONAWARD	Star Power Is RECOGNITION
Constant	1.540 (1.06)	1.234 (.86)	1.238 (.77)	1.250 (.78)
WONAWARD	1.117 (1.56)	N.A.	.529 (.99)	N.A.
RECOGNITION	N.A.	.225 (2.09)**	N.A.	−.069 (−.95)
G	−2.372 (−1.86)***	−2.679 (−2.11)**	−1.651 (−1.21)	−1.451 (−1.05)
PG	−.131 (−.19)	−.340 (−.49)	−.522 (−.47)	−.436 (−.39)
PG-13	−.818 (−1.54)	−.978 (−1.82)***	−.743 (−.69)	−.723 (−.67)
R	—ᵃ	—ᵃ	−.503 (−.49)	−.387 (−.38)
RELEASE	−1.358 (−.90)	−.779 (−.53)	1.331 (1.15)	1.212 (1.04)
SEQUEL	−.501 (−.63)	−.480 (−.61)	1.531 (1.56)	1.057 (1.10)
BUDGET	.053 (3.01)*	.047 (2.65)*	−.030 (−1.49)	−.017 (−.82)
SCREEN	.003 (10.97)*	.003 (11.09)*	.006 (19.03)*	.005 (19.00)*
WEEK	−.447 (−2.20)*	−.446 (−2.20)*	−.482 (2.23)*	−.480 (2.22)*
R²	.377	.380	.486	.487
Hausman test for random effects	M = 7.37*	M = 7.13*	M = 8.87*	M = 8.25*

* $p < .01$.

** $p < .05$.

*** $p < .1$.

a This set did not have any unrated films and thus dropped the R rating during estimation.

Notes: N.A. = not applicable; dependent variable is weekly revenue; method is time-series cross-section regression. The t-values are reported in parentheses.

DISCUSSION AND MANAGERIAL IMPLICATIONS

Critical reviews play a major role in many industries, including theater and performance arts, book publishing, recorded music, and art. In most cases, there is not enough data to identify critics' role in these industries. Are critics good predictors of consumers' tastes, do they influence and determine behavior, or do they do both? Our article sheds light on critics' role in the context of a film's box office performance. We further assess the differential impact of positive versus negative reviews and how they might operate jointly with star power and budget.

Our first set of results shows that for each of the first eight weeks, both positive and negative reviews are significantly correlated with box office revenue. The pattern is consistent with the dual perspective of critics (i.e., they are influencers and predictors). At the simplest level, this suggests that any marketing campaign for a film should carefully integrate critical reviews, particularly in the early weeks. If studios expect positive reviews, the critics should be encouraged to preview the film in advance to maximize their impact on box office revenue. However, if studios expect negative reviews, they should either forgo initial screenings for critics altogether or invite only select, "friendly" critics to screenings. If negative reviews are unavoidable, studios can use stars to blunt some of the effects by encouraging appearances of the lead actors on television shows such as *Access Hollywood* and *Entertainment Tonight* (*The Wall Street Journal* 2001).

Our second set of results shows that negative reviews hurt revenue more than positive reviews help revenue in the early weeks of a film's release. This suggests that whereas studios favor positive reviews and dislike negative reviews, the impact is not symmetric. In the context of a limited budget, studios should spend more to control damage than to promote positive reviews. In other words, there may be more cost effective options than spending money on advertisements that tout the positive reviews. First, studios could forgo critical screenings for fear of negative attention. For example, *Get Carter* and *Autumn in New York* did not offer advance screenings for critics, leading Roger Ebert (*Guardian* 2000) to comment that "the studio has concluded that the film is not good and will receive negative reviews." Second, studios could selectively invite "soft" reviewers. Third, studios could delay sending press kits to reviewers. Press kits generally contain publicity stills and production information for critics. Because newspapers do not run reviews without at least one press still from the film, withholding the kit gives the film an extra week to survive without bad reviews.

Our third set of results suggests that stars and budgets moderate the impact of critical reviews. Although star power may not be needed if a film receives good reviews, it can significantly lessen the impact of negative reviews. Similarly, big budgets contribute little if a film has already received positive reviews, but they can significantly lessen the impact of negative reviews. Therefore, in some sense, big budgets and stars serve as an insurance policy. Because success is difficult to predict in the film business (see, e.g., De Vany and Walls 1999), as is the quality of reviews, executives can hedge their bets by employing stars or by using big budgets (e.g., expensive special effects). These actions may not be needed and, on average, may not help returns; however, if critics pan the film, big budgets and stars can moderate the blow and perhaps save the executive's job (Ravid and Basuroy 2003).

Implications for other industries

Although the current analysis applies to the film industry, we believe the results may be applicable to other industries in which consumers are unable to assess the qualities of products accurately before consumption (e.g., theater and performance arts, book publishing, recorded music, financial markets). Critics may influence consumers, or consumers may seek out the critics who they believe accurately reflect their taste (i.e., the predictor role). For example, in urban centers, "theater and dance critics wield nearly life-or-death power over ticket demand" (Caves 2000, p. 189); for Broadway shows, critics appear both to influence and to predict consumers' tastes (Reddy, Swaminathan, and Motley 1998). Similarly, research in the bond market shows that there is little market reaction to bond rating changes when the rating agency simply responds to public information (i.e., the rating agencies simply predict what the public has done already). In contrast, if the rating change is based on projections or inside research, the markets react to the news (see Goh and Ederington 1993).

In addition to the role of critics, all the other issues that we have raised in this article (e.g., negativity bias, moderators of critical reviews) should be of significance in other industries as well. For example, bad reviews can doom a publisher's book (Greco 1997, p. 194), but as with films, readers' reliance on the book critics is reduced when the book features a popular author rather than an unknown author (Levin, Levin, and Heath 1997). When enough data are available, there is ample opportunity to extend our framework to assess the revenue returns of such similar creative businesses.

Notes

1   In investigating the role of budgets in a film's performance, we need to disentangle the effects of star power from budgets, because it could be argued that expensive stars make the budget a proxy for star power. However, in our data there is extremely low correlation between the measures of star power and budget, suggesting that the two measures are unrelated.
2   Although we report the results using one of the four possible definitions of star power, WON-AWARD, rerunning the regressions using the other three measures of star power does not change the results.
3   We thank an anonymous reviewer for this suggestion.
4   We thank an anonymous reviewer for this suggestion.

References

Assael, Henry (1984), *Consumer Behavior and Marketing Action*, 2d ed. Boston: Kent Publishing Company.
Austin, Bruce (1983), "A Longitudinal Test of the Taste Culture and Elitist Hypotheses," *Journal of Popular Film and Television*, 11, 157–67.
Baltagi, Badi H. (1995), *Econometric Analysis of Panel Data*. West Sussex, UK: John Wiley & Sons.
Boston Globe (2001), "Big Studios Get Creative with Film Promotion," (June 19), E1.
Business Week (2000), "Can Amazon Make It?" (July 10), 38–43.
Cameron, S. (1995), "On the Role of Critics in the Culture Industry," *Journal of Cultural Economics*, 19, 321–31.
Caves, Richard E. (2000), *Creative Industries*. Cambridge, MA: Harvard University Press.
Creative Multimedia (1997), *Blockbuster Guide to Movies and Videos*. Portland, OR: Creative Multimedia Inc.
De Silva, Indra (1998), "Consumer Selection of Motion Pictures," in *The Motion Picture Mega-Industry*, Barry R. Litman, ed. Needham Heights, MA: Allyn Bacon, 144–71.
De Vany, Arthur and David Walls (1999), "Uncertainty in the Movies: Can Star Power Reduce the Terror of the Box Office?" *Journal of Cultural Economics*, 23 (November), 285–318.
Einhorn, Hillel J. and Clayton T. Koelb (1982), "A Psychometric Study of Literary Critical Judgment," *Modern Language Studies*, 12 (Summer), 59–82.
Elberse, Anita and Jehoshua Eliashberg (2002), "Dynamic Behavior of Consumers and Retailers Regarding Sequentially Released Products in International Markets: The Case of Motion Pictures," working paper, The Wharton School, University of Pennsylvania.

Eliashberg, Jehoshua and Steven M. Shugan (1997), "Film Critics: Influencers or Predictors?" *Journal of Marketing*, 61 (April), 68–78.

Goh, Jeremy C. and Louis H. Ederington (1993), "Is a Bond Rating Downgrade Bad News, Good News, or No News for Stockholders?" *Journal of Finance*, 48 (5), 2001–2008.

Greco, Albert N. (1997), *The Book Publishing Industry*. Needham Heights, MA: Allyn Bacon.

Guardian (2000), "Hollywood Banishes the Critics That Bite," [available at http://www.guardian.co.uk/Archive/Article/0, 4273,4074671,00.html].

Hardie, Bruce G.S., Eric J. Johnson, and Peter S. Fader (1993), "Modeling Loss Aversion and Reference Dependence Effects on Brand Choice," *Marketing Science*, 12 (4), 378–94.

Holbrook, Morris B. (1999), "Popular Appeal Versus Expert Judgments of Motion Pictures," *Journal of Consumer Research*, 26 (September), 144–55.

Hsiao, Cheng (1986), *Analysis of Panel Data*. New York: Cambridge University Press.

Ito, Tiffany A., Jeff T. Larsen, Kyle N. Smith, and John T. Cacioppo (1998), "Negative Information Weighs More Heavily on the Brain: The Negativity Bias in Evaluation Categorization," *Journal of Personality and Social Psychology*, 75 (October), 887–901.

Jedidi, Kamel, Robert E. Krider, and Charles B. Weinberg (1998), "Clustering at the Movies," *Marketing Letters*, 9 (4), 393–405.

John, Kose, S. Abraham Ravid, and Jayanthi Sunder (2002), "The Role of Termination in Employment Contracts: Theory and Evidence from Film Directors' Careers," working paper, Stern School of Business, New York University.

Kahneman, Daniel and Amos Tversky (1979), "Prospect Theory: An Analysis of Decision Under Risk," *Econometrica*, 47 (March), 263–91.

Levin, Aron M., Irwin P. Levin, and C. Edward Heath (1997), "Movie Stars and Authors as Brand Names: Measuring Brand Equity in Experiential Products," in *Advances in Consumer Research*, Vol. 24, Merrie Brucks and Debbie MacInnis, eds. Provo, UT: Association for Consumer Research, 175–81.

Litman, Barry R. (1983), "Predicting the Success of Theatrical Movies: An Empirical Study," *Journal of Popular Culture*, 17 (Spring), 159–75.

—— and Hoekyun Ahn (1998), "Predicting Financial Success of Motion Pictures," in *The Motion Picture Mega-Industry*, Barry R. Litman, ed. Needham Heights, MA: Allyn Bacon, 172–97.

—— and L.S. Kohl (1989), "Predicting Financial Success of Motion Pictures: The '80s Experience," *Journal of Media Economics*, 2, 35–50.

MPAA (2002), "U.S. Entertainment Industry: 2002 MPA Market Statistics," [available at http://www.mpaa.org/useconomicreview/2002/2002_Economic_Review.pdf].

Neelamegham, Ramya and Pradeep Chintagunta (1999), "A Bayesian Model to Forecast New Product Performance in Domestic and International Markets," *Marketing Science*, 18 (2), 115–36.

The New York Times (1999), "Liking America, but Longing for India," (August 6), E2.

Prag, Jay and James Casavant (1994), "An Empirical Study of the Determinants of Revenues and Marketing Expenditures in the Motion Picture Industry," *Journal of Cultural Economics*," 18, 217–35.

Ravid, S. Abraham (1999), "Information, Blockbusters, and Stars: A Study of the Film Industry," *Journal of Business*, 72 (October), 463–92.

—— and Suman Basuroy (2003), "Beyond Morality and Ethics: Executive Objective Function, the R-Rating Puzzle, and the Production of Violent Films," *Journal of Business*, forthcoming.

Reddy, Srinivas K., Vanitha Swaminathan, and Carol M. Motley (1998), "Exploring the Determinants of Broadway Show Success," *Journal of Marketing Research*, 35 (August), 370–83.

Shaw, Steven A. (2000), "The Zagat Effect," *Commentary*, 110 (4), 47–50.

Skowronski, John J. and Donald E. Carlston (1989), "Negativity and Extremity Biases in Impression Formation: A Review of Explanations," *Psychological Bulletin*, 105 (January), 17–22.

Smith, S.P. and V.K. Smith (1986), "Successful Movies—A Preliminary Empirical Analysis," *Applied Economics*, 18 (May), 501–507.

Sochay, Scott (1994), "Predicting the Performance of Motion Pictures," *Journal of Media Economics*, 7 (4), 1–20.

Tversky, Amos and Daniel Kahneman (1991), "Loss Aversion in Riskless Choice: A Reference Dependent Model," *Quarterly Journal of Economics*, 106 (November), 1040–61.

Vogel, Harold L. (2001), *Entertainment Industry Economics*, 5th ed. Cambridge, UK: Cambridge University Press.

Walker, Chip (1995), "Word of Mouth," *American Demographics*, 17 (July), 38–44.

The Wall Street Journal (2001), " 'Town & Country' Publicity Proves an Awkward Act," (April 27), B1, B6.

Wallace, W. Timothy, Alan Seigerman, and Morris B. Holbrook (1993), "The Role of Actors and Actresses in the Success of Films," *Journal of Cultural Economics*, 17 (June), 1–27.

Weiman, Gabriel (1991), "The Influentials: Back to the Concept of Opinion Leaders," *Public Opinion Quarterly*, 55 (Summer), 267–79.

West, Patricia M. and Susan M. Broniarczyk (1998), "Integrating Multiple Opinions: The Role of Aspiration Level on Consumer Response to Critic Consensus," *Journal of Consumer Research*, 25 (June), 38–51.

Wyatt, Robert O. and David P. Badger (1984), "How Reviews Affect Interest in and Evaluation of Films," *Journalism Quarterly*, 61 (Winter), 874–78.

Yamaguchi, Susumu (1978), "Negativity Bias in Acceptance of the People's Opinion," *Japanese Psychological Research*, 20 (December), 200–205.

Chapter 29

JoEllen Shively

COWBOYS AND INDIANS: PERCEPTIONS OF WESTERN FILMS AMONG AMERICAN INDIANS AND ANGLOS (1992)

THE DOMINANT APPROACH TO understanding cultural products typically selects a particular popular genre for analysis in the hope of generating conclusions about the societal values expressed in the cultural product (some exceptions are Radway 1984; Griswold 1987; and Liebes and Katz 1990).[1] For example, Cawelti (1970, 1976), on the basis of his reading of Western novels, concluded that these novels are a vehicle for exploring value conflicts, such as communal ideas versus individualistic impulses, and traditional ways of life versus progress. Cawelti argued that Westerns are formulaic works that provide readers with a vehicle for escape and moral fantasy.

In the major sociological study of Western films, Wright (1977) used his own viewing of the most popular Western movies from 1931 to 1972 to argue that Westerns resemble primitive myths. Drawing on Levi-Strauss, Wright developed a cognitive theory of mythic structures in which "the receivers of the Western myth learn how to act by recognizing their own situation in it" (p. 186). Wright's main thesis is that the narrative themes of the Western resolve crucial contradictions in modern capitalism and provide viewers with strategies to deal with their economic worlds. The popularity of Westerns, Wright argued, lies in the genre's reflection of the changing economic system, which allows the viewers to use the Western as a guide for living.

These explanations of the Western's popularity attend to cultural texts but ignore the viewers, whose motives and experiences are crucial. The lack of solid data about audience interpretations of various formulas renders existing models of the cultural significance of Westerns and other genres speculative.

While growing up on an Indian reservation in the midwestern United States, I observed that fellow Indians loved Western movies and paperbacks. Subsequently, I observed this phenomenon on Indian reservations in Oregon and North Dakota, as well as among Indians who lived off the reservations. As scholars have noted (McNickle 1973; Cornell 1987; Snipp 1991), American Indians have always lived in a culturally, economically, and politically marginal subculture and are ambivalent about American values of achievement and acquisition of material wealth. Thus, it seemed unlikely that Indians who like Westerns would need them as conceptual guides for economic action as Wright alleged. The popularity of Westerns among Indians must be explained in other ways.

In an argument similar to Wright's, Swidler (1986) suggested that cultural works are tools used by people to contend with immediate problems. Swidler discussed "culture" in a broad sense as comprising "symbolic vehicles of meaning including beliefs, ritual practices, art forms, ceremonies as well as language, gossip, stories and rituals of daily life" (p. 272). Swidler was concerned with how culture shapes action and with how people "use" culture. Assuming that Western movies are a story or an art form, how do American Indians use this cultural product?

I address several issues that previous studies have made assumptions about, but have not addressed clearly. One issue is the general question of how different groups appropriate and find meaning in cultural products. In particular, does Wright's theory about the cultural use of Westerns hold true for American Indians watching a "cowboys vs. Indians" film? Is the mythic structure of a drama—the "good guy/bad guy" opposition in the Western—more salient than the ethnic aspect of the cultural product, or do Indians in the audience identify with Indians on the screen, regardless of who the good guys and bad guys are? Do Indians prefer Westerns that portray sympathetic and positive images of Indians, e.g., *Broken Arrow* and other movies described by Aleiss (1987) and Parish and Pitts (1976)? Do Indians like only Westerns that show a tribal group other than their own as the villains? Fundamentally, how do Indians link their own ethnic identity to the Western, or limit this identity so they can enter the narrative frame of the Western?

RESEARCH DESIGN

Matched samples of 20 Indian males and 20 Anglo[2] males living in a town on an Indian reservation on the Western Plains of the United States watched a Western film, *The Searchers*. Ethnically pure groups were assembled by one Anglo informant and one Indian informant who invited five ethnically similar friends to their homes to watch the film. Written questionnaires were administered immediately after the film, followed by focus-group interviews. An Anglo female conducted the focus-group interviews with Anglos; I conducted the focus-group interviews with Indians. (I am Chippewa.) (Transcripts of the focus interviews are available from the author on request.)

Respondents were asked why they liked or did not like *The Searchers* in particular and Western movies in general. Basic demographic questions included racial identification, including "blood quantum" for Indians.

The research site is the second largest town on the reservation and has a population of about 1,200. Equal numbers of Indians and Anglos live in the town.[3] According to the Tribal Headquarters Enrollment Officer (Bighorn, 12 May 1988), of the 600 Indians, approximately 40 percent are Sioux, 10 percent are Assiniboine, 10 percent are Indians of mixed Indian origins, and approximately 40 percent of the self-identified Indians are "mixed-blood," i.e., Indian and white ancestry. Because I wanted to avoid the possible ambiguity of asking how mixed-bloods understand Westerns, all Indians in my sample claim to be "full-blood" Sioux, and all Anglos claim to be white.[4] Because the Western genre is primarily about males, only males were included in the sample.[5]

The respondents did not constitute a representative sample, but were assembled in an effort to create roughly matched groups. I attempted to match Indians and Anglos on age, income, years of education, occupation, and employment status, but succeeded in matching mainly on age, education, and occupation, and was less successful on income and employment status.[6] In the analysis, neither employment status nor income appear to affect the dependent variables. Matching Indians and Anglos on education required me to exclude college-educated respondents.[7] All subjects were between the ages of 36 and 64 the average age of Indian respondents was 51, and the average age of Anglo respondents was 52. Most of the respondents were married.[8]

I chose *The Searchers* (1956) as the Western film to show because its major conflict is between cowboys and Indians. According to Wright (1977), *The Searchers* was one of the period's top-grossing films, a sign of mythical resonance. The film stars John Wayne—a critical advantage for a Western according to Indian and Anglo informants. Briefly, *The Searchers* is about Indian-hating Ethan Edwards's (John Wayne) and Martin Pauley's (Jeff Hunter) five-year search to find Debbie Edwards, Ethan's niece (Natalie Wood), who has been kidnapped by Comanche Chief Scar (Henry Brandon). In the end, Scar is killed, and Debbie, who was married to Scar, is taken back to the white civilized world.

FINDINGS

I began my research with the assumption that people understand movies based on their own cultural backgrounds. Therefore, the experience of watching Western movies should be different for Indians and Anglos, especially when watching scenes in which Indians are portrayed in distorted, negative ways. My most striking finding, however, is an overall similarity in the ways Indians and Anglos experienced *The Searchers*.

All respondents—Indians and Anglos—indicated that they liked Western movies in general. Furthermore, in the focus interviews, they said they wished more Westerns were being produced in Hollywood. I asked the respondents to rank the three types of films they most liked to watch from a list of 10 (musical, gangster, horror, and so on). All 40 subjects—both Anglo and Indian—ranked Westerns first or second; the Western was far and away the most popular genre. Seventy-five percent ranked Westerns first. Combat movies were a distant second, and science fiction movies were third.

On both the written questionnaires and in the focus interviews, all respondents indicated that they liked *The Searchers* and considered it a typical Western. One Indian and two Anglos reported that they had seen the film before.

In response to the question, "With whom did you identify most in the film?," 60 percent of the Indians and 50 percent of the Anglos identified with John Wayne, while 40 percent of the Indians and 45 percent of the Anglos identified with Jeff Hunter.[9] None of the Indians (or Anglos) identified with the Indian chief, Scar. Indians did not link their own ethnic identity to Scar and his band of Indians, but instead distanced themselves from the Indians in the film. The Indians, like the Anglos, identified with the characters that the narrative structure tells them to identify with—the good guys. In the focus-group interviews, both Indians and Anglos reiterated their fondness for John Wayne. For both audiences, the Indians in the film were either neutral or negative. What stood out was not that there were Indians on the screen, but that the Indians were the "bad guys." For example, in the focus groups respondents were asked. "Do you ever root for the Indians?" Both Indians and Anglos consistently responded, "Sometimes, when they're the good guys." Their responses suggest that there is no strong ethnic bias governing whom the respondents root for and identify with. Instead, antagonism is directed against the bad guys. The structure of oppositions that defines the heroes in a film seems to guide viewers' identification with the characters in the film and overrides any ethnic empathy.

The Indians' identification with the good guys in the film is similar to Jahoda's (1961,

p. 104) observations of African audiences reacting to films set in Africa that portray Africans as "rude, barbaric savages." Jahoda found that the majority of Africans did not identify with the Africans on the screen—only a minority of highly-educated Africans identified with the Africans.

Although Indians and Anglos relied on cues in *The Searchers* about whom to identify with, in other ways the fictional frame of the film did not completely capture these viewers. When discussing *The Searchers*, Indians and Anglos rarely used the main characters' story names. Instead they used the actors' names—John Wayne and Jeff Hunter—which suggests a strong "star effect." Although John Wayne plays different characters in different films, these audiences associated his "cowboy" personality with the off-screen John Wayne, not with specific movie characters. On one level, they saw the actor as embodying all his movie roles. For example, when asked, "Why do you think Ethan Edwards hated the Indians in this movie?" the Indians and Anglos responded in similar ways:

Indians

Well, John Wayne might have hated Indians in this movie, but in other movies he doesn't hate them. (Mechanic, age 51)

Well, they've killed his brother and his brother's wife. He doesn't hate Indians in all his movies. (Cook, age 56)

Anglos

John Wayne doesn't like the Indians here because they've killed his brother's family. But in other movies, he's on their side. He sticks up for them. (Foreman, age 56)

Sometimes he fights for the Indians like in Fort Apache. (Bartender, age 48)

Both Indians and Anglos reported that they liked all of John Wayne's movies, whether he played a boxing champion, a pilot, or a cowboy. In all of his films, they see the strong personality characteristics of "the Duke," or "Dude," as some of the respondents referred to him. For both Indians and Anglos on this reservation, being called "cowboy" or one of John Wayne's nicknames, often "Dude" or "Duke," is a token of respect. Indians often see themselves as "cowboys," greeting each other with, "How ya doing, cowboy?," or "Long time no see, cowboy," and refer to their girlfriends or wives as "cowgirls." Fixico (1986) described a similar emulation of the cowboy among reservation Indians in Arizona and South Dakota.

The respondents talked about John Wayne as if he were one of them and they knew him personally like a good friend. Believing in John Wayne the man is part of the charisma attached to the cowboy role. It is a self-reinforcing cycle: Because John Wayne always plays good guys characters with whom viewers empathize it is easy to identify with John Wayne and all he represents. Levy (1990) noted that, "because acting involves actual role playing and because of the 'realistic' nature of motion pictures, audiences sometimes fail to separate between players' roles onscreen and their real lives offscreen. The difference between life on and offscreen seems to blur" (p. 281). For respondents, John Wayne is the Cowboy, both in his movies and in real life. This focus on "John Wayne in real life" is similar to Liebes and Katz's (1990) finding that when retelling episodes of the TV series "Dallas," Americans and Kibbutzniks talk about the "real life" (behind-the-scene) personalities of the actors.

The real and the fictional: patterns of differences

Although Anglos and Indians responded in similar ways to the structure of oppositions in the narrative, the two groups interpreted and valued characteristics of the cultural product differently once they "entered" the narrative. The narrative was (re)interpreted to fit their own interests. Although both Indians and Anglos saw some aspects of *The Searchers* as real and others as fictional, the two groups differed on what, they saw as authentic and what they saw as fictional.

Table 29.1 shows how the two groups responded when asked to rank their three most important reasons for liking the film. The Kendall rank-order correlation coefficient of $\tau = .29$ indicates that Indians' and Anglos' reasons often differed. The two groups agreed on the importance of "action and fights," "it had cowboys and Indians," and "the scenery and landscape" as reasons for liking the film. They also agreed that "romance" was not an important reason for liking the film. But the differences between Indians and Anglos in Table 29.1 are striking: None of the Indians ranked "authentic portrayal of the Old West" as an important reason for liking the movie, while 50 percent of the Anglos ranked it as the most important reason.

The results in Table 29.1 suggest that the distinctive appeal of the Western for Indians has two elements: (1) the cowboy's way of life—the idealized Western lifestyle, seems to make this cultural product resonate for Indians; and (2) the setting of the film, the beauty of the landscape (Monument Valley) moves Indian viewers. When asked in the focus groups, "Why did you like this film, and what makes Westerns better (or worse) than other kinds of movies?" Indians reported: "Westerns relate to the way I wish I could live"; "The cowboy is free"; "He's not tied down to an eight-to-five job, day after day"; "He's his own man"; and "He has friends who are like him." What makes Westerns meaningful to Indians is the fantasy of being free and independent like the cowboy and the familiarity of the landscape or setting.

The setting also resonated for Anglos, but Anglos perceived these films as authentic portrayals of their past. In the focus groups, Anglos, but not Indians, talked about Westerns

Table 29.1 Ranks of reasons for liking *The Searchers*, by ethnicity

Reason	American Indians				Anglos			
	Ranked 1st	Ranked 2nd	Ranked 3rd	Weighted Sum of Ranks[a]	Ranked 1st	Ranked 2nd	Ranked 3rd	Weighted Sum of Ranks[a]
Action/fights	2	4	5	19	2	6	4	22
John Wayne	5	3	2	23	2	3	0	12
It had cowboys and Indians	6	5	3	31	3	2	5	18
Scenery/landscape	6	3	2	26	3	5	6	25
Humor	1	5	6	19	0	1	1	3
Romance	0	0	1	1	0	0	1	1
Authentic portrayal of Old West	0	0	0	0	10	3	3	39
Other	0	0	1	1	0	0	0	0

a Ranks are weighted: 1st $\times$ 3; 2nd $\times$ 2; 3rd $\times$ 1.

as accurate chronicles of their history. When asked, "Why did you like this film, and what makes Westerns better (or worse) than other kinds of movies?" Anglos said, "My grand-parents were immigrants and Westerns show us the hard life they had"; "Westerns are about my heritage and how we settled the frontier and is about all the problems they had"; "Westerns give us an idea about how things were in the old days"; and "Westerns are true to life." What is meaningful to Anglos is not the fantasy of an idealized lifestyle, but that Western films link Anglos to their own history. For them, Western films are like primitive myths: They affirm and justify that their ancestors' actions when "settling this country" were right and good and necessary.[10]

Indians seemed ambivalent about how the Old West was portrayed in *The Searchers*. In the focus groups, I asked Indians if the film was an authentic portrayal of the Old West and they responded:

> As far as the cowboy's life goes, it's real, but you don't get to know the Indians, so it's hard to say it's totally authentic. (Bartender, age 42)

> I think it's real in some ways, like when you see the cowboy and how he was. (Mechanic, age 51)

> The cowboys are real to me. That's the way they were. But I don't know about the Indians 'cause you never see much of them. (Farm worker, age 50)

> Yeah, the movie is more about the good guys than the bad guys. I mean, the bad guys are there, but you don't get to know them very well. Mostly the movie is about the cowboys, the good guys, anyway. (Carpenter, age 48)

For Indians, the film was more about cowboys than about Indians. This does not hinder their enjoyment of the film or make it less meaningful, because they did not view the Indians on the screen as real Indians. Both Indians and Anglos were asked, "Are Indians and cowboys in this film like Indians and cowboys in the past?" and, "Are they like Indians and cowboys today?" Anglos replied:

> I think the cowboys and the settlers are pretty much like those in the old days. It's hard to say if the Indians are like Indians in the past. (Mechanic, age 39)

> They're not like Indians today. (Foreman, age 56)

> Indians don't go around kidnapping white women and children these days. (Bartender, age 48)

> Probably they're similar to how some of the Indians were in the past, I mean Indians really did scalp white men. (Postal worker, age 49)

> Yeah, and they kidnapped white children and white women. My grandparents used to tell stories about how their parents told them to be careful when they played outside. They had to stay close to their homes, 'cause the Indians used to kidnap children. (Bus driver, age 49)

Anglos thought the cowboys in the Western were similar to cowboys of the past, and they suggested that Indians in the film were similar to Indians in the past. However, they did not think Indians today are like Indians in the film. When asked the same questions about whether Indians and cowboys in the film are like Indians and cowboys today and in the past, Indians replied somewhat differently:

The cowboys are like cowboys in the past. Maybe some Indians in the past were like the Indians in the films. (Bartender, age 58)

They're not like Indians today. I mean, the only time Indians dress up is for powwows. (Cook, age 60)

In this movie and other movies with Indians, you don't get to know them. I mean, they're not really people, like the cowboys are. It's hard to say they're like Indians in the past. For sure they're not like Indians today. (Bartender, age 42)

The Indians aren't at all like any of the Indians I know. (Unemployed factory worker, age 44)

Indians today are the cowboys. (Bartender, age 42)

The phrase "Indians today are the cowboys," means that contemporary Indians are more like cowboys than Anglos are, in the sense that it is Indians who preserve some commitment to an autonomous way of life that is not fully tied to modern industrial society. Indians want to be, and value being, independent and free—separate from society—more than Anglos do.

Because *The Searchers* portrays Indians not as human beings, but as "wild, blood-thirsty animals," Indians might be expected to report that the Indians on the screen are not like Indians they know today or like Indians in the past. How could they identify with the Indians on the screen when Indians are portrayed in such a caricatured fashion? The only connections that Indians made between the Indians on the screen and Indians of the past and present were with the costumes worn by the Indians on the screen.

On some deeper level, however, Indian respondents may have identified with the Indians on the screen. For example, when asked in the focus groups, "What's a bad Western like?" Indians reported that they like all Westerns except for films like *Soldier Blue*. All of the Indian respondents were familiar with this film. *Soldier Blue* is a 1970 film based on the Sand Creek massacre of 1864, when Colonel Chivington of the U.S. Calvary ambushed and slaughtered a village of peaceful Arapaho and Cheyenne children, women, and men in Colorado. In all of the Indian focus groups, this title was mentioned as one Western they did not like. This suggests that when films are too realistic and evoke unpleasant emotions, they are no longer enjoyable. This finding resembles Radway's (1984, p. 184) findings about "failed" romance novels. A "failed" romance is one that evokes overly intense feelings of anger, fear, and violence. Such novels are discarded by readers because they are not enjoyable. *Soldier Blue*, however, is sympathetic to the Indians, and the narrative leads the viewer to empathize with the Indians. Unlike the Indians, Anglos reported that they like all Westerns and could not think of an example of a bad Western.

Another striking difference revealed in Table 29.1 is that Indians cited "humor" as an important reason for liking the film, while Anglos did not. In the focus groups, Indians talked about several comic scenes in the film. When asked if humor was important in Western films, they all said, "Yeah." They reported that they liked humor and wit in Western movies and valued this trait in their friends. Humor is a source of joy for them—a gift.

Anglos, in contrast, never mentioned John Wayne's humor. Why did Indians and not Anglos respond to the humor? If Anglos perceived the film as an authentic story of their past, they may have concentrated on the serious problems in the film, i.e., getting the white girl back. Perhaps Anglos were so preoccupied with the film as an affirmation of their past that they were unable to focus on the intended humor, or at least other characteristics of the film were more important. On the other hand, Indians, who did not see the film as an authentic story of their own past, may have focused more on the intended humor in the film.

Ideal heroes

Indians and Anglos also valued individual traits of the cowboy differently. Table. 29.2 shows how the two groups responded when asked to rank the three most important qualities that make a good hero in a good Western. A Kendall rank-order correlation coefficient of $\tau = .167$ shows little agreement between Indian and Anglo rankings. Indians ranked "toughness" and "bravery" as the two most important qualities of a good hero in a good Western, whereas Anglos ranked "integrity/honesty" and "intelligence" as most important. Perhaps audiences look for exceptional characteristics in a good hero—qualities they would like to see in themselves. To live free and close to the land like Indians wish to live, exceptional bravery and toughness are necessary. Because Anglos do not want to live like cowboys, bravery and toughness are not as important. Responses of Indians in Table 29.2 are similar to responses in Table 29.1 and to the oral responses. For example, when the Indians described John Wayne as a reason why they liked *The Searchers*, they concentrated on John Wayne's toughness.

While the two groups differed on the qualities that make a good hero, Indians and Anglos tended to agree on the characteristics of a good Western. When asked what characteristics they liked in a good Western, a Kendall's rank-order correlation coefficient between Indian and Anglo responses was high, $\tau = .78$, i.e., there were no pronounced differences between Indians and Anglos. For both groups, the three most important characteristics of a good Western were: "a happy ending"; "action/fights"; and "authentic portrayal of Old West." Like the ranking of "a happy ending" as the most important ingredient in a good romance novel (Radway 1984, p. 59), Indian and Anglo viewers ranked "a happy ending" as the most desirable characteristic of a good Western. The essential happy ending for my respondents may be related to Cawelti's (1976, p. 193) "epic moment" when the villain is conquered, the wilderness is subdued, and civilization is established. The importance

Table 29.2 Ranks of qualities that make a good hero in a good western, by ethnicity

Quality	American Indians				Anglos			
	Ranked 1st	Ranked 2nd	Ranked 3rd	Weighted Sum of Ranks[a]	Ranked 1st	Ranked 2nd	Ranked 3rd	Weighted Sum of Ranks[a]
Bravery	8	6	4	40	3	4	1	18
Integrity/honesty	2	2	0	10	8	9	5	47
Independence	0	0	2	2	0	0	1	1
Toughness	8	8	4	44	0	0	0	0
Sense of humor	0	2	8	12	0	1	1	3
Strength	2	0	0	6	0	0	0	0
Loyalty	0	0	0	0	1	0	7	10
Intelligence	0	2	2	6	8	6	5	41
Other	0	0	0	0	0	0	0	0

a Ranks are weighted: 1st × 3; 2nd × 2; 3rd × 1.

of the "happy ending" may also support Wright's (1977) contention that the outcome of the Western narrative is important.

For Indians, the importance of a "happy ending" in a good Western film also reflects on their evaluation of *Soldier Blue* as a bad Western—*Soldier Blue* does not fulfill the "happy ending" criterion of a good Western. Although Indians like action or fights, they are discerning about what kinds of action or fights they enjoy. For both Anglos and Indians, the three least liked characteristics of a good Western were: "hero rides off into the sunset alone"; "Indians as bad guys"; and "romance between hero and woman." Both groups preferred that "the hero settles down." In some ways, the characteristics the respondents like to see in a good Western support Cawelti's assumptions about the cultural significance of the Western.[11]

THE POLITICS OF PERCEPTION

Some Indians do identify with the Indians in the Western and are not affected by the film's signals about whom to identify with. Before taking my research procedures into the field, I pretested them with 15 American Indian college students at a West Coast university (10 males, 5 females). Because Indians in the reservation sample differed in important characteristics from the Indians in the pretests (9 of the Indian students were "mixed-bloods"), systematic comparisons were not possible.

However, Indian students responded differently from Indians in the reservation sample. Ethnicity was a salient issue for the majority of the students. The narrative of *The Searchers* did not "work" for the students and they were unable to fully enter the drama. For example, unlike the reservation Indians, a majority of the Indian students identified with and rooted for Scar and his Indians or Debbie, the kidnapped girl. They thought Debbie should have been allowed to stay with Scar and that the search should not have taken place at all.

Like the reservation Indians, the college-educated Indians did not view *The Searchers* as an authentic portrayal of the "Old West" and were quick to point out stereotypical portrayals of Indians in the film. They reacted against the negative message in the film that "the only good Indian is a dead one." They also pointed out many inaccuracies in the film, such as the use of Navajos and the Navajo language for Comanche, "Comanche" Indians wearing Sioux war bonnets, and Indians sometimes wearing war bonnets while fishing. Neither the Indians nor the Anglos in the reservation sample mentioned any of these inaccuracies.

All students but one reported that they liked Westerns in general, but preferred Westerns whose plots are about "cowboys vs. cowboys" or "Indians vs. Indians," or a "cowboys vs. Indians" plot in which the Indian point of view is shown. Several male students indicated that they and their friends often rent Western videos and named the video stores nearest the university that had the best selection of Westerns.

None of the students particularly liked John Wayne. Like the reservation sample, the students talked about John Wayne in "real life" and referred to what they considered racist statements he made off-screen in various interviews.

I asked each student, "Do Indians back home on the reservation like Westerns?" and "Do they root for the cowboys?" All of them said, "Oh yeah, sure." One Sioux student said his father had most of John Wayne's films on video, and a Chippewa said that his uncle was named after John Wayne. One Navajo said of his reservation town, "Ever since they closed down the movie theater several years ago, every Friday night they show a movie in the cafeteria room at the high school, and most of the time it's a Western. Everybody goes."

The heightened ethnic awareness of the college students interferes with, or overrides, their responses to the Western so that they do not get caught up in the structure of oppositions in the narrative. Because they identify with their ethnic group, they see *The*

Searchers through a different lens. Education increases their awareness of anti-Indian bias in the film, producing a "revised eye" that frames these films in ethnic terms. In this context, ethnicity is a construct of a particular culture or subculture.

CONCLUSION

Although it would seem problematic for Indians to know which characters to identify with in *The Searchers*, it was not a problem for them at all—they identified with the cowboy and his lifestyle. Indians did not focus on the Indians, who are often portrayed on-screen as a faceless, screaming horde. Instead, they saw the cowboys as they want to see themselves—as the good guys.

What appears to make Westerns meaningful to Indians is the fantasy of being free and independent like the cowboy. In addition, the familiarity of the setting is important. Anglos, on the other hand, respond to the Western as a story about their past and their ancestors. The Western narrative becomes an affirmation of their own social experience—the way they are and what their ancestors strove for and imposed on the West are "good." Thus, for Anglos, the Western resembles a primitive myth. But it is not a myth in this sense for Indians—Indians do not view the Western as authentic.

Both Indians and Anglos find a fantasy in the cowboy story in which the important parts of their ways of life triumph and are morally good, validating their own cultural group in the context of a dramatically satisfying story. Perhaps this motive for ethnic group validation is more general and not peculiar to cowboy movies.

Oppositions in the Western narrative are important to viewers. Indians and Anglos both root for and identify with the good guys. The strength of the narrative lies in its Levi-Straussian oppositions, and Wright (1977) correctly focused on them. However, Wright's thesis, that viewers see their own economic situation in Westerns and use its messages to deal with their economic world, is not supported here. Both Indians and Anglos respond to "their own situation," but not in Wright's sense. Wright's sociological explanation of the cultural significance of Westerns does not entirely contradict Cawelti (1976). Although Cawelti's discussion is too nonspecific, and therefore more difficult to refute, my evidence is more compatible with Cawelti's argument that viewers use Westerns as a fantasy for exploring value conflicts (e.g., traditional ways of life versus progress) and to affirm the value of their ideals and way of life. Cawelti's nonspecificity and Wright's incorrect explanation may have resulted from their failure to ask viewers or readers why they like Westerns.

The Indian college students, who by attending college have opted for some of the values of white society, find other meanings in *The Searchers*. Because they are immersed in the intellectual world of the university, the symbolic importance of the film for them lies in its false representation of their ancestry and history.

Notes

1   Much work has involved literary and film studies. However, literary theories such as reader-response theory (Iser 1974; Fish 1980), pertain mostly to an "implied reader" within the text, and psychoanalyze what ethnicity, gender, religion, etc., in films mean (Friedman 1991). This work is interesting, but irrelevant for a study of how real audiences actually respond.

2   "Anglo" refers to non-Indian white Americans and does not include those of Spanish or Mexican descent.

3   Of the approximately 50,000 residents living on the 7 federally recognized reservations in this state in 1980, 48.5 percent are Indian and 51.5 percent are Anglo (Confederation of American Indians

1986, pp. 125–34). Under the 1887 General Allotment Act, more than 100 Indian Reservations on the Plains, along the Pacific Coast, and in the Great Lakes states, were divided up and allotted to individual Indians. The remaining land was declared "surplus" and opened up to white homesteaders. Under the terms of this Act, Indians were eventually dispossessed of almost 90 million acres (Talbot 1981, pp. 111–12). Today, whites continue to own land and live on these reservations where their land is "checker-boarded" between Indian-owned land. On some of these reservations, non-Indians own as much or more land than the tribe or Indians do, and the proportion white is equal to or higher than the proportion Indian. The research site is on one of these reservations.

4   I have observed that "mixed-blood" Indians acknowledge and respect both their Indian and white ancestries. To avoid speculation about whether the findings might be associated with the self-identified Indians' "Indianness" or "whiteness," I included only full-bloods.

5   My data show that the Western genre is popular among women, but because the major focus of this study is on racial differences and because I had a limited budget, I controlled for gender by looking at males only.

6   The median annual household income for the Indians was $9,000; the median annual household income for the Anglos was $13,000. Seven of the 20 Indian men were unemployed at the time of the research compared to 3 of the Anglo men. Of currently employed Indians, four were working part-time; three of currently employed Anglos were working part-time. There are no significant differences between the Indians in my study and the 1980 Census data on income and unemployment (U.S. Bureau of the Census 1986, Tables 9, 10, 25; U.S. Bureau of the Census 1988, Table 23–4). Occupations of the Indians included bartender, farm worker, mechanic, factory worker, carpenter, and food-service worker. Occupations of the Anglos included janitor, school bus driver, bartender, store clerk, factory worker, carpenter, mechanic, foreman, and postal worker.

7   Indians and Anglos differed in the proportion who completed high school, but this difference had no effect on the analysis. Among Indian respondents, 25 percent had completed high school and 60 percent had some high school. For Anglo respondents, 80 percent had completed high school and 20 percent had some high school.

8   To obtain matched 20-person samples, 11 groups comprising 30 Indians and 25 Anglos watched the film. Of these, 2 Indians and 3 Anglos had "some college education" and 8 Indians and 2 Anglos were mixed-blood. These respondents' questionnaires were not used and the respondents were not involved in the focus interviews.

9   One Anglo identified with Laurie, Jeff Hunter's girlfriend. It was difficult to tell why.

10   Describing the role of the myth among Trobriand Islanders, Malinowski (1948) wrote: "The myth comes into play when rite, ceremony, or a social or moral rule demands justification, warrant of antiquity, reality, and sanctity" (pp. 84–85).

11   I collected some data in the field on female reservation Indians and female Anglos. These data reveal gender differences as well as differences by ethnicity. For example, women identified with the women in the film, while the men did not. Women ranked "romance" as one of the most important reasons for liking the film, whereas the men ranked it as the least important reason. Women ranked "action/fights" as one of the least important reasons for liking the film, while the men ranked it as one of the most important reasons. Like Anglo men, Anglo women saw the film as an authentic portrayal of the past, while the Indian women, like the Indian men, did not. Indian women, like Indian men, also distanced themselves from the Indians on the screen.

References

Aleiss, Angela. 1987. "Hollywood Addresses Postwar Assimilation: Indian/White Attitudes in *Broken Arrow*." *American Indian Culture and Research Journal* 11:67–79.

Bighorn, Spike N. 1988. Personal communication with author. 12 May.

Cawelti, John. 1970. *The Six-Gun Mystique*. Bowling Green, OH: Bowling Green State University Popular Press.

Cawelti, John. 1976. *Adventure, Mystery and Romance*. Chicago: University of Chicago Press.

Confederation of American Indians. 1986. *Indian Reservations: A State and Federal Handbook*. Jefferson, NC: McFarland.

Cornell, Stephen. 1987. "American Indians, American Dreams, and the Meaning of Success." *American Indian Culture and Research Journal* 11:59–70.

Fish, Stanley. 1980. *Is There a Text in This Class?* Cambridge, MA: Harvard University Press.

Fixico, Donald L. 1986. "From Indians to Cowboys: The Country Western Trend." pp. 8–14 in *American Indian Identity: Today's Changing Perspectives*, edited by C. E. Trafzer. Sacramento, CA: Sierra Oaks Publishing Company.

Friedman, Lester D., ed. 1991. *Unspeakable Images: Ethnicity and the American Cinema*. Chicago: University of Illinois Press.

Griswold, Wendy. 1987. "The Fabrication of Meaning: Literary Interpretation in the United States, Great Britain, and the West Indies." *American Journal of Sociology* 92:1077–117.

Iser, Wolfgang. 1974. *The Implied Reader: Patterns of Communication in Prose Fiction from Bunyan to Beckett*. Baltimore, MD: Johns Hopkins University Press.

Jahoda, Gustav. 1961. *White Man: A Study of the Attitudes of Africans to Europeans in Ghana before Independence*. London: Oxford University Press.

Levy, Emanuel. 1990. *And the Winner Is . . .: The History and Politics of the Oscar Awards*. New York: Continuum.

Liebes, Tamar and Elihu Katz. 1990. *The Export of Meaning: Cross Cultural Readings of Dallas*. New York: Oxford University Press.

McNickle, D'Arcy. 1973. *Native American Tribalism: Indian Survivals and Renewals*. New York: Oxford University Press.

Malinowski, Bronislaw. 1948. *Magic, Science, and Religion and Other Essays*. Glencoe, IL: The Free Press.

Parish, James R. and Michael R. Pitts. 1976. *The Great Western Pictures*. Metuchen, NJ: The Scarecrow Press, Inc.

Radway, Janice A. 1984. *Reading the Romance: Women, Patriarchy, and Popular Literature*. Chapel Hill, NC: University of North Carolina Press.

Snipp, C. Matthew. 1991. *American Indians: The First of This Land*. New York: Russell Sage Foundation.

Swidler, Ann. 1986. "Culture in Action: Symbols and Strategies." *American Sociological Review* 51:273–86.

Talbot, Steve. 1981. *Roots Of Oppression: The American Indian Question*. New York: International Publishers.

U.S. Bureau of the Census. 1986. *1980 Census of Population. American Indians, Eskimos, and Aleuts on Identified Reservations and In The Historical Areas of Oklahoma*. Vols. 1–2. Subject Report prepared by the U.S. Department of Commerce. Washington, DC: U.S. Government Printing Office.

U.S. Bureau of the Census. 1988. 1980 *County and City Data Book*. Prepared by the U.S. Department of Commerce. Washington, DC: U.S. Government Printing Office.

Wright, Will. 1977. *Sixguns and Society: A Structural Analysis of the Western*. Berkeley, CA: University of California Press.

Chapter 30

Philippe Meers

"IT'S THE LANGUAGE OF FILM!": YOUNG FILM AUDIENCES ON HOLLYWOOD AND EUROPE (2007)

THIS CHAPTER, WHICH IS PART OF A larger research project on young film audiences in Belgium, examines the attitudes of young Flemish viewers towards Hollywood, European cinema and national cinema.[1] Inevitably, it engages with the issue that Thomas Elsaesser has described as 'the founding myth' of the discipline of film studies, the opposition between Hollywood and European cinema, which it views through the everyday life experiences and views of actual audiences in their social and cultural context.[2] In doing so, it considers the whole spectrum of film consumption, including television and video, something which is particularly important in considering Hollywood, since Hollywood films and their by-products in popular culture predominate in other media.[3] Broadening the field in this way helps to draw a richer picture of the kaleidoscopic experiences of film audiences, providing new insights on how audiences recreate and use discursive constructions of Hollywood, European and national cinema.

Some commentators have explained the hegemony of the US film industry over the European market as a form of cultural imperialism, while other scholars attribute Hollywood's success to its narrative and formal qualities.[4] Media reception scholars nuance both positions, but almost all these reception studies focus on television rather than film audiences.[5] The survey on which this chapter is based examines what Andrew Higson calls a 'national reception culture', using an approach that studies 'the activity of national audiences and the context within which they give meaning to the movies they watch'.[6] The audience examined is situated in Flanders, the Dutch-speaking part of Belgium, a fact that in itself problematises common definitions of 'national' cinema. Belgium is a small federal country in the heart of Europe. Its two main communities are Dutch-speaking Flanders and French-speaking Wallonia, with Brussels, the European capital, being bilingual. This ethnic and linguistic division has created significant differences in film culture between the two communities. On the level of production and policy, each has its own legislation and subsidy system. On the level of reception, there are related differences, mainly concerned with language issues, and the top ten box-office movies in the two parts of the country are very different. In Wallonia, most films are dubbed, whereas the only films not subtitled in Flanders are children's animation films; this holds true for films on television as well as in the cinema. Flanders has some of the biggest multiplexes, owned by the European-wide

Kinepolis Group; as in other parts of Europe, small town cinemas are well on the way to extinction. There are clear-cut distinctions between commercial multiplexes, arthouse cinemas (mainly in the big cities such as Antwerp, Ghent and Brussels), film museums (Antwerp and Brussels) and cultural centres screening films as part of their overall programming.

The range of films on offer to audiences includes an enormous number of Hollywood films in the multiplexes, a far smaller number of Flemish and Belgian films, some French films (especially in Brussels and the French-speaking community) and a few other European films. Hollywood films also feature prominently on prime-time television. Although the almost fully cabled Belgian television service offers more than thirty channels (Dutch, British, French, German, Spanish, Italian), the Flemish commercial and public channels are by far the most popular. Amongst these, the commercial channels VT4 and Kanaal 2 are aimed at a young audience and show primarily US films. Although Flanders is heavily dependent on US films, its geographical location makes it possible for the survey to study how young people interact with a cultural web in which not just American but French, German, Dutch, British and other films are available and accessible through various media channels.[7] The objective of the survey was

> to get a grasp of our contemporary media culture, particularly as it can be seen
> in the role of the media in everyday life, both as a topic and as an activity
> structured by and structuring the discourses within which it is discussed.[8]

Young people were selected as the focus for the survey because they are the core target group of contemporary mainstream (Hollywood) cinema. The survey's concern was with mainstream youth culture, rather than underground or marginal subcultures.[9] By taking a broader view of the role of film as a cultural product in young people's everyday lives, the survey offers insights into their cinematic preferences, patterns, opinions and attitudes.[10] It also encourages a detailed analysis of cross-cultural relationships in film reception, and a comparison of marketing and press discourses with those of the audience.[11] The survey illuminates the ways in which Hollywood is a formative part of popular film culture in Flanders, interacting with young people's national and regional identities.

In spring 2001, in depth interviews were conducted both with twenty-eight adolescents (seventeen girls and eleven boys with an average age of seventeen and a half) in their last year or second last year of secondary school, and also with their family members.[12] The educational level of those interviewed included students preparing for tertiary study (ASO), technical education (TSO), and those taking vocational courses (BSO). The level of film consumption varied widely within the sample, ranging from the rare filmbuff who watches films on a regular basis and collects film on video, to people who hardly ever go to the cinema or rent a video and for whom the experience of film is limited to watching films on television. Although the sample cannot be considered to be wholly representative of young people in Flanders, it does reflect an existing variety in class, gender, level of education and location.

Because interview data is never transparent, it inevitably poses problems when it comes to interpretation and evaluation. 'Interview talk is the rhetoric of socially situated speakers', remarks Thomas Lindlof, 'not an objective report of thoughts, feelings, or things out in the world'.[13] Every attempt has been made in this chapter to seek a balance, as Thomas Austin writes, between 'avoiding both the naive positivism of treating audience research as a source of unmediated access to film viewing experiences, and a defeatism that too readily abandons empirical inquiry'.[14] In summarising research findings, direct quotations are used to illustrate the points made while staying as close to the respondents' discourse as possible.[15]

HOLLYWOOD, EUROPE AND NATIONAL CINEMA: DISCURSIVE DICHOTOMIES

The survey's clearest finding was the overwhelming preference for Hollywood films displayed by a young mainstream audience, and the relative lack of interest in European and local Flemish films. For these audience members, as for the teenage boys studied by Martin Barker and Kate Brooks, Hollywood is 'a widely-shared mental construct which summarises a place of tinsel and tin, glamour, money and power' but also a site of power towards which interviewees feel ambivalence.[16] An analysis of young people's discourses brought to light a range of associations between particular notions of form, style and narrative and a particular style of American, European or Flemish film-making. While respondents paid little detailed attention to 'European' cinema as too abstract a category, a pattern of dichotomies between Hollywood and Flemish movies emerged on the levels of production, distribution, film characteristics and reception (see Table 30.1).

On the level of production, respondents knew that only Hollywood has the knowhow and the financing to make worldwide blockbusters. Big budgets have their own implications in terms of the use of special effects, settings and actions. On the level of distribution, Hollywood films are considered to be highly visible in the media, in the cinemas, in the videotheques and on television. This high visibility is associated with box-office success and a diverse audience range. Most respondents, however, focused on the differences in characteristics among the films. The most frequently articulated opposition was one of quality: Flemish films were considered 'low' quality while Hollywood meant 'high' quality. A comparable stylistic dichotomy emerged between 'primitive' national film and 'sophisticated' high-tech Hollywood. Some respondents contrasted the old-fashioned Flemish 'reality' with modern American 'fantasies'. A similar opposition also appeared in generic associations, where Flemish drama and historical film were perceived as very different from Hollywood's action, thriller and horror genres. National origin was, indeed, itself linked with the idea of genre. 'Hollywood cinema' was perceived by many as itself a broad genre, namely mainstream commercial cinema, as opposed to national cinemas, which were often dismissed as narrow or irrelevant. One respondent observed that 'Flemish film is not at all my film genre' and another confessed that 'I have never seen a real Belgian action movie, simply because they don't have the means to do that.' A film's setting was also understood as a generic element. Banal Flemish reality was often contrasted with Hollywood's attractive foreign, exotic settings, while the acting in Flemish films was considered amateurish and artificial in comparison to Hollywood's professional and spontaneous performances. Only Hollywood, some respondents believed, featured real movie stars. A similar contrast was constructed on more technical levels, such as sound and image, although the young people in the survey did not usually possess an adequate vocabulary to describe this difference and talked rather of 'ugly' and 'beautiful' images with special effects. Many connected the use of Dutch language to the notion of poor acting, regarding it as clumsy and artificial when compared to American English, the film language par excellence. Flemish movies were closely linked to daily reality, while Hollywood signified a fantasy world, but one considered more 'real' in that it was regarded as convincing within cinematic conventions. The young people surveyed constructed a clear-cut dichotomy between Hollywood as a sensational dream factory and Flemish film as small and not particularly attractive window on mundane reality. The existence of these attitudes has repercussions on the reception processes of both categories of film. Popular identification with Hollywood movies is much higher, entailing a higher suspension of disbelief. The horizon of expectation is much lower for Flemish film. Hollywood movies are consumed across all media, from cinema to the internet, while Flemish films are viewed mainly on television. The points of reference for Flemish movies

Table 30.1 Discourses on Flemish cinema vs Hollywood cinema: a schematic overview

Level	Subject	Local Flemish film	Hollywood film
Production	Budget	Cheap	Expensive
Distribution	Visibility	Low	High
	Success (box office)	Low	Blockbusters
Film characteristics	Quality	− Low + Good within a small budget	+ High − low considering the enormous budget
	Style	− Primitive, simple + Simple but OK	+ Sophisticated, high Tech,—Exaggerated
	Genre	− Drama, historical + Teenpics	Action, comedy, thriller, horror
	Subject	(Banal) reality Old fashioned	(Unreal) fantasy Modern
	Setting	(Banal) Flemish scenery	Attractive foreign setting
	Acting	Amateurish, artificial	Professional, spontaneous
	Actors	TV-celebrities	Movie stars
	Image and sound	Poor quality	High quality
	Language	Artificial	The film language
	Form	Ugly, grim	Beautiful, special effects
	Link with everyday life	High	Low
	Filmic/narrative realism	Low	High
Reception	Identification	Low	High
	Suspension of disbelief	Low	High
	Horizon of expectation	Low	High
	Context of exhibition	Multiplex	Multiplex
	Point of reference	Old films on television	Recent films in cinema
	Context of consumption	TV and rarely video	Cinema, video and TV

are 'not so recent' films shown on television while, for Hollywood, reference is usually to the latest blockbuster.

THE HOLLYWOOD BLOCKBUSTER AS CLASSIC

When audiences talk about 'American' film, they clearly mean mainstream Hollywood movies. Frequently, respondents did not distinguish between American cinema as a whole and Hollywood. This should come as no surprise, since only Hollywood fare reaches Flemish multiplex screens, and the rare US arthouse or independent production ends up in the kind of arthouse cinemas that few teenagers attend. Most young people explain the dominance of American cinema primarily in terms of Hollywood's enormous budgets, while more critical viewers point to its hegemonic presence in the Flemish media. Hollywood's supremacy also means that peer pressure forces viewers into watching such movies, in order to be able to talk about them.[17] This peer pressure is clearly linked to the hype created around blockbuster movies:

> *Marie* [eighteen-year-old school girl]: . . . thrillers such as *Scream* . . . I don't really like those films, but sometimes you have to because otherwise you're not up to date, what can you talk about if you haven't seen *Scream? . . . Hannibal* was the sequel of *Silence of the Lambs* and I hadn't seen it and then people said 'Oh no! you haven't seen it?'

For ordinary moviegoers, Hollywood occupies a category of its own 'mainstream cinema' somewhere between a genre and a style and with specific characteristics. The dichotomy between Hollywood and European film also involves a distinction revolving around genre:

> *Kristien* [eighteen-year-old school girl]: It's a different genre. Those American films, they mostly deal with issues, that's always action and violence. European films are less violent.

A more surprising element in the responses concerned the discussion of 'classic movies':

> *Marie* [eighteen-year-old school girl]: I'm not a film freak, but some films you just have to have seen them, otherwise it's a gap in your culture . . . Like *Jurassic Park* and *Star Wars*, those films, you know, classics . . .

People regularly use the word 'classic' to describe their favourite movies, referring more often than not to Hollywood movies of the 1980s and 1990s. For these young people, the most important criteria for a classic appear to be the repeated experience, the quality and the story. These films 'never lose their attraction', and the intensity of the experience remains high. To have watched these movies ten times is not exceptional, although many viewers have only seen the 'classics' on television or video. As with the cinephile video-collectors in the research of Uma Dinsmore-Tuli, people take pleasure in acquiring a detailed knowledge of the text, reciting the dialogue and song lyrics during the viewing process, and from the repeated discovery of new things in the same movie.[18] The distinction between regular films and classics also affects video collecting. While some cassettes are used for constant recording, others are reserved for collecting Hollywood 'classics':

> *Gert* [eighteen-year-old school boy]: I have a box or two full of cassettes with films I recorded the last years. I find it hard to erase those films, I want to keep them, those are good movies, the classics. For instance last week I recorded *The Godfather* series. I'm certainly going to keep them, those are classics, as a film fan I have to have them in the house.

Although there were no clear gender differences in the viewers' genre preferences, differences emerged in their discussion of 'classic' movies, with girls commonly citing *Grease* (1978), *Dirty Dancing* (1987) and *Pretty Woman* (1990). The identification of the classic was in some cases passed on from mother to daughter: one mother mentioned *Grease* and *Dirty Dancing* as her own favourites as well as her daughter's: '*Grease*, I went to see it four times a week, until they stopped playing it.' Boys, on the other hand, were more inclined to cite *The Matrix* (1999), *The Silence of the Lambs* (1991), *Hannibal* (2001) and *Star Wars: Episode One* (1999). *Braveheart* (1995) was a favourite for both sexes. The few highbrow or more alternative moviegoers preferred films such as *Festen* (1998), *Pulp Fiction* (1994) or *Gummo* (1997). In hardly ever mentioning directors when they talked about films, respondents resembled the US audiences researched by Tom Stempel.[19] For all the critical discussion and promotion of directors over the years, interviewees focused either on the movies themselves or on the actors. For Flemish young people, stars such as Julia Roberts, Bruce Willis and Steven Seagal epitomised Hollywood.

Although the positive discourse on Hollywood cinema was clearly dominant, there were also certain undertones of criticism. Mostly higher-educated people considered Hollywood film to be 'predictable, slick, superficial, exaggerated, over the top, form over content'. This minority vision injects a number of nuances into the straightforward Hollywood/European dichotomy:

> *Interviewer*: What is your typical Hollywood movie?
>
> *Christel* [nineteen-year-old school girl]: Big names, special effects, you notice there's a lot of money in it, probably also big-name directors. But since I prefer movies with content, I would rather watch the European films.
>
> *Interviewer*: And if you compare in general European films to American films?
>
> *Inge* [seventeen-year-old school girl]: Yeah that's a big difference. I find American films to be much more commercial, mostly with big budgets, and you notice it in the special effects and they use much more, so they are more successful. But if you peel off all that and just keep the story, it's just a simple story. I find European scenarios more original because with American movies. I often get the feeling I already know how it's going to end.

Other respondents expressed strong irritation at 'too promising' Hollywood trailers that turn the experience of watching the film itself into a disappointment:

> *Cor* [nineteen-year-old school boy]: They take five minutes of the movie, where all the action is, they push it in a trailer and show it. And that's what people go to see, and then most of the times the movie is disappointing, because the action is spread all over the movie and they squeeze it in five minutes and show it time and again. And the Americans have the money to show it over and over again.

The fact that films are frequently made to showcase particular actors disturbed some. The acting itself was often considered superficial:

> *Cor*: Most [American] films are built around actors, they put a big action giant there and then they build a film. Instead of making a film and then finding the best actor, they pick the actor first and then the movie.

It is important to keep in mind, however, that although some interviewees were critical of Hollywood cinema, they continued to consume a diet of primarily American movies.

EUROPEAN CINEMA: THE (IN)SIGNIFICANT OTHER

European cinema was at first a vague abstraction during the interviews. It was only after it was juxtaposed with Hollywood and specified as French, German or British that the concept became clearer. On the whole, however, young people displayed a combination of ignorance, indifference, dislike and even aversion towards European cinema:

Interviewer: What do you think of if you hear European film?

An [eighteen-year-old school girl]: Yeah, European film . . . if I think French film, I think boring. But it's probably the language, and German the same. But I really wouldn't know, like Spanish films or Italian films, I wouldn't know . . . if they exist [laughs].

The established view of European cinema as fundamentally art/auteur/intellectual cinema persists, creating an impression that it is difficult and less accessible: 'it forces you to pay attention and think'. There is also a clear association with particular arthouse cinemas:

Kristien [eighteen-year-old school girl]: European films are shown in smaller cinemas . . . there's much less advertising and they deal with subjects that don't interest everybody. American films are made for large audiences and European films are less easy for everybody and make you think.

Notwithstanding the negative attitudes towards European cinema, there also existed a minority opinion which viewed European cinema as a valid alternative to Hollywood. For some respondents, the technical and formal advantages of Hollywood cinema counted for little by comparison with the content of European cinema. Oppositions between form and content or predictability and originality were frequently mentioned, on the basis of a general cultural tendency to value auteur cinema rather than a range of exposure to European films. As in the marginal critical discourse on Hollywood, a respondent's level of education appeared to be an important factor in determining his or her attitude, although most interviewees showed an appreciation of the realities that led to the success of Hollywood films and the failure of European ones:

Gert [eighteen-year-old school boy]: European films are at a higher level, foreign films compared to Hollywood films. Hollywood films will have a weak story but great special effects. And because of the budget they can make a weak story popular, while European films have more content, and a deeper meaning, and they fail at the box office.

It is striking that this interviewee uses the term 'foreign' films in opposition to Hollywood, as if the US-centred discourse is already interiorised to such a degree that foreign simply means 'not American'.

Clichés about nationality – for example comments about 'the endless talking of the French' – were common in discussions of French cinema, which was considered to be the typical 'European' cinema:

Nora [seventen-year-old school girl]: Most French films are not interesting I think, always the same topic, very monotonous.

Interviewer: And what topic is that?

Nora: Well, mostly about relations and everyday life and the description of each day. There is a lot of talking and very little story in it.

Peer group attitude was an important influence. The few people who did like French films were met with incomprehension or rejection:

> *Inge* [seventeen-year-old school girl]: I don't know why but I like French films . . .
>
> *Interviewer*: And do you find it strange that you like them?
>
> *Inge*: I don't know, if I say to my friends, yeah, I rented two French movies, they say: 'What!? You rent French movies?'

School programmes dedicating time to film education typically discuss French film, but such analyses are, as one person comments, 'not applicable to the Hollywood movies I watch in the cinema'.[20] The association of European cinema, and French cinema in particular, with school not only fails to stimulate interest in a cinema that departs from the Hollywood mainstream, but also helps produce an active dislike of European cinema.

The importance of the language factor is highlighted by the fact that most French-speaking Belgian films such as *Rosetta* (1999) and *Le Huitième Jour* (1996) are often considered as French films. Furthermore, the 'raw realism' of the French-Belgian cinema is seldom appreciated, even by people who declare themselves to be open-minded towards European cinema generally. This is a different film language with which they are not familiar and do not appreciate, because it does not correspond to their definition of a pleasurable film experience:

> *Christel* [nineteen-year-old school girl]: We have often been forced to go to the cinema with the school. *Rosetta*, that was a bad film! . . . Maybe as cult film it was good. I mean, they filmed it this way and that way and it's different from the usual, but I came out and I felt so depressed. It was a beautiful day and I was depressed as hell. Maybe, probably even, this was the intention of the makers.
>
> *Kristien* [eighteen-year-old school girl]: French spoken Belgian films, I have seen a few, I usually find them a bit too negative . . . Like *Rosetta* or *La Promesse*, they're always in the same atmosphere, mostly poor people, I don't have anything against it, but they're often too negative.

The fate of other European national films was even worse. Except for a few mentions of *Lota Rennl* (1998), German cinema was completely unknown. Italian film shared the same fate. The *La Vita é Bella* (1997) effect had completely disappeared.[21] British film was a partial exception to the rule, but this had much to do with the language. Interviewees were also aware of the very limited offerings of European films that were available in the multiplexes. The most evident factor affecting cinematic tastes was the respondent's level of education, with more educated interviewees showing a slight inclination towards European films, although it would be fairer to describe this weak preference as displaying a less negative view of European film than that of other interviewees, rather than demonstrating a really positive attitude.[22]

LOCAL FLEMISH FILM AND MUNDANE REALISM

One might have expected a more positive view towards the local culturally specific Flemish films by comparison to non-domestic European cinema, but this was not the case. There is a very low level of consumption of Flemish film, almost exclusively on television. Most respondents had not seen more than one or two Flemish films in their lives, and usually referred to television showings of films such as *Daens* (1992), or to historical film adaptations of classical Flemish literature made in the 1970s and 1980s and depicting 'the peasant life', such as *Het gezin van Paemel* (1986). This image of Flemish cinema corresponds with the 'peasants in clogs' representation of Flanders in older television fiction.[23] Flemish cinema is perceived on the one hand as being too common in its depiction of everyday life, but at the same time too artificial in its acting and language. The budget was one of the main issues mentioned when it came to discussing differences in style between Hollywood or Flemish movies, In thinking about genre, style, setting and atmosphere, young people evaluate Flemish films in accordance with what they perceive as characteristic of Hollywood films: action, suspense and an intense cinematic experience. Key concepts were 'simple' and 'uncomplicated':

> *An* [eighteen-year-old school girl]: Maybe it [*Team Spirit*] was a bit silly and a bit simple, but I liked it, because Flemish films are more simple than American films but for me it's as good as an American film . . . for instance, when it's about football, in other movies, it's with a lot of fuss, and a huge stadium and a lot of blabla, and in a Flemish movie, it's just a small football field. This doesn't mean it's worse, it's just represented in a more unsophisticated way.

In commenting on the relatively small number of Flemish films they had seen, interviewees at times dismissed the acting as unprofessional and artificial. They also noticed a difference in image and sound quality, although they were unable easily to define them. They believed that a Flemish movie could be recognised through its particular atmosphere and its image. All these perceived characteristics resulted in an extremely low horizon of expectation. One of the most frequent comments was: 'It's not bad for a Flemish movie':

> *Kristien* [eighteen-year-old school girl]: Maybe because its Flemish, you think, it won't be much of a film . . . you know they don't have the means to make mass production, but that's not necessary, but they have less means and money to make films and mostly you know the actors from television. You don't go with mega expectations to the cinema, because you know how they act and you know the stories from the newspaper, so it's no big surprise. If it's good, it can be a nice surprise, because you don't have high expectations.

Finally, Flemish film has a limited generic range. Respondents did notice the complete lack of some genres – there are, for example, no Flemish action films. Discourses of comment and criticism, therefore, are consequently based on the interaction between genre preferences and genre availability. Many interviewees discriminated between different genres of Flemish films. The most striking example was *Team Spirit* (2000), a 'teenpic' by Flemish director Jan Verheyen and the only Flemish film that gained regular mention. This movie was constructed as a media event especially marketed for adolescents, with an *avant-première* for the contestants in the *Big Brother* (2000) house on commercial television channel Kanaal 2. *Team Spirit* was regarded by many as an atypical Flemish movie; one respondent described it as 'a Flemish movie with an American script'. Flemish cinema, like Hollywood cinema, was seen as a genre in itself with formal and content conventions. But, as one interviewee declared. 'Flemish cinema is not my genre'. Another thought that a Flemish film such as *Team Spirit* and a Dutch film such as *Costa* were successful because they appeared partly American. But she predicted that 'a real Flemish film, not like the Hollywood stuff, will have less success'.

As with European cinema in general, more positive reactions existed among a minority of respondents. Some young people recognised a number of specific characteristics of Flemish film and appreciated the quality, especially in the light of the many limitations that Flemish film-makers had to face. As one interviewee put it, 'In fact [they are] pretty good, if you look at the material and the capital that is invested in it, compared to American films, they can do a whole lot with a very small amount of money.'

LANGUAGE ON SCREEN

Language is a crucial factor influencing film appreciation. The survey found a clear equation between, on the one hand, the knowledge of a language and habit of listening to it and, on the other, the choice and enjoyment of film. American English was considered by interviewees to be the film language par excellence:[24]

Interviewer: And if you compare in general: European or American film?

Dirk [nineteen-year-old school boy]: Then American is better. The language, you start understanding it automatically, American . . . if you get English lessons, then you start talking English immediately. If you're used to it from the movies and stuff . . . it's the language of film.

Francine [eighteen-year-old school girl]: The way they act and talk, I think, in American [English], they have more effect than if you would say it in French or Dutch . . . because I really think that you can express yourself better in American than in Dutch. On the one side it's not so direct, because when you say for example 'Ik zie u graag' or 'Ik hou van u' while in American you just say 'I love you' or something . . . I find that easier . . . in French, it's a beautiful language, but I really don't have that feeling with it. And German, absolutely not.

Our respondents were used to American English, which sounded 'good, spontaneous, cool', whereas French was 'too fast, ugly' and Dutch sounded 'artificial'. One family preferred to watch the German film Das Boot (1981) on DVD with English language dubbing. When people do not possess an adequate level of knowledge of a European language, they are not able to enjoy films produced in that language. Failure to comprehend the dialogue does not merely reduce enjoyment in a particular film, it also promotes a negative attitude in general towards films in that language. The preference for a particular language is linked to respondents' familiarity with it and this frequently has to do with the social environment. People who have French-speaking friends (for example, those going to school in Brussels) are open to the language and also tend themselves to reach a certain level of expertise.

Arguments relating to levels of linguistic competence can, however, hardly be used for films in Dutch, the mother tongue in Flanders. The negative attitude found here derived more from the difference between the artificial standard Dutch and spoken (Flemish) dialects, the habituation to American English as the archetypal film language and the unusual nature of Dutch in film. Dutch was considered an ugly language, not appropriate for movies. The use of standard Dutch – in contrast to the informal dialects young people use – adds to the aversion.

Gert [eighteen-year-old school boy]: Flemish in a film sounds rather strange, amateurish because it's Flemish, it sounds so un-Hollywood-like, because of the language, so yes, I prefer American films to Flemish films.

The use of the interviewees' own language in this context, therefore, somewhat surprisingly is a disadvantage.

Respondents identified a clear link between acting and language. Both are usually perceived as either 'spontaneous and realistic' or 'artificial and affected':

> *Francine* [eighteen-year-old school girl]: In Dutch, it often does not give such a real impression, it seems more real when I watch an American film.

Dubbing and subtitling are equally linked with the language issue. Respondents attach great importance to subtitles. When English-language films are subtitled, they do not normally have to read them all, but subtitled French or German films often present them with difficulties in following the story. Even when Hollywood (animated) movies are dubbed into Dutch, the interviewees seem to have preferred the original English-language version. This was also true of television. The fact that foreign channels show dubbed (Hollywood) movies was regarded as reason enough for ignoring or changing away from the channel concerned:

> *Jakobien* [eighteen-year-old school girl]: James Bond or something, dubbed in French, that really is stupid, with those French voices, it destroys everything. And English or American is easier to understand, and the voices are better compared to French, or German, that's like an American film dubbed in German, not subtitled, its not at all the same, the voices. I prefer the original American.

From the survey, therefore, it seems that American English has become young people's *lingua franca* when it comes to film consumption. As one respondent put it bluntly: 'It doesn't matter where the film comes from, as long as it's English or American spoken, I don't care.' So far as respondents are concerned, other languages do not work on the screen. It is perhaps surprising that the mere sound of the language can have such an impact on the image of a country's cinema, even from people who may have studied up to four languages in school (Dutch, French, English, German or Spanish). A small number of these people say they are more open to different kinds of European film and that the precise language is not important. They claim that what matters is the story of the film itself. In practice, however, most of them also end up watching primarily Hollywood films too (and to much lesser extent French films) because so few films in other languages are actually available.

SCREEN LANGUAGE: REEL REALISM VS REALISTIC FANTASY

As well as highlighting a clear-cut opposition in young people's approach to language in film, the survey also foregrounded contrasting discourses on realism between Hollywood and European cinema. These discourses can be broadly divided in two main clusters. On the one hand, young people talk about the close link between films and the reality of everyday life, which we might call 'thematic realism'. On the other hand, another discourse focuses on the realistic and convincing character of the filmic narration, which we might call 'filmic realism'. The young people perceived Hollywood as creating a sensational but realistic fantasy world. By contrast, Flemish film offered a small and hardly attractive window on mundane reality:

> *Dirk* [nineteen-year-old school boy]: [Flemish film] is more weeping and moaning, Flemish films are more family dramas, a real family; someone runs away or is kidnapped. In America . . . there [is] something added, that normally never is [here],

Flemish films, television, is just what really happens. In America, there is a whole lot fantasised that you think normally is not possible, they like that, you know, loads of unreality added, fantasies.

Hollywood is on the one hand more exotic, fantastic, far away and remote from everyday reality. On the other hand, the narrative and the whole film language is so convincing that the level of spectatorial identification with the fantasy is higher. Thus it becomes a realistic — that is, a believable — fantasy. The narrative realism is articulated through 'cool', 'spontaneous', 'convincing' acting, lavish and exotic settings, fast pace and uncomplicated stories. The attractive exotic aura has much to do with the characteristics of the setting and the background that situates the narration far away, but at the same time makes it more convincing. This is related to the technical possibilities — for instance, when making a thriller or horror movie with 'realistic' special effects. The thematic realism of the Flemish film is regarded as 'mundane' and 'common' while the 'suspension of disbelief' is much higher in Hollywood cinema. The ambiguous relationship of these two concepts of realism, and how young people negotiate them, is illustrated in the following quote:

> *Patricia* [eighteen-year-old school girl]: American movies are more spectacular, terrorists and bomb attacks and plane crashes, and *Team Spirit*, that's just a simple football team they interview, the content is different, the stories, it's less spectacular and more kept to everyday life.
>
> *Interviewer*: And does that make it more interesting or less interesting?
>
> *Patricia*: It's something different, it's more interesting, because you know it's a movie, yeah, it's different from daily life, but if you watch a Flemish movie, then you say this is better because you can better identify with the movie, but you also say it's maybe worse because it's just what you experience everyday.

Ien Ang's concepts of 'emotional' and 'empiricist realism' are useful in this context.[25] Flemish film, representing local Flemish reality, provides an empiricist conception of realism, in which the emphasis is on the extent to which the representation corresponds to external reality. In emotional realism, the setting of the story is disregarded, and the focus is on whether the characters, models of action and conflict situations are believable within the context of one's own life-experiences. Hollywood film appears to offer mainly realism of this kind. As Geoffrey Nowell-Smith suggests, the realism of European cinemas that reflect their national-cultural distinctiveness is a mirror of everyday reality.[26] But this is not the kind of realism young audiences require of the cinema. Hollywood fantasy turns out to be much more entertaining and relaxing than European realism. This view is confirmed by the striking contrast between Flemish cinema and television. It is perhaps surprising that some of the most convinced fans of Hollywood blockbusters are equally fond of Flemish soap opera. On the small screen, however, they see this as a totally different genre, with other conventions, where the ties with everyday Flemish reality can be appreciated:

> *Interviewer*: On television you watch foremost Flemish series, and if you choose a film, it's mainly American?
>
> *Geertrui* [eighteen-year-old school girl]: Yes, but a film is different from a series, sometimes also unrealistic things happen in a series like in film, but it's different.
>
> *Interviewer*: And different in what sense?

Geertrui: I don't know, like *Thuis* [a popular Flemish soap opera] is Flemish and those are things that could happen here too. And in America, it's different, those things usually can't happen here.

INTERNATIONAL AUDIENCES, TRANSPARENT NARRATION AND CULTURAL DOMINANCE

Since Belgium has traditionally been seen as occupying a central position in Europe in geographical terms, and since a wide range of media windows for cinema are available there, it might be thought that young people would have a truly multinational experience of film. The findings of the survey on which this chapter is based do not, however, confirm this speculation. The analysis of young people's discourses on Hollywood, European cinema and Flemish cinema exposed a series of uniform discursive constructions centred on a number of oppositions between the clearly dominant Hollywood and its European and national counterparts. Hollywood is the one and only norm for cinematic experiences in Flanders, and is also paid considerable attention on television channels directed at teenagers. Hollywood blockbusters serve as markers for a new definition of the 'classic film'. European cinema is an insignificant Other: there is a general lack of knowledge and interest in it, and the few discourses on European cinema refer to its association with school and intellectual practice. The local Flemish film is seen as the discursive opposite of Hollywood, a rather unsophisticated form of film that only marginally touches upon the popular mainstream film culture.

As Thomas Elsaesser has noted, the Hollywood blockbuster plays an important role in the everyday film culture of European young people:

> The blockbuster as an event film becomes the engine of the contemporary media culture. We read about it, hear about it, get to see exciting trailers long before the exhibition, our experience is intensified and we have something to talk about and be a part of.[27]

Blockbuster movies are viewed in the cinemas, on video and television, and they intersect with other popular cultural phenomena and merchandising products. European and local films, on the other hand, are viewed almost exclusively on television and video. Moreover, because the quality or intensity of the viewing process differs, the fact that Hollywood blockbusters are seen in cinemas while, by and large, Flemish and other European movies are not, makes American cinema seem doubly dominant: young people watch more Hollywood films in general and especially more in the cinema, where the intensity is higher.

Since (American) English is regarded as the core film language, language performs an ambiguous role as a barrier for cultural product flows. In the distribution of European television fiction, linguistic and cultural affinity continue to play a decisive role in the success and appreciation of the programmes concerned.[28] But Hollywood is able to transcend such national boundaries. Indeed, young people's discourses are strikingly similar to those of the dominant Hollywood media industries and mainstream press institutions. As Janet Wasko and Eileen Meehan conclude in their cross-cultural reception study on Disney, film experiences and discourses remain largely demarcated by the industry.[29]

In the discursive dichotomy between Hollywood and Europe, many of the responses echo established distinctions in film criticism between mainstream Hollywood cinema and the European art film as its main stylistic and narrative opponent.[30] The contemporary vision of Hollywood on the part of Flemish young people strongly parallels David Bordwell, Kristin

Thompson and Janet Staiger's definition of the classical Hollywood cinema as 'an excessively obvious cinema' marked by a set of strict codes, an 'imperceptible and unobtrusive' narration, and a categorisation into well-defined genres that helps the audience to position the story and facilitates its comprehension. For Bordwell, Thompson and Staiger, these characteristics make Hollywood cinema accessible for audiences from different cultures, which in large part explains why it developed into the international standard.[31] In a more recent study, Kristin Thompson argues that contemporary Hollywood cinema still displays the classical narrative features of narrative clarity and coherence that assure high attractiveness.[32] For Thompson, the fact that Hollywood's international market has expanded in the 1990s demonstrates that the contemporary Hollywood film is not the fragmented post-classical object described by some post-modern film theorists:

> Could 'fragmented' Hollywood films appeal to audiences even in countries such as Iran, which nominally have cultures totally opposed to US values? The fact that such films are so easily comprehensible makes them more accessible . . . The films of countries like France, or Iran are, for better or for worse, the niche-audience product.[33]

The survey also suggests that Janet Staiger was right when she said that, considered from the perspective of reception studies, notions such as national cinemas become significant interpretative strategies.[34] Defining a film by its national production circumstances offers viewers as much a strategy for comprehending the movie as, for example, genre. In the case of Flemish movies, this results in a low horizon of expectation combined with little interest in the domestic films on offer, although on television European audiences prefer domestic soap opera, indicating a difference in the modes of experience and narrative between the two media. Cultural discount provides a disadvantage for European film, but a benefit for the small, everyday narratives of soap opera and television series. As in most media research, social context, cultural capital and education also play a significant role.

As Geoffrey Nowell-Smith argues, it seems as if 'much mouthed banalities about Hollywood as dream factory are not only true but important'.[35] Hollywood is the biggest 'fabricator of fantasy' and that remains its enormous and unchallenged strength. The perception of Hollywood as the norm for international cinema is reflected in the ways in which Flemish young people receive cinema. The survey also underlines a one-sided pattern of film consumption, and demonstrates Hollywood's hegemony in framing young people's cinematic fantasies. Narrative transparency thus does not exclude notions of cultural imperialism. Ultimately, the language factor – language in film and film language – is an issue of power. While the text may be transparent, issues of power relations and unbalanced media flows remain. The extremely efficient and sustained marketing efforts of the Hollywood majors in Europe are very well reflected in the discourses of young Flemish people on what cinema means for them.

Notes

1   Philippe Meers, 'De Europese film op zoek naar een publiek' ['European Cinema in Search of an Audience'], PhD thesis, Ghent University, 2003. Few studies have been published on contemporary audiences for Hollywood cinema, mostly focusing on one film, one genre or one particular audience group. See, for example, Jaqueline Bobo, 'The Color Purple: Black Women as Cultural Readers', in E. Deidre Pribram (ed.), Female Spectators: Looking at Film and Television (London: Verso, 1988), pp. 90–109; Valerie Walkerdine, 'Video Replay: Families, Films and Fantasy', in J. Burgin and C. Kaplan (eds), Formations of Fantasy (London: Methuen, 1986), pp. 167–99; Martin Barker and

Kate Brooks, *Knowing Audiences: Judge Dredd, its Friends, Fans and Foes* (Luton: John Libbey, 1998); Martin Barker, Jane Arthurs and Ramaswami Harindranath, *The Crash Controversy: Censorship Campaigns and Film Reception* (London: Wallflower Press, 2001); Annette Hill, *Shocking Entertainment: Viewer Response to Violent Movies* (Luton: John Libbey, 1997); Thomas Austin, *Hollywood, Hype and Audiences* (Manchester: Manchester University Press, 2002); Göran Bolin, 'Film Swapping in the Public Sphere: Youth Audiences and Alternative Cultural Publicities', *Javnost-The Public*, vol. 7, no. 2 (2000), pp. 57–73; Rajinder Kumar Dudrah, 'Vilayati Bollywood: Popular Hindi Cinema-going and Diasporic South Asian Identity in Birmingham', *Javnost-The Public*, vol. 9 (2002), pp. 19–36.

2   Thomas Elsaesser, 'Putting on a Show. The European Art Movie', *Sight and Sound*, vol. 4, no. 4 (1994), pp. 22–7.

3   Mark Jancovich, Lucy Faire with Sarah Stubbings, in their study of a century of film consumption in Nottingham, deliberately choose the term 'film consumption' because it is larger than just cinema-going, and includes other forms of distribution and exhibition: television (broadcast, satellite, cable), video rental and purchase, internet etc. It also is broader than the mere act of film watching: 'film consumption is about far more than simply the viewing of films'. *The Place of the Audience: Cultural Geographies of Film Consumption* (London: BFI, 2003), pp. 4–5. In *Hollywood, Hype and Audiences* (p. 8 n. 3), Austin also explicitly integrates films on video and television as part of popular film culture.

4   For a recent overview of the debate on Hollywood, see Toby Miller, Nitin Govil, John McMurria and Richard Maxwell, *Global Hollywood* (London: BFI, 2001); Scott Robert Olson, *Hollywood Planet: Global Media and the Competitive Advantage of Narrative Transparency* (Mahwah, NJ: Lawrence Erlbaum, 1999).

5   Ien Ang, *Watching 'Dallas': Soap Opera and the Melodramatic Imagination* (London: Methuen, 1985); Tamar Liebes and Elihu Katz, *The Export of Meaning: Cross-Cultural Readings of Dallas* (Cambridge: Polity, 1995); Daniël Biltereyst, 'Qualitative Audience Research and Transnational Media Effects. A New Paradigm?', *European Journal of Communication*, vol. 10, no. 2 (1995), pp. 245–70. One of the rare examples of cross-cultural research into film reception is Janet Wasko, Mark Phillips and Eileen R. Meehan (eds), *Dazzled by Disney: The Global Disney Audiences Project* (London and New York: Leicester University Press, 2001) on the reception of Disney in several countries.

6   Andrew Higson, 'The Concept of National Cinema', *Screen*, vol. 30, no. 4 (1989), pp. 36–46.

7   Els De Bens and Hedwig De Smaele, 'The Inflow of American Television on European Broadcasting Channels Revisited', *European Journal of Communication*, vol. 16, no. 1 (2001), pp. 51–76.

8   Pertti Alasuutari, 'Introduction: Three Phases of Reception Studies', in Alasuutari (ed.), *Rethinking the Media Audience: The New Agenda* (London: Sage, 1999), p. 6.

9   David Buckingham, 'Introduction', in Buckingham (ed.), *Reading Audiences: Young People and the Media* (Manchester: Manchester University Press), p. 12.

10   A similar approach is adopted to that of Charles Acland in considering everyday life outside the home context, focusing on the 'everyday' consumption of film in all its contexts. Charles Acland, 'Cinemagoing and the Rise of the Megaplex', *Television and New Media*, vol. I, no. 4 (2000), pp. 375–402.

11   We use the concept of 'audience', fully aware that, as Ien Ang has shown in *Desperately Seeking the Audience* (London: Routledge, 1991), the audience is as much a discursive as a social phenomenon, since individuals are constructed as audience members through industry attempts at marketing research, advertising, promotion, the décor of movie theatres, etc.

12   The respondents were selected out of a larger representative survey sample of young people. In a first quantitative survey (spring 2000), 1,088 secondary school students (aged sixteen to eighteen) in thirty-nine schools across Flanders and Brussels filled in a sixteen-page questionnaire on their media use, their leisure activities, their opinions on and experiences of film in different consumption contexts. The names of the twenty-eight respondents have been changed, due to the guarantee of anonymity offered respondents. The seventeen girls and eleven boys come from all five provinces of Flanders. They come from working-class (sixteen) and higher and lower middle-class (eleven) backgrounds. They live in villages or small towns (fifteen), middle-range towns (eleven) or large cities (two). They are all white. Questions of sexual orientation were not addressed. Their mother tongue is Dutch (with a Flemish accent). Only two are bilingual and speak French at home. All but one live at home with their parent(s).

13   Thomas Lindlof, *Qualitative Communication Research Methods* (Thousand Oaks and London: Sage), p. 165.

14   Austin, *Hollywood, Hype and Audiences*, p. 68.

15   Interviews were transcribed and analysed with NUD*IST, a software program for qualitative analysis, allowing systematic and precise selection and coding of statements.

16   Barker and Brooks, *Knowing Audiences*, p. 77.

17   Cf. Hill, *Shocking Entertainment*, p. 20.

18   Uma Dinsmore-Tuli, 'The Pleasures of "Home Cinema", or Watching Movies on Telly: An Audience Study of Cinephiliac VCR-use', *Screen*, vol. 41, no. 3 (2000), pp. 315–27.

19   Tom Stempel, *American Audiences on Movies and Moviegoing* (Lexington: University Press of Kentucky, 2001), p. 141.

20   This finding corresponds with the distinction made by students between films 'that can be analysed' and films 'for mere entertainment' based on the intentions of the producer in Naomi Rockler, 'Messages between the Lions: The Dominance of the Transmission Paradigm in Student Interpretations of *The Lion King*', *Journal of Communication Inquiry*, vol. 25, no.1 (2001), pp. 6–21.

21   In the survey conducted during the previous year, *La vita é bella* was an important factor in boosting the knowledge and appreciation of Italian film.

22   In interviews with parents, nostalgia for old popular European movies and stars tends to emerge: French action and thriller heroes such as Alain Delon and Jean-Paul Belmondo, comedy stars such as Fernandel and Louis de Funès.

23   Alexander Dhoesl, 'Peasants in Clogs: Imagining Flanders in Television Fiction', *Studies in Popular Culture*, vol. 23, no. 3 (2001), pp. 11–24.

24   Young audiences in Flanders, of course, are accustomed to seeing and hearing television fiction and films with subtitles.

25   Ang, *Watching 'Dallas'*.

26   Geoffrey Nowell Smith, 'Introduction', in Nowell-Smith and Steve Ricci (eds), *Hollywood and Europe: Economics, Culture and National Identity 1945–95* (London: BFI, 1998), pp. 1–18.

27   Thomas Elsaesser, 'De blockbuster als motor van de hedendaagse mediacultuur', in Elsaesser with Pepita Hesselberth (eds.), *Hollywood op straat: Film en Televisic in de hedendaagse mediacultuur* (Amsterdam: Vossiuspers AUP) pp. 27–44.

28   Daniël Biltereyst, 'Language and Culture as Ultimate Barriers? An Analysis of the Circulation, Consumption and Popularity of Fiction in Small European Countries', *European Journal of Communication*, vol. 7 (1992), pp. 517 40; De Bens and De Smaele 'The Inflow of American Television'.

29   Janet Wasko and Eileen R. Meehan, 'Dazzled by Disney? Ambiguity in Ubiquity', in *Dazzled by Disney*, pp. 329–43.

30   Cf. Bordwell, *Narration* and Wendy Everett, 'Introduction: European Film and the Quest for Identity', in Everett (ed.), *European Identity in Cinema* (Exeter: Intellect, 1996), pp. 7–12.

31   David Bordwell, Kristin Thompson and Janet Staiger. *The Classical Hollywood Cinema: Film Style and Mode of Production to 1960* (London: Routledge, 1985), p. 370; Bordwell, *Narration*, p. 157.

32   Kristin Thompson, *Storytelling in the New Hollywood: Understanding Classical Hollywood Narrative* (Cambridge, MA: Harvard University Press, 1999), p. 10 *et. seq.*

33   Thompson, *Storytelling in the New Hollywood*, p. 347.

34   Janet Staiger, *Interpreting Films: Studies in the Historical Reception of American Cinema* (Princeton: Princeton University Press, 1992), p. 95.

35   Nowell-Smith, 'Introduction', pp. 12–13.

Chapter 31

Francis L. F. Lee

CULTURAL DISCOUNT AND CROSS-CULTURE PREDICTABILITY: EXAMINING THE BOX OFFICE PERFORMANCE OF AMERICAN MOVIES IN HONG KONG (2006)

A MERICAN EXPORTS IN THE FORM OF FILM and tape rentals have increased substantially in the past 20 years (Scott, 2002, p. 970). Writing at the turn of the 20th century, Miller, Govil, McMurria, and Maxwell (2001, p. 3) noted that Hollywood owned between 40% and 90% of the movies shown in most parts of the world. More recently, Scott (2004) reported that the box office share of American films in year 2002 was 58.3% in France, 64.8% in Japan, and as high as 87.5% in Australia.

These figures show, on one hand, the general dominance of Hollywood movies around the world. But on the other hand, the figures also point to cross-country variations in the degree of Hollywood domination. Empirical studies have shown that domestically produced movies account for larger shares of total box office in countries with higher levels of GDP, consumer spending on movies, and investment in movies (Jayakar & Waterman, 2000; S. W. Lee, 2002; B. K. Lee & Bae, 2004; Oh, 2001). With the growth of movie industries in different parts of the world and the emergence of regional centers of media production, the dominance of Hollywood is by no means unchallenged.

For individual Hollywood movies, success outside America is even less certain. Globalization has not produced a homogeneous global culture (Tomlinson, 2001), and media studies have shown that media products moving across cultural boundaries are often subject to local reception processes (Ang, 1985; Liebes & Katz, 1986). *Local reception,* broadly understood as the ways in which meanings and values associated with media products are created within each local context, usually has been the subject of qualitative studies. But this article ties local reception to the concerns of media economics and examines two of its quantitative manifestations. First, a media product may be valued to a lesser extent by foreign audiences that lack the cultural background and knowledge needed for full appreciation of the product. This has long been discussed by media economists, who developed the concept of *cultural discount* (Hoskins & Mirus, 1988). Second, differences in aesthetic tastes, social and cultural values, language, and other factors may lead to different judgments of whether certain media products are better than others. The values of media products in a foreign market are not completely predictable by their performance in their original market. This study examines this concern with the concept of cross-culture predictability.

Both phenomena have seldom been the focus of empirical research, although cultural discount has featured in much theoretical discussions. This study provides an empirical analysis of the two phenomena by using box office data. Do different types of movies suffer from different degrees of cultural discount? Is lack of cross-culture predictability more serious among some types of movies than others? Answering these questions can further our understanding of the two concepts, which, in turn, would aid our understanding of how Hollywood movies (and media products in general) travel across cultures.

The following sections discuss the key concepts in the present study and explain how they can be examined with box office data. Contextual background and construction of the data set are then introduced. This is followed by the presentation of the analysis. The implications of the results are discussed at the end.

LOCAL RECEPTION, CULTURAL DISCOUNT, AND CROSS-CULTURE PREDICTABILITY

Audience reception studies in the past 25 years have established that meanings are created through the interaction between audiences and texts within contexts, with audiences bringing in their experiences and knowledge in the act of interpretation (Ang, 1985; Liebes & Katz, 1986; Morley, 1980; Radway, 1991). As a consequence, people from different social and cultural groups may come up with different understandings of the same media product. In the case of foreign media consumption, the result is local reception—the meanings of media products are produced within specific local contexts.

Media economists also have had a strong interest in how culture affects the appreciation of media products, although the main focus is more about economic values than about cultural meanings. More specifically, in an attempt to explain the dominance of American media products in the world market, Hoskins and Mirus (1988) coined the term *cultural discount* to refer to the phenomenon that a cultural product rooted in one culture "will have a diminished appeal elsewhere as viewers find it difficult to identify with the style, values, beliefs, institutions, and behavioral patterns of the material in question" (p. 500). Wildman (1994) also stated that "other things [being] equal, [viewers] would prefer films and programs produced in their native language. While foreign language productions can be subtitled or dubbed, something is always lost in translation" (p. 123). Although Wildman (1994, 1995) focused on language rather than on culture as the factor defining the boundaries of media markets, the idea of culture–language affecting audience evaluation is basically the same.

On the surface, the existence of a cultural discount means that, when an American cultural product is pitted against a local product with the same quality and sold at the same price, local people would opt for the latter. But as Hoskins and Mirus (1988) explicated, cultural discount actually helps American media products to dominate the world market. Assuming that the cultural discount rate is the same for media products flowing in either direction between two markets, market size would combine with the cultural discount rate to generate larger optimal production budgets for producers in the larger market (also see Hoskins & McFayden, 1991; Hoskins, Finn, & McFayden, 1997; Papandrea, 1998). It thus makes it very difficult for producers in the smaller market to generate products that can match their competitors in terms of both quality and price. This argument has been central to a microeconomic explanation of one-way media flow between media markets, regardless of whether the markets are regionally, nationally, culturally, or linguistically defined (Wildman & Siwek, 1988). Applying the argument to international media flows, the large U.S. domestic market size thus becomes crucial in explaining the domination of U.S. media.

However, no matter what advantages cultural discount gives to specific countries at the structural level, producers from any country should still want to reduce the cultural discount rate that their individual products would suffer from. Generally speaking, cultural discount could be reduced if a product were made less culturally specific. For example, take Hollywood movies. Non-Americans may not possess the knowledge about American history required to understand the political meanings encoded in *Forrest Gump*. But more people around the world can readily empathize with the romance in *Titanic* or enjoy the spectacle of *Jurassic Park*. In fact, researchers examining the strategies of American media corporations have pointed to the more or less conscious attempt to *universalize* the content of their products (e.g., J. M. Chan, 2002). The theory of "narrative transparency" also posits that American popular culture is highly popular around the world because of the universal stories they tell (Olson, 1999).[1] Although universalization may adversely affect the performance of the product domestically (Hoskins & McFayden, 1993), to the extent that foreign markets continue to rise in importance (Miller et al., 2001; Scott, 2004), the advantage the product gets from reducing cultural discount may turn out to outweigh the loss in the domestic market.

In addition to reducing cultural discount, universalization could also help the media product to counter the problem of lack of cross-culture predictability. *Cross-culture predictability* refers to the extent to which the performance of media products in a culture can be predicted by the performance of the same products in another culture. Lack of predictability is manifested in the fact that the media products most popular in one country are not necessarily the most popular in another country. Domestic success does not guarantee international success, or at least not to the same extent. For example, the Hollywood thriller *Speed* was the most popular U.S. motion picture in Hong Kong in 1994, but it ranked only eighth in the U.S. box office in the same year. *Forrest Gump*, which topped the U.S. box office in that year, ranked only third among U.S. productions in Hong Kong in the same year. The domestic success of a media product is a useful predictor of its international success only to a certain extent. And we may suggest that lack of predictability is likely to be more serious when cultural differences between two markets increase.

One way to understand lack of cross-culture predictability is to posit that different movies are subject to higher or lower levels of cultural discount because of their different degree of cultural specificity. For example, we may argue that *Forrest Gump* did not perform as well as *Speed* in Hong Kong because the former was discounted to a larger extent than the latter. However, though the metaphor of discount focuses exclusively on loss of values, lack of predictability can also be the result of some media products gaining added value as they travel across cultural boundaries. This possibility is becoming more important as media productions themselves have become more and more "international" in recent years. That is, media products are nowadays more and more likely to incorporate elements of more than one culture and inputs from more than one country. Disney's *Mulan*, John Woo's *Face Off*, or Chow Yun-fat's *Anna and the King* are not likely to merely suffer from discount as they travel from the U.S. to Hong Kong. Therefore, although cultural discount and cross-culture predictability are closely connected, it is useful to treat the two as distinct. Both are premised upon the existence of cultural differences and are likely to be reduced by universalization of media products. But cultural discount refers to loss of values rather than loss of predictability of values, and the two phenomena have their own empirical manifestations.

RESEARCH APPROACH AND QUESTIONS

This study uses box office data to empirically examine the phenomena of cultural discount and cross-culture performance predictability for Hollywood movies as they travel to a specific location, namely, Hong Kong. In fact, there has been a growing body of literature in the past decade examining the box office performance of movies. One stream of empirical research conceptualizes box office as the output generated by a combination of inputs, including, among others, star actors and directors, production budgets, and other qualities of the content (Albert, 1998; Bagella & Becchetti, 1999; De Vany & Walls, 1999; Sawhney & Eliashberg, 1996; Simonton, 2005). Others have analyzed the impact of advertising expenditures (Zufryden, 1996), Web promotion (Zufryden, 2000), critics' reviews (Basuroy, Chatterjee, & Ravid, 2003; Eliashberg & Shugan, 1997; Reinstein & Snyder, 2005), categorization of the movie (Zuckerman & Kim, 2003), and movie awards (Nelson, Donihue, Waldman, & Wheaton, 2001).

This study, however, differs from most other studies in the above literature in two ways. First, past studies have examined mainly the box office performance of movies in their domestic markets. There have been only a few studies addressing box office performance of movies in foreign markets (e.g., Hennig-Thurau, Walsh, & Bode, 2004). Second, the present study is not interested primarily in the modeling of box office performance or examining the effect of marketing or production factors. Rather, the primary aim is to use box office data to shed light on the phenomena of cultural discount and cross-culture predictability.

But how can we study cultural discount and cross-culture predictability with box office data? Cultural discount has seldom been directly examined with empirical data. In the works by Hoskins and his colleagues (Hoskins, Finn, & McFayden, 1997; Hoskins & McFayden, 1993; Hoskins & Mirus, 1988), cultural discount is used mainly as a metaphor that provides a plausible and coherent theoretical interpretation of phenomena in the international trade in media products. The goal was not to calculate the cultural discount rate. Certainly, it is very difficult, if not impossible, to specify the exact cultural discount rate from empirical data. When an American movie records a box office of US$15 million in the domestic market and only US$1.5 million in another country, the difference is clearly the result of many factors, such as differences in population size, differences in ticket prices, differing levels of consumer spending on movies, other general economic factors, and so on. Hence a simple box office ratio cannot represent the cultural discount. Nevertheless, when we focus on a single receiving country, what box office ratios could allow us to examine is "relative cultural discount," that is, whether certain types of movies suffer from a higher or lower discount relative to other types of movies when they travel to a specific place.

Similarly, cross-culture predictability has seldom been studied empirically, although in this case there is an obvious indicator available: the correlation between the box office figures of a set of movies in two different countries. It can be expected that the correlation would be positive, and a perfect correlation would mean that the relative box office performances of the movies in one country are completely predictable by their relative box office figures in the other country. The weaker the correlation, the weaker is the predictability of box office performance.

Again, it may be difficult or even misleading to interpret the meanings of one single correlation coefficient. Assume that we have found the correlation between the box office figures of a set of American movies in the United States and in another country to be .70, it would still be difficult for us to say whether it is high or low. But similar to the case of cultural discount, the coefficient provides a useful indicator for the purpose of comparison. What we can study is the relative degree of predictability over time or relative lack of predictability across different types of movies.

Given the above arguments, the present study examines whether certain types of Hollywood movies exhibit a higher degree of cultural discount and less cross-culture predictability than other types of movies when they are shown in Hong Kong. For movie types, this study focuses on the notion of genres, which are often examined as independent variables in research on box office data (e.g., Bagella & Becchetti, 1999; Sawhney & Eliashberg, 1996). More important, genres can be meaningfully discussed in relation to cultural differences. For example, it is widely agreed that humor is culturally specific (Palmer, 1995). Hence comedies are likely to suffer more from cultural discount than are movies of other genres. Action movies, on the contrary, are arguably less culturally specific. Hence they should be subject to cultural discount to a lesser degree.

However, this study does not set up specific hypotheses for individual genres. The large number of movie genres in the analysis makes such an endeavor inefficient. In addition, unlike comedies or action movies, for many movie genres there is no common agreement on whether they are culturally specific. For example, in discussing the case of American movies in Germany, Hennig-Thurau et al. (2004) argued that thrillers, at an abstract level, involve the universal formula of a confrontation between good and evil. But they also pointed out that, at a more concrete level, Hollywood thrillers often require the audience to use knowledge related to the American context. Given the existence of conflicting arguments and the lack of prior research on the same topic through the use of the same method, the present study adopts a more exploratory approach. The following two research questions are examined:

Q1: Do movies of certain genres exhibit a higher degree of cultural discount than movies of other genres? If yes, which genres suffer more from the problem of cultural discount?

Q2: Do movies of certain genres exhibit less cross-culture predictability than movies of other genres? If yes, which genres suffer more from lack of predictability? Are they the same genres that suffer more from the problem of cultural discount?

BACKGROUND AND METHOD

Because this study examines box office data in Hong Kong, some discussions about the movie industry and market in the city help contextualize the analysis. Hong Kong has long been an important regional center for movie production. Local Cantonese-based movies flourished particularly in the early 1980s in association with the "new wave cinema" in Hong Kong (Bordwell, 2000). However, Hong Kong was (and still is) only a small city with a small domestic market. Linguistically, the local dialect Cantonese is not widely used outside the Southern part of China, thus the Cantonese movie market is also not huge. Meanwhile, the role of the government in assisting the movie industry has been minimal (C. W. Chan, 2000, p. 9). The success of Hong Kong movies, therefore, has to be understood in terms of Hong Kong's role as a major movie exporter in Asia in the past. In the 1980s and early 1990s, because of the underdevelopment of the national movie industries in East and Southeast Asian countries, Hong Kong movies enjoyed huge popularity in the region (C. W. Chan, 2000, pp. 82–83).

Nevertheless, the movie industry in Hong Kong began to face a crisis in the late 1990s. The rise of movie industries in mainland China, Korea, and other Asian countries provided strong competition for Hong Kong movie producers. As the infrastructure for movie making has continued to improve in other Asian countries, the small domestic market size in Hong

Kong means that the movie industry in the city is distinctly disadvantaged (Hoskins & Mirus, 1988; Wildman & Siwek, 1988). As a result, the number of locally produced movies declined. According to the record maintained by the Hong Kong Film Archive, there were 134 locally produced movies shown in Hong Kong in 1991. The number dropped to 77 by 2003.[2] At the same time, though the total box office for local movies reached the historical high of about HK$1.2 billion in 1992, the figure declined to HK$345 million by 1999 (C. W. Chan, 2000, p. 7). This situation has led to discussions about the "death" of the Hong Kong movie industry in the local media.

Despite the decline, the presence of Hollywood movies cannot be regarded as having had a huge detrimental effect on the movie industry in Hong Kong. In fact, C. W. Chan (2000), who was writing in the late 1990s, still proclaimed that "Hollywood movies have never overtaken Hong Kong movies." Certainly, the continual decline of the local movie industry has probably made Chan's statement obsolete. Table 31.1 shows the number of Hollywood movies in the yearly Hong Kong box office top 10 and top 100 lists from 1989 to 2004. Hollywood movies indeed found it difficult to enter such lists in the late 1980s and early 1990s. But the number of Hollywood movies in the lists grew since then. By the beginning of the 21st century, Hollywood movies have constantly occupied 40% or more of the berths in the top 10 and top 100 lists.

Nevertheless, given the historical development of the Hong Kong movie industry, it is arguable that the seeming growth in Hollywood movies' popularity in Hong Kong as shown in Table 31.1 is primarily the effect rather than the cause of the decline of local movies—as there were fewer and fewer locally produced popular movies, more and more Hollywood movies came to occupy the berths in the top 10 and top 100 lists. Also, Hollywood movies are by no means dominating the Hong Kong market to an overwhelming extent. In recent years, much of the Hong Kong audience also turned to productions from other Asian countries, especially South Korea and Japan.

Table 31.1 Number of U.S. movies in top box office lists in Hong Kong

Year	T10	T100	Rank and Title of the Most Popular U.S. Movie	Average Box Office of U.S. Movies in the Top 100 List (in Hong Kong Dollars)
1989	1	14	5 (Indiana Jones and the Last Crusade)	9,080,807.9
1990	2	19	3 (Ghost)	10,951,459.7
1991	1	18	9 (Terminator 2)	7,287,718.3
1992	0	14	13 (Basic Instinct)	9,199,477.4
1993	1	21	1 (Jurassic Park)	12,707,119.6
1994	3	20	2 (Speed)	14,201,842.8
1995	3	35	5 (Die Hard With a Vengeance)	11,930,556.3
1996	5	48	2 (Independence Day)	9,769,055.2
1997	5	45	1 (Titanic)	12,800,936.2
1998	6	54	3 (Tomorrow Never Dies)	8,976,220.3
1999	3	46	3 (The Mummy)	8,053,305.3
2000	4	52	1 (Mission Impossible 2)	9,150,169.8
2001	4	51	2 (Harry Potter and the Sorcerer's Stone)	8,975,886.3
2002	6	46	2 (Harry Potter and the Chambers of Secrets)	8,354,839.5
2003	4	51	1 (Lord of the Rings)	7,319,739.0
2004	4	46	2 (The Day After Tomorrow)	8,167,965.6

Against this background, the following analysis examines the popularity of different types of Hollywood movies in Hong Kong, with cultural discount and cross-culture predictability as the conceptual foci. Various sources of information were used to construct a data set. Box office figures of American movies in Hong Kong were derived from the yearly box office top 100 list maintained by the Hong Kong Motion Picture Industry Association. The lists for year 1989 to 2004, originally available on the Web,[3] include the following information: title of the movie, country of origin, opening and closing dates of showing, total box office, and rating of the movie. The following variables were constructed on the basis of this information: (a) total box office in Hong Kong, (b) year of showing in Hong Kong, (c) total length of showing in cinema (in number of weeks), (d) a dummy variable representing movies rated as Category I, (e) a dummy representing movies rated as Category III,[4] (f) a dummy representing whether the movie was shown in cinema during Christmas holidays, and (g) a dummy representing whether the movie was shown in cinema during Lunar New Year holidays.

American box office figures for the movies were derived from data available at www.boxofficemojo.com, a Web site that maintains box office records of movies from the Motion Picture Association of America. Furthermore, following the suggestion by Hennig-Thurau et al. (2004), nominal variables for the genres of individual movies were derived from the Web site http://www.imdb.com. A research assistant went through the database to look for movie genres that appear relatively frequently (such that enough variance would exist for meaningful statistical analyses). In the end, nine movie genres were recorded: comedy, action, thriller, romance, science fiction, adventure, family, drama, and horror. Because one movie can belong to more than one genre, there are nine dummy variables for the nine genres respectively.

The data set, hence, contains basic information about all movies which originated in the United States and made the yearly top 100 list in Hong Kong. This research strategy may lead to underestimation of cultural discounts, as it is possible that the "flops" are excluded from the data set. But it should be noted that the top 100 lists in Hong Kong in the early 1990s usually began with movies with about or more than HK$40 million of box office receipts and ended with movies with only about HK$3 to 4 million. Into the 2000s, the few most popular movies could still earn more than HK$40 million, but the 100th movie on the list typically had box office receipts of below HK$2 million. Movies successful in the United States that performed this poorly in Hong Kong would constitute rare, extreme cases. Therefore, the bias should not be too substantial (and, in the end, the focus of the analysis is on a relative cultural discount rather than on a specific cultural discount).

There are a total of 580 movies from the 16-year period. It has already been pointed out that the number of U.S. movies entering the top 100 list in Hong Kong has increased over the years. However, the last column of Table 31.1 shows that the average box office of the U.S. movies in the list has actually shown signs of decline. The average box office of the 20 U.S. movies entering the list in 1994 was HK$14 million. The figure dropped to only HK$7.3 million in 2003.

ANALYSIS AND RESULTS

Relative cultural discount

Our first research question concerns the concept of cultural discount, or more precisely, relative cultural discount as discerned through box office figures. The interest is in whether movies of certain genres suffer a larger cultural discount when compared with movies of other genres. To tackle the research question, box office ratio was calculated by dividing the box office of a movie in the United States by the box office in Hong Kong. A larger box office ratio is an indication of a higher relative cultural discount.

Because one movie can belong to more than one genre, direct comparisons between movies of different genres are inappropriate. Instead, independent sample t tests were conducted to determine whether movies of a genre have an average box office ratio that is higher or lower than the ratio for movies not belonging to the genre.

Table 31.2 summarizes the results of such an analysis. Significant differences exist in four of the nine cases. As can be expected from the cultural specificity of humor (Palmer, 1995), the average box office ratio of comedies is significantly higher than that of non-comedies. Comedies are discounted to a larger extent than other types of movies.

Three genres demonstrate the opposite relationship with box office ratios. The average ratios for action movies, thrillers, and science fiction movies are significantly smaller than non-action, non-thrillers, and non-science fiction movies, respectively. This result is also consistent with the usual perception that such movies are relatively less culturally specific: The popularity of kung fu stars and the addition of kung fu elements in recent American productions is testimony to the universality of action; thrillers, as pointed out earlier, involve the universal formula of good versus evil at the abstract level; science fiction movies, on the other hand, are less rooted in specific cultural and historical traditions, as the idea of science and the scientific imagination are arguably universal in the modern world.

Table 31.2, of course, shows only the bivariate relationships between box office ratio and movie genres, but the movie genres themselves are not independent from each other. For example, 66% of the 97 science fiction movies (i.e., 64 of them) also belong to the genre of action, but only 36.4% of the 484 non-science fiction movies belong to the category of action. Therefore, multivariate analysis is needed to discern whether the significant relationships in Table 31.2 would survive after controlling for other genres.

Multiple regression analysis is used for this purpose. Instead of box office ratio, box office in Hong Kong is used as the dependent variable, with box office in the United States included as an independent variable. A significant coefficient for a genre variable, in this case, would mean that movies of the genre are generally more or less popular in Hong Kong after controlling for box office figures in the United States. This would serve the same purpose for

Table 31.2 Box office ratios for movies of different genres

Genre	Belong to the Genre	Not Belong to the Genre	t
Comedy (N = 204)	16.62	12.19	−4.01*
Action (N = 239)	11.78	15.12	3.39*
Thriller (N = 252)	11.90	15.16	3.42*
Romance (N = 99)	14.16	13.66	−0.39
Science fiction (N = 97)	9.54	14.59	6.10*
Adventure (N = 126)	13.22	13.89	0.63
Family (N = 69)	14.47	13.65	−0.54
Drama (N = 249)	13.18	14.17	1.01
Horror (N = 85)	11.79	14.08	1.66

Note. Entries are box office ratio: U.S. box office/Hong Kong box office. N refers to number of movies belonging to that genre.

* $p < .001$.

tackling Research Question 1. And in the context of multiple regression analysis, the use of Hong Kong box office as the dependent variable has the advantage that we can see the relationships between box office of U.S. movies in Hong Kong and other variables. The regression model also became the basis for the analysis addressing the second research question reported below.

In addition to genres and the U.S. box office, the year a movie is shown in Hong Kong and the two dummy variables for ratings were also included in the first regression model.[5] A second regression model was constructed by further including three time-related variables: number of weeks that a movie was shown in the cinema and the two dummy variables about whether the movies were being shown during the two major holiday periods in Hong Kong. These time-related variables were added only in the second model because not only do they influence box office figures but also they are themselves influenced by actual and/or expected box office. Whether a movie can survive in the cinema for a long period of time is dependent upon its initial box office performance (Walls, 1998), and it has been the usual practice for movie distributors in Hong Kong to reserve the major holiday periods for movies—both local and foreign—that are expected to be highly popular. To fully map the dynamics of a film's box office performance over time would require much more sophisticated analytical techniques and research design. In fact, in econometric studies, the use of three-stage least square regression is often preferred because of methodological concerns with the presence of endogenous variables (e.g., Elberse & Eliashberg, 2003). The present study, however, reports only ordinary least square regression because of a lack of suitable instrumental variables in the data set. The use of ordinary least square regression should be sufficient here because of two reasons. First, at least for the first regression model, endogeneity is not a huge problem. Second, the concern of the present study is not the precise modeling of box office but rather the examination of two specific conceptual phenomena. Small biases in estimation should not render the substantive conclusions and arguments invalid.[6]

Table 31.3 presents the results of the regression analysis. As already suggested by Table 31.1, the box office for Hollywood movies in Hong Kong registered a significant decline from 1989 to 2004. Movies that belong to Category I in the rating system (i.e., movies for which no parental guidance is needed) have lower box office figures after controlling for genre and the U.S. box office. More important, U.S. comedies are less popular in Hong Kong (again after controlling for genre); that is, the high relative cultural discount for comedies survives after controlling for films that combine comedy with other genres. Similarly, the low relative cultural discount for action and science fiction also persists. However, there is no significant relationship between thriller and box office in Table 31.3. It shows that the result regarding thriller in Table 31.2 is apparently a by-product of the overlapping between the genres of action and thriller.[7] Moreover, after controlling for ratings and combinations with other genres, "family" movies actually have higher box office figures in Hong Kong. It shows a low relative cultural discount in Hong Kong for U.S. movies targeted at family and children.

The results do not alter substantively when the three time-related factors are added. Not surprisingly, all three variables are significantly related to box office in Hong Kong. It is also notable that adding the three time-related factors substantially undermines the strength of the association between Hong Kong box office and U.S. box office. This is actually understandable. U.S. box office is probably one of the major indicators movie distributors use to determine how long a movie should be put on show and whether a movie should be placed in the holiday time periods. In this sense, the time-related factors are mediating the relationship between U.S. box office and Hong Kong box office.[8]

Table 31.3 Regression analysis of box office in Hong Kong

	Dependent Variable: Hong Kong Box Office (in HK$1,000)			
	Model 1		Time-Related Factors Added	
Variable	Unstandardized	Standandized	Unstandardized	Standandized
Constant	817589.5***		362229.7**	
U.S. box office	0.085***	.64	0.057***	.43
Year	−401.0***	−.17	−184.0**	−.08
Category I	−2715.3*	−.10	−1898.4	−.07
Category III	−520.2	.01	−1096.3	−.02
Comedy	−2166.4**	−.11	−1487.6*	−.07
Action	1797.1*	.09	2898.0***	.15
Thriller	326.5	.02	675.5	.03
Romance	1147.4	.04	107.3	.00
Sci-fi	2020.7*	.08	1926.9**	.07
Adventure	1371.8	.06	616.8	.03
Family	3046.1*	.10	2480.3*	.08
Drama	502.5	.03	−1045.5	−.05
Horror	759.8	.03	879.8	.03
No. of weeks	—	—	1352.7***	.42
Christmas	—	—	2021.4*	.06
New Year	—	—	3031.3**	.10

Note. $N = 580$. Model 1 Adjusted $R^2 = 45.3\%$***; Model 2 Adjusted $R^2 = 60.6\%$***. U.S. box office is in U.S.$1,000.

* $p < .05$. ** $p < .01$. *** $p < .001$.

Relative cross-culture predictability

The second research question deals with the relative degree of cross-culture performance predictability as manifested in the correlation between U.S. box office and Hong Kong box office. A weaker correlation is an indication of lower predictability. The analysis begins again at the bivariate level. As Table 31.4 shows, the U.S.–Hong Kong box office correlation is .56 for comedies, whereas for non-comedies the coefficient is .67. These two correlation coefficients differ from each other significantly at $p < .05$ (following Fisher's z transformation, see Cohen & Cohen, 1983, pp. 53–55). Hence we can argue that comedies are suffering from a relative lack of predictability. Combined with the findings from the previous section, the box office performance of U.S. comedies in Hong Kong has demonstrated the cultural specificity of humor through both relative cultural discount and relative cross-culture predictability.

Science fiction movies demonstrate the opposite pattern. Besides having a low degree of relative cultural discount, science fiction movies also have a higher degree of cross-culture predictability at the box office (science fiction: $r = .73$; non-science fiction: $r = .60$). However, although action movies were shown to exhibit a lower degree of cultural discount in the previous section, Table 31.4 shows that the box office correlation for action and non-action movies is basically the same. Instead, romance and horror movies exhibit relatively strong box office correlations. These latter findings show that cultural discount and lack of

Table 31.4 Relation between U.S. and Hong Kong box office for movies of different genres

Genre	Belong to the Genre	Not Belong to the Genre	z
Comedy (N = 204)	.56***	.67***	−2.03*
Action (N = 239)	.61***	.66***	−0.99
Thriller (N = 252)	.60***	.65***	−0.98
Romance (N = 99)	.80***	.59***	3.81***
Science fiction (N = 97)	.73***	.60***	2.09*
Adventure (N = 126)	.64***	.60***	0.64
Family (N = 69)	.67***	.63***	0.54
Drama (N = 249)	.62***	.64***	−0.39
Horror (N = 85)	.77***	.61***	2.65**

Note. Entries are Pearson correlation coefficients. The z score for testing the difference between two correlation coefficients was calculated using Fisher's z transformation procedure (see Cohen & Cohen, 1983, pp. 53–55). N refers to number of movies belonging to that genre.

* p < .05. **p < .01. ***p < .001.

cross-culture predictability are indeed empirically distinct. Movie genres that show higher or lower degrees of cultural discount do not necessarily show higher or lower levels of cross-culture predictability.

Multivariate analysis is conducted to further examine how robust the findings in Table 31.4 are. In the context of multiple regression, the interest is in whether there are interaction effects between the U.S. box office and the Hong Kong box office for specific movie genres. This can be addressed by adding individual interaction terms to the regression model in Table 31.3. However, the analysis here proceeds somewhat differently. Because the genre variables are binary, the movie sample was split into two subgroups and the regression model reported in the first column in Table 31.3 was conducted for the two subgroups separately. The coefficients in the two subgroups can then be compared following the usual t test procedure for comparing coefficients from two independent samples. The advantage of this latter approach is clearer presentation and interpretation of the findings.[9]

Table 31.5 summarizes the results. Only two (shown in bold) of the four significant differences shown in Table 31.4 remain. The regression coefficient for the U.S box office for non-comedies is significantly larger than the corresponding coefficient for comedies, and the coefficient for the U.S. box office for romance movies is significantly larger than for non-romance movies. The relationship between U.S. box office and Hong Kong box office for science fiction movies is still slightly stronger than that for non-science fiction movies, but the difference is not statistically significant. In other words, the finding in Table 31.4 regarding the relatively high degree of cross-culture predictability for science fiction movies is not robust enough to survive multivariate analysis.

DISCUSSION

In summary, this analysis has shown that certain movie genres are indeed suffering from relatively high cultural discount and/or lack of cross-culture predictability. Comedies, specifically, constitute the quintessential particularistic movie genre. Hollywood comedies not only suffer from a cultural discount that is relatively higher than movies of other genres, their box office performances in Hong Kong are also relatively less predictable by U.S. box office

Table 31.5 U.S. box office coefficients for movies of different genres

Genre	Belong to the Genre	Not Belong to the Genre
Comedy	.053*	**.097***
Action	.086*	.082*
Thriller	.083*	.087*
Romance	**.141***	**.073***
Science fiction	.094*	.082*
Adventure	.085*	.082*
Family	.068*	.089*
Drama	.094*	.079*
Horror	.095*	.081*

Note. With each genre variable, the sample was split into two groups, and the regression model in the first column of Table 4 (minus the genre variable used as the grouping variable) was conducted separately for the two subsamples. Entries are unstandardized regression coefficients for U.S. box office for the corresponding subsample. The entries in the first row, therefore, mean that the unstandardized regression coefficient for U.S. box office on Hong Kong box office among comedies is .053, whereas the coefficient among noncomedies is .097. *T* tests were conducted to examine if the coefficients for two subsamples divided by a genre variable differ from each other significantly. Significant differences are marked in bold.

* $p < .001$.

figures. This is in line with the generally held idea that humor is highly culturally specific (Palmer, 1995). It does not easily travel across cultures or survive the translation process.

In contrast, science fiction is close to being the quintessential universal movie genre. Hollywood science fiction movies have a relatively low cultural discount in Hong Kong, and their box office performance in Hong Kong is also relatively more predictable by U.S. box office figures. Although the latter finding is not robust enough to survive the multivariate test, the finding is still very interesting. When discussing the universalistic elements in movies and television, "sex and violence" are probably often the first things that come to mind. However, this study shows that the scientific imagination is as universal as, if not more universal than, sex and violence.

A few other genres exhibit a mixed pattern. Hollywood action and family movies enjoy a relatively low degree of cultural discount in Hong Kong, but they do not exhibit a higher or lower degree of cross-culture predictability than other genres. Romance movies, on the other hand, are not discounted particularly strongly or weakly, but their box office performance in Hong Kong is particularly predictable by box office performance in the U.S. (with the bivariate correlation as high as .80).

Generally speaking, the present study contributes to the analysis of the globalization of movie products by empirically examining, with box office data, the phenomena of cultural discount and (the lack of) cross-culture predictability as two manifestations of local reception. As pointed out earlier, local reception has long been studied as a problem of meaning construction with the use of qualitative research methods. But this study shows that specific manifestations of local reception can also be usefully examined quantitatively. More specifically, although cultural discount has seldom been directly tackled with empirical data, this study shows that analysis of box office performance can be usefully conducted in terms of relative cultural discount. At the same time, the analysis of box office correlation in terms of predictability of movie success across cultures is also fruitful.

The present study suggests that cross-culture predictability and relative cultural discount are related yet distinct phenomena. Although it is recognized that different cultural discounts applicable to different movies can be a major cause of lack of predictability, conceptually lack of predictability of value to consumers is still different from loss of value itself. Empirically, movies suffering from a relatively high cultural discount do not necessarily suffer also from low predictability.

The analysis also shows that genres are useful variables for such analysis. Not only do genres influence movies' box office performance (Bagella & Becchetti, 1999; Sawhney & Eliashberg, 1996), movies of different genres also differ in cultural specificity and thus are more or less subject to the problems of cultural discount and/or lack of cross-culture predictability.

Certainly, the present study is exploratory in some aspects and there are limitations that have to be rectified through further research. Most important, this study examines only one specific location, namely, Hong Kong. As Hong Kong has a relatively well-developed local movie industry that has nonetheless been in a state of crisis since the late 1990s, specific findings in the study may or may not be replicable in other countries. For example, the relatively high cultural discount suffered by comedies may be partially explained by the fact that comedies have long been the mainstay in the highly commercialized local movie industry in Hong Kong (Bordwell, 2000). In other words, Hollywood comedies may have found it difficult to enjoy popularity in Hong Kong not only because of the general cultural specificity of humor but also because of the existence of strong competition produced by local movie makers. On the contrary, science fiction movies were largely absent in the portfolio of the Hong Kong movie industry. Thus Hollywood science fiction movies were facing little local competition. In any case, the degree of generalizability of the findings from the present study can only be ascertained through similar research conducted in other contexts.

Second, a number of factors that have been found to influence box office performance, such as marketing and advertising, are absent in the present study (Nelson et al., 2001; Zufryden, 1996, 2000). Partially, it is because of the lack of a systematically maintained database for such data. Partially, it is because, as opposed to previous studies of box office performance, the present study is not interested in maximizing the predictive power of the empirical model. Yet future research can take additional factors into account. Given the concern with the movement of media products across cultures, of particular interest would be whether the marketing campaign for a movie is localized to suit the perceived tastes of local audiences has specific implications for cultural discounts and lack of predictability.

There are also other issues touched on by this study that deserve further analysis. One example is the relationship between the U.S. box office of Hollywood movies and the box office of such movies in other countries. Whereas we could expect at least a certain degree of correlation between such box office figures, a theoretical question would be whether U.S. box office is merely a predictor or actually an influencer.[10] In other words, we are not sure whether the U.S. box office is merely an indicator that can help us predict how popular specific movies could be in other places, or the U.S. box office figure is actually a piece of information that influences the movie-going behavior of audiences around the world.

This and other questions cannot be tackled in a single study. But the present analysis should have done enough to point to the importance of an area of study that deserves more research attention and effort.

Notes

1   The theory of narrative transparency thus posits that American movies are suffering from a cultural discount smaller than that suffered by movies of other countries. This point was also made by Hoskins and Mirus (1988), though by drawing on a different set of arguments.

2   The Hong Kong Film Archive was established by the government. A full record of all Hong Kong movies produced between 1913 and 2003 is available online at http://www.lcsd.gov.hk.

3   The lists were originally available at http://www.mpia.org.hk. The Web site is no longer in operation, but raw records of movie box office are kept at the Hong Kong Film Archive.

4   The Hong Kong government adopted a three-category rating system in the late 1980s. The Film Censorship Authority classified movies to be shown in cinema into Category I (suitable for people of all ages), Category II (not suitable for children and young persons), or Category III (exhibition only to people of 18 years old or above). In 1995, Category II was further subdivided into IIA and IIB. For the present analysis, the middle and broader Category II is used as the reference point for the construction of two dummy variables related to rating.

5   Movie categories are included because such categorization points to specific content elements to expect from the movies. The categories certainly correlate with genres. In fact, there is a significant degree of multicollinearity for the variable Category I for it relates rather strongly with the family genre. But the degree of multicollinearity is not extreme: Multiple R = .74 when Category I is used as the dependent variable to be explained by all other variables in the regression model. Most important, multicollinearity contributes to Type II instead of Type I error, that is, it contributes to the obscuring of actually significant relationships instead of the finding of significant relationships that are actually insignificant. Therefore, multicollinearity should not be a concern when the focus is on interpreting statistically significant relationships derived in Table 31.3.

6   In Elberse and Eliashberg's (2003) study, for example, the results derived from ordinary least square and three-stage least square regression do not differ in terms of whether specific variables are significant but rather in the exact strength of the coefficients and the overall explanatory power of the model.

7   In the current data set, 58.5% of thrillers are also action movies, but only 28.0% of non-thrillers are action movies.

8   To further analyze the data, the data set was split into two subsamples, with all the movies released during the two major holiday periods forming one subsample and all other movies forming the other. The regression model in the first column in Table 31.3 was run for each subsample. The results show that the correlation between U.S. box office and Hong Kong box office is significantly stronger for movies released during the holiday periods; that is, cross-culture predictability is relatively stronger for movies released during the holidays. At the same time, the results regarding relative cultural discount shown in Table 31.3 are slightly stronger among movies not shown during the holiday periods, although the relevant coefficients do not differ significantly across the subsamples. These results suggest that the two manifestations of local reception discussed in this article are both weaker among movies shown during the two holiday periods. One possible explanation for this phenomenon is that local distributors might be sensitive to factors that affect local reception and choose films subject to smaller discounts and loss of predictability for holiday releases. Another possibility is that the makeup of the audience is somewhat different during major holiday periods, which leads to differential degree of local reception. In any case, such further results show that timing of release is far from irrelevant to the study of local reception, but a full discussion of this issue is beyond the scope of this article, which focuses on the notion of movie genres.

9   In this study, there is no major difference between results derived from the two approaches.

10 In the literature on movie box office performance, this "predictor or influencer" question has been most frequently raised in relation to the role of critics' reviews (Basuroy, Chatterjee, & Ravid, 2003; Eliashberg & Shugan, 1997; Reinstein & Snyder, 2005).

References

Albert, S. (1998). Movie stars and the distribution of financially successful films in the motion picture industry. *Journal of Cultural Economics*, 22, 249–270.

Ang, I. (1985). *Watching Dallas: Soap opera and the melodramatic imagination*. London: Methuen.

Bagella, M., & Becchetti, L. (1999). The determinants of motion picture box office performance: Evidence from movies produced in Italy. *Journal of Cultural Economics*, 23, 237–256.

Basuroy, S., Chatterjee, S., & Ravid, S. A. (2003). How critical are critical reviews? The box office effects of film critics, star power, and budgets. *Journal of Marketing*, 67, 103–117.

Bordwell, D. (2000). *Planet Hong Kong: Popular cinema and the art of entertainment*. Cambridge, MA: Harvard University Press.

Chan, C. W. (2000). *The structure and marketing analysis of Hong Kong film industry*. Hong Kong: Hong Kong Movie Biweekly.

Chan, J. M. (2002). Disneyfying and globalizing the Chinese legend Mulan: A study of transculturation. In J. M. Chan & B. T. McIntyre (Eds.), *In search of boundaries: Communication, nation-states and cultural identities* (pp. 225–248). Westport, CT: Ablex Publishing.

Cohen, J., & Cohen, P. (1983). *Applied multiple regression/correlation analysis for the behavioral sciences*. Hillsdale, NJ: Lawrence Erlbaum Associates.

De Vany, A., & Walls, W. D. (1999). Uncertainty in the movie industry: Does star power reduce the terror of the box office? *Journal of Cultural Economics*, 23, 285–318.

Elberse, A., & Eliashberg, J. (2003). Demand and supply dynamics for sequentially released products in international markets: The case of motion pictures. *Marketing Science*, 22, 329–354.

Eliashberg, J., & Shugan, S. M. (1997). Film critics: Influencers or predictors? *Journal of Marketing*, 61, 68–78.

Hennig-Thurau, T, Walsh, G., & Bode, M. (2004). Exporting media products: Understanding the success and failure of Hollywood movies in Germany. *Advances in Consumer Research*, 31, 633–638.

Hoskins, C., Finn, A., & McFayden, S. (1997). *Global television and film: An introduction to the economics of the business*. New York: Oxford University Press.

Hoskins, C., & McFayden, S. (1993). Canadian participation in international co-productions and co-ventures in television programming. *Canadian Journal of Communication*, 18, 219–236.

Hoskins, C., & Mirus, R. (1988). Reasons for U.S. dominance of the international trade in television programmes. *Media, Culture & Society*, 10, 499–515.

Jayakar, K. P., & Waterman, D. (2000). The economics of American theatrical movie exports: An empirical analysis. *Journal of Media Economics*, 13, 153–169.

Lee, B. K., & Bae, H. S. (2004). The effect of screen quotas on the self-sufficiency ratio in recent domestic film markets. *Journal of Media Economics*, 17, 163–176.

Lee, S. W. (2002). An economic analysis of the movie industry in Japan. *Journal of Media Economics*, 15, 125–139.

Liebes, T., & Katz, E. (1990). *The export of meaning*. Oxford, England: Oxford University Press.

Miller, T., Govil, N., McMurria, J., & Maxwell, R. (2001). *Global Hollywood*. London: British Film Institute.

Morley, D. (1980). *The nationwide audience: Structure and decoding*. London: British Film Institute.

Nelson, R. A., Donihue, M. R., Waldman, D. M., & Wheaton, C. (2001). What is an Oscar worth? *Economic Inquiry*, 39, 1–16.

Oh, J. (2001). International trade in film and the self-sufficiency ratio. *Journal of Media Economics*, 14, 31–44.

Olson, S. R. (1999). *Hollywood planet: Global media and the competitive advantage of narrative transparency*. Mahwah, NJ: Lawrence Erlbaum Associates.

Palmer, J. (1995). *Taking humor seriously*. London: Routledge.

Papandrea, F. (1998). Protection of domestic TV programming. *Journal of Media Economics*, 11, 3–15.

Radway, J. (1991). *Reading the romance*. Chapel Hill, NC: University of North Carolina Press.

Reinstein, D. A., & Snyder, C. M. (2005). The influence of expert reviews on consumer demand for experience goods: A case study of movie critics. *Journal of Industrial Economics*, 53, 27–51.

Sawhney, M. S., & Eliashberg, J. (1996). A parsimonious model for forecasting gross box-office revenues of motion pictures. *Marketing Science*, 15, 113–131.

Scott, A. J. (2002). A new map of Hollywood: The production and distribution of American motion pictures. *Regional Studies*, 36, 957–975.

Scott, A. J. (2004). Hollywood and the world: The geography of motion-picture distribution and marketing. *Review of International Political Economy*, 11, 33–61.

Simonton, D. K. (2005). Cinematic creativity and production budgets: Does money make the movie? *Journal of Creative Behavior*, 39, 1–15.

Tomlinson, J. (2001). *Globalization and culture*. Chicago: University of Chicago Press.

Walls, W. D. (1998). Product survival at the cinema: Evidence from Hong Kong. *Applied Economics Letters*, 5, 215–219.

Wildman, S. S. (1994). One-way flows and the economics of audiencemaking. In J. S. Ettema & D. C. Whitney (Eds.), *Audiencemaking: How the media create the audience* (pp. 115–141). Thousand Oaks, CA: Sage.

Wildman, S. S. (1995). Trade liberalization and policy for media industries: A theoretical examination of media flows. *Canadian Journal of Communication*, 20, 367–388.

Wildman, S. S., & Siwek, S. E. (1988). *International trade in films and television programs*. Cambridge, MA: Ballinger.

Zuckerman, E. W., & Kim, T. Y. (2003). The critical trade-off: Identity assignment and box-office success in the feature film industry. *Industrial and Corporate Change*, 12, 27–67.

Zufryden, F. S. (1996). Linking advertising to box office performance of new film releases: A marketing planning model. *Journal of Advertising Research*, 36, 29–41.

Zufryden, F. S. (2000). New film website promotion and box-office performance. *Journal of Advertising Research*, 40(1–2), 55–64.

Chapter 32

Rosemary J. Coombe

THE CELEBRITY IMAGE AND CULTURAL IDENTITY: PUBLICITY RIGHTS AND THE SUBALTERN POLITICS OF GENDER (1992)

WHO AUTHORS THE CELEBRITY? Where does identity receive its authorization? I shall argue that the law constructs and maintains fixed, stable identities authorized by the celebrity subject. In so doing, however, the law also produces the possibility of the celebrity signifier's polysemy. The celebrity image[1] is a cultural lode of multiple meanings, mined for its symbolic resonances, and, simultaneously, a floating signifier, invested with libidinal energies, social longings, and political aspirations.

Focusing upon cultural practices that engage, reproduce, ironize, and transform the meaning and value of celebrity personas to assert alternative gender identities, I shall argue that the celebrity is authored in a multiplicity of sites of discursive practice, and that in the process unauthorized identities are produced, both for the celebrity and for her diverse authors. Through its prohibitions the law produces the means by which unauthorized identities are both engendered and endangered.

I will very briefly summarize the legal doctrine of publicity rights[2] and argue that the rationales traditionally offered for recognizing and protecting rights to the celebrity persona cannot be supported and do not justify the extent of the protections legally afforded celebrities, their estates, or their assignees. The social and cultural value of the celebrity image will then be addressed.

Popular cultural practices that engage celebrity images in innovative fashions will then be explored to demonstrate the vibrant role played by these cultural icons in the self-authorings of subaltern social groups. Gay male appropriations of female stars in camp subculture, lesbian reworkings of James Dean, and middle-class women's use of the *Star Trek* characters in the creation of fan magazines (fanzines) are practices that rewrite media imagery in subversive but politically expressive fashions. Investing celebrity personas with new and often oppositional meanings, these subordinate groups assert unauthorized gender identities. They thereby affirm both community solidarity and the legitimacy of their social difference by empowering themselves with cultural resources that the law deems the properties of others.

Liberal notions of freedom of expression fail to grasp the nature of contemporary cultural politics, I suggest, because they are held hostage by the philosophical conceits of the Enlightenment. In conclusion, I propose that we situate these practices in an enlarged vision of contemporary democracy that considers the political as dialogic cultural practices of articulating the social world and authoring politically salient forms of difference. In this context, we can begin to consider the political costs of granting the celebrity exclusive rights to authorize her (own) image.

THE LEGAL PROTECTION OF THE CELEBRITY PERSONA

Anglo-American legal jurisdictions recognize the right of individuals to protect publicly identifiable attributes from unauthorized and unremunerated appropriation by others for commercial purposes or economic benefit.[3] Originally developed primarily to deal with an unauthorized use of a person's name or picture in advertising that suggested the individual's endorsement of a product, the right of publicity has been greatly expanded in the twentieth century. It is no longer limited to the name or likeness of an individual, but now extends to a person's nickname, signature, physical pose, characterizations, singing style, vocal character-istics, body parts, frequently used phrases, car, performance style, mannerisms and gestures, provided that these are distinctive and publicly identified with the person claiming the right. Although most cases still involve the unauthorized advertising of commodities, rights of publicity have been evoked to prohibit the distribution of memorial posters, novelty souvenirs, magazine parodies, and the presentation of nostalgic musical reviews, television docudramas, and satirical theatrical performances. Increasingly it seems that any publicly recognizable characteristic will be recognized to have a commercial value that is likely to be diminished by its unauthorized appropriation by others.

The right is recognized as proprietary in nature and may therefore be assigned, and the various components of an individual's persona may be independently licensed. A celebrity could, theoretically at least, license her signature for use on fashion scarves, grant exclusive rights to reproduce her face to a perfume manufacturer, her voice to a charitable organiza-tion, her legs to a pantyhose company, particular publicity stills for distribution as posters or postcards, and continue to market her services as a singer, actor, and composer. The human persona is capable of almost infinite commodification, because exclusive, non-exclusive, and temporally, spatially, and functionally limited licenses may be granted for use of any aspect of the celebrity's public presence. Furthermore, the right of publicity has been extended beyond the celebrity, her licensees, and assignees, to protect the celebrity's descendants and their licensces.[4]

THE VALUE OF THE CELEBRITY IMAGE

In an age of mass production and mass communications technologies, the celebrity persona is a potent force with which to market goods (Sudjic). Celebrities clearly have an interest in policing the use of their personas to insure that they don't become tainted with associations that would prematurely tarnish the patina they might license to diverse enterprises. This potential commercial value is generally offered as reason in itself to protect the star's control over his identity through the allocation of exclusive property rights; because such interests have market value, they deserve protection. Others, like myself, see this as "a massive exercise in question begging" (Lange 156). Market values arise only after property rights have been established and enforced; the decision to allocate particular property rights is a prior question of social policy that requires philosophical and moral deliberations[5] and a consideration of social costs and benefits.[6]

Publicity rights are justified on the basis of the celebrity's authorship, but star images must be made, and, like other cultural products, their creation occurs in social contexts and draws upon other resources, institutions, and technologies. Celebrity images are authored by studios, the mass media, public relations agencies, fan clubs, gossip columnists, photographers, hairdressers, body-building coaches, athletic trainers, teachers, screen-writers, ghostwriters, directors, lawyers, and doctors. Even if we only consider the production and dissemination of the star image, and see its value solely as the result of human labor, this value cannot be entirely attributed to the efforts of a single celebrity author.

Moreover, as Richard Dyer shows, the star image is authored by its consumers as well as its producers; the audience makes the celebrity image the unique phenomena that it is (*Heavenly Bodies, Stars*). Selecting from the complexities of the images and texts they encounter, they produce new values for the celebrity and find in stars sources of significance that speak to their own experience. These new meanings are freely mined by media producers of the star's image to further enhance its market value. To quote Marilyn Monroe's last recorded words in public, "I want to say that the people – if I am a star – the people made me a star, no studio, no person, but the people did" (qtd. in MacCannell 115).

The star image is authored by multitudes of persons engaged in diverse activities. Moreover, stars and their fame are never manufactured from whole cloth – the successful image is frequently a form of cultural *bricolage* that improvises with a social history of symbolic forms. Consider the Marx Brothers. Clearly their characterizations involved creative activity, but, as David Lange points out,

> . . . what we cannot know in fact . . . is how much the characters created by the Marx Brothers owe to the work of tens, scores, perhaps hundreds of other vaudeville and burlesque performers with whom they came into contact. . . . What we do not know, in short, is how much of these characters the Marx Brothers themselves appropriated from others. All that is certain is that they created themselves, individually and collectively, as a kind of living derivative work. That much Groucho himself has told us. . . . To be sure, the Marx Brothers became celebrities as most vaudevillians did not. But surely we are not rewarding them on that ground alone. (162)

Publicity rights enable stars to "establish dynasties on the memory of fame" (162). In Groucho Marx Productions, Inc. v. Day and Night Co., Inc., those who held rights in the Marx Brothers made a successful publicity rights claim against the creators of the play *A Day in Hollywood, A Night in the Ukraine*. The play's authors intended to satirize the excesses of Hollywood in the thirties and evoked the Marx Brothers as characters playfully imagined interpreting a Chekhov drama. The defendants were found liable and their first amendment claim was dismissed on the ground that the play was an imitative work.

The Marx Brothers *themselves* might be seen as imitative or derivative works, whose creation and success as icons in popular culture derives from their own creative reworkings of the signifying repertoire of the vaudeville community. Contemporary stars are authored in a similar fashion. How much does Elvis Costello owe to Buddy Holly, Prince to Jimi Hendrix, or Michael Jackson to Diana Ross? Take the image of Madonna, an icon whose meaning and value lies partially in its evocation and ironic reconfiguration of several twentieth-century sex-goddesses and ice-queens (Marilyn Monroe obviously, but also Jean Harlow, Greta Garbo, and Marlene Dietrich) that speaks with multiple tongues to diverse audiences. Descriptions of the Madonna image as semiotic montage abound,[7] but this extract from the *Village Voice* is my favorite:

> What Madonna served up in the name of sexuality was not liberation as I'd known it, but a strange brew of fetishism and femininity. Only later would I understand that the source of her power is precisely this ambiguity. It's a mistake to think of any pop icon as an individual. . . . Madonna is a cluster of signs, and what they add up to is precisely the state of sex in the culture now: torn between need and rage and unable to express one without the other. . . . Madonna raids the image bank of American femininity, melding every fantasy ever thrown onto the silver screen and implanting them in the body and voice of every-babe. (Goldstein 36)

In an era characterized by nostalgia for the golden age of the silver screen and an aging baby boom generation's fascination with the television culture of its youth, successful images are often those which mine media history for evocative signifiers from our past. This is not to deny that such appropriations are creative endeavors; it is to stress emphatically that they *are* and to assert that such authorial processes ought not to be frozen, limited, or circumscribed by the whims of celebrities or the commercial caprice of their assignees.

If the Madonna image appropriates the likenesses of earlier screen goddesses, religious symbolism, feminist rhetoric, and sadomasochistic fantasy to speak to contemporary sexual aspirations and anxieties, then the value of the image derives as much, perhaps, from the collective cultural heritage on which she draws as to her individual efforts. But if we grant Madonna exclusive property rights in her image, we simultaneously make it difficult for others to appropriate those same resources for new ends, and we freeze the Madonna constellation itself. Future artists, writers, and performers will be unable to draw creatively upon the cultural and historical significance of the Madonna montage without seeking the consent of the celebrity, her estate, or its assigns, who may well deny such consent or demand exorbitant royalties. As Lange argues, the proliferation of successful publicity rights claims occurs at the expense of our rights to the public domain (163). Consequentially, access to the public domain is choked, or closed off, and the public "loses the rich heritage of its culture, the rich presence of new works derived from that culture, and the rich promise of works to come" (165).

Some celebrity images seem so deeply embedded in the North American social imaginary that they might be said to constitute parts of a collective cultural heritage. Such images should not be subject to control by the parochial interests of celebrity's estates. Elvis Presley provides an apt example. In the recent film *Mystery Train*, director and producer Jim Jarmusch explores the cultural and psychological significance of Presley in the depressed economy of Memphis, Tennessee, and in the consciousness of those who live on its social margins. The film also addresses his charisma for those in other countries whose fascination with American media images manifests itself in pilgrimages that have turned Memphis into a late twentieth-century Mecca. The possibility that Elvis Presley's estate *might* seek to prohibit the production and/or distribution of a film such as this[8] while simultaneously arranging to market cologne designed "for all the King's men"[9] indicates the parameters of the problem. The opportunity for the celebrity's assignees to behave this way has, in fact, been seized. When the City of Memphis decided to erect a bronze statue to memorialize Elvis as part of a city redevelopment scheme, a nonprofit city corporation offered pewter replicas of the King in return for donations to finance the monument. Owners of rights to commercially exploit the Presley likeness were quick to seek and obtain an injunction (Memphis Development v. Factors).[10]

The traditional liberal justification for bestowing property rights in the celebrity image is inadequate to establish a right to receive the full market value of the star persona or to support exclusive rights to control its circulation and reproduction in society. Liberal values protecting individual freedom guarantee the possession and use only of the product of one's personal labors and only insofar as the exercise of this right does not harm the rights of others. Enabling celebrities, their estates and assigns to exercise absolute rights to authorize the circulation of the celebrity image may have adverse consequences, both for the preservation of our collective heritage and for our future cultural development.

The social value and cultural meaning of the celebrity image has its genesis in the same historical conditions that created the possibility of its economic value. In his illuminating essay "The Work of Art in the Age of Mechanical Reproduction," Walter Benjamin suggested that technologies of mechanical reproduction and systems of mass production changed modes of human perception and evaluation, fundamentally altering our aesthetic responses. These changes, I argue, are integrally related to the cultural value of the celebrity image in contemporary social life.

Benjamin's reflections on the work of art and the decline of its aura may help us to understand the cultural significance of the celebrity image. Here I want to go beyond Benjamin's own disjointed observations of the screen actor as one who has his performance fragmented by the camera, is alienated from his audience, deprived of his corporeality, and dissolved into flickering images and disembodied sounds (228–29). He sees the effect of film as engaging the whole living person but destroying its aura and replacing the actor's aura with an artificially produced "personality" that is only the "phony spell of the commodity." Benjamin alludes to the possibility of another, alternative understanding of the celebrity with his reference to "the cult of the movie star" – one that suggests that celebrities may represent residual vestiges of the "auratic" in contemporary mass culture (231).

If the work of art's aura derived from its unique, embodied, or tangible presence in time and space, an individual history, and a situation in a cultural tradition, then it is difficult to deny the aura of the celebrity. However often a celebrity's likeness is reproduced, there remains a social knowledge of the celebrity as an individual human being with an unapproachable or distant existence elsewhere, a life history, and a mortal susceptibility to the processes of heartache, injury, illness, aging, and ultimately, death. It is difficult to envisage Elvis Presley without conjuring up images of health, vibrancy, and sexual energy followed by self-inflicted harm, gluttony, corpulence, and decay. Arguably, the celebrity evokes the fascination she does because however endlessly her image is reproduced, her substantive duration, that is, her life, never becomes wholly irrelevant. She never loses her autonomy from the objects that circulate in her likeness.

Moreover, the star is historically situated and lives her life in historical and social conditions that give her image its meaning, resonance, and authority. The celebrity image's value might also be seen to reside in its character as a particular human embodiment of a connection to a social history that provokes its beholder to reflect upon her own relationship to the cultural tradition in which the star's popularity is embedded. We all consider celebrities from different social positions; as a feminist and social democrat, for example, I cannot perceive Marilyn Monroe without reflecting upon my own troubled relationship to male definitions of female sexuality, the femininity of sexual innocence, the Playboy tradition, the Cold War, and Monroe's own left-wing politics.[11] Celebrity images, I would contend, always maintain their aura because they bind subjects in affective and historically mediated relationships that preclude their appropriation as pure objects.[12]

Stewart Ewen sees the power of the celebrity image as rooted in photography's simultaneous affinity to reality and fantasy (90), and as a cultural response to modern social experiences of alienation and anomie. The celebrity is an icon of the significance of the personal and the individual in a world of standardization and conformity – embodying the possibility of upward mobility from the mass, "celebrity forms a symbolic pathway, connecting each aspiring individual to a universal image of fulfillment: to be someone, when 'being no one' is the norm" (95–96).

The seductive power of celebrity auras and their ubiquity in contemporary social life make the star persona a compelling compilation of signifiers in our cultural fields of representation. Simultaneously embodying the fantastic and the real, utopian ideals and quotidian practices, and the realization of popular aspirations for recognition and legitimacy, the celebrity form attracts the authorial energies of those for whom identity is a salient issue and community an ongoing dilemma.

"DOING GENDER": THE CELEBRATED BODY AND THE POLITICS OF POSTMODERNISM

What meaning do particular celebrities have in people's own social experiences? It is necessary to make these arguments about the cultural losses contingent upon the commodification of the celebrity image historically concrete. In so doing, the political dimensions of this foreclosure on the use of cultural resources come into relief. Marginal social groups are continually engaged in nascent constructions of alternative identities. The celebrity image plays a central role in many of these cultural practices.

The practices I will examine are those of gay male camp subculture in the pre-liberation era, lesbian refashionings of pop icons, and finally, middle-class women's engagement in the reading, writing, and circulation of *Star Trek* fanzines. These practices involve the redeployment of celebrity images – an aspect of that rearticulation of commodified media texts that has been defined as the essence of popular culture (Foster). Theorists of postmodernism assert that contemporary cultural theory must come to terms with "the textual thickness and the visual density of everyday life" (McRobbie 165) in societies characterized by pervasive media imagery and commodified forms of cultural representation. A central dimension of the study of postmodernism has therefore been a concern with the ways in which people "live and negotiate the everyday life of consumer capitalism" (Ross, *Universal Abandon* xv)[13] and use mass culture in their quotidian practices. Cultural consumption is increasingly understood as an active use rather than a passive dependence upon dominant forms of signification. As Michel de Certeau and Paul Willis argue, consumption is always a form of production and people continually engage in cultural practices of *bricolage* – resignifying media meanings, consumer objects, and cultural texts in order to adapt them to their own interests and make them fulfill their own purposes. These practices are central to the political practices of those in marginal or subordinated social groups, who forge subcultures with resources foraged from the mediascape.[14]

Subcultural practices involve improvisational cultural appropriations that affirm emergent cultural identities for those in subordinate social groups (Connor 186).[15] Angela McRobbie argues that the frenzied expansion of mass media enables new alliances and solidarities across traditional spatial, racial, and cultural boundaries and resources for producing new meanings and new identities:

> Sontag's linking [of camp] with . . . gay men, is instructive because she shows how a relationship evolved around a social minority making a bid for a cultural form in which they felt they could stake some of their fragmented and sexually deviant identity. The insistence, on the way, on both style and pleasure made the product attractive to those outside as well as inside. . . . [S]he is describing

how forms can be taken over, and re-assembled . . . [which] often means outstripping their ostensible meaning . . . And if media forms are so inescapable . . . then there is no reason to assume that consumption of pastiche, parody or high camp is, by definition, without subversive or critical potential. Glamour, glitter, and gloss, should not so easily be relegated to the sphere of the insistently apolitical. (174–75)

Mass media imagery provides people who share similar social experiences to express their similarity by imbuing with emotional energy a range of cultural referents that media communications have afforded them shared access. It also enables them to author/ize their difference by improvising with those images to make them relevant to their social experiences and aspirations.

If the celebrity is an image that is both fantastic and real, embodying the realization of widespread aspirations for public affirmation, it is especially likely to attract the authorial energies of those in marginal groups for whom recognition, legitimacy, and positively evaluated identity are compelling issues. Although the "recoding" of celebrity images is in no way limited to a concern with gender identity, I will focus upon practices which question traditional formulations of gender and express desires to construct alternatives.

The concept of alternative gender identities is borrowed from Judith Butler's pathbreaking work *Gender Trouble* in which she suggests that a feminist politics requires an inquiry into the political construction and regulation of gendered identities, a radical critique of the limitations of existing categories of identity, and an exploration of practices in which alternatively gendered worlds are imagined. The practices I will be exploring are active performances of gender "that disrupt the categories of the body, sex, gender, and sexuality and occasion their subversive resignification and proliferation beyond the binary frame" (xii).

Identity is always a practice of articulation from within existing cultural forms; gender is performative, a doing and constituting of the identity it is purported to be. These performances are always constructed within the terms of discourse and power, and thus engage heterosexual cultural conventions (Butler 25–30).[16] Butler is interested in modes of "doing" gender that evoke but do not constitute simple reproductions of the terms of power but subvert the very constructs they mobilize, "displacing those naturalized and reified notions of gender that support masculine hegemony and heterosexist power" (33). For example, "numerous lesbian and gay discourses . . . [position themselves] in resignificatory relationships to heterosexual cultural configurations" (121). This repetition of heterosexual cultural forms may be the site of their denaturalization, bringing "into relief the utterly constructed status of the so-called heterosexual original" (31).

Celebrity images provide important cultural resources for many practices of "doing" gender that subvert and reconstruct dominant forms of gender identity. The denaturalization of heterosexual cultural forms is readily apparent in gay camp subculture, a phenomenon I have already alluded to as involving an engagement with media disseminated celebrity images. Andrew Ross argues that gay camp has had a significant influence on changing social definitions of masculinity and femininity from the late fifties, working "to destabilize, reshape and transform the existing balance of accepted sexual roles and sexual identities" (*No Respect* 159). Whatever its ultimate cultural effects, however, its origins must be understood in the context of gay urban life in the pre-liberation period.

In the nineteen fifties and sixties a sophisticated gay male subculture evolved around a fascination with classical Hollywood film stars like Judy Garland, Bette Davis, Mae West, Greta Garbo, and Marlene Dietrich. In an age when their ability to be open about the fact that they were gay was circumscribed, gay men's use of certain star images constituted a kind of "going public" or "coming out." Camp contained a kind of commentary on the ongoing feat "of survival in a world dominated by the tastes, interests, and definitions of others" (*No Respect* 144).

The biggest "camps" were drag queens – homosexual men performing the social character of "women" (that is, the signs and symbols of a socially defined American category) by artificially creating the image of glamour (Newton 3). The most popular stars in the camp pantheon, subject of most frequent impersonation, were "glamorous" in highly mannered ways that indicated an awareness of the artifice in which they were engaged. This celebration of the personas of those who subtly mocked the "corny flamboyance of femaleness . . . defetishized the erotic scenario of woman as spectacle" (*No Respect* 159). Thus they explored the relation between artifice and nature in the construction of sexuality and gender long before these were recognized as political issues.

Camp lost its appeal with the arrival of a militant gay politics that asserted the "natural" quality of homosexuality, revived "masculine" styles, and sought to undermine the "effeminacy" of the stereotypical gay image. The finale of Michel Tremblay's acclaimed 1974 play *Hosanna* well illustrates the new attitude towards camp. Hosanna, an aging drag queen who identifies with, and projects her identity upon Elizabeth Taylor, is humiliated and forced to renounce her attachment to the star, and disarm herself of her Taylor impersonation. Stripped naked, he declares "I'm a man," and (at long last, it is implied), allows his lover to embrace his "true" "masculine" self. Camp has, however, enjoyed something of a resurgence in the 1980s, confluent, perhaps, with the influence of Michel Foucault, poststructuralism, and a revival of the credibility of the notion of the socially constructed subject.

Lesbian engagement with celebrity images is a less documented and more recent phenomena. One lesbian challenge to the "truth" of sex, gender, and desire and the restrictions of a binary sexual economy is given voice and celebrated by Sue Golding, in her discussion of a performative gender identity she calls lesbian hermaphrodism. This "erotic sensibility" (49) worn, felt, and enacted by a number of lesbians is a "fictionalized sexuality" (50) that finds its performative significations in mass media icons which it replicates in ironic, playful, and assertive reconfigurations:

> I know you've seen the type: no tits, no cock, oozing with a kind of vulnerable "masculinity," sheathed in a 50's style black-leather motorcycle jacket. Or to put it slightly differently, it's James Dean, with a clit. . . . What emerges is the "virile girl," the butch baby, full of attitude but not of scorn, lots of street smarts and a bit of muscle. This new hermaphrodite embodies forever the image of the destructive adolescent dramatically and in one being, teeming with a creative, raw energy, and beckoning with the possibility of a new era. (49)

This gender rebel performs with her body an erotic identity that is an embodied performative – "the defiant aesthetic of the erotic masculine shot through with the voluptuousness of the female sexual organs" (52). An "erotic mutant," "a fractured playfulness of social icons [like the Dean image, although Elvis Presley offers other possibilities] copied over and over again" (52), the lesbian hermaphrodite exemplifies the sex/gender/desire/ practice matrix as a performatively enacted signification that parodies, proliferates, and subverts gendered meanings. "Doing gender," however, is not the exclusive preserve of gays and lesbians (although their social experiences are more likely to incline them to contest hegemonic norms of gender identity). This is illustrated by the authorial activities of *Star Trek* fanziners, who construct communities and articulate new gender identities by literally re-writing their favorite television series characters.

Star Trek fans constitute a social and cultural network that is international in scope.

Within this community, there are distinct groups of fans that organize around the production, circulation, and consumption of fanzines.[17] This subculture is explored with great sensitivity by Camille Bacon-Smith in her sparkling ethnography *Enterprising Women*. The fanzine community is almost exclusively female and predominantly heterosexual. It involves middle-class women who work as housewives and in nursing, teaching, clerical, and service occupations.[18] Fans exchange letters, distribute newsletters, create artworks, make videotapes, and produce and circulate fanzines that contain original fiction, poetry, and illustrations written by women across North America, Britain, and Australia.[19] In 1988 it was estimated that there were 300 publications that enabled fans to explore aspects of television series, 120 of them centered on *Star Trek* (Jenkins 89), a number which no doubt *underestimates* the production of fan literature because it doesn't include literature circulated only in photocopy circuits or more covertly circulated publications.[20]

In their creative endeavors, fanzine contributors employ images, themes, and characters from a canonized set of mass culture texts (the *Star Trek* television series episodes, films, and commercially produced novels), to explore their own subordinate status, voice frustration and anger with existing social conditions, envision alternatives, share new understandings, and express utopian aspirations. In so doing, they force media texts to accommodate their interests, to become relevant to their needs, and thereby empower themselves with mass culture images. Issues of gender roles, sexuality, and the tension between family obligations and professional ambition are explored in the *Star Trek* future world – one which holds out the promise of opportunities for nontraditional female pleasures, active involvement in central decision-making roles, and a state of sexual equality in which emotional needs and professional responsibilities are taken seriously by men and women alike (Jenkins 93–97).

In most stories women are engaged in rewriting the masculine gender rather than in imagining alternative feminine ones. Many stories involve male friendships, and two significant genres of fanzine fiction are "Slash" (or homoerotic) and "Hurt-Comfort"[21] stories, both of which center on relationships between the male characters. In all of these stories the links between anatomy, gender, desire, and sexual practice are sundered. In the male friendship stories the male characters are alternatively engendered; stripping them of a rationalist, ego-centered individualism, the fans imbue them with emotionality and empathy, knitting them into close family and community relationships as well as intimate caring friendships which nurture and support them in their adventures (Bacon-Smith 745–47).

In "Slash" fiction, women write erotic stories and draw illustrations depicting a love relationship between Kirk and Spock.[22] Fearing social ridicule, loss of employment, and possibly legal repercussions,[23] fanzine writers often write such stories under pseudonyms. Much of this literature circulates only through complex subterranean photocopying networks in order to evade exposure outside of the group (Bacon-Smith 209–16).[24] So well hidden is the circuit that only the most experienced readers and writers have access to it. Bacon-Smith describes a number of tasks performed by the homoerotic romance and rejects the idea that the male characters are surrogate women – an idea popularized by Joanna Russ when she argued that because of the overriding importance of touch, to the slow thoroughness and sensitization of the whole body, the sexuality expressed is female (cited in Bacon-Smith 242–45). She asserts that these women are writing consciously and deliberately about men, exploring who men are and reconstructing them into people with whom it might be more comfortable to share life, love, and sexual relationships. These women want to explore relationships between powerful equals while tearing "down the very institution of hierarchical power that constructs men as individuals" – reconstructing power itself as an integrated union of mutuality with full and open communication (Bacon-Smith 249–50).

In all of these stories the "male" characters are given a combination of gender traits – Kirk's "feminine" traits are matched to Spock's "masculine" ones and vice versa. Each shares aspects of traditional gender roles. In this way, new genders are inscribed on "male" bodies and new desires, experiences, feelings and practices may therefore proliferate.[25] As well as being alternatively engendered, the male characters are freshly embodied; their bodies are inscribed with ranges of sensitivity, expanded zones of erogeneity and a heightened receptivity to tactile pleasures and physical comfort (Bacon-Smith 195–96). Their heroes' pain, decontextualized in the mass media, is re-united by fanzine writers with both physical and psychological suffering. The male characters then, are reconstructed as fully emotional and sentient beings. Arguably, the fanzine writers perform the most thorough practices of "doing gender" that have been examined. Constructing new connections between novel (male?) bodies, new (masculinities?), erotic desires, and sexual practices, they simultaneously situate these newly engendered creatures in personal and social relationships, empowering themselves and their community as they do so.

JURIDICAL PRODUCTIONS OF CULTURAL SPACE(S)

Cultural studies theorists rarely consider law when they study popular cultural practice.[26] At first these subcultural practices seem distant, if not divorced from the legal regime of publicity rights, but they occupy a space intersected by a multiplicity of relations between law and cultural form. I am concerned here, not simply with law as a set of prohibitions, but rather with law as it is imbricated in the everyday life of cultural practice.[27]

The risks these people run under legal regimes of prohibition are real enough. So are the ethical risks of writing about their practices.[28] Juridical powers, however, are productive as well as prohibitive; the law is generative of knowledges, spaces, categories, identities, and subjectivities.[29] The law of publicity rights, by prohibiting reproductions of the celebrity image for another's advantage, promotes the mass circulation of celebrity signifiers by ensuring that they will have a market value; if the image were freely available for mass reproduction, there would, presumably, be less of an incentive to engage in the investments necessary to disseminate it through media channels. Ironically, then, the law creates the cultural spaces of postmodernism in which mass media images become available for signifying practice. It produces fixed, stable identities authored by the celebrity subject, but simultaneously creates the possibility of places of transgression in which the signifier's fixity and the celebrity's authority may be contested and resisted. Authorized and unauthorized identities are both, therefore, engendered in relation to this juridical regime. The law, however, lends its authority only to those meanings that the celebrity wishes to appropriate, attributing these to her own efforts, and denies that cultural value may be produced elsewhere.

Power may produce resistance in the Foucauldian sense, but it does not determine the form or the content of the practices that transgress its strictures. Through its prohibitions the law may produce the means by which unauthorized identities are both engendered and endangered, but these practices are not simply effects or consequences of juridical regimes. People's interests and inclinations to engage in the construction of alternative gender identities are shaped by multiple hegemonies. Performative enactments of erotic identity are unlikely to be univocal direct statements of opposition to any singular structure of power; more often they may engage multiple forms of cultural "resistance" to multiple instances of power. Through irony, mockery, parody, pastiche, and alternative modes of appreciation, activities of creative appropriation enable fans to comment indirectly on gender ideology, law, and the commodity form.

Such commentary is especially cogent in the fanzine context. Fans don't see *Star Trek* as something that *can* be reread but something that *must* be rewritten in order to make it more responsive to their needs and a better producer of personal and community meanings (Jenkins 87). According to Henry Jenkins, fans expressly reject the idea that the *Star Trek* texts or the Kirk/Spock characters are a privileged form of exclusive property but at the same time they have developed a complex moral economy[30] in which they legitimize their unorthodox appropriation of the media texts, characters, and personas. Despite the potential for legal prosecution, they see themselves as loyalists, fulfilling the inherent promise and potential of the series — a potential unrealized or betrayed by those who "own" the intellectual property rights in it. Fans respect the original texts, and regularly police each other for abuses of interpretive license, but they also see themselves as the legitimate guardians of these materials, which have too often been manhandled by the producers and their licensees for easy profits. As one fan writes: "we have made *Star Trek* uniquely our own, so we have all the right in the world . . . to try to change it for the better when the gang at Paramount starts worshipping the almighty dollar as they are wont to do" (Jenkins 100). Fan writers exercise an ethic of care with regard to the characters — a care they fear that commercially motivated parties frequently do not share.[31]

Although fanziners, gay camps, and lesbian hermaphrodites are not engaged in practices in direct opposition to the law (however they may unintentionally violate it), the law of publicity rights informs their performative activities. The knowledge that the cultural icons with which they express themselves do not belong to them, however affectionately they are adopted, is constitutive of these practices. The relationship of fans to the commodification of the signifiers whose meanings they create may be one of admiration or antagonism, irony, parody, fear, or complicitous critique.[32] In any case, the law generates the space for a proliferation of politics as well as identities, polities as well as genders, as people create their own ethical distinctions between expression and theft. Communication always involves borrowing the images of alterity. Only recently has it become a form of theft.

INFINITE DIVERSITY IN INFINITE COMBINATION: DEMOCRACY AS DIALOGIC PRACTICE

The cultural politics of constructing alternative gender identities through improvisations upon the celebrity image, are not readily appreciated using current juridical concepts or easily encompassed by the liberal premises upon which legal categories are grounded. The reasons for these difficulties, I believe, can be located within the contradictions, instabilities, and ambiguities of liberal legal discourse itself — contradictions that are becoming increasingly apparent in the condition of post-modernity.[33]

Liberal legal discourse addresses the expression of identity, community, and political aspiration under the rubric of free speech or freedom of expression, a field of doctrine that clings tenaciously to Enlightenment concepts in the face of late-capitalist realities. As Owen Fiss notes, the constitutional protections of freedom of speech rest on increasingly anachronistic premises that do not address the salient characteristics or challenges of capitalist mass communications systems in North America. Pre-supposing that the biggest threat to public discourse is the silencing of the individual speaker by the state, "the Free Speech Tradition can be understood as a protection of the street corner speaker" (1408). Assuming a natural division between public and private actors, it simply protects all "private" actors, regardless of their power, against the evils of state intervention, notwithstanding that in an age of mass media conglomerates, threats to the autonomy of speech and public debate are more likely to come from extremely powerful "private" actors who control the most influential circuits and contents of communication (1410–13). Increasingly, a person's right to political speech may encroach upon another's rights of property (the need to picket in shopping malls, for example) and property rights generally prevail unless the property-holding citizen is understood to hold the property for public use (and thus to exercise a "governmental" function so that she must be treated like a state).

Critics on the left argue that the public/private and state/citizen dichotomies of freedom of speech law mystify and distort our understanding of contemporary political life

> because government is implicated in all activity that occurs within its territorial jurisdiction. As sovereign, the government is as responsible for its active decisions not to intervene and regulate as it is for its decisions to act affirmatively . . . the retention of an existing situation is also due to the efforts and actions of the state. . . . The protection of private property and the enforcement of private contracts by the government attests to the strong and necessary presence of government in private transactions . . . property and contract are creatures of the state and support for these allocative regimes is neither more or less politically neutral or activist than opposition to them. The question is not whether government should intervene, but when and how. (Hutchinson 21)

When "public" speech interests come up against "private" property interests, the latter almost invariably triumph, ensuring that "the law insulates vast sectors of the social hierarchy from official scrutiny and public accountability" (22). Those who hold "private" property are not required to consider the "public" interest in free speech in their exercise of exclusive property rights. Once we break down this untenable distinction, however, and recognize the state's role in creating and enforcing property rights, "the question of whose entitlements are to be protected from whose interference becomes a contested matter of political choice rather than the correct application of abstract principle" (22).

Laws commodifying the celebrity image inevitably come up against concerns about freedom of expression, but they do so sporadically, yielding inconsistent and confused rationales that reveal the inadequacies of liberal discourse in the cultural conditions of postmodernism. It is generally accepted that rights of publicity must yield to social interests in freedom of expression, "when first amendment principles outweigh the celebrity's interest in compensation" (Lawrence 332). But when will this be the case? To answer this question, or to understand the cultural world in which this question is a sensible one, we must detour through yet another alternative universe – that of contemporary jurisprudence.

Courts routinely assert that the First Amendment protects publication of news of a celebrity but does not protect commercial uses of celebrity images.[34] Often this seems to be premised on a distinction between fact and fiction – factual accounts about celebrity behavior do not violate their publicity rights because celebrities are the subject of legitimate news (Garner). Newspapers, films, and documentaries are not understood to be engaged in commercial purposes when they publish news, notwithstanding that their production, distribution, and exhibition is a large commercial enterprise carried on for private profit (University of Notre Dame v. Twentieth Century Fox). Distinctions between fact and fiction, publishing news about a celebrity and commercially exploiting her image, are notoriously difficult to maintain in the promotional culture[35] of postmodernity. The courts' efforts to employ and maintain such distinctions yield contradictory and sometimes ludicrous results, as the following cases, drawn from the same jurisdiction, illustrate.

Ann Margret sued *High Society* magazine for a violation of publicity rights for the unauthorized use of a semi-nude photograph taken from one of her films. The court dismissed the action on the basis that the photograph was newsworthy and its use protected. The same year, a model brought legal action for the unauthorized use of a nude photograph in the same magazine. The court rejected the defendant's claim that the First Amendment protected use of the photos because the model was not shown participating in a newsworthy event; the photographs, therefore, were not a matter of public interest (Hansen). When a couple found their nude photographs in a commercially distributed mass market guide to nude beaches, a court denied them relief and upheld the publisher's right to disseminate information of public interest; the photographs were not being used for commercial purposes (Creel).

Law students are trained to rationalize and distinguish such cases to show how categories like disseminating information in the public interest and commercial exploitation of another's name and likeness are rational, desirable, and necessary. Celebrities and the media industries will reward them handsomely for their efforts. Even the most determined law student, however, might have difficulty supporting a decision which held that the unauthorized use of "before and after" photos of a girl in a teen magazine – replete with the brand names of the products used to effect the transformation – was a newsworthy use of her name and likeness rather than a commercial exploitation (Lopez).

The underlying distinction between fact and fiction that is meant to provide the scaffolding for this conceptual structure becomes increasingly fragile in postmodernity as societies become saturated with signification and the value of the hyperreal accelerates. Courts have found it harder and harder to distinguish truth from falsity, and fact from fiction, or to limit First Amendment protection to objective renderings that correspond to some knowable reality. However, they maintain the philosophical edifice of "the mirror of nature" by developing ever more distinctions within distinctions to keep its structure intact.

Accommodating the immense potential value in fictionalizing the lifestyles of the rich and famous has provoked courts to articulate new distinctions within the fact and fiction dichotomy. A New York court held that a right of publicity will not be recognized where a fictionalized account of a public figure's life is depicted in such a way that the audience knows (truly?) that the events are false (Hicks). However, another New York bench decided that allowing the publication of a known fictional bibliography of a (factual) baseball player would take freedom of expression too far given the defendant's "limited research" efforts to verify his story. The book was seen as a clear case of "a commercial exploitation" (Spahn).

Attempting to limit freedom of speech defenses in publicity rights claims to the dissemination of factual information in the name of newsworthiness is conceptually boggling, culturally untenable, and politically pernicious. We value freedom of expression not as a means of spreading verifiable information about a world of brute fact, but as the activity with which we culturally construct worlds, create social knowledges, forge ethics, and negotiate intersubjective moral truths whose credence is never established by a measurable correspondence to an objective reality. Self, society, and identity are realized only through the expressive cultural activity that reworks those cultural forms that occupy the space of the social imaginary.

Political theorists of the postmodern condition point to the necessarily cultural character of contemporary politics. The social and political orders in which we live are contingent creations that we ourselves discursively construct. It is through creative cultural practices of articulation that the social world is given meaning, and, hence, it is always contestable and open to re-articulations.[36] Ernesto Laclau and Chantal Mouffe, in particular, see practices of articulating social difference as central to democratic politics.[37]

All knowledges of social identity are symbolic systems of difference, and representational structures of difference are, by their very nature, incapable of achieving closure. No structure of differential identity is ever final; new forms of difference are always emergent, and new social identities continually assert their legitimacy and presence. Indeed, advances in the democratization of Western societies are dependent upon "autonomous initiatives starting from different points within the social fabric" (Laclau and Mouffe,

"Post Marxism" 105), as new groups constitute themselves politically. Laclau and Mouffe refuse to privilege any particular subject positions, seeing the contemporary political world as one of multifaceted struggles amongst peoples continually articulating new social identities from discursive resources. Democratic politics is essentially a dialogic process whereby social identities are continually emergent in political articulation. A radical and plural democracy must maintain optimal conditions for encouraging such articulations.

Articulations of identity are possible only in conditions of polysemy, symbolic ambiguity, and a surplus of meaning, where the necessary cultural resources for contesting meaning and asserting identity are freely accessible. In the condition of postmodernity, our cultural resources are increasingly the properties of others, and meaning is the monopoly of an elite who control the commodified texts that pervade our social lives. These are the cultural images with which politically salient forms of difference may increasingly be shaped. Whose identities will be authorized and whose authorship will be recognized? As the cultural cosmos in which we live becomes increasingly commodified, we will need to define and defend the cultural practices of articulation with which we author the social world and engender our identities.

Notes

1   I will use the term "celebrity image" to designate not only the celebrity's visual likeness, but rather, all elements of the complex constellation of visual, verbal, and aural signs that circulate in society and constitute the celebrity's recognition value. The term "persona" will also refer to this configuration of significations. I will also use the terms celebrity and star interchangeably.

2   I use the umbrella term publicity rights to encompass the tort of appropriation of personality as it has developed at common law, the proprietary right of publicity that has developed in American law, and rights to prevent the appropriation of (inter alia) names and likenesses that have been enacted in provincial and state statutes as well as federal trademark legislation.

3   In Canada and Britain this right developed at common law into a distinct cause of action known as the tort of appropriation of personality. In the United States, the right of publicity arose as a category of the right of privacy which protects the individual against misappropriations of her name or likeness (among other things), and is recognized as a common law tort. Various states have also incorporated these rights in privacy statutes and state constitutional provisions. The literature detailing the origins and developing scope of these rights is so voluminous that a 256-page *bibliography* of relevant American literature was published in 1987 (Lawrence). Today the literature is even more extensive, and I make no effort to summarize all the nuances of the field here. For an insightful discussion of some of the landmark cases in American law from a cultural studies perspective see Gaines.

4   American courts are divided on the issue of whether a right of publicity survives the individual's death and in what circumstances. Some courts have refused recovery for the relatives or assignees of a decedent where the name or likeness has been appropriated for commercial purposes on the grounds that an individual's personal right of privacy does not survive his death. Others have allowed recovery for invasion of privacy in similar circumstances. Decisions predicated upon rights of publicity range from those that hold that the right survives death in all circumstances, those that require the celebrity to have engaged in some form of commercial exploitation during her life before the right will be descendible, and those which unconditionally oppose descendibility in any circumstances. The tendency, however, has been towards greater recognition of the descendibility of publicity rights and state legislatures have also inclined towards statutory recognition of the descendibility of such rights. The issue has yet to be determined or even seriously addressed in Canadian or British courts because the right is still considered a personal rather than a proprietary one.

5   See Radin for one philosophical discussion of the factors we need to weigh in determining if commodification is an appropriate mode of valuation.

6   Publicity rights are justified on the basis of the celebrity's authorship – her investment of time, effort, skill, and money in the development of the image. Such claims, however rhetorically persuasive, are rarely supported by any empirical data. How much of a star's celebrity and its value is

due to the individual's own efforts and investments? Clearly individual labor is necessary if the persona is to have value and we could not appreciate stars without their expenditure of effort. But, as Edwin Hettinger argues, "it does not follow from this that all of their value is attributable to that labor" (37).

7   For one example, see Podlesney, who argues that "the blonde" is the perfect post-WWII product and the ultimate sign of US global supremacy, white patriarchy, and the triumph of American mass media and mass production. Madonna, she suggests, is the blondest blonde ever, "with forty years of the blonde phenomenon informing her every move" (82). As Podlesney also notes, Madonna has frequently been "heralded for (mis) (re)appropriating the iconography of the blonde bombshell in a cynical defiance of the rules of sexuality codified by patriarchy" (84).

8   I have no idea whether Jarmusch sought the consent of the Presley estate or the corporate owners of his publicity rights and, if so, what royalties he agreed to pay. Nor do I know whether the Presley estate ever sought to enjoin the film's production or to demand royalties. The very possibility of such an injunction and its desirability is what is at issue here. Celebrities or their estates are not obliged to grant licenses for the use of their image regardless of the artistic or social merit of the work in which they are employed, and may withhold consent on any pretext. In this hypothetical scenario, *Mystery Train might* be privileged under the First Amendment but then again, it might not. In a longer version of this argument, I discuss some of the problems with the concept of freedom of speech in intellectual property contexts in the postmodern era. See "Publicity Rights and Political Aspiration: Mass Culture, Gender Identity, and Democracy." Forthcoming in *New England Law Review* 27 (1992).

9   A party launching the Elvis Presley cologne was held at the New York club Hot Rod in early October of 1990. Reported in Musto.

10 Presley's relatives, however, are not necessarily realizing the profit or controlling the uses to which the image is put. Prior to his death, Presley had conveyed the exclusive right to exploit his name and likeness to a corporation controlled by Colonel Tom Parker, his manager, in exchange for royalties. Factors Etc., Inc. is an assignee corporation controlled by Parker who is presumably free to exploit the Presley image in any manner.

11 See McCann for an extended elaboration of a male feminist's reflections on his relationship to the Monroe persona, and Dyer, *Heavenly Bodies*, for an insightful discussion of her position in newly emergent discourses of sexuality in the 1950s. Monroe's ongoing dynamic presence in contemporary sexual politics is addressed in MacCannell, a perceptive and scathing review of biographies written by Norman Mailer, Gloria Steinem, Anthony Summers, and Roger G. Taylor.

12 I am grateful to Kathleen Robertson for clarifying this point and expressing it so cogently.

13 See Coombe, "Encountering the Postmodern" and "Postmodernity and the Rumor"; Hutcheon; and Willis.

14 The concept of the mediascape is borrowed from Appadurai. He asserts that we need to consider the complexity of the global flow of cultural imagery as producing new fields he defines as ethnoscapes, technoscapes, finanscapes, mediascapes, and ideascapes.

15 Dick Hebdige, for example, describes the manner in which music styles like rap and hip hop deploy existing cultural forms using principles of parody, pastiche, and irony to articulate and negotiate mixed, plural, or transitional identities for social groups at the margins of national or dominant cultures. See *Cut'N'Mix*.

16 Butler's position here is congruent with my stance in "Room for Manoeuver," where I argue that subjectivity is always constructed within the discursive forms of prevailing structures of power, through the creative process of *bricolage* – cultural practices that deploy existing cultural forms in ever-emergent new fashions that may transform structures of power even as they evoke its significations.

17 For a discussion of the social and institutional structures of fan communities see the second chapter of Bacon-Smith.

18 See Bacon-Smith (322); Jenkins; and Penley, "Brownian Motion" and "Feminism, Psychoanalysis, and Popular Culture." These two essays are adapted from "To Boldly Go Where No Woman Has Gone Before: Feminism, Psychoanalysis, and Popular Culture," a lecture delivered at the conference "Capital/Culture," Toronto, 24 Apr. 1990, and at "Cultural Studies Now and in the Future," Univ. of Illinois at Urbana-Champaign, 5–9 Apr. 1990.

19 Usually produced out of women's homes, fanzines are generally mimeographed or photocopied productions but some have become more sophisticated with the introduction of computerized desktop publication technology; few issues are less than a hundred pages long. As Bacon-Smith writes:

for statistical information about the product created within the community, I turned to Roberta Rogow's *Trexindex*. Rogow, a children's librarian in Northern New Jersey, has been indexing the writings and graphic arts that have appeared in the community's fanzines since 1977. The *Trexindex* has some limitations . . . By design it considers for inclusion only those items created on the *Star Trek* theme, or items created about other media sources that appear in fanzines highlighting *Star Trek* materials. The *Trexindex* does not include fanzines devoted to other source products, nor does it include material not printed in the fanzines, such as literature passed by photocopy, hanging art, or costume. In spite of its limited goals, as of 1988, Rogow's *Trexindex* does list over 34,000 items, produced by more than ten thousand community members from the United States and English-speaking countries, and from countries such as Japan, German, and Italy . . . (322)

20   In her public lecture ("To Boldly Go") Constance Penley estimated that there were three to five hundred publishers of homoerotic fanzines alone (which would include those featuring characters from *Blake's 7, Miami Vice, The Professionals, Simon and Simon, Starsky and Hutch*, as well as the *Star Trek* characters). These publications are sold at cost, relying upon subscriptions and often pre-payment to finance production and distribution costs (Bacon-Smith 4); producers are motivated more by the desire to express identity and establish community than any monetary interest and often operate at a loss.

21   Hurt-Comfort stories are those in which one male character is hurt and suffers and the other comforts and nurses him. See discussion in chapter ten of Bacon-Smith.

22   Erotic fiction is also written about the characters in *Starsky and Hutch, Blake's 7*, and *The Professionals*.

23   Constance Penley told me in conversation that Lucasfilm threatened legal action (most likely an injunction on copyright grounds) when they discovered that fanzine writers had depicted Luke Skywalker and Han Solo in an erotic relationship. Bacon-Smith also notes that the fandom has had an uneasy relationship with Lucasfilm but does not elaborate (171n5).

24   Not all *Star Trek* fans share the same attitudes to this fiction. Some fans oppose these stories on religious or moral grounds, others find them "untrue" to the source or canon, some find them too explicit, and others worry about exposing the original actors to ridicule (Bacon-Smith 222–24).

25   This would help to explain why fans don't necessarily see the sexual relationship between Kirk and Spock as a homosexual one (Penley, "Feminism, Psychoanalysis, Popular Culture" 486–88n3). As some fans see it, there are forms of love that defy description; the sexual orientation of Kirk and Spock is irrelevant because their love is a matter of cosmic destiny (487). For similar reasons, fans don't see even the most sexually graphic material as pornographic. Such categories are simply inappropriate in these alternative universes (Bacon-Smith 243).

26   A significant exception here is the important work of Jane Gaines.

27   For longer discussions of this approach to thinking about law, see Gordon; and Coombe, "Room for Manoeuver."

28   Bacon-Smith, Jenkins, and Penley have been very careful not to reveal details about or examples of particular fanzine writing, filming, and drawing practices or the identities of practitioners. I respect their circumspection and similarly will not, as a matter of ethical principle, delineate the precise ways in which fanzines or performers in gay and lesbian subcultures could be held to violate publicity rights (as well as the copyright and trademark rights held by the commercial producers of the media products on which they draw). To do so would be to provide the legal resources with which to prosecute them, or with which they might be threatened with potential legal action.

29   Foucault argued that juridical regimes must be understood as productive rather than merely prohibitive — producing what they purport merely to represent. For a general discussion of the socially constitutive character of law see Harrington and Yngvesson. For a discussion of the juridical production of class and gender subjectivities in the transition to industrial capitalism see Coombe, "Contesting the Self."

30   The term is borrowed from E.P. Thompson, "The Moral Economy of the English Crowd in the 18th Century," *Past and Present* 50 (1971): 76–136.

31   Bacon-Smith also illuminates the complexities of the attitudes fanwriters hold with regard to the legal status of the source product. On the one hand they are aware that the characters, plots, films, television episodes, videos, logos, and dialogues with which they work are the properties of others. On the other hand, they take quite seriously the philosophy of "IDIC" (Infinite Diversity in Infinite Combination), propagated by Gene Roddenberry, the originator of *Star Trek*. They respect the legal

prohibition against profiting from their writing, tape-making, and artistic activities, but the possibility that their activities might still be enjoined on copyright, trademark, or publicity rights grounds does not appear to operate as a serious deterrent. These women know they assume risks of legal prosecution but legal risks are only a very few and possibly the most distant of the risks they face; indeed, Bacon-Smith implies that the assumption, management, and shared exploration of risk is the central ethos of the community, and constitutive of the construction and reconstruction of culture in which they engage (203–98).

32   For a discussion of complicitous critique as an attitude symptomatic of postmodernism, see Hutcheon.

33   I explore these in more detail in "Publicity Rights and Political Aspirations."

34   See, for example, Grant v. Esquire, Inc., Rinaldi v. Village Voice, Garger v. Triangle Publications.

35   The concept of promotional culture is developed by Wernick, who suggests that North American culture has come to present itself at every level as an endless series of promotional messages. Advertising, besides having become a most powerful institution in its own right, has been effectively universalized as a signifying mode.

36   For a discussion that draws upon Mikhail Bakhtin's theory of dialogism to argue the political necessity of appropriating legally commodified cultural forms in late-capitalist democracies see Coombe, "Objects of Property."

37   See Laclau and Mouffe, *Hegemony* and "Post Marxism"; and Mouffe, "Radical Democracy." See also Dallmayr, "Hegemony" and *Margins*; and Macdonald.

Works cited

Ann Margret v. *High Society Magazine* 498 F. Supp. 401, 6 *Media Law Reporter* (BNA) 1774 (S.D.N.Y. 1980).

Appadurai, Arjun. "Disjuncture and Difference in the Global Cultural Economy." *Global Culture: Nationalism, Globalization, and Modernity*. Ed. Mike Featherstone. London: Sage, 1990. 295–310.

Bacon-Smith, Camille. *Enterprising Women: Television, Fandom, and the Creation of Popular Myth*. Philadelphia: U of Pennsylvania P, 1992.

Benjamin, Walter. "The Work of Art in the Age of Mechanical Reproduction." *Illuminations*. Ed. Hannah Arendt. Trans. Harry Zohn. New York: Schocken, 1969. 217–52.

Butler, Judith. *Gender Trouble: Feminism and the Subversion of Identity*. New York: Routledge, 1990.

Certeau, Michel de. *The Practice of Everyday Life*. Trans. Steven F. Rendall. Berkeley: U of California P, 1984.

Coombe, Rosemary J. "Contesting the Self: Negotiating Subjectivities in Nineteenth Century Ontario Defamation Trials." *Studies in Law, Politics, and Society* 11 (1991): 3–48.

——— . "Encountering the Postmodern: New Directions in Cultural Anthropology." *Canadian Review of Sociology and Anthropology* 28 (1991): 188–205.

——— . "Objects of Property and Subjects of Politics: Intellectual Property Laws and Democratic Dialogue." *Texas Law Review* 69 (1991): 1853–80.

——— . "Postmodernity and the Rumor: Late Capitalism and the Fetishism of the Commodity/Sign." *Jean Baudrillard: The Disappearance of Art and Politics*. Ed. William Chaloupka and William Stearns. New York: St. Martin's, 1991. 98–108.

——— . "Room for Manoeuver: Toward a Theory of Practice in Critical Legal Studies." *Law and Social Inquiry* 14 (1989): 69–124.

Connor, Steven. *Postmodernist Culture: An Introduction to Theories of the Contemporary*. London: Blackwell, 1989.

Creel v. Crown Publishers, 115 A.D. 2d 414, 496 N.Y.S. 2d 219, 12 Media Law Reporter (BNA) 1558 (1985).

Dallmayr, Fred. "Hegemony and Democracy: On Laclau and Mouffe." *Strategies: A Journal of Theory, Culture, and Politics* 1 (1988): 29–49.

——— . *Margins of Political Discourse*. Albany: SUNY P, 1990.

Dyer, Richard, *Heavenly Bodies: Film Stars and Society*. New York: St. Martin's, 1986.

——— . *Stars*. London: BFI, 1979.

Ewen, Stewart. *All Consuming Images: The Politics of Style in Contemporary Culture*. New York: Basic, 1988.

Fiss, Owen. "Free Speech and Social Structure." *Iowa Law Review* 71 (1986): 1405–25.

Foster, Hal. *Recodings: Art, Spectacle, Cultural Politics*. Seattle: Bay, 1985.

Foucault, Michel. *History of Sexuality Volume I: An Introduction*. Trans. Robert Hurley. New York: Pantheon, 1980.

Gaines, Jane. *Contested Culture: The Image, the Voice, and the Law*. Chapel Hill: U of North Carolina P, 1991.

Garner v. Triangle Publications, 97 F. Supp. 546 (S.D.N.Y. 1951).

Golding, Sue. "James Dean: The Almost Perfect Lesbian Hermaphrodite." *Sight Specific: Lesbians and Representation*. Ed. Dionne Brand. Toronto: A Space, 1988, 49–52.

Goldstein, Richard. "We So Horny: Sado Studs and Super Sluts: America's New Sex Tude." *Village Voice* 16 Oct. 1990: 35–37.

Gordon, Robert. "Critical Legal Histories." *Stanford Law Review* 36 (1984): 57–126.

Grant v. Esquire, Inc., 367 F. Supp. 876 (S.D.N.Y.).

Groucho Marx Productions, Inc. v. Day and Night Co., Inc., 523 F. Supp. 485 (S.D.N.Y. 1981) 689 F. 2d. 317 (2d Cir 1982).

Hansen v. *High Society Magazine*, 5 *Media Law Reporter* (BNA) 2398 (N.Y. Sup. Ct.), rev'd, 76 A.D. 2d 812, 429 N.Y.S. 2d 552, 6 *Media Law Reporter* (BNA) 1618 (1980).

Harrington, Christine, and Barbara Yngvesson. "Interpretive Social Research." *Law and Social Inquiry* 15 (1990): 135–48.

Hebdige, Dick. *Cut 'N' Mix: Culture, Identity, and Caribbean Music*. London: Routledge, 1987.

Hettinger, Edwin. "Justifying Intellectual Property." *Philosophy and Public Affairs* 18 (1989): 31–52.

Hicks v. Casablanca Records, 464 F. Supp. 426, 4 *Media Law Reporter* (BNA) 1497, 204 U.S.P.Q. (BNA) 126 (S.D.N.Y. 1978).

Hutcheon, Lynda. *The Politics of Postmodernism*. London: Routledge, 1989.

Hutchinson, Alan. "Talking the Good Life: From Free Speech to Democratic Dialogue." *Yale Journal of Law and Liberation* 1 (1989): 17–30.

Jenkins, Henry. "Star Trek Rerun, Reread, Rewritten: Fan Writing as Textual Poaching." *Critical Studies in Mass Communication* 5 (1988): 85–107.

Laclau, Ernesto, and Chantal Mouffe. *Hegemony and Socialist Strategy: Towards a Radical Democratic Politics*. London: Verso, 1985.

——. "Post Marxism Without Apologies." *New Left Review* 166 (1987): 79–106.

Lange, David. "Recognizing the Public Domain." *Law and Contemporary Problems* 44.4 (1981): 147–78.

Lawrence, Lisa. "The Right of Publicity: A Research Guide." *Hastings Comm/Ent Law Journal* 10 (1987): 143–389.

Lopez v. Triangle Communications 70 A.D. 2d 359, 421 N.Y.S. 2d 57, 5 *Media Law Reporter* (BNA) 2039 (1979).

MacCannell, Dean. "Marilyn Monroe Was Not a Man." *Diacritics* 17 (1987): 114–27.

Macdonald, Bradley. "Towards a Redemption of Politics: An Introduction to the Political Theory of Ernesto Laclau." *Strategies: A Journal of Theory, Culture, and Politics* 1 (1988): 5–9.

McCann, Graham. *Marilyn Monroe: The Body in the Library*. New Brunswick: Rutgers UP, 1988.

McRobbie, Angela. "Postmodernism and Popular Culture." *Postmodernism: ICA Documents*. Ed. Lisa Appignanesi. New York: Columbia UP, 1989.

Memphis Development Foundation v. Factors Etc., Inc., 441 F. Supp. 1323 (W. D. Tenn. 1977).

Mouffe, Chantal. "Radical Democracy: Modern or Postmodern?" Ross, *Universal Abandon?* 31–45.

Musto, Michael. "La Dolce Musto." *Village Voice* 26 Oct. 1990: 44.

Newton, Esther. *Mother Camp: Female Impersonators in America*. Chicago: U of Chicago P, 1979.

Penley, Constance. "Brownian Motion: Women, Tactics, and Technology." *Technoculture*. Ed. Constance Penley and Andrew Ross. Minneapolis: U of Minnesota P, 1991, 135–62.

——. "Feminism, Psychoanalysis, and Popular Culture." *Cultural Studies*. Ed. Lawrence Grossberg, Cary Nelson, and Paula Treichler. New York: Routledge, 1992, 479–500.

——. "To Boldly Go Where No Woman Has Gone Before: Feminism, Psychoanalysis, and Popular Culture." Lecture. Toronto, 24 Apr. 1990 and Univ. of Illinois at Urbana-Champaign, 5–9 Apr. 1990.

Podlesney, Theresa. "Blondes." *The Hysterical Male: New Feminist Theory*. Ed. Arthur and Marilouise Kroker. London: St Martin's, 1991. 80–90.

Radin, Margaret. "Market Inalienability." *Harvard Law Review* 100 (1987): 1849–1937.

Rinaldi v. *Village Voice* 79 Misc. 2d 57, 359 N.Y.S. 2d 176 (1974) modified 47 A.D. 2d 180. 365 N.Y.S. 2d 199 cert. denied 423 U.S. 883 (1975).

Ross, Andrew. "Introduction." *Universal Abandon? The Politics of Post-modernism*. Ed. Andrew Ross. Minneapolis: U of Minnesota P, 1988. vii–xviii.

——— . *No Respect: Intellectuals and Popular Culture*. New York: Routledge, 1989.

Russ, Joanna. "Another Addict Raves About K/S." *Nome* 8 (1985): 28–32.

Spahn v. Julian Messner, Inc., 43 Misc. 2d 219, 250 N.Y.S. 2d 529 (1964).

Sudjic, Deyan. *Cult Heroes: How to be Famous for More than Fifteen Minutes*. New York: Norton, 1989.

Tremblay, Michael. *Hosanna*. Trans. John Van Burek and Bill Glassco. Vancouver: Talon, 1974.

University of Notre Dame v. Twentieth Century Fox, 22 A.D. 2d 452, N.Y.S. 2d 301 (1965).

Wernick, Andrew. "Promotional Culture." *Canadian Journal of Political and Social Theory* 15 (1991): 260–84.

Willis, Paul. *Common Culture*. Philadelphia: Open University P, 1990.

Chapter 33

Thomas H. Guback

GOVERNMENT SUPPORT TO THE FILM INDUSTRY IN THE UNITED STATES (1987)

THE ECONOMIC PLIGHT OF SMALL, independent film and video producers and distributors frequently raises the question whether some form of federal government support should exist to insure their well-being. There have been isolated moments as well during the last three decades when financial problems have prompted similar concerns for the Hollywood filmed entertainment industry itself.

There are, of course, federal aid programs that have existed since 1965. The National Endowment for the Arts seeks to encourage new work by artists of exceptional talent, and to assist its exhibition in theaters or on television. The National Endowment for the Humanities supports film projects that explore human cultures and experiences. Traditionally, though, filmed entertainment in the United States has been financed by investment from the private sector. Because of this, it is easy to believe that the private and public sectors have been at arm's length, and that the film industry has been unconcerned about using state assistance to improve its own financial posture.

Capitalist relations of production, and the making of commodities for the purpose of valorizing capital, are the context for almost all cinematic activity in the United States. It makes no difference whether the enterprises are large or small, they subscribe to the same economic premises that guide their behavior. Production, distribution, and exhibition take place within a capitalist framework, and it is in this framework, therefore, that the question of government financial support must be situated and analyzed.

Elsewhere (8, 9, 10), I have described the rationale, development, and operation of film aid programs in west European countries. Rather than up-dating their myriad relevant details. I want to turn my attention to the United States and to consider in a more general way the meaning and practice of state support for the film industry in a private enterprise system. This reveals to us an important aspect of the political economy of the film establishment, while illuminating how the state responds to a specific private interest.

Some general observations are in order before the peculiarities of the filmed entertainment business can be considered.

PRIVATE ECONOMY AND PUBLIC STATE

The dispensing of financial aid by the public sector to the private sector represents a significant step in the evolution of industrial capitalism. It would be safe to conclude, looking historically at the matter, that more, rather than less, of such assistance will be proposed for the future. The significance of this development exists in what it tells us, not only about the nature of the economic system itself, but also about the terms on which the state and private business relate to each other in an era of monopoly capitalism.[1]

Two centuries ago, when capitalism achieved supremacy in several countries in Europe, it was premised on the assumption that certain natural laws of economics existed. These could be discovered by rational humans who, in responding to them, would fulfill society's needs in an efficient manner. In place of religious, governmental, and guild regulation of economic conduct, competition was to keep the system in check and encourage acceptable behavior from all engaged in economic pursuits—which meant sellers as well as buyers. Church and political strictures were anathema to this system, as was any kind of favouritism or intervention by these authorities. The whole idea was to allow the demand for profit, rather than social need, to govern the allocation of economic resources. Unquestionably, this involved some risks, but the market place was supposed to be the final, objective arbiter in this matter. The state, consequently, was relegated to a mere protector of productive private property, and was mandated to stay out of economic processes so that unbridled competition could sort things out. The economic system, so it was claimed, was inherently efficient and self-correcting, if left to itself.

Without reviewing the details of the last couple of centuries, suffice it to say that capitalist economies, when left to themselves, have demonstrated a repeated proclivity for crises, uneven development, and the negation of what was supposed to be the basic regulating mechanism: competition. Concentration and centralization of productive resources, including industrial and bank capital, have called into question the basic assumptions of the system. Indeed, if it were not for a few brakes on this process, such as the antitrust laws, there would be even greater degrees of concentration and centralization throughout all economic sectors (see 4).

These features have meant that, particularly within the last several decades, the state has been called upon to use its power to avert major economic calamity and widespread breakdown (18). Whereas two centuries ago, it was in the interest of the dominant economic class to render the state impotent, it is more and more the necessity of that class and the system to demand state intervention as a means of self-preservation. This has taken many forms, and has been rationalized by creative rhetoric, but the underlying imperatives are quite uniform. While there might be disagreements among segments of the private sector about the best way to use state power to avoid economic crisis, a constant result has been the enlargement of state power. The state has been obliged to move from a posture of laissez-faire, and to take, first, remedial action and, then, creative action to deal with problems of the economic system in general, and with those of certain sectors, and even companies, in particular.

A notable aspect of state intervention is that it seeks to maintain the integrity of the economic system as a whole, rather than considering alternatives to it. In this way, the state demonstrates that it is hardly a neutral institution, but one that actively works to facilitate capital reproduction and accumulation, and consequently to facilitate the broad interests of the private sector. As an institution, the state is not merely a passive reflection of private economic interests. In addition to being a political instrument, the state is an economic instrument. A disturbing aspect of all this is that we continue to use the rhetoric and slogans of an economic system that has been largely superceded.

This background is essential for putting into context the issue of federal support for the filmed entertainment business, or particular segments of it. This is not a new question, by the way; it has been discussed for at least a quarter of a century in the United States. But more importantly, the question is certainly not an isolated one. It reflects a general malaise that permeates innumerable economic sectors. It is perennial because it is systemic.

STATE INTERVENTION IN THE PRIVATE ECONOMY

The subject of state aid for film and video usually is addressed in two ways: Should such aid exist? and, What particular form should it take? I would suggest that the issue needs to be reformulated, because as it now stands, state aid seems to be a solution in search of a problem. It would be more appropriate to ask: *who* has a problem? *what* is the problem? what are the *causes* of the problem? It seems to be shortsighted and a questionable practice to apply remedies without investigating and understanding these causes, and without clearly distinguishing causes from symptoms. In its most stark form, the question ought to be: What causes of problems is state intervention being asked to eradicate or alleviate? Framed in this way, the question naturally leads to another: Is state intervention capable of eliminating the causes, or will it be a mere palliative?

The basic problem that state intervention throughout the economy has been asked to confront is one of capital reproduction and accumulation, although the problem is never stated in clear terms like that. The source of difficulty is the inability of the private economic system to maintain a suitable average rate of profit for firms and sectors in it. Additionally, because of exigencies of the system, there is a broad inability of market mechanisms to satisfy many kinds of needs. Usually, these are conveniently labelled "minority" demands, which, unfortunately, camouflages what is really involved: the profit imperative's supremacy over social needs. Calling them "minority" demands, also tends to excuse the system's inability to handle them, and makes this seem to be at most a minor aberration.

In addition to direct bolstering of capital accumulation, state intervention has been summoned to blunt the edges of antagonisms, not just between classes, but within them as well. Those who feel threatened by the evolution of the economic system, and who feel especially powerless to affect it, can become volatile elements.[2] Their demands need to be heard, and they have to be assuaged, if it seems that doing so could contribute to the stability of the system as a whole. In this regard, contests between small and large business[3] frequently have necessitated state intervention in the market place, usually to protect the small from being engulfed by the large or, at minimum, to assure a basic economic return that would keep the small afloat.[4]

State intervention, then, and particularly financial support, is a device to protect an economic sector from its own internal weakness and contradictions, as well as from pressures of a systemic nature originating in the economy at large. This principle is quite evident in the film business. The way it has been translated there warrants closer attention.

STATE AID FOR THE PRIVATE FILM BUSINESS

Considering only the United States, it is possible to discern three arguments that have been advanced in favor of some form of state intervention to correct ills of the picture business. All three arguments called for subsidization of production, that is, an additional increment of revenue to producers beyond that traditionally obtainable from rentals paid by exhibitors.

In addition, all three arguments originated in the capitalist sector, demonstrating again that state intervention is eagerly sought when it can benefit private interests.

One argument has at its foundation the position that theatrical motion pictures produced in the United States are subject to inevitable commercial pressures, and that these result in content that is, among other things, sexually explicit and gratuitously violent. Film producers can do better than that, this argument contends, but only if they are relieved of the irresistible imperative to make commodities that make profit. "[S]ince the film industry—unlike any other manufacturer of saleable commodities—is capable of a tremendous and vital contribution to our humanistic environment, those members of the film community who want to embark on ventures of cultural benefit should be able to do so, independent of the profit system." According to this argument, "[t]he only way to advance film as an art form in America would be by some form of government subsidization" (6, pp. 155–156). The state already aids the arts, and there is no reason why film should be excluded. Film is an industry too, and government subsidization of agriculture, transportation, petroleum and mineral industries provide ample precedents for assisting film production.

There are several difficulties with this argument, but let me point only to a couple. First, the obvious source of the problem is the economic system to which film is subjected, but subsidization in this proposal treats only a symptom, not the cause. Second, such a plan would absolve the private sector of even the most rudimentary responsibility for "culturally beneficial" production. Since that obligation is economically unprofitable, the task can be discarded and handed over to the state, while the private sector is allowed to devote its resources to the production of profit. According to this plan, the state supports deficit activities at public expense, whereas private business retains activities that facilitate capital reproduction and accumulation.

A second argument, prevalent as far back as the early 1960s, took as its starting point so-called runaway production, that is, the flight of film making from California to England, Italy, France, Spain, and elsewhere as well.[5] This argument contended that producers were deserting Hollywood because they were attracted to foreign countries by production subsidy programs cunningly devised by governments abroad to stimulate employment in their own nations' film industries.[6] To eradicate runaway production and bring it back to California, according to this argument, the United States needed a subsidy plan of its own that would erase the competitive advantage of other countries.

This general line of thought did not bother to acknowledge that subsidy programs abroad were initiated at the insistence of foreign film businesses (chiefly producers and distributors) as a way of providing them financial support in the face of massive film exportation from the United States. Moreover, in the post war decades, the withdrawal of earnings of American films was partially blocked in many countries because of general economic difficulties, and this created pools of funds that American companies decided to use for production abroad. Wage rates were quite favorable overseas, too. Taken together, these factors served to stimulate what amounted to capital export from the United States, because comparatively higher rates of return could be anticipated from production abroad than from production in California. In other words, there were better opportunities for capital reproduction when films were produced overseas because costs could be reduced while revenues could be increased artificially by the subsidy.

The implicit purpose of the subsidy advocated by this argument was to increase the opportunities for capital reproduction in this country, and thereby to entice U.S. companies back to the U.S. It is perfectly clear, though, that capital knows no nationality, and that capital flight can occur whenever important differences appear in comparative rates of return. This continues to be painfully obvious in other industries, as manufacturing and services are shifted from the north-eastern states to the sun belt, or from the United States to the Far East.

A third argument for state intervention, heard most often in the 1960s and early 1970s, drew inspiration from the decline of theatrical film production and concomitant rise of unemployment among film industry workers. Because runaway production was less of an issue by this time, and certainly this was true by the early 1970s,[7] it was apparent that other forces beyond foreign subsidies were at work to reduce production of theatrical films in the United States. It also was clear that theater screens were not being flooded by imported films, and television had shown virtually no imported programming, so foreign producers could not be blamed for stealing the American market. That chronic unemployment characterized industrial sectors throughout the country, and therefore was systemic rather than peculiar to film making, somehow fell out of view when Congressional hearings were held in 1971 on joblessness in the motion picture business (25). The state was urged to "do something" to save this important industry that had helped to display American institutions, and particularly the benefits of the private enterprise system, to the rest of the world.[8] That state aid is fundamentally inconsistent with the ideology of private enterprise was something else that fell out of view. In any case, advocating public subsidization of private business became an even more acceptable position to take, and industry leaders lost no time convincing the state that this was the American way. The campaign for a subsidy was well orchestrated around the theme of creating jobs and putting Americans back to work. While one might feel uncomfortable about subsidizing business people, raising objections to giving jobs to workers seemed more disrespectful than stepping on the flag.[9] (But note that creating jobs in the private profit sector is deemed acceptable, while creating jobs in the public non-profit sector is treated as "make-work" nonsense.[10])

There were problems with the proposed solution, though. As grave as it was, unemployment was only a symptom. Workers were eager to return to their jobs, but they could not do that because they did not control their jobs. They were dependent upon owners of productive resources, and upon centers of finance with whom owners have a community of interest. There was no doubt that theatrical film production was declining,[11] and yet exhibitors, the principal source of demand, were complaining that they wanted *more* films. The roots of this contradiction were in the comparative rates of return that could be achieved from capital invested in film versus other fields, and in the necessity imposed on many film companies by lenders and major investors to reduce long term debt and to increase profitability. Because capital is largely indifferent to where it finds its return, capital was attracted less by manufacturing motion pictures and more by fields in which rewards were at least as good, or better, given the level of risk. We hardly need to recall that the long period of financial crisis in Hollywood culminated, in the late 1960s and early 1970s, with substantial changes in ownership and control of most major film production and distribution companies.[12] This signalled a broad attempt to shape-up the industry, to safeguard loans, to insure repayment of debts, and to revitalize financial returns. In an oligopolistic industry, where conduct of a few dominant firms has significant impact on business patterns as a whole, it takes only a handful of large companies engaging in parallel behavior to create a shortage of product. The general effect of limiting supply is the raising of price, and this, in turn, facilitates capital reproduction.

Seen in these terms, unemployed workers and their jobs became hostages of the private sector. The ransom was a higher rate of return on capital to be achieved either by reducing production and raising price, or by underwriting production through some form of state subsidy that would channel public funds into private coffers. The second alternative may have given jobs to some workers, although no explicit guarantees ever were offered on that account. That is not surprising because the *fundamental* problem of the system was not creating jobs but creating profit, and profit can come from greater productivity of labor power not necessarily more labor power.

In this case, as in the ones previously mentioned, state intervention in the guise of subsidization was trying to come to grips with some nasty fallout from the private sector, to clean up the debris as it were, and to make sure this debris did not impede the smooth functioning of that sector. In political terms, these pro-subsidy arguments represent a kind of reformism that admits the inherent shortcomings of the private system and the need for state intervention, provided the intervention benefits owners of capital and facilitates expansion of capital. By concentrating on symptoms, rather than examining causes, these arguments call only for cosmetic treatment. But perhaps nothing more can be expected because, in a capitalist society, the function of the state is to protect private interest and not to throw it into question.

PLANS FOR STATE ASSISTANCE

Having examined three arguments that favor state subsidization, I would like to review briefly some attempts to launch financial aid programs for film production in the United States. My description and analysis hardly constitute an extended discussion, a task that should command future attention because it is an undeveloped aspect of the film industry's political economy and history. The need is not just to accumulate and set down the facts, but more importantly to put them into a framework for explaining relations between the state and the private sector. (U.S. subsidiaries have benefitted from subsidy programs in western Europe that were designed to encourage indigenous artists and companies, but that subject is beyond the present discussion.)

One of the earliest plans was drafted in 1964 and circulated at a meeting of the Association of Motion Picture and Television Producers (26). It would have added a few cents to the price of each ticket, the proceeds being shared by production companies according to some formula that was not revealed publicly at the time. This proposal was superficially similar to the Eady scheme in the United Kingdom to the extent that both were based on a ticket surcharge. The difference was that the British plan operated by government authority, whereas the American proposal was to be run by the industry. This would have amounted to a private tax levied on spectators—taxation without representation. The proposal was said to have evolved from one that would have channeled to film production a small share of the federal tax then imposed on theater admission tickets.[13] That an industry-operated system had to be proposed suggests that the idea to divert a part of the federal admission tax did not elicit much support, or was simply impractical on its face. In any case, the private plan would have required the voluntary cooperation of theater owners, who would have had to set their ticket prices higher, collect the money, and then make regular payments to some central agency. Producers and distributors obviously would have had to agree to the principle of the plan and, most importantly, to the basis on which the money pool would be divided. Should financially unsuccessful pictures be supported? Or should already successful pictures receive further rewards? Should artistic and cultural quality be criteria for judgment? The dilemmas are obvious.

A surcharge or tax on tickets, with rebates to production companies, seemed simple in principle, but would have been complex in practice. Because the subsidy fund was to be consumer-fed, the manufacturing sector, which it was designed to aid, would have continued to be susceptible to all the uncertainties of the retail side of the business. Admissions, in particular, were declining during this period. For these kinds of reasons, the 1964 plan made little headway, and as long as production companies could enjoy foreign subsidies and lower labor costs, there seemed little motivation to deal with obstacles to a domestic plan.

Unemployment among production workers continued to be a problem throughout the 1960s. As late as December 1970, several thousand workers rallied under the auspices of the Hollywood Film Council (AFL) to protest jobless rates and to demand more production in the United States. California Governor Reagan endorsed the principle of tax incentives for American-made films[14]—or more accurately, for the companies that make them—and hinted that import tariffs might be necessary on foreign-made films, although it still is hard to see how they had anything to do with unemployment.[15] Representative John Dent, meanwhile, said Congressional hearings would look into the problem.

In March 1971, a group of 21 California Congressional representatives introduced the Domestic Film Production Incentive Act (HR 6069). This legislation avoided the difficulties of the 1964 plan and proposed welfare for producers through another mechanism. For computing federal income tax, the Act would have allowed a tax payer to exclude 20 percent of the gross income earned by feature films made in the United States, provided that at least 80 percent of the labor cost was paid to U.S. citizens.[16] The Act applied to revenue received by production as well as distribution companies. Thus, a firm earning $1 million from a picture made in the U.S. could exclude $200,000 of that amount when calculating its federal income tax.

A month after this legislation was introduced, two dozen labor and employer representatives met with President Nixon to urge his support. He reportedly expressed sympathy for the industry, but refused to make a personal commitment because the House Committee on Ways and Means was then reviewing a broad overhaul of taxes in order to stimulate the sagging domestic economy.

Hearings on the Incentive Act were held in October 1971 by the Committee on Education and Labor (25), but these centered more on unemployment in Hollywood than on the legislation's provisions. The Act made no perceptible headway, and finally died in committee at the end of the Congressional session. Its death was hardly memorialized with deep mourning because behind this public pageant to secure subsidization was another campaign that was much quieter and more discreet.

Before turning to it, two additional points need to be brought out about the Domestic Film Production Incentive Act. First, its benefits would not have been much use for films that were box office flops, those that earned very little revenue. This would become all the more serious for flops with great negative costs and release expenses. If the implicit objective of subsidization was to facilitate capital reproduction, the Act's provisions did little to compensate companies for losses stemming from poor box office receipts. In this respect, the Act would not have accomplished the task that capital required.

Its greatest shortcoming, though, was that it would have supported only theatrical production, while doing nothing for TV series and made-for-TV production. The latter, of course, had become an important business line for many companies, which were shifting capital from theatrical to television production. Inasmuch as the principle of welfare for the film industry seemed rather established, it made little sense to settle for half a loaf when more was within reach. The imperative to bring television program production under the umbrella of federal financial aid obviously was one reason why the Incentive Act was allowed to slip into its grave while a better alternative was sought.

The solution to this problem had to be cut loose from an idea implicitly imbedded in both the 1964 and 1971 plans—namely that financial aid should be connected in some way to box office receipts, which is the way European plans operate (5, 21). The solution had to be disassociated from the concept that films were products consumed by paying theatrical spectators. The alternative had to be based on the notion that filmed entertainment involved capital outlays that bought equipment, raw materials, and labor power, which were used by owners to create value. In this context, the manufacturing of filmed entertainment for theater or television was analogous to other industrial activities and, for financial aid purposes, could be treated similarly. Consequently, the solution that was pursued made no distinction between investment in filmed entertainment and investment in other undertakings (an acknowledgement that capital is indifferent to where it finds its return).

The answer existed in the Revenue Act of 1971 (HR 10947) that was being considered throughout the year in slightly different versions by the House and Senate. Both versions, though, proposed to restore a 7 percent tax credit for business investment that had been repealed in 1969. Production of theatrical motion pictures and television programs had never been eligible for this tax credit. However, lobbying by the Motion Picture Association of America persuaded the House and Senate to include them in the Revenue Act of 1971, which became law later that year. The Act was approved by substantial margins in both chambers, but there was a common criticism, summed up best by Representative Charles Vanik. The "tax credit," he said, "appears more likely to increase corporate profits than to create jobs for unemployed workers" (20, p. 102).

Since 1971, therefore, it has been public policy in the United States to provide welfare to filmed entertainment production companies, and to support their activities with a tax advantage. The word "subsidy" is scrupulously avoided, of course, yet a subsidy is what it is: a grant from the state to assist private business undertakings. The film industry, as we have seen, is just one industrial sector among many to benefit from this state largess, which is designed to facilitate capital reproduction and accumulation. The tax credit system is quite distinct from various tax shelter schemes developed in the 1970s by creative attorneys and accountants for investors in film making. The Internal Revenue Service has been monitoring abusive tax shelters and closing them down (see 19, 24).

The Revenue Act of 1971 permits companies to reduce their income tax in proportion to their investment in tangible property, which includes theatrical films and television programs. The tax credit amounts to 7 percent of the cost of eligible property that has a useful life of at least 7 years.[17] In practice, this means that a company investing $50 million in the production of theatrical features or TV programs can reduce its federal income tax that year by $3.5 million.

No matter how unsuccessful the product, it still generates a tax credit. Indeed, the tax credit is like profit from a permanent ancillary market, but one that involves no selling costs and one that can be counted on to pay the same rate year after year. The tax credit, like other sources of earnings, is factored by production companies into the revenue-expense-income equation. As an example, Taft Broadcasting Company explained to investment analysts in 1979 how the tax credit significantly limited its downside risk on the series *Man From Atlantis*, produced for NBC (23). Total production cost was about $10 million, the eligible tax credit was $600,000, which resulted in a net cost of about $9.4 million. Against that, revenue consisted of $7.9 million from the network, $1.4 million from foreign sales, and $200,000 from licensing fees, for a total of $9.5 million. Thanks to the tax credit, the series at that point was showing a profit of $100,000. Similarly, Metro-Goldwyn-Mayer executives revealed in 1980 that "even the financial results of an unsuccessful series can be rewarding because of the substantial investment tax credits generated by television production . . ." (12). The mid-season cancellation of *Executive Suite* normally would have resulted in a loss, had it not been for foreign sales and the tax credit.

The Revenue Act of 1971 allows a company to deduct from its tax bill an amount up to 7 percent of qualified investment in film and television production—and in other business lines as well, if it is a diversified company. How does this translate into value at tax time? The tax credit method means that a company might be able to cut upwards of a quarter, a half, or even more, from its federal income tax. Metro-Goldwyn-Mayer in 1975 was able to reduce its statutory tax rate of 48 percent to an effective rate of 37 percent. In 1980, its statutory rate of 46 percent came down to 27 percent, and in 1982 it fell to only 3 percent. Columbia Pictures Industries in fiscal year 1980 lowered its rate from the statutory 46 percent to 24 percent, thanks to tax credits. From 1979 through 1983, MCA's average effective tax rate was less than 22 percent, while the statutory rate was 46 percent. Other examples abound. Percentages, of course, do not reveal the whole story. More interesting are the actual dollar figures, which could be recited for film companies for each of the last dozen or so years. A few samples from 1983 should suffice. Thanks to tax credits, these companies cut their bills by the following amounts: Disney, $10 million; MCA, $27.6 million; and Warner, $42.5 million (2).

Exhibition companies, as businesses, can qualify for tax credits just as do other enterprises.[18] Since exhibitors customarily are not involved in financing production, their credits are derived from other kinds of investment in tangible property, often totally unrelated to filmed entertainment. This is especially true for diversified companies, such as General Cinema. Yet, even exhibition companies with no other business lines manage to benefit from the system. AMC Entertainment Inc., the third largest theater circuit in the United States, had tax credits totalling $2.7 million from 1979 through 1984 (1).

Some sidelights on the investment tax credit system are worth noting. One concerns how companies treat tax credits in the financial accounts for their productions. The tax credit received by a studio, as we know, can improve its profit. But for the purposes of a studio's contacts that allow stars a participation in the profit of a particular production, the credit is not considered to be income, and is not shared with them (11). Second, MCA filed a tax refund suit in 1975 contending that it was entitled retroactively to credits on certain theatrical films and television programs for the years 1962 through 1970. The company subsequently amended its claim to include an additional group of theatrical features. In 1979 and 1980, the two claims were resolved in MCA's favor at a value of $52 million. Third, carry-forward provisions of the tax law allow a company to stockpile credit. As a result, Orion Pictures Corporation was able to report to its owners in 1983 that it had accumulated tax credits of $13 million that could be used to reduce future federal income tax, before those credits began expiring in 1990. Finally, because of tie-ins between the film and music industries, we should note that, under the Economic Recovery Tax Act of 1981, costs of creating record masters now qualify for a 10 percent investment tax credit. This is likely to be a further benefit to MCA and, especially, Warner.

Investment tax credits certainly have been a bonanza for film industry companies.[19] This subsidization has meant the redistribution of money into the hands of those who already have it—welfare for the wealthy. Other public doles to this class were written into the Tax Reduction Act of 1975 and the Tax Reform Act of 1976. These permitted a company to establish an Employee Stock Ownership Plan (ESOP). Under this program, a company can claim an *additional* tax credit of one percent of qualified investment against federal income tax if the amount is contributed to an ESOP. Such contributions are used to purchase shares of the company's common stock on the open market. Under the ESOP program, MCA was able to claim additional tax credits of $30.4 million from 1979 through 1982. The ESOP program, of course, has nothing to do directly with film production, but it is still another example of how the state assists already-privileged classes.

The investment tax credit system initiated in 1971 has been a windfall for owners, but it has done little to increase production and relieve unemployment in the film industry. Those alleged benefits were the sweet rationalizations that made the plan palatable and saleable. Indeed, in 1976, when Congress considered still another wave of tax reform legislation, a parade of witnesses reiterated the catalog of sour economic conditions on the film industry that had become so familiar by then. In particular, the president of the Screen Actors Guild pointed out that unemployment was great throughout skills and crafts, and that production of films and television programs was languishing (17, 21). Obviously, the 1971 tax credit scheme had not come to grips with those problems. Yet labor's solution to massive jobless-ness in the filmed entertainment industry was to call for expanded federal relief *for the owners*. This was another example of the trickle-down theory, which claims that helping the unfortunate can be done by first helping the fortunate.

A sidelight needs to be mentioned about film industry aid. We will recall that the Domestic Film Production Incentive Act of 1971 died in committee when tax credit eligibil-ity was extended to film and television production. But the incentive plan was resuscitated and introduced again in January 1973 by Representative Thomas Railsback of Illinois. Its fate was no better that time. Normally such a tiny detail of history is not worth dwelling upon, except in this instance. During his tenure in the House, Congressman Railsback was a friend of film industry interests, particularly on cable and copyright legislation. In January 1983, he was hired as an executive vice president of the Motion Picture Association of America.

CONCLUDING OBSERVATIONS

I would like to draw my conclusions around four points. First, contrary to popular belief, American filmed entertainment production companies already are subsidized, and have been for some time. For more than three decades, their branches in western Europe have been able to draw from state supported programs that were designed originally to benefit Europe's own domestic production companies. In the United States, as we have seen, theatrical and television production has received assistance since 1971, and even before then, if we use the example of MCA. One difference, though, between the European and American models is that the European market was overrun by exported American pictures. Nothing even remotely similar has happened in the United States. A second difference is that, in the United States, filmed entertainment is not state supported for its own intrinsic nature. It is not singled out because it is *film*. Financial aid is premised on the fact that a company manufacturing films or door knobs makes investments in tangible property that is put into service by that company. The end result, nonetheless, is that production of filmed enter-tainment is a supported undertaking. It is public policy to treat film production as other forms of economic activity. This bypasses the entire debate about whether film is art, and whether it ought to be financially assisted if it benefits society. Of course, there are legitimate questions about that. But there are no questions about film being a business.

Second, if one strips away the rationalizations, the rhetoric, and the appeals to higher purposes, the fundamental reason for state support in a capitalist economy is to stimulate and underwrite production of profit, to put a floor under (and increase) rates of return on capital. That this is the real objective, and that the state has to intervene to help business attain that goal, demonstrates that the private economy is no longer capable of functioning by itself. The private system has been in a continuous condition of crisis. Incentives from the state have been a means, not just to prevent breakdown, but also to insure that the dominant class can continue to secure its rewards.

Third, that subsidization is an established principle throughout the economy, and not just in the film industry, raises the question why this public support has not been contingent upon reorganization and democratic public control.[20] By forgiving some tax imposed on film production companies, the public is participating economically in the industry. Yet decisions about how resources are used continue to be entirely in a very small circle of private hands.

Finally, if a symptom to be addressed is the strangulation of small, or independent film and video businesses (and they can benefit from the investment tax credit system, too), then trying to keep them solvent at additional public expense may not be an appropriate answer. A life-support system like that is not a cure. Historically, the trend of American capitalism over the last century in all fields has been precisely the eradication of the little business person, the self-employed enterpreneur or artisan, and the enormous growth in the concentration and centralization of economic resources.

The beginning of a solution needs to be found in rethinking primary causes, and *that* is an issue much larger than the film industry.

Notes

1   Classical liberalism's concept of the pluralist state, an impartial body that sorts out inputs from co-equal groups in society, has been called into question by empirical evidence of how the state actually operates, and by Marxist theories about the function and role of the state in a capitalist society (see 7, 13, 14).

2   A case in point in the 1970s was the opposition of the National Association of Theatre Owners to the relaxation of restraints on the growth of pay television. NATO initially took its case to the Federal Communications Commission, which ruled that exhibitors had no standing on this matter. Subsequently, NATO "tried to persuade" Congress that deregulation of pay television was not in the public interest. Theater owners, of course, were not the only parties to oppose expansion of pay television. Much more vigorous opposition came from the commercial television networks.

3   A typical example was the contest between independent exhibitors and major distributors, which was substational enough to provoke a couple of rounds of Congressional hearings thirty years ago (15, 16). In the mid-1970s, the problem erupted again, but this time in a number of private antitrust suits in which major distributors and major theater circuits were defendants.

4   The condition of the Canadian film industry could be studied in some detail. One need only recall that the Council of Canadian Filmmakers, meeting in Winnipeg in 1975, urged the federal and provincial governments to cooperate on a plan for nationalizing one of the major theater circuits so that Canadian made features would have a chance to be exhibited.

5   A contemporary problem facing California is the exodus of film making from that state to other locations around the country, and the flow of money to those locations as well.

6   In House committee hearings on this subject, the thrust of testimony by industry spokespeople, reiterated by some Congressional representatives, was that the U.S. film companies were not to blame for runaway production, that they had been subjected to "tremendous economic pressure by foreign governments" (25, p. 8), and the "producers were forced to go into foreign markets" (25, p. 102). Throwing the blame overseas absolved U.S. business from any responsibility for its own decisions and actions, and created the illusion that it was the harmed party that merited sympathy and concessions.

7   To some extent, the devaluation of the U.S. dollar tended to offset the economic attractiveness of western Europe as a production site.

8   A statement by Representative James Corman of California was submitted for the hearing record. He declared: "We must make it our national policy to save this vital American industry without further delay. The motion picture industry is, after all, the industry which has 'sold America' to the world by a graphic display of the American system, and of the productivity of free, competitive enterprise. It is the motion picture industry which has opened up new vistas of international communication and it is most directly responsible for much of the development of art and culture in this century" (25, p. 17).

9   Of course, creation-of-jobs is not sufficient reason in itself to support something out of hand without first critically examining the nature of the thing that is supposed to create those jobs. The creation-of-jobs argument does more to mystify, rather than clarify, the economic processes that are at work. The argument is advanced by business to justify a wide range of policies that would work in its immediate favor, such as relaxing environmental controls, health and safety standards in the work place, etc. We only need to recall that arson, vandalism, child pornography, and war create jobs, too.

10   Until February 1983, President Reagan had opposed expansion of federal aid to the jobless. His change of position was conditioned on the belief that only the private sector could create jobs that

mattered, while the public sector (and particularly the federal government) merely created "make work" jobs that had little significance or use.

11   According to data from the Motion Picture Association of America, there was an average of 212 theatrical films released annually by national distributors in the 1975–1979 period. For the comparable period a decade earlier, the annual average was 261 films.

12   Among the changes in ownership and control during this period, we can note the following acquisitions: Paramount by Gull & Western Industries in 1966, United Artists by Transamerica Corporation in 1967, Warner Bros Seven Arts Ltd. by Kinney National in 1969, Metro-Goldwyn-Mayer by Kirk Kerkorian in 1969, and Columbia Pictures by Herbert Allen interests in 1974. The acquistions of Paramount and Warner Bros, were assisted by the Chase Manhattam Bank. The financial status of these and other companies was none too solid, as long term debt figures reveal Metro-Goldwyn-Mayer, $62.5 million in 1969; United Artists Corporation, $68.9 million in 1971; Columbia Pictures, $122.6 millions in 1973. The interest payments by these companies are worth noting: Metro-Goldwyn-Mayer, $7.6 million in 1969; Artists Corporation, $6.7 million in 1971, and Columbia Pictures $20.9 million in 1974.

13   Note the similarity to proposals in the early 1980s for increasing the revenue of companies that own copyrights to motion pictures transmitted by television stations, cable systems, or pay TV services. Such films can be recorded at home quite easily. HR 5705, introduced in March 1982, would have imposed a compulsory royalty charge (a euphemism for a use tax) on video cassette recorders and blank cassettes. The fees were to be deposited by merchants with the Copyright Royalty Tribunal, which would then distribute them to owners of film copyrights.

14   In 1971, Governor Reagan wrote to President Nixon about "the need for immediate action by the U.S. Government" to overcome "the tragedy of our film industry" (25, p. 8).

15   The public record on this issue often is considerably confused, resulting from a failure to distinguish between films made abroad by subsidiaries of U.S. companies and those made by foreign companies. The latter, as a group, never have had any significant share of the U.S. domestic market, and their dollar earnings have been negligible compared to the earnings of U.S. films overseas.

16   According to the Act, a domestic film was defined as one in which "[n]ot less than 80 percent of the total remuneration paid or payable for services performed in the production of the film is paid or payable to persons who are United States persons at the time the services are performed. In determining such total remuneration, any remuneration which is contingent upon receipts or profits of the film shall be excluded; and there may also be excluded amounts paid or payable as remuneration for services performed by any two individuals, neither of whom was a United States person while performing such services." The Act also provided that the aggregate playing time of portions of the film photographed outside the United States must not exceed 20 percent of the total playing time.

17   Under the tax credit system, the taxpayer can receive an investment credit for tangible property that is placed in service by the taxpayer. For full credit, the property placed in service must have a useful life of at least seven years. If the property has a useful life of at least five years, but fewer than seven, the credit is two thirds of the full credit. If the property has a useful life of at least three years but fewer than five years, the credit is one third. The tax credit is available only for investments in "qualified films," which are motion pictures or videotapes created primarily for public entertainment or educational purposes. The credit is calculated on the basis of "qualified United States production costs," which are direct costs incurred for making, processing and distributing in the United States.

18   Exhibition companies also have been trying to re-qualify for financial assistance from the Small Business Administration, from which they have been barred since 1978. At that time, the SBA declared that theaters were subject to the "opinion molder rule," an administrative policy under which the SBA can deny assistance to small businesses engaged in the creation or dissemination of ideas, values, thoughts, or opinions. The National Association of Theatre Owners has been working for some years to reverse this policy, and was an active supporter of HR 1157, introduced in February 1983 by Representative Joseph Addabbo. The bill, which would have restricted the SBA's power to enforce the opinion molder rule, had not been passed by the end of 1984.

19   We should not overlook another form of assistance to motion picture production. On the state government level, there are some tax credit plans that allow companies using locations or production facilities within the state to receive benefits for state income tax purposes. Beyond that, there are dozens of state film commissions that actively court film production for their states by scouting locations and assisting the companies in numerous other ways. The public expense of

running these commissions is supposedly offset by the money production companies spend in the host state.

20   I am not suggesting by this that limited public input, such as in a managerial form, is going to correct the ills of particular companies, industrial sectors, or the entire economy for that matter. But arguments that propose inauguration of limited public control need to be critically examined because they represent an attempt to deal with, by reform, the most serious deficiencies of a private enterprise economy (see 3). Reform, of course, does not change the structural relations of production. Private ownership with some kind of limited public decision-making input is still private ownership, even though its attendant problems may be cosmetically camouflaged.

References

1.   AMC Entertainment Inc. *Common Stock Prospectus*. August 18, 1983, and *1984 Annual Report*.
2.   Annual reports of the companies cited.
3.   Carnoy, Martin and Derek Shearer. *Economic Democracy*. Armonk, New York: M. E. Sharpe Inc., 1980.
4.   Compaine, Benjamin. Christopher Sterling, Thomas Guback, and J. Kendrick Noble Jr. *Who Owns the Media?*, 2nd edition. White Plains, New York: Knowledge Industry Publications Inc., 1982.
5.   Degand, Claude. *Le Cinéma, Cette Industrie*. Paris, Editions Techniques et Economiques, 1972.
6.   Fadiman, William. *Hollywood Now*. New York: Liveright, 1972.
7.   Gold, David, Clarence Lo, and Erik Olin Wright. "Recent Development in Marxist Theories of the Capitalist State." *Monthly Review* 27 (5), October 1975, pp. 29–43 and 27 (6), November 1975, pp. 36–51.
8.   Guback, Thomas. "Cultural Identity and Film in the European Economic Community." *Cinema Journal* 14 (1), Fall 1974, pp. 2–17.
9.   Guback, Thomas. *The International Film Industry*. Bloomington, Indiana: Indiana University Press, 1969.
10.   Guback, Thomas. "Les Investissements Américains dans l'Industrie Cinématographique Européenne." *Cinéthique*. January–February 1970, pp. 33–40.
11.   *Hollywood Reporter*. "Concept of 'Net Profits' Still Vexes Hollywood Community." April 30, 1981.
12.   Metro-Goldwyn-Mayer Inc. *Report of Stockholders' Annual Meeting*. January 5, 1980.
13.   Miliband, Ralph. *The State in Capitalist Society*. London: Quartet Books, 1973.
14.   Mosco, Vincent and Andrew Herman. "Communication, Domination and Resistance." *Media, Culture and Society*, (2) 1980, pp. 351–365.
15.   *Motion Picture Distribution Trade Practices*. Hearings before a subcommittee of the Select Committee on Small Business, U.S. Senate, 83rd Congress. 1st Session. Government Printing Office, 1953.
16.   *Motion Picture Distribution Trade Practices—1956*. Hearings before a subcommittee of the Select Committee on Small Business, U.S. Senate, 84th Congress, 2nd Session. Government Printing Office, 1956.
17.   Nolan, Kathleen, president, Screen Actors Guild, statement in *Tax Reform Act of 1975*. Hearings before the Committee on Finance, U.S. Senate, 94th Congress, 2nd Session. Government Printing Office, 1976.
18.   O'Connor, James. *The Fiscal Crisis of the State*. New York: St. Martin's Press, 1973.
19.   *Proposals Relating to Tax Shelters and Other Tax-Motivated Transactions*. Prepared by the staff of the Joint Committee on Taxation, Committee on Ways and Means, U.S. House of Representatives, February 17, 1984. Government Printing Office, 1984.
20.   *Revenue Act of 1971*. Report of the Committee on Ways and Means, U.S. House of Representatives, 92nd Congress, 1st Session, September 29, 1971. Government Printing Office, 1971.
21.   *Screen Actor*. "Motion Picture Industry Joins Forces to Retain Tax Incentives." April–May 1976, pp. 16–17.
22.   Sieklucka, Catherine. *Les Aides à l'Industrie Cinématographique dans la Communauté Economique Européenne*. Paris, Presses Universitaires de France, 1967.

23. Taft Broadcasting Company. Presentation to the Entertainment Group of the New York Society of Security Analysts, November 15, 1979.

24. *Tax Shelters: Movie Films*. Prepared by the staff of the Joint Committee on Internal Revenue Taxation for the use of the Committee on Ways and Means, September 10, 1975. Government Printing Office, 1975.

25. *Unemployment Problems in American Film Industry*. Hearings before the General Subcommittee on Labor of the Committee on Education and Labor, U.S. House of Representatives, 92nd Congress. 1st Session. Government Printing Office, 1972.

26. *Variety*, " 'Subsidy': Three-Penny Opus; MPAA Promotes a Yank 'Eady' " and "Opinion of Craft Leaders Favors. Some Showmen Cautious On. 'Subsidy.' " April 15, 1964, p. 3.

Chapter 34

Kelly Gates

WILL WORK FOR COPYRIGHTS: THE CULTURAL POLICY OF ANTI-PIRACY CAMPAIGNS (2006)

> No nation can lay claim to greatness or longevity unless it constructs a rostrum from which springs a 'moral imperative' which guides the daily conduct of its citizens.
>
> (Valenti 2003)

INTRODUCTION

HOLLYWOOD IS IN THE PROCESS OF reasserting the legitimacy and moral justification for its dominant control over the production and distribution of virtually all film and entertainment television content in the United States. In the 1970s, the emergence and proliferation of the video-cassette recorder challenged the Hollywood intellectual property regime and instigated a major effort on the part of copyright owners to secure control over filmed-entertainment content using mechanisms in the marketplace, the court system and the legislature (Bettig 1996). Peer-to-peer (P2P) file-sharing technology, combined with the spread of expanding bandwidth, has presented yet another technological challenge to established production and distribution arrangements, once again raising legal and moral questions about why and how a media oligopoly should maintain such a stranglehold over culture. P2P technology has introduced a crisis of legitimacy of sorts for intellectual property owners in the culture industries, forcing them to reassert and even reformulate arguments for why they are the rightful proprietors and purveyors of culture. This project has been taken up as a central charge of the Motion Picture Association of America (MPAA).

At the same time, the information technology sector has focused concerted effort on a similar set of problems surrounding software piracy. Through cooperative efforts among information technology companies, such as the work of the Business Software Alliance (BSA), the computer software industry and its hardware partners have been working to govern software production, distribution, and use in a way that maintains and reproduces the established dominance of the main industry players. Like Hollywood, the software industry recognizes this problem as a matter not only of legislative concern, although strong copyright law remains central, but also as a matter of cultural policy, a set of strategies for governing the conduct of citizens outside the formal realm of the law, and either beyond or at the extended reach of the state.

Following but inverting Rosemary Coombe's (1998) cultural approach to the study of intellectual property, this essay examines not the culture of law but the laws of culture, not the way that the law works to shape culture but the way that cultural policies outside the formal doctrine of law work to shape the conduct of citizens. Specifically, I examine the cultural policy of copyright protection by considering two overlapping forms of "cultural labor" invoked in the MPAA and BSA anti-piracy campaigns. First, both the MPAA and BSA make labor-related appeals as part of their strategies to combat film and software piracy. The MPAA rather disingenuously encourages moviegoers to empathize with the "ordinary working people" involved in film and television production whose livelihoods are threatened, as the MPAA's argument goes, by film and television piracy. For its part, the BSA makes a cynical attempt to capitalize on disenfranchised workers' desire for revenge against their employers by asking these workers to report companies that use unlicensed software. These seemingly different strategies have at least one fundamental similarity: both exploit the economic insecurity of workers to make their anti-piracy appeals. In addition, both of these strategies are presented as empowering to workers: the MPAA gives screen workers visibility where they are typically invisible, and the BSA fulfills disgruntled workers' revenge fantasies. In fact, these so-called worker-friendly anti-piracy strategies serve to further disempower workers by individualizing them and severely limiting the way in which the threat to their economic security is constructed and addressed.

The second form of cultural labor addressed in this essay involves the work of cultural citizenship. The two industry associations discussed here, themselves non-state-governing institutions engaged in programs of cultural policy, have devised strategies for "outsourcing" the work of copyright protection not only to workers, as in the cases just mentioned, but also to teachers, parents, and students. Both the MPAA and the BSA have designed and distributed pre-packaged curricula aimed involving teachers and parents in indoctrinating students into industry-defined standards of online conduct, with a special emphasis on respect for copyrighted material. In other words, the culture and software industries are working to strengthen their control over intellectual property through explicit strategies and programs for enlisting parents and teachers to teach children how to govern themselves and others in the interest of "the cultural-capitalist polity" (Miller 1993, p. ix). In this way, parents, teachers, and children represent a new cultural labor force for the copyright industries.

CULTURAL POLICY, CULTURAL CITIZENSHIP, AND INTERNET GOVERNANCE

In the introduction to their Critical Cultural Policy Studies reader, Justin Lewis and Toby Miller (2003) define cultural policy as the site where cultural citizens are produced, to a great extent outside the limits of formal laws or conventional political participation. The culture industries have a central governing role to play in the process of producing cultural policy and governing cultural citizens, not simply in the representations that they circulate, but in the rationales for particular types of conduct that they instruct and prescribe. Taking guidance from the assertion of Karl Marx that the moral force of policy must be formulated in supplemental organic laws outside the formal bounds of the Constitution, Lewis and Miller set an agenda for the study of cultural policy that involves critical investigations of the culture industries in their role as governing institutions. As ex-bomber pilot and MPAA chairman Jack Valenti's comments introducing this essay attest, the culture industry brokers concern themselves emphatically with matters of producing loyal citizen subjects, in the name of cultural capitalist national renewal. Miller diagnoses a "determinate indeterminacy" at the heart of this process of producing loyal citizens, "an ethical incompleteness, which cultural subjects are encouraged to see in themselves and then remedy" (1993, xii). This incompleteness is fed by a perpetual tension between the selfless individual concerned with public good and community, and the selfish and self-serving consumer at the center of his/her own needs and desires. As we will see, the cultural industries' current anti-piracy initiatives make productive use of these tensions in their attempts to fashion guidelines and prescriptions for appropriate online conduct.

The Internet not only poses public policy challenges for legislators, jurists, and state agencies; it also poses cultural policy challenges for the state and culture industries. Diagnoses regarding the Internet's unruly and ungovernable environment, while not entirely accurate characterizations, nevertheless have been accompanied by a litany of moral panics. Efforts to govern "cyberspace" through cultural policy have taken a variety of forms, some more systematic and orchestrated than others. In the cultural policy initiatives for Internet governance examined here, a sense of urgency underlies descriptions of the seemingly new forms of information exchange that it enables. The so-called "freedom" of cyberspace necessitates the formulation of guidelines for governing oneself in one's actions as a free "cyber citizen," including instructions for positive behaviors that good online citizens are compelled to perform, and prohibitions against those behaviors that should be avoided. As a means of gaining control over the unruly domain of cyberspace, governing institutions have worked to yoke certain bad online behavior onto newly villainized problem identities. Helen Nissenbaum charts how legislative bodies, the courts, and the popular media transformed hackers from "heroes to hooligans" over a period of four decades (2004, 198). In the 1960s and 1970s, popular conceptions of hackers saw them as a bit fanatical and unsavory but otherwise dedicated techies on the cutting edge of computer innovation; government officials grudgingly admired them and "not only turned a blind eye to unofficial hacker activities but indirectly sponsored them" (Nissenbaum 2004, 198). Today, hackers are conceived as "miscreants, vandals, criminals, and even terrorists" (Nissenbaum 2004, 195). As Nissenbaum argues, demonizing hackers has served regulatory efforts to control computer-mediated transactions, providing an image of the abnormal against which to define good behavior, while also offering justification for ongoing investments in security measures and new deployments of Internet control strategies.

The current scramble over online intellectual property protections should be understood in the context of these wide-ranging efforts to control the types of communicative transactions that occur over the Internet. In short, the intellectual property debates are an integral component of larger debates over Internet governance. While "Internet governance" means different things in different contexts, I deploy the term from the perspective of Foucault's notion of governmentality and the empirical scholarship that it inspired on the study of political rationality. As Nikolas Rose (1999) explains, this work is concerned with gaining a purchase "on the forces that traverse the multitudes of encounters where conduct is subject to government: prisons, clinics, schoolrooms and bedrooms, factories and offices, airports and military organizations, the marketplace and shopping mall," and much more (Rose 1999, 5). The Internet, or "cyberspace," can and must be added to this list. While current copyright issues extend beyond the online environment to include all things digital, and the distinction between the online and offline worlds is an indeterminate one, the challenge the Internet poses to the intellectual property regime plays centrally in virtually every discussion on the matter. Of scholars informed by Foucault's work on governmentality, Andrew Barry (2001) has explored the question of intellectual property and its centrality to the "government of a technological society." In other words, Barry maintains that current political preoccupations center on technical concerns, and efforts to determine the indeterminate subjects and objects of intellectual property rights represent central problems of government. In the realm of intellectual property protection, governmental concerns take not only legislative and judicial, but also technical, forms, as copyright owners wield their influence to shape technology standards. Extending Barry's analysis, it is useful to consider how this problem of government manifests itself in the cultural policy programs of the culture and software industries.

"WHO MAKES MOVIES?"

> The movie industry is laboring to find rebuttals to piracy.
>
> (Valenti 2003)

As noted at the outset of the essay, the MPAA is a primary channel through which Hollywood has taken on the battle to intensify intellectual property protections. As part of this effort, the MPAA launched a new initiative in the summer of 2003, a public relations strategy centered on convincing moviegoers that downloading free copies of movies was morally wrong. Devised by the MPAA Public Relations council, a body consisting of the MPAA's Public Affairs team and senior Public Relations representatives from the seven major studios, the aim of this new public relations campaign was "to build consumer awareness about the growing threat of digital piracy to the entertainment industry, its employees and consumers themselves" (MPAA 2003). As part of this effort, 20th Century Fox created a series of public service announcements (PSAs) aimed at showcasing the "real victims" of film piracy: the production laborers. The MPAA began airing these spots on 35 network and cable television outlets the evening of 24 July, each network donating a 30-second slot in the first commercial break during prime time (MPAA 2003). This television "roadblock," as the MPAA referred to it, would lead into a lengthier run of anti-piracy PSAs shown as trailers before movies in over 5,000 US theaters. Like the free television time, every major US exhibitor agreed to air the PSAs *pro bono*. The MPAA's original plan would rotate a different trailer through theaters every three months, with each new spot featuring a single individual who works in some aspect of movie production. A third venue for the new anti-piracy PSAs would be the Internet itself: audiences could view the PSAs at a new website created as part of the campaign (www.respectcopyrights.org). The site, noted an MPAA press release, "will show how easy it is to enjoy high-quality entertainment online in ways that both protect American families and the interests of creators" (MPAA 2003). The content of the site eventually would include not just the trailers, but also "resources to help teachers, children, university administrators, and corporations participate in the Industry's anti-piracy initiatives" (MPAA 2003).

A central theme of the campaign focused on portraying the unauthorized reproduction and distribution of movies as a threat to the livelihoods of people working in the film industry. The aim was to turn attention away from the copyright owners and major beneficiaries of the intellectual property regime, and to focus the lens on below-the-line laborers, "ordinary working people" with whom ordinary consumers could identify. As Fox Filmed Entertainment Chairman Jim Gianopulos explained at ShoWest in Las Vegas, "People must be taught that the so-called victimless crime of downloading movies has the power to cost real people real jobs—*not just executives like me* . . . but hundreds of people who are involved" in the process of making and distributing movies (quoted in Kilday 2003; emphasis added). "We feel strongly about the need to communicate that piracy has the power to cost real people real jobs; and that illegally downloading movies is a blow to creativity, *not corporate might*," declared Peter Chernin, Chairman of the Fox Group (quoted in MPAA 2003; emphasis added).

While the original MPAA announcements promised a series of PSAs, it appears that only two spots made their way to theaters, onto the "respectcopyrights" website, and into the collective memory of US moviegoers. One featured a stuntman named Manny Perry and another a set painter named David Goldstein, both of whom became minor celebrities in their own right as a result of the widespread screen time the spots received. The spots opened with the question "Who Makes Movies?," which, after their testimonial, was answered with "David Goldstein Makes Movies." In an effort to personalize the copyright issue, the MPAA trailers portrayed Perry and Goldstein as hardworking men who loved their jobs and sincerely felt that film piracy presented a serious and direct threat to their liveli-hoods. In keeping with the central campaign message, Goldstein claimed that the effect of piracy on big-time Hollywood producers is "minuscule to the way it affects me—the guy working on construction, the lighting guy, the sound guy—because we're not million-dollar employees . . . We're lucky if we can put together twelve straight months." The spot tried to visually convey digital downloads by freezing shots of actors and sliding them off the screen. In Perry's testimonial he emphasized how much time, energy, and effort screen laborers invest in their work—noting that in his case he puts his life on the line. Both spots interspersed images of the men with scenes from films they worked on, concluding by appealing to viewers to "Put an end to piracy," because "Movies. They're Worth It." The spots represented a rather obvious effort to encourage film audiences to identify with working-class movie laborers, since moviegoers could hardly be expected to have sympathy for losses incurred by wealthy Hollywood producers and investment bankers.

The MPAA carried their piracy-threatens-the-livelihoods-of-screen-workers message through other aspects of their public relations campaign, including efforts to take the "respect copyrights" initiative into schools. Together with Junior Achievement, an organiza-tion with a mission "to ensure that every child in America has a fundamental understanding of the free enterprise system" (Junior Achievement n.d.), the MPAA designed and distrib-uted lesson plans in a packet of materials titled "What's the Diff? A Guide to Digital Citizenship for Volunteers and Teachers."[1] At a cost of a mere $100,000, the MPAA launched the campaign in the fall of 2003, planning over the next two years to reach 36,000 classrooms and 900,000 children in Grades 5–9 (Regardie 2003).

The MPAA-sponsored curriculum, administered by Junior Achievement volunteers in cooperation with middle-school teachers, encourages students to connect personally with the copyright issue and to become morally invested in strong intellectual property rights. For example, "What's Fair?" draws analogies between downloading copyright material and things like having one's homework stolen and passed off as someone else's work. Another lesson, "Patents and Progress," centers on a story about the essential role the Bell patents played in the development of the telephone, presenting a decidedly rosy image of the Bell monopoly. Another lesson assigns roles to students, such as producer, actor, key carpenter, and file-swapping computer user, and asks them to speak about the copyright issue from that perspective, strongly suggesting that they identify with each of the roles except for the file-swapping computer user, whose attitudes and behavior they are meant to criticize. In "Starving Artist," students gather in groups and play the role of a new band signed by a record label. After coming up with the name of their band, the type of music they play, their message and their CD cover, students are informed that their album has been downloaded and shared among Internet users, and the record company is thus no longer interested since it could not possibly recoup its investment. Lessons conclude by encouraging students to ask themselves a set of questions about their online behavior, such as whether their real activities online are fair to everyone and how their online behavior makes them feel about themselves.

In addition to these lessons, the MPAA designed a contest for Junior Achievement students, called "Xcellent Xtreme Challenge," whereby students could win prizes for developing an organized and viable campaign plan for teaching their peers that downloading copyrighted materials is not only illegal, but unethical. Prizes include cash awards for the winners' schools and a trip to Hollywood. In addition, teachers whom the MPAA and Junior Achievement deem outstanding in their efforts to convey the anti-piracy message to students also win prizes, including a Sony DVD player, DVDs, and a year's worth of movie passes.

This MPAA program of cultural policy operates on multiple levels. In these strategies and tactics for strengthening the moral ground of copyright, the MPAA, and the groups and individuals compelled to offer their labor to advance this cultural policy program, are engaged in a process of "translation" (Rose 1999, 48). "In the dynamics of translation," writes Nikolas Rose, "alignments are forged between the objectives of authorities wishing to govern and the personal projects of those organizations, groups and individuals who are the subjects of government" (1999, 48). The alignments formed in the MPAA cultural policy program are perhaps most obviously manifest in the "What's the Diff?" curriculum, as it translates the interests of cultural industries to control film and television distribution into the interests of teachers to provide lessons for their classrooms. By employing the labor of teachers (paid for by the state in the case of public schools) and translating its anti-piracy agenda into the language and practice of middle school education, the MPAA can produce desired effects at a relatively minuscule financial investment (provided at least some of the children actually abide by the code of ethics and refrain from unauthorized copying). In addition, the curriculum program enlists the labor of parents and students themselves by translating copyright protections into good parenting skills as well as student learning and self-styling activities. And of course, the "Xcellent Xtreme Challenge" is designed to offload the labor of devising effective, age-appropriate anti-piracy strategies onto students themselves, who are incentivized to offer their free labor with the promise of recognition and possibly a trip to Hollywood.

The MPAA's message about the threat that piracy poses to the livelihoods of ordinary working people involves a more complex process of translation. Perhaps more so than other ethical appeals for appropriate copyright-respecting conduct, the appeal for empathy with individual culture industry workers invokes the "ethical incompleteness" ever present in the production of good cultural citizens (see Miller 1993). The worker-friendly message asks individuals to refrain from the bad consumer behavior of file-sharing movies; not because it infringes on the profit potential of the culture industry's copyright owners, but because it injures other individuals. Consumer-citizens are asked to resist their selfish impulses for free access to culture and to equate Hollywood's intellectual property rights with the public good because Hollywood employs people. Consumers are encouraged to distinguish "individuals" from the "industry" and to identify with the former, specifically not seeing these individual screen workers as spokespersons for organized labor groups.

What is particularly manipulative about this strategy is not so much the message that workers at all levels of cultural production are dependent on the intellectual property regime. What clearly demonstrates the self-serving nature of this strategy on the part of Hollywood's copyright owners is their glaring silence regarding other, no doubt more significant threats to livelihoods of US screen laborers. As a perusal of the Teamsters' Motion Picture and Theatrical Trade Division website suggests, the piracy issue does not register as their number one priority. What gets considerably more attention in their Spring 2003 newsletter, for example, is "the problem that keeps 'going away' "—not unauthorized movie reproduction and distribution, but runaway production. As long as this problem persists, "members are in a fight for their economic lives" (Teamsters Motion Picture & Theatrical Trade Division 2003). The Film and Television Action Committee (FTAC), a single-issue organization formed in 1998 to address the problem of runaway production, offers the following definitions of the problem: "1. those U.S. productions which are developed and are intended for initial release, exhibition, or broadcast in the U.S. and appear to be made in the U.S., but are actually filmed in another country," and "2. that hissing sound you hear as $10 billion drains out of the U.S. economy each year" (About FTAC n.d.). A favorite example is the Hollywood blockbuster *Chicago*, much of which was filmed not in the windy city but in and around Toronto. As Miller et al. explain, Hollywood creates and exploits an international division of cultural labor that "links productivity, exploitation, and social control" (2001, 52). The studios move production around from country to country in order to elude organized labor and capitalize on employment instability.[2]

Clearly, runaway production presents an arguably more significant and immediate threat to the livelihoods of US screen workers, but it fails to register as part of the ethical appeal in industry-defined guidelines for appropriate consumer conduct. Thus, under the guise of showcasing the contribution of individual below-the-line workers to the process of film production, and empowering these individuals to speak about their work and their position on the copyright issue, this seemingly "worker-friendly" message in fact narrowly defines the threats to their economic security, and, by extension, the range of possible action that might alleviate those threats. Just as Hollywood sells a rosy global image of itself as universal storyteller while orchestrating an international network of control over film and television production (Miller et al. 2001), so it offers up sentimental references to the dedication of Yanki screen workers even as it directly undermines their job security by moving production to sites where labor is cheaper. This strategy of exploiting the economic insecurity of workers as a matter of cultural policy has parallels in the anti-piracy initiatives of the software industry.

"DUMPED WORKERS FIND REVENGE"[3]

> Parting gift ideas for your old employer: $150,000 fine for unlicensed software. (Business Software Alliance, online advertisement) Accessed 2 March 2005 from: www.theonion.com/news/index.php?issue=4109&n=1

Like the MPAA, the BSA, an international trade association representing the big players in the software industry, similarly engages in public relations or "public education" campaigns aimed at guiding appropriate online conduct in the name of strong intellectual property protections. The BSA's obvious concern is software piracy (as opposed to film piracy), a problem it defines in stark economic terms: $6.5 billion lost to software piracy in 2003, with 22% of software in the United States unlicensed (BSA 2005). The BSA anti-piracy cultural policy initiatives represent a significant part of its multi-pronged global strategy to strengthen intellectual property rights in the interests of its members. Its goal is to guide public policy on a global scale, but also to govern software production, distribution, and use through other, non-legislative means. As BSA's website indicates, its mission "is to promote a long-term legislative and legal environment in which the business software industry can prosper" (BSA n.d.a). In addition to policy advocacy, it "achieves its goals through global education on software management and copyright protection" and other commercial software issues (BSA n.d.a). BSA also engages in surveillance and enforcement activities, conducting investigations and auditing company computer networks in response to complaints about potential software piracy. Its archive of press releases is full of headlines announcing six-figure cash settlements from companies exposed for various forms of software piracy.

In its role as a private software copyright enforcement agency, the Business Software Alliance has faced the challenge of how to monitor private companies and identify potential infringers, especially as a non-state actor with no legally sanctioned authority. One strategy that the organization has employed to identify potential users of unlicensed software has involved appeals targeted at disgruntled employees. These direct appeals to angry workers urge them to report their employers, or ex-employers, to the BSA for installation and use of unlicensed software on company networks. As early as October 1996, the BSA launched an advert campaign called "Nail Your Boss," targeting employees who were seeking revenge against their superiors (Thompson 1996). Soon thereafter, the BSA began reporting the results: among other hits, whistleblowers helped the organization collect $400,000 from Marketing Management Inc., in Forth Worth, Texas, $121,610 from the City of Philadelphia, and $120,000 from a law firm in New Orleans (Ornstein 1997).

By the summer of 1999, the BSA had changed the name of the disgruntled worker campaign to something a bit tamer, calling it "Worker Bee," but the objective remained the same: urging workers to turn in their employers for unauthorized software on company computers (BSA 1999). In New York, the "Worker Bee" campaign included a billboard in Times Square, live radio spots on Howard Stern, advertisements on subway cards, and a direct mail campaign to thousands of the city's "worker bees." In July 2001, Wired News online reported that the BSA was noting a marked increase over the past year in reports filed by ex-employees against technology companies, which Bob Kruger, BSA vice president for enforcement, attributed to the high rate of layoffs in the technology sector (Delio 2001). Kruger offered a warning to companies that they were "only one disgruntled employee away from a full-blown BSA investigation" (Delio 2001). Most recently, a BSA online advertisement, quoted at the beginning of this section, has appeared periodically at the Onion spoof news website (www.theonion.com), inviting disgruntled employees to "Do the Right Thing" and "Report Software Piracy NOW." Clicking on the advert hyperlinks the Onion website visitors to a piracy reporting form at the BSA website. Individuals may also call 1-888-NO-PIRACY in the United States, or find a number among a list of different piracy reporting hotlines in about 50 other countries. According to the BSA, most of the investigations and audits they conduct begin with calls to their hotline or reports submitted through their online reporting form (BSA 2004a). In 2004, a single BSA press release reported "$2.2 million in settlements with 25 companies nationwide" as a result of BSA investigations of company computer networks (BSA 2004a).

In addition to employing disgruntled employees as (unpaid) software surveillance agents, BSA's anti-piracy program includes efforts aimed at parents and teachers to educate children about "the importance of cyber ethics and respect for intellectual property" (BSA 2004b). Based on US Census data, their own commissioned research, and reports from other industry sponsored nongovernmental organizations, the BSA determined that most US school children had computer access, that high-speed Internet access among children was on the rise, and that a large portion of adults engage in some form of software piracy (BSA 2002b). Thus they deemed critical the need for "early cyber education" as an integral part of student development, emphasizing instructions regarding authorized versus unauthorized use of copyrighted software. In April 2002, the BSA announced its release of a packaged curriculum for elementary and middle schools in the United States and Canada (BSA 2002a). Like MPAA's "What's the Diff?" lesson plans, the BSA curriculum prescribed a code of ethical conduct regarding appropriate online behavior, emphasizing "the importance of strong copyright protection for creative works like computer software" (BSA 2002a).

To create the curriculum, the BSA worked with Lifetime Learning Systems, Inc., a company that designs education materials. Lifetime Learning Systems, Inc. educational tools are sponsored by major corporations, trade associations, non-profits, and government agencies, and are distributed free to teachers. BSA's free curriculum, entitled "Play it Safe in Cyberspace," was distributed to 25,000 US schools and made available online (www.playitcybersafe.com).

According to the BSA, the "Play it Safe in Cyberspace" curriculum is designed to assist both parents and teachers in having conversations with children about responsible cyber behavior. Classroom activities and discussions are intended to help students "become better online citizens" and gain an understanding of "cyber ethics, piracy and proper software use" (BSA 2002b). The notion of "playing it safe in cyberspace" suggests a connection between the governance of children vis-à-vis software copyrights and their protection against the dangers that the unruly Internet environment poses. In particular, both the BSA and the MPAA consistently yoke piracy to tropes about the Internet as a hotbed of pornography and pedophilia. Anti-piracy public education campaigns lump online copyright violations together with all manner of insidious online activities. Children's access to "inappropriate or offensive online material" and the "temptation to download illegal software, music, games, and other creative works" are conceived as one and the same problem (BSA 2002b).

As part of the "Play it Safe" curriculum, students are invited to sign "The Cyber-Ethics Champion Code" certificate pledging to abide by seven principles guiding their online conduct. Principles include the signatories' commitments to "look for the copyright symbol (#) whenever I add a new program or game to my computer," and to "know that the copyright owner gets to decide how many times a software program can be copied" (BSA n.d.b). The code also includes types of prohibited conduct that students should commit to eliminating from their repertoire of action; for example, pledges not to make unauthorized copies of one's games or computer programs for friends, not to download copyrighted software programs from Internet "file-sharing" networks, and not to use software programs that appear to have been copied. Six of the seven principles deal specifically with copyright, while the seventh principle urges kids to keep their passwords and personal information, like their address and phone number, to themselves, again connecting unauthorized software copying to the more seedy dangers lurking for kids in cyberspace. Once students agree to follow the code, they are instructed to sign the certificate and post it near their computers (BSA 2003).

These components of the BSA's cultural policy program targeting disgruntled workers and distributing pre-packaged classroom activities to schools resemble similar initiatives of the MPAA. Like the MPAA, the BSA campaign attempts to translate the objectives of the software industry into the personal projects of individuals and groups whose actions the industry seeks to govern. For disgruntled workers, the BSA offers a direct line of action to fulfill their desires for revenge against their employers. For teachers, the BSA-sponsored curriculum provides ready-made lessons for instructing students, and for students it taps into their personal project of educational development (although students may not always receive and internalize the message as intended). The intention of these initiatives is to translate the needs of workers, teachers, and students so that these individuals will provide the necessary cultural labor for protecting intellectual property of the software industry.

In the case of disenfranchised workers, this cultural labor takes the form not so much of appropriate online conduct, but of industry-serving surveillance activities. Certainly individuals who have lost their jobs may get a certain satisfaction from making their employer the target of a software piracy investigation. But the very intelligibility of such a motivated action implies a highly individualized form of labor, the lone worker disconnected from other individuals with shared interests, managing his/her own risks, and acting on his/her own impulses to address psychic needs that do nothing to address the problem of unemployment and economic insecurity. It is a particularly cynical strategy given its aim to capitalize on worker dissatisfaction and disposability, the destructive effects of workforce flexibilization and weakening social safety nets. Dismissing its own culpability for the morally questionable basis of this strategy, the BSA suggests that the disgruntled worker should "do the right thing" by reporting software piracy. Since the software piracy is morally wrong, apparently the ends of identifying offenders justify the means used to "nail" them. Of course, the Internet users of the world include among their ranks many individuals with just the right mocking sense of humor to retort to such cynical approaches to piracy problem.

RESPECT BOOTLEGGERS AND THE PUBLIC DOMAIN

It would be a mistake to assume the cultural policy initiatives examined here work entirely according to the intentions of the authorities that orchestrate them. But while there certainly exist various forms of "resistance" to these initiatives—not least in the form of ongoing "piracy" itself—cautious analysis avoids attributing too much agency to popular copyright-defiant actions. It is too easy to interpret them as "merely the obverse of a one-dimensional notion of power as domination" (Rose 1999, 279). And the BSA's "Nail Your Boss" strategy demonstrates well the easy appropriation of such dichotomous conceptualizations of domination versus resistance. Nevertheless, some of the oppositional responses to anti-piracy discourse deserve measured recognition.[4]

In particular, the MPAA's effort to take on file sharing with its "save the worker" message did not fall on deaf ears. Rather, it was received by the computer culture that Thomas Streeter has astutely characterized as "a deeply contradictory but politically powerful fusion of 1960s countercultural attitudes" and "a revived form of political libertarianism" (2003, 161). Through various means of online expression, members of the libertarian computer counterculture answered back to Hollywood's duplicitous call to "respect copyrights" in the name of screen workers. For example, a video at a website called respect-bootleggers.org featured testimonial from a bootlegger worried about how he would make a living in the face of the impending intensification of copyright enforcement. The site received sympathetic coverage at Wired News online. Another site created to directly respond to the MPAA's anti-piracy message (respectthepublicdomain.org) offered a more earnest source of counter-information. The site explained the concept of the "public domain" and criticized the culture industries' successful legislative efforts to extend the length of copyright protections beyond the intended limits of the US Constitution. The site encouraged moviegoers to shout out "respect the public domain!" in movie theaters when the MPAA trailers appear, as well as to write to their senators and representatives in Congress in opposition to lengthy copyrights, and to release their own creative works under the less restrictive "founder's copyright" administered by Creative Commons, an organization dedicated to less restrictive copyright laws.

Bloggers also took to ridiculing the MPAA spots. At www.lowculture.com, "matt" commented on "those incredibly annoying respectcopyright.org ads that run before the trailers at movies lately":

> Let's leave aside how offensive it is that the highly paid producers, studio heads, and chairmen of the entertainment conglomerates are using these ordinary working Joes to guilt us out of pirating movies. What I found really offensive was that one spot, the one with stuntman Manny Perry . . . features clips from *Enemy of the State* (directed by A.O. Scott's namesake and doppelganger, Tony Scott). This movie was produced by Jerry Bruckheimer, whom *Entertainment Weekly* recently deemed the most powerful man in Hollywood . . . Is Jerry Bruckheimer in any position to tell us how we're mistreating Hollywood's

underlings? What's next, a commercial with Scott Rudin's assistants telling us we're making their lives a living hell? Maybe a spot with some Korean animators telling us how we're destroying Disney?

("One of these men" 2003)

Another blogger known as the "Defamer" (www.defamer.com) captured a similar sentiment in a post entitled "Defamer Call To Arms: No More 'Respect Copyrights' Propaganda!" The blogger noted a "chorus of groans" rising up from the audience as one of the trailers began at a recent movie. The post also quoted a "representative sample" among his readers' many expressions of frustration: "if I have to sit through [Manny Perry's] miserable lispy rant one more time I'm going to start a second career hocking bootlegs outside Roscoe's on Pico" ("Defamer call to arms" 2004).

Perhaps the MPAA should have anticipated such dismissive responses to their worker-friendly message, given the long tendency of Hollywood films to villainize labor unions, and, although occasionally portraying individual workers sympathetically, generally offering portraits of working-class individuals "as salt-of-the-earth but easily manipulated dupes" (Ross 2001, 88–89). Of course, a more systematic survey would be necessary to determine the extent of popular ridicule of the MPAA's "piracy hurts workers" message. Predictably, the MPAA's own surveys suggested that their PSAs were effective. Shortly after that campaign began, the organization reported reaching more than 72 million television viewers and moviegoers in less than a week (Cohen 2003). According to an online survey conducted by Digital Market Services, 20 percent of 600 13–24 year olds reported learning that downloading movies was illegal from the MPAA PSAs (Sperling 2003). But learning that the practice is illegal does not mean refraining from the activity. As the MPAA seemed to recognize with subsequent strategies, they would no doubt need to dissuade current and potential film pirates with the threat of judicious and punitive enforcement tactics. Efforts to instill in people a sense of moral obligation to consider the "ordinary working people" involved in film production were joined by more ominous warnings in new campaign slogans such as "you can click but you can't hide" and in an explicit connection between file-sharing and "illegal trafficking." In addition, the influence they continue to wield over the legislative process and the development of technology standards provides them with considerable ammunition in their efforts to enforce their copyrights and maintain control over the production, distribution, and uses of culture.

CONCLUSION

This essay has examined the cultural policy programs of the culture and software industries, specifically with regard to their anti-piracy initiatives. For these industries, no less than the state, the so-called "freedom" of cyberspace poses a problem of government, particularly to the extent that new digital technologies and expanding bandwidth threaten to dislodge established controls over the production and distribution of commodified forms of culture and information. Recognizing that they cannot win the current battle against "piracy" through legislative, judicial, and technical channels alone, the brokers of these industries have adopted strategies for winning hearts and minds, prescribing codes of appropriate online conduct. These cultural policy programs have aimed to forge alignments between the objectives of copyright owners and the personal self-fashioning activities of individual workers, consumers, teachers, parents, and students, a process that enlists these individuals as cultural laborers working to produce and enforce the meaning and legitimacy of the intellectual property regime. To fashion good cyber-citizens, appropriately respectful of copyrights, these cultural policy programs encourage individuals to connect recognition of the rights of copyright owners to their own projects of self-betterment. Where the MPAA asks individuals to respect copyrights in the name of an ethical regard for others, the BSA invites disenfranchised workers to respond to their selfish psychic impulses. These somewhat conflicting messages in fact speak to the "ethical incompleteness" of cultural subjects (see Miller 1993). Of course, the messages have another unifying principle: the manner in which they exploit the economic insecurities of an individualized workforce under the pretext of empowering individual workers.

No one can claim to have a simple resolution to the current digital copyright debacle. Despite the U.S. Supreme Court's decision in favor of the copyright industries in MGM v. Grokster, thousands of bad cyber citizens are still risking legal repercussions by using P2P software to download free copies of copyrighted material. While the music industry has already incurred heavy losses (although some have argued that file sharing is not entirely to blame), Hollywood has yet to fully feel the wrath of the unfolding broadband revolution. As the scope and tenor of the MPAA's current anti-piracy campaign suggests, the beneficiaries of Hollywood's copyright privileges have no intention of getting fiscally broadsided by high school kids with laptops and ipods—the demographic that MTV executives so fondly refer to as "super savvy navigators," or their "base." However, if successive generations of MTV viewers respond cynically to the copyright industries' ethical cyber citizenship appeals, those industries in part have MTV, and themselves, to thank.

Notes

1   These materials are accessible at www.respectcopyrights.org. However, it should be noted that the cover page of the document indicates that "The text of this publication, or any part thereof, may not be reproduced or transmitted in any form or by any means, including photocopying, recording, storing in an information retrieval system, or otherwise except in the course of conducting a registered Junior Achievement class or with the permission of the publishers."

2   Unfortunately, in their fight against runaway production the screen labor unions also have difficulty pointing the finger at their employers. The source of the runaway production problem, according to the organizations such as Teamsters and the FTAC, lies not with the studios but with foreign subsidies on screen labor, such as those offered by the Canadian government to lure Hollywood film production from California. The FTAC advocates an investigation into these foreign subsidies as unfair trade practices, with possible initiation of dispute settlement proceedings at the World Trade Organization. However, the organization insists that it does not oppose shooting films outside the United States for creative purposes, and that it supports "the concept of world labor solidarity between the film workers of all nations, and the healthy development of national film industries" (About FTAC n.d.).

3   "Dumped Workers Find Revenge" is the headline of an article on the Business Software Alliance at Wired News online.

4   There is a vast and growing literature in critical legal studies, cultural policy studies, communications, and related fields that offer thorough and detailed critiques of copyright law. I do not address this literature here, but it can certainly be viewed as part of the oppositional response to the anti-piracy campaigns of the culture industries. See Bettig (1996), Boyle (1997), Coombe (1998), Lessig (2004), Litman (2001), McLeod (2001, 2004), and Vaidhyanathan (2003).

References

About Film and Television Action Committee. n.d. [Accessed 14 February 2005]. Available from from http://www.ftac.net/html/about.html; INTERNET.

Barry, Andrew. 2001. *Political machines: Governing a technological society*. New York: Athlone.

Bettig, Ronald V. 1996. *Copyrighting culture: The political economy of intellectual property*. Boulder, Co.: Westview Press.

Boyle, James. 1996. *Shamans, software, and spleens: Law and the construction of the information society*. Cambridge, Mass.: Harvard University Press.

Business Software Alliance. n.d.a. Membership details [accessed 6 March 2005]. Available from http://www.bsa.org/usa/about/Membership-Details.cfm; INTERNET.

——. n.d.b. The cyber-ethics champion code [accessed 3 March 2005]. Available from http://www.playitcybersafe.com/resources/EthicsCode.pdf; INTERNET.

——. 1999. BSA creates a "buzz" about software piracy in New York City [accessed 6 March 2005]. Available from http://www.bsa.org/usa/press/newsreleases/BSA-Creates-A-Buzz-About-Software-Piracy-In-New-York-City.cfm; INTERNET.

——. 2002a. New software use, cyber ethics curriculum announced [accessed 6 March 2005]. Available from http://www.bsa.org/usa/press/newsreleases/New-Software-Use-Cyber-Ethics-Curriculum-Announced.cfm; INTERNET.

——. 2002b. Software industry teams with weekly reader to educate youth about cyber ethics and software piracy. [accessed 6 March 2005]. Available from http://www.bsa.org/usa/press/newsreleases/Software-Industry-Teams-Wit-Weekly-Reader-to-Educate-Youth-About-Cyber-Ethics-and-Software-Piracy.cfm; INTERNET.

——. 2003. New e-tools available for parents, educators to teach children about online copyrights [accessed 6 March 2005]. Available from http://www.bsa.org/usa/press/newsreleases/NEW-ETOOLS-AVAILABLE.cfm; INTERNET.

——. 2004a. In it's first "$2 Million Tuesday," BSA collects nearly $500,000 from companies in the Southeast Region [accessed 6 March 2005]. Available from http://www.bsa.org/usa/press/newsreleases/2-Million-Tuesday-Southeast-Region.cfm; INTERNET.

——. 2004b. Majority of youth understand "copyright," but many continue to download illegally [accessed 6 March 2005]. Available from http://www.bsa.org/usa/press/newsrelease/Majority-of-Youth-Understand-Copyright.cfm; INTERNET.

——. 2005. California companies settle software piracy claims [accessed 27 2005]. Available from http://www.bsa.org/usa/press/newsreleases/California-Companies-Settle-Software-Piracy-Claims.cfm; INTERNET.

Cohen, David S. 2003. MPAA reaches out. Video Business, p. 28 [accessed 17 January 2005]. Available from Lexis-Nexis Academic database; INTERNET.

Coombe, Rosemary J. 1998. *The cultural life of intellectual properties: Authorship, Appropriation, and the Law*. Durham, N.C.: Duke University Press.

Defamer call to arms: No more "Respect Copyrights" propaganda! 2004. [Accessed 17 January 2005]. Available from http://www.defamer.com/topic/defamer-call-to-arms-no-more-respect-copyrights-propaganda-020264.php; INTERNET.

Delio, Michelle. 2001. Dumped workers find revenge. *Wired News* [accessed 22 February 2005]. Available from http://www.wired.com/news/culture/0,1284,44906,00.html; INTERNET.

Junior Achievement. n.d. Corporate identity standards [accessed 6 March 2005]. Available from http://www.ja.org/about/about_res_stan.shtml; INTERNET.

Kilday, Gregg. 2003. All-star Fox piracy PSA heads for movie screens. *The Hollywood Reporter* [accessed 17 January 2005]. Available from Lexis-Nexis Academic; INTERNET.

Lessig, Lawrence. 2004. *Free culture: How big media uses technology and the law to lock down culture and control creativity*. New York: Penguin.

Lewis, Justin, and Toby Miller. 2003. Introduction. In *Critical cultural policy studies*, edited by J. Lewis and T. Miller. Malden, Mass.: British Film Institute. 1–10.

Litman, Jessica. 2001. *Digital copyright: Protecting intellectual property on the Internet*. Amherst, N.Y.: Prometheus.

McLeod, Kembrew. 2001. *Owning culture: Authorship, ownership and intellectual property*. New York: Peter Lang.

——. 2004. *Freedom of expression: Overzealous copyright bozos and other enemies of creativity*. New York: Doubleday/Random House.

Miller, Toby. 1993. *The well-tempered self: Citizenship, culture, and the postmodern subject*. Baltimore, Md.: Johns Hopkins University Press.

Miller, Toby, Nitin Govil, John McMurria, and Richard Maxwell. 2001. *Global Hollywood*. Malden, Mass.: British Film Institute.

Motion Picture Association of America. 2003. Film/TV industry launches public service announcements as part of nationwide awareness campaign on the impact of digital piracy [accessed 13 January 2005]. Available from http://www.mpaa.org/jack/2003/2003_07_22a.pdf; INTERNET.

Nissenbaum, Helen. 2004. Hackers and the contested ontology of cyberspace. *New Media and Society* 6(2):195–217.

"One of these men is the most powerful man in Hollywood. Two are chumps." 2003. [Accessed 17 January 2005]. Available from http://www.lowculture.com/archives/ 001577.html; INTERNET.

Ornstein, Charles. 1997. Software piracy group announces fine on Forth Worth, Texas, firm. *The Dallas Morning News* [accessed 6 March 2005]. Available from Lexis-Nexis Academic database; INTERNET.

Regardie, Jon. 2003. Putting the fear of Valenti into your kids heads. *Variety*, 8 December, p. 68.

Rose, Nikolas. 1999. *Powers of freedom: Reframing political thought*. Cambridge: Cambridge University Press.

Ross, Steven J. 2001. American workers, American movies: Historiography and methodology. *International Labor and Working-Class History* 59:81–105.

Silverman, Jason. 2004. Anti-piracy campaign gets a laugh. *Wired News* [accessed 9 February 2004]. Available from http://www.wired.com/news/digiwood/0,1412,62197, 00.html; INTERNET.

Sperling, Nicole. 2003. MPAA bowing 2nd PSA to combat piracy. *The Hollywood Reporter* [accessed 16 January 2005]. Available from from Lexis-Nexis Academic database; INTERNET.

Streeter, Thomas. 2003. "That deep romantic chasm": Libertarianism, neoliberalism, and the computer culture. In *Critical cultural policy studies*, edited by J. Lewis and T. Miller. Malden, Mass.: Blackwell. 161–71.

Teamsters Motion Picture & Theatrical Trade Division. 2003. Canada increases labor subsidies [accessed 13 February 2005]. Available from http://www.teamster.org/divisions/motionpix/ newsletters/motpixSP2003.htm; INTERNET.

Thompson, Rory J. 1996. Do the right thing – by phone. *InformationWeek* [accessed 6 March 2005]. Available from Lexi-Nexis Academic database; INTERNET.

Vaidhyanathan, Siva. 2003. *Copyrights and copywrongs: The rise of intellectual property and how it threatens creativity*. New York: New York University Press.

Valenti, Jack. 2003. Consumer privacy and government technology mandates in the digital media marketplace: Hearing before the Senate Commerce Committee, United States Senate. Testimony to the 108th Congress [accessed 27 January 2006]. Available from http://www.commerce.senate.gov/ hearings/testimony.cfm?id=919& wit_id=2587; INTERNET.

3D GLOBALIZATION

Chapter 35

_____

Tom O'Regan

CULTURAL EXCHANGE (2004)

> A film . . . circulates in a sphere which can be described as transnational with none of
> the specificity so desired by nationalists. It does so because its mode of communication
> doesn't rely exclusively on the local or the national for success.
>
> Ron Burnett, "The National Question in Quebec"

I T ALMOST GOES WITHOUT SAYING that what distinguishes the cinema
from a good proportion of broadcasting and book publishing is that it is from inception
international (McQuail 1994: 16–20). In most cinema markets and those parts of the
television schedule dedicated to movies, including pay-TV movie channels, international
productions dominate. Films circulate across national, language, and community boundaries
reaching deep into social space. Audiences, critics, and filmmakers appropriate, negotiate,
and transform this international cinema in various ways. It is in cinema's nature to cross
cultural borders within and between nations, to circulate across heterogeneous linguistic and
social formations. This is an internationalism in production and in reception, in the making
of films and in their consumption. And if we agree that an internationalism is intrinsic to the
cinema then what must underwrite this are systems of cultural exchange. We can say then
that cultural exchange is fundamental to cinema at every level.

Cultural exchange is intrinsic to the cinema's production, circulation, and uptake.
A normal – even unexceptionable – feature of the film milieu, cultural exchange can be
found in filmmaking and film criticism, film reception, and film marketing. Processes of
cultural exchange are intrinsic to the circulation of filmmaking across national and cultural
borders – among and within states. They facilitate the lending and redisposition of cultural
materials from one filmmaking and cultural tradition to another. A powerful force for
innovation in filmmaking and the development of international understanding and misunderstanding alike, cultural exchange is a critical component of wider processes of cultural
identity formation and cultural development. Cultural exchange matters to processes of
cultural definition, loss, reconstruction, and renewal. It is constitutive of the cinema and
of culture and identity more generally. As such, it is both unexceptional and controversial.
In this chapter I establish and evaluate the ways filmmaking and film studies alike have
conceptualized and ordered the compelling evidence for cultural exchange.

By cultural exchange we mean the circulation – the giving, receiving, and redisposition – of cultural materials among differentiated socio-cultural formations. The component parts of the cultural exchange process – from the distribution mechanisms to the materials circulated and the formations that send and receive – are immensely varied in incidence, form, and purpose.

The central disputes within film studies about cultural exchange turn on how we identify its nature and how we evaluate its standing and direction. At issue here is not whether such exchange either does or should take place, as everyone agrees that it is a structural given at some level and is indeed committed to at least some forms of international, intercultural, or intercommunal cultural exchange. How we describe and judge cultural exchange is tied up with our very notions of culture, identity, and exchange itself. Our theoretical and normative positions on these concepts determine not only the range of cultural-exchange practices and processes in the cinema that are selected for investigation and discussion, but also the kind of position on cultural exchange that we adopt.

A vocabulary has built up within film studies to attempt to capture the various modalities of this handling of exchange. We speak of film, filmmakers, and audiences alike indigenizing, adapting, appropriating, poaching, resisting, coopting, and remaking films, filmmaking styles, practices, and technologies drawn from other filmmaking traditions – national and otherwise. We speak of filmmakers entering into a dialogue with the dominant international cinema and other cinema traditions. We speak of the cross-cultural reception of film and television. We speak of too little and too much cultural exchange, of unequal and reciprocal exchanges.

To discuss these matters we need to grasp the sheer dimensions of cultural exchange in terms of the materials that are exchanged, the peculiar standing of cultural exchange in the cinema in its broader contexts, the cultural communities involved in that exchange, and the economics of cultural exchange.

1 THE MATERIALS OF CULTURAL EXCHANGE

The cultural materials involved in this exchange can be diverse. They can be films like *Titanic* (James Cameron, 1997), circulating almost wherever films are screened commercially in theaters around the world. They can be concepts for films, as when the French film *Trois hommes et un couffin* (Coline Serreau, 1985) was remade in Hollywood as *Three Men and a Baby* (Leonard Nimoy, 1987). Filmmakers routinely draw on stories from other cultural traditions: how many times have Shakespeare's plays been remade or used as concepts for stories in various cultural traditions from the Russian to the Japanese to the American? They can be the adjustments made to films with the explicit purpose of facilitating international circulation: this impinges on the selection of content (is it too parochial?), of actors and directors (are they known in other territories?), and even of accents and dialogue (will they be comprehensible?). The original *Mad Max* (George Miller, 1979) was dubbed from Australian into American English to facilitate its circulation; and the children's film *Babe* (Chris Noonan, 1995) strove for accents that would be acceptable to North American school children. Such factoring in of international circulation and therefore a film's potential for cultural exchange is a consistent consideration for investors, producers, directors, and scriptwriters.

The cultural materials can be filmmaking practices. Italian neorealist aesthetics and production practices of the late 1940s – particularly the enthusiasm for location shooting and the use of nonprofessional actors – evident in films such as *Roma: Citta aperta* (Roberto Rossellini, 1945, *Rome: Open City*) and *Ladri di biciclette* (Vittorio de Sica, 1951, *Bicycle*

Thieves) were diffused among a variety of other national cinemas over the late 1940s and 1950s. These aesthetics created critical expectations as to what the cinema (generally) should look like.

The materials can be the reception of films and filming, which in turn inform those who produced the films in the first place. Provocatively, Thomas Elsaesser claims that the New German Cinema of Rainer Fassbinder, Wim Wenders, Werner Herzog, Volker Schlöndorff et al. was "discovered and even invented abroad, and had to be reimported to be recognised as such" within Germany (1989: 300). Such refashioning is part of the general circulation of any national cinema as it "travels" outside its domestic context and enters new contexts. Elsaesser writes of how:

> European films intended for one kind of (national) audience or made within a particular kind of aesthetic framework or ideology, for instance, undergo a sea change as they cross the Atlantic and on coming back find themselves bearing the stamp of yet another cultural currency. (1994a: 25)

Audiences routinely take up and reshape films made in other places, from other times, and yoke them to their purposes. They can create "imaginary Americas," turning film's purposes in alternate directions, creating aberrant interpretations and the like. Non-American audiences, John Caughie writes, routinely "play at being American" in their consumption of Hollywood movies. There is, he claims, a curious game of identification and nonidentification being played by audiences, such that the non-American "plays at being American" with all the "tactics of empowerment" and "games of subordination" that this implies (1990: 45). As Alison Butler observes:

> the refunctionalization of texts is not just a manifestation of occasional resistances, but the very condition of possibility of such border crossings. Productive – and indeed unproductive – misreading is perhaps the paradigmatic operation which governs the reception of films outside – and sometimes inside – their original national contexts. (1992: 419)

Identifying much the same processes, Henry Jenkins writes of fans raiding "mass culture, claiming its materials for their own use, reworking them as the basis for their own cultural creations and social interactions" (1992: 18). Fans like Caughie's non-American are situated "outside" but reconstruct this status so as to inscribe themselves within that creative process.

The cultural materials can also include our ways of conceiving cinema itself. These consist of ideas about what cinema is, what it can be, how it can be important, in what ways its study should be approached. André Bazin (1967, 1971) and his colleagues at *Cahiers du cinéma* in the 1950s and 1960s developed ideas about the cinema of great international significance. Their ideas arguably underwent something of a sea-change also, as they were refashioned into the auteurist criticism of Andrew Sarris in North America and in that circulation helped found contemporary Anglo-American film studies.

People can be cultural materials too, as skills honed and developed in one cultural milieu are redisposed in another. Film directors often contribute to a number of national cinemas. Luis Buñuel made Spanish, Mexican, US, and French films. For his part Joseph Losey, "compelled to leave America at the time of Senator McCarthy . . . had to digest the mores of a new environment and struggle to obtain work" in the UK (Thomson 1980: 358). There he made classics of British cinema such as *The Servant* (1963) and *The Go-Between* (1971). The peripatetic Hungarian, Emeric Pressburger, worked in the film industry in Germany, then France, before settling in England, becoming one half of British cinema's most creative partnership, "Powell & Pressburger" (see MacDonald 1994). And it was he more than his collaborator who was responsible for the extraordinary wartime propaganda film *The 49th Parallel* (1941), aimed at shoring up wavering American public opinion for involvement in World War II. Pressburger's contributions did not end with his British involvements. In the 1960s he wrote the script from England for an Australian film, *They're a Weird Mob* (Powell, 1966).

Such freewheeling internationalism for actors, cinematographers, and directors is now an ordinary, even customary, way of inhabiting a film milieu. This experience of crossing borders is often driven by the needs of the receiving culture. Australian director Fred Schepisi is on record as saying that the Americans "want you [meaning non-Americans like him] to be original within formula frameworks" (Koval 1992: 43). They want "your original-ity but not for original films, they want it applied to their kind of films" (42) – in his case the results include *Russia House* (1990), *Roxanne* (1987), and *Six Degrees of Separation* (1993).

The cultural materials exchanged include particular technologies of exhibition, produc-tion, and marketing. Film festivals, for example, provide a machinery for films of various local cinemas to, in Bill Nichols's words, "circulate globally, within a specific system of institutional assumptions, priorities and constraints" (1994: 68). Screened at film festivals, these films are "never only or purely local"; instead they "circulate, in large part, with a cachet of locally inscribed difference and globally ascribed commonality." Film festivals as a distribution mechanism allow for the recognition of "the uniqueness of different cultures and specific filmmakers," while at the same time affirming "the underlying qualities of an 'international cinema.' "

Another example of cultural materials in circulation is provided by the adoption of different cinema exhibition venues. Take the example of the multiplex – the phenomenon of multi-screen theatrical exhibition spaces. It begins in Canada in the late 1950s, is extended to the US over the 1960s, and from there becomes dispersed around the world. Or take the siting of exhibition venues in giant shopping malls in the US and their slow spread throughout the global system since the late 1970s and into the twenty-first century. Here developments in real estate, site management, and city-planning are part of the diffusion of cinema developments internationally.

Exchangeable cultural materials are also of a more generalized character – such as the ideas, practices, and conceptions of everything from modernity to the role and functions of the state – and flow across cultural borders impacting upon film form, content, and the very organization of the cinema. John Orr, for example, identifies a "neo-modern moment" which "has its origin in the national cinemas of Western Europe and the United States where it engages with Western capitalist modernity" and has been extended to other cinematic traditions (1993: 6). John Tomlinson argues that a feature of the contemporary period is one where the "the simultaneous advantages and demerits of 'modernity' are being extended to powerful and impoverished nations alike" (1992: 175; see also Downing 1996: 223). In this context the cinema is, as Hamid Naficy has pointed out, one of those institutions of modernization, as "Third World" filmmakers, "wooed to cinema by Western films," trained in many cases in Europe, the US, and to a lesser extent the USSR, upon return made "films that critiqued the West and attempted to create a national identity in contradistinction to it" (1996: 4).

Another instance of such general exchanges is in policy models, where the ideas, the phrases, the arguments are borrowed and redisposed. Not long after the publication of the South African Film White Paper in 1996 (see Tomaselli and Shepperson 1996), Zimbabwe released its own film "white paper" which bore a remarkable resemblance to the South African document. The South Africans involved in the original white paper were surprised by these similarities. Although the Zimbabweans seem to have had no other agenda than to use an available African-based policy, one consequence of this kind of ad hoc borrowing is that it aligns, mirrors, and therefore helps integrate various regional film industries. Such policy-learning is important internationally. And it happens everywhere. Canadian film policy-making of the late 1960s and early 1970s directly impacted on Australian film policy development in the same period, with Canadian officials advising their Australian counterparts. The prevalence of the overseas "fact-finding mission" is a more general instance of this on most government horizons. It is replicated by the obligatory visit of previously domestic filmmakers to international festivals, not only to learn the festival system but to assimilate the prevailing international standards of everything from imaging standards to deal-making.

Such cultural materials provide the glue holding together the more-or-less integrated international film system of production, circulation, distribution, and exchange.

2 THE COMMUNITIES FOR CULTURAL EXCHANGE

Alongside the various cultural materials that can be exchanged and the mixed standing of this exchange we also need to recognize the various partners involved – the community terrain on which cultural exchange takes place. The cultural formations involved are as varied as are the cultural materials of the exchange and generate distinctive cultural-exchange dynamics.

They can be smaller and larger, richer and poorer nations. They can be groupings of nations, as in Europe, Africa, Latin America, as in the North and the South, as in the developed and the underdeveloped world, as in the Occident and the Orient. They can be communities of language-speakers of varying size and collective wealth – francophones, Zulu-speakers, Japanese-speakers, and anglophones. They can be religious communities embracing groups of nations, as in the so-called Islamic and Catholic countries. Such faith communities, like their language-community counterparts, can exist within and across a number of nations. The nation states involved in cultural exchange can be of various types. There are the "new world," neo-European nations of the Americas and Australasia defined by settler invasions and the dispossession of indigenous populations; there are the "old world" nations of Europe with their predominantly indigenous populations; and there are the postcolonial nations of Africa and South-East Asia.

The cultural formations involved in exchange also include smaller and larger sub-groupings within nation states. They might be the various "national communities," such as the Quebeckers and the Inuit "first nation" in Canada. They include the various minorities defined by ethnicity, region, sub-culture, sexual orientation, and gender. And they include the various cultural communities within national borders and those – such as various diasporic communities – who persist across national borders.

The cultural communities can be at greater or lesser cultural distance from each other. Some can be partly derived from each other and share a common language, such as the US, Canada, Australia, New Zealand, and South Africa, which are all former British colonies. Unsurprisingly, Hollywood has some of its best markets in English-speaking territories, leading to the perennial complaint of Britons, Australians, and English Canadians that they are cursed with sharing the English language with the dominant international cinema and wearing the consequences of this cultural proximity. Some national communities, like the Scandinavian and Benelux countries, are particularly open to cultural exchange. As small countries these nations look to a variety of import sources for television and cinema as a means of maintaining a sense of a distinctive identity, whereas bigger countries like Britain, France, and Germany look principally to their own local productions to secure these same objectives (Sepstrup 1990: *passim*). Smaller countries tend to regard imports in a different way from big countries, seeing in them advantages as much as disadvantages and often putting effort into diversifying the sources of film and program imports. Other national communities are remarkably closed, with international productions making up a negligible amount of the US box office and television schedules (but this negligible amount is enough to make the US Britain's best television and cinema export market).

The communities involved in cultural exchange can operate at a large cultural distance from each other – think of the gap between, say, a small Pacific Island nation such as Vanuatu and the People's Republic of China. And this large gap may be replicated within a nation, as when we compare traditional Aboriginal communities in central Australia with their "mainstream" European and increasingly Asian equivalents. Underwriting the complexity of cultural exchange are systems of mutual attraction and repulsion. We might assume that culturally contiguous communities would be more likely to be involved as partners in cultural exchange than communities at some distance from each other. But this does not always hold. In situations of conflict or histories of invasion, such communities may prefer, as a matter of policy, more culturally distant materials. Croatians prefer German and Hollywood filmmaking to that of their Serbian neighbours; Pakistan prefers Western programming over that of its neighbour India. Sometimes, among diasporic refugee communities, the films and television-programming of a proximate community are preferred to the local cultural materials of a homeland still under a despised political dispensation.

Sometimes this cultural exchange can be equal: French and German cultural trade is roughly balanced and both have larger populations. Mostly, however, cultural exchange is unequal. Some countries – like the US, Japan (in television at least), and India – are cultural producers, others cultural importers. Studies of the flow of cinema and television have quantified this cultural exchange, indicating the largely one-way cultural flows from the richer to the poorer, from the developed to the underdeveloped, from the North to the South, from the English language to other languages, from the larger language groups to the smaller ones, from the US to the rest of the world (Varis 1988). Such studies have also indicated the substantial role in cultural exports of highly populated countries in Europe (France, Germany, and Italy), Latin America (Mexico and Brazil), the Middle East (Egypt), and Asia (India, Japan, and Hong Kong/China) and the minor but significant role played by more sparsely populated countries such as Australia and Canada (see Sinclair et al. 1996).

This unequal character of cultural exchange is longstanding. In 1946 Gordon Mirams concluded his study of New Zealand filmgoing with the observation that "if there is any such thing as 'a New Zealand culture,' it is to a large extent the creation of Hollywood" (cited in Lealand 1988: 83). *The Moving Picture World* (Jan 7) of 1922 observed: "The American control of foreign market with respect to motion pictures is approximately the following: South America, 95%; Australian 90%; continental Europe, 85%; Britain, 85%; Far East, 8%" (quoted in de Usabel 1982: xv). Even in the world's second largest economy, Japan, international productions make up half the cinema box office (though negligible amounts on television).

Such unequal cultural-exchange dynamics have their origins in the structural dynamics of the cinema – its system of scale production with mass distribution and exhibition – requiring expensive technology, specialized screening venues, continuously improving standards of image-making and large-scale administrative coordination (Tunstall 1977). The international film industry is, unsurprisingly, dominated by a handful of major transnational corporations. Such multinationals conduct a largely unequal relationship with weaker domestic producers, exhibitors, and policy-makers. This industry is geographically concentrated in a handful of wealthy film centers, and its international scale shapes the production possibilities and contexts of peripheral film industries, nations, peoples, and centers

(Guback 1969; Thompson 1985). The international industry is both dominant and predatory. It is predatory in that it is naturally expansive. It seeks new markets, new personnel
for its productions (many national cinemas – British, Australian, Canadian, Dutch, and
New Zealand – have their most talented directors for only so long), new commercial
opportunities (in theme parks, product tie-ins, new media). And it seeks to extract the
maximum benefit from its productions by, for example, forcing cinema-, video-, and
television-buyers to take a package of products, whether sight unseen to get continuous
access to valued products or in order to purchase that handful of productions that are most
desired. As Janet Wasko notes, "it seems undeniable that the media business has increasingly
become even more concentrated and unified" with "corporate mergers and diversification
activities" intensifying this trend (1994: 18).

Yet this same Hollywood cinema, along with the other dominant international cinemas,
plays an important role in cinema capacity-building globally, providing the incentive to
invest in building or renovating exhibition infrastructures. For these reasons, much national
cinema policy-making, while wanting to do much more to redress the imbalance, ends up
leaving substantially intact the exhibition, distribution, and production nexus which aids the
dominant international cinemas. Typically there is some fiddling at the edges through various
national cinema supplements – based sometimes on minor imposts on the distribution and
exhibition sectors, but mostly on various government-funded production support mechanisms. The commercial order of the cinema is one where unequal exchanges, dominance,
hierarchies, the size and length of the multinational and national exhibition and distribution
networks rule. It is onto this basic structure that various governments and local industries
graft their local filmmaking activities.

The partners to cultural exchange in the cinema come to that exchange on an undeniably and permanently unequal basis with disparities of language, wealth, size, resources,
infrastructures, and culture. Few film relations are based on free and open exchange. There
are many one-way cultural flows and little reciprocity. There are two broad ways in which
community agents and film critics have understood the economic domination of cinema
exchange by the larger players and in particular Hollywood. In the first, they see it as
evidence of fundamental and structural inequality in the international system amounting
to discriminatory economic dynamics (Schiller 1969; Mattelart et al. 1984). In the second, it
is a pragmatic and improvised economic response to a set of given cultural conditions
(Wildman and Siwek 1988). In one, Hollywood's dominance represents the distortion of
markets, and in the other, a response to market conditions.

What the concentration on audiovisual flows and distribution dynamics tends to neglect
is the use made by communities of the cultural materials that are exchanged. Clearly the
producers and viewers in this international cultural exchange system only weakly share
cultural resources. Both are required to negotiate cultural cleavages to create meanings. Eric
Michaels suggests that this circumstance has had important textual consequences: it has
encouraged Hollywood producers to adopt a "highly complex rhetorical stance which makes
it quite difficult to say what the intended meaning of many programs might be" (1990: 19).
In other words, the "conversation" between producers and audiences is designed to minim-
ize obstacles to local and international participation alike on the part of potential audiences.
But this strategy of incorporation is achieved through a communicative inefficiency (which is
exploited most efficiently): as propositional contents are bent further, opportunities for
partial misunderstanding are increased and even encouraged. And this is not a problem.
For Hollywood, it does not particularly matter that wildly divergent or astonishingly con-
vergent interpretations are routinely accomplished by audiences through Hollywood's global
circulation so long as tickets are sold and videos rented. But equally, as Michaels elsewhere
contends:

It would seem difficult to see in the introduction of imported video and television programs the destruction of Aboriginal culture. Such a claim can only be made in ignorance of the strong traditions and preferences in graphics, the selectivity of media and contents, and the strength of interpretation of the Warlpiri. (1994: 95)

Heterogeneous cultural communities of region, race, and ethnicity make for various kinds of internal cultural exchange dynamics which can be profoundly unequal, dysfunctional, and to the disadvantage of the weaker party to the exchange. Taking the USA as an example, the cultural communities involved in this exchange include the "mountain" communities that are the subject of J. W. Williamson's study *Hillbillyland* (1995), which has as its subtitle *What the Movies Did to the Mountains and what the Mountains Did to the Movies*. In this exchange, the mountains, with their associations of inbreeding, mental degeneration, and quaintness, become ciphers for a metropolitan imagination exercising its cultural power.

Similar unequal dynamics sustain many representational politics. Film scholarship speaks to the systematic and questionable representational dynamic involving African-American, Amerindian, and other minority populations in the content and practices of mainstream cinema, in its institutions, and among its mainstream white audiences (see Bogle 1973; Bataille and Silet 1980). Cultural exchange is routinely condemned here for the distorted lens it provides, leading to calls for the taking over of the representation of minorities to the mainstream by the minorities themselves so as to fashion a more inclusive image. Such internal cultural diversity is itself a leitmotif in much cultural studies and contemporary screen scholarship. It shifts attention to contingent processes of integration, differentiation, and assimilation of the cultural materials of the host and minority culture by minorities themselves, displacing the mainstream from its assumed center stage. So we find Hamid Naficy's Iranian immigrant viewers of film and television in California adapting aspects of their Persian heritage and taking on elements of American culture to construct composite, hybrid identities in symbolic cultural practices which simultaneously disavow and recognize their difference (1993: 86). Homi Bhabha's immigrant and marginal diasporic communities further make a claim for the centrality of their experience to the constitution of the nation itself: "the Western metropole must confront its postcolonial history, told by its influx of postwar migrants and refugees, as an indigenous or native narrative internal to its national identity" (1994: 6). For their part, gay and lesbian communities interacting with a filmmaking largely premissed on heterosexual orientations produce not only their own resistances but proactive readings and filmmaking, including notions of a queer nation internal to the nation itself (see Brasell 1995). Equally important is the concomitant stress placed on the imaginative consequences of cultural diversity upon majority groups. In this context Kobena Mercer poses the question: "what is going on when whites assimilate and introject the degraded and devalued signifier of racial otherness into the cultural construction of their own identity?" (1992: 21). Julian Stringer, answering this question, argues that white appropriations of blackness and Chineseness are qualitatively different: "the racial economy in the white imagination of *True Romance* (dir. Tony Scott, writer Quentin Tarantino) is clear: you can have the Chineseness; but you can be black" (1996/7: 60). Stringer asks: "what is it that makes him [Tarantino] want to be black but not really Chinese?"

Cultural exchange mechanisms can, as these examples demonstrate, be located at macro and micro levels alike, suggesting that cultural exchange is both a constitutive component of culture itself and involves matters of cultural and economic power. As Michael Schudson observes:

The intertwinings of local, regional, national, and global cultures are now complex beyond reckoning. Cultures flow in, out, around, and through state borders; within states, centres radiate to peripheries but peripheries influence centres, too; in the world system the same phenomenon is repeated and culture flows in many directions. (1994: 42)

In such circumstances the critical issue is the *handling* and *standing* of such cultural exchange by agents in various cultural formations. In this both the senders and receivers, the exporters and the importers, the foreign and the host cultures are implicated. At issue is how cultural exchange mechanisms enter into and shape cultural milieux, including identities and the culture itself.

3 THE STANDING OF CULTURAL EXCHANGE

A mixed standing to cultural exchange in the film milieu and beyond is an inevitable consequence of both this sheer diversity and scope of cultural materials exchanged and the variety of levels at which such cultural exchange operates – from policy to ideas, from the circulation of people to the extension of practices, from reception contexts to industry development. Cultural exchange is part of the very furniture of the film milieu, a taken-for-granted given. And it is something very much in the foreground of consideration as some aspects of cultural exchange are made into substantive political, critical, and ethical issues by film critics, filmmakers, activists, and governments.

Our film politics, our film policy-making, our film appreciation, and our film criticism are deeply ambivalent about cultural exchange. We take it for granted, embrace it, and repel it in equal measure. We simultaneously see cultural exchange as an ordinary and integral part of the very constitution of the cinema, and as something so extraordinary as to require urgent critical and policy remedy. On the one hand we appreciate it and evolve strategies for more of it, and on the other we formulate policies designed to ensure less of it, including campaigns to diminish or enhance its standing. This ambivalence about cultural exchange is a consequence of how we encounter – remark upon or simply take for granted – the standing of cultural exchange.

Cultural exchange can have standing as simply an unexceptionable process in the film milieu, as when Kristin Thompson writes of how national cinemas are, as a matter of course, shaped by the "influences film-makers and audiences picked up from the presence of American films" (1985: ix). Describing and judging this sort of cultural exchange cuts across every facet of film study. The study of film auteurs needs to assess, for example, the influence of the British creative duo Michael Powell and Emeric Pressburger on the work of Martin Scorsese. Lesley Stern, for example, writes that "*Raging Bull* (Scorsese, 1980) bears an imprint, can be read in terms of *The Red Shoes* (Powell & Pressburger, 1948); it is as though *The Red Shoes* has bled subliminally into *Raging Bull*" (1995: 11). A strand of national cinema analysis embeds the national cinema in question into a larger international cinema, such that comparing one's own national cinema to others becomes a way to understand it. Darrell William Davis notes how one strand in the discussion of Japanese cinema "emphasises its similarities and differences to other works, usually from Western cinema" (1996: 19). The result aimed for is that of "an intertextual conversation of allusion and influence that conveys the dialectic of artistic process" within Japanese cinema (19). Cultural exchange functions here as a catalyst for understanding and reinvigorating local traditions.

Cultural exchange can be of such a character that it is not even noticed as a form of exchange. Geoff Lealand notes the naturalizing of the Hollywood screen presence on the cultural horizons of ordinary New Zealanders:

The stories of Hollywood that persist have been long naturalised into New Zealand popular culture, so that *E. T.* seems no more alien to New Zealanders than to Americans. The images we [New Zealanders] have embraced, as well as having been naturalised, have also been "neutralised"; no longer perceived as threats to the cultural integrity of New Zealand. They are deemed as something else – "entertainment", "escapism", "fantasy", universal stories with universal appeal. (1988: 90)

Here cultural exchange is part of the wallpaper – a cause for neither celebration nor denigration, it is simply something we are to attend to if we want to understand the cinema before us and the everyday transnational conversations of which it seems a part. Its standing is literally that of any other naturalized part of the film milieu. Cultural exchange seems here to be part of us, who we are, what we think. We can no more disaggregate and disentangle it than catch the air.

Something of the mundane character of this cultural exchange can be seen in the gestation and critical uptake of Alex Proyas's recent feature film *Dark City* (1998). Proyas, whose previous feature was the cult classic *The Crow* (1994) featuring the late Brandon Lee, made *Dark City* in his native Australia in a studio part-owned by the Fox Corporation – a major Hollywood studio and multi-national film distributor. In keeping with the emerging logic of global film production that Toby Miller has explored (1996, 1998a, 1998b), *Dark City* is simultaneously a Hollywood film made in Australia, an Australian film (the studio in question was developed in conjunction with support from federal and state [provincial] governments), a film with an international cast and crew, and a film whose story coordinates are claimed by its director in French comics, sci-fi literature and the German Expressionist cinema of the 1920s (Barber and Sacchi 1998; Helms 1998).

For their part, film critics typically made sense of this film through an orgy of comparison. It was judged to be a commentary on *and* an extension of classic films as diverse as *Nosferatu, eine Symphonie des Grauens* (1922), *Metropolis* (1926), *La Bête humaine* (1938), *The Wizard of Oz* (1939), *Zardoz* (1973), *Phenomena* (1984), *Hellraiser* (1987), *Delicatessen* (1991), *The Hudsucker Proxy* (1994), *The Crow* (1994), and *La Cité des enfants perdus* (1995).[1] The reviews on the Internet proliferated resemblances. Some critics declaimed its derivativeness. Paul Tatara (1998) claimed a "dead lift" from *Brazil* (1985): "Think of a loud, unimaginably confused (visually as well as narratively) *Brazil* with absolutely no sense of humor." Others found in its cinematic references a rich intertextual space. Roger Ebert (1998) noted that: "Its villains, in their homburgs and flapping overcoats, look like a nightmare inspired by the thugs in *M*, but their pale faces would look more at home in *The Cabinet of Dr. Caligari* (1919)."

The filmmakers and audiences (insofar as critics are indicative of the audience) alike saw the film adapting, appropriating, poaching, and remaking films, filmmaking styles, practices, and technologies drawn from various filmmaking traditions. Proyas's film was clearly entering into a dialogue with the cinema – past and present, the dominant international cinema, art cinema, and traditions of comics.

The film has no discernible Australian precedent, nor can any influence be claimed from previous Australian films, and yet it is likely to significantly impact on Australian production (Venkatasawmy and O'Regan 1998). It is a film with decidedly international precedents. While not an Australasian art film along the lines of Jane Campion's *The Piano* (1993), it takes up aspects of art cinema hitherto unexplored in its imagining of other possible worlds, its plays with the logic of representation, and its studio-based rather than location-based film practice.

With *Dark City* cultural exchange is fundamental to its very constitution in production, circulation, and significance. The debating point is the quality of this exchange. Few doubt whether it should exist (they might want less of it but could not imagine none of it) or if this is the right kind of cultural exchange (to do so would query a line of filmmaking that begins with Fritz Lang's *Metropolis*). The issue is rather if it is any good at what it does in its own terms and in terms of the sci-fi, expressionist, and film-noir traditions on which it draws. Is it parasitic on them? Does it adequately contribute to them? At issue is its cinema, not its cultural authenticity or the appropriateness of an Australian creating an American noir city in a Sydney backlot. This film and this filmmaker are not making a statement about Australia or his Greek-Australian identity. They are participating in the cinema, and this film is produced, circulated, and criticized in a transnational space.

Cultural exchange is often publicly embraced as a good thing in circumstances where the line between self and other – the domestic national cinema and the international cinema – is clearer. The public championing of cultural exchange is often tied up with how generations (of audiences, filmmakers, and critics) step in the face of their predecessors by actively seeking and lionizing certain kinds of cultural exchange as a matter of active policy. Such a searching out of available international models of film and living was part of a purposive rejection of a local film and socio-political situation by the emerging filmmakers of the New German Cinema from the 1960s. Anton Kaes contends that a "unifying force of New German Cinema since the 1960s has been the 'uncompromising rejection of the [fascist] National Socialist film tradition" (1989: 8). He cites directors such as Wim Wenders looking to American directors such as John Ford "for stylistic inspiration"; Volker Schlöndorff going to France "to learn filmmaking," and Herzog identifying himself with "the tradition of German Expressionism of the 1920s."

The local situation need not be as drastic as a fascist past; typically many a national filmmaker will publicly reject his or her own domestic production traditions in favor of the seemingly more expansive, even liberating, horizons and models available in the international cinema. Devaluing the national cinema and admitting to the value of Hollywood is part of how filmmakers like Australia's Baz Luhrmann (*Strictly Ballroom*, 1992) declare their "newness," "relevance," and "importance" in the local milieu. Hollywood enacts what the national cinema holds out, at least potentially, as its preserve – namely a natural and direct relation with the local audience. As Kim Schroder and Michael Skovmond celebrate it, "by breaking away from traditional, class-based notions of good taste, [it] could be absorbed by the actual tastes and desires of large numbers of working-class people" (1992: 7).

Governments the world over promote the educational and cultural value of international understanding in their cultural policies. They inaugurate programs for intercultural dialogue, which include the support of film festivals and the encouragement of coproductions. Indeed one of the functions of national public broadcasters in the latter part of the twentieth century – particularly in their niche and minoritarian variants – was to provide expanded opportunities for seeing and appreciating more of the world's cinema and television programming than they would otherwise have had available to them through the commercial dynamics of free-to-air broadcasting. So it is, for example, that Australia's national public broadcaster, SBS-TV, broadcasts 50 per cent of its programming in languages other than English drawn from around the world and maintains a "world movies" pay-TV channel. In a similar fashion the UK's Channel 4 has been an important screening venue and production catalyst for feature films, documentaries, and series television exploring local and international cultural diversity and including a variety of international production partnerships.

Sometimes moments of cultural exchange become defining moments for a film community and enable cultural communities to reorient their appreciation, criticism, and sense of the purposes and possibilities of filmmaking, as happened in France in the 1950s and early

1960s. Like so many of his generation, Henri Agel encountered as a revelation the American cinema largely denied him under German occupation after World War II:

> It was in the course of these nights, glistening with all the fires of the music hall, through swarming carnivals worthy of the early Rouault, in smoke-filled halls oozing with all the effluvia of Pigalle, that for some an American enchantment was born. A magic, doubtless impure and at times closer to a junkie's high, a magic too tied up with tinsel and vulgarity of the Boulevard not to be ambiguous. And even so, in the trip from the icy Palace to the last metro for Etoile, everything began to decant, to regroup along certain lines of force that in the course of those weeks etched a more precise and more dense image of Hollywood, no longer the one that our professors pronounced with their lips pursed, but a crucible perpetually on the boil in which was blended fear and laughter and eroticism and violence and tenderness. Surely we were mixing thus the best and the worst. (1963: 12–13; quoted in Routt 1992: 61)

This cinema became a vehicle for both a cinephilia – a love of and commitment to the cinema – and a highly particular French "romance Americaine." In Agel's case this desire and love for a specifically American cinema is simultaneously embedded with unambiguously French landmarks and cultural references.

Love and desire are as indiscriminate here as elsewhere. The desire may just as likely be for an art cinema, a political cinema, an experimental cinema seemingly unavailable in one's own local cinema as for a popular vernacular cinema like Hollywood. (Indeed in English-speaking countries this desire for cultural exchange is more likely to manifest itself publicly in a desire for something other than Hollywood vernacular and the Anglo-American quality film, including its Australasian and Canadian variants.)

Just as cultural exchange can be so appreciated, loved, and desired, cultural exchange can be repulsed, actively and trenchantly resisted. Indeed desire and repulsion are part of the very public provenance of cultural exchange, as we see in the Agel quote. One person's (foreign or simply Other) love object is another's hate object. Agel's love for Hollywood and the cinema is matched by his professors' disdain for American cinema and "the movies." Often desire and repulsion for the same cinematic phenomena are to be found among the same people. The *Cahiers du cinéma* film critics who espoused American cinema in the 1950s and early 1960s had adopted a far less sympathetic tone toward Hollywood by the mid-1960s as directors facing American competition.

Resisting cultural exchange has long been a very public matter and has its origins in the profoundly unequal cultural flows of the international audiovisual system mentioned above. As these unequal cultural exchanges flow from capitalist dynamics which have concentrated the "power over communications" into a handful of multi-nationals, resistance to them becomes a public matter. François Mitterrand, as French President, railed against this nexus in 1982:

> The distribution of information developed and controlled by a few dominant countries could mean for others the loss of their history or even their sovereignty, thus calling into question their freedom to think and decide. (cited in Mattelart et al. 1988: 19)

Various cultural, educational and religious elites make a political issue of *too much distributed cultural exchange*. The desire for cultural exchange readily turns to repulsion when it rubs up against, and is seen to compromise through sheer scale, cultural transmission and routines of identity formation. Many a Briton, Frenchman or woman, and Australian has worried publicly about the consequences for cultural maintenance, transmission of heritage, and allegiance even to the nation and community of a youth brought up on other people's pictures, knowing more of the 4th of July and apple pie than 1066, the storming of the Bastille, or Gallipoli. These worries are often registered in a public anti-Americanism, anti-market, or anti-transnational-corporation position on the part of various elites and popular movements, given Hollywood's role as the primary international cinema and the US's role as the world's leading economy.

Cultural exchange with the US is actively resisted for the threats it poses to the transmission of local cultures from generation to generation. In film criticism we speak of films and filmmaking traditions being swamped by other cultural traditions. In the case of Australian and Canadian audiences and filmmakers, they not only "feel second best . . . forced to second guess what their authentic indigenous culture should be" but they produce a "neo-colonial 'second cinema' that consciously and unconsciously strives to reproduce the Hollywood models of production and circulation, counterfeiting the local sense of historical reality" (Dermody and Jacka 1988: 20, 23). Hollywood's effects are experienced not only in the perverted complexion of markets and investment but in the perversion of the national subject itself, the value and identity of a nation's citizens. America's offense is psychical: they are the privileged group, globally enforcing their world-view. People the world over respond by becoming identified with this American point of view, and in the process their identity, history, and culture are devalued. Agents locate an abjection among audiences and filmmakers to explain why a positive relation between the local audience and their national cinema is so difficult to achieve. Under such conditions of distorted cultural exchange film-making milieux can seem to become predominantly neocolonial (Dermody and Jacka 1988: 23). Repulsion is integrally tied up with matters of national pride and sour grapes: too much cultural exchange becomes a measure of national failure for the local product not only to own its domestic market but to count internationally.

There are powerful political reactions on the part of political and cultural elites to the unequal cultural exchange implicit in the international audiovisual system. Perceiving too much of one kind of cultural exchange, such as largely one-directional cultural flows, these reactions acquire a modular form. Film critics in English-speaking countries routinely lament too much American influence on local filmmakers and call for a greater openness on their part to to other cultural influences like Asian or European cinema (see, for example, Berry 1992: 48). Film agents – from critics to lobbyists – around the world call for and attempt to implement protectionist measures, including the expulsion of "foreign bodies" to recover a being, a space before "contamination": in 1975 an Australian government report claimed its legitimate business as protecting local locations from exploitation by predatory international filmmakers (Interim Board of the Australian Film Commission 1975: 36). Mainland and Taiwanese critics routinely lambast Hong Kong cinema for being "un-minzu" – for being un-Chinese in its adoption of "Western" modes of filmic expression. Domestic film-industry spokespersons routinely regard the loss of their domestic audience to Hollywood (or another dominant international cinema) as a consequence of predatory and colonizing behaviors. Sometimes resistance to cultural exchange has been exhibited in political disturbances, including acts of arson and threats accompanying the opening of the South Korean market to Hollywood films and American distributors.

Repulsion need not be founded on the schoolmaster's elitism with its implicit assumptions of low versus high culture, elite versus popular art, Europe versus America. It may instead be founded on resolutely populist and even tribalist positions. Indigenous community leaders (see Michaels 1994: 20–46) are concerned at the cultural impact of a readily available cinema, television, and video on traditional life – rituals, mores, observances, and practices – and the respect for cultural authority. But even here indigenous people are typically not against cultural exchange per se. They are more often concerned to guard against its excesses and to attempt to turn it toward community-building and cultural enhancement. Classification and censorship regimes "protect citizens" from materials that would give cultural or religious offense.

Whether this is a genuinely felt cultural need, an informed response to objective conditions of concentration and control over transmission, or simply opportunist industry posturing to secure its own advantages, such reactions license both policy programs designed to foster a local filmmaking ecology and political rhetorics aimed at reclaiming symbolicly a tradition in danger of extinction. On grounds of the cultural threat and cultural erosion following from exchange, a panoply of measures have developed internationally to inhibit, limit, and channel it. These inhibitions include a variety of governmental instruments from public policy to film-censorship regimes, from film-importing practices to curricula adjustment.

Nations around the world and jurisdictions such as the Canadian province of Quebec "use the law as a vehicle for the protection of [their] identity" (Burnett 1996: 250). So we have had long histories of regulated box office quotas and levies on films, introduced and sustained over the 1930s stretching through to the 1980s as a means of ensuring a viable local supplement alongside a vigorous international cinema. Quebec legislators, as part of their efforts to encourage the public use of French and protect a distinctive identity, have mandated not only street signage in French but also that English-language films can only "play for between eight and twelve weeks before a French dubbed version must appear in the theatres" (Burnett 1996: 257).

Various content regimes, first in the cinema and later in television, mandate amounts of local cinema and television product or specify upper limits on foreign content. Such content regimes are designed to encourage particular kinds of cultural exchange and production sources for the people's cinema enjoyment. In 1928 the New Zealand government mandated that 20 per cent of films imported into New Zealand should be British, justifying this measure on the grounds that it would "give our people, particularly the younger ones, a clearer idea of British history, of British countries and British customs and ideals" (cited in Lealand 1988: 91). Lest the colonial dominion relation evident here be seen as something of the past, just substitute for British "European" and you have the basis for much of the same supra-nation-state discourse of the contemporary European Community. For his part, the French cultural minister of the 1980s, Jack Lang, denounced multi-national and, by implication, American dominance of the international cultural exchange system in remarks that occasioned diplomatic exchanges with the Americans (cited in Mattelart et al. 1988: 19–20). Against this cultural imperialism he was concerned to construct counter-measures in a Latin audiovisual space (see Mattelart et al. 1984: passim).

The reactions to too much exchange of a certain kind reach into general societal reactions to perennial issues such as screen (cinema and TV) violence and classification issues. Because these controversies were associated in Australia, from the late 1950s to the mid-1970s, with imported product, the importing of that product became a political issue, whereas in the US the issue was one of influencing Hollywood's generation of product. Controversies over the same programs and films in Australia carried an additional weight in that Australian children were not just being affected by violence, they were also being "Americanized." Social and educational elites in Australia found themselves supporting Australian production as a quality alternative. Quality film and television meant non-US television and screen drama. This is quite typical. Moral crusaders the world over transpose US concerns about the effects of movie and television violence on civic, social, and family life into similar concerns couched in terms of the circulation of specifically American cinema and programming. Sometimes these reactions can become populist movements dedicated to purging the foreign presence and identifying the movies and entertainment more generally as a primary target, as in Iran under Khomeini. The standing of cultural-exchange dynamics is obviously implicated in systems and relations of power within the cinema and society more generally. And this power is not only exercised by the stronger cultural producer against the weaker cultural receivers and producers, but also by the power of domestic elites to co-determine with international distributors the shape, form, and trajectory of the cultural exchange that does take place.

This mixed standing of cultural exchange when coupled with the diversity of materials for cultural exchange has encouraged film and cultural studies alike to seek to classify it – to distinguish types and kinds of cultural exchange, and to disclose the effects of the operation of these various types of cultural exchange on different film milieux, filmmakers, and film-reception contexts. And in classifying cultural exchange, film and cultural studies have been concerned to make judgments about it. We have been concerned with "what ought to be the case" and we have therefore expressed preferences for and aligned ourselves with some rather than other forms of cultural exchange, assiduously seeking to praise and locate the best and most appropriate. We have lauded those who resisted the power dynamics of the international cinema, articulating a "third cinema" – "a cinema of research and experimentation, equidistant from both mainstream and auteurist cinema" (Stam 1993: 242). And conversely we have been vitally concerned to search out and warn of the worst excesses of cultural exchange – circulation and imitation that is destructive, whether of indigenous traditions or simply of sensibility itself. Consequently critics, like their filmmaker and policy-maker counterparts, routinely find some kinds of cultural exchange good, and others bad. We use our identification of whether cultural exchange is good or bad to figure out the standing and therefore the value of films, filmmaking traditions, and film-production entities like particular companies and indeed whole countries. Cultural exchange is consequently alternately valued and criticized, embraced and combatted. Film studies' attempts to classify and evaluate cultural exchange are irrevocably shaped not only by the communities concerned and the standing of that exchange but by the very notions of culture, identity, and exchange deployed. It is to these notions we must now turn.

4 CULTURAL EXCHANGE AND CULTURAL IDENTITY

Our deliberations above inevitably lead us to the conclusion that cultural-exchange processes are simultaneously a blessing and a curse; they enable cultural development and identity formation and they disable the same. They help define one's own pictures and are integral to substituting other people's pictures for one's own. Cultural exchange is double-faced. It is part and parcel of the mechanisms that establish a sense of collective identity; and, equally importantly, it is part of disestablishing the same. It is inextricably tied to our notions of cultural identity, national identity, diasporic identity – for peoples and for the cinema in, for example, a national cinema. Cultural exchange is an intrinsic part of the self-same process that makes our cultural and political identities so provisional.

Insofar as identity involves notions of cultural integrity and autonomy, ideals of cultural becoming and cultural wholeness including a sense of destiny as a people, cultural exchange mechanisms diminish these. The integrity and autonomy of a culture and an identity formed in auto-identificatory fashion (constructing an identity in relation to itself rather than in relation to another) seem compromised by processes which, by definition, must question, even corrode, the bounded, coherent, and placed character of a cultural formation (adopted from Morley and Robins 1995: 122). Such cultural-exchange processes emphasize the interrelatedness and hybridity of cultural formations producing cultural fragmentation under the impact of imports as the audience for the local cultural product is fractured and seemingly "lost" to other cultures.

Such processes are often held to contribute to a perceived failure to achieve an identity. This is the classic anxiety over the incompleteness of various national and sub-national identities. We can worry whether we are sufficiently other (or even have an identity or separate culture). We are concerned about unrealized or weak identities whose very weakness is a product of the encounter with other, hegemonic cultural traditions. A leitmotif in these discussions is the recognition that the domestic cinema, the culture, and the identity under conditions of cultural exchange are decentered, unbounded, incoherent, and placeless. So it is that Susan Dermody and Elizabeth Jacka talk of how:

> Second-world countries like Canada and Australia are riddled with post-colonial ambiguity and anxieties. . . . Our identity becomes both clamorous and permanently obscure. . . . For where do "we" end and the "other" begin? Who is the other by which we define our difference, ensuring "us"? Britain? America? How are "they" to be satisfactorily disentangled from what we have internalized and hybridized from them? (1988: 20)

Sometimes film critics see this as a self-inflicted national failure – a product of cultural and social dysfunction, immaturity, and underdevelopment of cinema and other institutions. More commonly however, this failure is located elsewhere in colonial histories and neocolonial power relations embodied in critical conceptions of cultural imperialism and varieties of oppression and incapacity. These circumstances make one susceptible to other people's pictures and projections that are not one's own, and even lead to pathological and dysfunctional identities for a culture and its cinema. In the field of cultural power, we routinely speak of overpowering and vulnerable identities as some cultural identities are more powerful than others. But this is not the whole story.

Cultural-exchange processes also pose an alternative mechanism for founding a cultural identity – one that is based on the recognition of the relational and hybrid character of identity and culture. As Edward Said maintains, a culture, a self, a national identity is always produced in relation to its "others":

> the development and maintenance of every culture requires the existence of another different and competing alter ego. The construction of identity . . . whether of Orient or Occident, France or Britain . . . involves establishing opposites and "others" whose actuality is always subject to the continuous interpretation and reinterpretation of their differences from "us". (1995: 332)

Cultural-exchange processes clearly contribute to identity and culture formation at fundamental and basic levels. Identity is also intrinsically relational and cultures are themselves hybrid mixes. Such processes enter into the very story-telling of the vulnerable party. Olle Sjogren observes that, as a "small country," Sweden in its films and TV programs:

> is forced to transform its culturally weak position into a comedic national virtue. Comedy becomes a funny mirror for reflecting upon one's cultural weakness. It allows one to admit that one longs for a more exciting life without threatening the life one is leading. Through parodies one can indulge one's fascination with another, more exciting culture, while simultaneously dismissing the indulgence as a joke. (1992: 157)

Cultural-exchange processes show us how "we" are different from "them"; they let us know who we are through showing us who we are not. Such processes also illuminate and clear spaces for identities other than "ourselves." As Philip Schlesinger observes:

> How we define the other and how the other simultaneously defines us are part of the unavoidable game of identity politics. We are defined, in part at least, by being different from how they are. (1994: 27)

For Schlesinger this process of hetero-identification is part of all identity politics, whether it is staged at international, national, or sub-national level. Cultural exchanges are the ordinary stuff of cultures and identities. The Canadian and Australian condition is not then special but an ordinary condition of identity formation. The difference is more one of inflection: these cultural formations routinely problematize their identities, often as a matter of civic and ethical principle (Hutchinson 1994: 164–97).

Ron Burnett details some of the issues at stake when discussing the case of Quebeckers Celine Dion and Denys Arcand, the director of *Jésus de Montréal* (1989), both of whom have been "closely identified with the nationalist wing of Quebec culture" yet want, in the case of Dion, to be successful musically in the American market and, in the case of Arcand, to become known as "an international filmmaker":

> Celine Dion and Arcand have understood that specificity as such can best be identified from the outside and that the distinctions which we so arbitrarily use to maintain our sense of identity rarely survive without being affirmed by observers from other cultures. (1996: 260)

Cultural exchange is critical to any meaningful identity. It also carries the risk of substituting local culture with that of another. International contamination becomes a necessary risk, and identity a balancing act. It's not unusual for national cultural formations to oscillate between periods where public discourse emphasizes the line between self and other and other periods where it embraces a deliberate mixing, blurring, and preparedness to confuse itself with the world. Ross Gibson, for example, acknowledges that "the audience for Australian cinema . . . is now perhaps more interested in the world rather than the boundaries that could theoretically separate the nation from the remainder of the international community" which it was so preoccupied with in the 1970s (1992: 81).

Burnett seems to be suggesting continuous processes of cultural interpenetration and exchange which precede the advent of the cinema and are subsequent to it. In this scenario attention is shifted to cultural–transfer processes and the relation between them. Its premise is that there is, in Davis's words, "an international consciousness inseminating the film industries of all countries from the moment of their inception" making the cinema "an institution that is profoundly, inescapably international" (1996: 19). In such circumstances there is no original or authentic local culture or national cinema – every national cinema is consequently " 'always already' touched by other cultures" (20). National cinemas become, in Elsaesser's words, "relations": " 'National cinema' makes sense only as a relation, not as an essence, being dependent on other kinds of filmmaking, to which it supplies the other side of the coin" (1994a: 25 6).

When Richard Collins notes the "productivity of US cultural influences . . . on the Nouvelle Vague, the New German Cinema, or on Italian filmmakers like Sergio Leone or . . . Gianni Amelio" (1990: 157), he is finding Hollywood positively in the constitution of the national cinema product. This not only questions the idea of contamination; it suggests an informed dialogue with Hollywood. To be sure this is an asymmetrical dialogue, but a dialogue nonetheless.

But the cinema disposing the Other to produce a sense of Self raises the question as to whether the Other is displayed for him or herself or simply as a cipher to establish ourselves. Such dynamics hardly matter if the Other is a culturally stronger First-World Other, as when people of a European descent (usually Americans and Britons) and African-Americans are depicted as villains in Hong Kong cinema (such representation was aided by Hong Kong censorship under British control, which was more concerned to police representations of the mainland for fear of giving offense to a capricious People's Republic of China than to police the representation of themselves and the West). Where those Others are weaker, racially, religiously, and ethnically different, and comparatively voiceless, film critics worry about the representation of these Others functioning as "metaphors for . . . [a] sense of collective identity" (Berry 1994: 33). Obviously and throughout history preceding and subsequent to the cinema, such forms of hetero-identification have been typically discriminatory and prejudiced. A blackness helps define a whiteness; the Africans and Asians help define the European; women help define men, and so on.

But with the contemporary critical attention currently paid to diasporas, migrants, intercultural exchange, exile, and marginal, minority communities defined either by ethnicity and race or by sexual preference (it is now common to talk of the "queer" nation [Berlant and Freeman 1992]), a literature on hetero-identification has developed which has moved from denouncing an in-principle opposition to forms of hetero-identification to distinguishing between negative and positive self/other dynamics. On the one hand there is the attention paid to colonialist representational logics (Young 1990) and accompanying notions of Eurocentrism (Shohat/Stam 1994); on the other hand this has been accompanied by a deal of attention to locating and celebrating good, productive, life and identity-affirming practices. Here hybridity and intersubjective encounters are celebrated and endorsed. So it is that Chris Berry, in writing of Denis O'Rourke's fiction documentary *The Good Woman of Bangkok* (1992), talks of a "postcolonial encounter" at the Rose Hotel between the prostitute Aoi and the filmmaker, which has also become an "intersubjective space":

> What is enacted in the intersubjective exchanges in the Rose Hotel, on the other hand, is the encounter of two very different entities, each internally incoherent and split in its own way, each caught in larger patterns. Furthermore, these entities are caught up in the unequal relationships that the hybrid, syncretic space of their own interaction creates; in the Rose Hotel they create a space that is far from utopian but is different from what went before. And what is the nature of this particular intersubjective exchange, this particular deal in Bangkok? Symbolized in the form of her rice farm, Aoi gets to exert agency, and symbolized in the haunting form of his film O'Rourke gets to be in Asia and gets Asia in him. (1994: 55)

Exemplary filmmaker theorist figures such as Trinh T. Minh-ha (1992) exemplify what ought to be in such exchanges. Theirs is a hybridity of form and function in filmmaking and film criticism. They perform an avowedly indeterminate identity – refusing any fixed identity as American or Vietnamese, for example. They insist on process rather than outcome, a becoming rather than an arriving. They occupy a space that, in being neither one thing nor another, is a liminal "in between" space appropriate to the crossing of territorial and other borders in their work and its reception. They are seen to be both "outsider-in" and "insider-out."

Culture under a dispensation that takes both national societies as its unit and various communities within and across it is routinely and inevitably a hybrid phenomenon made of past and present cultural exchanges. It cannot be an ideal purity corrupted through inappropriate cultural exchange or an ideal purity to be achieved at some point in the future. Cultures under conditions of cultural exchange are made from nonoriginary, nonorganic characteristics. They are hybrid, they are contingent, they are in process. The faultlines within film studies are centered on how we describe this international contamination and the standpoints we take on cultural exchange, and most particularly where we draw the line as to its desirable and undesirable components.

Our very ways of discussing cultural exchange and identity here make it tempting to find two models of culture: an older organic model rooted in tradition and heritage and auto-identification, and another contemporary version for our globalizing times based on hetero-identification and hybridity. But if we go back to some of the founding analyses of culture and national cultures by Herder (1993), for instance, we find the same sense of culture being formed by interactions with others – through invasions, cultural transfers, migrations, and so on, alongside the more organic nativist constructions. The issue is not then a matter of choosing between one or the other but the relation between the two – the interpenetration of auto-identificatory processes with hetero-identificatory ones. The fault-lines within film studies over cultural exchange emerge over the weighting given to each and therefore the angle of incidence taken on these processes.

Embedded in this discussion is a way of understanding the double-edged character of culture itself, cultural exchange and its relation to cultural identity. Such exchange is critical to defining and transforming the self, to defining the culture and redefining it; it is also critical to processes of cultural denaturing, of eroding the culture and the sense of self, of compromising it, of ruining it, reducing it to a form of sameness. This simultaneous character of cultural exchange – both as a means for us to determine who and what we are and a powerful corrosion of who and what we are – is fundamental to cultural exchange in the cinema and bedevils film studies and the wider film milieu.

An emerging perspective in film studies has it that we need a change from *normative* approaches to cultural exchange toward *normalizing* the cultural-transfer processes intrinsic to such cultural exchanges. Film studies, at least in part, is moving from principled objections to unequal cultural exchange to a careful attention to the variety, shape, and interrelatedness of the various cultural-exchange processes. This attention focusses on the negotiation of cultural transfers by the receiving culture.

5 NEGOTIATION OF CULTURAL TRANSFERS

Regardless of these various asymmetries, the international film and television milieu is configured by flows and transfers (of concepts, genres, styles, texts, fashions, etc.) which shape filmmaking, criticism, and consumption in a variety of ways. Soviet semiotician Iouri Lotman (1990) has made cultural transfers central to his understanding of national cultural formations. Elsewhere I have applied this model to thinking about Australian national cinema and cultural-transfer/exchange processes more generally (see O'Regan 1996).

For Lotman cultural transfers play a significant role in the formation of cultures. They are central to culture and cultural development generally. A culture cannot turn itself into a sending culture without being at some point a receiving culture. He distinguishes processes of cultural transfer and provides a way of linking these as the successive stages involved in the unfolding story of any culture's development. These are: a first stage where imported texts "keep their strangeness" and are valued more than those of the home culture; a second stage where "the imported text and the home culture . . . restructure each other" (so, for example, Rolf de Heer's *Bad Boy Bubby* [1994] indigenizes the Eastern European art film in an Australian context); a third stage where "a higher content is found in the imported world-view which can be separated from the national culture of the imported texts" and attached to the local product (so local films become better films than their original Hollywood exemplars); a fourth stage where "imported texts are entirely dissolved in the receiving culture" (as with Italian neorealism or the Nouvelle Vague); and a fifth stage where "the receiving culture . . . changes into a transmitting culture directing its product to other, peripheral areas of the semiosphere" (so British films such as Mike Newell's *Four Weddings and a Funeral* [1994] and Hugh Hudson's *Chariots of Fire* [1981] circulate the length and breadth of the international system) (Lotman 1990: 146).

For Lotman, national cultures need to pass through these five stages. Cultures cannot become transmitting cultures without passing through the earlier stages. As a professional historian and semiotician of culture, it makes no sense to Lotman to oppose these stages to one another, as they are part of a general and larger process. Both the abject home culture of stage one and the confident producing culture of stage four are not only part of a continuum of cultural exchange but are organically interconnected. Such natural semiotic processes are not to be criticized as such but are rather to be identified for what they are – part of the general condition of any culture and not just antipodal ones. It is also the case that these stages are co-present at any one time.

In the first stage identified by Lotman, "[t]he texts coming in from the outside keep their 'strangeness' " such that they are "read in the foreign language (both in the sense of natural language and in the semiotic sense)." Also, "[t]hey hold a high position in the scale of values, and are considered to be true, beautiful, of divine origin" (1990: 146). If Australians routinely hold Hollywood filmmaking, British cinema and television, and the European and now Asian cinema in higher esteem than the local product, they are matched by those in France like Henri Agel or Naficy's "third world audiences" wooed to the cinema by Hollywood. Industry people – distributors, filmmakers, and exhibitors – regularly report that audiences, from their perspective, are unwarrantedly resistant to quality local product, so inured are they by the almost divinized imported product. For the cinephile, American, not one's own national cinema, is "the cinephile's heaven" (Martin 1988: 92). Theirs is a loving regard for modes of filmmaking often not their own. Filmmakers can often insist upon the cultural appropriateness in other contexts of the Hollywood imaginary, berating those who would accentuate what is different about local speech and life styles and ignoring what is imaginatively held in common. For Lotman:

> Knowledge of the foreign language is a sign of belonging to "culture," to the elite, to the best. Already existing texts in "one's own" language, and that language itself, are correspondingly valued lowly, being classed as untrue, "coarse," "uncultured." (1990: 146)

Variously, the Hollywood cinema, American independents, European and Asian art films, the avant-garde, exploitation, political, multi-cultural, or feminist cinema can show up the limits and inadequacies of the local product. The film critic calls on this international repertoire to introduce to the local cinema some film-performance style, genre, or social problematization. Audiences are often animated by similar concerns, as when John Baxter reported how viewing local films left him:

> disturbed rather than glowing with national pride rather like a Catholic hearing mass said for the first time in English rather than Latin. There was only one proper place for making films and that was America: I didn't care to see fantasies enacted right on my doorstep. It was a common reaction. (1986: 22)

During this stage, Lotman suggests there is a "dominant psychological impulse . . . to break with the past, to idealize the 'new,' i.e. the imported world-view, and to break with tradition, while the 'new' is experienced as something salvific" (1990: 146). Instances of this stage abound in criticism, filmmaking, and film policy development. The need for a new start is undergirded by a recognition of the worthless character of the National Socialist tradition in Germany or the cinema of papa for the French New Wave. The devaluation of British-produced culture and elevation of Hollywood and the continental international art cinema is a natural part of the British experience of the cinema and culture more generally. Hence the common conception of British cinema as a kind of cardigan (Medhurst 1995: 16).

Sometimes this first stage is referred to retrospectively and disparagingly as the "cultural cringe," where anything imported is valued, come what may. The standpoint of later stages reconstructs this stage as a false consciousness to rail against. But Lotman's first stage is essential to the introduction of new formats, critical paradigms, and combinations of filmmaking. Without it there can be no system regeneration, no second stage of indigenizing the imported culture from which to begin. It also encourages a healthy disrespect for the local product and enables people to dream of an outside from which to reposition the local.

The second stage, where the "imported texts and the home culture restructure each other," is evident in the many film-concept remakes. It is present in criticism when critics take the different theories developed for other cultural formations and sometimes apply them with only minor changes to their own context. And it is an important component in documentary cinema traditions where the substantially local character of much documentary circulation makes the original neither as publicly available nor as valued as the local copy, thus permitting often rudimentary concept remakes.

Typically, feature-filmmakers and television-drama producers operate in the more advanced stage of a full-blown adaptation – as the Hollywood, British, and European originals already have a market presence. In this second stage, Lotman insists, "translations, imitations and adaptations multiply" and "the codes imported along with the texts become part of the metalingual structure." This second stage gives rise to a relatively strict division of labor: the local is the content, the flavor, the accent, and the social text, while the international provides the underlying form, values, narrative resolutions, etc. The products of this second stage are subject to Mattelart et al.'s criticism that in them "cultural identity [is] reduced to a national label stuck on what is essentially a transnational copy" (1988: 22).

This stage also includes "a predominant tendency to restore the links with the past, to look for roots" (Lotman 1990: 147). The new is now interpreted as "an organic continuation of the old, which is thus rehabilitated." Peter Weir's *Picnic at Hanging Rock* (1975) makes sense not just as a lush and quirky European art film or a classy horror film but in its connections with longstanding Australian storytellings, based as it is upon a screen adaptation of Joan Lindsay's novel. It was connected with nativist ideas about the threatening bush and tall stories and ghost stories about child disappearance and horror met with in the bush. Lotman notes that ideas of organic development come to the fore at this stage. Films can become part of a larger narrative of a culture undergoing development and flowering maturity.

Lotman's third stage stresses:

> a tendency . . . to find within the imported world-view a higher content which can be separated from the actual national culture of the imported texts. The idea takes hold that "over there" these ideas were realized in an "untrue," confused or distorted form and that "here," in the heart of the receiving culture

they will find their true, "natural" heartland. The culture which first relayed these texts falls out of favour and the national characteristics of the texts will be stressed. (146)

The third stage crucially involves perceptions. It reevaluates the home culture's product in a situation of assumed international comparison. The establishment of a film's international credentials, like success and awards at the Cannes and Berlin film festivals, establishes its domestic credentials as an exemplary local product of international standard. Lotman's third stage opens out onto the heartfelt pride many producers and filmworkers feel about the quality and innovation of their product in an international frame. It is evident in the appreciation of films such as Luc Besson's *La Femme* (1990). This film reveals the complete mastery of the thriller genre. It is appreciated for its technical virtuosity and its aggressive and exuberant vitality, and its standing is confirmed by its concept remake in Hollywood.

The fourth stage assimilates the imported matrices, making them entirely its own: "the imported texts are entirely dissolved in the receiving culture." For Lotman:

> During this stage . . . the culture itself changes to a state of activity and begins rapidly to produce new texts; these new texts are based on cultural codes which in the distant past were stimulated by invasions from outside, but which now have been wholly transformed through the many asymmetrical transformations into a new and original structural model. (1990: 146)

Whether it be the Japanese cinema of the 1950s and early 1960s, the French New Wave, Italian neorealism of the 1950s and the cinema of the 1960s, German Expressionism of the 1920s, or the New German Cinema from the 1960s, this cinema is related to but not beholden to its distant "debts." There are limits to participation at this fourth stage. For some film-producing countries it happens regularly, as with the larger countries of Europe. For the vast bulk of countries, which are small- or medium-sized in population terms or are comparatively impoverished in terms of film-production funding and circulation, we can be looking at "one-person" film industries. There is not the level of production activity to sustain it, nor is there the dominance of local "symbolic" culture at the box office and on the television schedule.

In the fifth stage:

> The receiving culture, which now becomes the general centre of the semio-sphere, changes into a transmitting culture and issues forth a flood of texts directed to other, peripheral areas of the semiosphere. . . . As with any dialogue, a situation of mutual attraction must precede the actual contact. (Lotman 1990: 146)

Of course the prospect of any but the larger countries being at the center of the international audiovisual semiosphere is largely chimerical. Although individual films from countries other than the US do regularly become "dominant entertainment forces" (this is particularly so if they are produced in the English language or can be dubbed into English effectively, as with Bruce Lee's Kung Fu films of the early 1970s), these tend to be the exception, not the rule. Nonetheless there is an ambition within just about every reach of cinema and criticism not only to be particular and local but also to be universal and to speak to the world. The trajectory of many actors, cinematographers and directors to Hollywood, to Hong Kong, and to the larger film industries of Europe – France for francophone Africa, for example – makes sense in this context. The move to Hollywood completes the cycle: think of how many filmmakers continued to make "their" films in Hollywood. There is, obviously, a good case to be made that Alfred Hitchcock continued to make British films throughout his Hollywood career. For Elsaesser, Hitchcock's cinema revealed "the peculiar complexion of the British dandy" (1994b: 21), while for Ken Mogg, Hitchcock remained till the end "a British filmmaker" (1995: 21).

6 CONCLUSION

Lotman's schema provides support for a widely held position within film theory to put more flexible and open-ended conceptions of cultural exchange at the heart of its study. These conceptions are predicated on conceptions of culture that see it as always already hybrid – products of border-crossings and other features. Lotman would agree with Davis that "an international consciousness" inseminates "the film industries of all countries from the moment of their inception" (1996: 19). He, too, would see not only the cinema as "an institution that is profoundly, inescapably international" but that every national cinema, every national or marginal cultural community is " 'always already' touched by other cultures." And he would add that this is not new but the very historical condition of culture. Clearly the normalization, divinization, and demonization of cultural exchange noted above are themselves naturally occurring features of the cultural-exchange cycle.

By normalizing cultural transfers we can shift our attention from moments of cultural exchange to its broader dynamics. In so doing analysis moves from valorizing one type of cultural exchange over others to understanding the larger cultural-exchange processes that link these moments. Lotman's own emphasis upon the cyclical character of cultural exchange makes him sanguine about it. For this historian of culture we should not take sides too quickly or take up the teleological invitation of seeing five sequential stages in which the latter stages are superior. We can afford to give each stage its due, particularly if we want system regeneration to occur and if we want to create the conditions for the cultural exchanges we prefer to occur (Lotman shows we need those other aspects of cultural exchange we might sometimes abhor). Filmmaking methods, ideas, concepts are also transformed in the encounter with local traditions. In this way cultural exchange facilitates the adaptation and reinvigoration of tradition.

Such a position not only has practical consequences for how we might secure "cultural futures," in Michaels' happy phrase (1994: 99), but also has ethical and normative consequences for our practice as policy-makers and critics alike. Burnett warns us of the dangers inherent in our very conduct of cultural exchange:

> The necessity of the other . . . makes policy necessary for culture but only if policy itself is seen as a cultural product and thus as open to change and reevaluation as any cultural production might be. Any transformation of policy into law in this regard closes off the very channels of discourse and exchange which have made the creation of culture possible in the first place. (1996: 260)

For Burnett, as for Lotman, our policies, our plans of action, our very critical vocabulary need to remain flexible and open lest they inhibit and deny the very cultural adaptations so critical to cultural maintenance and growth. Working out the contours of this practice is a central issue facing contemporary film studies, whether it focusses on cultural exchange between or within societies.

Note

1   These titles are listed as links with other titles in the Internet Movie Database pages on the film. See
     http://us.imdb.com/Title?Dark+City+(1998). Accessed August 11, 1998.

References

Agel, Henri. 1963. *Romance americaine*, 7th edn, art 35. Paris: Les Editions du Cerf.

Barber, Lynden, and Marco Sacchi. 1998. "Shadow Player." *The Australian Magazine Supplement, Weekend Australian* (May 16–17): 32–4.

Bataille, Gretchen, and Charles Silet, eds. 1980. *The Pretend Indians*. Ames: Iowa State University Press.

Baxter, John. 1970. *Australian Cinema*. Sydney: Pacific Books.

——— . 1986. *Filmstruck: Australia at the Movies*. Sydney: Australian Broadcasting Corporation.

Bazin, André. 1967, 1971. *What Is Cinema? Vols 1 & 2*. Essays selected and trans. Hugh Gray. Berkeley: University of California Press.

Bell, Philip, and Roger Bell. 1993. *Implicated: The United States in Australia*. Melbourne: Oxford University Press.

Berlant, Lauren, and Elizabeth Freeman. 1992. "Queer Nationality." *boundary* 2, 19 (spring): 149–80.

Berry, Chris. 1992. "Heterogeneity as Identity." *Metro* 91 (spring): 48–51.

——— . 1994. *A Bit on the Side: East—West Topographies of Desire*. Sydney: EM Press.

Bhabha, Homi. 1994. *The Location of Culture*. London: Routledge.

Bogle, Donald. 1973. *Toms, Coons, Mulattoes, Mammies and Bucks*. New York: Viking Press.

Brasell, R. Bruce. 1995. "Queer Nationalism and the Musical Fag Bashing of John Greyson's *The Making of 'Monstors.'* " *Wide Angle* 16, 3: 26–36.

Burnett, Ron. 1996. "The National Question in Quebec and Its Impact on Canadian Cultural Policy." In *Film Policy: International, National and Regional Perspectives*. Ed. Albert Moran. London: Routledge. 249–61.

Butler, Alison. 1992. "New Film Histories and the Politics of Location." *Screen* 33, 4 (winter): 413–26.

Caughie, John. 1990. "Playing at Being American: Games and Tactics." In *Logics of Television*. Ed. Patricia Mellencamp. Bloomington: Indiana University Press, 44–58.

Collins, Richard. 1990. *Television: Culture and Policy*. London and Cambridge: Unwin Hyman.

Davis, Darrell William. 1996. *Picturing Japaneseness*. New York: Columbia University Press.

Dermody, Susan, and Elizabeth Jacka. 1988. *The Screening of Australia Vol. 2: Anatomy of a National Cinema*. Sydney: Currency Press.

De Usabel, Gaizka S. 1982. *The High Noon of American Films in Latin America*. Ann Arbor: UMI Research Press.

Downing, John. 1996. *Internationalizing Media Theory*. London: Sage.

Ebert, Roger. 1998. "Dark City." *Chicago Sun Times* (March 11). <http://www.suntimes.com/ebert/ebert_reviews/1998/02/022704.html> Accessed Aug. 14, 1998.

Elsaesser, Thomas. 1989. *New German Cinema: A History*. London: BFI/Macmillan.

——— . 1994a. "Putting on a Show: The European Art Movie." *Sight and Sound* 4 (April): 22–7.

——— . 1994b. "The Dandy in Hitchcock." *Maguffin* 14: 15–23.

"Foreign Market." 1922. *The Moving Picture World* (Jan. 7): 30.

Gibson, Ross. 1992. *South of the West*. Bloomington and Indianapolis: Indiana University Press.

Guback, Thomas. 1969. *The International Film Industry*. Bloomington: Indiana University Press.

Helms, Michael. 1998. "Dark City" Interview with Andrew Mason and Alex Proyas. *Cinema Papers* 124 (May): 18–21, 45.

Herder, Johann. 1993. *Against Pure Reason: Writings on Religion, Language, and History*. Trans. and ed. Marcia Bunge. Minneapolis: Fortress Press.

Hutchinson, John. 1994. *Modern Nationalism*. London: Fontana Press.

Interim Board of the Australian Film Commission. 1975. *Report of the Interim Board of the Australian Film Commission*. Canberra (February).

Jenkins, Henry. 1992. *Textual Poachers*. London: Routledge.

Kaes, Anton. 1989. *From Hitler to Heimat: The Return of History as Film*. Cambridge: Harvard University Press.

Koval, Ramona. 1992. *One to One*. Sydney: ABC Books.

Lealand, Geoff. 1988. *A Foreign Egg in Our Nest? American Popular Culture in New Zealand*. Wellington: Victoria University Press.

Lotman, Iouri M. 1990. *The Universe of the Mind: A Semiotic Theory of Culture*. Trans. Ann Shukman. Bloomington and Indianapolis: Indiana University Press.

MacDonald, Kevin. 1994. *Emeric Pressburger: The Life and Death of a Screenwriter*. London: Faber and Faber.

McQuail, Denis. 1994. *Mass Communication Theory: An Introduction*, 3rd edn. London: Sage Publications.

Martin, Adrian. 1988. "Nurturing the Next Wave: What Is Cinema?" In *Back of Beyond: Discovering Australian Film and Television*. Ed. Peter Broderick. Sydney: Australian Film Commission, 90–101.

Mattelart, Armand, Xavier Delcourt, and Michèle Mattelart. 1984. *International Image Markets: In Search of an Alternative Perspective*. Trans. David Buxton. London: Comedia Publishing Group in association with Marion Boyars.

——. 1988. "International Image Markets." In *Global Television*. Ed. Cynthia Schneider and Brian Wallis. New York: Wedge Press. 13–34.

Medhurst, Andy, 1995. "Inside the British Wardrobe." *Sight and Sound* (March): 16–17.

Mercer, Kobena. 1992. "Skin Head Sex Thing: Racial Difference and Homoerotic Imaginary." *New Formations* 16 (spring): 1–23.

Michaels, Eric. 1990. "A Model of Teleported Texts (With Reference to Aboriginal Television)." *Continuum: The Australian Journal of Media and Culture* 3, 2: 8–31.

——. 1994. *Bad Aboriginal Art: Tradition, Media and Technological Horizons*. Sydney: Allen and Unwin; Minneapolis: University of Minnesota Press.

Miller, Toby. 1996. "The Crime of Monsieur Lang: GATT, the Screen and the New International Division of Culture Labour." In *Film Policy*. Ed. Albert Moran. London: Routledge. 72–84.

——. 1998a. "Hollywood and the World." In *The Oxford Guide to Film Studies*. Ed. John Hill and Pamela Church Gibson. Oxford: Oxford University Press.

——. 1998b. *Technologies of Truth: Cultural Citizenship and the Popular Media*. Mineapolis: University of Minnesota Press.

Mogg, Ken. 1995. " 'How about I Pump Hitler?': Hitchcock's *Foreign Correspondent* (1940) and Its Sources." *Maguffin* 16: 11–26.

Morley, David, and Kevin Robins. 1995. *Spaces of Identity: Global Media, Electronic Landscapes and Cultural Boundaries*. London: Routledge.

Naficy, Hamid. 1993. "Exile Discourse and Televisual Fetishization." In *Otherness and the Media: The Ethnography of the Imagined and the Imaged*. Ed. Hamid Naficy and Teshome H. Gabriel. Longhorne: Harwood Academic Publishers.

——. 1996. "Theorizing 'Third World' Film Spectatorship." *Wide Angle* 18, 4: 3–26.

Nichols, Bill. 1994. "Global Image Consumption in Late Capitalism." *East–West Film Journal* 8, 1: 68–85.

O'Regan, Tom. 1996. *Australian National Cinema*. London: Routledge.

Orr, John. 1993. *Cinema and Modernity*. Cambridge and Oxford: Polity Press.

Routt, William D. 1992. "L'Evidence." *Continuum: The Australian Journal of Media and Culture* 3, 2: 40–67.

Said, Edward. 1995. *Orientalism*. Ringwood, Melbourne: Penguin Books.

Schiller, Herbert. 1969. *Mass Communications and American Empire*. New York: Augustus M. Kelley.

Schlesinger, Philip R. 1994. "Europe's Contradictory Communicative Space." *Daedalus* 123, 2: 25–52.

Schroder, Kim Christian, and Michael Skovmond. 1992. "Introduction." *Media Cultures: Appraising Transnational Media*. Ed. K. C. Schroder and M. Skovmond. London and New York: Routledge.

Schudson, Michael. 1994. "Culture and the Integration of National Societies." In *The Sociology of Culture*. Ed. Diane Crane. Cambridge and Oxford: Blackwell.

Sepstrup, Preben. 1990. *Transnationalization of Television in Western Europe*. Academic Research Monograph 5. London: John Libbey.

Shohat, Ella/Robert Stam. 1994. *Unthinking Eurocentrism: Multiculturalism and the Media*. London and New York: Routledge.

Sinclair, John, Elizabeth Jacka, and Stuart Cunningham, eds. 1996. *New Patterns in Global Television*. Oxford and New York: Oxford University Press.

Sjogren, Olle. 1992. "The Swedish Star-Spangled Banner: An Essay on Blended Images in Film." In *Networks of Americanization*. Ed. R. Lurden and E. Asard. Abstract by Richard Holm, pp. 156–60. Uppsala and Stockholm: Almqvist and Wiksel International.

Stam, Robert. 1993. "Review Essay: Eurocentrism, Afrocentrism, Polycentrism: Theories of Third Cinema." In *Otherness and the Media: The Ethnography of the Imagined and the Imaged*. Ed. Hamid Naficy and Teshome H. Gabriel. Langhorne: Harwood Academic Publishers. 233–54.

Stern, Lesley. 1995. *The Scorsese Connection*. London and Bloomington: BFI/Indiana University Press.

Stringer, Julian. 1996/7. "Problems with the Treatment of Hong Kong Cinema as Camp." *Asian Cinema* 8, 2: 44–65.

Tatara, Paul. 1998. "Someone in *Dark City* Needs to Lighten up." *CNN Interactive* (10 March). <http://cnn.com/SHOWBIZ/9803/10/dark.city.review/> Accessed Aug. 14, 1998.

Thompson, Kristin. 1985. *Exporting Entertainment: America in the World Film Market 1907–1934*. London: BFI.

Thomson, David. 1980. *A Biographical Dictionary of the Cinema*. London: Secker and Warburg.

Tomaselli, Keyan, and Arnold Shepperson. 1996. "Misreading Theory, Sloganising Analysis: The Development of South African Media and Film Policy." *South African Theatre Journal* 10, 2: 161–75.

Tomlinson, John. 1992. *Cultural Imperialism*. Baltimore: Johns Hopkins University Press.

Trinh T. Minh-ha. 1992. *Framer Framed*. London and New York: Routledge.

Tunstall, Jeremy. 1977. *The Media Are American: Anglo-American Media in the World*. London: Constable.

Varis, Tapio. 1988. "Trends in International Television Flow." In *Global Television*. Ed. Cynthia Schneider and Brian Wallis. New York: Wedge Press. 95–108.

Venkatasawmy, Rama, and Tom O'Regan. 1998. "Only One Day at the Beach: *Dark City* and Australian Filmmaking." *Metro* 117 (November).

Wasko, Janet. 1994. *Hollywood in the Information Age*. Cambridge: Polity Press.

Wildman, Steven, and Stephen Siwek. 1988. *International Trade in Films and Television Programs*. Cambridge: Ballinger Publishing.

Willemen, Paul. 1994. *Looks and Frictions: Essays in Cultural Studies and Film Theory*. London and Bloomington: BFI/Indiana University Press.

Williamson, J. W. 1995. *Hillbillyland: What the Movies Did to the Mountains and What the Mountains Did to the Movies*. Chapel Hill: University of North Carolina Press.

Young, Robert. 1990. *White Mythologies*. London: Routledge.

Chapter 36

Scott R. Olson

THE GLOBALIZATION OF HOLLYWOOD (2000)

THERE WAS A TIME NOT LONG AGO THAT Hollywood was the apotheosis of indigenous, authentic culture, and that view is still held by cultural elites in many countries. In the last round of the GATT talks, France famously tried to limit the amount of American media programming allowed into its borders (Moerk and Williams, 1993). Most of the fear of American media is based on the premise that American values are being exported within the media like soldiers in a Trojan Horse, but recent studies have found indigenous cultures to be quite resilent in their interpretations of Western media (Liebes and Katz, 1993; Gillespie, 1995a & 1995b; Roome, 1999). The era of throwing up barricades in resistance to imported media has for all practical purposes passed, however. The effective hybridity or interstitiality of contemporary cultures is of increasing interest to scholars (Bhabha, 1999; Davis, 1999; Naficy, 1999; and Nagel, 1999). The essence of Hollywood is now too ephemeral and omnipresent a foe for a barricade to keep it out.

The reason for the holes in this wall are simple. Hollywood has become an aesthetic, and is no longer just a place in California. That aesthetic has been increasingly adopted by other media production centers in other countries around the world. Contrary to what is commonly reported, Hollywood is not particularly an *American* aesthetic, at least not anymore. Hollywood is a global aesthetic, and that in a nutshell sums up its transnational appeal.

"Going Hollywood" no longer means packing up and moving to Los Angeles, nor does it mean adopting a certain disaffected personal deportment, the sunglasses and espadrilles and deconstructed jackets that served as mock signifiers for a high status within the film industry. "Going Hollywood" now means joining Brazil, Hong Kong, and other production centers in the scramble for global audiences. It means adopting a certain way of engaging audiences with media texts, a way that allows vastly different kinds of audiences to make sense of the same media texts. Hollywood has so transcended geography that its name has been appropriated and is now used to describe media capabilities in countries outside the United States: for example, the film production center in India is now commonly called *Bollywood* and in Hong Kong it is called *Dongfang Haolaiwu*, or "Hollywood of the East."

THE GOLDEN MEAN OF IMAGES

Understanding how this Hollywood aesthetic diaspora evolved can best be illustrated by a metaphor. Early in this decade, an interesting research project was conducted at the University of Texas at Austin by Judith Langlois and at the University of Arkansas by Lori Roggman (Bower, 1990). Langlois and Roggman took photographs of 32 different faces representing a mix of ethnicities, used computer imaging technology to "morph" these images into a single face (that is, to blend the features of each into a new coherent whole), resulting in a new synthetic image in addition to the 32 real, original faces. These 33 images were then shown to individuals who were asked for their assessment of the images' attractiveness: which face was the most beautiful?

Interestingly, the raters were overwhelmingly most attracted to the composite face, which to them seemed warmer, softer, prettier, and more familiar. Part of its beauty must have been in the fact that we could all see ourselves in her—that her face was a microcosm of all our faces. Langlois and Roggman concluded that averageness[1]—features normed across an entire population or even the human race—must in part form the basis for attractiveness (Bower, 1990).

A study since then by Perrett, May, and Yoshikawa (Bower, 1994) found that a certain amount of cultural distinctiveness combined with the averageness led to optimal attractiveness, but the scientific consensus remains that averageness is the basis of attraction (Rhodes, Sumich, & Byarr, 1999). One need not be a behavioral scientist to see the metaphoric significance of these findings. For those interested in culture, the message is fairly clear: appealing images have a prevailing norm underneath the surface, the coming together of diverse idiosyncrasies to form an attractive and familiar whole. This metaphor says something about what is attractive in the movies and television programs that cross national boundaries and succeed in the international marketplace. In order to be intelligible, they have underneath them a normative mode of communicating. They are appealing because we see a part of ourselves in them. A motion picture like *Titanic* functions like that 33rd face because there is a golden mean for images.

Why are some national media industries more successful than others at creating international markets for their products? There are usually two explanations given in answer to this:

(1)   International political pressure by superpowers forces movies and television programs into countries that might not otherwise have wanted them. Media programming is not without ideology, and the indigenous media production capacity of colonies and other areas have been hamstrung before, such as during events leading up to the American Revolutionary war.

(2)   Unfair pricing and other economic incentives make it difficult or impossible for local sovereignties to resist media imports and undermining the local production of film and television programs. This has certainly been the case in some African countries.

But while both of these are true to some extent, they don't account for the success of non-superpowers, such as Hong Kong or Brazil, in media exporting, nor do they account for the enthusiasm shown in many countries for the imported product. Audiences around the world are sincerely attracted to *Titanic* and *Walker: Texas Ranger*, choosing them over competing media imports.

Consequently, a third explanation is required. It is not exclusive, nor intended to replace the other explanations, but rather to examine cultural reasons that work independently of the political and economic reasons used by the other two schools of thought:

(3)   There are textual reasons why some media are successfully exported—that is, the film or television program itself exhibits traits that make it easier or more popular to consume, in the same way we might prefer a Toyota to an indigenously produced automobile. The text itself exerts a force leading to its acceptance and success.[2]

It is the argument of this paper that if success in the global media has at least in part a textual basis, these textual differences must stem from attributes of the producing culture. Further, those countries that are particularly successful in exporting film and television are so because they are microcosms of international audience taste. The United States, Hong Kong, and Brazil (among others) are "culture factories" producing a product with culturally transparent attributes.

HOLLYWOOD'S MARKET ADVANTAGE

The best way to begin to understand how texts might be produced for export by "culture factories" is by applying Michael Porter's (1990) theory of "national competitive advantage" to film and television production. Porter's question was: Why are certain countries strong in certain industries? For example:

- Sweden is particularly strong in the production of mining equipment
- Japan is particularly strong in the production of consumer electronics
- Italy is particularly strong in the production of ceramic tiles (Porter, 1990).

Porter argues that specific factors present in the nation combine to enable preeminence, to give that nation a competitive advantage. These factors include:

- The availability of natural resources
- Favorable regulatory policies
- Uniquely educated and configured workforce
- Unusual industry structure
- Blind luck.

These factors combine in a fortuitous way to make such a nation what he calls a "home base" (Porter, 1990) for successful global competitors in a particular industry. The home base is the nation in which the essential competitive advantages of the enterprise are created and sustained. Porter doesn't spend any time on it, but Brazil, Hong Kong, and the United States are three areas with a home base advantage in the global media.

Porter does not argue that nations have some sort of generalized and deterministic advantage which enables them to do well in whatever industry they choose, such as that the British are industrious and frugal and therefore successful at whatever they do. On the contrary, the very things that make the British successful at producing and exporting pop music may make them unsuccessful at pharmaceuticals.

For Porter (1990), competitive advantage emerges in one of two types:

- "Factor-based" competitive advantage, which results from an abundance of cheap labor or natural resources. This type of advantage is hard to sustain because lower cost labor or more abundant resources can frequently be found elsewhere.

- "Differentiation" advantage, which results from conferring on a product attributes that make it more desirable to consumers even though it might be more expensive than a competitor. Those differentiations include:

    1. Product quality or perceived quality (e.g., Coca-Cola);
    2. Special features (e.g., Macintosh computers);
    3. After-sale service (e.g., Lexus automobiles).

The differentiation approach has typically been the route to sustainable competitive advantage. It certainly characterizes the appeal of the American media: Hollywood films and television have little factor-based advantage of this sort due to huge production costs, yet are differentiated in such a way in the marketplace that they have an inherent desirability.

Sustainable home base advantage is created through what Porter (1990) calls the "diamond" of four interrelated national attributes:

1. Factor conditions—the labor force, natural resources, infrastructure, capital, and knowledge capital available in a certain national industry. Specialized labor is the most significant of these factors for the film and television industry;

2. Related and supporting industries—the suppliers, subassemblers, distributors, and other companies in a value chain. In the film and television industry, this refers to supplier industries, special effects firms, costume design shops, production insurance firms, post-production houses, film laboratories, studio space, specialized photographic equipment, writers, and acting talent, all within commuting distance of each other. Los Angeles certainly shows this level of integration, but then so does Rio de Janeiro, where the $250 million "Projeto Jacarepagua" studio complex resides;

3. Firm strategy, structure, and rivalry—the way firms in a particular country organize themselves and compete with each other, and how that competition can lead to global predominance. Porter (1990) reasons that if the toughest competitors are domestic, international competitors will prove easier to defeat. The close quarters of head-to-head studio competition in California are increasingly matched by studio competition over telenovela production in Brazil and over action film production in Hong Kong (where studio rivalries can even turn violent);

4. Demand conditions—the type of domestic consumer and what they expect from the product. The more demanding the domestic consumer, the better for the industry.

When these four advantage categories are applied to the film and television industry, it is easy to see why success concentrates in a few areas, such as Hollywood, Brazil, Hong Kong, and India. While the factor conditions, supporting industries, and industry structure are all important to the success of media industries, the most significant factor of all is consumer expectations. Increased exposure to global media has produced increasingly sophisticated global audiences who have come to expect the Hollywood aesthetic. The success of that aesthetic is its similarity to the 33rd face.

THE HOLLYWOOD AUDIENCE

The most important aspect of competitive advantage in Brazil, Hong Kong, and the United States relates to the nature of domestic demand there. The domestic audience has come to expect the "Hollywood" aesthetic, an aesthetic that has definable attributes. The audience does not necessarily expect products from California, because "America is . . . just another brand name" (Yoshimoto, 1994, p. 195).

Domestic media consumption patterns in the United States are somewhat different than in other parts of the world. Audiences are complicated and segmented, of course, but the following generalizations about the US media audience have some basis in their consumption patterns:

- The US audience is parochial—inward looking and generally uninterested in imported media, the one significant exception being children's programming.[3] What this means is that in spite of all the sensations they seek from the media, they also want the familiar—hence the success of sequels that basically retread the original plot.
- The US audience's primary expectation for the electronic media is that they be pleased and entertained.
- The US audience expects to get what it *wants* from the electronic media, and gives fairly little thought to what it *needs*, problematic though that distinction is. Of very little interest to the general US audience is what cultural élites feel might be in the audience's best interest.
- The US audience shares many elements in common with the American audience that Alexis De Tocqueville observed in 1850, audiences born of a culture that was:

  1. Preoccupied with commerce and practical matters instead of science, art, or literature;
  2. More attracted to the tangible and the real than to tradition and to formalism;
  3. Focused on gratifying the body instead of the mind.

- The contemporary US audience is also, according to Baudrillard (1988), primitive, ahistorical, and utopian.
- Finally, and most importantly, as to the question of how Hollywood became a global aesthetic, the US audience is multicultural, a mix of indigenous and immigrant peoples, cultures, customs and languages. The extent of ethnic diversity in media consumption in the United States has changed significantly since the time of the invention of motion pictures, paralleling the increasing diversity of American society generally.

The electronic media will, of course, go where the audience is, and these psychographic attributes govern the way films and television programs are produced in California, still the dominant center for the Hollywood aesthetic. Studios in California, seeking to capture as much of the audience as possible, will obviously develop products conducive to audience tastes. Attracting that domestic audience means the adoption of conventions which satisfy its longing for the familiar, for entertainment, for practical and tangible matters, and for the primitive and utopian, but for doing so in a way that is attractive to the full range of cultural diversity. Films like *Titanic* found a way to appeal to African-Americans, Italian-Americans, Korean-Americans, and Latin Americans.

Given an audience that has specific expectations for the electronic media but are themselves extremely diverse in cultural background, there are only a few ways to craft programs for them. Elsewhere (Olson, 1999) I have argued that successful electronic media succeed by linking to *mythotypes* designed to overcome what Blumenberg (1985) called "the absolutism of reality." By this phrase, Blumenberg means the existential dread that our lives might be short, meaningless, and ultimately ephemeral, the very things that myth and religion try to negate. This negation is most easily accomplished by appealing to those emotions that block out the absolutism of reality: wonder, awe, purpose, and participation (Olson, 1999). That can be done in a culturally particularized fashion, but the psychographic pathology of domestic audience demand in the United States necessitates the adoption of certain conventions by Californian film and television studios:

- A simple "good guys" vs. "bad guys" plot, with clear division of appearance, behavior, and objective between protagonist and antagonist;
- Resistance to the idea of film as art;[4]
- Middle class sentiments (see Wright, 1995);
- Formulaic and emotional stories with happy endings (see Cawelti, 1976);
- Stories with clear, simple, and predictable affect: e.g., thrills, laughter, tears (see Gitlin, 1990);
- Obsession with beauty (see Douglas, 1995 on what she calls the "bionic bimbo");
- Action (Gitlin, 1990);
- Hope and optimism.

While these conditions are not conducive to "art" films, they are conducive to textual *transparency*—a property whereby media are perceived to be indigenous by the viewing audience (see Olson, 1999). Ultimately, it is in transparency that all the demand factors create a transportable media text. By virtue of their ethnic diversity, the United States (and for similar reasons, Brazil and Hong Kong) produces media programming that is differentiated within and anticipatory of global market tastes. Economic modeling has enabled even more sophisticated predictors of global taste in media programming (Neelamegham & Chintagunta, 1999).

THE GLOBAL TEXT

Think of what makes a myth or legend or fairy tale work, the storytelling that enables tales like "Cinderella" to transcend time and space. The same basic devices enable media programming to connect to diverse audiences. These devices have been identified (Olson, 1999) and revolve around commonly found mythic themes:

1. Circular stories—tales that begin where they end, or return to the same equilibrium as existed at the beginning of the tale. Every episode of a situation comedy, for example, restores itself to the pre-conflict state of affairs.
2. Archetypal characters—familiar stock heroes, villains, and incidental characters that keep story lines within the comfort zone of audiences. The similarities between Luke Skywalker and King Arthur or between Obi-Wan Kenobi and Merlin are a case in point.
3. Open-ended plots—stories that lend themselves to endless cycling, renovation and recapitulation. The Mahabharata is a classic example; *Star Trek* a more contemporary example.
4. Inclusion strategies—devices that pull audiences into the action and help them feel involved. The point-of-view shot, a standard device in the Hollywood omniscient style (well described in Arijon, 1991), is one example; it literally places the viewer into the perspective of a character in the narrative.
5. Negentropy—the process by which the electronic media assure audiences that life is not fundamentally chaotic, but rather orderly and purposeful (see Kubey & Csikszentmihalyi, 1990). *Titanic* was a good example of this because it reaffirmed true love and triumph over death.

6.   Awe—spectacle that inspires the audience. In the case of the Hollywood aesthetic, this is primarily instilled by high production values that present majestic vistas, lavish sets, and lush costuming. This is more common in theatrically released motion pictures than in television programming, but HDTV may change that soon. New digital production techniques, exhibited in *Star Wars: The Phantom Menace* and elsewhere, further enhance the audience awe.

7.   Omnipresence—saturation of the human environment by electronic media stimulation. This creates a condition in which being an audience member is a common and frequent experience in numerous venues, from shops to restaurants to sports bars. Synergy, the marketing technique of creating additional iterations of a media narrative through apparel, toys, games, computer products, and spin-offs in other media, is one aspect of omnipresence.

These attributes of global media texts do not describe most national cinemas. They do not describe the French cinema, or the Swedish cinema, or the Chinese cinema. Those cinemas are not part of the Hollywood aesthetic.[5] *The aesthetic of the global text is analogous to the aesthetic of the 33rd face, a type of beauty that is accessible because it is familiar; open, reassuring, inclusive, and everywhere.*

The domestic US audience is not the only one receptive to the aesthetics of the global Hollywood text. Similarities between American and Brazilian audience demand demonstrates how that aesthetic has international appeal. It is not surprising that the domestic audience in these two countries should be similar. Both the United States and Brazil are former colonies with large and diverse indigenous populations, populated with many races and a history of slavery, with vast geographic and demographic differences and a frontier, both democracies, both hailed as the wave of the future. Home demand in these two countries has these things in common:

1.   The domestic audiences in Brazil and the US are large;
2.   The domestic audiences in Brazil and the US are a significant percent of world market share;
3.   The domestic audiences in Brazil and the US have a voracious appetite for the media;
4.   The domestic audiences in Brazil and the US are receptive to synergy, to product merchandising and marketing spin-offs;
5.   The domestic audiences in Brazil and the US have high expectations for the production values of cinema and television, and share the desire for a spectacle.[6]

Telenovelas are a good example of a global text, and of how the Hollywood aesthetic has escaped California: they are crafted to domestic demand in Brazil, but are also amazingly transparent, rendering them universally exportable and comprehensible. As with the Langlois and Roggman's 33rd face (Bower, 1990), telenovelas are convivially familiar and conventional in the way the golden mean of images appeals to its audience. Even so, telenovelas still have a slight veneer of cultural peculiarity glued on top of the global text.

Telenovelas are big business. In Mexico, 30 to 40 telenovelas are produced every year, totaling more than 4500 hours of programming, and generating $500 million in revenue annually. Venezuelan telenovelas are exported to 30 countries, generating sales of $20 million/year. Finally, Brazil's TV Globo network produces eight telenovelas a year, worth $31 million through exports to seventy countries. *Salsa e Merengue* and *Rei do Gado* are two examples (Margolis, 1997). So while Brazilian cinema has historically been a "national allegory" (Xavier, 1997), and in other words quintessentially Brazilian, Brazilian television has been multinational in appeal and identity—a global text crafted within the Hollywood aesthetic.

Brazil's telenovelas are popular throughout the world and can attribute their success to the Hollywood aesthetic devices used therein. Soap operas in general stick to easily exportable human themes, such as self-reliance, good defeating evil, and romantic love. Brazilian telenovelas differentiate themselves in the marketplace due to their high production values, use of location shooting, mix of genres (comedy, parody, politics, as well as the essential melodrama), clever use of theme to generate interest (e.g. *Explode Coracao*), and synergy (CDs, apparel, toys, etc.).

When it comes to soap opera the Hollywood aesthetic is deployed better in Brazil than it is in the United States. Some (for example Wasser, 1995) go so far as to say that telenovelas embody nothing of the originating culture—that while Brazilian cultural values are scarcely being exported, telenovelas "undermine the autonomy of their own national culture" (p. 425). For Wasser, Hollywood isn't "American" anymore and TV Globo isn't Brazilian. They cater too much to international tastes to be domestic, and their domestic audience is effectively international. Both are part of a global culture. The same pattern has been repeated in other cultures successful at exporting media, from Japanese video games and *anime* to Hong Kong action pictures to British pop music.

To repeat this argument in a nutshell, economic and political explanations of global media don't tell the whole story. Textual explanations for global media success must be taken into account. If there are textual differences that account for the success of certain national film and television industries, they originate in the culture, and can be explained through home demand. Home demand in Brazil and the United States is similarly demanding and multicultural and encourages the development of transparent texts. That transparency is seen in the narratological devices of circular storytelling, archetypal characters, open-ended narratives, audience inclusion strategies, negentropy, high production values, and omnipresence. Telenovelas are just one example of transparent texts becoming international successes.

The face of a telenovela, or *Pokemon*, or *Titanic* embodies a little bit of all our faces. Like the 33rd face, the morphed golden mean of 32 real faces, the global text is a composite, born of the necessity of making sense to a culturally complex domestic market. That face and those texts combine the slightly exotic with the mostly familiar. The successful global media text is a transparent microcosm of the audience watching it because it embodies all of us. We see ourselves in it. The face in the audience and on the screen in Brazil and in the United States is the 33rd face, and is a microcosm of the complex multicultural planet we live in.

The developed world is so interdependent that media programming produced almost everywhere looks less and less culturally idiosyncratic and more and more global, gravitating to a global mean of images. The face on our television is the 33rd face. Like it or not, from the inside out, not as a product of cultural imperialism but as a matter of aesthetic choice, we're *all* going Hollywood.

If the world is going Hollywood, what of those pure cultures, those that are untouched by outside influence, virgin identities unadulterated by foreign media?

Going . . .

going . . .

gone.

Notes

1 When referring to facial appearance, the word "average" in English has a connotation of plain or even dull looks. That use should not be confused with this more scientific use. By "average," Langlois and Roggman meant the most normal nose, the most normal eyes, etc., which, it turns out, tends to be a quite attractive visage.

2 By "text" in English we mean any site of negotiated understanding, any place where a producer enters meaning and a consumer decodes it. It could be a book, but also a film, billboard, postcard, or dance. A face can be a text, too, such as the 33rd face. The meaning is negotiated there, which means that the reader or consumer has as active a role in determining its meaning as the producer of the object.

3 *Pokemon* and *The Power Rangers* are the two best examples of non-American media programming that succeeded in the United States. Their success is due in part to the ability to dub voices easily—in the case of *Pokemon* due to the animation and in the case of *Power Rangers* due to the masks worn by the characters. Segments of *Power Rangers* in which the characters are unmasked are actually restaged and reshot in the United States with American actors.

4 Until quite recently, studios paid little attention to the maintenance of original film negatives, and in the early days of cinema, acetate was routinely bleached to retrieve the silver from the emulsion and make way for new motion pictures. There was little conception of them as an art form worthy of preservation. The recent establishment of a national register of historic films has ensured that at least some film classics will be preserved as works of art.

5 This is by no means a criticism of those national cinemas. Some of the greatest films have come from them. On the other hand, whatever their "artistic" accomplishments, they are far from formidable players in global media market share.

6 This change in audience demand exemplifies the shift in Brazil from focussing on a "national cinema" (and therefore a largely domestic market) to producing global texts using the "Hollywood" aesthetic. In the history of cinema. Brazil is primarily regarded as the cradle of *Cinema Novo*, which had the minimalist anti-Hollywood aesthetic of "a camera in the hand and an idea in your head" or what Glauber Rocha called "the aesthetics of hunger" (Xaiver, 1997). These scarcely describe the telenovelas of the 1990s.

References

Arijon, D. (1991). *Grammar of the Film Language*. Los Angeles, CA: Silman-James Press.

Baudrillard, J. (1988). *America*. Trans. C. Turner. New York, NY: Verso.

Bhabha, H. (1999). Arrivals and departures. In H. Naficy, Ed. *Home, Exile, Homeland: Film, Media, and the Politics of Place*, pp. vii–xii. New York, NY: Routledge.

Blumenberg, H. (1985). *Work on Myth*. Trans. R. Wallace. Cambridge. MA: MIT Press.

Bower, B. (1990). "Average attractions: Psychologists break down the essence of physical beauty." *Science News*, *137* (19): 298–299.

Bower, B. (1994). "Facial beauty may lie more than skin deep." *Science News*, *145* (12): 182.

Cawelti, J. (1976). *Adventure, Mystery, and Romance*. Chicago: University of Chicago Press.

Davis, J. (1999). "Questions of identity." *The Hedgehog Review: Critical Reflections on Contemporary Culture*, *1* (1): 5–8.

De Tocqueville, A. (1945a). *Democracy in America*. Volume 1. New York, NY: Vintage.

Douglas, S. (1995). *Where the Girls Are: Growing Up Female with the Media*. New York, NY: Times Books Random House.

Gillespie, M. (1995a). *Television, Ethnicity, and Cultural Change*. New York, NY: Routledge.

Gillespie, M. (1995b). "Sacred serials, devotional viewing, and domestic worship: A case-study in the interpretation of two TV versions of *The Mahabharata* in a Hindu family in West London." In R. Allen, Ed. *Speaking of Soap Operas*. . . . New York, NY: Routledge, pp. 354–380.

Gitlin, T. (1990). "Down the tubes." In M. Miller, Ed. *Seeing Through Movies*. New York, NY: Pantheon Books.

Kubey, R. and Csikszentmihalyi, M. (1990). *Television and the Quality of Life: How Viewing Shapes Everyday Experience*. Hillsdale, NJ: Lawrence Erlbaum Publishers, Inc.

Liebes, T. and Katz, E. (1993). *The Export of Meaning: Cross-Cultural Readings of Dallas*. Cambridge, MA: Polity Press.

Margolis, M. (1997). "Soaps clean up—special report: Latin TV." *Latin Trade*, 5 (4): 46–52.

Moerk, C. and Williams, M. (1993, December 20). "Moguls swat GATT-flies: Recession and Eurocrats can't nix global ties." *Variety*: A1.

Naficy, H. (1999). "Between rocks and hard places: The interstitial mode of production in exilic cinema." In H. Naficy, Ed. *Home, Exile, Homeland: Film, Media, and the Politics of Place*, pp. 125–150. New York, NY: Routledge.

Nagel, J. (1999). "The rise and decline of ethnicity: Native American ethnic revival." *The Hedgehog Review: Critical Reflections on Contemporary Culture*, 1 (1): 55–62.

Neelamegham. R. and Chintagunta, P. (1999). "A Bayesian model to forecast new product performance in domestic and international markets." *Marketing Science*, 18 (2): 115–136.

Olson, S. (1999). *Hollywood Planet: Global Media and the Competitive Advantage of Narrative Transparency*. Mahwah, NJ: Lawrence Erlbaum Associates.

Porter, M. (1990). *The Competitive Advantage of Nations*. New York, NY: Free Press.

Rhodes, G., Sumich, A., and Byatt, G. (1999). "Are average facial configurations attractive only because of their symmetry?" *Psychological Science*, 10 (1): 52–58.

Roome, D. (1999). "The serious 'consequences' of comedy: Negotiating cultural change and difference through humor." Unpublished paper delivered to the National Communication Association Annual Convention, Chicago, November 4–7.

Wasser, F. (1995). "Is Hollywood America? The trans-nationalization of the American film industry." *Critical Studies in Mass Communication*, 12 (4): 423–437.

Wright, J. (1995). "Genre films and the status quo." In B. Grant, Ed. *Film Genre Reader II* Austin, TX: University of Texas Press.

Xavier, I. (1997). *Allegories of Underdevelopment: Aesthetics and Politics in Modern Brazilian Cinema*. Minneapolis: University of Minnesota Press.

Yoshumoto, M. (1994). "Images of empire: Tokyo Disneyland and Japanese cultural imperialism." In Smoodin, E., Ed. *Disney Discourse: Producing the Magic Kingdom*. New York, NY: Routledge, pp. 181–199.

Chapter 37

Bill Grantham

AMERICA THE MENACE: FRANCE'S FEUD WITH HOLLYWOOD (1998)

HOLLYWOOD AND FRANCE ARE THE feuding hill-billy dynasties of world culture, mired in a conflict so ancient and obscure that few can explain what, exactly, it's about. Yet, it appears impossible for more than a few months to go past without some person—who should know better—declaiming about the God-given right of the people of France to view some forgettable special-effects extravaganza, or of the urgent need to protect the gossamer-fragile civilization of Racine, Flaubert, and Proust from the cultural depredations of Bruce Willis and Leonardo DiCaprio.

If all of this were just background noise, it might not matter. However, the war of words between French and American culture is also a policy issue. The existence of quotas on the importation of American television programs into Europe—an issue of minuscule importance in terms of the global economy—almost wrecked the Uruguay Round GATT talks in 1993. Within Europe, France is unflagging in the diplomatic efforts that it has maintained for more than a decade to persuade its neighbors of the need to hold the line against the flood of American cultural imports. And, in the United States, the lobbying power of the American cultural industries, notably Hollywood, can still distract administrations, Democratic or Republican, into believing that the policy ramifications of this cultural posturing actually affect vital interests.

Most of us have short memories, so we treat these issues as if they are newly minted. In fact, the cultural animosity between France and America long predates the cinema. And the use of the movies as a battleground for enacting this dispute has lasted almost as long as there has been a motion picture industry. Indeed, since 1908, there has been an explosion of Franco-American cinema animosity roughly every 20 years. (The one exception in this otherwise constant cycle is 1968, a year in which the French were otherwise occupied—although they did find time to indulge in a significant gesture against the international cinema establishment, by occupying and closing down the Cannes film festival.) The historical, cultural and—dare one say it—atavistic underpinnings of these disputes have been insufficiently recognized by French and American policymakers. One consequence of this is that, all too frequently, they have come up with the wrong policies.

LOATHING—AND LOVING—AMERICA

It is not difficult to trace French animosity toward America back more than a century and a half. A standard dictionary dates the use of the word "Americanize" in the French language (*s'américaniser*) to the year 1851. In a tactful note for wary users, it adds the observation, "often pejorative." Barely half a century into its existence, the young American republic was already getting a bad rap in France. The poet Charles Baudelaire declaimed that the "poor man" who became "Americanized" would lose "the idea of the differences which characterize the phenomena of the physical world and of the moral world, of the natural and of the supernatural." Baudelaire was accordingly stuck with the problem of what to do with Americans who palpably were not so lost. His solution: de-Americanize them. Thus, according to Baudelaire, the America of one of his heroes, Edgar Allan Poe, was "a vast cage, a great accounting establishment," in which the great *poète maudit* "made feeble efforts to escape the influence of this antipathetic atmosphere."

America's problem for the Old World, even in the nineteenth century, was that it was the avatar of modernity. Baudelaire's contemporary, Karl Marx, saw the burgeoning American capitalism of the mid-century as a promising early candidate for the inevitable upheaval of revolution.

The combined energy and rootlessness of American culture seemed for the French, as for many Europeans, to mark a decisive rupture—a threatening one for the partisans of the *ancien régime*. Of course, this rupture was not really between the physical Old and New Worlds but between the ideological ones, between the forces of those loaded concepts "progress" and "reaction." Thus, American culture had huge appeal to those who embraced Victorian invention and entrepreneurism, who attended trade fairs and exhibitions and marveled at Buffalo Bill Cody's Wild West shows, a form of mythopoeia that married the wonders of modernity to the elemental and essential lure of the frontier.

The crowds of nineteenth-century Europeans that flocked to this ineradicably American entertainment were also sampling the commercialization of entertainment and, with it, culture. Show business, wrote P. T. Barnum, was an "art" that was "merchantable." Our world, he claimed, "is a trading world of men, women and children, who cannot live on gravity alone, need something to satisfy their gayer, lighter moods and hours, and he who ministers to this want is in a business established by the Author of our nature." Barnum would not be the last show business mogul to claim that the American style of entertainment was the inevitable product of the natural world, although, perhaps, he remains alone in suggesting that it owes its existence to God himself.

EXPELLING THE FRENCH

The group of competing inventors striving to solve the technical problems of the moving picture at the end of the nineteenth century were not particularly concerned with the potential of the nascent cinema either for art or for entertainment. In France, the Lumière brothers, whose public demonstrations of films in 1895 are usually taken as the starting point of the modern cinema, initially shot banal, informational subjects: workers leaving the Lumière factory, or a train arriving at a railway station in Provence. But these early pioneers quickly grasped the narrative and diversionary qualities of the new medium. In 1898, at the time of the Spanish-American War, the Vitagraph director J. Stuart Blackton filmed *Tearing Down the Spanish Flag*, a short subject where, as its title suggests, the foreign flag was removed from its staff and replaced by the Stars and Stripes. According to Blackton, "the people went wild." In France, Georges Méliès, arguably the first important film director, graduated from filming street scenes to filming stage illusions and conjuring tricks, drama-documentaries on subjects such as the Dreyfus affair, fairy and fantasy tales (including the celebrated *Voyage to the Moon*), and even what would today be called "adult" movies.

Thanks to people such as Méliès, France was the creative leader of the early cinema. But it was also the industrial leader that, effectively, invented the modern studio system, a vertically integrated, globally implanted web of production and distribution offices that achieved substantial economies of scale and market power. The leader of this French cinematic conquest was the Pathé Frères company. Pathé manufactured the cameras that were used to make and project films, sold film stock, produced movies, and distributed them through its international distribution network. By 1908, when the cinema "industry" was just 13 years old, French film releases, led by Pathé, had captured up to 70 per cent of the American market.

In the era of robber barons, this French hegemony was an affront to American industrialists. Indeed, as early as 1896, just one year after their original demonstrations in France, the Lumière brothers found themselves thwarted in their attempts to present their system in the United States. Confronted by boycotts, confiscations by customs, and the "inexplicable" cancellation of demonstrations—all inspired, they believed, by owners of rival cinema systems—the Lumières gave up their efforts. Other French companies who stayed the course found themselves under similar attack, however.

The industrial attack centered on patents—the intellectual property protection afforded the camera and projection systems on which the competing industrialists depended. As in the early days of home video, when the mutually incompatible Betamax, vhs, and Philips 2000 fought each other for market leadership, the pioneering days of the cinema were marked by bitter battles between systems. In order to run a cinema, it was necessary to ally oneself with one or another competing industrialist. Once that decision was made, the cinema owner could only show films made using that industrialist's system: everybody else was effectively locked out. In order to drive the French out of the American market, a group of patent holders, led by Thomas Edison, pooled their various camera and project patents and formed the Motion Picture Patents Co. (MPPC), the main purpose of which was to exclude foreign competition.

The creation of the MPPC had an instant impact on the French movie businesses, driving most of them out of the American market. In just two months, the foreign share of short films in release fell by 25 percentage points. However, two leading French producers, including Pathé, managed to obtain MPPC licenses and thereby become part of the cartel.

The cartel itself could not be sustained. First, one of its essential patents, dealing with the crucial system for threading film through a camera, was struck down by the courts. Then, the nascent federal antitrust laws were successful in busting the cartel. Unfortunately, this came too late for the French companies that had been excluded from the United States by Edison and his cronies. Pathé's affiliation with the MPPC did it little good, either. By the outbreak of the First World War, foreign films were down to just over 15 percent of the American market.

FATAL DECISIONS

There is a paradox here. *All* French film companies declined in America, and not just those that were kept outside the MPPC cartel. Although it would be comforting for some to view the decline of the French film industry before the First World War as the unique product of American perfidy, this is only partly true. Equally important was the mismanagement of the world leader, Pathé Frères. Pathé took a fatal strategic decision to stick to making short films when everybody else was getting into full-length feature production. Moreover, in general, the company was not very well run. In consequence, and despite having an American subsidiary that should have shielded it from the lack of market access imposed by the conditions of the world war, Pathé's American subsidiary failed in 1921, and was taken over by its stockholders and management.

There was another aspect to France's cinematic decline: its moviemakers began to diverge stylistically from their American counterparts. American directors such as Edwin S. Porter and D. W. Griffith developed a narrative style that critical admirers such as Sergei Eisenstein observed was rooted in the technique of the nineteenth-century novel and its linear storytelling methods. In France, the best early directors, such as Abel Gance, Marcel L'Herbier, and Louis Delluc, eschewed this style (which would became known as "narrative continuity") in favor of approaches that in the words of one British critic, Roy Armes, left them "marginalized in terms of world cinema."

Another factor leading to France's cinematic decline was geopolitical. For all the European combatants, waging the First World War was immensely costly, sucking in national economic resources at unsustainable rates. At the same time, the imperial nations, such as France, neglected their empires and the markets upon which they depended. The United States, on the other hand, did not enter the war for nearly three years during which its government, as a matter of policy, determined to enter the international markets— including the cinema—evacuated by the warring European powers. By the time of the Armistice, the American film industry, already identified with Hollywood, was booming. After the war, the United States, undiminished economically by the costs of the conflict, was poised to expand internationally: between 1918 and 1921, film exports grew by 300 percent.

These four factors—the MPPC cartel, Pathé's managerial weakness, the divergence of French cinema from the stylistic mainstream, and the catastrophe of the First World War— all had combined by the early twentieth century to topple France from the industrial and creative pinnacle it had occupied in 1908. By 1927, Hollywood films represented more than 60 percent of all films submitted to the French censor for pre-exhibition approval, while the domestic market revenue share of French producers had fallen below 40 percent.

INDUSTRIAL PROTECTIONISM AND CULTURAL ANIMOSITY

France was not the first country to respond to Hollywood's cinematic hegemony by introducing quotas on American films. Germany, citing both cultural and industrial reasons, limited the importation of foreign films in 1921, followed over the next few years by Britain, Italy, Hungary, and Austria. In February 1928, the French education minister, Edouard Herriot, set up a national quota system of Byzantine complexity, introduced, he said, in "the interests of good order, and of public morality," "internal and external state security," and "safe-guarding [French] customs and national traditions." While the quotas were aimed at all foreign films, including those from the increasingly successful film industry in Germany, the main target was Hollywood.

For the French in 1928, as now, the American movie business represented a combination of economic muscle and cultural aggression that had to be withstood. As always, there was some truth in the claims. No less a person than Herbert Hoover, while serving as secretary of commerce, had spoken of "the significance of motion picture exporting both as a straight commodity trade and as a powerful influence in behalf of American goods and habits of living." The movies, in other words, were not just a source of income; they induced audiences to buy *other* American goods and promoted the American way of life. Anecdotes supported this claim: Hollywood was said to have been responsible for the introduction of the bungalow to Brazil, while businesses generally reported that demands for American styles and brands in products as diverse as shoes, clothes, cars, and furniture was due to the exposure of foreign audiences to American films.

In France, nationalists such as Charles Pomaret, a parliamentarian who ultimately served as a minister in the Vichy government, railed against Hollywood's alleged predatory practices—raids on European acting and directing talent, monopolization of movie theaters, boycotts of independent exhibitors, and even alleged stifling of European films (by buying them up and then giving them only limited releases).

The economic critique of Hollywood went hand in glove with a cultural attack on the values of its output. However, this critique was married to a fundamental antipathy to American industrial society and the "zoocratic" tendencies deplored, 80 years earlier, by Baudelaire. In 1930, Georges Duhamel published a dystopian novel titled *Scènes de la vie future*, (published in the United States, lest the lesson be lost, as *America the Menace*). Among the targets of Duhamel's anti-American rage were the luxury picture palaces that had sprung up in the previous decade. For him, they had "the luxury of some big bourgeois brothel—an industrialized luxury made by soulless machines for a crowd whose own soul seems to be disappearing." The American cinema, he railed, was "a diversion for Helots, a pastime for the illiterate, for miserable creatures, stupefied by their drudgery and their cares."

The narcotic effect of the mass media was not a theme unique to Duhamel: one thinks of the "feelies" in Aldous Huxley's *Brave New World*, or the tireless mind control exerted by movies, television programs, dime novels, and cheap music in George Orwell's *Nineteen Eighty-Four*. However, only in Duhamel is the theme so explicitly linked to an attack on America's cultural and industrial impact.

This combination of economic fear and cultural loathing informed the French quota policy in 1928 (as it does today). Then, as now, the issue for policymakers should have been: did the quotas work? The answer is unclear, but the evidence suggests that they did not. In 1929, the number of French-made films submitted for censorship actually fell by nearly one-half. The arrival of talking pictures stimulated demand for new films, and raised French production levels by the early 1930s. But this rise was not sufficient to meet the demand for new movies. Instead of booming, French studios went out of business in the 1930s. As a result, the number of cinemas in France, which had roughly tripled in the decade after 1918, fell by one-sixth between 1929 and 1937.

The impact of the Depression and the high cost of wiring theaters for talking pictures undoubtedly exacerbated the movie industry's problems. However, in the United States, it overcame these hurdles. In France, despite being forced to loosen its quota regime twice in the 1930s, the protected film industry underwent serious decline.

SPLENDID ISOLATION

As so often happens, this did not prevent people from drawing the wrong conclusions. This fact was exacerbated by the experience of the French cinema during the Second World War, when Hollywood films disappeared and the local industry prospered. At Liberation, the artistic and popular success of such films as Marcel Carné's *Les enfants du paradis* and *Les visiteurs du soir*, and Robert Bresson's debut features, *Les anges du péché* and *Les dames du Bois de Boulogne*, suggested to many that a film industry isolated from the insidious influences of Hollywood could be a great statement of national culture. This was a position attractive to both right and left. On the right, nationalists could use the Vichy experience to advance the cultural agenda which, as we have seen, dated back a century. On the left, the cultural argument was taken up at the dawn of the Cold War to create a broader context for anti-Americanism.

At the same time, there was a huge backlog of American movies waiting to be shown in France. Young *cinéphiles* such as André Bazin, the father of postwar film criticism, eagerly awaited the arrival of unseen films from the Hollywood directors they admired (while deploring the industrial system within which these masters worked). The French public longed to see the American spectaculars that they had not been allowed to see during the war, notably *Gone With the Wind*. At the same time, the system of support that enabled the French industry to thrive during the war years collapsed at the Liberation. Apocalyptic voices—of which there have always been many—proclaimed the death of French cinema, swept away by a wave of inferior Hollywood films.

While left and right united to attack Hollywood, the French government went about the business of rebuilding the French economy. An agreement with the United States for $1 billion worth of credits was struck in 1946 by the acting French prime minister Léon Blum and James F. Byrnes, the Truman administration's secretary of state. Tied to the deal was an agreement to reopen the French market to Hollywood films. Although the deal basically revived the prewar quota system with modifications made at the request of the French, the so-called Blum–Byrnes Accords, while modified in 1948 and largely forgotten elsewhere, lingered in the collective memory of the French cinema as the moment when Hollywood destroyed the Vichy renaissance.

Of course, this was not true. While Hollywood had undoubtedly lobbied for the reopening of the French market, as it did with respect to all European markets after the war, it did not seek to dismantle the prewar quota system. Moreover, the threatened avalanche of unreleased American films was short-lived and effectively over by 1948.

However, the French experience of the Edison cartels, the Herriot quota decrees, and the Blum–Byrnes quotas coalesced to create a powerful national myth: The Americans used dirty tricks to defeat a world leader that was French. Quotas were the only means to stem the tide of American films that represented both a menace to the domestic industry and an alien cultural onslaught. And, when threatened, the American film industry would deploy all its economic and political muscle to defeat the French.

FORGETTING THE LESSON

All these issues resurfaced in the 1980s and 1990s, when the member-states of the European Community (now the European Union) attempted to limit the volume of American films and programs shown on European television screens. The spur for this was the spectacular redrawing of the European televisual landscape that occurred in the mid-1980s when the arrival of frontier-breaching satellite television combined with an ideological shift in favor of consumer markets to create an avalanche of new, mainly private, television channels in countries previously accustomed to a nearly exclusive diet of public service broadcasting.

The first factor—cross-border transmission—created legal and supervisory voids that called for regulatory action on a pan-European level. The second factor—new channels—created another problem. The startup television services, still building their audiences to the levels at which they could achieve significant earnings from advertising or subscriptions, looked for sources of plentiful, cheap, and watchable television, and found them, to nobody's great surprise, in the United States.

In France, it seemed like Blum–Byrnes all over again. Just at the moment when it appeared that the television sector was on the verge of significant expansion, the Americans were ready to sweep in and take the spoils. France led the diplomatic charge in Europe for quota barriers to be erected against the importation of non-European (that is, American) television programs, backed by a sustained rhetoric bordering on paranoia. French leaders, including the culture minister Jack Lang, railed against American hegemony and the "social dumping" of cheapjack foreign culture. The director Bertrand Tavernier—one of the most sophisticated French historians of the American cinema—proclaimed that American intentions toward the French cinema were equivalent to its treatment of the Indians: "If we're very good, they will give us a reservation."

At the same time, critics denounced the EuroDisney theme park near Paris as another symptom of the Hollywoodization of France, a "cultural Chernobyl," a "construction of hardened chewing gum and idiotic folklore taken straight out of comic books written for obese Americans" and a "world that will have all the appearance of civilization and all the savage reality of barbarism."

The reality was more nuanced. The campaign to curb television program imports ignored an axiom of television scheduling, namely that national audiences overwhelmingly prefer national programming. Imported programs have the advantage of being cheap, because television accounting practices mean that the costs of their production have been substantially recouped by the sale of the programs to television networks in their home country prior to export. Importing networks accordingly use (inexpensive) foreign programs to free up money to produce their own (expensive) domestic shows, which command bigger audiences (and therefore income).

This rule applied with equal vigor in Europe: indeed, once the new wave of private television networks became established, national programming became paramount once more. By 1998, the Hollywood studios were noting that in the rich, highly competitive German market, their programs were close to being squeezed out altogether by local fare.

Back in the 1980s, this rule was known but largely ignored. As a result of sustained French pressure, in 1989 Europe adopted quotas under a policy called, with a completely straight face, Television Without Frontiers. However, the quotas were set at or around the level that foreign programs would probably have achieved in a free market had the quotas not existed at all. In other words, the policy, founded in the rhetoric of the past and ignorant of the realities of the present, was ultimately cosmetic rather than effective.

DO QUOTAS MATTER?

However, this reality—that the quotas did not really matter—was lost on the target of the quota policy, Hollywood. For years, since the U.S. government became interested in motion picture exports during the First World War, Hollywood has been an effective lobbyist on its own behalf in Washington. Under its colorful chief lobbyist, Jack Valenti, Hollywood launched its onslaught against the European quotas and, in time, found a sympathetic ear in the Clinton administration. The forum for the anti-quota struggle became the efforts to extend the General Agreement on Tariffs and Trade (GATT) to cover services, including entertainment services such as movies and television programs. To the United States, it seemed clear that free trade in services could not tolerate the existence of quotas. To France, this was just another piece of barbarism from the "giant accounting establishment," an unacceptable attempt to reify culture into P. T. Barnum's "merchantable art."

This is not the place to discuss in detail what happened in the GATT negotiations, except to make two observations. First, ultimately, France won: the issue of quotas was not addressed in the 1993 agreement. Second, it didn't matter: Europe's television landscape developed with the quotas much as it would have done without them, and Hollywood's sales of programs to Europe were scarcely affected by the Television Without Frontiers policy.

This zero-sum policy game had little to do with the empirical merits of the issues, but everything to do with the baggage the two sides carried to the table. What is important about these vignettes of cultural and industrial history is the way in which the French attack on Hollywood appears to have drawn its strength as much from a continuum of aesthetic and even psychological themes rather than from a measured appraisal of genuine industrial, economic and, yes, cultural questions. If the reality is that Pathé would have declined anyway; that the Herriot quotas harmed French cinema; that Blum–Byrnes didn't matter; and that the Television Without Frontiers quotas were irrelevant—then policy conclusions drawn from the reverse of these truths must, self-evidently, be suspect.

We are accustomed to the atavistic and irrational as factors in the making of policy. But we do not usually think of them as significant to the dull matters of trade negotiations and market barriers. At times, French politicians and intellectuals speak of Hollywood the way Greece talks about Turkey or Gerry Adams refers to the British government, with the rhetoric of war. That, to say the least, is an odd way to talk about *Baywatch*.

It's plausible to see in the gulf that separates the two sides the same features that informed cultural anti-Americanism in the nineteenth century—a fundamental lack of comfort with the constantly changing apparatus of the modern world. It's the same impulse that led the French president, Jacques Chirac, to dismiss the Internet recently as "an Anglo-Saxon network." How convenient to have someone to blame for unwelcome or uncontrollable change, and Hollywood fits the bill quite well.

Nonetheless, the issue of quotas on Hollywood's output is still on the cultural agenda in Europe, although, despite France's continuing efforts, it is a waning one. American movies take the lion's share of the box office in France, and will doubtless continue to do so. Yet, at the same time, France is by far Europe's biggest producer of movies, each year making more than 100 films, including vernacular hits that do as well in the home market as the most successful Hollywood fare. American television programs on French networks take second place to well-made, locally produced police dramas, soaps, children's programs, and game shows.

Yet the strange psychohistory of Franco-Hollywood animosity remains powerful, providing an available, useable rhetoric in stressful times. Here, as with any feud, fighting words are great for getting people riled up—but not much good for anything else.

Index